CONTEMPORARY CIVIL LITIGATION

ASPEN PUBLISHERS

CONTEMPORARY CIVIL LITIGATION

Stephen C. Yeazell
David G. Price & Dallas P. Price Professor of Law
UCLA School of Law

Wolters Kluwer
Law & Business

AUSTIN   BOSTON   CHICAGO   NEW YORK   THE NETHERLANDS

Aspen Publishers
Attn: Permissions Department
76 Ninth Avenue, 7th Floor
New York, NY 10011-5201

To contact Customer Care, e-mail customer.care@aspenpublishers.com, call 1-800-234-1660, fax 1-800-901-9075, or mail correspondence to:

Aspen Publishers
Attn: Order Department
PO Box 990
Frederick, MD 21705

Printed in the United States of America.

1 2 3 4 5 6 7 8 9 0

ISBN 978-0-7355-6246-2

Library of Congress Cataloging-in-Publication Data

Contemporary civil litigation / Stephen C. Yeazell.
    p. cm.
  Includes bibliographical references and index.
  ISBN 978-0-7355-6246-2 (alk. paper)
  1. Civil procedure — United States. 2. Practice of law — United States. I. Yeazell, Stephen C.

  KF8839.C56 2009
  347.73'5 — dc22

                                                          2009036192

This book contains paper from well-managed forests to SFI standards.

About Wolters Kluwer Law & Business

Wolters Kluwer Law & Business is a leading provider of research information and workflow solutions in key specialty areas. The strengths of the individual brands of Aspen Publishers, CCH, Kluwer Law International and Loislaw are aligned within Wolters Kluwer Law & Business to provide comprehensive, in-depth solutions and expert-authored content for the legal, professional and education markets.

CCH was founded in 1913 and has served more than four generations of business professionals and their clients. The CCH products in the Wolters Kluwer Law & Business group are highly regarded electronic and print resources for legal, securities, antitrust and trade regulation, government contracting, banking, pension, payroll, employment and labor, and healthcare reimbursement and compliance professionals.

Aspen Publishers is a leading information provider for attorneys, business professionals and law students. Written by preeminent authorities, Aspen products offer analytical and practical information in a range of specialty practice areas from securities law and intellectual property to mergers and acquisitions and pension/benefits. Aspen's trusted legal education resources provide professors and students with high-quality, up-to-date and effective resources for successful instruction and study in all areas of the law.

Kluwer Law International supplies the global business community with comprehensive English-language international legal information. Legal practitioners, corporate counsel and business executives around the world rely on the Kluwer Law International journals, loose-leafs, books and electronic products for authoritative information in many areas of international legal practice.

Loislaw is a premier provider of digitized legal content to small law firm practitioners of various specializations. Loislaw provides attorneys with the ability to quickly and efficiently find the necessary legal information they need, when and where they need it, by facilitating access to primary law as well as state-specific law, records, forms and treatises.

Wolters Kluwer Law & Business, a unit of Wolters Kluwer, is headquartered in New York and Riverwoods, Illinois. Wolters Kluwer is a leading multinational publisher and information services company.

For Owen and Emmet, my contemporary sons

SUMMARY OF CONTENTS

CONTENTS

3 SETTLEMENT: THE LAW AND STRATEGY OF LITIGATION RISK CONTROL

ACKNOWLEDGMENTS

Stephen Yeazell gratefully acknowledges the superb assistance of the Darling Law Library at UCLA, whose librarians and student assistants have tracked down publications, verified references, and moved this project forward at critical times. He thanks as well several generations of UCLA law students, whose enthusiasm and patience helped shape the course — including its title, which was the winner of a contest sponsored when one class came to him explaining, "This is a really interesting course, but no one will ever take it if you keep calling it Advanced Civil Procedure." I would like to thank the following authors and publishers for kindly granting permission to reproduce excerpts of, or illustrations from, the following materials:

American Civil Liberties Union (ACLU), About the ACLU, http://www.aclu.org/about/index.html (last visited Sept. 14, 2009). Copyright © 2009 by the American Civil Liberties Union (ACLU). Reprinted with permission.

American Judicature Society, Judicial Selection in Mississippi: An Introduction, http://www.ajs.org/js/MS.htm (July 6, 2005). Copyright © 2005 American Judicature Society, http://www.ajs.org/js/MS.htm (July 6, 2005). Courtesy the American Judicature Society.

Baker & McKenzie, Our Firm, http://www.bakernet.com/BakerNet/Firm+Profile/default.htm. Copyright © 2009 by Baker & McKenzie. Reprinted with permission.

Begue, Yvette, and Candice Goldstein, *How Judges Get into Trouble: What They Need to Know About Developments in the Law of Judicial Discipline*, 26 Judges' J. 8 (1987). Yvette Begue, formerly a staff attorney with the Center for Judicial Conduct Organizations of the American Judicature Society, currently serves as Deputy General Counsel for the Massachusetts Department of Telecommunication and Energy. Reprinted with permission.

Berenson, Alex, *Analysts See Merck Victory in Vioxx Deal*, N.Y. Times, Nov. 10, 2007. Copyright © 2007 The New York Times. All rights reserved. Used by permission and protected by the Copyright Laws of the United States. The printing, copying, redistribution, or retransmission of the Material without express written permission is prohibited.

Bernstein, Lisa, and Daniel Klerman, *An Economic Analysis of Mary Carter Settlement Agreements*, 83 Geo. L.J. 2215 (1995). Reprinted with permission of the publisher, Georgetown Law Journal © 1995.

Brooks, C. W., *Pettyfoggers and Vipers of the Commonwealth: The "Lower Branch" of the Legal Profession in Early Modern England* 233, 236 (1986). Reprinted with the permission of Cambridge University Press.

Carson, Clara N., *The Lawyer Statistical Report: The U.S. Legal Profession in 2000* (2004). Copyright © 2004 by American Bar Foundation. Reprinted with permission.

Center for Individual Rights, Fighting for Individual Rights, http://www.cir-usa.org (Jan. 5, 2005). Reprinted with permission of the Center for Individual Rights.

Cummings, Scott, *The Politics of Pro Bono*, 52 UCLA L. Rev. (2004). Copyright © 2004. Reprinted with permission of the author.

Deja, Daniel, *How Judges Are Selected: A Survey of the Judicial Selection Process in the United States*, 75 Mich. B.J. 904 (1996). Reprinted with permission from the September 1996 issue of the Michigan Bar Journal.

Deutsch, Linda, *Kozinski Declares Mistrial in L.A. Obscenity Case*, Associated Press, June 16, 2008. Copyright © 2008 by the Associated Press. Reprinted with permission.

Engler, John, and Lucille Taylor, *Judicial Selection: A View from the Governor's Perspective*, 75 Mich. B.J. 910 (1996). Reprinted with permission from the September 1996 issue of the Michigan Bar Journal and the authors.

Friedenthal, Jack, *Secrecy in Civil Litigation: Discovery and Party Agreements*, 9 J.L. & Poly. 67, 67-71, 76-77, 78, 81-83, 85, 87, 90, 92, 94, 95, 96, 97-98 (2000). Copyright © 2000. Reprinted with permission.

Glater, Jonathan, *Study Finds Settling Is Better Than Going to Trial*, N.Y. Times, Aug. 8, 2008. Copyright © 2008 The New York Times. All rights reserved. Used by permission and protected by the Copyright Laws of the United States. The printing, copying, redistribution, or retransmission of the Material without express written permission is prohibited.

Goldberg, Barbara, and Kenneth Mauro, *Utilizing Structured Settlements*, Practising Law Institute/Litigation and Administrative Practice Course: A Handbook Series, 658 PLI/Lit 31 (2001). Reprinted with permission.

Gray, Cynthia, *Judicial Discipline in 2003*, 87 Judicature 193 (2004). Judicature, the journal of the American Judicature Society. Reprinted with permission.

Heinz, John, *The Changing Character of Lawyers' Work*, 32 Law & Socy. 751 (1998). Copyright © 1998 by Blackwell Publishing. Reprinted with permission.

JAMS, Mediation, http://www.masadr.com (July 7, 2005). Reprinted with permission. Copyright 2009 JAMS. All rights reserved.

Jones Day, Firm Overview: One Firm Worldwide, http://www.jonesday.com/firm/overview (Feb. 23, 2009). Reprinted with permission.

Jones, Ashby, *More Law Firms Charge Fixed Fees for Routine Jobs*, Wall St. J., May 2, 2007, at B1. Copyright 2007 by Dow Jones & Company, Inc. Reproduced with permission of Dow Jones & Company, Inc. in the format Textbook via Copyright Clearance Center.

West, from Weil & Brown, *California Practice Guide: Civil Procedure Before Trial* (TRG 2006), Chapter 12 Part II. All rights reserved.

Wollschlager, Christian, *Exploring Global Landscapes of Litigation Rates*, in Soziologie Des Rechts: Festschrift Fur Erhard, Blankenburg Zum 60 Geburstag, 587 (J. Brand & D. Stempel eds., 1998). Reprinted with permission.

Yeazell, Stephen C., Brown, *The Civil Rights Movement, and the Silent Litigation Revolution*, 57 Vand. L. Rev. 1975 (2004). Copyright © 2004 by Vanderbilt Law Review. Reprinted with permission.

Yeazell, Stephen C., *Getting What We Asked For, Getting What We Paid For, and Not Liking What We Got: The Vanishing Civil Trial*, 1 J. Empirical Legal Stud. 943 (2004). Copyright © 2004 by Blackwell Publishing. Reprinted with permission.

Yeazell, Stephen C., *The Misunderstood Consequences of Modern Civil Process*, 1994 Wis. L. Rev. 631. Wisconsin Law Review; Copyright © 1994 by The Board of Regents of the University of Wisconsin System; Reprinted by permission of the Wisconsin Law Review.

Yeazell, Stephen C., *Refinancing Civil Litigation*, 15 De Paul L. Rev. 183, 190-193 (2001). Copyright © 2001 De Paul Law Review. Reprinted with permission.

CONTEMPORARY CIVIL LITIGATION

INTRODUCTION

A. GOALS AND MEANS

These materials explore two bodies of law and two sets of institutional practices, all four of which have central importance in contemporary U.S. civil litigation. They will assume basic familiarity with the civil litigation process and will focus on issues arising at the beginning and the end of lawsuits: identifying the client, financing the lawsuit, selecting the judge, and settling the case. We shall approach these problems from three perspectives: one demographic, one doctrinal, one institutional.

Demographically, we'll look at three populations — of lawyers, of lawsuits, and of judges — and ask how many, where, and what kind of each. The demography matters not only because it enables us to think clearly about the profession, about civil litigation, and about the judiciary, but also because all have changed over the last half century.

Doctrinally, we shall look at the law of representation and the law of settlement. The law of representation describes what lawyers can do — and what they must not do — to and for clients; this law comes from professional ethics, from rules of procedure, and from the law of legal malpractice. The law of settlement explores the ways in which lawyers can effectuate settlements arrived at through the process of litigation and negotiation; these doctrines lie at the intersection of contracts and civil procedure.

Institutionally, we shall examine litigation finance and judicial selection, recusal, and discipline. We shall first examine how the financing of lawsuits affects the course of litigation; that is, how do contingency fees, litigation budgets, insurance practices, and firm finance affect the course of lawsuits? These questions will take us into the worlds of finance and banking, and of the organization both of for-profit and non-profit practice groups. The second institutional focus — on judicial selection and retention — will take us into the world of politics as well as law, as we examine the ways in which those who control the alternative to settlement (i.e., adjudication) are chosen.

All four topics critically matter to litigating lawyers. How lawsuits are paid for affects their start, their progress, and their conclusion. The last 50 years have seen fundamental changes in the financing of litigation: the "plaintiffs' bar" is far batter capitalized than it was in 1950; the "defense bar" operates under much tighter budgetary controls than it did at the same time; and

1

insurance is a central factor in a high proportion of civil litigation. Changes in the structure of legal practices have vastly increased the likelihood that even in ordinary litigation lawyers will find themselves in circumstances of conflict with clients. Moreover, recent developments have made such conflicts a matter not only for ethical reflection and a remote possibility of professional discipline, but also of disqualification motions and malpractice liability.

Suppose the lawyer avoids the pitfalls of conflict, and after some factual investigation and procedural maneuvering reaches a proposed settlement satisfactory to all concerned. How does the lawyer effectuate that settlement? Answering that question requires a consideration beyond the basic principles of res judicata and of contractual drafting. Recent years have seen an increase in the subtlety of such consensual ending of litigation. Because trial is both expensive and risky, both sides seek to control their risks and hedge their litigation investments. These practices begin to blur the lines between transactional and litigation practices.

The law of settlement has grown in a second way as well. When a plaintiff sues more than one defendant, settlement issues become immensely more complicated because, to be effective, the settlement must resolve matters not only between plaintiff and defendant—the obvious goal—but also between defendant and defendant. This second aspect of settlement arises because in many situations the substantive law of contribution or indemnity will give one defendant a right to recover some of the damages from the other defendant. To achieve an effective settlement between any two parties, the two settlers must either gain the consent of the third or find another method that will bind the non-settling party.

Matters between client and lawyer and between parties to a settlement are in many respects private matters regulated by contracts negotiated against the background of professional regulation and substantive legal rules. Their prominence reminds us of how much U.S. litigation is "private" rather than "public" law. But because we are exploring litigation, not contractual negotiation, there is always a 700-pound gorilla lurking in the background—the judge. Most litigators will tell you that next to the substantive merits of the case, the single most important factor in the outcome is the identity of the judge to whom the case is assigned. Not surprisingly, lawyers are intensely interested in affecting the identity of the judge. They express this interest in quite different ways—through challenges and recusal motions and through participation in judicial selection and election. We shall explore both—the first a developing area of doctrine, the latter a contested political arena in which recent developments suggest that the intensity will grow.

B. THIS COURSE AND THE REST OF LAW SCHOOL

You've had courses in civil procedure, torts, contracts, and property—the building blocks with which most civil litigation is constructed; if you're in your fourth or later semester of law school, you've had a number of other courses as well. But if you talk to lawyers who focus on civil litigation, you quickly find that they are interested in many things that don't find any obvious place in law school curriculums — in any year. They'll be interested, for example, in exactly what insurance coverage the parties have, in the identity of the judge, in the practice organization from which the lawyer(s) on the other side come, in forms of settlement that might mitigate some of the risk inherent in litigation, in whether the addition of a new party to the suit may "conflict" them out of representation. And, because they're now embedded in their careers, they'll be very interested in the ways that practice is changing.

The materials in this chapter try to make sense out of such matters. They start where your courses in substantive and procedural law leave off, assuming your familiarity with those building blocks and using them to help you see how contemporary litigation is constructed. If you look at the table of contents, the first thing you may notice is that most of the source materials aren't cases or statutes or law review analyses. You'll look at some of those, but most of the materials are drawn from sources less common in law school courses. First, the chapter will present some data: How many lawsuits are there in an average year? How much do lawyers really earn? Are most judges contributors to the campaigns of whoever appointed them? This data forms the background for another kind of reading, press accounts — both the "trade" press (newspapers and magazines addressed to the bench and bar) and some similar accounts addressed to the general public. Both the data and the press accounts are inherently unanalytical — they're either statistical compilations or accounts of something recent the journalist and her editor thought readers would be interested in. For the student, that's good news and bad news.

The good news is that most of these make for much quicker (and maybe more interesting) reading than do most cases and statutes. The bad news is that you have to do the heavy lifting: *you* (with a little help from your teacher) have to figure out how this fits into what you already know and into the possibilities and constraints created by the other materials in this course. Why do lawyers care how the other side is paying for the lawsuit? What does it mean that the typical U.S. lawyer is no longer a solo practitioner? What difference does the average duration of a lawsuit ending in trial make? Why do judges care about what lawyers think of them? How much malpractice insurance should a particular practice organization carry? Why would a lawyer recommend a settlement that, instead of saving her client the cost of trial, guaranteed the case would go to trial? Connecting these dots will make the course work for you. It may also help you to think about where you want to fit into a profession that seems to be undergoing rapid evolution. But that's most likely to happen if you remember that, in most of these materials, the question is not, "What did the court hold?" but rather, "Why did the lawyers (or judge, or practice organization) do that, and how will it affect this and other lawsuits? Enjoy.

C. SOME HYPOTHETICAL CASES

Each of the following cases occurs in the setting of relatively routine litigation: no class actions, no multidistrict orders, no conflict of laws or knotty issues of supplemental federal jurisdiction, not even a plausible question of whether the court has personal jurisdiction over the defendant. In the same vein they involve no difficult questions of evidence or motions for a new trial because in only one of these cases will there ever be a trial (and even that trial will occur *because of* not *instead of* a settlement). In that sense these hypothetical cases are typical of most lawsuits, which do not present complex doctrinal issues. They do, however, present some very difficult legal problems, problems whose contours we shall explore this term. Each hypothetical explores the following questions: What is going on? What problem does it present the lawyer with? What response is appropriate?

1. You're halfway through your second year of law school and thinking seriously about Life After Graduation. You're pretty sure you want to practice, and you think you want to be involved in litigation; but after that things are a little hazy. A lot of large firms hold interviews at your law school, and most of your classmates seem to be focusing on those opportunities. You don't have anything against such a practice — and some friends seem happy in them — but you'd also like to have a better idea of what else is out there. Some classmates seem to be focusing on public interest or non-profit practices, and these hold some attractions for you — if only you knew better what was out there. You think you might be happy in a small firm, with a dozen or so lawyers, but you've discovered they don't conduct interviews at your placement office, and you have no idea how to get information about, much less a job offer at, such a firm. Nor do you know how they pay, what their practices and "cultures" are like, and whether you'd fit in. Does anyone have this information?

2. After a few years in a firm, you and a classmate have struck out on your own, establishing a small practice. You finance the operation on your charge cards and loans from your great-aunt for a month or two, but soon realize that to survive you will need a line of credit to pay the rent and staff until the cases you have in hand ripen into fees. After calling around town, you find a bank willing to consider such a line of credit. You fill out forms and more forms. One day the bank calls and tells you the head of the legal lending division wants to interview you and your partner that afternoon. You and your partner have lunch — out of a paper bag — in your "conference room" (a large former utility closet) and try to figure out what the banker will want to know? What questions should you expect and what answers would be the "right" ones?

3. You have just graduated from law school and are intent on becoming a top-flight litigator. Having attended lots of placement workshops, you understand that an excellent litigator must be able credibly to threaten to take a case to trial. But in contemporary practice there aren't many trials, so a young litigator has a hard time gaining the experience that makes such a threat credible. Fortunately for you, you have found a job in a small firm that specializes in insurance defense, a firm the insurers like because it takes most of its cases to trial and wins a high percentage of them. After some orientation and a little second-chair work with your seniors, you get your first "solo" case — a small claim for soft-tissue personal injuries of the sort that are both common and easily faked. You believe your case falls into the latter category. The insurer has decided, as a matter of company policy, not to settle such cases, so you're looking forward to your first trial. You interview the defendant-driver, Andrea

Anderson, and are delighted to hear that her version of the accident corroborates your sense that the plaintiff has a very weak case on liability and injury. At the end of the conversation, you make a vague but hopeful remark that you hope to mount a convincing defense. Ms. Anderson responds cheerfully, "That's good; when I returned the car to my brother he was really miffed that I hadn't asked his permission to use it! So I'm sure glad that there won't be any blotches on his insurance record!"

4. You return from a well-deserved post–bar-examination vacation to begin as an associate in a large firm with an active litigation and securities practice. Feeling well-prepared for this challenge as a result of your specialization in the business curriculum at law school and a pretty substantial number of clinical courses, you look forward to your first case. U$$$.com, a successful Internet firm, has managed to go public on a recent stock market bounce and is grateful to your firm for its help during the sometimes tense legal and financial maneuvering that occurs in this period. So the company turns immediately to the firm when it gets a telephone call from the federal Securities and Exchange Commission (SEC) asking for an appointment to make what are described as "routine inquiries" regarding trading in U$$$.com's stock by various of the company's officers and chief stockholders. The person who got the phone call knew enough to realize that there is almost never any such thing as a "routine" inquiry by the SEC, and immediately called a partner at your new firm. Swamped with other work, the partner can't realistically schedule any time with the company for several weeks, but he doesn't want to wait that long for reasons both of client relations and of concern that there might be something that requires a quicker response. So this partner calls you in, makes a conference call to the company's CEO, to whom he describes you as "one of our best young securities litigators" (you're prepared to agree with the "young" part of the description), and says you'll be there the next day to conduct some preliminary interviews so "we can see what we might need to think about." After the call, the partner speaks with you. He asks you to talk at least with the officer who got the call and with whomever keeps track of the forms required for SEC filings. He wants you to ask questions not so much about substance — did any insiders trade? — as about systems and record keeping: what mechanisms the company has for reminding insiders about regulations, what records are kept, and the like. He reminds you to keep your eyes and ears open but to be agreeable: "This is a good and potentially important client." He tells you his secretary will set up as many appointments with as many people as possible for the next day. You spend the rest of the afternoon frantically brushing up on the law of insider trading. As you lie in bed that night, you begin to wonder how you should handle the coming interviews.

5. Uncomfortable with large practices and filled with a spirit of adventure, you hang out your shingle solo. For the first year you eke out a living and get lots of experience drawing wills for relatives, handling simple divorces for your former law school classmates, and taking an occasional referral from a friend at a large firm that's been conflicted out of a case. Then come first one, then two, then three personal injury cases. You throw yourself into the work and get pretty good results: no headline-grabbing verdicts but a string of good-sized settlements at the upper end of what more experienced colleagues say they

would expect. Then one day Marge Starkweather limps into the office with a case that you will long remember. She was rather badly injured in a three-car auto collision: medical damages are high, as are lost wages, and the claim is real (no imaginary soft-tissue injuries here). You estimate the special damages, excluding pain and suffering, to be in the neighborhood of $500,000. Even better, both of the other drivers are more than solvent and both turn out to be well-insured, with excess liability policies on top of the standard auto policies. And the case for liability seems strong: intersection photos suggest that one or perhaps both of the prospective defendants ran a red light. So you are not surprised when, shortly after notifying the two insurance carriers of your representation, you get a call from a claims adjuster for one of the drivers, offering to talk about a quick settlement. The insured involved is the driver against whom the evidence of liability is weaker (it's not clear he ran the light) and who, given the circumstances of the accident, is probably responsible for less of the harm to your client. He is, however, the better-insured of the two: his combined excess and basic liability policies amount to $5,000,000 (versus $1,000,000 for the other driver). The adjuster rehearses some doubts about the evidence against his insured but ends by offering an immediate settlement of $50,000. You consult with some more experienced lawyers who tell you that this is a relatively generous amount, given all the circumstances. Your client is prepared to accept it. You draw up a general release, get it signed by your client, and take her the check, less your agreed fee. She is pleased and says this will help with living expenses as you pursue the case against the other driver. Did you make the right call in recommending settlement?

6. The case against the other driver continues. You work with experts on the medical expenses, lost wages, changed earning capacity, and the like, learning more than you ever imagined about actuarial assumptions. Pursuant to local rules, you exchange experts' reports with your opposing counsel and, following that, conduct mutual depositions of the experts. You are pleased with the case as it is developing—not without some soft spots but generally strong. You're therefore pleased, but not surprised, when opposing counsel suggests you get together to talk about "resolving the case." Even better, as you spar a bit, it becomes clear that you and she have reached essentially the same conclusions about the likely outcome—both of you figure a recovery (discounted by the possibility of a defense verdict) of about $700,000. (This figure includes an allowance for some pain and suffering.) That's in line with your earlier guesses. Even better, the defendant is prepared to settle for almost that amount—$600,000. Elated, you telephone Ms. Starkweather. The telephone call ends the elation. Your client absolutely refuses to accept such a settlement: she points out that she has $500,000 in "special" damages, and that a mere $100,000 in pain and suffering is, given her injuries, almost an insult. In vain you point out that litigation is not a science, that juries regularly render defense verdicts even in relatively strong cases, and that even if she recovered a verdict of more than $600,000, it might well come years from now. She flatly refuses the settlement. Worse, she accuses you of abandoning her case and says she has lost faith in you and plans to report you to the state bar. What should you do?

7. You represent the driver and insurance company on the other side of the Starkweather case. After new counsel has been substituted in, the case proceeds

through a bit more discovery. You are not prepared to make a substantially higher settlement offer, and Ms. Starkweather makes clear to her new lawyer that she insists on going to trial. Shortly before trial, however, you begin to become nervous about the possibility of a runaway plaintiff's verdict. Can you reduce this risk?

8. Just before the Starkweather trial, the judge to whom it has been assigned retires from the bench, and a new judge is assigned. Asking around about her reputation, you are disheartened: she was a prominent member of the plaintiffs' bar, best-known for making fire-breathing speeches denouncing insurance companies at bar association meetings. Even worse, at the first pre-trial conference, held just after lunch, the odors of alcohol emanating from the judge seemed to fill the chambers and the garbled questions she asks confirms your worst fears. Stuck in traffic on the way back to your office you wonder (a) how she got appointed to the bench and (b) whether there is any way you can get her off your case.

CHAPTER 1

LAWYERS, CLIENTS, AND CIVIL LITIGATION

INTRODUCTION

Most of us come to law school with a set of things we "know" about law, lawyers, and litigation — only some of which turn out to be true. In substantive courses we learn that some promises we would have thought were enforceable contracts weren't, and that other promises we didn't think were "contracts" (maybe because they weren't in writing) were, in the law's eyes, entirely enforceable. Many of us have a similar set of background beliefs about the legal profession and about litigation. Maybe we "know" that civil litigation is increasing by leaps and bounds. Maybe we "know" that once a tort plaintiff gets her case before a jury, the plaintiff's verdict will be large. Before we came to law school we "knew" that the most important attribute of a law school was its ranking and that lawyers who had graduated earned fabulous sums. Maybe after a few months in law school we "know" that large firms are the only viable forms of practice, although maybe we also "know" that most lawyers in such firms lead miserable lives.

This chapter tries, first, to confront such "knowledge" with data. It looks at the demography of the legal profession — a demography that has changed substantially over the past few decades, as the entry of women and members of minority groups has reshaped the bar. It looks at data about how lawyers feel about their practices and lives and about the challenges they face in balancing the two. It looks at the incidence of litigation: how much there is and what happens to these cases. It looks at the way in which the laws that govern lawyers — ethical rules, malpractice suits, rules of procedure — shape lawyers' behavior in litigation. Lawyers who don't understand this legal framework (or who ignore it) find themselves disbarred, sued by their clients, and sanctioned by courts. To understand contemporary civil litigation, the lawyer needs to understand how her choices are constrained by this legal framework.

Beyond the legal framework, however, all lawyers face a persistent problem that flows from their being lawyers, from their being people who act as fiduciaries and agents for their clients. All agents — plumbers, physicians, accountants, house painters, as well as lawyers — face a problem. They have expert knowledge that a client—their *principal*—has asked them to deploy in ways that will fulfill the client's goals. But these lawyer-agents may have other goals, and behave in ways that fail to serve the client. In the realm of professional ethics, one such failure occurs when the lawyer has other clients, whose aims conflict. And an elaborate set of ethical constraints tell the lawyer she must withdraw from one of those representations—or, in some circumstances, obtain an informed waiver from both clients. But the ethical dilemmas of conflicts and disqualification don't begin to exhaust the ways in which agency problems are part of professional life. Behind much civil litigation in the United States lies insurance, and the insurer-lawyer-client triad creates another agency problem: to whom does the lawyer, paid by the insurer but representing the insured, owe a duty? And how should he behave when information uncovered in the course of representation casts doubt, for example, on whether the insured really is insured? And how should the law guard against an insurer's temptation to conduct the litigation—for which it is paying—in ways that benefit the insurer's long-term interests rather than the immediate interests of the insured? On the other side of the representational "v," the plaintiff's lawyer, perhaps working on a contingent fee, faces a different agency problem: suppose that these lawyers prefer not to strip defendants of all their available assets but to rely instead on insurance coverage; are they thereby failing to serve their clients?

Taken individually, the readings in this chapter explore the incidence and outcome of civil litigation in the United States and a set of rules and practices that constrain and channel lawyers' conduct in that litigation. Taken together, these readings explore what in another setting one might describe as the "ecology" of contemporary civil litigation—what we know about its environment and the opportunities and constraints that environment entails. In the process, we'll be confronting a number of the things most of us thought we "knew" about civil litigation, a number of which turn out *not* to be true. As a byproduct of this survey, students should gain a more accurate picture of the professional world they are about to enter. The goal is to help readers see modern civil litigation with clearer eyes, as well as to help them think about some of the professional challenges they will face as participants in such litigation.

A. LAWYERS: WHO WE ARE, HOW WE MAKE A LIVING

INTRODUCTORY NOTE

The next few readings seem at first glance to betray the promise made in the introduction: they do not appear to be about "how they really do things in practice." Instead, you may feel as if you have wandered by mistake into an undergraduate offering in sociology or demography. But keep reading—and keep thinking: there is a payoff. These readings offer baseline facts from which many of the most fundamental aspects of contemporary practice flow: Where do lawyers practice? How many of us are there? Where do we go for our first jobs? How much do we earn? Are we happy with our careers? Did I make a mistake in choosing my law school? What special challenges might women and minority lawyers face? How many lawsuits are out there anyway? How does the United States compare with other societies—are we wildly litigious (and how would one know how to answer that question?)? What happens to lawyers who mess up? What's with legal malpractice? How do clients find lawyers? How do lawyers find clients? With the answers to these questions, you'll have a set of keys that will unlock puzzles in cases, professional disputes, and maybe even some career choices that lie ahead of you.

1. THE ORGANIZATION AND STRUCTURE OF THE PROFESSION

John Heinz, The Changing Character of Lawyers' Work

32 Law & Society Review 751 (1998)

This article compares findings from two surveys of Chicago lawyers, the first conducted in 1975 and the second in 1995. The earlier study indicated that the Chicago bar was then divided into two broad sectors or "hemispheres," one serving large corporations and similar organizations and the other serving individuals and small businesses. Analyses of the structure of co-practice of the fields of law indicate that the hemispheres are now less distinct. The fields are less tightly connected and less clearly organized—they became more highly specialized during the intervening 20 years and are now organized in smaller clusters. Clear indications of continuing separation of work by client type remain, however. Estimates of the amount of lawyers' time devoted to each field in 1975 and 1995 indicate that corporate practice fields now consume a larger share of Chicago lawyers' attention, while fields such as probate receive a declining percentage. Growth is most pronounced in the litigation fields, especially in business litigation. The organizational contexts within which law is practiced both reflect and contribute to these changes. The scale of those organizations has increased greatly, and the allocation of work within them has been divided along substantive, doctrinal lines. As a result, there is a greater disaggregation of work and work-groups within the profession today.

A Hypothesis that the urban bar is essentially divided into two distinct sectors or areas of practice was propounded in *Chicago Lawyers: The Social Structure of the Bar* (Heinz & Laumann 1982):

> [W]e have advanced the thesis that much of the differentiation within the legal profession is secondary to one fundamental distinction—the distinction between lawyers who represent large organizations (corporations, labor unions, or government) and those who represent individuals. The two kinds of law practice are the two hemispheres of the profession. Most lawyers reside exclusively in one hemisphere or the other and seldom, if ever, cross the equator. (P. 319)

The two sectors of the legal profession thus include different lawyers, with different social origins, who were trained at different law schools, serve different sorts of clients, practice in different office environments, are differentially likely to engage in litigation, litigate (when and if they litigate) in different forums, have somewhat different values, associate with different circles of acquaintances, and rest their claims to professionalism on different sorts of social power. . . . Only in the most formal of senses, then, do the two types of lawyers constitute one profession. (P. 384)

Following the publication of *Chicago Lawyers*, the two-hemispheres hypothesis became a frequent point of reference in the scholarly literature, but the survey on which that book was based was conducted in 1975. There have since been important changes in the legal profession — women entered the bar in large numbers (Hagan & Kay 1995), the overall size of the profession almost doubled while the size of the organizations within which law is practiced grew even more rapidly (Galanter & Palay 1991; Sander & Williams 1992), the management practices of those organizations became more formal and intrusive (Abel 1989:199-202), and there were substantial changes in the level of demand for particular types of legal services, some increasing while others declined. Many of these changes may well have affected the organization of lawyers' work and thus have altered the degree of separation (or lack thereof) of the two hemispheres of law practice.

The purpose of this article is to compare the Chicago findings from 1975 with more recent data concerning patterns of co-practice among the fields of law and the extent of specialization by field in order to determine whether the distribution of lawyers' work has changed — that is, whether there is a clear separation between two broad sectors of practice, one serving large organizations and the other serving individuals and small businesses.

[Heinz and Lauman in 1975 found that lawyers who attended "national" law schools tended to be children of well-educated parents and to spend their professional careers representing entities (often business entities) and working in associations that contained a number of lawyers (often firms). By contrast, lawyers who attended local or regional law schools tended to come from blue collar families and to spend their professional careers representing individuals, usually working alone.]

* * *

1995 Patterns of Co-Practice

. . . . In these 1995 data, however, it appears that the organization of work is subdivided into smaller, more highly specialized clusters that are less clearly separated by the broad distinction between corporate and personal client types. . . .

It appears that substantive or skill-type specialization plays a greater role in this structure than was the case in the 1975 analyses. . . .

In general, the 1995 data concerning organization of work appear to be less orderly than was the case in 1975. This might be attributable to a higher degree of specialization in 1995. In such a situation, there would be less overlap among the fields, the clustering analyses would be working with less variance, and this might create instability — essentially random events would have greater impact on the results. Thus, we turn next to an analysis of specialization.

Specialization by Field

Table 1. Rank Order of Fields by Specialization Index (SI), 1975 and 1995[a]

	1975		1995	
	Rank	Mean SI	Rank	Mean SI
Criminal (prosecution)	1	.785	1	.859
Patents & trademarks	2	.664	2	.717
Labor (unions)	3	.650	14	.560
Public utilities & administrative	4	.621	23	.499
Environmental (plaintiffs)	5	.591	11	.580
Business tax	6	.586	4	.681
Business real estate	7	.561	12	.575
Labor (management)	8	.559	5	.628
Business litigation	9	.559	6	.625
Personal injury (defendants)	10	.546	3	.694
Municipal	11	.543	10	.601
Criminal (defense)	12	.536	8	.612
General corporate	13	.485	21	.511
Securities	14	.482	15	.559
Civil rights	15	.480	24	.491
Antitrust (plaintiffs)	16	.478	9	.605
Probate	17	.469	27	.469
Personal injury (plaintiffs)	18	.460	7	.622
Banking	19	.455	18	.533
Personal tax	20	.454	20	.524
Antitrust (defense)	21	.447	25	.486
General litigation	22	.445	16	.550
Personal real estate	23	.443	22	.502
Divorce	24	.443	26	470
Family	25	.436	19	.532
Environmental (defendants)	26	.426	13	.572
Commercial (including consumer)	27	.417	17	.543

[a]Rank order correlation: Pearson's $R = .57$ ($p < .01$).

In 1975, of 687 practicing lawyers responding, 22.7% worked in only one field. In 1995, in spite of the fact that respondents were presented with a longer, more detailed list of fields (42 field categories were used in 1995 vs. 30 in 1975), 32.6% of 675 practicing lawyers indicated that they worked in only one field. Thus, specialization appears to have increased substantially over the 20 years. . . . The fields that increase most markedly are personal injury plaintiffs work, which moves from 18th in the rank order to 7th place; environmental work for defendants, which moves from 26th to 13th; and commercial, which moves from last place to 17th. In sum, specialization increased both substantially and quite generally over the 20-year period. Note, also, that the corporate fields are not necessarily the most specialized — for example, banking and antitrust defense have a relatively low degree of special-ization at both times, and general corporate is in 13th place in 1975 and 21st in 1995. But family law and divorce — both of which are personal client fields — are also consistently near the bottom of the list. . . .

Client Differentiation by Field

Table 2. Percentage of Business Clients by Field of Practice, 1995 (Fields with 10 or More Lawyers at 25% or More Time)

	Mean %
High group:	
Environmental defense	91
Banking	87
Commercial (including business bankruptcies)	86
Patents, trademarks & copyright	84
Securities	83
Insurance	81
Civil litigation (corporate clients)	81
General corporate	80
Personal injury defense	79
Business real estate	75
Corporate tax	72
Public utilities & administrative	68
Employment (management)	67
Middle group	
Personal tax	58
Environmental plaintiffs	53
Municipal	45
Residential real estate	45
Civil litigation (personal clients)	45
Probate	43
Civil rights	37
Low group	
Divorce	23
Employment (unions)	22
General family practice	21
Personal injury plaintiffs	15
Criminal defense	8
Criminal prosecution	5

[T]he degree of client differentiation among the fields is quite striking. Table 2 presents the mean percentages of business clients by field. Note that, as one would expect, fields dealing with the personal problems of individuals ("personal plight" fields) tend to be the quintessential personal client fields. This is especially true when the field often represents poor people or persons of moderate means, as in criminal defense and personal injury plaintiffs work. When the clients are more likely to have some money — as, for example, in probate or residential real estate — there is a greater likelihood that the practitioner may represent businesses as well. At the other extreme of the distribution, we find fields that are likely to represent the largest corporations — environmental defense, banking, and patents and trademarks.

But note that some fields of practice serve a more varied mix of clientele. Thus, on the average, 45% of the clients served by lawyers who do municipal law work are businesses, while those same lawyers also do a considerable amount of work for local government. Note that 58% of the clients of respondents who do personal tax work are businesses and that 72% of the clients of those who do corporate tax are businesses. The lawyer who prepares the corporate tax returns for the Smedley Corporation may do the returns of Mr. and Mrs. Smedley as well. As indicated in Table 2, instead of "two hemispheres," we see three broad clusters of fields. Six fields are practiced by lawyers who serve relatively few businesses, while respondents in a larger group of fields (half of the 26) report that two-thirds or more of their clients are businesses, and the remainder of the fields serve a more varied mix of clientele. Thus, the distribution of client types among the fields in 1995 does not show a clear separation between "two hemispheres" of practice. Rather, a middle group of fields appears to bridge the extremes. In a similar analysis of the 1975 data, we find a greater tendency for the fields to divide into two broad clusters, separated by client type.

Allocation of Time in 1975 and 1995

. . . [A]s the number of lawyers doubled, the total amount of time devoted to almost all of these fields has increased — to varying degrees. The only fields on the list in which the amount of lawyers' effort actually decreases, in absolute terms, are probate and public utilities (which were also among the fields that moved down markedly in the specialization rank order). The biggest increases are seen in the litigation fields. Business litigation shows by far the largest increase, but the increase in general litigation is also substantial. In percentage terms, we see decreases in general corporate work (from 11% to 6%) and in divorce (from 6% to 3%). As to the former, corporate work has apparently become more specialized, so that it is less often assigned to the general, undifferentiated category and more often to particular specialties — such as environmental work. The decrease in the percentage of divorce work probably reflects the fact that the rate of increase in business activity has been far greater than that of the Chicago-area population.

Overall, the corporate client fields have grown much more rapidly than the personal client fields, and the "hemispheres" are now even more unequal in size. In the 1975 data, the estimate is that 53% of lawyers' time was allocated to the corporate fields (including work for non-business organizations such as unions and governmental entities), while 40% was devoted to the personal client fields and another 7% was not clearly assignable or was spread across a variety of small fields. By 1995, the disparity between the two sectors had increased considerably. As we can see in Table 3, the corporate sector consumed more than twice the amount of Chicago lawyers' time devoted to personal and small business client work in 1995 (64% vs. 29%). The "large corporate" cluster of fields increased most — from 18% of the total in 1975 to 32% in 1995 — while the "personal business" and "personal plight" clusters both declined.

Changes in Practice Organizations

The growth of the corporate sector of practice and the decline in the percentage of personal and small business legal work has been paralleled by a corresponding realignment of the organizational contexts within which law is practiced. In the 1975 survey, 23% of the respondents were in private law firms with 2 to 10 lawyers; in 1995, only 14% worked in firms of that size. At the same time, the percentage of lawyers working in firms with more than 30 lawyers nearly doubled — from 15.7% in 1975 to 29.3% in 1995. The average number of lawyers in the private law firms represented in the 1975 sample was 27; by 1995, the average number per firm had grown to 141.24 The largest private law firm in our 1995 sample employed 1,800 lawyers.

The percentage of lawyers practicing alone has been declining for as long as data are available. The national Lawyer Statistical Report found that in 1960 solo practitioners constituted 64% of all lawyers, but by 1991 the proportion of the nation's lawyers in solo practice had decreased to 45% (Curran & Carson 1994:7). In large cities, that percentage is smaller. In the 1975 Chicago survey, 19% of the respondents practiced alone, and by 1995 only 13% did. Thus, more lawyers are now in partnership with other lawyers and the size of those partnerships has increased very substantially.

Even in the personal and small business sector of practice, legal work is increasingly concentrated in larger organizations. Some routine, high-volume matters — such as divorce, simple wills, and consumer bankruptcies — are now handled by franchise legal service companies and group legal service plans such as Jacoby & Meyers and Hyatt Legal Plans, which employ lawyers at relatively low wages (Van Hoy 1997; Seron 1996). We should not overstate the case, however. Although the *percentage* of solo practitioners within the Chicago bar declined from 1975 to 1995, given the doubling in the size of the lawyer population our estimate is that the *number of solos* increased substantially.

Other organizational contexts in which lawyers work have had similar patterns of growth. The average size of "house counsel" offices (i.e., lawyers employed within corporations and other private organizations) in the 1975 sample was 17, while by 1995 the average number of lawyers in each such office had grown to 55. Government law offices averaged 64 lawyers each in 1975, but the average increased to 399 in 1995. The office of the State's Attorney for Cook County (Chicago and some suburbs) employed 850 lawyers in 1995.

As the organizations grow, they are more likely to adopt a clear division of labor, so that they become organized along lines of formal rationality rather than in traditional hierarchies. In the older, smaller firm model, a relatively small number of powerful senior partners presided over their own hierarchies within the firm (Nelson 1988). These workgroups, consisting of associates and junior partners working under the supervision of one or more seniors, typically served the needs of a particular, limited group of clients. The law firm's relationships with these clients were tended and nurtured by the seniors, and the workgroup often dealt with the full range of the clients' problems — commercial transactions, antitrust, securities regulation, real estate acquisition, and so on. In the newer, larger firm model, specialized departments replace the personal hierarchies. Instead of being built around dominant seniors, these departments are defined by substantive expertise or skill types — for example, tax, litigation, real estate, mergers and acquisitions. Typically, the allocation of work in each department is managed by a chairman, assisted by a second level of supervisors.

Specialization of work changes the lines of communication within the profession — some lines are severed, some are reconstituted. If each lawyer deals with a broad range of doctrinal legal categories, then the set of lawyers brought together to handle a problem is likely to be determined by availability and by client affinities, and thus the set will change from case to case. But if work is organized by departments that are defined by doctrine or skill type, lawyers will spend most of their time talking with fellow specialists. Thus, when "general corporate work" evolves into securities, antitrust, corporate tax, and intellectual property, this results in a decoupling of fields of law (and sets of practitioners) that were formerly brought together by their work. The increase in the scale of the profession — both in the organizational units and in the size of the overall bar — has a similar effect. That is, as the numbers grow, the probability of chance transactions between any given pair or any given sets of lawyers decreases. Since individual lawyers' circles of acquaintance are unlikely to expand at the same rate or to the same extent as the growth of the bar, there will be an increasing number of their fellow lawyers with whom they have no ties. Thus, communication among Chicago lawyers is likely to be restricted to more narrow slices of the whole. The bar, therefore, becomes more diverse and less well integrated.

The changes in the organizations where law is practiced are closely analogous to the restructuring of medical service organizations (Starr 1982). Management has become so central in medicine that the product is referred to as "managed care." What were formerly "doctors' offices" are now "health care delivery systems." In part, this is attributable to the contagion of jargon, but another part of it is a real change. Many not-for-profit hospitals have been taken over by profit making hospital corporations, such as Humana and Columbia/HCA, and doctors are now marshaled by HMOs instead of practicing alone or in small partnerships. In the legal profession, the consolidation of services does not appear to have progressed quite as far as it has in medicine, but the bureaucratization of the bar has advanced sufficiently that the trend is clear and the effects are felt by most lawyers.

Conclusion

The separation of American lawyers into functional categories has a long history. Early in this century, a report sponsored by the Carnegie Foundation recommended the creation of an "inner bar" that would handle complex business transactions and would be separate from the "general body of practi-tioners" handling smaller cases and personal problems. The two sorts of law-yers were to be trained in different schools, with different curricula. The report was not favorably received, but a similar division of practice evolved, de facto, although the educational channels are still not as distinct as had been con-templated. Lawyers who handle the divorces and automobile accidents of a neighborhood clientele might also draft wills and close the sales of homes, but they are unlikely to work on mergers of large companies or to deal with the tax problems of major real estate developers. Moreover, the specialization of practice tends to create boundaries for professional relationships among lawyers. The kinds of work that lawyers do, the style of their work, and the places in which they do it differ greatly.

But the bar has changed greatly since the 1970s. One of the most important of the changes, surely, is the sheer growth. The number of lawyers in the United States increased from about 355,200 in 1970, one for every 572 persons in the population, to about 805,900 in 1991, one per 313 persons. In Cook County, the number of resident lawyers increased from 19,072 in 1976 to 35,704 in 1994, an increase of 87%, while the county's population decreased modestly. The population of the greater Chicago metropolitan area, however, grew by 7.8% from 1975 to 1995, and thus the demand for divorces, wills, personal injury settlements, residential real estate closings, and other personal legal services presumably grew at a similar rate. But the demand for corporate law services increased far more during the two decades than did demand for lawyers' services to individuals and small businesses. Overall, expenditures on legal services in the United States increased by 309% between 1972 and 1992. This rate of increase was twice that of the gross national product during the same period and even exceeded the percentage increase in spending for health services.

A large share of the new lawyers are women. Historically, the American bar—like medicine and other elite professions—included few women. In the 1975 survey of Chicago lawyers, the random sample was composed of 30 women and 747 men. Though women had started to enter law schools in substantial numbers in the early 1970s, not many had yet entered practice by 1975. The picture is much different today. The official count of Illinois lawyers does not include an enumeration by gender at the city or county level, but women amounted to 26% of the statewide total in 1995. Nationally, in 1970 only 2.8% of the nation's lawyers were women, and this percentage had remained steady since the mid-1950s. By 1991, the percentage of women had burgeoned to 20%—but it was still far from the percentage among law school graduates, which was over 40%.

Thus, the face of the bar has changed. Gender and racial diversity within the bar, rare before, is now seen in many contexts within the profession, but the mix differs with the context. Women and minorities are disproportion-ately concentrated in certain types of practice, and these readily perceived differences accentuate lines of demarcation.

Although demand for legal services to corporations and other large orga-nizations has grown far more rapidly than demand for services to individuals and small businesses, entry into the market is easier in the latter types of practice. That is, any lawyer can hang up a shingle and seek clients in auto accident or refrigerator repossession cases, but it is difficult for lawyers to obtain access to the venues where corporate legal services are delivered. Therefore, since demand was expanding in the types of practice where entry is difficult but growing only much more slowly in the areas where entry is easy, lawyers in the former tended to prosper while those in the latter languished. Sander and Williams (1989:449-51) estimate that from 1972 to 1982 the real incomes of lawyers in solo practice decreased by 46%. Thus, the increasing gap between rich and much less rich within the bar has also accentuated the differences among the types of practice.

There are, then, several reasons to suppose that Chicago lawyers might be less cohesive in the 1990s than they were in the 1970s, and urban lawyers may now have become subdivided into smaller clusters. But the division between the two classes of clients — between large organizations, on the one hand, and individuals and small businesses, on the other — endures. Note that this distinction, unlike wealth, for example, is conceived of as a dichotomy. If the difference were between lawyers representing more wealthy and less wealthy clients, then the clients (and, presumably, their lawyers) could be arrayed along a continuous scale. Of course, size of client is also a matter of degree, but the distinction between organizations and individuals (and the small businesses owned by individuals) is a matter of both form and substance. One might argue that small corporations, even publicly held ones, are more akin to partnerships than they are to large corporations, but the difference in form has important legal content, and it alters the nature of the lawyers' work and the relationship between lawyer and client. Because corporations are owned by shareholders, their lawyers' relationships with management are more difficult and ethically complex than are lawyers' relationships with owner-operators. Corporations pay corporate tax, and the rules and procedures differ from those that apply to the taxation of individuals. Corporations also issue securities, and they are subject to a multiplicity of reporting requirements at the federal, state, and local levels. Other large organizations — governmental institutions, labor unions, trade associations, professional organizations — are also subject to special rules and reporting requirements, and the character of lawyers' relationships with these clients is more like their relationships with corporations than like those with individual clients.

Lawyers employed by large law firms do, of course, handle legal work for individuals — often for the individuals who are officers of their corporate clients. Some large law firms have probate departments, many handle individual income tax problems for favored clients, and a few will even work on clients' divorces. To the extent that this occurs, the corporate and the personal client sectors of the bar are drawn closer. But there is a division of labor within these law firms, and the lawyers who do the corporate work may not be the same ones who handle personal matters. If lawyers' work has become increasingly specialized — if lawyers who do securities work are now less likely to do probate or commercial law as well — this will tend to separate the two sectors of the bar. Fewer lawyers will cross the boundary.

Is the legal profession still divided into hemispheres? Well, "hemi" means "half," and it is now hard to argue that the two parts are of approximately equal size, at least in Chicago (and probably in other large cities). Work for corporate clients is a much larger part of the profession than is work for individuals or small businesses. The amount of Chicago lawyers' time devoted to corporate fields and to fields serving other large organizations is more than twice that devoted to personal client fields. But the relative size of the two parts is probably not a very important part of the thesis — this will vary with the size and character of the jurisdiction in any event — and we have not assessed in this article the degree of socioeconomic, ethno-religious, educational, and political separation of practitioners in the two sectors. Within each of the broad parts, the fields are now more distinct, more clearly separated than they were 20 years ago. In this respect, there is greater disaggregation of work and workgroups within the profession today. On the other hand, the increase in scale of law firms and other practice organizations may mean that the specialties are to some extent reintegrated within overarching structures. The departmentalization of the firms, however, appears to result in workgroups that are more narrowly defined than was previously the case. Our finding that specialization has increased markedly in most fields, especially in the corporate sector, suggests this. We think it unlikely that the present organizational structures provide enough interchange among the specialties to produce a bar that functions as a community of shared fate and common purpose.

CLARA N. CARSON, THE LAWYER STATISTICAL REPORT: THE U.S. LEGAL
PROFESSION IN 2000 (EXCERPTED)

American Bar Foundation 2004

Total number of Lawyers in the U.S.: 1,066,328 with 73% (or 778,268) being male.

The median age: 45 years.

In 1951, the number of lawyers was 221,605 and the population/lawyer ratio was 695/1. In 2000, there were 1,066,328 with a ratio of 264/1.

Top 10 states ranked by Lawyer Population (2000):

1. New York (142,487)
2. California (133,846)
3. Texas (67,642)
4. Florida (60,008)
5. Illinois (53,209)
6. District of Columbia (50,914)
7. Massachusetts (43,396)
8. Ohio (42,727)
9. Pennsylvania (41,811)
10. New Jersey (36,474)

Top 10 states ranked by Population/Lawyer Ratio (2000):

1. District of Columbia (11/1)
2. New York (133/1)

3. Massachusetts (146/1)
4. Connecticut (191/1)
5. New Jersey (231/1)
6. Illinois (233/1)
7. Alaska (237/1)
8. Colorado (245/1)
9. California (253/1)
10. Hawaii (257/1)

Employment for lawyers is expected to grow 11% between 2006 and 2016, about the average for all occupations for that time period.

In 2006, the median annual earnings for all wage and salaried lawyers was $102,471. The middle half of the occupation earned between $69,910 and $145,600.

Earnings in particular industries:

Management of companies and enterprises: $128,610
Federal Government: $119,240
Legal Services: $108,100
Local Government: $78,810
State Government: $75,840.

Median salary 9 months after graduation:

Of all graduates: $60,000
Private Practice: $85,000
Business: $60,000
Government: $46,158
Academic/Judicial Clerkships: $45,000

STATE BAR OF CALIFORNIA, 2006 MEMBERSHIP SURVEY

Available online at http://calbar.ca.gov/calbar/pdfs/reports/
2006_State-Bar-Survey.pdf

[The state bar periodically hires a firm to survey its members on a variety of issues; the data below is based on such a survey of about a thousand randomly selected members; the polling firm asserts that the data should be accurate within a +/−3% range.]

Among the findings of the survey are:

- In general, the demographic makeup of the State Bar continues to diversify, though not uniformly across all lines.
- There is now a greater percentage of female and LGBT (Lesbian, Gay, Bisexual, Transgender) members than there was five years ago. Females make up nearly half of the attorneys 35 and younger and have also made some gains in income and partnership.
- There are now more members at each end of the economic spectrum with increases in those making under $50,000 and those making over $300,000 from their law practice compared with five years ago.

CA Lawyers by Practice Type

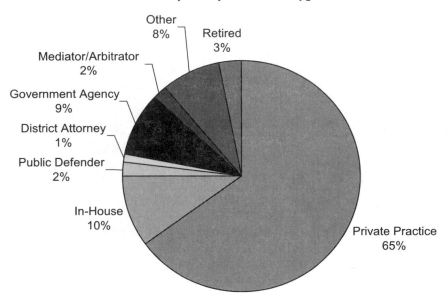

Other
8%

Retired
3%

Mediator/Arbitrator
2%

Government Agency
9%

District Attorney
1%

Public Defender
2%

In-House
10%

Private Practice
65%

CA Lawyers by Practice Group Size

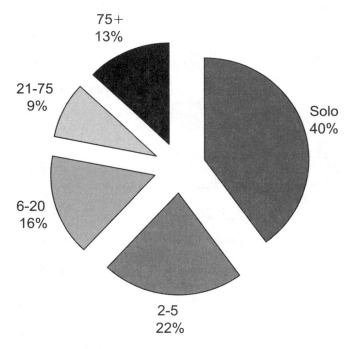

75+
13%

21-75
9%

6-20
16%

Solo
40%

2-5
22%

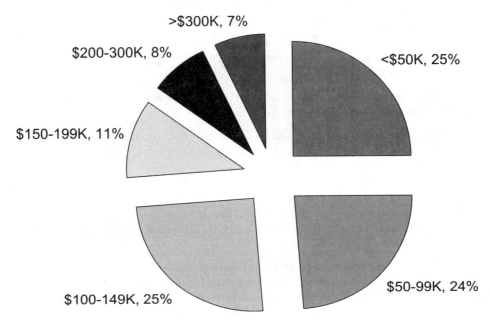

Income from Practice — 2006

>$300K, 7%

$200-300K, 8%

<$50K, 25%

$150-199K, 11%

$100-149K, 25%

$50-99K, 24%

NOTE ON LEGAL DEMOGRAPHY

Consider how the readings you have encountered so far relate to each other:

1. Explain how Heinz's study of Chicago lawyers makes sense of the fact that the District of Columbia has more lawyers per capita than any other jurisdiction.

2. Consider California's lawyers, as discussed in the state bar's survey. About two-thirds of them report that they are in private practice, and 40 percent of those report that they are in solo practices.

> a. California is a populous state, most of whose people live in three major metro centers. Do its lawyer statistics suggest that Heinz's generalizations may be valid nationally (although, of course, as a careful sociologist, he would warn us not to generalize from a specific study)?
>
> b. The solo practice percentage for California, after dropping for several years to the low 30s, ticked up in the most recent survey, running counter to the trend Heinz and others have been observing for several years. Anecdotal evidence suggests that some lawyers have found that emerging technology — online access to legal libraries, ease of producing complex documents by modifying digitally available forms, and the like — have made it possible for some lawyers to

practice this way. It's not clear whether this will be a national trend or just a momentary blip in the decades-long decline in solo practice as a viable option.

   c. *If* Heinz's and others' data about solo practice incomes holds true for California, where in the income distribution would you expect solo practitioners to fall?

3. The next selection looks at a single-year snapshot of the placement statistics for a single U.S. law school.

   a. Again, consider how its data fits with that on the Chicago lawyers. Where does the Heinz taxonomy of Hemisphere I/Hemisphere II law schools put this school?

   b. Is that taxonomy consistent with the fact that most of UCLA's students entered private practice?

   c. Is that taxonomy consistent with the fact that more than two-thirds of this school's recent graduates entered practice in private firms with more than 100 lawyers?

4. The reading following the UCLA data suggests that many applicants to U.S. law schools have intuitively grasped the Hemisphere I/Hemisphere II division of law schools — even when it may not apply to their own situations and ambitions. How might one present this information to prospective law students?

UCLA Law Graduates, Class of 2007: A Comparison Cohort

UCLA Office of Career Services, available online at http://www.law.ucla.edu/home/index.asp?page=1307

2007 Employment Categories

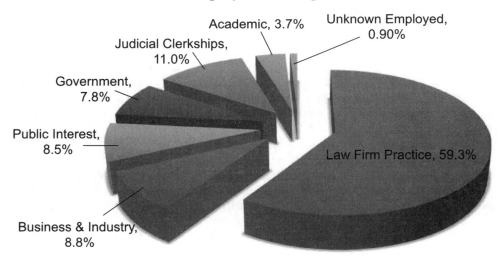

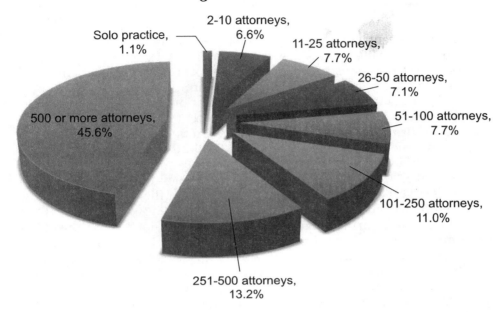

2007 Categories in Private Practice

Category	Salary Range	Salary Median
TOTAL PRIVATE SECTOR	**$50,000-$145,000**	**$130,000**
Self-employed	N/A	N/A
2-10 Attorneys	$60,000-$140,000	$ 78,000
11-25 Attorneys	$50,000-$160,000	$ 80,000
26-50 Attorneys	$50,000-$135,000	$ 85,000
51-100 Attorneys	$70,000-$160,000	$135,000
101-250 Attorneys	$95,000-$160,000	$145,000
251-500 Attorneys	$88,000-$160,000	$160,000
501 or more Attorneys	$90,000-$160,000	$160,000

Category	Salary Range	Salary Median
TOTAL GOVERNMENT SECTOR	**$43,000-$72,421**	N/A
Judicial Clerkship	$43,000-$65,748	$58,262
Military	N/A	N/A
Other Government	$45,000-$72,421	$59,142

Category	Salary Range	Salary Median
TOTAL BUSINESS SECTOR	**$66,000-$170,000**	**$110,000**

Category	Salary Range	Salary Median
TOTAL PUBLIC SECTOR	**$34,800-$78,000**	**$51,245**

Leigh Jones, Top Law Schools Tighten Their Hold on NLJ 250 Firms

National Law Journal, April 14, 2008

A bigger percentage of students graduating from top law schools in 2007 took jobs at NLJ 250 law firms than those graduating in 2006.

Columbia Law School landed in the No. 1 spot again as the school that sent the greatest portion of graduates to NLJ 250 law firms, with nearly 75 percent of its students in 2007 taking jobs among the nation's largest law firms. The school ranked No. 1 last year, when 69.6 percent of its graduates went to NLJ 250 law firms. Boston College Law School rounded at the list of the top 20 go-to law schools, with 36.8 percent of its 261 juris doctor graduates in 2007 heading for full-time jobs at NLJ 250 law firms.

All together, the top 20 law schools that NLJ 250 law firms relied on most to fill their first-year associate ranks sent 54.9 percent of their graduates to those firms, compared with 51.6 percent in 2006. . . .

Making a big jump in its percentage of graduates accepting positions at NLJ 250 firms was Northwestern University School of Law. It took the No. 2 spot, compared with No. 11 the year before. Some 73.5 percent of its 2007 graduates went to NLJ 250 firms, or 172 graduates out of a total of 234. The year before, 143 graduates out of 265 went to NLJ 250 firms, which equaled 54 percent.

"We've made a tremendous effort to reach out to employers," said David Van Zandt, Northwestern's dean. The school has also focused on enrolling students with significant postgraduate work experience, which makes them attractive to law firm recruiters, he said. And the school has worked to accept students in recent years from geographically diverse areas, with an emphasis on those from the Northeast, which has helped to boost recruiting from NLJ 250 firms, he said.

Another school with a big increase was University of Southern California Gould School of Law, which jumped from the No. 20 spot to No. 14 this year. Of its 195 J.D. graduates in 2007, 85 of them, or 43.6 percent, took jobs with NLJ 250 firms. Of its 215 J.D. graduates in 2006, 36.3 percent began working full time for NLJ 250 law firms.

Two schools dropped four spots compared with the ranking for 2006 graduates. Stanford Law School had 51.4 percent of its 2007 graduates go to NLJ 250 law firms, compared with 54.9 percent of its 2006 graduates. The school dipped to the No. 12 spot, from No. 8 the year before. Boston College Law School, ranked No. 20, sent 36.8 percent of its 2007 graduates to NLJ 250 firms, compared with 39.1 percent the year before. It was ranked No. 16 last year.

New to the List

Two law schools were new to this year's top 20 list, driving two schools off the list. Earning a spot was the University of California at Los Angeles School of Law, which ranked No. 17. NLJ 250 law firms hired 39.1 percent of its 320 graduates in 2007. Michael Schill, the UCLA law school dean, also attributed his school's popularity among NLJ 250 firms to an increased effort to geographically diversify the student body. "We're being more aggressive," Schill said. In addition, Boston University School of Law, ranked No. 18, was new to the list. It sent 113 of its 291 graduates in 2007 to NLJ 250 firms.

Dropping from the list of top 20 schools was University of Texas School of Law, ranked No. 19 last year. . . .

Law firms ranked the highest on the NLJ 250 consistently recruited from the top 20 go-to law schools. . . .

WILLIAM HENDERSON & ANDREW MORRISS, WHAT LAW SCHOOL RANKINGS DON'T SAY ABOUT COSTLY CHOICES

National Law Journal, April 16, 2008

Deciding where to go to law school is a difficult decision for many applicants. Law school is expensive and becoming more so each year, making the choice of where to go often the biggest investment decision an applicant has made in his or her life. Yet many prospective law students lack knowledge about the entry-level legal market or even what different types of lawyers do in their daily lives.

Despite its many flaws, the annual *U.S. News & World Report* law school ranking is cheap and easy to use, making it an important source of information for prospective students weighing their options. Unfortunately, the utility of these rankings is often distorted by an Internet-based echo chamber, where anonymous posters brag about their admissions to elite schools and job prospects at big firms.

To further complicate students' decisions, many law schools are engaged in vigorous competition to lure students who will boost the schools' status in key *U.S. News* metrics, such as median LSAT score or selectivity. All too often, the results are expensive, bad decisions about law school.

Based upon our combined 21 years of experience as legal educators and our empirical study of rankings, we think students rely on law school rankings as a rough guide to their future employment prospects. Yet the *U.S. News* rankings would be far less influential, and produce fewer bad choices, if students had better sources of information. Providing prospective law students with better information is the purpose of this special guide.

During the last three decades, the size and geographic dispersion of the global economy has dramatically increased the demand for sophisticated corporate legal services. In contrast, the demand for personal-services legal work—wills and estates, personal injury, family law, simple business contracts, etc.—has grown at roughly the rate of population growth.

These dynamics have resulted in a "bimodal" income distribution, in which there is a heavy concentration of salaries in two distinct ranges, based on salary figures provided by NALP. At the high end are the large corporate firm starting salaries that so interest the media. In 2006, salaries in the largest firms in major markets jumped from $125,000 to $135,000 to $145,000. Thus out of 22,684 starting salaries reported for 2006, 4,809, or 21.2 percent, were in the $125,000 to $145,000 range. (In 2007, this mode moved further to the right due to associate "salary wars.") Yet prospective lawyers need to remember that most new lawyers do not earn $160,000 a year at a large firm. Many earn $40,000 to $55,000 per year in small to midsize firms and solo practice. In 2006, 8,577 reported salaries, or 37.8 percent, were in this range out of the 22,684. The payments on $100,000-plus worth of law school debt look quite different to someone earning $50,000 than they do to someone earning $160,000 a year.

Why are large firm salaries rising so dramatically? In large part, it is due to the post–World War II spread of the "Cravath system" of law firm organization (originally designed by New York–based Cravath, Swaine & Moore). Under this model, the best students are recruited from the best schools and (in theory) provided with the best training to attract the best clients. After an eight- to 10-year apprenticeship period — some call it a "tournament" — the best associates are promoted to partner, and the others depart for less elite firms or take a job with corporate legal departments.

As the amount of corporate legal work has grown, the large elite law firms have bid up the starting salaries of entry-level associates in an effort to recruit a sufficient number of students with top grade point averages (GPAs) from the elite law schools. Because demand for these top graduates has far outstripped supply, the hunt for the best students has, gradually, encompassed a much broader array of law schools. But outside of a small number of national law schools (we put this number at fewer than 20), only the highest-ranked students at a broad swath of regional law schools can hope for access to these high-paying jobs.

This dynamic is summarized by considering the percentage of graduates from the classes of 2005, 2006 and 2007 who took jobs among the nation's 250 largest law firms, as ranked by the *National Law Journal* (the NLJ 250). Although the proportion of NLJ 250 jobs correlates strongly with *U.S. News* rank, the probability of a large-firm job drops off very quickly. Big increases in hiring in 2006 and 2007 reveal the importance of pedigree for many of the largest firms. With demand for elite graduates outstripping supply, many chose to recruit deeper into the classes at elite law schools.

For the vast majority of students who are not admitted to top-tier national law schools, these figures lead to a simple conclusion: Slavishly following the *U.S. News* rankings will not significantly increase one's large-firm job prospects. And the excess debt that students incur is likely to undermine their career options.

Drawing upon our research and detailed data made available by the NLJ, ALM Research and the 2008 American Bar Association–Law School Admission Council "Official Guide to ABA-Approved Law Schools," we offer some additional information to help prospective students decide whether to enroll (or not) in law school, and where.

Debt and High-Paying Jobs

For most prospective law students, the most important question is whether law school is worth $100,000 in debt plus three years of lost earnings. In purely financial terms, elite law schools offer a high degree of certainty: Although corporate law is not everyone's preferred calling, the $160,000 per year salary plus bonus provides ample earning power to pay off student loans quickly. For many students at elite schools, the lure of money, prestige and power is overwhelming.

Yet, even among highly ranked law schools, large-firm jobs are available to a relative small proportion of students. The full chart of employment trends for law school graduates summarizes the most recent employment outcomes data for ABA-accredited law schools. This information is taken from the class of 2005 nine months after graduation, the most recent class for which such information is available. Drawing upon additional data supplied by ALM Research and the NLJ, we ordered the chart based on the top 100 law schools for NLJ 250 employment. ("Other firms" was calculated by subtracting the school's number of NLJ 250 jobs from the total count for "employed in law firms." "Graduate school" means "pursuing graduate degrees," and "Academia" means "employed in academia.")

Although the ordering of top NLJ 250 feeder schools is strongly correlated with *U.S. News* rankings, movement within the top of the hierarchy provides a much larger employment payoff than an equivalent change does for a school ranked in the middle or the bottom.

For example, between schools No. 25 (William & Mary) and No. 5 (Columbia), NLJ 250 employment rose from 21.9 percent to 54.5 percent, an increase of 32.6 percentage points. This change actually understates the employment payoffs because highly ranked schools also send a larger proportion of their graduates to federal judicial clerkships. In turn, at the end of the clerkships, large firms often pay hiring bonuses to these graduates. Conversely, between schools No. 45 (Brigham Young) and No. 25, the increase in large-firm employment was only 8.4 percentage points, with fewer judicial clerkships. And between No. 65 (Louisville) and No. 45, the increase in large-firm employment is a mere 4.3 percentage points.

Below school No. 26 (Emory), a graduate has a less than one in five probability of starting his or her career at a large law firm. If 80 percent of law school applicants are convinced that they will make that 20 percent cutoff, three out of four are destined to be disappointed. With these numbers, does it really make economic sense to go to the highest-ranked school one can get into? In many cases, the answer is no.

DEBT, EMPLOYMENT, GRANTS, TRANSFERS

School attribute	Top 14	Tier 1	Tier 2	Tier 3	Tier 4
Average debt of graduate, 2006	$98,746	$72,254	$77,119	$73,207	$79,545
Students with debt	82%	83%	84%	87%	85%
Students with NLJ 250 jobs	49%	19%	7%	3%	1%
Employed within state	35%	58%	77%	70%	73%
Receiving full tuition grant aid	2%	4%	4%	6%	4%
Receiving half-to-full grant aid	12%	12%	12%	14%	11%
Total receiving grants	45%	52%	43%	44%	39%
Net Transfers (Average per school)	+34	+9	+5	-5	-28

Sources: ABA-LSAC Official Guide; U.S. News & World Report, March 2008; ALM Research

An equally important question is whether to go to law school at all. A ranking of 50 law schools by the percentage of students who either flunked out or are unemployed or unaccounted for nine months after graduation includes many schools in tiers two, three and four of the 2007 *U.S. News* rankings. Thus law school does not guarantee lucrative, or even gainful, employment. Moreover, over-reliance on the *U.S. News* rankings can be damaging to a law student's financial health.

How Law Schools Price Tuition

Law schools obsess about rankings as much or more than do prospective students. In terms of admissions, the conventional law school playbook is pretty simple: Provide steep tuition breaks to students with LSAT scores and undergraduate GPAs above this year's target medians and make up for the lost revenue by charging closer to full tuition for students who do not boost the school's numbers — especially transfer students who are hungry for the more prestigious J.D.

The table [above] summarizes some key statistics based on the *U.S. News* rankings. (Note we include a Top 14 category because the same schools have occupied the Top 14, occasionally switching positions, since the first *U.S. News* ranking in 1987. These schools all have national cachet in the entry-level legal markets.)

As the data reveal, the vast majority of students finance their legal education through debt. Some may be surprised to learn, however, that high-rank schools, all with large endowments, are not especially generous with scholarships. In general, their graduates have the highest debt loads. Because of the ready access they provide to lucrative corporate jobs, these schools enjoy enormous market power. They can raise tuition, reduce teaching loads, poach scholars from lower-ranked schools and tweak their course offerings to please tenured faculty.

Yet it is not just high-rank schools that are exercising market power. Among all law schools, the percentage of students receiving scholarship money hovers in the vicinity of 50 percent; by definition, grants to more than 50 percent of enrollment do not optimize a school's *U.S. News* inputs because LSAT scores and undergraduate GPAs are calculated from a school's median figures, and schools tend to offer tuition breaks only to those students whose scores are above the median. In recent years, our conversations with law school admissions officers and administrators suggest that virtually all law school financial aid has been redeployed in the service of law school rankings.

This system of cross-subsidies means that many students will graduate with debt loads far above the school's average. At a high-rank law school, a recent graduate can pay off that debt with a job at a large law firm — though he or she may not enjoy the work or the hours. But an even worse scenario is high debt — because the graduate enrolled in the highest-ranked school he or she was able to get into — and limited job prospects at a non-elite school.

This data also reveals another key distortion of rankings that combine all 194 ABA-approved law schools: With the exception of a few national firms, the vast majority of legal employment is regional. For T14 schools, 35 percent stay in state upon graduation, versus 58 percent for the rest of Tier 1 and 70 percent to 77 percent for tiers two through three.

What does it take to become a successful lawyer? A degree from an elite law school may get one's foot in the door at a big firm, but the prestige and money are no guarantee of happiness. Most young lawyers who start at big firms leave within a few years. But regardless of the pedigree of one's degree, every lawyer's long-term success depends upon the development of key professional skills: time management, interpersonal skills, teamwork, excellent written and oral communication, emotional intelligence and the elusive intangible of "judgment."

AFTER GRADUATION

Employment outcomes for graduates of ABA-approved schools, including academic attrition

	%	Cumulative %
NLJ 250	12.3%	12.3%
Other law firms	35.2%	47.6%
Clerkship	8.7%	56.3%
Government	9.9%	66.2%
Public interest	3.9%	70.1%
Business	10.8%	80.9%
Graduate school	2.1%	83.0%
Academia	1.4%	84.4%
Transferred to another school	2.3%	86.7%
Unemployed	6.7%	93.4%
Unknown	3.0%	96.4%
1L academic attrition	3.6%	100.0%

Sources: ABA-LSAC Official Guide to ABA-Approved Law Schools (2008 ed.), ALM Research

Based on our experience with many extremely successful alumni, all of these qualities can be developed (sometimes better and faster) in smaller firms, state court clerkships, government practice or public interest jobs. Yet the key is avoiding the financial vise of excessive law school tuition.

A Regional Approach

For many prospective lawyers, the best strategy may be a careful evaluation of the regional job market in the area of the country where they want to work. If they are not competitive for admission into a national law school — or are sure they are not interested in corporate law — they can use their entering credentials to negotiate for a substantial tuition discount. By focusing on price rather than rankings, they will have the financial freedom to pursue jobs that will build valuable professional skills and mentoring relationships or leave the law altogether, without debt, to pursue other life ambitions. Further, if prospective law students still want a shot at large corporate law practice, their best bet may be to focus on regional schools in major legal markets that will provide them with substantial scholarships. Virtually all large firms routinely interview at regional law schools in close proximity to major branch offices while ignoring higher-ranked schools farther away . . .

In today's competitive law school environment, the numbers (LSATs and undergraduate GPAs) that will get someone admitted to an Ivy League school with $120,000 in debt can get the same person a free ride at one of the Tier 1 schools in the table. Likewise, numbers that would get someone into the bottom of the *U.S. News* Tier 1 (at $100,000 in debt) can get that person a full ride at an excellent regional school with a strong alumni base in his or her dream city.

Finally, if no law school is willing to substantially underwrite a prospective law student's education, he or she needs to understand the financial realities of the job market. Based on our calculations using data from the 2008 ABA-LSAC "Official Guide" (see the table on page 31), roughly 13.3 percent of all students at ABA-accredited schools either flunk out as 1Ls or are unemployed or unaccounted for nine months after graduation. And at 44 schools, flunked out, unemployed or unaccounted for comprise 20 percent of all outcomes.

Bad outcomes lurk in other categories. Among the 10.8 percent of students who are employed in "business," students need to understand that this category includes in-house legal work, investment banking, selling insurance, waiting tables and driving a cab. Overall, there is a strong inverse relationship between a school's placement in large-firm jobs and its placement in the business category, which suggests that many nonlegal jobs out of law school are not very lucrative.

We provide regional breakdowns for all ABA-accredited law schools. In compiling this data, we attempt to avoid two pitfalls of *U.S. News*.

- Because the vast majority of the legal market is regional, we categorize schools based upon location in the same state or metropolitan area as one of the 10 largest NLJ 250 markets. These markets include the metropolitan areas of New York, Washington, Los Angeles, San Francisco, Chicago, Boston, Atlanta, Dallas, Houston and Philadelphia. Thereafter, we summarize the remaining ABA-accredited law schools by state.

- We don't rank; neither should prospective students. Within regional markets, many schools will have similar outcome profiles. The question to ask is whether marginally better employment outcomes — for example, 12 percent large-firm employment versus 6 percent — is worth the additional law school debt. Often a prospective student choosing a school ranked higher in *U.S. News* will join a more competitive student body, making it harder to earn higher grades. This could cancel out the 6 percent gain in big-firm employment, but not the additional $60,000 in debt.

William D. Henderson is an associate professor at Indiana University School of Law–Bloomington. Andrew P. Morriss is the H. Ross and Helen Workman Professor of Law and Business at University of Illinois College of Law.

2. WHERE DO I FIT INTO THIS PICTURE—AND WILL I LIKE IT?

MARCIA RUBEN, GETTING THEIR DUE: IT'S NEVER BEEN AS EASY AS IT IS TODAY TO BE A FEMALE LAWYER, BUT A FEW HURDLES REMAIN

San Francisco Recorder, Jan. 8, 2003, at 4

Former Attorney General Janet Reno, speaking at a California Women Lawyers' dinner at the California State Bar meeting in September 2001, recalled that while at Harvard Law School in the early 1960s, the dean asked what she planned to do with her degree, as if unsure what a woman could accomplish with this credential.

At that time, it was unusual for women to attend law school, and even more unlikely for them to actually practice law. It was inconceivable that a woman could become the attorney general of the United States. Reno recounted that just after her confirmation as attorney general in 1992, she reminded the dean of that previous conversation, much to his chagrin.

The former managing partner at a major law firm in San Francisco reminisced about a moment early in her career, more than 20 years ago, when she was appearing in the courtroom of a recently appointed female federal judge. The judge took a moment to pause and point out that all those with a role in her courtroom for that motion were women: the clerk, deputy, law clerks, court reporters and both attorneys. This was remarkable because just a few years earlier, most or all of these representatives would have been male. . . .

Retention among female attorneys is a pressing issue for the legal profession. All groups interviewed in the study, from senior male and female partners to female associates, indicated that the struggle to balance work and home life is real.

The women emphasized that anyone who says it is easy to raise a family and have a full-time career is not telling the truth. Many in the sample said that while large firms talk about the importance of life balance, they do not "walk the talk," and attorneys are expected to work evenings and weekends. It is not unusual for attorneys in large firms to work 60-80 hours a week. Women who leave large firms and/or the profession often do so because they feel torn between the competing demands of their career and their personal lives. . . .

The legal profession is at a turning point. More women than men are choosing the law as a career. Yet, at the same time, talented female associates and partners are leaving their firms, and even the profession, because they don't feel that their needs are being met. In corporations, the loss of key talent can cost millions of dollars in recruitment expenses, work put on hold, loss of clients and lowered morale and productivity. Firms invest a great deal to develop new attorneys. The return on that investment depends on creativity in addressing issues of concern to women. . . .

KAREN ASNER, COMMENTARY: WHERE THE WOMEN ARE

Special to Law.com, July 6, 2006, at 52

While the number of women in law schools now roughly equals the number of men, the same, unfortunately, does not hold true when it comes to women partners in law firms. The National Association for Law Placement reports that about 17 percent of partners at major law firms are women, up from 13 percent 10 years ago. While that's progress, the numbers are not increasing as quickly as most of us would like.

Most law firms these days recognize the importance of recruiting and retaining top talent—regardless of gender—particularly in an increasingly competitive job market. Thus, the problem isn't that law firms aren't willing or eager to make their women lawyers partners—it's that so many of the women leave before such promotions can even take place. Studies show that the number of first-year associates at major law firms is generally split evenly between women and men. But beginning in the fourth or fifth year, women depart law firms in greater numbers than men, leaving fewer of them in the partnership pool.

The Mommy Track

Part of the problem stems from the fact that just about the time when an associate begins taking on increasing responsibility is also generally a woman's prime childbearing years.

As a commercial litigator who also acts as our firm's global administrative partner and is the mother of three, I know firsthand the challenges of trying to balance professional and personal obligations. And while most women lawyers would like to keep working once they become mothers, the expectations placed on them at most major law firms sometimes can be overwhelming, so it's not surprising that some female lawyers make the decision to cut back on their hours if they can or leave a firm all together.

Female associates may be reluctant to voice concerns about juggling various commitments for fear they will be seen as not committed to the firm or their clients and automatically be "mommy-tracked." Rather than ask for a temporary leave of absence or a more flexible schedule, a female associate simply will overextend herself to the point of burnout, inevitably leaving the firm that much sooner. Firms therefore need to take a hard look at their flextime policies (assuming they even have one) to ensure that the policies are well designed, well understood and well implemented.

Dissatisfaction

Beyond that, however, key issues remain. A 2001 study of top law school graduates by think tank Catalyst revealed that while women clearly struggle with work-family obligations, the biggest reason women lawyers leave a firm is because they are dissatisfied with work itself or feel stalled in their careers.

Why do women feel dissatisfied? The Harvard Center for Work-Life Policy study found that only 20 percent of highly qualified female lawyers cited "a powerful position" as a very important career goal. Yet the percentage of women who said that "helping others" or "improving society" was one of the most important factors in picking a career was double that of men. Thus, if women feel the client work they are tackling is not advancing a "greater good," they may indeed be less satisfied with their jobs, prompting them to depart sooner.

Women also may be more apt to downplay their abilities and accomplishments than their male counterparts. A study done by Harvard Law School revealed that 33 percent of male students considered themselves in the top 20 percent of their class in legal reasoning, but only 15 percent of the women did. Note that this is not how the law students were actually ranked but rather how women perceived themselves. Other studies have shown that women are more likely to share credit for a completed project than men, so supervising partners may erroneously perceive that a male associate is actually contributing more to a project's success, rewarding him with more responsibility.

The issues surrounding retention of top female associates are admittedly complex, but it seems apparent that these factors help shape how women associates interact in the law firm environment. If they are less likely to view themselves as top performers or take full credit for their work, they are less likely to be singled out for exciting, cutting-edge assignments. And it's the cutting-edge, high-profile work that gets the attention of firm management and leads to partnership promotions.

What Firms Can Do

These issues are at the heart of why some firms have embraced women's networks as well as other retention and development tools geared specifically for women. . . .

Just as there's rarely one simple solution for a complex legal problem, there's no easy answer on how to increase the number of women partners. What we do know, though, is that simply hiring an entering class that is half women isn't getting us where we need to be. We need to continue to find solutions that meaningfully increase the number of women who stay in the running for partnership. Fifty percent of the talent pool — and, by definition, the future of law firms — depends on it.

Karen Asner is a commercial litigator and an administrative partner at White & Case LLP in New York, where she oversees all administrative aspects of the firm's 36 offices and helps shape firm culture, policies and strategic business objectives.

KELLIE SCHMITT, GOT KIDS? THESE CLIENTS DON'T CARE

San Francisco Recorder, April 24, 2006, at 1

So much for sisterhood.

Women juggling kids and careers in private practice might expect some sympathy, maybe even a little slack, from female clients. After all, the thinking goes, they can relate.

Or not.

Last week, a panel of in-house counsel at a National Association of Women Lawyers event in Los Angeles told the crowd to keep their personal lives out of the equation: Clients should come first.

"If there's a family crisis or something with the kids or other clients, we don't care about it — get the job done," Linda Louie, general counsel for the

National Hot Rod Association, told an audience of about 100 women Wednesday. "You are a commodity to us—show me how you can solve a problem."

Panelist Elizabeth Atlee, a senior counsel for BP American Inc., doesn't have a problem with lawyers leading balanced lives—so long as that's not an excuse to blow off client demands.

Don't answer the phone if you're putting kids to bed, Atlee told the audience, but call back with your full attention as soon as you've done so—and skip the blow-by-blow: "I don't want to hear about your kids," she said. "I'll tell you if I do—don't tell me."

Though those sentiments may sound extreme, Joan Williams, director of the Center for WorkLife Law at Hastings College of the Law, said it's not all that unusual.

"There's a generation gap between baby boomers who played by the old rules and Gen X men and women who want to establish new rules," Williams said. "When women my age entered law, if we had done anything different than men, we would have been out so fast our heads would have been spinning." . . .

Louie, who has children of her own, said she's always sought to separate her work from her personal life. Unfortunately, she said, some of the outside lawyers she's worked with don't draw that line.

"Maybe it's because I was trained mostly by men when it wasn't as cool to have kids," Louie offered. "When my clients call me, they expect 100 percent of my attention, and I expect to give 100 percent, no matter what I am doing." . . .

Angela Bradstreet, the creator of the San Francisco Bar Association's No Glass Ceiling Initiative, said it's important for women to take a businesslike approach to clients and be careful about interjecting too much that's personal. Business and time are valuable commodities, especially to in-house clients who are also held accountable, said Bradstreet, a partner at San Francisco's Carroll, Burdick & McDonough.

"Sometimes we can be more preoccupied with creating a relationship with someone, and we have a comfort level talking about personal issues as opposed to business issues," she said. "Sometimes, it's not appropriate to start talking about whatever personal issues one has."

Joan Haratani, president of the Bar Association of San Francisco, said that what's appropriate is often the client's call: "When you're the client, you have the right to hire folks whose priorities comport with yours."

Haratani is working with a task force to come up with ways lawyers can strike a healthier work-life balance while still satisfying the most demanding of clients.

"It's a difficult issue, and it's becoming more pronounced as more women enter the legal field," she said. . . .

"Folks are paying close attention," she said, "not only for recruiting and retention but also in terms of succession planning."

Haratani said she hopes the survey results, due in September, offer some solutions. "I think everyone agrees you want your talented folks to stay, and folks also agree a lot of people choose to have lives outside of work. So how do you make those coexist?"

EDITORS OF *CALIFORNIA LAWYER* & POINT BY POINT PUBLISHING,
LOVIN' IT: A NEW POLL OF CALIFORNIA'S LAWYERS FINDS WIDESPREAD
CONTENTMENT WITH THEIR WORK

California Lawyer, July 2005, at 21

The CALIFORNIA LAWYER Reader Poll

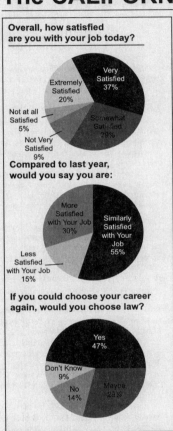

Overall, how satisfied are you with your job today?

- Very Satisfied 37%
- Somewhat Satisfied 29%
- Extremely Satisfied 20%
- Not Very Satisfied 9%
- Not at all Satisfied 5%

Compared to last year, would you say you are:

- Similarly Satisfied with Your Job 55%
- More Satisfied with Your Job 30%
- Less Satisfied with Your Job 15%

If you could choose your career again, would you choose law?

- Yes 47%
- Maybe 29%
- No 14%
- Don't Know 9%

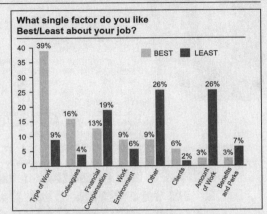

What single factor do you like Best/Least about your job?

BEST / LEAST

- Type of Work: 39% / 9%
- Colleagues: 16% / 4%
- Financial Compensation: 13% / 19%
- Work Environment: 9% / 6%
- Other: 9% / 26%
- Clients: 6% / 2%
- Amount of Work: 3% / 26%
- Benefits and Perks: 3% / 7%

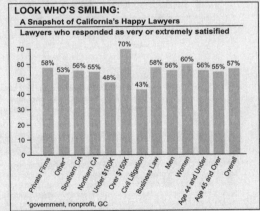

LOOK WHO'S SMILING:

A Snapshot of California's Happy Lawyers

Lawyers who responded as very or extremely satisfied

- Private Firms: 58%
- Other*: 53%
- Southern CA: 56%
- Northern CA: 55%
- Under $150K: 48%
- Over $150K: 70%
- Civil Litigation: 43%
- Business Law: 58%
- Men: 56%
- Women: 60%
- Age 44 and Under: 56%
- Age 45 and Over: 55%
- Overall: 57%

*government, nonprofit, GC

AT A GLANCE: Who Responded to Our Poll

TIME IN PRACTICE

20 years or more	37%
10 to 19 years	26%
5 to 9 years	22%
0 to 4 years	16%

EMPLOYER

Private firm, 1 to 5 attorneys	22%
Private firm, 6 to100 attorneys	28%
Private firm, >100 attorneys	22%
Government	12%
Corporate counsel	7%
Nonprofit, other	9%

TYPE OF LAW

Civil litigation	30%
Business litigation	17%
Business transactions	16%
Appellate	8%
Employment	8%
Estates, trusts	8%
Family	8%
Real property	8%
Criminal	7%
Intellectual property	6%
Environmental	5%

GENDER

Male	53%
Female	47%

TOTAL ANNUAL LAW-DERIVED COMPENSATION

>$300K	10%
$200K to $299K	12%
$150K to $199K	13%
$100K to $149K	33%
<$100K	33%

AGE

55 and over	21%
45 to 54	35%
35 to 44	27%
34 and under	19%

RACE/ETHNICITY

White non-Hispanic	80%
Asian	8%
Hispanic	6%
Black non-Hispanic	3%
Other (biracial, multiracial)	3%

WORK LOCATION*

Los Angeles & Orange Counties	38%
San Francisco Bay Area	26%
San Diego County	15%
Fresno County	3%
Sacramento County	3%
Other	19%

*Multiple responses

epending on whom you ask—and on what day you're asking—being a lawyer is either the best or worst job imaginable. Demanding clients are balanced by intellectual stimulation and a desire to advance the common good. But are lawyers any more or less happy with their jobs than other professionals? CALIFORNIA LAWYER wanted to know.

In the fall of 2004 the editors of CALIFORNIA LAWYER conducted an email poll of lawyers across the state. Those responding provided their perspectives on their job satisfaction and what they like and dislike about their chosen career.

The upshot? Fully 57 percent of responding lawyers said they're extremely or very satisfied with their jobs. Another 29 percent said they are somewhat satisfied, which makes a

---

"You get to help people truly in need and work with others who share your passion. What could be better?"

---

whopping 86 percent who are content with what they do for a living. What's more, 30 percent are more content at work today than they were a year ago. California lawyers do indeed seem to be a happy group.

Respondents overwhelmingly said the type of work they did was what made them most happy to be lawyers. "Intellectually

challenging," said one respondent. "Fascinating," said another. Many expressed their satisfaction at being able to help clients and advocate for their communities. "Working as a public defender is the best legal job there is," said one. "You get to help people truly in need—and you work for an agency with 200 lawyers who share your calling and your passion. What could be better than that?"

Then there's the money. Although financial compensation was mentioned as one of the best aspects about being a lawyer in California, it was also considered by many to be the worst. One lawyer summed up the issue: "It is absurd for starting lawyers on the East Coast to be making two-thirds of what I and other senior partners [in California] make. It's also absurd that partners get pounded endlessly by firm management about their billable-hour requirements while junior attorneys are not hassled, have the same billable-hour requirements, and receive lockstep pay raises.... But I like the intellectual game of commercial litigation, so I'll probably be doing this ten years from now in the same firm."

Other lawyers mentioned negatives about the job such as stress, long commutes, unpredictable workloads, and administrative pressures. But when asked their plans for the next year, only 15 percent of our respondents thought it was very or extremely likely they would search for a new job.

Although the respondent base was too small to make statistically valid conclusions about which types of lawyers are the most satisfied, we were able to derive some insights from the data. Lawyers who make more than $150,000 had the highest level of satisfaction. At the same time, lawyers who work in organizations other than private law firms seemed to have the greatest increase in job satisfaction over the past year.

A recent nationwide study by the Conference Board, a New York–based business research group, found only half of Americans are happy with their jobs. Our findings indicate that California's stimulating legal environment makes the state's lawyers happier than most American workers.

Perhaps this metric is the best indicator of happiness: When asked whether they would choose law if they had to choose their career again, only 14 percent said no.

—*Maryann Jones Thompson*

ABOUT THE POLL

The CALIFORNIA LAWYER poll covered degree of job satisfaction, reasons for job satisfaction, and plans to change jobs. Respondents were guaranteed that their responses would be kept confidential. Data tabulation and analysis were conducted by Point by Point Publishing, an independent analysis and editorial services firm in the Bay Area. Percentages are based on the number of respondents answering each question. Data distributions may not total 100 percent due to rounding or multiple answers.

The questionnaire was sent to a representative sample of 700 California lawyers; every attempt was made to have the survey recipients mirror the geographic and gender composition of the State Bar. In fact, our 17 percent response rate reflected State Bar membership geographically and demographically, except in one category: gender. According to a 2001 California Bar Journal Survey conducted by Richard Hertz Consulting of Petaluma, the State Bar at that time was 68% male and 32% female. Although our survey went out to State Bar members in that proportion, our respondents were 53% male and 47% female.

B. LITIGATION: HOW MUCH, ABOUT WHAT, AND WITH WHAT OUTCOME?

NOTE ON LITIGATION STATISTICS

This section moves from lawyers to lawsuits. And, as with lawyers, we look first at the topic statistically: how much litigation is there (in the United States and elsewhere)? What does that mean? What do the composition and trends reveal: does it involve auto accidents, contract disputes, or civil rights claims? Is litigation increasing or decreasing? How do those suits end and with what results? Who wins, who loses, and how much? And how have the answers to these questions changed over recent decades? As with our survey of the legal profession, our goal is to get a sense of the ocean in which each lawsuit swims — to understand how that environment will affect the individual suit.

The opening reading is a piece of comparative law that tries to answer a question that regularly surfaces in the U.S. political debate: is the United States a pathologically litigious society, drowning in its disputes and poisoning political discourse with litigation? Or, more neutrally put, what generates the U.S. litigation rate, and would we be happy with the changes that would reduce that rate?

1. GLOBAL CIVIL LITIGATION

CHRISTIAN WOLLSCHLÄGER, EXPLORING GLOBAL
LANDSCAPES OF LITIGATION RATES

In Soziologie des Rechts: Festschrift fur Erhard Blankenburg zum
60 Geburstag, 587 (J. Brand & D. Stempel eds., 1998)

Usually flowers are presented on the occasion of anniversaries. If a socio-legal scholar's birthday is celebrated, a colorful bunch of litigation rates seems to be more appropriate. . . . The latter include former socialist countries, Africa, South America, Asia, and Oceania. These parts of the world are widely unknown in the comparative literature on civil litigation.

The following study attempts to broaden the view towards a global perspective. The feasibility of worldwide comparison of judicial statistics is discussed and data from 35 nations are analyzed in an exploratory manner. Taken together, they outline the diversity and the range of national demands for civil justice. The title deliberately draws on Marc Galanter's vision of a "landscape of disputes." Judicial statistics indeed reveal a variety of litigation rates — as wide and bewildering as the outdoors, which are the random result of many interacting forces. Disputes, however, do not shape this landscape (maybe the foothills). They are a minority of all cases reported by statistics. In the contemporary scenery, the peaks of court business consist of debt collection cases. Uncontested money claims determine the international rank order of litigation rates. As a consequence, it is suggested here that economic development and its impact on social relations have the strongest influence on the civil caseloads of trial courts in our time. . . .

In spite of these limits, global coverage of judicial statistics seems to be feasible. In nearly all nations, the judicial branch of government maintains a system of self-observation that monitors input and output of the court system. The caseload per capita allows [us] to study the demand for civil justice. Judicial statistics thus provide a quantitative measure of law in Donald Black's theoretical framework. No other variable is available for socio-legal research in similar worldwide dimensions.

Data and Methodology

The United Nations counts 185 members. Many of these are subdivided into federal states with independent judiciaries. This adds at least 200 jurisdictions where individual court structures and rules of civil procedure can exist. Given the practical impossibility to cover all, a selection must suffice. This can be representative in a loose sense only. Litigation rates are calculated here on the basis of annual filings in courts of first instance per 1000 total population. The study embraces the upper and lower extreme cases of all jurisdictions for which recent figures (dating from 1996 back to 1987) could be found. Each of the world's major regions is illustrated by several countries. The most populous nations are included, such as China, the former Soviet Union, the US, and India (if only represented by one federal state). Altogether the data cover approx. 45% of the world population. Sophisticated methodology is hardly applicable to these handpicked data. A rank order provides strong clues as to the operation of demographic, economic, and other factors which determine the demand for civil justice. One has to be aware, though, that international comparison of judicial statistics cannot be as detailed as social science normally requires. If different legal systems are involved, crude measures are available only. These are meaningful in spite of inevitable inaccuracies, because the range of litigation rates is so wide that margins of error are tolerable. The findings here start from 2 cases per 1000 total population up to well over 100. The range corresponds well to the dynamics found in historical series of civil litigation. German rates, e.g., range from 7 units or less in the 18th century to a climax of 215 during the Great Depression in 1931. The societal demand for civil justice at large is a macrophenomenon. It cannot be analyzed with the same precision as in micro-social research. Orders of magnitude count here, not single percentage points.

Courts and Cases in International Comparison

Nations have been ranked on the basis of a special unit of count which is necessary for a meaningful international comparison of judicial statistics. The "adjusted total" of civil cases, as it is used here, comprises not only ordinary "lawsuits" as defined by the national law of civil procedure. It includes conciliation and simplified debt collection procedures. It is not limited to courts; court-like institutions, as e.g., the Chinese People's Mediation Committees, are also included.

This method of count relies on a functional method of international comparison. All institutions and types of procedure are included which serve judicial functions, regardless of the organizational and procedural form by which government performs its duty to render justice. Dunning procedures, e.g., are applicable for uncontested money claims in many European jurisdictions as well as in Japan. The duty of courts to enforce creditor's rights is performed herewith. Settlement is a judicial function, too. If it is performed by special institutions or in separate procedures, these cases cannot be omitted. The Chinese People's Mediation Committees do not constitute formal courts at all. Their caseload is shown here because mediation is de facto mandatory. The regular courts reject cases which have not been processed by the committees. So the business of the latter represents the Chinese demand for civil justice. Some nations have empowered administrative law enforcement agencies — similar to bailiffs or marshals — to collect private debts without preceding court action. In the course of Swedish history, e.g., jurisdiction in these matters has been shifted back and forth between both branches of government. This cannot matter in international comparison. The actual organizational solution by which legislators satisfy creditors' demand for law enforcement should be irrelevant there.

In general, a functional approach is required because the various means of judicial remedies substitute for one another. As a rule, creditors may choose between ordinary and special types of procedure. For this reason, the number of regular civil cases is determined by the availability of procedural alternatives. The societal demand for civil justice has to be measured by the total input into the court system. The total of different case types represents all incidents in which private citizens submit particular facts to the judicial branch of government asking to enforce their claims. This macro-variable can be meaningfully compared between nations and over time as an object of socio-legal inquiry.

International Litigation Rates (1987-1996)
Civil Cases Filed in Courts of First Instance per 1000 Population.
Data and Sources in Appendix.
Civil Litigation and Development

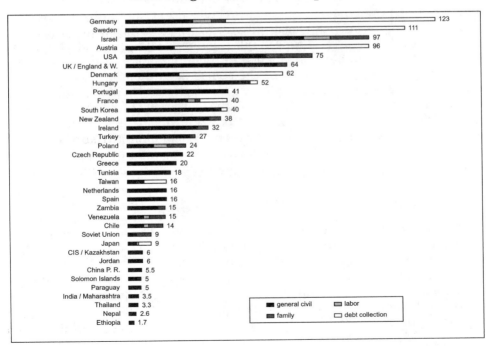

The resulting rank order immediately illustrates the validity of the constructed unit of count. A plausible sequence of litigation rates emerges. Demand for civil justice is obviously related to socio-economic development. The upper and lower extremes reflect the contrast between industrialized and developing nations. The low litigation rates of Ethiopia (1.7 cases per 1000 population), Nepal (2.6), Paraguay (4.9), or the Solomon Islands (5.1) can be easily attributed to economic underdevelopment. "Civil law varies directly with development," one might conclude in Donald Black's laconic language. Or: "law increases," as he puts it even shorter himself.

"Development" is here taken as a shorthand to denote a bundle of causes that contribute to modernization. Economic growth plays a major role, accompanied by a rising volume of credit in consumer relations. Urbanization and social mobility are the social corollaries of development. Both result in individualism, estrangement, and juridification of personal relations. Development has been observed most often by the urban-rural dichotomy variable, i.e. the fact that urban litigation rates exceed those of agrarian regions. The present study shows that this well-known causal factor operates on the international level, too.

Before this is illustrated in more detail, the importance of a proper method of count should be noted. The ranking would be quite different, if only regular civil lawsuits in the meaning of the national law of civil procedure were counted. Israel would be on top, followed by the US, England, and Hungary. The leaders would drop to the neighborhood of former socialist countries, not too far from the even lower levels of underdeveloped regions. The common method of counting regular lawsuits only is indeed inadequate. It conceals the socio-economic causes of the demand for civil justice. It is particularly distorting for jurisdictions where no special debt collection procedures are available, namely the Anglo-American legal systems, which include Israel, the Spanish "legal family," and East European jurisdictions. The result of the cross-sectional analysis can be easily applied in the longitudinal perspective. Civil litigation has a tendency to rise in the course of further "development". In 1989 Erhard Blankenburg firmly placed a question mark behind "Prozeßflut?" (Floods of Litigation?) — the title of a volume on the civil business of European courts. Nine years later and in the light of worldwide data, it seems that the question mark should be replaced by an exclamation mark. The largest distance on our scale has to be explained by economic development. This factor has the strongest explanatory power, however ambiguous the term may be.

Consumer Credit Relations

Uncontested money claims constitute the bulk of cases. Wherever statistical sources permit to single out debt collection cases, these take the largest share of the total. They determine the rank order at the upper end of industrialized nations (Germany, Sweden, and Austria). The volume of consumer credit relations and the use of courts by businessmen to collect debts are the dominant causes of civil caseloads. In Germany, Sweden, and Austria, a block of 75-85 debt collection cases per 1000 population is processed by the courts. Urbanization and prosperity thus make for the highest litigation rates in the world. Former socialist nations including East Germany give evidence to the same effect. If separate rates are calculated for both parts of Germany, which were united in 1990, the East comes out with 53 units less than the West (79 vs. 132 units in 1996). The difference arises from the number of dunning cases alone, whereas the rates of general civil and family cases are equal. In the sixth year after unification, East German business, which was completely restructured, has evidently not yet fully adopted the Western habits of court use. . . .

Family Relations

Family matters constitute the second largest field of court activity. Here the US take[s] the lead with a rate of 18 domestic relations cases per 1000 population, followed by Israel (15 units). At the other extreme, namely in Nepal, the per capita rate (0.8 units) is a fraction of the top values, although family cases constitute a sizable share of court business there, too (31%). The data show family relations as another expanding sector of judicial activity. In traditional societies they used to be the most intimate — up to the point where the family was out of reach for any kind of law (as, e.g., in Ancient Rome or traditional Japan). Urbanization and social mobility brought about estrangement in personal relations. Patriarchal family structures disintegrated. So the need to dissolve marriages increased together with the need to protect children's rights where parental care failed. The juridification of the family is an ongoing process — pushed by population growth. There is an inverse relation between the use of law and the proper functioning of personal relations.

This aspect of development, too, can be demonstrated by international judicial statistics. Most developed nations exhibit rates of 4 to 6 family cases per 1000 population; that is one third or less of the two leaders in this field. The majority includes Western European nations as well as the Soviet Union, Poland, Latin American nations and New Zealand. The distance to the top shows the causal relation once more. The US and Israel are both ethnic melting pots where social ties are loosening. In the US, this may be due to high social mobility. Israel has not yet been socially integrated in her 50 years of existence, particularly as the population grew constantly by waves of immigrants from different countries. The bonds of long-standing traditions and informal norms do not seem to have emerged thus far. Disruptive family relations as well as strained business-consumer relations seem to be the consequence. Both result in high litigation rates.

Labor Relations

In labor litigation, Israel ranks on top with a rate of 11 labor cases per 1000 population. Her special situation is illustrated again by the distance to other nations, whose median value is only about 2 labor cases per 1000 population. The basic mechanism of development is at work here, too. Underdeveloped nations do not report labor cases at all. This has structural causes; it is no deficiency of statistics. There are so few labor cases that there is no need for special procedures or separate courts as they have been established in most European countries (including former socialist countries) and South America. . . . In earlier agrarian economies labor relations were primarily patriarchal. Workers were subordinate, relying on the benevolence of the patron. Ideally there was no need for law, just as in parent-child relations. Socioeconomic development has loosened this bond. Labor relations participate in the general process of juridification. This adds a significant sector of judicial business, with a median share of 6% of the total workload. Although it is not the largest, it is certainly one of those fields where future development will require more judicial intervention.

Conclusion

The exploration has focused on the big effects of development as they appear in the results of judicial statistics. Economic growth and rising individualism in personal relations contribute most strongly to an increasing use of civil courts. International litigation rates show the global operation of the same causes of litigation that have been found in national or micro-regional studies. An overall tendency to rise emerges particularly in consumer credit relations, family matters, and labor litigation. Theoretical orientation in the landscape of litigation rates was obtained from the catch-all concept of "development" and from Donald Black's theory. These proved to be useful for a description of the most prominent features of the ranking scale. As the data were analyzed neither strictly nor completely, some qualifications should be added. Earlier criticism of evolutionary concepts, as I pronounced it under Erhard Blankenburg's guidance, seems to be weakened in the light of worldwide data. However, underwriting to Black's blunt thesis that "law increases" means no return to linear evolutionary concepts.

Civil caseloads have many causes. The actual outcome of their interplay is hard to predict. Historical statistics show nations where civil caseloads have stagnated or declined for decades, even for a whole century. Industrialized and wealthy Japan obviously does not fit the interpretive line of economic development. Her low litigation rate is far below Western levels. This suggests that social attitudes and cultural values may influence the demand for civil justice even more strongly than the economy. On the other hand, Japan is still by no means non-litigious, as many believe. In other nations, judicial activity is even less, particularly in the least developed countries. This requires a more detailed discussion. In the global context, Japan appears to be an exception rather than the rule. The present state of the world, as it is reflected in our cross-sectional data, seems to be that the law-expanding forces of socio-economic development are the most effective. More refined international comparison is certainly needed to see this more clearly. If socio-legal research intends to live up to theoretical expectations of universal validity, the global perspective should no longer be ignored.

International Litigation Rates*

Region	Nation	Year	Litigation Rate per 1000 Population					Source
			Total	Gen. Civil	Labor	Family	Debt Coll.	
Africa	Ethiopia	1990/91	1.7					Stat. Yearb. 1992
	Tunisia	1993/94	17.8					Stat. Yearb. 1994
	Zambia	1987	15.0	12.8		2.2		Jud. Stats. 1987
Americas	Chile	1989	13.7	7.4	1.4	4.9		Stat. Yearb. 1992
	Paraguay	1994	4.9	4.6	0.3			Stat. Yearb. 1994
	USA	1995	74.5	56.1		18.4		Supra note 26
	Venezuela	1994	14.5	7.2	2.2	5.1		Stat. Yearb. 1994
Asia, East	China P.R.	1994	5.5	5.5				Stat. Yearb. 1994
	Japan	1994	9.3	4.3		0.7	4.3	Jud. Stats. 1994
	South Korea	1995	39.8	37.7		2.1		Stat. Yearb. 1996
	Taiwan	1995	16.9	7.3			9.6	Jud. Stats. 1995
Asia, South	India/Maharashtra	1992	3.5	1.8				Jud. Stats. 1992
	Nepal	1990/91	2.6					Stat. Yearb. 1993
Asia, S. E.	Thailand	1994	3.3					Stat. Yearb. 1995
Asia, West	CIS/Kazakhstan	1991	5.9					EC report 1993
	Israel	1995	96.8	71.2	10.6	15.1		Stat. Yearb. 1996
	Jordan	1992	5.6	5.4		0.1		Stat. Yearb. 1992
	Turkey	1993	27.3	25.4	1.9			Stat. Yearb. 1995
Europe, East	Czech Republic	1995	22.3					Stat. Yearb. 1995
	Hungary	1994	52.4	49.6	2.7			Stat. Yearb. 1994
	Poland	1994	23.5	10.9	5.7	6.9		Stat. Yearb. 1995
	Soviet Union	1988	9.4	3.6	0.7	5.1		SU in Figures 1988
Eur. Union	Austria	1995	95.9	95.9			41.3	Jud. Stats. 1995
	Denmark	1995	62.5	21.2			11.0	Stat. Yearb. 1996
	France	1994	40.3	24.4	2.9	2.1		Stat. Yearb. 1997
	Germany	1995	123.2	26.5	7.7	5.6	83.4	Jud. Stats. 1995

International Litigation Rates* (Cont'd)

Region	Nation	Year	Litigation Rate per 1000 Population					Source
			Total	Gen. Civil	Labor	Family	Debt Coll.	
	Greece	1993	19.8					Stat. Yearb. 1994
	Ireland	1994/95	32.7	28.7		4.1		Stat. Yearb. 1995
	Netherlands	1995	16.0					Stat. Yearb. 1997
	Portugal	1994	40.7	39.7	0.2	0.8		Stat. Yearb. 1995
	Spain	1992	15.5					Jud. Stats. 1993
	Sweden	1992	111.2	25.7			85.5	Jud. Stats. 1993
	UK/England & Wales	1993	64.4	60.7		3.7		Jud. Stats. 1993
Oceania	New Zealand	1990	37.7	32.7		5.0		Min. of Justice
	Solomon Islands	1989	5.1					Stat. Yearb. 1993

*A detailed list of data and sources is available from the author at Universität Bielefeld, Postfach 100131, D-33501 Bielefeld, Germany.

2. CIVIL LITIGATION IN THE UNITED STATES: THE BIG PICTURE

NATIONAL CENTER FOR STATE COURTS, CIVIL FILINGS IN STATE
COURTS BY TYPE OF LITIGATION

Compiled from Examining the Work of State Courts, 2006, available online at
http://www.ncsconline.org/D_Research/csp/CSP_Main_Page.html

Civil Filings in 45 State Courts of General Jurisdiction 1996-2005

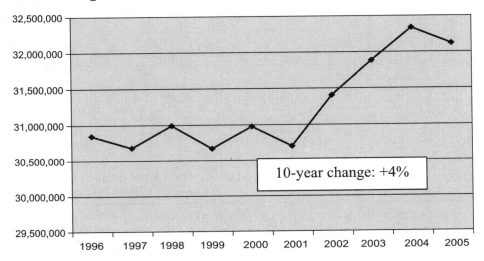

Contract Filings in 13-State Sample

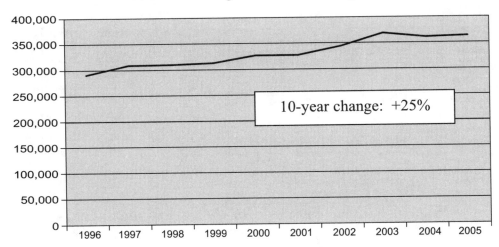

Tort Filings—30-State Sample

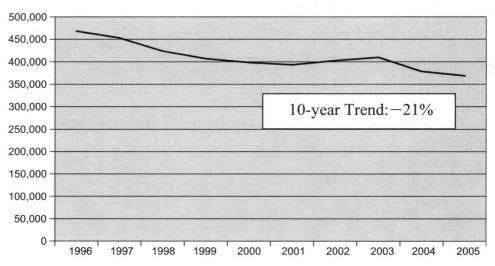

10-year Trend: −21%

NATIONAL CENTER FOR STATE COURTS, CIVIL FILINGS IN STATE
COURTS BY TYPE OF LITIGATION

Compiled from State Court Caseload Statistics, 2003, available online at
http://www.ncsconline.org/D_Research/csp/1998_Files/1998_SCCS.html
(last visited March 16, 2006)

Incoming General Civil Caseload Composition in 22 Unified and General Jurisdiction Courts, 2003

State	Incoming General Civil Cases	General Civil Composition
Unified Courts		50%
North Dakota	10,590	
Missouri	165,029	
Kansas	162,351	
Minnesota	36,844	
Puerto Rico	55,780	
Iowa	23,753	
Connecticut	65,853	
Total	**520,200**	
General Jurisdiction Courts		
Utah	90,834	
Oregon	62,041	
Mississippi	26,256	
Wyoming	2,202	
Colorado	37,811	
Arkansas	26,876	
New Jersey	510,321	
New Hampshire	4,331	
New Mexico	22,953	
Arizona	26,765	
Hawaii	3,262	
Washington	59,638	
Texas	73,027	
Tennessee	21,194	
Massachusetts	19,134	
Total	**986,645**	

■ Contract   ■ Tort   ■ Real Property

- Certain tort case types (e.g., medical malpractice, product liability) dominate civil reform debates. However, as the bars in the figure at left indicate, contract cases are often the majority of general civil caseloads.

- Contract percentages ranged from a low of 28 percent in Massachusetts to a high of 94 percent in North Dakota. Incoming tort cases exceeded incoming contract cases in only five of these 22 courts.

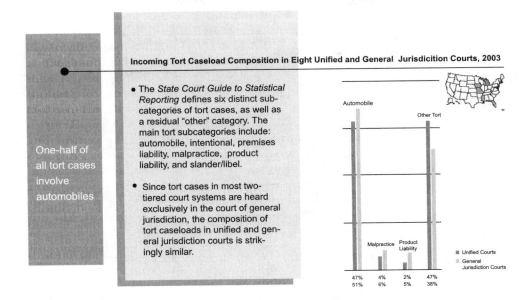

One-half of all tort cases involve automobiles

Incoming Tort Caseload Composition in Eight Unified and General Jurisdicition Courts, 2003

- The *State Court Guide to Statistical Reporting* defines six distinct subcategories of tort cases, as well as a residual "other" category. The main tort subcategories include: automobile, intentional, premises liability, malpractice, product liability, and slander/libel.

- Since tort cases in most two-tiered court systems are heard exclusively in the court of general jurisdiction, the composition of tort caseloads in unified and general jurisdiction courts is strikingly similar.

Automobile | Other Tort | Malpractice | Product Liability

Unified Courts
General Jurisdiction Courts

47% 4% 2% 47%
51% 6% 5% 38%

LYNN LANGTON & THOMAS H. COHEN, U.S. DEPARTMENT OF JUSTICE, BUREAU OF JUSTICE STATISTICS SPECIAL REPORT, CIVIL BENCH AND JURY TRIALS IN STATE COURTS, 2005

Special Report, revised December 18, 2008, available online at http://www.ojp.usdoj.gov/bjs/pub/pdf/cbjtsc05.pdf

State courts of general jurisdiction disposed of approximately 26,950 general civil cases—tort, contract, and real property—through a jury or bench trial in 2005. These trials were a small percentage of the reported 7.4 million civil claims filed in all unified and general jurisdiction state courts nationwide.[1] Among jurisdictions that provided totals for both trial and non-trial general civil dispositions in 2005, trials collectively accounted for about 3% of all tort, contract, and real property dispositions in general jurisdiction courts.

Civil bench and jury trials are rare but important events. Records from civil trials are the primary source of information on civil cases in general. The terms of settlement agreements and other key information for civil cases resolved prior to trial may not be reported to the court or may not be publicly available.

---

1. Approximately 7.4 million civil claims were filed in general jurisdiction and unified jurisdiction courts in 2005, with 4.5 million of those claims filed in courts of general jurisdiction and 2.9 million civil cases filed in states with a unified court structure. See LaFountain, R., Schauffler, R., Strickland, S., Raftery, W., & Bromage, C. *Examining the Work of State Courts, 2006: A National Perspective from the Court Statistics Project* (National Center for State Courts 2007).

Figure 1

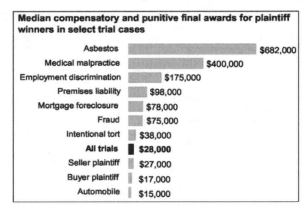

Median compensatory and punitive final awards for plaintiff winners in select trial cases

Asbestos	$682,000
Medical malpractice	$400,000
Employment discrimination	$175,000
Premises liability	$98,000
Mortgage foreclosure	$78,000
Fraud	$75,000
Intentional tort	$38,000
All trials	**$28,000**
Seller plaintiff	$27,000
Buyer plaintiff	$17,000
Automobile	$15,000

Major findings from the 2005 Civil Justice Survey of State Courts include —

- A jury decided almost 70% of the approximately 26,950 general civil trials disposed of in 2005.
- About 60% of the general civil trials included in the survey involved a tort claim and about a third involved contractual issues.
- Plaintiffs won in almost 60% of trials overall.
- The median damage award for plaintiffs who won monetary damages in general civil trials was $28,000 (figure 1).
- Punitive damages were awarded to 5% of plaintiff winners in general civil trials in 2005.
- In the nation's 75 most populous counties, the number of general civil cases disposed of by jury or bench trial declined by about 50% from 1992 to 2005.

The Civil Justice Survey of State Courts (CJSSC) examines tort, contract, and real property trials disposed of in general jurisdiction courts. It provides information such as the types of litigants involved in trials, who wins in civil trials, compensatory award amounts, punitive damages, and case processing times. The 2005 CJSSC was the first time that the series examined general civil trials concluded in a national sample of urban, suburban, and rural jurisdictions. Prior iterations of the CJSSC focused on general civil trial litigation in the nation's 75 most populous counties.

Motor Vehicle Accident Cases Accounted for Over a Third of Civil Trials in 2005

The majority (61%) of the nation's civil cases disposed of by trial involved a tort claim, in which the plaintiff(s) alleged injury, loss, or damage from the negligent or intentional acts of the defendant(s) (table 1). Contract cases, concerning an alleged breach of a contractual agreement, accounted for 33% of all civil trials in state courts in 2005. Real property cases, involving disputes over land ownership, accounted for 6%.

Table 1. Civil Trials in State Courts by Case Type, 2005

Case Type	Total Trials*		Percent Disposed Through Jury Trial
	Number	Percent of Total Trials	
All cases	26,948	100.0%	68.3%
Tort cases	16,397	60.8%	90.0%
Motor vehicle	9,431	35.0	92.1
Medical malpractice	2,449	9.1	98.7
Premises liability	1,863	6.9	93.8
Intentional tort	725	2.7	78.3
Other or unknown tort	664	2.5	71.6
Conversion	378	1.4	46.3
Product liability	354	1.3	93.5
Asbestos	87	0.3	95.5
Other	268	1.0	92.7
Slander/libel	187	0.7	64.2
Professional malpractice	150	0.6	59.9
Animal attack	138	0.5	80.6
False arrest, imprisonment	58	0.2	63.9
Contract cases	8,917	33.1%	36.0%
Seller plaintiff	2,883	10.7	16.6
Buyer plaintiff	2,591	9.6	44.1
Fraud	1,114	4.1	50.2
Rental/lease	605	2.2	19.2
Other employment dispute	558	2.1	62.9
Employment discrimination	319	1.2	91.2
Mortgage foreclosure	249	0.9	3.5
Other or unknown contract	245	0.9	52.2
Tortious interference	152	0.6	61.7
Partnership dispute	119	0.4	32.3
Subrogation	82	0.3	7.4
Real property cases	1,633	6.1%	26.4%
Title or boundary dispute	963	3.6	15.0
Eminent domain	542	2.0	50.7
Other or unknown real property	129	0.5	9.0

Note: Detail may not sum to 100% because of rounding.
*Trial cases include all bench and jury trials, trials with a directed verdict, judgments not withstanding the verdict, and jury trials for defaulted defendants. See *Methodology* for case type definitions.

The most common types of civil cases disposed of by trial were motor vehicle accident cases (35%), followed by seller plaintiff cases involving payments owed for the provision of goods or services (11%). Buyer plaintiff cases, in which the purchasers of goods or services sought the return of money, accounted for 10% of all civil cases disposed of by trial in 2005. Medical malpractice cases, involving the allegation of harm caused by a doctor, dentist, or other heath care provider, accounted for 9%, and premises liability cases, concerning an alleged harm from inadequately maintained or dangerous property, accounted for 7% of the civil trials. Employment discrimination and product liability cases each accounted for less than 2% of all civil trials in 2005.

Nine of Every 10 Tort Trials Resolved by Juries in 2005

Civil trials involving tort claims of personal injury or damaged property were most often heard before a jury (90%), rather than a judge (10%). Medical malpractice (99%), alleged illness or harm due to asbestos (96%) or some other product (93%), premises liability (94%), and motor vehicle accident (92%) cases were among the most likely tort claims to be tried by a jury in 2005.

Judges decided a greater percentage of business-related civil trials—contract (64%) and real property (74%) cases—than juries. Litigants waived their rights to a jury trial and had their cases decided by a judge in more than 80% of contract cases involving seller plaintiff, mortgage foreclosure, rental lease agreement, and subrogation issues. In the category employment discrimination, the majority (91%) of contract trials were decided by a jury.

Judges Hear Business Litigation More Often than Juries

Civil cases tried before juries and judges in state courts differed in terms of the litigants, plaintiff win rates, damage awards, and case processing times (table 2). Bench trials (57%) had a higher percentage of business litigants than jury trials (39%) and were likely to be decided in less time than jury trials. Judges were more likely than juries to find for plaintiffs. Plaintiffs won in 68% of bench trials, compared to about 54% of jury trials.

The median damage awards in 2005 were statistically similar for both jury and bench trials overall. Contract cases tried before a jury ($74,000), however, had significantly higher median final awards than contract cases decided by a judge ($25,000).

Table 2. Bench and Jury Trials in State Courts, by Selected Characteristics, 2005

	Jury	Bench
How many civil trials were decided by a Jury or Judge?	18,404	8,543*
Who were the litigants?[a]		
Individual vs. individual	45.5%	33.7%*
Individual vs. business	30.4	22.2*
Business vs. individual	1.8	17.9*
Business vs. business	6.4	16.8*

Table 2. (Cont'd)

	Jury	Bench
Who won?[b]		
Plaintiffs overall	54.4%	68.0%*
Plaintiffs in torts	52.8	60.8
Plaintiffs in contracts	61.6	70.1*
What was the median final award?[c]		
In all cases	$30,500	$24,000
In tort cases	24,300	21,100
In contract cases	74,000	25,000*
What percent of prevailing plaintiffs were awarded $1 million or more?		
In all cases	6.3%	1.6%*
In tort cases	5.7	3.7
In contract cases	8.7	1.0*
What percent of plaintiff winners seeking punitive damages were awarded punitive damages?[d]	34.0%	19.6%
What percent of cases were terminated within two years?[e]	56.9%	76.0%*

*Jury-bench difference is significant at the 95% confidence level.
[a]Data on litigant pairings were available for 99.8% of jury and 99.7% of bench trials. Bench and jury percentages do not add to 100% due to the exclusion of hospital and government litigants.
[b]Data on plaintiff winners were not applicable to real property trials. Data were available for 99.7% of tort and contract jury trials and 99.4% of tort and contract bench trials.
[c]There were 9,376 jury and 4,794 bench trials in which the plaintiff won an award. Median award amounts were calculated for plaintiff winners in tort and contract cases.
[d]Includes only the 1,824 plaintiff winners who sought punitive damages. Data were available for 96.6% of trials.
[e]Case processing data were available for 99.9% of jury and 99.5% of bench trials.

Table 3. Primary Litigants in Civil Trials in State Courts, by Case Type, 2005

Litigant by Case Type[a]	Total	Primary Litigant			
		Individual	Business[b]	Government[c]	Hospital[d]
All cases					
Plaintiff	100%	80.5	17.3	2.1	0.1
Defendant	100%	50.1	38.1	6.0	5.8
Tort					
Plaintiff	100%	95.8	4.0	0.1	/
Defendant	100%	55.0	29.3	7.0	8.8

Table 3. (Cont'd)

Litigant by Case Type[a]	Total	Primary Litigant			
		Individual	Business[b]	Government[c]	Hospital[d]
Contract					
Plaintiff	100%	55.0	43.3	1.3	0.3
Defendant	100%	36.9	58.4	3.3	1.4
Real property					
Plaintiff	100%	64.6	9.4	25.9	/
Defendant	100%	73.8	15.7	10.5	/

Note: Plaintiff or defendant type for each case is whichever type appears first in this list: 1. hospital/medical company, 2. governmental agencies, 3. corporate/business, and 4. individuals. A case with a hospital defendant was categorized as such even if a business, individual, or government was also a defendant in the case.
/No cases reported.
[a]0.1% of plaintiff types and 0.2% of defendant types are unknown.
[b]Includes insurance companies and other businesses not involved in the medical industry.
[c]includes government organizations and law enforcement agencies.
[d]Includes any organization or medical practice that provides health care and dental treatment. Individual doctors are counted as individuals.

Individuals Accounted for the Majority of Plaintiffs in Tort Trials; Businesses Were More Heavily Represented as Plaintiffs in Contract Disputes

In 2005, individuals accounted for the largest percentage of plaintiffs (81%) and defendants (50%) in civil trials (table 3). This held true in both tort and real property trials. For contract trials, the majority of defendants were businesses (58%). Also in contract trials, a larger percentage of plaintiffs were businesses (43%) than in tort (4%) or real property (9%) cases.

Real property cases involved the highest percentage of government plaintiffs (26%) and defendants (11%). A hospital or medical company was the plaintiff in less than 1% and the defendant in less than 6% of all civil bench and jury trials in 2005.

Seventy Percent of Civil Trials Involved Individuals Suing Other Individuals or Businesses; 40% of Trials Involved One Plaintiff and One Defendant

The most common civil trials involved an individual suing either another individual (42%) or a business (28%) (table 4). Businesses sued other businesses in about 10% of all civil trials. In 2% of all civil trials, a government entity initiated the lawsuit.

Table 4. Civil Trials in State Courts, by Litigant Pairings, 2005

Litigants	Number of Total Trials[a]
All trials	26,984
Individual versus —	
Individual	11,224
Business	7,472
Hospital	1,546
Government	1,383
Business versus —	
Individual	1,852
Business	2,604
Hospital	9
Government	198
Hospital versus[b] —	
Individual	13
Business	16
Hospital	7
Government versus[b] —	
Individual	384
Business	151
Government	22

[a]Litigant data were available for 99.7% of trials.
[b]There were no reported cases in which a hospital/medical company filed against the government or in which the government filed against a hospital/medical company.

Excluding class action lawsuits, almost 86,000 litigants were involved in general civil trials in 2005. Forty percent (10,800) of all civil trials disposed of in state courts in 2005 involved one plaintiff and one defendant. Almost half (47%) of all civil bench and jury trials in 2005 had multiple defendants, and more than a quarter (29%) had multiple plaintiffs (not shown in a table).

Plaintiffs Won in the Majority of Tort and Contract Trials

Plaintiffs won in more than half (56%) of all general civil trials concluded in state courts (table 5). In 2005, a higher percentage of plaintiffs won in contract (66%) than in tort (52%) cases.

Among tort trials, plaintiffs were most likely to win in cases involving an animal attack (75%), followed by motor vehicle accident (64%), asbestos (55%), and intentional tort (52%) cases. Plaintiffs had the lowest percentage of wins in medical malpractice trials (23%), product liability trials that did not involve asbestos (20%), and false arrest or imprisonment trials (16%), compared to plaintiffs in other tort cases.

In contract cases, plaintiffs won in the majority of trials for all case types except subrogation (28%), which involves an insurance company seeking to recover the amount paid on behalf of a client. Mortgage foreclosure cases, in

Table 5. Percent of Plaintiff Winners in Civil Trials in State Courts, by Case Type, 2005

Case Type	Total Trials	
	Number	Plaintiff Winners*
All cases	23,445	56.4%
Tort cases	15,428	51.6%
Animal attack	125	75.2
Motor vehicle	8,844	64.3
Product liability (asbestos)	82	54.9
Intentional tort	609	51.6
Conversion	296	48.3
Other or unknown tort	606	41.1
Slander/libel	175	39.4
Professional malpractice	143	39.2
Premises liability	1,827	38.4
Medical malpractice	2,397	22.7
Product liability (other)	265	19.6
False arrest, imprisonment	58	15.5
Contract cases	8,016	65.6%
Mortgage foreclosure	245	89.4
Seller plaintiff	2,610	74.6
Partnership dispute	102	65.7
Rental/lease	531	62.5
Buyer plaintiff	2,252	62.3
Employment discrimination	307	60.9
Tortious interference	146	60.3
Other or unknown contract	214	59.3
Fraud	1,041	59.1
Other employment dispute	519	50.9
Subrogation	51	27.5

Note: Data on plaintiff winners were not applicable to real property cases. Data on plaintiff winners were available for 99.6% of all tort and contract trials.

*Includes cases in which both the plaintiff and defendant won damages and the plaintiff award amount was greater than the defendant award amount. Excludes the 1,884 bifurcated trials in which the plaintiff litigated only the damage claim.

which the plaintiff was either a mortgage company or other financial lending institution, had the highest percentage of plaintiff winners (89%) of all tort and contract cases in 2005.

Over 60% of Plaintiff Winners Were Granted Final Awards of $50,000 or Less

Plaintiff winners in civil bench and jury trials were awarded an estimated sum of $6 billion in compensatory and punitive damages in 2005 (not shown in a table). Among the 14,000 plaintiffs awarded monetary damages, the median final award amount was $28,000 (table 6). Contract cases in general had higher median awards ($35,000) than tort cases ($24,000).

Table 6. Plaintiff Award Winners in Civil Trials in State Courts, by Case Type, 2005

Case Type	Number of Trials with Plaintiff Winner[a]	Median Final Award Amount[b]	Percent of Plaintiff Winners with Final Awards				
			<$10,000	$10,001- $50,000	$50,001- $250,000	$250,001- $1 Million	>$1 Million
All cases	14,170	$28,000	28.7%	33.0%	24.1%	9.9%	4.4%
Tort cases	8,455	$24,000	32.7%	30.6%	21.3%	10.4%	5.0%
Product liability	99	567,000	4.0	17.2	13.1	35.4	30.3
Asbestos	47	682,000	2.1	0.0	19.1	53.2	25.5
Other	52	500,000	5.8	32.7	7.7	17.3	36.5
Medical malpractice	584	400,000	0.7	5.3	29.1	43.8	21.1
False arrest, imprisonment	8	259,000	37.5	0.0	12.5	12.5	37.5
Professional malpractice	63	129,000	3.2	31.7	22.2	28.6	14.3
Premises liability	666	98,000	5.6	30.9	32.9	23.3	7.4
Other or unknown tort	305	83,000	36.1	8.9	27.2	12.5	15.4
Intentional tort	429	38,000	28.7	23.8	36.1	7.0	4.4
Conversion	148	27,000	24.3	31.8	37.2	4.1	2.7
Slander/libel	80	24,000	22.5	40.0	2.5	22.5	12.5
Animal attack	107	21,000	37.4	32.7	29.0	0.9	0.0
Motor vehicle	5,964	15,000	40.0	34.8	17.7	5.4	2.1
Contract cases	5,715	$35,000	22.7%	36.5%	28.3%	9.1%	3.5%
Employment discrimination	183	175,000	3.3	7.1	70.5	14.8	4.4
Tortious interference	90	169,000	8.9	12.2	34.4	24.4	20.0
Partnership dispute	82	120,000	7.3	24.4	41.5	22.0	4.9
Mortgage foreclosure	222	78,000	1.4	15.3	71.6	10.4	1.4

Table 6. (Cont'd)

Case Type	Number of Trials with Plaintiff Winner[a]	Median Final Award Amount[b]	Percent of Plaintiff Winners with Final Awards				
			<$10,000	$10,001-$50,000	$50,001-$250,000	$250,001-$1 Million	>$1 Million
Fraud	660	75,000	16.1	24.1	34.1	18.3	7.4
Other employment dispute	282	45,000	8.9	45.7	26.6	13.1	5.7
Rental/lease	293	35,000	25.6	38.2	27.3	7.8	1.0
Subrogation	44	30,000	25.0	70.5	4.5	0.0	0.0
Other or unknown contract	134	30,000	21.6	29.9	20.9	11.2	16.4
Seller plaintiff	2,177	27,000	23.0	45.2	24.9	4.9	2.0
Buyer plaintiff	1,549	17,000	34.2	35.6	19.9	8.2	2.1

Note: Data on plaintiff winners were not applicable to real property cases.

[a]Excludes bifurcated trials in which the plaintiff won on the liability only claim. Includes cases in which both the plaintiff and defendant won damages and the plaintiff award amount was larger. Also includes damages only trials in which the plaintiff was awarded a greater damage amount. Number of plaintiffs awarded damages may be different from the number of plaintiffs who successfully litigated the case. This difference is primarily due to the exclusion of plaintiff winners who receive no award because of award reductions and to the inclusion of bifurcated damage trials.

[b]Award data rounded to the nearest thousand. Median amounts calculated for compensatory plus punitive damage awards, after adjustments for contributory negligence, prior settlement, high/low agreement and damage caps but prior to post-trial activity and appeals.

Almost two-thirds (62%) of all plaintiff award winners were awarded $50,000 or less. A small percentage (about 4%) of all plaintiff award winners were awarded $1 million or more. Plaintiff winners in asbestos cases tended to win the highest award amounts. The median final award in asbestos cases was almost $700,000. More than three-quarters of all award amounts in asbestos cases were greater than $250,000.

Cases with median final awards over $150,000 included other product liability ($500,000), medical malpractice ($400,000), false arrest or imprisonment ($259,000), employment discrimination ($175,000), and tortious interference ($169,000).

Motor vehicle accident cases accounted for more than 40% of all plaintiff award winners in 2005. The median award in motor vehicle accident cases was $15,000. Forty percent of plaintiff winners in motor vehicle accident trials were awarded $10,000 or less.

Punitive Damages Were Awarded to 5% of Plaintiff Winners in General Civil Trials in 2005

Punitive damages are awarded to punish and deter the defendant. Punitive damages were sought in 13% of the approximately 14,000 general civil trials with plaintiff winners in 2005 (table 7). Plaintiffs were awarded punitive damages in 700 of the 14,000 trials (5%).

The median overall punitive damage amount awarded to plaintiff winners was $64,000. About a quarter (27%) of the punitive damage awards in 2005 were over $250,000 and 13% were $1 million or more. Of the approximately 450 contract cases in which punitive damages were awarded, plaintiffs were awarded punitive amounts of $250,000 or more in 40% of the trials.

Tortious interference ($6,900,000) and medical malpractice ($2,800,000) cases had among the highest median punitive damage awards for specific contract and tort case types. During 2005, there were less than 20 of each case type in which punitive damages were awarded. Among the case types in which punitive damages were awarded most frequently—intentional torts, fraud, and buyer plaintiff cases—the median punitive damage awards were $100,000 or less.

Largest Damage Award Was $172 Million

Of the civil trials sampled in state courts nationwide in 2005, the largest damage award was granted to approximately 116,000 California employees who brought a class-action lawsuit against a large retail corporation.

The lawsuit was originally filed in 2001 by several former employees and was expanded to cover California employees working for the retailer between 2001 and 2005. The employees claimed that the retailer had violated a California state law requiring that employees working six hours or more be given a 30-minute, unpaid lunch break. Under the law, if an employee was not permitted the break, the company was required to pay a full hour's wages in compensation. The employees maintained that they were owed more than $66 million plus interest.

After four months of testimony and three days of deliberation, an Alameda County jury awarded the plaintiffs $57 million in general damages and $115 million in punitive damages.

Table 7. Plaintiff Winners Who Sought and were Awarded Punitive Damages in Civil Trials, by Selected Case Types, 2005

Case Type	Number of Plaintiffs Who Sought Punitive Damages[a]	Punitive Damages Awarded[b]		Number of Cases with Punitive Damages	
		Number	Median Amount	Over $250,000	$1 Million or More
All cases	1,823	700	$64,000	191	93
Tort cases[c]	822	254	$55,000	59	43
Medical malpractice	56	6	2,835,000	5	5
Intentional tort	141	126	81,000	13	4
Conversion	31	12	50,000	5	2
Slander/libel	38	24	13,000	9	6
Motor vehicle	417	67	7,500	9	8
Animal attack	23	0	/	/	/
Contract cases[c]	1,001	446	$69,000	132	50
Tortious interference	42	18	6,888,000	12	11
Employment discrimination	84	10	115,000	1	1
Fraud	259	151	100,000	67	7
Seller plaintiff	88	14	86,000	2	0
Buyer plaintiff	372	138	53,000	20	3
Other employment disputes	93	86	10,000	12	10

/No cases reported.
[a]Data on punitive damages sought are available for 99.9% of total trial cases with a plaintiff winner.
[b]Data on punitive damages awarded are available for 97.5% of total trial cases with a plaintiff winner. Median amounts are reported prior to adjustments, post-trial activity, or appeals and are rounded to the nearest thousand.
[c]Specific case types will not sum to tort and contract totals because not all case types are shown in the table.

Punitive Damages Exceeded Compensatory Awards in Over Half of the Cases in Which They Were Awarded

In a number of cases since 1996 the United States Supreme Court has examined the issue of what constitutes a *grossly excessive*[3] ratio between plaintiff compensatory and punitive damage award amounts. In 2003, the Supreme Court opined that "few awards exceeding a single-digit ratio between punitive and compensatory damages . . . will satisfy due process."[4]

---

3. In BMW of North America, Inc. v. Gore, the U.S. Supreme Court ruled that the punitive damages of more than 500 times the amount of compensatory damages was *grossly excessive* and unconstitutional (517 U.S. 559, May 20, 1996).
4. State Farm Automobile Insurance Company v. Campbell (123 S. Ct. 1513:1524, April 7, 2003).

Table 8. Award Amounts for Plaintiffs Who were Awarded Punitive Damages in Civil Trials in State Courts, by Case Type, 2005

	Cases with Plaintiff Winner Awarded Punitive Damages	Sum Total of Damage Award Amounts (in Thousands)			Percent of Punitive Damage Cases with Punitive Awards		
		Total*	Punitive	Compensatory*	Greater than Compensatory Damage Awards	At Least 2 Times Greater than Compensatory Awards	At Least 4 Times Greater than Compensatory Awards
All cases	700	$2,170,338	$1,231,764	$914,371	52.8%	38.2%	26.1%
Tort cases	254	$802,227	$335,550	$454,781	37.4%	20.8%	8.3%
Contract cases	446	1,368,111	896,214	459,589	61.7	48.2	36.1

Note: Punitive and compensatory damage data will not sum to total because costs, fees, and interest have been excluded.
*Compensatory and total award damages do not include post-trial activity or appeals. Total award damage amounts include adjustments for contributory negligence, damage caps, high/low agreements and prior settlements. Compensatory amounts are adjusted to reflect award amounts after any counterclaim damage awards have been subtracted.

In 2005, punitive damages exceeded compensatory awards in 37% of tort and 62% of contract trials (table 8). Punitive awards were at least four times greater than compensatory awards in 26% of all applicable trials. In 17% of applicable trials, punitive awards exceeded compensatory awards by a ratio of 10 to 1 or greater (not shown in table).

Damage Awards Were Adjusted in About 16% of All Civil Trials

The initial compensatory and punitive damage amounts awarded to plaintiff winners were adjusted prior to trial end in about 16% of all trials (not shown in a table). Of the approximately 2,300 adjusted awards, over half (56%) were reduced due to findings of contributory negligence on the part of the plaintiff. A small percentage (about 1%) were adjusted because of damage caps. Thirty percent of the adjustments were due to miscalculation of cost, payment of additional fees, set-off claims, collateral source reductions, and other reasons.

Jury Trials Lasted Two Days Longer on Average than Bench Trials

In 2005, jury trials for general civil cases lasted almost four days on average (table 9). Bench trials lasted almost two days. Thirteen percent of jury trials and 70% of bench trials were completed within one day (not shown in a table). Among bench and jury trials, contract cases lasted slightly longer on average than both tort and real property cases.

Table 9. Case Processing Time and Days in Trial, by Case and Trial Type, 2005

Case Type	Mean Days in Trial		Mean Months from Filing to Disposition*	
	Jury	Bench	Jury	Bench
All cases	3.9	1.7	26.1	20.3
Tort cases	3.7	1.5	26.0	20.6
Contract cases	4.8	1.7	26.2	20.6
Real property cases	2.9	1.6	30.4	18.8

Note: Data on the number of days in trial were available for 94% of jury trials and 96% of bench trials. Data on the number of months from complaint filing to case disposition were available for 99.9% of jury trials and 99.5% of bench trials.
*Disposition refers to the date the verdict was rendered for jury trials and the date the decision was announced for bench trials.

Asbestos jury trials tended to take the most time, averaging 13 days in trial. Although less than 10% of employment discrimination, medical malpractice, and other product liability cases were bench trials, these cases took the longest for judges to hear and dispose (about three days). The longest trial recorded in the 2005 CJSSC sample was a premises liability case, in which the trial lasted for 69 days (not shown in a table).

Majority of Bench and Jury Trials Were Disposed Within Two Years of Filing

Cases heard before a jury took more time from filing of the complaint to rendering of the verdict than those heard before a judge. On average, the processing of a case required an additional half year for a jury trial (26 months), compared to a bench trial (20 months). About three-quarters (76%) of bench trials and more than half (57%) of jury trials were disposed of within two years of filing.

Overall, there was little difference in the average number of months needed for tort and contract case processing. Real property jury trials took about four months longer from filing to verdict than tort and contract jury trials. Real property bench trials took two months less time on average to process, compared to other general civil bench trials. Among jury trials, mortgage foreclosure (47 months), false arrest and imprisonment (40 months), and tortious interference (36 months) cases took the longest to process on average. Partnership dispute cases averaged the longest time from filing to bench trial judgment (43 months) (not shown in a table).

Litigants Filed Notices of Appeal in Nearly 1 in 5 Civil Trials

Litigants who seek to overturn or modify a verdict or judgment that they believe does not comply with state law have the option of filing a notice of appeal. Appeals were filed with the trial court in 17% of general civil trials concluded in 2005 (not shown in a table).

The rate of appeal for civil bench and jury trials varied depending on the case outcome. Plaintiffs filed appeals in 5% of general civil trials in which they prevailed, and in 15% of civil trials in which they did not win any monetary award (not shown in a table). Defendants gave trial court notice of appeal in 12% of civil trials with a plaintiff winner, and in 2% of trials in which the plaintiff did not receive an award.

In the Nation's 75 Most Populous Counties, the Total Number of Civil Trials Declined by Over 50% from 1992 to 2005

Prior to the 2005 CJSSC, BJS funded three surveys that examined general civil trial litigation. The surveys focused on general civil trials concluded in a sample of the nation's 75 most populous counties in 1992, 1996, and 2001.

For the purpose of discussing trends in this report, this section focuses on civil trial litigation in the nation's 75 most populous counties rather than on the national sample examined in 2005. The trends analyses has been restricted to the nation's 75 most populous counties as data from previous BJS civil justice surveys cannot be used to generate national level estimates.

In the nation's 75 most populous counties, the number of civil trials decreased 52%, from 22,451 in 1992 to 10,813 in 2005 (table 10). Tort cases decreased the least (40%), while real property (77%) and contract (63%) cases registered the largest declines. Among tort cases, product and premises liability experienced the sharpest declines, while decreases in medical malpractice cases were not statistically significant from 1992 to 2005. In terms of contract trial litigation, seller plaintiff cases saw the largest declines (73%) and the number of fraud and buyer plaintiff cases dropped by about 50%.

Data from the two most recent BJS civil trial surveys showed stabilization in the number of general civil trials. From 2001 to 2005, the number of general civil trials concluded in the nation's 75 most populous counties declined by 9%, a decrease that was not statistically significant.

NOTE ON CIVIL LITIGATION IN FEDERAL COURTS

The statistics above focus on state courts, where 98% of U.S. civil litigation occurs. The analogous federal data is gathered by the Administrative Office of the United States Courts, whose most recent report appears online at http://www.uscourts.gov/judbus2008/contents.cfm. Those data tell a story first of a much smaller number of civil filings — between 250,000 and 300,000 a year over the past few years (compared to 10 million state filings). The number of filed civil cases declined modestly from 2004 to 2005. About a third of federal civil cases *could* have been filed in state courts because the sole basis of jurisdiction was diversity, as to which state and federal courts share jurisdiction. About 17% of federal filings come to federal court because the United States is a party: these comprise everything from multibillion dollar disputes over defense contracts to claims for injuries involving postal trucks and suits seeking to collect on unpaid student loans. Unlike the state cases, where contract claims dominate, tort claims predominate on the federal civil docket, comprising about 23% of the docket. The next two categories, contracts and civil rights, each account for about 12% of the filings.

The median time to termination for these civil filings was, in 2009, eight months. As with state courts most cases end quickly, often without any court action, in less than six months. Judicial involvement increases the time to termination (not because judges gum up the works, but because the cases that require judicial involvement are the cases where the parties cannot agree). If one disregards one massive block of asbestos cases in the 5th Circuit that took almost 14 years to conclude, even cases requiring a trial took about two years.

C. CLIENTS: REPRESENTATION AS THE HINGE OF LITIGATION DYNAMICS

NOTE ON REGULATION OF THE LEGAL PROFESSION

With this section we move from the global and statistical to the professional and "legal." Those yearning for the doctrinal material typical of law school courses will be relieved: we're back on familiar ground, with statutes, rules, and cases. The topic is the special obligations required of lawyers because they are lawyers and the consequences of failing to fulfill those obligations. Those consequences can include both discipline by the state bar (up to and including disbarment) and, on a parallel track, liability for legal malpractice. Both are expanding fields. In recent decades state bars, in response to public pressure, have increased the scope of their "prosecutorial" functions. At the same time legal malpractice is booming: both the number of cases brought and the average size of the recoveries has trended steadily upward in recent decades. In fact, both the prosecution and defense of state bar actions and legal malpractice claims have emerged as growing niche practices in their own rights.

As you absorb these materials, keep the preceding sections in mind. For example, consider whether bar discipline and legal malpractice claims are alternative tracks — one characterizing Heinz's Hemisphere I lawyers, the other his Hemisphere II lawyers. Why would this be? What kinds of problems would be most likely to emerge in what forms of practice? Consider as well how the various configurations of practitioners might try to help their colleagues avoid such pitfalls.

1. DUTIES OF LAWYERS AS LAWYERS

a. The Formal Structure: Selected Model Rules of Professional Conduct

---
Rule 1.1: Competence

A lawyer shall provide competent representation to a client. Competent representation requires the legal knowledge, skill, thoroughness and preparation reasonably necessary for the representation.

Rule 1.3: Diligence

A lawyer shall act with reasonable diligence and promptness in representing a client.

Rule 1.5(e): Fees

(e) A division of a fee between lawyers who are not in the same firm may be made only if:

(1) the division is in proportion to the services performed by each lawyer or each lawyer assumes joint responsibility for the representation;

(2) the client agrees to the arrangement, including the share each lawyer will receive, and the agreement is confirmed in writing; and

(3) the total fee is reasonable.

Compare: California Rule of Professional Conduct 2-200

(A) A member shall not divide a fee for legal services with a lawyer who is not a partner of, associate of, or shareholder with the member unless:

(1) The client has consented in writing thereto after a full disclosure has been made in writing that a division of fees will be made and the terms of such division; and

(2) The total fee charged by all lawyers is not increased solely by reason of the provision for division of fees and is not unconscionable as that term is defined in rule 4-200.

Rule 1.6: Confidentiality of Information

(a) A lawyer shall not reveal information relating to the representation of a client unless the client gives informed consent, the disclosure is impliedly authorized in order to carry out the representation or the disclosure is permitted by paragraph (b).

(b) A lawyer may reveal information relating to the representation of a client to the extent the lawyer reasonably believes necessary:

(1) to prevent reasonably certain death or substantial bodily harm;

(2) to prevent the client from committing a crime or fraud that is reasonably certain to result in substantial injury to the financial interests or property of another and in furtherance of which the client has used or is using the lawyer's services;

(3) to prevent, mitigate or rectify substantial injury to the financial interests or property of another that is reasonably certain to result or has resulted from the client's commission of a crime or fraud in furtherance of which the client has used the lawyer's services;

(4) to secure legal advice about the lawyer's compliance with these Rules;

(5) to establish a claim or defense on behalf of the lawyer in a controversy between the lawyer and the client, to establish a defense to a criminal charge or civil claim against the lawyer based upon conduct in which the client was involved, or to respond to allegations in any proceeding concerning the lawyer's representation of the client; or

(6) to comply with other law or a court order.

Rule 1.7: Conflict of Interest: Current Clients

(a) Except as provided in paragraph (b), a lawyer shall not represent a client if the representation involves a concurrent conflict of interest. A concurrent conflict of interest exists if:

(1) the representation of one client will be directly adverse to another client; or

(2) there is a significant risk that the representation of one or more clients will be materially limited by the lawyer's responsibilities to another client, a former client or a third person or by a personal interest of the lawyer.

(b) Notwithstanding the existence of a concurrent conflict of interest under paragraph (a), a lawyer may represent a client if:

(1) the lawyer reasonably believes that the lawyer will be able to provide competent and diligent representation to each affected client;

(2) the representation is not prohibited by law;

(3) the representation does not involve the assertion of a claim by one client against another client represented by the lawyer in the same litigation or other proceeding before a tribunal; and

(4) each affected client gives informed consent, confirmed in writing.

Rule 1.8: Conflict of Interest: Current Clients: Specific Rules

(a) A lawyer shall not enter into a business transaction with a client or knowingly acquire an ownership, possessory, security or other pecuniary interest adverse to a client unless:

(1) the transaction and terms on which the lawyer acquires the interest are fair and reasonable to the client and are fully disclosed and transmitted in writing in a manner that can be reasonably understood by the client;

(2) the client is advised in writing of the desirability of seeking and is given a reasonable opportunity to seek the advice of independent legal counsel on the transaction; and

(3) the client gives informed consent, in a writing signed by the client, to the essential terms of the transaction and the lawyer's role in the transaction, including whether the lawyer is representing the client in the transaction.

(b) A lawyer shall not use information relating to representation of a client to the disadvantage of the client unless the client gives informed consent, except as permitted or required by these Rules.

(c) A lawyer shall not solicit any substantial gift from a client, including a testamentary gift, or prepare on behalf of a client an instrument giving the lawyer or a person related to the lawyer any substantial gift unless the lawyer or other recipient of the gift is related to the client. For purposes of this paragraph, related persons include a spouse, child, grandchild, parent, grandparent or other relative or individual with whom the lawyer or the client maintains a close, familial relationship.

(d) Prior to the conclusion of representation of a client, a lawyer shall not make or negotiate an agreement giving the lawyer literary or media rights to a portrayal or account based in substantial part on information relating to the representation.

(e) A lawyer shall not provide financial assistance to a client in connection with pending or contemplated litigation, except that:

(1) a lawyer may advance court costs and expenses of litigation, the repayment of which may be contingent on the outcome of the matter; and

(2) a lawyer representing an indigent client may pay court costs and expenses of litigation on behalf of the client.

(f) A lawyer shall not accept compensation for representing a client from one other than the client unless:

(1) the client gives informed consent;

(2) there is no interference with the lawyer's independence of professional judgment or with the client-lawyer relationship; and

(3) information relating to representation of a client is protected as required by Rule 1.6.

(g) A lawyer who represents two or more clients shall not participate in making an aggregate settlement of the claims of or against the clients, or in a criminal case an aggregated agreement as to guilty or nolo contendere pleas, unless each client gives informed consent, in a writing signed by the client. The lawyer's disclosure shall include the existence and nature of all the claims or pleas involved and of the participation of each person in the settlement.

(h) A lawyer shall not:

(1) make an agreement prospectively limiting the lawyer's liability to a client for malpractice unless the client is independently represented in making the agreement; or

(2) settle a claim or potential claim for such liability with an unrepresented client or former client unless that person is advised in writing of the desirability of seeking and is given a reasonable opportunity to seek the advice of independent legal counsel in connection therewith.

(i) A lawyer shall not acquire a proprietary interest in the cause of action or subject matter of litigation the lawyer is conducting for a client, except that the lawyer may:

(1) acquire a lien authorized by law to secure the lawyer's fee or expenses; and

(2) contract with a client for a reasonable contingent fee in a civil case.

. . .

Rule 1.9: Duties to Former Clients

(a) A lawyer who has formerly represented a client in a matter shall not thereafter represent another person in the same or a substantially related matter in which that person's interests are materially adverse to the interests of the former client unless the former client gives informed consent, confirmed in writing.

(b) A lawyer shall not knowingly represent a person in the same or a substantially related matter in which a firm with which the lawyer formerly was associated had previously represented a client. . . .

(c) A lawyer who has formerly represented a client in a matter or whose present or former firm has formerly represented a client in a matter shall not thereafter:

(1) use information relating to the representation to the disadvantage of the former client except as these Rules would permit or require with respect to a client, or when the information has become generally known; or

(2) reveal information relating to the representation except as these Rules would permit or require with respect to a client.

Rule 1.10: Imputation of Conflicts of Interest: General Rules

(a) While lawyers are associated in a firm, none of them shall knowingly represent a client when any one of them practicing alone would be prohibited from doing so by Rules 1.7 or 1.9, unless the prohibition is based on a personal interest of the prohibited lawyer and does not present a significant risk of materially limiting the representation of the client by the remaining lawyers in the firm.

(b) When a lawyer has terminated an association with a firm, the firm is not prohibited from thereafter representing a person with interests materially adverse to those of a client represented by the formerly associated lawyer and not currently represented by the firm, unless:

(1) the matter is the same or substantially related to that in which the formerly associated lawyer represented the client; and

(2) any lawyer remaining in the firm has information protected by Rules 1.6 and 1.9(c) that is material to the matter.

(c) A disqualification prescribed by this rule may be waived by the affected client under the conditions stated in Rule 1.7.

(d) The disqualification of lawyers associated in a firm with former or current government lawyers is governed by Rule 1.11.

b. Informal Exhortations

STATE BAR OF CALIFORNIA, CALIFORNIA ATTORNEY GUIDELINES OF CIVILITY AND PROFESSIONALISM

Adopted by the Board of Governors of the California State Bar, July 20, 2007, available online at http://calbar.ca.gov/calbar/pdfs/reports/ Atty-Civility-Guide.pdf

Introduction

As officers of the court with responsibilities to the administration of justice, attorneys have an obligation to be professional with clients, other parties and counsel, the courts and the public. This obligation includes civility, professional integrity, personal dignity, candor, diligence, respect, courtesy, and cooperation, all of which are essential to the fair administration of justice and conflict resolution.

These are guidelines for civility. The Guidelines are offered because civility in the practice of law promotes both the effectiveness and the enjoyment of the practice and economical client representation. The legal profession must strive for the highest standards of attorney behavior to elevate and enhance our service to justice. Uncivil or unprofessional conduct not only disserves the individual involved, it demeans the profession as a whole and our system of justice.

These voluntary Guidelines foster a level of civility and professionalism that exceed the minimum requirements of the mandated Rules of Professional Conduct as the best practices of civility in the practice of law in California.

The Guidelines are not intended to supplant these or any other rules or laws that govern attorney conduct. Since the Guidelines are not mandatory rules of professional conduct, nor rules of practice, nor standards of care, they are not to be used as an independent basis for disciplinary charges by the State Bar or claims of professional negligence. . . .

Section 7 — Service of Papers

The timing and manner of service of papers should not be used to the disadvantage of the party receiving the papers.

For example:

a. An attorney should serve papers on the attorney who is responsible for the matter at his or her principal place of work.
b. If possible, papers should be served upon counsel at a time agreed upon in advance.
c. When serving papers, an attorney should allow sufficient time for opposing counsel to prepare for a court appearance or to respond to the papers.
d. An attorney should not serve papers to take advantage of an opponent's absence or to inconvenience the opponent, for instance by serving papers late on Friday afternoon or the day preceding a holiday.
e. When it is likely that service by mail will prejudice an opposing party, an attorney should serve the papers by other permissible means.

Section 8 — Writings Submitted to the Court, Counsel or Other Parties

Written materials directed to counsel, third parties or a court should be factual and concise and focused on the issue to be decided.

For example:

a. An attorney should not make ad hominem attacks on opposing counsel.
b. Unless at issue or relevant in a particular proceeding, an attorney should avoid degrading the intelligence, ethics, morals, integrity, or personal behavior of others.
c. An attorney should clearly identify all revisions in a document previously submitted to the court or other counsel.

Section 9 — Discovery

Attorneys are encouraged to meet and confer early in order to explore voluntary disclosure, which includes identification of issues, identification of persons with knowledge of such issues, and exchange of documents. Attorneys are encouraged to propound and respond to formal discovery in a manner designed to fully implement the purposes of the Civil Discovery Act. An attorney should not use discovery to harass an opposing counsel, parties, or witnesses. An attorney should not use discovery to delay the resolution of a dispute. For example:

a. As to Depositions:
   1. When another party notices a deposition for the near future, absent unusual circumstances, an attorney should not schedule another deposition in the same case for an earlier date without opposing counsel's agreement.
   2. An attorney should delay a scheduled deposition only when necessary to address scheduling problems and not in bad faith.
   3. An attorney should treat other counsel and participants with courtesy and civility, and should not engage in conduct that would be inappropriate in the presence of a judicial officer.

4. An attorney should remember that vigorous advocacy can be consistent with professional courtesy, and that arguments or conflicts with other counsel should not be personal.

5. An attorney questioning a deponent should provide other counsel present with a copy of any documents shown to the deponent before or contemporaneously with showing the document to the deponent.

6. Once a question is asked, an attorney should not interrupt a deposition or make an objection for the purpose of coaching a deponent or suggesting answers.

7. An attorney should not direct a deponent to refuse to answer a question or end the deposition without a legal basis for doing so.

8. An attorney should refrain from self-serving speeches and speaking objections.

b. As to Document Demands:

1. Document requests should be used only to seek those documents that are reasonably needed to prosecute or defend an action.

2. An attorney should not make demands to harass or embarrass a party or witness or to impose an inordinate burden or expense in responding.

3. If an attorney inadvertently receives a privileged document, the attorney should promptly notify the producing party that the document has been received.

4. In responding to a document demand, an attorney should not intentionally misconstrue a request in such a way as to avoid disclosure or withhold a document on the grounds of privilege.

5. An attorney should not produce disorganized or unintelligible documents, or produce documents in a way that hides or obscures the existence of particular documents.

6. An attorney should not delay in producing a document in order to prevent opposing counsel from inspecting the document prior to or during a scheduled deposition or for some other tactical reason.

c. As to Interrogatories:

1. An attorney should narrowly tailor special interrogatories and not use them to harass or impose an undue burden or expense on an opposing party.

2. An attorney should not intentionally misconstrue or respond to interrogatories in a manner that is not truly responsive.

3. When an attorney lacks a good faith belief in the merit of an objection, the attorney should not object to an interrogatory. If an interrogatory is objectionable in part, an attorney should answer the unobjectionable part.

c. The Consequences

JOHN CAHER, PROPOSAL GIVES HIGHER PENALTIES TO FAKE LAWYERS

New York Law Journal, February 6, 2006, at 1

The New York state Senate Judiciary Committee last week approved a bill that would make the unauthorized practice of law a felony on par with statutory rape, stalking, insurance fraud, identity theft and inciting a riot.

It would also make the penalty for unlawful practice a maximum of four years in state prison, the same potential punishment faced by doctors, accountants, architects and certified shorthand reporters who ply a professional trade without the appropriate license.

"Licenses and registration ensure the public that a certain level of competency has been achieved to practice within a profession," the bill's sponsor, Charles Fuschillo Jr., R-Long Island, said in his justification memo. "Certainly, the unlawful practice of law should constitute a crime equivalent to the unauthorized practice of a profession."

Fuschillo said the aim of the law is to "provide consistency" within the profession. He noted that under Education Law §6512, anyone who wrongly presents himself as a professional in a field requiring a license is guilty of a Class E felony. His bill would amend §485 of the Judiciary Law, which describes the unlawful practice of law as a misdemeanor. §1865 is a new bill that has not previously been introduced during a legislative session. It would take effect 60 days after passage.

State Bar President A. Vincent Buzard declined to take a position on whether unauthorized practice should be a felony. However, he recognized that unauthorized practice is a "significant problem," and one that prompted him to appoint a task force to study the issue. The task force's report is expected in March.

The problem varies around the state, said Buzard, of Harris Beach in Rochester. "In New York City, it more relates to immigration law, whereas upstate it is more of a real estate practice issue. But it is . . . a consumer protection issue."

Buzard said part of the problem is that local district attorneys often lack the time and resources to aggressively pursue sham lawyers. Senate Judiciary Committee Chairman John A. DeFrancisco, R-Syracuse, has for several years introduced legislation that would give the attorney general jurisdiction over unauthorized practice cases. That legislation, however, has failed to gain traction in the Legislature.

Hawes v. State Bar of California

797 P.2d 1180 (Cal. 1990)

The Review Department of the State Bar Court (review department) has recommended that petitioner William Ray Hawes be suspended from the practice of law in California for five years, that execution of the suspension order be stayed, and that he be placed on probation for five years upon conditions that include actual suspension from the practice of law for three years. Petitioner's main contention is that the recommended discipline is excessive because his misconduct resulted in significant measure from a mental disturbance, bipolar affective disorder that is now controlled by medication, and also from related alcoholism and drug abuse that he has now overcome. We agree.

Facts

. . .

A. Evidence Relating to Misconduct

[Petitioner began having professional problems when he left his government position and became a solo practitioner. This case arises out of petitioner's actions in six different matters. Among the many instances of misconduct were: unavailability to clients (in one matter, the client could not reach petitioner for four years); failure to reply to former clients' new counsel and to the state bar; failure to respond to and to propound discovery; failure to contact clients and to keep appointments with them; submitting incomplete and unverified interrogatory answers; failure independently to investigate a case; omitting opening and closing statements at trial; failure to attempt to negotiate settlement; and refusal to return a client's file.]

B. State Bar Findings

The hearing panel made these findings: (1) in each instance, petitioner failed to use reasonable diligence to accomplish the purpose for which he was employed . . . ; (2) . . . petitioner withdrew from employment without taking reasonable steps to avoid foreseeable prejudice to his clients' rights; (3) . . . petitioner failed to return unearned fees . . . ; (4) . . . petitioner failed to cooperate in the State Bar investigation . . . ; (5) . . . petitioner demonstrated a lack of support of state law . . . ; (6) . . . petitioner showed disrespect to the court . . . ; and (7) petitioner demonstrated a pattern of misconduct.

The review department adopted each of these findings.

C. Mitigating Circumstances

Petitioner presented evidence of the following circumstances in mitigation: At the time of the misconduct, petitioner was abusing alcohol and methamphetamines. Petitioner began to take methamphetamines under prescription to control his weight, and there is no evidence he ever obtained methamphetamines illegally, but he evidently became dependent on the drug and took it for purposes other than that for which it was originally prescribed.

Petitioner was first diagnosed as having bipolar affective disorder, previously known as manic-depressive illness, in January 1984. Lithium carbonate was prescribed to control the disorder, but at a dosage that proved insufficient. Petitioner ceased taking the medication on his own accord shortly after it was prescribed, and he resumed his use of alcohol and methamphetamines.

In October 1984, petitioner was convicted of contempt of court in a matter unrelated to this proceeding. He was placed on probation on certain conditions, including that he abstain from the use of alcohol and controlled substances, that he participate in an Alcoholics Anonymous or a Narcotics Anonymous program, and that he take part in a drug monitoring program with regular blood or urine analysis. Between October 1984 and September 1986, petitioner violated his probation at least three times by taking methamphetamines. As a result, the period of probation was extended from two to four years.

In September 1986, petitioner was referred to The Other Bar, an alcohol counseling program for attorneys, as a result of which he entered an inpatient recovery program. While in this program, petitioner's bipolar affective disorder diagnosis was confirmed and he was again placed on a regimen of lithium carbonate, this time at an adequate dosage. Since his discharge from the program in October 1986, petitioner has been regularly taking his medication and has totally abstained from alcohol and methamphetamine use.

In the opinion of his treating physician, petitioner has become a completely changed, normal and stable person.

The hearing panel, however, concluded "there is no assurance that [petitioner's] present stable condition will continue." The panel noted that the period of petitioner's abstinence from alcohol and methamphetamines, as well as control of his mental disorder through medication, was at that time less than *two* years; that during this time he was subject to regular blood or urine testing as a condition of his probation in the contempt matter; and that he previously had suffered relapses during which he discontinued medication or resumed alcohol and drug abuse. The review department adopted the hearing panel's conclusion after correcting it to recite that the period of demonstrated rehabilitation was then less than *one* year.

In addition, the hearing panel made these findings, which were also adopted by the review department, regarding mitigating circumstances: petitioner has no prior record of discipline; none of the clients affected by petitioner's misconduct was seriously harmed; and during the period of his misconduct, petitioner's marriage was the subject of a dissolution proceeding that was very stressful for him, but he has since remarried and established a stable home life.

D. Discipline Recommended by the State Bar

The hearing panel noted that disbarment was authorized under the State Bar's Standards for Attorney Sanctions for Professional Misconduct . . . It concluded, however, that the factors in mitigation were more compelling than those in aggravation, and recommended that petitioner be suspended for five years, that execution of the suspension is stayed, and that petitioner be placed on probation for five years subject to specified conditions, including actual suspension of one year. . . .

Discussion . . .

Because petitioner has furnished us with persuasive evidence, not available to the review department, that he has successfully completed a meaningful and sustained period of rehabilitation, we conclude that the discipline recommended by the review department is excessive and that the purposes of attorney discipline are better served by imposing one year, rather than three years, of actual suspension from the practice of law.

We order that William Ray Hawes be suspended from the practice of law for five years from the date this opinion is final but that execution of the suspension order be stayed and that he be placed on probation for five years on all the conditions of probation adopted by the review department at its June 16, 1988, meeting, except that he shall be actually suspended for only the first year, rather than the first three years, of the probationary period.

It is further ordered that William Ray Hawes comply with the requirements of rule 955 of the California Rules of Court [Duties of disbarred, resigned, or suspended attorneys] . . . (under §6126, subd. (c), failure to comply with rule 955 of the California Rules of Court may result in imprisonment), and that he take and pass the Professional Responsibility Examination given by the National Conference of Bar Examiners within one year of the effective date of this order.

This order is effective upon finality of this decision in this court.

IN RE DALE: IN THE MATTER OF JOSHUA M. DALE, A MEMBER OF THE STATE BAR

4 Cal. State Bar Rptr. 798 (2005)

Opinion on Review

Respondent, Joshua M. Dale, compromised the integrity of the criminal justice system when he systematically befriended and then cajoled Darryl Geyer, an incarcerated 22-year-old with a 10th grade education, into giving a confession about an arson fire at an apartment building. Geyer had previously confessed to the police about the fire, and the voluntariness of that confession was the key issue upon which he was appealing his second degree murder conviction. Respondent, who was representing the tenants in a negligence lawsuit against the apartment owner arising from the same fire and was facing the owner's summary judgment motion, needed Geyer's statement about the condition of the premises when he set the fire.

Respondent knew that the declaration he obtained from Geyer could be used as evidence at Geyer's re-trial if his conviction were reversed on appeal. Geyer's trial and appellate attorneys refused respondent's requests to contact Geyer, and they advised Geyer not to speak with respondent. Nevertheless, respondent intentionally used his status as an attorney to gain access to Geyer while he was in jail and to meet with him in private. He skillfully took advantage of Geyer's vulnerability and exacerbated Geyer's dissatisfaction with his attorneys. Respondent offered his services to represent Geyer at his parole hearing if he would sign the incriminating declaration, and Geyer acquiesced. Even after obtaining the declaration, respondent continued to curry favor with Geyer so that he would make himself available as a percipient witness at the civil trial. Respondent ultimately obtained a $400,000 settlement in his civil case.

The hearing judge found respondent culpable of violating rule 2-100 of the Rules of Professional Conduct by improperly communicating with a represented party; committing acts of moral turpitude in violation of Business and Professions Code section 6106; and breach of a fiduciary duty owed to a non-client in violation of section 6068, subdivision (a). She recommended, inter alia, four months' actual suspension. For the reasons set forth below, we modify her culpability determinations, but we nevertheless adopt her disciplinary recommendations. . . .

MIKE MCKEE, BAD NEWS FOR BAD LAWYERS: BAR LEADERS
WANT MISCREANTS TO FOOT THE TAB FOR DISCIPLINE

San Francisco Recorder, August 19, 2004, at 1

Getting bad lawyers out of the legal profession isn't cheap. Just ask State Bar of California officials who have calculated that policing their own puts the agency in a financial hole to the tune of about $600,000 a year.

But that might be changing soon as agency leaders push aggressive new measures that could force errant attorneys to pay a substantial portion of the costs of their own prosecution in State Bar Court.

Legislation went into effect this year that lets the State Bar go to court to seek civil judgments for certain costs assessed against disciplined lawyers. And Bar leaders are now reviewing a proposal that would force attorneys to pay several other costs, including prosecutors' hourly fees.

"The goal isn't to collect more money," says Roderick McLeod, one of the Bar governors backing the idea, "but rather to force these lawyers to shoulder more of these costs. We are trying to get attorneys that are causing the problems to share the burden."

Even so, the idea remains controversial — even within the State Bar itself. Some feel that the move would come across as an attack on solo practitioners and small-firm lawyers, while others believe it's an overly harsh punishment and very likely uncollectible. . . .

Adds Diane Karpman, a Los Angeles lawyer who represents attorneys: "Many of these lawyers wind up flipping burgers or selling clothes at Macy's. They are barely making it economically, and I would anticipate that this would result in less money being recovered."

Floundering lawyers might choose not to return to the law rather than to make payments beyond their means, some Bar staff agree. . . .

[Under current law] the State Bar recovers only about $350,000 to $400,000 of its $950,000 to $1 million in discipline costs each year.

The committee considered, and rejected, a couple of other proposals that were deemed too harsh. One was to raise the filing fees to apply for reinstatement from $900 to more than $11,000. The committee settled on $2,000 as a more reasonable sum. The other proposal would have allowed the State Bar to fine lawyers on top of suspending or disbarring them. The committee dismissed the idea entirely. . . .

Bar officials are too lenient on bad lawyers, [another bar governor asserted.] "They are not going after attorneys who face discipline problems tooth and nail. They want to give them every benefit of the doubt.

"It's almost like they have a sensitivity for the fallen," he adds. "And yet I don't see the same sensitivity for the upstanding, the people who don't get into trouble." . . .

STATE BAR OF CALIFORNIA, CLIENT SECURITY FUND

Available at State Bar of California Web site, http://www.calbar.ca.gov

The Client Security Fund is a public service of the California legal profession. The State Bar sponsored the creation of this fund to help protect consumers of legal services by alleviating losses resulting from the dishonest conduct of attorneys.

The fund may reimburse up to $50,000 for theft committed by a California lawyer. It covers the loss of money or property resulting from lawyer dishonesty (but not because the lawyer acted incompetently, committed malpractice or failed to take certain actions).

To qualify for reimbursement, you must be able to show that the money or property actually came into the lawyer's possession and that the loss was caused by the lawyer's dishonest conduct.

The types of dishonest conduct that may lead to reimbursement from the fund are:

- Theft or embezzlement of money or the wrongful taking or conversion of money or property;
- Refusal to refund unearned attorney fees paid to the lawyer in advance where the lawyer performed no services whatever, or such an insignificant portion of the services the lawyer agreed to perform such that the lawyer may be regarded at the time payment was made as having lacked the intention of performing the work;
- The borrowing of money from a client without the intention or reasonably anticipated ability to repay the money;
- Obtaining money or property from a client by representing that it would be used for investment purposes when no investment is made; and
- An act of intentional dishonesty or deceit that directly leads to the loss of money or property that actually came into the lawyer's possession.

The fund may reimburse fees you paid the lawyer, but only in very limited cases. Fees are not reimbursable simply because you are dissatisfied with the services, or because the work was not completed.

Since you will need to prove the attorney dishonestly took your money or property, you must first file a complaint against the attorney with the Attorney Discipline System before seeking reimbursement from the Client Security Fund.

NOTE ON REMEDIES FOR CLIENTS

All states appear to have some form of client protection fund, a fund typically created by bar dues. Notice two features of the California fund, which are widely replicated. Besides the absolute cap on recovery ($50,000 in California), the funds do *not* protect against ordinary malpractice — the topic of the next section. They permit clients to recover only for what amounts to lawyer theft. Further, note that to recover from the fund the client must file a complaint with the State Bar. As one would discover if one trolled further through the California site, the bar disciplinary authority must find that the lawyer had in fact stolen the client's money or failed to provide services before the client can recover from the fund. One suspects that the hope of such a recovery caused clients to complain of the acts of William Hawes, whose case appears above. Suppose a client was thus wronged by a lawyer. After reading the next section consider when you would expect the client to sue for malpractice and when you would expect her to take the Client Protection Fund route.

2. DUTIES OF LAWYERS AS PROFESSIONALS

JOHN LEUBSDORF, LEGAL MALPRACTICE & PROFESSIONAL RESPONSIBILITY

48 Rutgers Law Review 101 (1995)

Scholars and courts have not given much attention to legal malpractice law. They should. As claims multiply, firms suffer huge settlements and judgments, and malpractice insurance rates rise, the practical importance of malpractice law to lawyers increases. So does its broader significance for the legal profession.

The time has come to consider legal malpractice law as part of the system of lawyer regulation. In recent decades, that system has been transformed. Increasingly, professional ideals have been turned into enforceable law, and self-regulation by the organized bar has become regulation by courts and legislatures. The civil liability of lawyers obviously has a role to play in promoting the goals of this regulatory system. These goals include ensuring that lawyers fulfill their fiduciary duties to clients, restraining overly adversarial behavior which is harmful to non-clients, and promoting access to legal services. Yet legal malpractice law has rarely been considered in the light of such goals.

Scholars of the legal profession have tended to concentrate their attention on the rules promulgated by courts and enforced through disciplinary proceedings. The actual frequency of enforcement of those rules, however, is still not very high despite invigoration of the disciplinary system. Lawyer civil liability, by contrast, is neglected, receiving only a few pages of attention in standard coursebooks. . . .

Courts deciding malpractice cases tend to treat them as standard tort suits, at least on the surface. (As will appear below, the reality is quite different.) In part, this standard treatment is justifiable. One could hardly expect courts to develop new principles of causation, for example, just for legal malpractice suits. On the other hand, judges have been reluctant to acknowledge that special rules are appropriate for lawyers even when that is the case. Judges are not the only ones to seek refuge in the generalities of the law of torts; the proposed Restatement of the Law Governing Lawyers does the same thing.

The neglect of legal malpractice law contrasts strangely with the attention devoted to its big sister, medical malpractice law. The latter has received much attention from empirical investigators, analysts, and legislators. That may be because health and the health industry are more important than law and the law industry, because the attitudes of the medical profession differ from those of the legal profession, or for other reasons. Unfortunately, although some medical malpractice literature suggests interesting comparisons with legal malpractice, the two fields pose quite different problems. . . .

This article will demonstrate how legal malpractice law relates to three important functions of the law of lawyers, namely, delineating the duties of lawyers, creating appropriate incentives and disincentives for lawyers in their dealings with clients and others, and providing access to remedies for those injured by improper lawyer behavior. Most of the controverted issues in legal malpractice law can better be resolved if analyzed in light of these functions, rather than under the tort law scheme currently employed by courts. This article will discuss not only the traditional action for negligence — although the propriety of describing a malpractice action as one for negligence is one of the matters to be elucidated — but also other civil claims against lawyers arising from the practice of law. My focus, however, will be on the traditional action, for the nontraditional claims asserted against lawyers nowadays embrace every sort of civil wrong that a defendant could commit or a plaintiff's advocate could conceive.

I. Specifying Lawyers' Duties

One of the most striking ways in which medical and legal malpractice differ concerns the role of the courts in outlining standards for practice. Although courts properly fashion medical malpractice rules protecting patient rights, such as the informed consent doctrine, no sensible person wants courts to decide how doctors should practice medicine. When a court started down that road in Helling v. Carey,[21] the state legislature and the commentators quickly rejected its holding. Even when medical practice is clear, courts rarely seek to freeze it by imposing it as a matter of law. Rather, they leave the decision as to what constitutes malpractice to future juries, guided by future experts. This approach is proper: courts lack medical expertise, medicine evolves, and physicians should not shape medical procedures by consulting legal precedents.

Courts hearing legal malpractice cases should pursue a very different course. Judges are lawyers and usually have practiced law although their experience may be limited to litigation or another specialty. Moreover, judges themselves are the main authors of the changes affecting the law of lawyering. They promulgate professional rules, albeit drawing heavily on the proposals of the bar. They construe those rules, in disciplinary proceedings and otherwise, and resolve constitutional challenges to them. Judges frequently decide issues arising in litigation, such as motions to disqualify counsel, invocations of the attorney-client privilege, and attorney fee disputes. They have been responsible for the demolition of the bar's bans on advertising, unhindered price competition, and group practice. In most states, judges wield the inherent power to regulate the bar.

The standards of lawyer conduct applied in legal malpractice suits should parallel the standards courts apply in other contexts. Any other course would compromise the enforcement of the standards and subject lawyers to conflicting obligations. Malpractice actions, moreover, offer opportunities to elucidate standards that are generally accepted, such as the duties to keep a client informed and not to misuse a client's confidential information, as they apply to important and difficult situations. Such opportunities may not arise in disciplinary proceedings, which tend to involve gross misconduct.

Finally, legal malpractice cases offer courts an unusual opportunity to effectuate the rules they promulgate by influencing lawyers' conduct. Lawyers read malpractice decisions, and will heed the possibility of personal liability. Indeed, the evidence indicates that medical malpractice law has a substantial impact on the conduct of physicians, who are less likely than lawyers to learn of and follow legal precedents.

Nevertheless, courts have often failed to recognize the relevance of the judicial role in regulating the legal profession to basic, recurring issues of legal malpractice law. Those issues include the standard for malpractice, the relation between malpractice and breach of fiduciary duty, the relevance to malpractice of breaches of professional rules, and the role of expert witnesses.

---

21. 519 P.2d 981 (Wash. 1974) (holding that the failure to give a patient under forty the pressure test for glaucoma was malpractice regardless of the reported contrary medical practice).

A. What Is Malpractice?

Courts seeking to define the care that lawyers owe clients typically rely on combinations of reasonableness and norms of professional practice. Each of these definitions has its strengths; yet neither is sufficient alone or in combination.

1. Reasonableness

Reasonableness is the usual standard for negligence, either in its traditional "reasonable person" form or under the Learned Hand formula that calls on the judge or jury to balance the cost of precaution against the risk averted multiplied by its probability. Those who prefer to derive the malpractice action from an implied contractual duty of care — a derivation usually relevant only to the selection of a statute of limitations — reach the same test from that contractual basis.

2. Professional Practice

Courts decide medical malpractice cases under a standard based on sound professional practice. Some courts have applied a similar standard to legal malpractice cases. In medical cases, this standard reflects the obvious superiority of medical knowledge over legal insight as a guide for physicians.

Whatever its merits in medical malpractice cases, a professional practice test simply will not work for legal malpractice except in a very few areas where procedures are standardized as in real estate closings. Otherwise, we have no information about how most lawyers deal with most of the problems that arise in malpractice cases. A lawyer called as an expert witness will know of the practice in his or her firm and possibly also that of a few other firms. He or she cannot possibly know how most of the thousands of lawyers who practice in a typical jurisdiction handle a specific problem. Even were such knowledge available, it is unclear whose practice would set the standard. Some courts refer to the "average" lawyer, which implies that much of the bar is routinely committing malpractice. Speaking of the "ordinary" lawyer is no better. If we base the standard on the least competent lawyer who is not actually committing malpractice, we have simply rephrased the question at issue: what is malpractice?

Setting a standard requires considering what lawyers should do, not merely looking to what they actually do. Of course, the standard must be one that ordinary lawyers can meet. Moreover, any available evidence of common practice should be weighed heavily. Ultimately, however, courts must turn to prescriptive rather than descriptive sources.

Some prescriptive sources will come from within the profession. These include statements of professional standards, ABA ethics opinions, and recognized practice books. Even in medical malpractice cases, authoritative professional sources probably play a greater role than evidence of actual practice in setting the standard of care. Courts adjudicating legal malpractice cases, however, should not be limited to such materials in deciding how a lawyer should behave. They can turn to their own decisions in other malpractice cases and in cases dealing with such matters as ineffective assistance of counsel, disqualification for conflict of interest, and attorney fee forfeiture.

They can use professional rules and cases construing them. They can rely on general principles of fiduciary duty and agency law and on general understandings of the proper roles of lawyers.

Legal malpractice, in short, should be defined as failure to provide a client the services that a lawyer of ordinary knowledge, skill and diligence reasonably should provide. Both reasonableness and professional practice count importantly in this standard. The ultimate question, however, is whether the lawyer in question has done what a lawyer should do in light of all relevant concerns and authorities.

B. Breach of Fiduciary Duty

One part of the law regulating lawyers with which legal malpractice law should be integrated is the law defining and enforcing lawyers' fiduciary duties. Unfortunately, this integration has not yet been accomplished. . . .

The study of fiduciary duties should provide a useful bridge between traditional malpractice law and disciplinary rules and foster the integration of the two. Fiduciary duties are like traditional malpractice law in that they are enforced through civil actions by injured parties: the beneficiaries of the fiduciary relationship. They are like the obligations to clients set forth in disciplinary rules in that they articulate a relatively detailed regulatory scheme, based on the vulnerability of clients. At the same time, the invocation of fiduciary duty summons up the law and scholarship that deals with the duties of fiduciaries other than lawyers, such as trustees, corporate officers and directors, and agents. Ultimately, legal malpractice in the narrow sense should be considered just one form of actionable breach of fiduciary duty; breach of fiduciary duty should not be viewed as a peripheral subject area that must somehow be squeezed into legal malpractice. The action for legal malpractice in the narrow sense enforces duties of diligence and competence. These duties are themselves fiduciary in nature, classifiable as duties of care. But lawyers also owe duties of loyalty that are likewise enforceable by injured clients. Although distinctions between the enforcement of different duties will sometimes make sense, in general duties of care and of loyalty should be treated similarly for purposes of civil liability. From a client's point of view, it makes little difference whether a lawyer lost the case by failing to obtain vital information or by disclosing protected information to the opposing party.

Again, therefore, we are led to a unitary concept of legal malpractice, one that focuses on what lawyers should do and derives its standard from regions extending beyond traditional negligence law. That concept can help us analyze malpractice problems in a more specific and useful way. More importantly, it can help make malpractice liability a consistent part of lawyer regulation.

C. The Relevance of Professional Rules

By this point, the proper role of professional rules in legal malpractice actions should be clear. Although these rules are promulgated as bases for lawyer discipline, judges and juries should rely on them in delineating the details of lawyers' duties to their clients.

Because courts and scholars have given so much attention to professional rules, the role of those rules in malpractice actions has been litigated and discussed with desirable results. Courts have generally approved the use of professional rules as evidence of what the standard of care requires of a lawyer, with some holding that rules define that standard as a matter of law. Commentators likewise support use of the rules either as evidence of the standard or the standard per se. On the other hand, courts have rejected assertions that violation of a professional rule by itself gives rise to a cause of action, particularly in cases where a non-client sues a lawyer.

Using the professional rules makes sense. Not only do these rules reflect a broad consensus among courts and bar committees about how lawyers should behave, they also constitute law that lawyers must obey. Courts deciding whether to discipline a lawyer or whether to hold one liable for malpractice should seek to apply consistent standards of conduct.

Any other approach would threaten lawyers with inconsistent standards of conduct. When, for example, the disciplinary rules require a lawyer to withdraw from a representation, it would be intolerable to hold the lawyer liable in damages for abandoning a client. This result would be equally intolerable even if the rules permitted withdrawal, because such permission is usually based on important grounds of public policy. Similarly, when the rules forbid the lawyer to withdraw but the lawyer nevertheless does so, it is hard to imagine a situation in which the lawyer should be able to avoid malpractice liability by claiming that withdrawal was consistent with the duties a lawyer owes a client.

The argument for ignoring the rules in devising malpractice standards is based almost entirely on assertions by the American Bar Association, in the preambles to the Model Rules and Model Code, that the Rules and Code do not augment damage liability. Some state supreme courts did not include these disclaimers when they promulgated versions of the Rules or Code in their states. In any event, courts do not authorize the use of professional rules as evidence of professional standards because the rules themselves so provide, but because of the need for consistent, knowable principles for lawyers to follow. These, of course, are the same concerns underlying the traditional use by courts of criminal and other statutes to fill in the negligence standard, often by treating violations as negligent per se. Nor will using professional rules in malpractice suits discourage rule-makers from raising lawyer standards. Those who draft the rules already proceed on the assumption that they will inevitably affect civil suits, and indeed sometimes shape them for that purpose. And civil liability decisions in turn influence the drafting of rules.

Disciplinary rules cannot be a complete or infallible guide in malpractice actions. Some rules are too vague to provide much help. Other rules seek to protect non-clients and do not prescribe the duties that a lawyer owes to a client. Under accepted tort principles, violations of such rules are not evidence of a lawyer's negligence to a client, although they may sometimes indicate imprudent overzealousness likely to backfire against the client.

Most importantly, professional rules are not the only source of legal malpractice law. They must be harmonized with existing law on the civil liabilities of lawyers and other relevant law and should be considered in light of overall regulatory goals. Here again, harm to an opposing party furnishes an example: holding lawyers liable to such a party may unwisely dilute their loyalty to their clients, and must be considered with that in mind. This and other related problems of balancing incentives will be considered in Part II of this article.

D. The Role of Expert Witnesses

Lawyers and courts have used expert witnesses to fill the gaps left by the courts' failure to define with sufficient specificity what duties a legal malpractice action enforces. Courts have ordinarily required malpractice plaintiffs to produce an expert witness in order to go to the jury, except in the rare case in which it is plain that the acts alleged constitute malpractice. When the plaintiff introduces the testimony of one or more experts, the defendant usually replies in kind. Some of the more celebrated professional responsibility scholars often appear as experts, and have become like the Roman jurisconsults: private persons authorized to give legal opinions.

On what are the experts expert? Typically, on just the matters that I have been contending should be the responsibility of courts: how lawyers should act in various circumstances. . . .

II. Adjusting Lawyer Incentives

Many of the problems of lawyers' professional responsibility, and also of malpractice law, arise from the numerous impacts of lawyer behavior. Lord Brougham said that a lawyer knows — that is, should know — but one person in all the world, his client. The inescapable reality is that every lawyer is at the center of a web, affecting other people's lives with his or her behavior.

The central problem to which this reality gives rise is that of adversariness. To what extent are lawyers privileged to pursue the interests of clients at the expense of others? Another problem concerns lawyer independence from a client. To what extent may or must a lawyer act or advise on the basis of the lawyer's own values, even if a client might prefer a different course? A third group of problems, just beginning to be considered, involves law firms, house counsel offices, and other professional settings in which lawyers practice. To what extent should a lawyer be responsible for the conduct, or subject to the decisions, of colleagues?

Although these problems reappear in the law of legal malpractice, they fail to be recognized as familiar problems of professional responsibility. Instead, they are usually handled with the ungainly tools of negligence law. These problems, of course, are involved in the definition of a lawyer's duties to clients, which has already been discussed. Once a lawyer's duties are defined, however, recognizing the right of a client or non-client to sue for any violation gives rise to further difficulties.

These difficulties concern the clashing incentives liability may foster. Every cause of action encourages the prospective defendant to act to avoid liability. This is often desirable and is indeed a major reason for imposing liability. The incentive, however, may be too great or unfocused, leading to undesirable behavior. Such misincentives are particularly likely to arise from lawyer liabilities because a lawyer's acts often affect people with conflicting interests. Holding lawyers liable to clients increases the incentive to abuse non-clients; holding lawyers liable to non-clients increases the incentive to laxity in representing clients.

In this respect, medical malpractice differs from legal malpractice. Physicians may affect the lives of non-patients. The ethical problem of curing a murderer, for example, has long been recognized. Nonetheless, physicians do and should disregard these effects, receiving a privilege even broader than that of a lawyer to consider the well-being of one person alone. The exceptions are few and strictly limited. Although the drain one expensive case can cause on society's resources has led to increasing social concern, it receives only slight recognition in medical law. Furthermore, the medical profession and others have generally disregarded conflicts between doctors' interests and the interests of their patients. Hence, analysts of legal malpractice law should focus on professional responsibility rather than seeking help that medical malpractice law cannot provide.

A. Lawyer Liability to Non-clients

The traditional tort battleground of privity furnishes poor terrain to determine when lawyers should be liable to non-clients. Traditional approaches furnish flexibility but offer few clues to the difficult problems. One can always extend liability by relying on vague Californian formulas stressing the foreseeability that a defendant's acts will harm others. In actions against lawyers, it has often been foreseeable that negligence by a lawyer could harm non-clients. Rendering lawyers liable to non-clients, however, may improperly hamper their efforts to look out for clients. This problem is distinct from the fears of unlimited liability and subjective claims of damage that have led many courts to restrict negligence liability in other situations.

Courts, when determining whether a non-client has a cause of action against a lawyer, should balance the possible incentive to lawyers not to serve their own clients properly and the need of the non-client for protection from lawyer misconduct. This calls for particularized inquiries, with an emphasis on such factors as whether the non-client is represented by counsel or otherwise protected. Some examples follow.

1. Recovery by Opposing Litigant

The arguments against allowing recovery by a non-client are strongest when a litigant sues opposing counsel. The adversary system, the judge, and the litigant's own counsel furnish considerable (albeit incomplete) protection against opposing counsel's misconduct. Subjecting a lawyer to suit by an opposing party, who has directly contrary interests and is already embroiled in litigation with the lawyer's client, could discourage the lawyer's protection of the client's interests. Recognizing a claim by a non-client would be less likely to discourage adversarial excess by lawyers than to multiply it by allowing the obstreperous to sue opposing counsel. . . .

Turning to the law of civil procedure, however, we often find courts holding lawyers liable under Federal Rule of Civil Procedure 11 and similar provisions in ways that are inconsistent with the tort rules. Before the 1993 amendments, an opposing litigant could institute Rule 11 proceedings against a lawyer with prospects (at least in some Circuits) of obtaining a substantial monetary award, even though courts insisted that the award was deterrence rather than compensation. The grounds for recovery—asserting a claim or defense without reasonable factual investigation or reasonable legal foundation—were hard to distinguish from negligence. Since it is unthinkable to recognize a tort duty of due care running between a lawyer and an opposing litigant, it is difficult to justify attorney liability under former Rule 11. . . .

2. Actions by Will Beneficiaries

At the opposite extreme from a litigant's suit against opposing counsel is one by a frustrated will beneficiary against a lawyer who drafted the will for a client and supervised its execution, but negligently failed to make it valid. Here, allowing the suit gives lawyers an added incentive to comply with the directives of their clients. Indeed, because the defect only appears after the client's death, the prospect of a suit by the beneficiary probably is the only civil damage incentive available. . . .

3. Claims by a Beneficiary Against Lawyers Who Represent Trustees and Executors

It is not surprising that courts disagree whether the lawyer for a trustee or executor owes a duty of care to the beneficiaries under the trust or will. Often it is unclear how such lawyers should act and what incentives are appropriate. Because the clients are themselves fiduciaries, they must act in the best interests of others. That limits the proper behavior of their lawyers, who may assist their clients only toward those clients' lawful ends. Beneficiaries are often the logical persons to enforce those limits. Yet in many situations trustees and executors may properly disagree with one or more beneficiaries, and in doing so they are entitled to the assistance of counsel, which should not be hindered by their lawyers' fear of suits by non-clients. . . .

4. Claims by Parties to Commercial Transactions Encouraged to Rely on Another Party's Lawyer

A buyer and a seller are usually persons with conflicting interests, despite their common interest in completing the sale. As with opposing litigants, allowing one party to sue the other's lawyer for lack of due care[135] could undermine that lawyer's service to his or her own client. Yet amid the great variety of commercial transactions, there are exceptions.

Courts thus have permitted suit for negligence when a lawyer or party has encouraged the opposing party to rely on the lawyer's words or acts. For example, a plaintiff may have insisted on the lawyer's opinion letter as a condition of the transaction. In other cases, a lawyer has volunteered advice or help to an unrepresented person at a real estate closing.

Recognizing non-client claims in such limited situations does not undermine services a client can properly expect from a lawyer. The client benefits from the non-client's reliance on the client's lawyer because that reliance facilitates the consummation of the transaction. Looking at the situation ex ante, the client benefits from the non-client's right to sue the lawyer for negligence

---

135. Intentional misrepresentation, by contrast, is actionable. *E.g.*, Hartford Accident & Indem. Co. v. Sullivan, 846 F.2d 377, 383-85 (7th Cir. 1988); Zafiris, Inc. v. Moss, 506 So. 2d 27, 28 (Fla. Dist. Ct. App. 1987).

because the existence of that right encourages non-clients to rely on lawyers in similar situations. No doubt some clients would benefit even more if they could use the reliance of a non-client without their lawyers' following through; but clients have no right to that benefit.

B. Lawyers and Clients

Legal malpractice law should give lawyers an incentive to pursue the best interests of clients. That seems simple enough, but courts have not always recognized it. Moreover, liability should sometimes be limited to protect the proper independence of the bar, among other reasons. Here, as elsewhere, courts should shape malpractice law to meet the concerns of professional responsibility law, not through unthinking application of tort law norms.

1. Damages for Emotional Distress

Although some courts routinely allow emotional distress damages in malpractice actions, other courts either regard them as a kind of punitive damages, granted only to punish egregious lawyer misconduct, or take intermediate positions. The hesitation to award such damages probably results from comparing malpractice claims arising from economic disputes to contract claims, in which emotional distress damages are rarely allowed. It also reflects fear of padded claims.

At a minimum, a party should be entitled to emotional distress damages upon a proper evidentiary showing when other damages are normally unavailable. Otherwise, lawyers would have a diminished incentive to exercise care in such situations. . . .

2. Malpractice in Criminal Defense

A number of courts have allowed a convicted criminal defendant to recover for malpractice only on a showing, not just that he or she would have been acquitted but for malpractice, but also that he or she was in fact innocent, or has received post-conviction relief setting aside the conviction. Such holdings reflect a fear of overstimulated defense lawyers or overlitigious convicts.

In my opinion, there is more reason to fear that defense lawyers will do too little than too much. . . . With great respect for the many dedicated and able criminal defense lawyers who continue to strive in difficult circumstances to make defendants' rights a reality, and with regrets for making their lives still harder, there is no reason to exempt the defense bar from the malpractice remedy considered salutary for other lawyers.

3. A Lawyer Independence Defense

One way to deal with the possibility that malpractice liability will push lawyers, whatever their field of practice, into abusively adversarial behavior is to recognize as a defense to malpractice claims a lawyer's refusal to perform an act reasonably believed to be unlawful or immoral.

Some authority supports this lawyer independence defense. Were courts and commentators to enunciate the defense more explicitly, they would make it more effective in reinforcing the willingness of lawyers to resist pressures to pursue a client's interest beyond proper limits.

4. Client Contributory Fault

One cannot hope to apply properly such defenses as contributory or comparative negligence in legal malpractice cases without considering the unusual relationship between client and lawyer. That relationship, of course, is not a joint venture in which each participant owes comparable duties to the other. Rather, it is the lawyer's task to seek a client's welfare, remedying within limits some omissions by the client—for example, failure to read or understand a document—that might in other situations constitute negligence. There is no Code of Client Responsibility. A client's enforceable duties to a lawyer are limited, with rare exceptions, to paying the lawyer's fee and compensating the lawyer for certain expenses caused by the client.

Nevertheless, legal malpractice law does recognize contributory fault defenses. With such recognition, the law offers clients an incentive to help themselves while only marginally limiting the incentive of lawyers to provide legal counsel. Thus, if a client deprives his lawyer of essential information, he cannot censure the lawyer for a resulting undesirable outcome. . . .

5. Defensive Practice

Excessive incentives for lawyer care might lead to excessive care, for which the public ultimately would pay. Physicians frequently assert that medical malpractice law has had this result. Some argue that excessively stringent professional rules in the area of conflicts of interest, for example, could also have similar impacts.

Although this remains a danger to beware in the future, current professional literature on avoiding malpractice suggests that malpractice law today provides few deleterious incentives for lawyers. Unlike medical patients, most legal clients pay their own bills and thus are more likely to resist unneeded services. . . .

C. Lawyers in Firms: Vicarious Liability

When lawyers practice in groups, legal malpractice law should seek to provide at least two further incentives. First, the law should spur lawyers to monitor and improve each other's practice. Second, it should encourage lawyers to resist peer pressure to behave improperly.

Although civil liability has important roles in providing these incentives, the relevant liability is usually not for legal malpractice. Giving lawyers causes of action against their firms or (in the case of house counsel) against their employers can help them resist attempts to induce unprofessional behavior and discourage potential defendants from resorting to such pressures. Malpractice liability may have the same impact or a contrary one, depending on whether the unprofessional behavior in question hurts or helps clients.

The essential impact of malpractice law on behavior within firms stems from the vicarious liability of the firm itself and its partners, which gives all of them the incentive to make sure that other lawyers in the firm do not commit malpractice. When a firm is organized as a partnership, partnership law provides this vicarious liability. Liability, however, also implements the professional principle that the firm and each of its partners take responsibility for the practice of every lawyer in the firm. Thus, vicarious liability has sometimes been recognized for professional corporations. . . .

III. Access to Remedies

Although facilitating access to remedies is an important goal throughout the legal system, three concerns give it special importance for legal malpractice. First, the need for protection of clients that justifies making lawyers fiduciaries likewise warrants smoothing the way for clients to seek redress when they believe lawyers have taken advantage of their vulnerability. Second, lawyers have more advantages in defending litigation against them than other fiduciaries. A lawyer defendant retains and communicates with counsel more easily than a non-lawyer plaintiff. A client, believing himself to have been injured by his lawyer, may have special difficulties in finding and trusting another lawyer qualified to sue the first one. This is true even in a jurisdiction where malpractice lawyers abound and is especially true where lawyers are few and chummy. Third, because access to competent counsel is essential to the rule of law, it becomes crucially important to provide access to remedies that reinforce the reliability of lawyers.

When it comes to access to legal malpractice remedies, medical malpractice provides an example of what to avoid. Starting in the nineteenth century, the medical profession sought to protect itself from malpractice claims by discouraging doctors from testifying against each other. In response, courts spurred the growth of a market in expert testimony by relaxing the locality rule, under which doctors were judged only by the standard of competence where they practiced. More recently, the profession has responded to growing litigation and rising insurance premiums by securing the adoption of statutes of varying merit in an effort to reduce the cost of malpractice litigation.

So far, the legal profession has escaped a comparable history. The locality rule was never widely recognized for lawyers. Recent authority, to the extent it considers the issue at all, opts for a statewide or even a nationwide standard. The bar has not yet sought restrictive legislation, other than limitations on vicarious liability of law firm partners. Indeed, the professional rules promote access to malpractice remedies by forbidding advance waivers of malpractice liability and by limiting settlements with unrepresented parties. Nevertheless, there is much room for improvement. . . .

A. Some Current Problems

. . .

2. The Case Within a Case

Much of the expense of legal malpractice litigation results from the "case within a case" doctrine. This doctrine requires a client claiming malpractice in the conduct of another action to relitigate that other action to prove that the client would have prevailed but for the lawyer's malpractice. Aside from its expense, the doctrine gives a client the task of litigating a former case against the client's own former lawyer, who knows the strengths and weaknesses of the case, perhaps from the client's own confidences. Furthermore, the doctrine puts a lawyer in the unseemly position of contending that a case he or she agreed to bring was hopeless.

One plausible substitute for trying the case within a case would be the loss-of-a-chance approach, which has been adopted in England and France, and in medical malpractice actions in the United States. Under this approach, the plaintiff obtains compensation for losing the chance of recovery, whose value is measured by the probability of prevailing and the likely damages. This approach may call for less precision than the case within a case approach and may be less costly. Courts, however, have not accepted it in the rare instances in which litigants proposed it in legal malpractice cases. Perhaps judges find it easier to accept the unpredictability of medical matters than that of litigation.

A related approach would grant plaintiffs relief based on the settlement value of their claims. Most civil claims are settled and settlement occurs even after trial begins. Courts have allowed clients to recover from their former lawyers for failure to settle and for negligently making inadequate settlements. Because settlement is always probable, courts should extend these rulings by presuming that when a lawyer commits malpractice and loses the case, it would otherwise have been settled. The presumption would be especially plausible in cases in which the lawyer's negligence caused a client's case to die before trial, for example, through a default judgment or through failure to satisfy the statute of limitations. Under established principles of damages law, a defendant who has made it impossible for anyone to be sure what would have happened but for the defendant's wrong should bear the resulting risk of error. . . .

C. New Directions

A regulatory perspective suggests methods to foster access to malpractice remedies beyond tinkering with current doctrine. Besides the attorney fee recovery proposal just discussed, two other regulatory measures deserve mention.

1. Compulsory Malpractice Insurance

Only one state requires lawyers in private practice to obtain malpractice insurance although a number of foreign nations impose such a requirement. . . .

2. Compulsory Arbitration

When all is said and done, which often happens in malpractice litigation, a lawsuit is a cumbersome way to remedy malpractice. Most malpractice claims are for less than a thousand dollars, making litigation wholly impractical for all except those able and willing to proceed pro se in a small claims court.

An obvious solution is to require lawyers to submit to arbitration of malpractice claims against them. Arbitration could be modeled on methods used in many states for client fee grievances, and this would be appropriate because malpractice and fee claims often intertwine. As is true with fee arbitration rules, the client should not be required to submit to arbitration. The client should be able to pursue a remedy in court. This will help ensure an adequate supply of legal malpractice precedents, and will protect the right of clients to bring their claims before a judge and jury, hence preserving the role of judge and jury in regulating the profession.

IV. Conclusion

Commentators and courts have not been sufficiently willing to recognize that the problems of legal malpractice law are substantially the same as the traditional problems of professional responsibility. Defining the duty of due care enforced by a malpractice action is just one means that courts and other regulators should use to define and enforce lawyer fiduciary duties to clients. Adjusting lawyer incentives by deciding when non-clients can sue lawyers for malpractice is just one part of deciding how far lawyers should be free to promote their clients' interests at the expense of others. Providing access to malpractice remedies is just part of providing potential clients with access to competent and responsible legal representation.

Putting legal malpractice issues in their proper context will not resolve them because the problems of professional responsibility are themselves difficult and contested. However, if malpractice issues are recognized as issues of professional responsibility, courts will consider the relevant issues instead of masking them with tort law formulas. Perhaps malpractice issues will also receive more attention from those of us who interest ourselves in professional responsibility. After all, if one thing is certain about malpractice law, it is that those who practice law, as well as their clients, will be thinking about it more and more.

The professional responsibility context of legal malpractice can also direct our attention to broader regulatory issues. Should society entrust an important role in regulating the bar to lay juries? Will the current legal malpractice boom simply lead, as has been alleged of its medical counterpart, to an increase in insurance costs ultimately borne by clients, without raising the quality of representation? Would a further investment in the invigoration of the lawyer disciplinary system be a better way to enforce professional norms than the malpractice system, or can each system make a distinctive contribution? Do both systems suffer from the same weakness — excessive reliance on client complaints with consequent failure to address situations where lawyers injure non-clients or where clients do not detect malpractice? Will legal malpractice litigation simply give wealthy and sophisticated clients, who already receive good service, a means of securing still more zealous representation, to the detriment of non-clients and of the proper independence of the bar? Will it make client and lawyer adversaries by encouraging clients to respond to fee claims with malpractice claims and lawyers to respond to malpractice claims with counterclaims against the malpractice lawyers advancing them? How will its effects differ for lawyers in large firms, in small firms, and in other practice settings?

Scholarly attention and empirical research are urgently needed to answer questions such as these. Meanwhile, legal malpractice law has an important and neglected role to play in regulating the legal profession.

NOTE ON MALPRACTICE CASES

The three cases that follow display lawyers accused of malpractice. In reading them consider what act or failure to act the plaintiff holds up as proof of malpractice and what the court says about that act or omission. Just as important for this course, consider what features of the contemporary legal world *produced* the malpractice; what in the setting of practice led the lawyer astray? The point of the second question isn't to absolve the lawyers involved of responsibility, but to focus your attention on how a lawyer who might have been well-meaning could have wandered into this mess.

Following the malpractice cases are several selections in which lawyers incur liability, not to clients, but to third parties whom they have harmed by being *too* loyal to their clients, or, more properly speaking, by pursuing their clients' goals by forbidden means. Consider these accounts in light of the point made by Leubsdorf in the article above—that malpractice liability rarely extends beyond clients.

WALDMAN V. LEVINE

544 A.2d 683 (D.C. Cir. 1988)

ROGERS, J.

Appellants [Waldman and Steven] . . . are attorneys who represented appellee [Swann] in an action for medical malpractice arising out of the death of her daughter. . . . Swann . . . sued appellants for legal malpractice, alleging that they had been negligent in representing her in the medical malpractice action. Appellants principally appeal the jury verdict on the grounds that (1) Swann's legal expert distorted the standard of care for attorneys in medical malpractice actions, and (2) Swann's evidence of legal malpractice was factually and legally insufficient. Appellants appeal from the dismissal of their third-party complaint against Swann's successor counsel, appellee [Levine], and a directed verdict on the issue of Levine's alleged negligence in failing to file a motion to set aside the settlement and vacate the dismissal of the medical malpractice case as an intervening cause of Swann's loss. We hold that the trial court did not err in denying appellants' motion for judgment notwithstanding the verdict or a new trial since the expert's testimony was properly admitted and Swann presented sufficient evidence from which the jury reasonably could find that appellants were negligent. We further hold that the motions judge did not err in dismissing the third-party complaint since application of the normal rules of indemnity for an alleged successor, independent tortfeasor is incompatible with the attorney-client relationship when successor counsel must choose between alternative courses of action. Accordingly, we affirm.

I.

[Swann's daughter] died . . . twelve days after giving birth to her fourth child. The cause of death was determined to be pelvic thrombophlebitis. [During an exploratory surgery the day of decedent's death, a blood clot broke away and caused decedent's death]. Swann, the decedent's mother, subsequently retained appellant[s] Waldman [and Steven] to file a wrongful death and survival action for medical malpractice. . . .

A. The Medical Malpractice Action . . .

[Appellants contacted numerous medical professionals and experts to review the case. All those consulted advised appellants that they would need to consult an OB/GYN to both review the files and to testify as an expert at trial. After searching for an OB/GYN over a two year period, appellants were still unable to locate one who would testify on Swann's behalf. Upon deposing an internist, appellants decided that her testimony undermined Swann's medical malpractice claim. Nonetheless, appellants proceeded with the action, deposing the defendant physicians and obtaining a continuance of the trial. Appellants decided that based on one of the defendant's deposition testimony, they no longer believed that there had been any medical negligence. Therefore, appellants decided to consider negotiating a settlement, and they informed Swann that defendants would only settle for funeral and attorneys' costs. Swann refused to settle.

Swann and appellants did not thereafter communicate until a pretrial hearing at which the continuance was denied and appellants moved to withdraw as Swann's counsel. Swann, believing she had no other option than to settle, agreed to have her action dismissed with prejudice in exchange for $2,200 for funeral and out-of-pocket expenses. The dismissal was entered, but the judge never ruled on appellants' motion to withdraw.

The following month, Swann's new counsel Levine contacted appellants to inform them that Swann was seeking to have the dismissal set aside. At Levine's and Swann's request, appellants sent Levine a writ to effect their withdrawal from the matter, in order that Levine could enter his appearance as Swann's counsel and move to set aside the dismissal. The writ was never filed with the court, and Levine never entered his appearance. Swann then sued appellants for legal malpractice.]

B. The Legal Malpractice Action

In the legal negligence action, Swann alleged that appellants had breached their fiduciary duty to her, fraudulently misrepresented both their investigation and the status and quality of the medical malpractice action, and had negligently failed to prosecute her case with diligence. She relied on evidence that appellants had failed to consult with an OB/GYN expert before recommending that she settle her case for expenses, had failed to obtain an economist to prepare and testify about the damages resulting from her daughter's wrongful death, and had failed fully to advise her of her options and unjustifiably refused to seek the continuance that she had requested.

Before trial, appellants filed a third-party complaint against Levine alleging that Swann's damages were caused by Levine's negligent failure to take the steps necessary to have the dismissal set aside. Levine moved to dismiss the complaint. After a hearing, [the judge] granted the motion, ruling that the third-party complaint failed to state a claim upon which relief could be granted since appellants had not been the intended beneficiaries of Levine's legal services, the injury allegedly caused by Levine was distinct from that allegedly caused by appellants, and public policy precludes any claim for contribution or indemnification because of the potential conflict of interest it would create in the representation of a plaintiff by successor counsel.

At trial, Swann presented the testimony of attorney Thomas P. Meehan as an expert on the standard of care for lawyers in wrongful death and medical malpractice cases. Meehan stated that in formulating his opinion as to the appropriate standard of care, he had considered certain provisions of the Code of Professional Responsibility for lawyers. Meehan testified that in failing to consult an OB/GYN specialist in preparing the medical malpractice case, appellants' conduct fell below the minimum standard of care for attorneys in medical malpractice cases. In his view, consultation with an OB/GYN was essential in order to get an opinion with respect to an obstetrical/gynecological problem. . . .

Meehan also testified that in his opinion the standard of care required that an economist or similarly situated expert . . . testify in the wrongful death/ survival action on the economic loss suffered by the decedent's estate and her minor children. . . . In his experience, attorneys in all wrongful death/ survival cases in the District of Columbia would have an economist testify.

The jury returned a verdict for Swann in the amount of $643,493.88. . . .

II.

A.

Appellants first argue that the trial court improperly permitted Swann's legal expert to testify that their failure to consult or secure expert testimony from an OB/GYN specialist and from an economist violated the standard of care for attorneys in medical malpractice/wrongful death cases. Appellants contend that caselaw in the District of Columbia has established that the standard of care for attorneys in medical malpractice actions does not require that an attorney retain a medical expert witness having the same specialization as the medical malpractice defendant. They assert that in the District a physician may testify as a medical expert even if he is not a specialist in the particular field of which he speaks. . . . Therefore, they argue, because their presentation of Dr. Dimitroff's testimony would have presented a legally sufficient case of negligence, their handling of the medical malpractice action *a fortiori* conformed to the standard of care. They view the standard of care as irrelevant to consultations that do not provide the basis for testimonial evidence.

Appellants' argument misconceives the issue before us. The question is not whether [the internist's] testimony would have withstood the test of admissibility or would have permitted appellants to present a *prima facie* case of medical negligence. Rather, the question is whether appellants' conduct of the lawsuit met the standard of care for attorneys in medical malpractice/wrongful death actions. . . . The requisite care is that which a reasonably prudent person would have exercised under the same or similar circumstances. . . . This standard is equally applicable to actions involving negligence by professionals, such as attorneys and physicians. . . . "Their conduct must comport with that degree of care reasonably expected of other medical [or legal] professionals with similar skills acting under the same or similar circumstances, *i.e.*, they must adhere to the standard of reasonable care." . . .

. . . The medical experts whom appellants consulted advised of the necessity of consulting with experts in these medical fields. Yet no consultations occurred over more than a three year period. To suggest that under these circumstances a jury could not reasonably find that an attorney preparing a medical malpractice case was negligent if the attorney failed to consult with an OB/GYN, or failed to be certain as to the nature of any other specialists' consultations with an

OB/GYN, prior to recommending that the client settle for costs, strikes us as a manifestly untenable position, particularly when appellants' own legal expert testified that his notes of their conversations indicated that appellants recognized the need to consult with such an expert. . . . [W]hether the failure to consult an OB/GYN breached the attorney's standard of reasonable care to the client presented a factual issue. A jury finding of negligence does not, as appellants urge, interfere with the attorney's exercise of professional judgment, but rather is a determination that there are minimum actions required of any attorney in the exercise of reasonable care in these circumstances; nor is such a finding at odds with the principle that the selection of one among several reasonable courses of action does not constitute malpractice. . . .

If the judgment is allowed to stand, appellants argue, this court will be imposing a *per se* rule that attorneys in medical malpractice actions must obtain testimony from a medical expert having the same specialization as the medical malpractice defendant, or the attorneys will necessarily be liable to their clients for negligence. Our holding will have no such effect, nor could it. . . .

Our holding remains faithful to the single negligence standard of reasonable care under the circumstances. . . . [The court discusses previous rulings that held that] the degree of reasonable care and skill appropriate to the particular case was a matter to be established for the trier of fact through the use of expert testimony [but that] some situations did not require expert testimony on the standard of care and that an attorney's negligence could be established as a matter of law. . . . Insofar as appellants complain about Meehan's testimony, however, the standard of care to be exercised by appellants was a matter for jury determination based upon the testimony of experts presented at the trial. . . . While the general standard of conduct is an invariable legal rule — it requires an attorney to exercise that degree of reasonable care and skill expected of members of the legal profession under the same or similar circumstances, . . . — the specific standard of conduct required under a given set of factual circumstances is a question to be answered by the trier of fact on a case-by-case basis with the assistance of expert testimony, in most instances, adduced at trial. . . .[3]

Moreover, expert testimony is not binding on the trier of fact . . . and the trier of fact is given considerable latitude in determining the weight to be given to such evidence. . . . Therefore, an expert's testimony as to the standard of care does not conclusively establish the standard of care; it is only evidence of that standard. *Cf. District of Columbia v. Barriteau, 399 A.2d 563, 569 (D.C. 1979)* (expert economic testimony on impact of future inflation is only evidence of future inflationary trends). The expert may, of course, be cross-examined and his testimony may be rebutted by that of other experts. . . .

Accordingly, we find no error by the trial court in permitting Meehan to testify that in his opinion the standard of care for attorneys in medical

---

3. As explained by Prosser, the *general* standard of conduct "is a legal rule, from which the jury are not free to deviate, it is a matter of law, and is to be applied by the court." W. Keeton, D. Dobbs, R. Keeton, & D. Owen, Prosser & Keeton on the Law of Torts §37, at 236 (5th ed. 1984) (hereinafter Prosser & Keeton). Because of the infinite variety of circumstances which may arise, it is impossible for courts to prescribe in advance *specific* standards of conduct establishing the particular standard of care in every given situation. Thus, the details of the standard of care must be filled in each case. Prosser & Keeton, *supra*, §37, at 237.

malpractice/wrongful death actions required consultation with an OB/GYN specialist. Meehan did not testify that the standard required appellants to present an OB/GYN witness at trial. In any event, Meehan's testimony was nothing more than evidence of the standard of care. Appellants were entitled to cross-examine him and to present contrary expert testimony of their own, and they did both. Appellants may disagree with Meehan's opinion of what the standard of care required, and the jury apparently accepted his assessment, but their disagreement presents no grounds for reversal.

B.

For similar reasons we reject appellants' argument that the trial court erred in permitting Meehan to testify to the need for an economic expert witness at trial of the wrongful death and survival claim.

> This court has observed that arriving at a sum representing future loss of earnings often involves a complicated procedure. To arrive at a reasonable figure the trier-of-fact must have evidence pertaining to the age, sex, occupational class, and probable wage increases over the remainder of the working life of the plaintiff. For this reason, . . . "the task of projecting a person's lost earnings lends itself to clarification by expert testimony because it involves the use of statistical techniques and requires a broad knowledge of economics."

. . . Given this observation it is not surprising that the expert witness on medical malpractice and wrongful death cases testified that appellants' failure to have an economic expert witness on behalf of Swann in her case against the Hospital constituted a failure to meet the standard of care required under the particular circumstances. . . . Appellants were free to point out the error of his opinion through cross examination and presentation of their own expert witness, and they did. The trial court properly instructed the jury that the law did not require an economist or similar expert to testify in Swann's case, and that the issue before it was whether appellants had breached their standard of care under the circumstances.

C.

Appellants further object to the trial court's admission of Meehan's testimony that he had considered various provisions of the Code of Professional Responsibility for Lawyers in determining what was the appropriate standard of care for an attorney in appellants' circumstances. Appellants contend that because the Code provides no private cause of action for its violation, any testimony about it was both irrelevant to appellants' liability for negligence and extremely prejudicial.

Although it may be true that the Code provides no private cause of action for its violation, . . . a question we need not decide, the issue is whether the standards set by the Code are relevant to establishing the standard of care governing an attorney's conduct. A number of courts have held that although the Code does not attempt to delineate the boundaries of civil liability for the professional conduct of attorneys, its provisions constitute some evidence of the standards required of lawyers.

It is an obvious proposition that the Code of Professional Conduct provides a gauge by which to determine the competency of the Bar. . . . A legal expert's use of the Code in determining the standard of care required in a legal malpractice case is not unlike the use of practice codes in other negligence contexts . . . The testimony in the instant case was extremely limited in scope. Meehan did not testify that the appellants had violated the provisions he cited and expressed no opinion at all upon that question. He merely stated that certain Code provisions had served as guides in his determination of the standard of care. We hold that this testimony was properly admitted.

III.

Appellants next challenge the factual and legal sufficiency of Swann's evidence. They assert that Swann failed to prove that she would have prevailed in the underlying medical malpractice action, and that therefore she is precluded from recovery in the suit for legal malpractice. . . . Appellants attack the testimony of Swann's medical expert, arguing that it was based upon serious factual errors. They contend that the decedent's death could not have been caused by manipulation of the blood clot mass during surgery. . . . The defendants in the medical malpractice action presented expert testimony [tending to show that the death might not have been caused in the manner Swann alleged. Since the experts hadn't discussed certain other factors, however, it was the jury's task to weigh the evidence,] and it apparently credited the testimony of Swann's expert as to the cause of death.

. . .

IV.

Finally, appellants contend that their third-party complaint against Levine was improperly dismissed. They argue, in essence, that Levine's negligence in failing to have the dismissal set aside was either an intervening or contributing cause of Swann's injuries. Specifically they contend that Levine prevented them from taking any action after Swann changed her mind about settlement and that Swann's injury was not established until the time had passed during which action could have been taken to set aside the settlement and vacate the dismissal order.

No court in this jurisdiction has yet had occasion to consider the potential liability of successor counsel to predecessor counsel for indemnification or contribution of damages caused to a client by the successor counsel's alleged negligence. In other jurisdictions the courts have focused on whether the client's injury continues to accrue after successor counsel takes over the client's case, whether the action to be taken by successor counsel is mandated and counsel fails to act, or whether the action involves a choice among alternatives requiring the exercise of professional judgment. . . . Where there is a choice to be made, successor counsel has no duty to the client to take action which would lessen the damages resulting from predecessor counsel's negligence, and is not liable to predecessor counsel for contribution. . . . The line drawn in these jurisdictions permits successor counsel to act in the client's best interests without concern that a lawsuit will be filed by predecessor counsel for indemnification or contribution. Because we conclude that a client's successor counsel should not be required to choose between a course of conduct which is in the best interest of the client and the course best suited to insulate successor counsel from a third-party complaint by predecessor counsel, we hold that the dismissal was proper.[8]

Accordingly, the judgment is affirmed.

CENTURY MEDIA CORP. V. CARLILE PATCHEN MURPHY & ALLISON

773 F. Supp. 1047 (S.D. Ohio 1991)

SMITH, J.

[The court is reviewing a motion for summary judgment brought by defendants.]

Facts

. . . In this matter the plaintiff alleges that the defendants, through their actions, inactions, conduct and misconduct, acted negligently in their representation of the plaintiff [in a prior matter]. . . . To fully understand the instant case it is necessary to digress to the facts of the WKBN v. Wendy's . . . case. [There,] the plaintiff and the defendants in the instant case were co-defendants. As co-defendants a joint and several judgment was taken which has given rise to the case currently before this Court.

. . . Wendy's Food Systems, Inc., contacted Century Media Corp. to obtain advertising "air time". Wendy's . . . operates Wendy's Restaurants in the Youngstown, Ohio area. Century secured the requested advertising "air time" from various broadcasting companies, including WKBN Broadcasting Corp. Century contracted directly with the broadcasting stations for the advertising, and when the bill was not paid the broadcasting companies filed suit against both Wendy's and Century.

. . . Attorney Igoe was requested by Domenic Federico, a defendant in the instant case and a principal in Wendy's Food Systems, Inc., to enter a defense on behalf of Wendy's and Century. Wendy's and Century had entered into an agreement wherein Wendy's agreed to "defend the Action on Century's behalf, by counsel of Wendy's designation, . . ." . . .[2]

---

8. We leave for future resolution whether public policy would prohibit a third-party complaint against successor counsel where successor counsel does not face a choice among alternative courses of action. Cf. Parker v. Morton, 117 Cal. App. 3d 751, 763, 173 Cal. Rptr. 197, 204 (1981) (third-party complaint permitted where successor counsel's duty did not involve exercise of professional judgment).

2. The Agreement between Wendy's and Century essentially provided as follows:

This will confirm our understanding pursuant to which, in consideration of your forebearance (sic) of asserting a cross-claim against us in the Action and for other good consideration, the receipt and sufficiency of which is hereby acknowledged, we have agreed as follows:

1. [Wendy's] hereby indemnifies and agrees to hold [Century], its officers, directors, stockholders, agents, employees, legal and personal representatives, harmless from and against any and all loss, cost, expense, claims, demands and liabilities, (including reasonable counsel fees and disbursements) in any way arising out of or relating to the Action.
2. Wendy's shall defend the Action on Century's behalf, by counsel of Wendy's designation, and shall pay all costs and fees incurred by said counsel.

[Igoe undertook the defense of both Wendy's and Century in the under-lying action. He claims that Century's attorney-representative told him that he didn't wish to be bothered by the case details.] . . . Igoe claims that it is for that reason that he did not copy Attorney Tofel nor inform him of pleadings, pro-gress, and other relevant information with relation to the underlying suit. Tofel vehemently denies having made such a statement.

[Plaintiffs] in the underlying case propounded interrogatories to Wendy's and Century by serving a copy upon Attorney Igoe at CPM&A. . . . Igoe did not forward copies of the interrogatories to Century. Instead, by the direction of Federico, on behalf of Wendy's, the interrogatories went unanswered.

[T]he plaintiff[s] in the underlying case filed a motion to compel answers to the interrogatories. Again . . . Igoe did not respond to the interrogatories nor did he respond to the motion to compel. According to . . . Igoe, he was of the under-standing that Wendy's was simply going to pay the outstanding debt, thereby rendering the underlying case and the pending interrogatories moot. Further-more, he was allegedly told that since the bill would be paid shortly he was to keep his legal fees down by limiting his activity on the matter. . . . Igoe admits that he did not inform Century of the motion to compel that had been filed.

. . . Again, . . . Igoe did not see fit to either file answers or inform Century of his failure to do so. Instead, he simply disregarded a direct order of the court.

[Then,] plaintiffs in the underlying action filed a Rule 11 motion for sanc-tions for the failure to comply with the court's order. A response to the motion was not filed, Century was not notified as to the most recent revelation and still, the interrogatories went unanswered. The Common Pleas Court granted the motion for sanctions and declared that the facts sought to be established by the interrogatories were deemed established.

[After plaintiffs moved for summary judgment and Igoe again failed to respond, the court entered summary judgment for plaintiffs against Wendy's and Century.]

The day before the judgment was entered, Wendy's Food System, Inc., filed a petition in bankruptcy. . . . Presumably based upon Wendy's bankrupt sta-tus, the plaintiffs attempted to execute the judgment against Century. It was not until September 8, 1987, that . . . Igoe informed Century that a judgment was currently pending against them.

Century retained new counsel shortly after receiving knowledge of the pending judgment against them. This was done in an effort to have the judg-ment set aside. The new counsel was successful in setting aside the judgment[;] however, the judge ordered that a bond in the amount of the judgment be posted. . . . [T]he bond was not posted and the judgment was reinstated. . . .

. . . [P]laintiff Century alleges legal malpractice in Count One; breach of a fiduciary duty in Count Two; misrepresentation and/or fraud in Count Three; and breach of contract in Count Four. . . .

Standard of Review

. . .

Analysis

In the adjudication of civil law suits there is no case more difficult, com-plex and taxing than a claim of legal malpractice. In such a case the Court is often times faced with the task of not merely sitting in judgment of the case before it, but the Court must also weigh and determine the probable outcome of an underlying cause of action upon which the malpractice was allegedly performed. That is precisely the situation this Court has been confronted with for purposes of the three pending summary judgment motions. "The procedural tool for demonstrating trial level malpractice has been given the popular name of a 'suit within a suit.' ". . . .

In order to show legal malpractice the plaintiff is required to prove as follows:

1. There was an attorney-client relationship.
2. There were sufficient facts to show that the attorney's alleged misconduct caused the plaintiff's injury.
3. The attorney had breached his duty to provide competent legal services.
4. The damages which the plaintiff sustained were the proximate result of the attorney's alleged misconduct.

. . . Furthermore, as each party has noted, an attorney is required to exercise the knowledge, skill, and ability ordinarily possessed and exercised by members of the legal profession similarly situated. . . . The Court will first turn its attention to Defendant . . . Igoe and CPM&A's motions for summary judgment.

I. Motions of Defendant Michael E. Igoe and Carlile Patchen Murphy & Allison for Summary Judgment

The defendants have set forth two defenses to the plaintiff's claims upon which they argue summary judgment should be granted. Specifically, the defendants argue that there was no act of negligence because the attorney was acting pursuant to the instructions of the client, Wendy's. The defendants further argue in the alternative, that even assuming, arguendo, that the attorney's conduct was negligent, summary judgment is still appropriate because any alleged negligence did not directly and proximately cause any damages to plaintiff. Essentially, the argument is that the plaintiff did not possess any defense to the underlying action and therefore would have eventually been jointly and severally liable regardless of any deficiencies in the representation by counsel. The Court will first address the issue of the attorney having merely acted pursuant to the directives of his client.

As previously stated, the defendants wish to argue that Attorney Igoe was merely following the client's instructions and as such cannot be found to have acted negligently as a matter of law. This Court disagrees. Surely when Century agreed to permit Wendy's choice of counsel to also represent their interests they assumed there would be continued active representation beyond the simple filing of an answer to the complaint. This they had every right to assume. At the very least, . . . Igoe should have advised Century, as the situation grew progressively worse for both them and Wendy's, that his inactivity was adversely affecting their position and that a potential conflict of interest existed. He should have further advised Century that it would be in their best interest to retain independent counsel. He failed to do either of these things, and instead opted to do absolutely nothing.

Disciplinary Rule 5-105(B) provides as follows:

(B) A lawyer shall not continue multiple employment if the exercise of his independent professional judgment on behalf of a client will be or is likely to be adversely affected by his representation of another client, or if it would be likely to involve him in representing differing interests, except to the extent permitted under DR 5-105.

Although . . . violation[s] of disciplinary rules are not a per se indication of malpractice, they do provide each individual attorney a general stricture under which to tailor his or her actions. DR 5-105(B) specifically provides that multiple representation, as found here when both Wendy's and Century were represented by a single attorney, must not continue when it impinges upon the attorney's ability to make independent professional decisions on behalf of each client without adversely affecting the other client.

Attorney Igoe must have known that his repeated failure to respond to the propounded interrogatories was adversely effecting both Wendy's and Century[;] however, only Wendy's had given dispensation for this lackadaisical approach. Defendants' argument in support of . . . Igoe's inaction on behalf of Century was an alleged conversation with Attorney Tofel, where he allegedly stated that he did not want to be bothered with the "details" of the lawsuit. Although the issue of whether this statement was ever even made is in contention, the facts dictate that the circumstances surrounding the lawsuit had eroded to a point that there were no longer mere "details."

Furthermore, it surprises this Court that an attorney and an officer of the court would outright disregard a direct order of the Common Pleas Court that demanded that the interrogatories be filed. Clearly the attorney was in a position where the client's direct instructions and the Court's direct order were dichotomous. This however does not abrogate the attorney's responsibility to follow the order of the Court or at least advise the Court as to his reasoning for his inaction.

The defendant contends his actions were appropriate based upon the directive of his client to not work on the case. Defendant supports this position by citing McInnis v. Hyatt Legal Clinics Services, 10 Ohio St. 3d 112, 461 N.E.2d 1295 (1984), which the Defendant states provides that an attorney is negligent when he disobeys the specific instructions of a client even if the attorney undertakes to do what the law requires.

In the McInnis case, the attorney was being sued by a former client because the attorney served process through newspaper publication after having promised the client that the legal matter would "not be in the paper." In McInnis the Supreme Court of Ohio adopted the appellate court's conclusion that "when the defendant attorney elected to cause publication notice of the pendency of the instant divorce, without notice to his client, he disobeyed the lawful instruction of his client, breached the terms of his employment agreement, and is culpable to the extent of losses following from his breach and acts." . . .

The Court relied, at least in part, upon Ethical Canon 7-8 of the Code of Professional Responsibility, which provides in relevant part as follows:

A lawyer should exert his best efforts to insure that decisions of his client are made only after the client has been informed of relevant considerations.

The lawyer should always remember that the decision whether to forego legally available objectives or methods . . . is ultimately for the client and not for himself. . . .

The Court concluded that the attorney should have informed the client of the legal necessity of obtaining service of process through publication. McInnis stands for the proposition that when an attorney is confronted with a legal necessity that is in direct contradiction with the client's expressed declarations, the attorney must seek the client's direction after advising the client of the necessary action.

When the Court . . . [ordered] . . . that the interrogatories be filed, that underlying case and consequently this case, became distinguishable from McInnis[, which] did not deal with a case where the attorney was balancing the interests of two separate clients. . . . Igoe's professional judgment was to be in the best interest of both Wendy's and Century. It is apparent from the facts that Wendy's instructed . . . Igoe in how they wished for him to proceed. In most cases such an arrangement would be uneventful[;] however, Wendy's instructions were patently unconventional and iconoclastic and as such should have brought attention to the fact that their method of defending the lawsuit may not be shared by Century.

What McInnis may tell us is that at that point the attorney should have advised his clients of the court's order. His failure to do so may give rise to negligence[;] however, whether that coupled with the numerous other failures to bring to Century Media's attention other revelations in the underlying suit give rise to negligence is a genuine issue of material fact for a jury to decide. For these reasons the defendants' argument that the plaintiff would be unable to show negligence at trial is not well taken. . . .

The second part of the test requires a finding that there were sufficient facts to show that the attorney's alleged misconduct caused the plaintiff's injury. This question thrusts the Court into the very crux of this matter, in that it raises the question of whether the plaintiff was injured by . . . Igoe's handling of the underlying matter. The plaintiff argues that the defendants' conduct caused Century to lose the underlying case[—]specifically, that had the defendant properly forwarded an agency defense, they would not currently have a judgment for over $70,000 against them.

The agency argument, the plaintiff contends, would have prevailed in the underlying action, absolving them of any liability under the agreements to purchase air time. In the alternative, the plaintiff argues that even if an agency relationship is not shown to have existed, the plaintiff was still damaged by the attorney's conduct. The plaintiff explains that if . . . Igoe had informed Century of the growing potential for divergent interests between Wendy's and Century, this would have enabled Century to retain independent counsel to negotiate a settlement more favorable than a judgment for the entire amount.

In reviewing the supplemental memoranda filed by the respective parties, it becomes apparent that there existed a legitimate agency issue available to Century in the underlying case. That is not to say that Century would necessarily have prevailed on the issue[;] however, Century was certainly due the opportunity to set forth the argument and permit a jury to decide whether Century should have been exonerated from all liability. At this time, this Court can only speculate as to the result of a trial had it been held. Nonetheless, this underlying agency issue raises a genuine issue of fact that must be placed before a jury to decide.

It should further be noted, that as the plaintiff points out, the agency issue is not dispositive of the entire case. The plaintiff could very well set forth damages, although an amount would be very difficult to ascertain, which would reflect the harm done by not permitting Century to utilize independent legal acumen to attempt to negotiate a more favorable settlement than a summary judgment for the entire amount. . . . For the above stated reasons, the Defendants['] Motion for Summary Judgment is hereby *DENIED*.

II. Motion of Plaintiff for Summary Judgment on Liability Only

Plaintiff argues that as a matter of law, Attorney Igoe's actions in representing the parties gave rise to negligence. Specifically, the plaintiffs state that the defendants were advised of the agency defense and were instructed to assert it, yet the defendants failed to raise any defense whatsoever. Plaintiff states that the defendants' inaction lost the opportunity to defend the case on any basis.

The plaintiffs cite Howard v. Sweeney, 27 Ohio App. 3d 41, 499 N.E.2d 383 (1985) and Belfer v. Spiegel, 18 Ohio App. 3d 64, 480 N.E.2d 825 (1984), asserting that in a malpractice action, the plaintiff must prevail when it is proven that the plaintiff possessed a valid defense or claim which would have been successful had the attorney not been negligent. While this Court does not disagree with such a holding, I do not believe that the plaintiffs have proven that an agency argument conclusively would have prevailed before the common pleas court. Clearly there exist genuine issues of material fact as to the capacity with which Century contracted with the broadcasting companies. As such the plaintiff's motion for partial summary judgment on liability only is hereby *DENIED*.

Mosier v. Southern California Physicians Insurance Exchange

74 Cal. Rptr. 2d 550 (Cal. Ct. App. 1998)

Hastings, J.

This case presents a unique fact situation involving a courtesy defense provided to Dr. Neil Jouvenat, an uninsured physician, by appellant, Southern California Physicians Insurance Exchange (hereinafter SCPIE). . . .

[Jouvenat, an uninsured physician, was sued for medical malpractice. SCPIE tendered him a courtesy defense in the action, which was brought against Jouvenat and two other doctors, both of whom were insured by SCPIE. The jury in the underlying action found that Jouvenat was 70 percent liable for the malpractice. Jouvenat subsequently filed bankruptcy and prosecuted an action alleging that SCPIE defrauded him by inducing him to accept the defense and that SCPIE conspired to breach fiduciary duties that the defense attorneys owed to Jouvenat. The jury in that action concluded that Jouvenat was only 40% liable in the underlying malpractice case.]

A judgment was subsequently entered against SCPIE, directing it to pay Mosier, an interim trustee for the bankruptcy estate of Jouvenat, $4,221,078.90

in compensatory damages, $14 million in punitive damages and $24,311.82 in costs.

SCPIE appeals, raising numerous issues. After a thorough review of the record, while we conclude there is sufficient evidence to support the findings of the jury relating to fraud and breach of fiduciary duty, we conclude there is insufficient evidence to support a finding that Jouvenat was injured or that the compensatory damages are causally related to SCPIE's breaches of duty.

Statement of Facts

. . .

Background Facts

[The underlying action arose from the delivery of a baby in which Jouvenat used a forceps procedure not authorized by the hospital. The baby was born with severe spinal injuries and is a quadriplegic.]

[The present action was brought on the basic theory] that SCPIE, having the goal of paying as little as possible on behalf of [the two insured defendant physicians], agreed to retain Forgey, an attorney it knew and trusted, to carry out a litigation strategy devised by SCPIE to have the jury place greater blame on Jouvenat than on SCPIE's insureds, Hsu and Wu, all without the knowledge of Jouvenat. Forgey, Mosier alleged, continued to meet and plan trial strategy with SCPIE as if SCPIE were his client. At issue were several of the decisions Forgey had made during the medical malpractice action: the decision to have Jouvenat admit liability and present a joint defense with Hsu and Wu; the decision not to call a designated expert witness, a Dr. Martin, who may have been helpful in Jouvenat's defense; the decision not to assign Jouvenat's rights to a bad faith action against SCPIE after the verdict had been rendered; the decision not to oppose the post trial motion of Hsu and Wu to credit the judgment with the amount of the pretrial settlements; and the prodding of Jouvenat to file bankruptcy.

At trial, various SCPIE personnel testified about their involvement in the matter. All of them denied there had been a plan to use Jouvenat to deflect liability from Hsu and Wu. . . .

[Among the detailed testimony of SCPIE's employees, it was revealed that Jouvenat wasn't told that he had a right to choose his own attorney. One lawyer wrote in a memorandum to another lawyer that he assumed the *Cumis* situation had been discussed with Jouvenat and that no problems existed.]

At trial, Forgey was asked about [some] memoranda and what discussions he had had with Bolger about them. He testified he did not believe this was a *Cumis* situation, he never considered doing any research on the *Cumis* issue, and he did not seek or obtain a *Cumis* waiver from Jouvenat. With regard to [a] comment by Susan Robins, Forgey had asked for her impressions of the client. She forwarded a memorandum to him . . . which was read to the jury. The relevant portion states: "Oh yes, I certainly do remember Dr. Jouvenat (sp)! The case is in a rather interesting posture — plaintiff's OB expert — Mac Wade — had almost no criticisms of Dr. Jouvenat, because Bruce [Fagel] was trying to set the case up against codefendants with insurance or assets. . . . He can be called by Bruce, if Bruce decides to play it that way."

Forgey admitted that Jouvenat desired to testify at trial but that Forgey had dissuaded him. While Jouvenat did not believe that he had been negligent, and had recently begun putting his life back together, he "expressed a desire to get on the stand and basically make a mea culpa and say: Yes, I did have problems with drugs and alcohol." Forgey was concerned about the effect the admission of drug and alcohol use may have had on the jury. He was concerned that an award of punitive damages or a finding of willful misconduct might result in a non-dischargeable judgment in bankruptcy[;] therefore, he opted to advise Jouvenat to admit liability.

[Among evidence introduced at trial was a memorandum written by an SCPIE employee describing "Plan B":]

". . . I proposed that we initiate Plan 'B' at this time, that being to offer a courtesy defense to the uninsured . . . [Jouvenat]. *This will enable us to maintain control and mitigate the impact of negative testimony anticipated from [Jouvenat].*

[The court continues summarizing evidence that Mosier submitted at trial relating to Jouvenat's standard of care in the incident that gave rise to the medical malpractice action.]

Neither Forgey nor Breitbarth ever discussed with Jouvenat a potential conflict of interest with SCPIE and its insureds. Forgey did not advise him there were two medical theories regarding Ashley's injuries: one which related to Jouvenat's negligence in delivery, and the second which involved aggravation of the injuries caused by Hsu and Wu. Forgey also did not advise him that an expert had been designated on his behalf (Dr. Martin) by Jouvenat's prior attorney, McDonald, who could have helped Jouvenat on the issue of contribution "for the injuries versus Hsu and Wu." He did recall that Forgey suggested a "united defense" with the other defendants and that they would "work all together to try to get this case resolved." Later, Forgey advised him to admit liability in an attempt to avoid punitive damages because of his past history of drug and alcohol abuse. He reluctantly agreed to do so. He testified he had told Forgey about his financial situation at their original meeting but never gave Forgey consent to discuss this subject with SCPIE, assuming that what he told Forgey was privileged.

Mosier's medical experts, Drs. Menkes and Moosa, the same doctors who had testified in the personal injury action on behalf of Ashley, testified that had Hsu and Wu promptly and correctly diagnosed Ashley's spinal cord injury, and Ashley been treated with steroids, as recommended by a leading pediatric textbook, Ashley would not be ventilator dependent. Dr. Perry Lubens, a pediatric neurologist who had also testified at Ashley's trial, gave testimony consistent with his testimony in the prior case and on the same subjects: the difference between care necessary for a ventilator dependent quadriplegic and care necessary for a non-ventilator-dependent quadriplegic, and the standard of care in 1987 with regard to use of steroids in cases similar to Ashley's.

Mosier called Steven Prater, a professor and author of treatises on insurance law, former general counsel for an insurance company, expert witness, and lecturer. He generally explained what liability insurance was; explained the *Cumis* case; the legislative history of Civil Code section 2860; and defined the term "reservation of rights." He discussed the concepts of good faith and fair dealing, defined the nature of a fiduciary relationship, the duties of retained counsel in relation to the insured versus the insurer, the need for full disclosure between retained counsel and the insured, and waiver by the insured of potential conflicts. He described the industry practice of hiring counsel to represent the insured from the same basic pool of attorneys, and discussed the concept of a "courtesy defense," stating that, based on his knowledge of the industry and the legal research he had performed, it was an unusual arrangement. He also explained the reason for the principle established in the *Cumis* case and codified in section 2860: When a carrier provides a defense but asserts no duty to indemnify, a potential conflict of interest arises because of conflicting economic motives between the insured and the insurer.

Specifically with regard to the facts of this case, Prater agreed with SCPIE that it was not *obligated* to provide insurance coverage to Jouvenat, but concluded that the arrangement agreed to was a type of "insurance contract" between SCPIE and Jouvenat. He explained that within the insurance industry there are insurance contracts to pay only for legal fees which resemble standard contracts of insurance. According to Prater, the concept of good faith and fair dealing and a "fiduciary-like duty" was implied in the "contract" between Jouvenat and SCPIE, and therefore SCPIE had an obligation to "tell the truth and be up front with" Jouvenat about the arrangement, including potential conflicts of interest and the theories and issues pertaining to the defense of Hsu and Wu and of Jouvenat.

Prater further . . . opined that the situation presented a conflict of interest which would be well known in the insurance industry. He explained that while there was nothing wrong with SCPIE providing an attorney to Jouvenat, communications between SCPIE and Forgey should have been limited to billing matters. . . . In particular, he was asked to look at that portion of the document titled "Plan B" which indicated that SCPIE was giving a courtesy defense to Jouvenat "enabling us to maintain control" of the litigation. He opined that, under the facts presented, this violated the duty owed by the carrier under the principles encompassed within *Cumis* and Civil Code section 2860. . . .

The Verdict

The jury returned a special verdict which reflected the following findings: (1) SCPIE made a representation as to a material fact to Jouvenat in obtaining his consent to accept Darrell Forgey as his attorney for the Ashley Hughes trial; (2) the representation was false; (3) the agents of SCPIE knew that the representation was false when it was made; (4) the agents of SCPIE made the representation with the intent to defraud Jouvenat; (5) Jouvenat was not aware of the falsity of the representation made by any of the agents of SCPIE when he accepted Forgey as his attorney; (6) Jouvenat acted in reliance upon the truth of the representation; (7) Jouvenat was justified in relying on the representation; (8) Jouvenat acted to his detriment in relying upon the representation; (9) SCPIE participated in a conspiracy to breach the fiduciary duty owed by Forgey to Jouvenat by its actions in connection with providing Forgey as an attorney; (10) Jouvenat, Hsu and Wu were all negligent; (11) the negligence of each of them was a legal cause or aggravation of injury to Ashley; (12) the percentage of negligence attributable to Jouvenat was 40 percent, and the percentage attributable to Hsu and Wu was 60 percent; and (13) there was clear and convincing evidence that SCPIE's conduct constituted oppression, malice and fraud.

. . .

The punitive damage phase took place the following day. The jury returned with a special verdict indicating that punitive damages in the amount of $65 million should be assessed against SCPIE. This amount was reduced by the trial court to $14 million following a new trial motion by SCPIE, and the judgment was entered.

Discussion

. . .

Duty and the Relationship Between SCPIE and Jouvenat

The evidence is uncontroverted that Jouvenat was not insured by SCPIE for the underlying personal injury action and SCPIE owed him no defense. Thus, prior to offering Dr. Jouvenat the courtesy defense, the only duty SCPIE owed with regard to that action was to its insureds, Hsu and Wu, to conduct itself in good faith for their benefit.

We conclude that SCPIE's voluntary action of providing a defense to Jouvenat created a relationship giving rise to a duty on behalf of SCPIE towards Jouvenat based on the principle that one who voluntarily comes to the aid of another, having no initial duty to do so, becomes bound to exercise due care in the performance of the duties it undertakes to provide. . . .

The reason this situation is analogous to that mentioned in *Cumis* is that while SCPIE was providing a defense to Jouvenat, it insisted that it would not indemnify him; that duty only reached to SCPIE's insureds, Hsu and Wu. While a joint defense may have been beneficial to a certain point, as urged by SCPIE and conceded by respondent, it does not require much sophistication to understand the conflict which existed: SCPIE was in a position to mold the outcome of the underlying litigation to benefit its own financial interests by diminishing the liability of its insureds at the expense of Jouvenat. . . .

[The court affirmed a judgment of liability on these grounds, but reversed on the jury's calculation of damages:]

The measure of damages in a case predicated on legal malpractice "is the difference between what was recovered and what would have been recovered but for the attorney's wrongful act or omission. Thus, in a legal malpractice action, if a reasonably competent attorney would have obtained a $3 million recovery for the client but the negligent attorney obtained only a $2 million recovery, the client's damage due to the attorney's negligence would be $1 million—the difference between what a competent attorney would have obtained and what the negligent attorney obtained." . . . Mattco Forge, Inc. v. Arthur Young & Co. (1997) 52 Cal. App. 4th 820, 834 [60 Cal. Rptr. 2d 780] [trial-within-a-trial is the standard of proof to determine damages actually caused by a professional's negligence]; Travelers Ins. Co. v. Lesher, supra, 187 Cal. App. 3d at p. 197 ["'An attorney malpractice action . . . involves a suit within a suit, a reconsideration of the previous legal claim, and only by determining whether or not the original claim was good can proximate damages be determined.' [Citation.]"].)

The parties correctly proceeded on the theory of trial within a trial and the jury reapportioned fault. However, we cannot accept the mere fact that the jury reapportioned fault as evidence of damage. It is not inconceivable that different juries viewing the same facts independently will reach differing conclusions on apportionment of fault. It is necessary that substantial evidence exist which legally supports the difference in apportionment. We therefore review the two trials and focus on the issue of apportionment. . . .

While we sympathize with the tragic circumstances which gave rise to the original suit, and the fact that Ashley will be precluded from recovering any additional damages, the unfairness is not a result of the breaches of duty by Forgey and SCPIE, but the fact that Jouvenat was not insured to begin with and was forced to elect bankruptcy after rendition of the underlying judgment.

We conclude that there is no substantial evidence to support reallocation of fault other than the desire of the second jury to remedy a perceived unfairness generated by Jouvenat's bankruptcy.

Disposition

The judgment is reversed. The parties are to absorb their own costs.
Vogel C. S., P.J., and Epstein, J., concurred.

NOTE ON *WALDMAN, CENTURY MEDIA, MOSIER*

1. First consider *Waldman, Century Media Corporation*, and *Mosier* as a group.

- a. What acts or omissions did the plaintiff in each case allege as evidence of malpractice?
- b. Which case presents the most egregious case of malpractice, and why?
- c. Which case presents the most understandable (in the sense that you could imagine yourself doing the same thing) case of malpractice, and why?
- d. As Leubsdorf points out in the article preceding the cases, in each malpractice trial, there is a case within a case. After demonstrating that the lawyer-defendant's work fell below a reasonable level of professional care, the malpractice plaintiff then has to prove that *but for* this failing he would have prevailed in the original case. In each case be prepared to identify the act of malpractice and the links in the plaintiff's chain of causation ("if my lawyer had not failed me in this way, then . . ."). In which case does plaintiff win on negligence but lose (at least partially) on causation?
- e. One can roughly divide malpractice cases into those involving disloyalty by the lawyer and those involving a lawyer who is loyal but fails to do a good enough job. Which cases fall into which category?

2. Now consider the cases separately.

- a. *Waldman* can be read as a case about lack of diligence and competence — the plaintiff's original lawyers didn't find a specialist to evaluate the case. Why? The lawyers say they tried, in which case, the appellate court essentially says they didn't try hard enough. Consider another explanation: in 2009 one can find both in print and online extensive directories of experts willing to testify — for a fee — in an astounding variety of fields. If we assume that such directories existed at the time of the case, the plaintiff's lawyers' inability to find an obstetrical expert begins to look like a problem not of diligence but of capital: were they unable or unwilling to invest the additional amount to have the case evaluated by an obstetrician rather than a general practitioner? If that's the problem, the case poses an interesting question: when does a lawyer's inadequate capitalization amount to malpractice? (Stay tuned for the finance section.)

b. *Century Media* appears, at first blush to be about simple negligence: Igoe, the plaintiff's principal lawyer, failed to respond to several motions and court orders, thereby causing plaintiff to lose the case. Suppose you were able to talk to Igoe: what superficially reasonable story might he tell about why he ignored the several motions and orders? The rules and codes of professional responsibility permit a lawyer to represent two clients jointly, provided they agree and, after being properly informed, waive any conflicts of interest resulting from the joint representation. Would that have worked in these circumstances?

c. Is *Mosier* more like *Waldman* or like *Century Media*? Forgey comes off as the fall guy; could he tell a story that casts him in a more flattering light?

3. An experienced legal malpractice defense lawyer has asserted that in legal malpractice cases the single most important factor in predicting the outcome before a jury is whether the lawyer gave the client his undivided loyalty. In this lawyer's view the jury isn't sure about what level of competence a reasonable lawyer should have (you're probably not either, and you know a lot more than most jurors about it). But, this lawyer continues, what a jury can completely understand is when a lawyer has divided loyalties. If loyalty is divided and the outcome of the matter (case or transaction) is bad, this lawyer asserts, malpractice liability looms. To what extent do these cases bear out that observation? Would he think the next reading — the case of Duane Morris — bore out his observation?

GINA PASSARELLA, DUANE MORRIS DEFEATS CLAIM OF MALPRACTICE

Legal Intelligencer, February 14, 2008

A Philadelphia jury Wednesday cleared Duane Morris of a claim of legal malpractice for its representation of a former client in settlement negotiations, according to attorneys in the case.

The eight-member jury found the firm did not breach the standard of care or breach any fiduciary duty when its client signed a settlement agreement that provided no security, the attorneys said. . . .

Joseph K. Adlerstein sued Duane Morris in 2004 after he failed to receive $1.6 million of a $1.8 million settlement with his former company, Spectru-Medix. He claimed the firm committed legal malpractice by failing to ensure the settlement agreement included some form of security in the event SpectruMedix didn't pay up.

The case, *Adlerstein v. Duane Morris*, was filed a year after Duane Morris sued Adlerstein for not paying more than half of his $480,000 legal bill. He had paid the firm $200,000 — the only portion of the settlement with SpectruMedix he actually received. . . .

Duane Morris' counsel, Nicholas M. Centrella of Conrad O'Brien Gellman & Rohn, said in court that it was Adlerstein's fault for walking away from an earlier settlement agreement that would have guaranteed $800,000 to be paid in five days. He made a second mistake, Centrella had said, when he signed the agreement for the $1.8 million even after he allegedly knew there was no security. . . .

NOTE

Contrast the next two selections with the malpractice cases. The first seeks to make bar disciplinary proceedings more effective, presumably so fewer clients will be harmed by malpractice. The selection following that — concerning the lawyers facing RICO charges — presents a quite different problem. Be prepared to explain why a malpractice action would not have been appropriate under the circumstances.

MARY PAT GALLAGHER, NJ COURT RULES LAWYERS MUST REPORT COLLEAGUES' KNOWN MISDEEDS

New Jersey Law Journal, April 25, 2008

A lawyer has a duty to blow the whistle on another lawyer's wrongdoing of which he has knowledge, even if the victim is not a client, a New Jersey appeals court ruled on Wednesday.

"We hold that a reporting duty in such circumstances is mandated by principles of legal ethics, tort law, and public policy, so long as the attorney is shown to have had actual knowledge of the other lawyer's wrongdoing," the judges held in *Estate of Spencer v. Gavin*, A-0424-06.

But the panel stopped short of deciding whether something less than actual knowledge can trigger a duty to report misconduct to ethics authorities.

The ruling allows a claim to go forward against Dean Averna, a lawyer who is alleged to have known that another lawyer, Daniel Gavin, stole money from three estates for which he served as the executor/administrator. The estates were still open when Gavin died of cancer in 1995. A substitute administrator discovered Gavin had stolen $400,000 to $500,000 in the year before his death. . . .

Averna and his law partner Michael Gardner rented office space from Gavin in the same Woodbridge building where Gavin conducted his own law practice, as did several other attorneys.

There was evidence that Averna and Gavin had a close working relationship, and that Gavin was grooming Averna to take over his practice when he retired. . . .

Averna also denied knowing of Gavin's defalcations.

"Nonetheless, there is considerable proof in the record that, if believed by a factfinder, circumstantially indicates that Averna was not ignorant of Gavin's misdeeds," [Judge] Sabatino wrote.

The "principal source of this counterproof" was deposition testimony by Toni Marcolini, another of Gavin's lawyer-tenants, that Averna told her at some point before Gavin's death that Gavin was "raping and pillaging" Kathryn's estate, Sabatino noted. . . .

The court went on to hold that Averna had a duty to all three estates, even if none of them was his client, because they all "implicitly relied upon Averna to be faithful to their best interests, and not to turn a blind eye if he learned that the executor was plundering estate funds." If Averna knew about it, he was obliged to report it, said Sabatino . . .

That duty was likely to be satisfied by contacting the Office of Attorney Ethics and if feasible, the affected client, though there was no preclusion on informing the police as well, stated Sabatino.

He emphasized there was no unfairness in imposing a duty on a lawyer in Averna's shoes to turn in a colleague, while acknowledging it might not be easy or pleasant and could carry professional and personal repercussions. . . .

The Lawyers Fund for Client Protection has reimbursed $322,570 of the loss, and the estates have recovered additional amounts from other parties. . . .

Lisa Siegel, Lawyers Face Civil RICO Charges

Connecticut Law Tribune, May 16, 2005, at 1

A civil RICO suit filed against two Connecticut attorneys in federal court in Hartford has survived the lawyers' summary judgment motions and is set to begin trial next week. Attorneys Leonard A. Fasano and Todd R. Bainer are accused of committing wire, mail and bankruptcy fraud in a conspiracy to shield their client's assets from a judgment creditor.

Fasano is a partner with the New Haven firm of Fasano, Ippolito & Lee as well as a former Republican state senator and assistant minority leader. Bainer practices law in Branford. Their alleged misconduct dates back to 1998, when Cadle Co., a national debt-purchasing business, tried to collect a $90,747 federal judgment against Fasano's client Charles Flanagan in connection with Flanagan's default on a $75,000 loan. . . .

U.S. District Judge Alfred V. Covello's May 2 summary judgment ruling in *Cadle Company and D.A.N. Joint Venture Ltd. v. Charles Flanagan et al.* left little doubt that the judge has few, if any, questions of fact about the attorneys' liability in the case. Viewed in the light most favorable to Cadle for the purposes of summary judgment, Covello found that the pattern of allegedly fraudulent conduct by Fasano and Bainer "far exceeds the rendering of legal advice." . . .

In a bid to collect the judgment owed by Flanagan, Cadle served a writ of execution on him and Thompson & Peck in January 1998. In response to Fasano's objection and statement to the court that Thompson & Peck held no property of Flanagan's other than wages, Covello ordered Flanagan to submit to the court for in camera inspection documents pertaining to his assets. Covello also enjoined Flanagan from transferring his assets. . . .

Flanagan . . . never furnished any documents to the court concerning his other assets.

. . . . The alleged misconduct included fraudulently mischaracterizing proceeds that Flanagan received from Thompson & Peck in relation to a court settlement.

Before the writ was served, the money had been treated as settlement proceeds. Nevertheless, Fasano and Bainer represented to the court that the money was wages and, therefore, was untouchable by the writ, according to evidence cited by Covello. Other evidence, the judge emphasized, showed that the attorneys knew they risked a civil conspiracy claim for their conduct. . . .

Fasano claimed Cadle "brought [the RICO] action as a failed attempt to bully and retaliate against the principal defendant, Charles Flanagan," and characterized the allegations as a "ludicrous" mischaracterization of protected legal advice.

But Covello concluded that the civil RICO charge — often considered the ultimate weapon in litigation — was apt in this case and deserved to be put to a jury. . . .

JEFF BLUMENTHAL, SURVEY: MORE FIRMS USING THEIR OWN GC

Legal Intelligencer, June 1, 2005, at 1

With the number and stakes of legal malpractice cases on the rise along with the size of lawyer headcounts and geographic expanse, more law firms are asking partners to serve as in-house general counsel.

According to a recent Altman Weil survey, the percentage of Am Law 200 firms that have designated a general counsel has increased from 63 percent in 2004 to 69 percent in 2005, with 92 percent being partners and none from outside the firm.

The survey also says that 32 percent were serving full time in the position, compared to 26 percent last year. Those who are part time spend 36 percent of their total hours on the general counsel function, averaging 753 hours per year, down from 43 percent and 775 hours the year before. Average total cash compensation for law firm GCs ranged from $250,000 to $1.3 million, averaging $493,292. That figure is up dramatically from an average of $386,875 in 2004.

As for areas in which general counsel serve or advise their firms, 96 percent consult on firm management, 88 percent on engaging outside counsel, 86 percent on professional liability issues, 84 percent on representing the firm in disputes, 82 percent on professional responsibility issues such as conflicts and client privilege, 65 percent on partnership issues and employment matters such as discrimination, and 63 percent conduct in-house ethics education. . . .

[One Philadelphia law firm] has used Alfred "Chub" Wilcox as general counsel since 1996. He retired from the partnership two years ago but still remains active as of counsel. He said he believes it is wise for law firm general counsel to steer clear of serving in other management roles such as the compensation committee.

"You want people to come to you sooner rather than later with potential problems," Wilcox said. "And you don't want to create an impediment such as the possibility that you might rat the lawyer out to the compensation committee." . . .

3. DUTIES OF LAWYERS AS LITIGATORS

Federal Rule of Civil Procedure 11

(a) Signature. Every pleading, written motion, and other paper shall be signed by at least one attorney of record in the attorney's individual name, or, if the party is not represented by an attorney, shall be signed by the party. Each paper shall state the signer's address and telephone number, if any. Except when otherwise specifically provided by rule or statute, pleadings need not be verified or accompanied by affidavit. An unsigned paper shall be stricken unless omission of the signature is corrected promptly after being called to the attention of attorney or party.

(b) Representations to Court. By presenting to the court (whether by signing, filing, submitting, or later advocating) a pleading, written motion, or other paper, an attorney or unrepresented party is certifying that to the best of the person's knowledge, information, and belief, formed after an inquiry reasonable under the circumstances, —

(1) it is not being presented for any improper purpose, such as to harass or to cause unnecessary delay or needless increase in the cost of litigation;

(2) the claims, defenses, and other legal contentions therein are warranted by existing law or by a nonfrivolous argument for the extension, modification, or reversal of existing law or the establishment of new law;

(3) the allegations and other factual contentions have evidentiary support or, if specifically so identified, are likely to have evidentiary support after a reasonable opportunity for further investigation or discovery; and

(4) the denials of factual contentions are warranted on the evidence or, if specifically so identified, are reasonably based on a lack of information or belief.

(c) Sanctions. If, after notice and a reasonable opportunity to respond, the court determines that subdivision (b) has been violated, the court may, subject to the conditions stated below, impose an appropriate sanction upon the attorneys, law firms, or parties that have violated subdivision (b) or are responsible for the violation.

(1) How Initiated.

(A) By Motion. A motion for sanctions under this rule shall be made separately from other motions or requests and shall describe the specific conduct alleged to violate subdivision (b). It shall be served as provided in Rule 5, but shall not be filed with or presented to the court unless, within 21 days after service of the motion (or such other period as the court may prescribe), the challenged paper, claim, defense, contention, allegation, or denial is not withdrawn or appropriately corrected. If warranted, the court may award to the party prevailing on the motion the reasonable expenses and attorney's fees incurred in presenting or opposing the motion. Absent exceptional circumstances, a law firm shall be held jointly responsible for violations committed by its partners, associates, and employees.

(B) On Court's Initiative. On its own initiative, the court may enter an order describing the specific conduct that appears to violate subdivision (b) and directing an attorney, law firm, or party to show cause why it has not violated subdivision (b) with respect thereto.

(2) Nature of Sanction; Limitations. A sanction imposed for violation of this rule shall be limited to what is sufficient to deter repetition of such conduct or comparable conduct by others similarly situated. Subject to the limitations in subparagraphs (A) and (B), the sanction may consist of, or include, directives of a nonmonetary nature, an order to pay a penalty into court, or, if imposed on motion and warranted for effective deterrence, an order directing payment to the movant of some or all of the reasonable attorneys' fees and other expenses incurred as a direct result of the violation.

(A) Monetary sanctions may not be awarded against a represented party for a violation of subdivision (b)(2).

(B) Monetary sanctions may not be awarded on the court's initiative unless the court issues its order to show cause before a voluntary dismissal or settlement of the claims made by or against the party which is, or whose attorneys are, to be sanctioned.

(3) Order. When imposing sanctions, the court shall describe the conduct determined to constitute a violation of this rule and explain the basis for the sanction imposed.

(d) Inapplicability to Discovery. Subdivisions (a) through (c) of this rule do not apply to disclosures and discovery requests, responses, objections, and motions that are subject to the provisions of Rules 26 through 37.

CHRISTIAN V. MATTEL

286 F.3d 1118 (9th Cir. 2003)

McKEOWN, Circuit Judge.

It is difficult to imagine that the Barbie doll, so perfect in her sculpture and presentation, and so comfortable in every setting, from "California girl" to "Chief Executive Officer Barbie," could spawn such acrimonious litigation and such egregious conduct on the part of her challenger. In her wildest dreams, Barbie could not have imagined herself in the middle of Rule 11 proceedings. But the intersection of copyrights on Barbie sculptures and the scope of Rule 11 is precisely what defines this case.

James Hicks appeals from a district court order requiring him, pursuant to Federal Rule of Civil Procedure 11, to pay Mattel, Inc. $501,565 in attorneys' fees that it incurred in defending against what the district court determined to be a frivolous action. . . .

Mattel is a toy company that is perhaps best recognized as the manu-facturer of the world-famous Barbie doll. Since Barbie's creation in 1959, Mattel has outfitted her in fashions and accessories that have evolved over time. . . . Mattel has sought to protect its intellectual property by registering various Barbie-related copyrights, including copyrights protect-ing the doll's head sculpture. Mattel has vigorously litigated against puta-tive infringers.

In 1990, Claudene Christian, then an undergraduate student at the University of Southern California ("USC"), decided to create and market a collegiate cheerleader doll. The doll, which the parties refer to throughout their papers as "Claudene," had blonde hair and blue eyes and was outfitted to resemble a USC cheerleader. . . .

In the complaint, which Hicks signed, Christian alleged that Mattel obtained a copy of the copyrighted Claudene doll in 1996, the year of its creation,[2] and then infringed its overall appearance, including its face paint, by developing a new Barbie line called "Cool Blue" that was substantially sim-ilar to Claudene. Christian sought damages in the amount of $2.4 billion and various forms of injunctive relief. . . .

Two months after the complaint was filed, Mattel moved for summary judgment. In support of its motion, Mattel proffered evidence that the Cool Blue Barbie doll contained a 1991 copyright notice on the back of its head, indicating that it predated Claudene's head sculpture copyright by approximately six years. Mattel therefore argued that Cool Blue Barbie could not as a matter of law infringe Claudene's head sculpture copyright. . . .

At a follow-up counsel meeting required by a local rule, Mattel's counsel attempted to convince Hicks that his complaint was frivolous. During the videotaped meeting . . . Hicks declined Mattel's invitation to inspect the dolls and, later during the meeting, hurled them in disgust from a conference table.

Having been unsuccessful in convincing Hicks to dismiss Christian's action voluntarily, Mattel served Hicks with a motion for Rule 11 sanctions. . . . Hicks declined to withdraw the complaint during the 21-day safe harbor period provided by Rule 11, and Mattel filed its motion. . . .

The district court granted Mattel's motions for summary judgment and Rule 11 sanctions. The court ruled that Mattel did not infringe the 1997 Clau-dene copyright because it could not possibly have accessed the Claudene doll

---

2. The United States Copyright Office issued a certificate of registration on November 20, 1997, for "Claudene Doll Face and Head." The certificate specified the work's nature as "sculpture," and the "nature of authorship" as "3-dimensional sculpture."

at the time it created the head sculptures of the Cool Blue (copyrighted in 1991) and Virginia Tech (copyrighted in 1976) Barbies. . . .

As for Mattel's Rule 11 motion, the district court found that Hicks had "filed a meritless claim against defendant Mattel. A reasonable investigation by Mr. Hicks would have revealed that there was no factual foundation for [Christian's] copyright claim." Indeed, the district court noted that Hicks needed to do little more than examine "the back of the heads of the Barbie dolls he claims were infringing," because such a perfunctory inquiry would have revealed "the pre-1996 copyright notices on the Cool Blue and [Virginia Tech] Barbie doll heads."

Additionally, the district court made other findings regarding Hicks' misconduct in litigating against Mattel, all of which demonstrated that his conduct fell "below the standards of attorneys practicing in the Central District of California." The district court singled out the following conduct:

- Sanctions imposed by the district court against Hicks in a related action against Mattel for failing, among other things, to file a memorandum of law in support of papers styled as a motion to dismiss and failing to appear at oral argument;
- Hicks' behavior during the Early Meeting of Counsel, in which he "toss[ed] Barbie dolls off a table";
- Hicks' interruption of Christian's deposition after Christian made a "damaging admission . . . that a pre-1996 Barbie doll allegedly infringed the later created Claudene doll head. . . ." When asked whether the prior-created Pioneer Barbie doll infringed Claudene, Christian stated, "I think so . . . [b]ecause it's got the look. . . ." At that juncture, Hicks requested an immediate recess, during which he lambasted his client in plain view of Mattel's attorneys and the video camera.
- Hicks' misrepresentations during oral argument on Mattel's summary judgment motion about the number of dolls alleged in the complaint to be infringing and whether he had ever reviewed a particular Barbie catalogue (when a videotape presented to the district court by Mattel demonstrated that Hicks had reviewed it during a deposition);
- Hicks' misstatement of law in a summary judgment opposition brief about the circuit's holdings regarding joint authorship of copyrightable works.

After Mattel submitted a general description of the fees that it incurred in defending against Christian's action, the court requested Mattel to submit a more specific itemization and description of work performed by its attorneys. Mattel complied.

The district court awarded Mattel $501,565 in attorneys' fees. . . .

The district court did not abuse its discretion in concluding that Hicks' failure to investigate fell below the requisite standard established by Rule 11. . . .

Hicks argues that even if the district court were justified in sanctioning him under Rule 11 based on Christian's complaint and the follow-on motions, its conclusion was tainted because it impermissibly considered other misconduct that cannot be sanctioned under Rule 11, such as discovery abuses, misstatements made during oral argument, and conduct in other litigation.

Hicks' argument has merit. While Rule 11 permits the district court to sanction an attorney for conduct regarding "pleading[s], written motion[s], and other paper[s]" that have been signed and filed in a given case, Fed. R. Civ. P. 11(a), it does not authorize sanctions for, among other things, discovery abuses or misstatements made to the court during an oral presentation. . . .

The orders clearly demonstrate that the district court decided, at least in part, to sanction Hicks because he signed and filed a factually and legally meritless complaint and for misrepresentations in subsequent briefing. But the orders, coupled with the supporting examples, also strongly suggest that the court considered extra-pleadings conduct as a basis for Rule 11 sanctions. . . .

The laundry list of Hicks' outlandish conduct is a long one and raises serious questions as to his respect for the judicial process. Nonetheless, Rule 11 sanctions are limited to "paper[s]" signed in violation of the rule. Conduct in depositions, discovery meetings of counsel, oral representations at hearings, and behavior in prior proceedings do not fall within the ambit of Rule 11. Because we do not know for certain whether the district court granted Mattel's Rule 11 motion as a result of an impermissible intertwining of its conclusion about the complaint's frivolity and Hicks' extrinsic misconduct, we must vacate the district court's Rule 11 orders.[10]

We decline Mattel's suggestion that the district court's sanctions orders could be supported in their entirety under the court's inherent authority. To impose sanctions under its inherent authority, the district court must "make an explicit finding [which it did not do here] that counsel's conduct constituted or was tantamount to bad faith." Primus Auto. Fin. Serv., Inc. v. Batarse, 115 F.3d 644, 648 (9th Cir.1997) (internal quotation marks omitted). We acknowledge that the district court has a broad array of sanctions options at its disposal: Rule 11, 28 U.S.C. §1927,[11] and the court's inherent authority. Each of these sanctions alternatives has its own particular requirements, and it is important that the grounds be separately articulated to assure that the conduct at issue falls within the scope of the sanctions remedy. *See, e.g.,* B.K.B. v. Maui Police Dep't, 276 F.3d 1091, 1107 (9th Cir.2002) (holding that misconduct committed "in an unreasonable and vexatious manner" that "multiplies the proceedings" violates §1927); Fink v. Gomez, 239 F.3d 989, 991-992 (9th Cir.2001) (holding that sanctions may be imposed under the court's inherent authority for "bad faith" actions by counsel, "which includes a broad range of willful improper conduct"). On remand, the district court will have an opportunity to delineate the factual and legal basis for its sanctions orders. . . .

---

10. We emphasize that the district court's underlying order regarding summary judgment is not affected by this opinion. Nor do we disturb the district court's finding that Hicks filed "a case without factual foundation" or its other findings as to Hicks' misconduct.

11. Section 1927 provides for imposition of "excess costs, expenses, and attorneys' fees" on counsel who "multiplies the proceedings in any case unreasonably and vexatiously."

D. CLIENTS FINDING LAWYERS, LAWYERS FINDING CLIENTS

1. A PROBLEM SEEN FROM TWO SIDES

a. Client Ignorance

You have likely already had the experience of a relative or friend approaching you to ask you to recommend a lawyer for some matter. If so, you have witnessed a basic problem for most individuals who need legal help. Because, as individuals, we are not in the regular market for legal services, we don't know which providers are out there and which are competent in which fields. Entities that use legal services repeatedly develop some skill in such matters, but most individuals do not.

b. Lawyer Ignorance

Lawyers have a version of the same problem. Clients come in many varieties and degrees of honesty, candor, and financial responsibility. It is every lawyer's nightmare to find herself in the middle of a representation (from which she cannot withdraw without harming the client and violating an ethical duty) only to find that her client has (a) lied to her about important underlying facts, (b) told the truth but only very selectively and has thus omitted critical information, or (c) is failing to pay the lawyer. Ethical responsibilities forbid the lawyer from telling the judge or the other side that her client is lying, and the same responsibilities often forbid the lawyer from withdrawing from the case on the grounds that the client has stopped paying the bills. So the key for the lawyer is careful investigation and thought about whether to begin representing any particular client.

2. SOLUTIONS FOR CLIENTS

a. Information

SHERI QUALTERS, CONTROVERSIAL LAWYER-RATING SERVICE TO EXPAND

National Law Journal, April 7, 2008

The controversial lawyer-rating Web site run by Avvo Inc. is bringing its rating system to the Florida and Massachusetts legal markets.

The Seattle-based Avvo announced that its Avvo Ratings and Avvo Profiles will now include every attorney in those two states. With the expansion, Avvo said it rates and profiles about 60 percent of licensed U.S. attorneys and is available in 11 states and the District of Columbia.

Consumers are increasingly turning to the Internet to find and research lawyers, said Avvo CEO Mark Britton, who was previously general counsel at online travel reservation company Expedia Inc.

"Avvo makes it easy for lawyers to take advantage of this shift by giving every lawyer a free online presence where they can showcase their work and attract new clients," Britton said.

Not all lawyers welcomed Avvo's launch last June. Lawyers were rankled by a rating system that categorized lawyers from "extreme caution" to "average" to "good" to "superb."

In December, a federal judge in the Western District of Washington dismissed a class action case filed against the company by two Seattle lawyers. Browne v. Avvo, No. 2:07-cv-00920 (W.D. Wash.).

Britton said the thousands of lawyers who used Avvo's services far outweigh the two attorneys who filed the lawsuit.

Dan Levine, California Bar Votes to Require Client Disclosure on Malpractice Insurance

San Francisco Recorder, May 20, 2008

If it's true that the measure of any successful compromise is that few are fully satisfied, then the California State Bar's Board of Governors cooked up a good deal on malpractice insurance.

The board voted 16-4 on Friday to finally approve new rules on coverage disclosure, an issue that's been festering there for two years. Under the compromise—which still must be approved by the state Supreme Court—lawyers who expect to bill a client for more than four hours must pipe up if they aren't covered for malpractice.

The disclosure idea rankled some small firm and solo practitioners, who thought it put them at a disadvantage vis-a-vis larger-shop lawyers, who are more likely to be covered. In 2006, the *California Bar Journal* printed an estimate that 20 percent of the state's lawyers in private practice don't carry insurance.

While some governors would have preferred no disclosure at all, the compromise gained support from them because they felt it better than more far-ranging alternatives.

Auburn, Calif., solo John Dutton supported the deal after he voted against an earlier slew of more aggressive disclosure requirements recommended by a task force. Those proposals included noting a lawyer's insurance status on his or her Bar Web page. . . .

The four-hour exception was designed to assuage concerns that casual solicitations for advice—say, at a cocktail party—would turn comically formal when the lawyer says he can't answer without issuing a coverage letter. . . .

But some on the board were happy. State Bar President Jeffrey Bleich said the compromise merely reflects an old statutory system that required insurance disclosure, but had lapsed. . . .

b. Referral and Advertising

LEIFF CABRASER HEIMANN & BERNSTEIN WEB SITE

Available online at http://www.lieffcabraser.com (site visited October 2007)

LIEFF CABRASER HEIMANN & BERNSTEIN
●●●● LLP

Attorney Advertising
Re: Referral of Medtronic Defibrillator Lead Personal Injury Cases
October 30, 2007

Dear Counsel:

Lieff Cabraser Heimann & Bernstein, LLP, with offices in San Francisco, New York and Nashville, is one of the largest law firms in America dedicated solely to advancing the rights of plaintiffs.

Since our founding thirty-five years ago, we have been committed to achieving justice for investors, consumers, employees and patients, promoting safer products and fair competition, protecting our environment and remedying violations of the civil rights of citizens worldwide. For the past five years, *The National Law Journal* has selected Lieff Cabraser as one the top plaintiffs' law firms in the nation.

Our personal injury attorneys possess decades of experience in litigating defective medical device cases. Assisted by a team of in-house legal nurse consultants, our attorneys provide each client with high-level, individual representation.

Currently, we are dedicating substantial resources to the Sprint Fidelis defibrillator lead litigation. Leads are thin insulated wires connected to a defibrillator that carry electric impulses to the heart. On October 15, 2007, due to reports of at least five patient deaths, Medtronic withdrew its line of Sprint Fidelis defibrillator leads from the market.

Our firm was aware of injury reports concerning this medical device and commenced an in-depth investigation of the product earlier this year. On the same day the recall was announced, with co-counsel, patients represented by Lieff Cabraser filed the first lawsuits against Medtronic. Our clients suffered repetitive and devastating electrical shocks as a result of their leads fracturing.

You can learn more about the Medtronic recall at medtronicheartle adrecall.com, a website created and operated by Lieff Cabraser.

Lieff Cabraser is committed to entering into competitive referral arrangements. If you wish to discuss the Medtronic litigation please contact attorney Wendy R. Fleishman in New York at 212-355-9500 or wfleishman@lchb.com, Mark P. Chalos in Nashville at 615-313-9000 or mchalos@lchb.com, or Heather A. Foster in San Francisco at 415-956-1000 or hfoster@lchb.com.

Very truly yours,
Elizabeth J. Cabraser
Wendy R. Fleishman
Mark P. Chalos
Heather A. Foster

JOEL STASHENKO, SUIT OVER NY RULES ON LAWYER ADVERTISING GOES TO TRIAL

New York Law Journal, April 17, 2007

A federal judge on Friday declined to dismiss a challenge to the constitutionality of New York state's new rules on attorney advertising. . . .

The new rules, adopted by the presiding justices of the four Appellate Divisions, went into effect Feb. 1. They are being challenged by the personal injury firm Alexander & Catalano of Syracuse and Rochester, that firm's co-founder James L. Alexander and Public Citizen Inc., a Washington, D.C.-based advocacy group founded by Ralph Nader in 1971. . . .

The complaint argues that the guidelines' prohibition against the portrayal of a judge in ads, the use of a nickname by a firm that implies a special ability to get results or the use of elements designed to "obtain attention" that are not relevant to a consumer's selection of counsel inhibit flamboyant marketing themes that Alexander & Catalano has spent "significant" sums developing over the past decade. . . .

Alexander & Catalano had billed itself in most of its advertisements as "heavy hitters" but has abandoned the motto for fear of running afoul of the rules' prohibition against implying the ability to obtain results. It and Public Citizen argue, however, that "heavy hitter" means only that the firm is expert in its area of practice—personal injury and wrongful death cases—and is not a boast that it is more apt to win settlements. . . .

According to the complaint, the Alexander firm received more than 42,000 calls between 2001 and 2006 from potential clients. Fewer than 10 were complaints about the firm's splashy TV commercials. . . .

As to Alexander & Catalano's heavily run commercials, the state's memorandum says they are rife with "patent falsities" and "absurdities."

"Irrespective of whether Plaintiffs intend their commercials to be humorous, it cannot be denied that there is little likelihood that they were retained by aliens, have the ability to leap tall buildings in a single bound, or have stomped around downtown Syracuse, Godzilla-style," the state argues.

Among the "disturbing misrepresentations" in the Alexander & Catalano ads, the memorandum says, is one in which an alien says it was told there was "no way" an insurance company would cover damages to its space ship. Alexander then appears, saying, "Then we'll get them to say 'yes, way.'" . . .

3. SOLUTIONS FOR LAWYERS, INCLUDING AT LEAST ONE ILLEGAL ONE

Although rules of professional responsibility give lawyers many duties once they have undertaken to represent a client, those rules do not require that lawyers represent any particular client. And many lawyers report that carefully selecting clients is among the most important things they do. But that freedom has limits.

JAMES MCELHANEY, SPOTTING THE LOSERS
_____

ABA Journal, June 2005

Bill Brickman — who is a very solid lawyer — walked over to the corner table in the Brief Bag, tired and disheveled. He dropped himself in a chair and looked around. "I'm in trouble," he said. "Bad trouble. I'm in way over my head."

"What's wrong?" said Mike Pirelli. "You been indicted?"

"Nothing that simple," said Bill. "My practice is out of control. I stayed up all night evaluating every active file in my office, taking notes on what needed to be done. At about 5 o'clock this morning I came to a terrible realization. A year ago, I left Randolph & Wheeler — a perfectly fine law firm — to try to get some control over my professional life. To march to my own drummer. Now here I am, a solo practitioner, and I'm not even in charge of my own office. So every day I just get mired deeper in the pit."

"What's the real problem?" said Beth Golden. "Are you overwhelmed with too many cases, or are you stuck doing stuff you just can't stand?"

"Kind of a combination of the two," said Bill. "While I've got about two dozen cases that I feel on top of . . ."

"Congratulations," said Myra Hebert. "I wish I were on top of any of my cases."

"Anyway," said Bill, "I've got another dozen that make me feel seriously inadequate. Some because I'm too far behind, or because I don't really have a grasp of the facts or the law.

"But others are genuine dogs. Losers. Cases I never should have taken. They sit in piles scattered throughout the office, starting to compost like old piles of leaves. Except for what absolutely has to be done, I neglect them — and I know it. The clients call, wanting to know what's happening in their cases. I've even begun waking up in the middle of the night, worrying about them. I've got piles of cases in my office that are absolutely flea-ridden, mangy dogs, and I need to figure out how to get rid of them."

"Don't worry," said Flash Magruder. "It's in the great tradition of the practice of law. All the lawyers I know have albatross files — cases that weigh them down."

"What Bill needs is a strategy for how to deal with them," said Angus.

"Like they have at Mason & LeClerq," said Margaret Anderson. "My first day in the office, I had a pile of files on my desk a foot-and-a-half tall — I measured it. Every case was a dog. And every one had been on at least one other lawyer's desk before it got to mine. Some had been kicking around the office for years. I was able to deal with a couple of them. The rest I passed on to someone else a few months later. That's how you handle it — just dump your problem cases on the next lawyer to join the firm."

"Somehow I don't think that's going to work for a solo practitioner like me," said Bill.

Resorting to Legal Triage

"What you need to do," Angus said, "is a serious triage."

"Like the battlefield medics?" said Bill.

"Right," Angus said. "They would divide the wounded into three basic groups. The first ones were beyond hope. All the medics could do was give them some morphine and try to make them comfortable. Second were the walking wounded, the ones who could wait for medical attention. And then there were the genuine emergency cases — the gravely wounded soldiers who might be saved if they got immediate medical attention.

"You've got to do something like that with the cases you have," said Angus. "You're the only doctor in your office, and you don't have unlimited time to give to every case. But when you conduct your legal triage, the groups are a little different.

"First are the genuine losers. They're the ones that — after some discovery and legal research — you realize don't have the facts or the law that would let them win. But that doesn't mean you throw them out in a heap next to your door. Call the client into your office and explain the situation, treating the client with the respect he or she deserves — whether or not you charge for the time you spent on the matter.

"And be careful how you send people away. Tell them they're welcome to get a second opinion, especially if it's a doubtful area of the law or if they have a technically valid claim that you feel doesn't have much economic value.

"Otherwise, some other lawyer may figure a way to make the case pay after the statute of limitations has run by making you the defendant in a malpractice suit. So it's a good idea to write a letter explaining that your client is welcome to a second opinion and suggesting prompt action so the statute of limitations won't run out first."

Carefully Sift Cases from the Start

"The second group is made up of misplaced cases. When the little corporate case came into the office, you were sure this was an area you would enjoy. Only you missed signing up for that great seminar on close corporation battles. And when that real estate acquisition dispute walked in the door, it looked like the perfect opportunity to expand your practice in that direction. But now that you're so busy learning about defending age discrimination cases, you don't have the time or inclination for it.

"Dogs are in the eyes of the beholder," said Angus. "These cases would be fine in the hands of the right lawyers, but not in your office. So your job is to help this kind of case find a good home and then talk to the client about you dropping out."

"Wait," Bill said. "I've got a question: If you send a case like this to someone else, do you ask for a referral fee?"

"Some do," said Angus, "but not me. I'm a lawyer, not a broker. I only take money for work I've actually done that benefits the client. That does not include finding another lawyer. Period."

"Fool," said Myra Hebert under her breath, which made Beth Golden give Myra a look and toss her head with a sniff.

"The third group is the troubled or difficult cases that present special problems but may well be worth your effort," Angus said. "These are the ones that might profit from a creative approach to proving some key facts or new way—for you, at least—to argue the case or make the evidence come alive. After all, you took the case because you thought you could do something with it. Now is the time to brainstorm it looking for some fresh ideas."

"That's impressive," said Bill. "I almost feel like going back to the office right now."

"Wait," Angus said. "There's more to albatross files than just conducting a triage on the cases you already have."

"Prevention is still more valuable than cure," said Angus. "Start picking your cases more carefully. Understand that every time you commit yourself to take on a case, you are evaluating the facts, the law, the client and yourself.

"Lots of cases depend on facts you may not be able to prove. So there are times when you should make it clear from the beginning that whether you will stick with a case may be contingent on what you learn in trial preparation and discovery.

"The same is true when the case depends on what happens on the cutting—or sometimes raggedy—edge of the law. When the appellate court suddenly changes the rules, you need to re-evaluate the situation.

"Then there's the client and you. Lots of clients are difficult people— which is how they got involved in disputes like the ones that brought them to see you. Can you stand to work with this person in a demanding relationship that may last for years and requires trust, confidence and patience?

"Finally, don't carry any of these ideas to excess. There are some law firms that have the reputation of taking only 'perfect' cases with wonderful clients who never act difficult and who always make a good impression with the judge and jury. Some of these firms never take on a hard case or represent an annoying client for any reason. They are lawyers who never know the satisfaction of having made a contribution to the development of the law, or never feel the pride of having given some of their time to make the world a little more fair.

"Not every deserving case is a popular cause or earns a big fee," said Angus. "There are times when you need to take the albatross that walks in your office just because it's the right thing to do."

CALIFORNIA RULE OF PROFESSIONAL CONDUCT 2-400

Added by order of Supreme Court, effective March 1, 1994

Prohibited Discriminatory Conduct in a Law Practice . . .

(B) In the management or operation of a law practice, a member shall not unlawfully discriminate or knowingly permit unlawful discrimination on the basis of race, national origin, sex, sexual orientation, religion, age or disability in:

(1) hiring, promoting, discharging, or otherwise determining the conditions of employment of any person; or

(2) accepting or terminating representation of any client.

(C) No disciplinary investigation or proceeding may be initiated by the State Bar against a member under this rule unless and until a tribunal of competent jurisdiction, other than a disciplinary tribunal, shall have first adjudicated a complaint of alleged discrimination and found that unlawful conduct occurred. Upon such adjudication, the tribunal finding or verdict shall then be admissible evidence of the occurrence or non-occurrence of the alleged discrimination in any disciplinary proceeding initiated under this rule. In order for discipline to be imposed under this rule, however, the finding of unlawfulness must be upheld and final after appeal, the time for filing an appeal must have expired, or the appeal must have been dismissed.

Discussion

In order for discriminatory conduct to be actionable under this rule, it must first be found to be unlawful by an appropriate civil administrative or judicial tribunal under applicable state or federal law. Until there is a finding of civil unlawfulness, there is no basis for disciplinary action under this rule. . . .

MICHAEL PARRISH, LEADING CLASS-ACTION LAWYER PLEADS GUILTY TO CONSPIRACY

New York Times, October 30, 2007

LOS ANGELES, Oct. 29 — William S. Lerach, 61, a former partner at the law firm now known as Milberg Weiss, pleaded guilty to conspiracy on Monday.

Mr. Lerach pleaded guilty to conspiracy to obstruct justice, specifically for concealing his secret, illegal payments to Dr. Steven G. Cooperman, who was a plaintiff in the class-action lawsuits for which the firm became famous.

Dr. Cooperman, 64, of Fairfield, Conn., has already pleaded guilty to participating in the scheme. Sentencing for Mr. Lerach was set for Jan. 14. Mr. Lerach, 61, of Rancho Santa Fe, Calif., admitted to a role in an arrangement in which the firm pursued companies with class-action lawsuits when their share prices dropped.

The criminal cases against Mr. Lerach; his former partner, Melvyn I. Weiss; several other former partners; and the firm itself are based on how prosecutors say these parties gained an illegal advantage over other firms filing similar suits. Mr. Lerach and the others, prosecutors said, gave kickbacks of about

10 percent of the firm's share of settlements to individuals who remained on call to act as lead plaintiffs.

Having Dr. Cooperman and others in place allowed the firm to file suits faster, giving it a lead position in cases, which generally led to higher legal fees. Prosecutors said that in more than 150 cases, from the 1970s to 2005, the law firm earned more than $216 million in legal fees, paying $11 million in kickbacks.

Mr. Lerach agreed earlier in the morning to put up a $50,000 unsecured bond and not to leave the country. The terms of his plea agreement include forfeiture of $7.75 million to the government, a $250,000 fine, one to two years in federal prison without parole and three years of supervised release. Mr. Lerach has not agreed to cooperate with the government.

In Los Angeles, Judge John F. Walter of Federal District Court asked Mr. Lerach whether he was pleading guilty because he was in fact guilty.

"I am," replied Mr. Lerach, dressed in a black suit and subdued yellow and black tie. His wife, in a black pantsuit and heels, sat with an entourage of supporters in the audience. As Mr. Lerach, his wife and lawyers walked from the courtroom, he declined to comment, saying, "We'll see you again another time."

The agreement leaves as defendants the existing law firm, Milberg Weiss; Mr. Weiss; and Paul T. Selzer, 66, of Palm Springs, Calif., a lawyer who is accused of being an intermediary, laundering money between the firm and the on-call plaintiffs.

Prosecutors have confirmed that they are in "serious discussions" with Mr. Selzer, presumably about a plea agreement. Mr. Lerach and Mr. Weiss broke up their partnership in 2004, with Mr. Lerach opening a practice on the West Coast.

E. LAWYERS AS AGENTS: THE PROBLEM OF DIVIDED LOYALTIES

1. "CONFLICTS": A PROFESSIONAL PROBLEM AND A LITIGATION TACTIC

a. The Problem Defined and Illustrated

GEOFFREY HAZARD, SUSAN KONIAK, & ROGER CRAMTON,
THE LAW OF ETHICS AND LAWYERING

575-577 (3d ed. 1999)

Lawyers are exposed to two primary categories of conflicts: conflicts between clients and conflicts between lawyer and client. . . .

Conflicts between clients can be divided into two major subcategories: concurrent and successive representation. . . .

The rules governing conflicts of interest in concurrent representation address two situations: when the interests of one client run (or have the potential to run) counter to those of another client and when the antagonism between two clients is great. As to the first problem, diverging interests, it is easiest to imagine the problem if you contemplate two clients who seek representation jointly as a matter of common purpose, for example the city of New York and one of its police officers seeking a common defense against a civil rights suit caused by the officer's actions in causing the person's death. Some defenses available to the city involve implicating the officer. The interests of the two clients in the lawyer investigating the facts to develop those defenses . . . diverge. It is in the city's interest, but not in the interests of the officer. . . . The more the interests of the two clients diverge . . . , the more the lawyer's representation of each client is restricted by her duty not to harm the other client. This is the problem of diverging interests.

As to the second problem, antagonism, . . . [i]magine a lawyer representing corporation X in a suit brought against it by one of its employees alleging sex discrimination. That lawyer is now approached by corporation Y which wants to sue corporations X and Z for conspiring to restrain trade. The interests of X in the first suit . . . and the interests of Y in the second suit are not divergent. . . . Given that the two matters (the sex discrimination case and the antitrust suit) are completely unrelated to one another, the problem of representing divergent interests does not arise. But were the lawyer to accept Y's invitation to sue its own client, X, the lawyer would be taking as antagonistic a stance against one of its own clients as it is possible to take. After being sued by its own lawyer, would it be reasonable for corporation X to trust that lawyer . . . ?

MARIE-ANN HOGARTH, CONFLICTS CAUSE FORMER WINSON SONSINI PARTNER TO CUT SHORT HIS STAY AT KIRKLAND

San Franciso Recorder, March 10, 2006 at 1

Former Wilson Sonsini Goodrich & Rosati securities litigator Bruce Vanyo, who encountered conflict issues a month after starting a new job at Kirkland & Ellis, was in Chicago Wednesday signing up with his third law firm of the year, Katten Muchin Rosenman.

He joins the firm's Los Angeles office and will co-chair its securities litigation practice. He will also serve as a member of the firm's board of directors.

Vanyo said he contacted Katten Chairman David Kistenbroker as soon as he realized he faced conflict issues at Kirkland with both current and prospective clients. . . .

Vanyo, one of Wilson's most highly compensated partners, joined Kirkland's Los Angeles office on Feb 2. He declined to provide details on the nature of the unanticipated conflicts and said he couldn't recall when the conflicts first arose.

"[Kirkland] is a wonderful firm," he said. "It is just that stuff came up that none of us expected to come up. It's a big law firm with a lot of clients and relationships, and I have a significant practice." . . .

Vanyo said he cleared a conflict check at Katten within 24 hours. He added that he presented a list of "a lot" of clients and cases going back three years. He declined to provide details about his current clients.

Recruiter Larry Watanabe, who brokered both the Kirkland and Katten deals for Vanyo, said the scope and size of major law firms were causing greater uncertainty in the lateral hiring process.

"While firms make every attempt to clear conflicts before commencement, the nature of business is ongoing, and sometimes matters like this are simply unavoidable," Watanabe said.

Christopher Hockett, who heads the litigation department at Bingham McCutchen, nonetheless said it's unusual for a firm to be surprised by a late-breaking conflict issue. "There is a very thorough conflicts check that we do as part of our due diligence," he said.

"Still it is possible that something gets missed, and perhaps that is what happened here," Hockett added.

b. Two "Simple" Examples

WESTINGHOUSE ELEC. CORP. v. KERR-MCGEE CORP.

580 F.2d 1311 (7th Cir. 1978)

[Kirkland & Ellis represented two clients. One, Westinghouse, made generators for nuclear power plants and supplied those plants with uranium fuel, under contracts with a number of electric power utilities. In 1975 Westinghouse announced that the continued supply of uranium had become "commercially impracticable," as that term is defined in the UCC and that it was abrogating its contracts with the utilities as a result. The utilities sued for breach, and as part of its defense to the utilities, Westinghouse impleaded more than twenty suppliers of uranium, claiming they had unlawfully conspired to restrain trade (and thus make Westinghouse's performance of the utility contracts impracticable). Kirkland had about half a dozen of its lawyers involved in representing Westinghouse in these utility-Westinghouse-uranium supplier cases.

At about the same time, the Washington DC office of Kirkland had taken on a lobbying/reporting task for the American Petroleum Institute (API). Congress was considering legislation to break up the oil companies, which were resisting. As part of their efforts, API hired Kirkland to write a report — which was to be based on information it collected confidentially from API's members, who, except when they were combining for lobbying purposes, competed with each other. To get this information, Kirkland promised that its information would be kept strictly confidential, not to be disclosed to any other company or even to the API. A team of Kirkland lawyers collected this information, which included information about the general energy market — including uranium mining — and wrote the report, which took the general position that there was in fact real competition in the uranium industry.

The problem and the case arose because several of the oil companies also engage in uranium mining — and were some of the defendants in the Westinghouse uranium antitrust case. Those defendants (Gulf Oil, Kerr-McGee Mining, and Getty Oil) moved to have Kirkland disqualified from representing Westinghouse in the uranium antitrust case. The trial court denied the motion, citing the complete independence of the two representations, the elaborate security provisions within Kirkland that prevented the exchange of information, and the changes in the practice of law (including the growth of large firms), that called for a different application of the rules concerning conflicts. The oil companies appealed and the Seventh Circuit reversed, ordering Kirkland's disqualification. It found that:

- The oil & mining companies were Kirkland's "clients" although it never directly engaged the firm and paid none of its bills directly (API was the client and bill-paying entity);
- The confidentiality and "wall" provisions did not solve the imputed knowledge rules, which attribute to all a firm's lawyers knowledge held by any of them.]

E. F. HUTTON & CO. v. BROWN

305 F. Supp. 371 (S.D. Tex. 1969)

NOEL, District Judge.

I. Preface

A. Introduction

Plaintiff E. F. Hutton & Company, Inc. ("Hutton"), a national brokerage firm, brought this action against defendant John D. Brown, its former Houston regional vice-president, for alleged negligence and breach of fiduciary duty to the corporation. Jurisdiction exists under 28 U.S.C. §1332 as to the entire case, and under 28 U.S.C. §1331 as to a portion of the case. . . .

In this litigation Hutton is represented by a Houston law firm (hereinafter called "the Houston firm"), which appears as Hutton's counsel of record. Hutton's corporate general counsel, Cahill, Gordon, Sonnett, Reindel & Ohl of New York City (hereinafter called "the New York firm") has not entered a formal appearance and does not appear "of Counsel" on the pleadings filed by the Houston firm on Hutton's behalf, but (as will be show later in more detail) has participated in the investigation of Hutton's claim against Brown and in Hutton's prosecution of this litigation. Defendant Brown has moved to disqualify both of these firms from continuing to represent or to advise Hutton in connection with this litigation and to enjoin them from turning over certain information in their files to Hutton or to new counsel whom Hutton may retain.

[The reported case is one of several government actions and private lawsuits surrounding the collapse] of Westec Corporation in August, 1966. In late July or early August, a man named John Hurbrough approached Brown seeking a substantial loan from Hutton to be secured by Westec common stock. After negotiations, Brown authorized and made a loan to Hurbrough in the amount of $650,000, and caused Hutton to lend that sum to Hurbrough upon receipt of the collateral. Shortly after the loan was completed, however, the American Stock Exchange and the Securities and Exchange Commission (SEC) suspended trading in Westec stock. In due course, Brown and other Hutton personnel were asked by the SEC to testify in a formal investigation into the internal affairs of Westec and into trading in Westec stock. Subsequently, these same personnel were asked to testify at public hearings instituted by Westec's trustee in bankruptcy. In accordance with its usual practice in such cases, the New York firm dispatched one of its members (hereinafter called 'the New York partner') to accompany Brown to each hearing. A member of the Houston firm (hereinafter called 'the Houston partner') also accompanied Brown to the bankruptcy hearing.

[With the collapse of the stock, Hurbrough's creditors also became alarmed and Westec declared bankruptcy. As Hutton began to investigate, it also became disturbed by the actions of Brown, its officer, who approved the original loan. Ultimately, Hutton fired and sued Brown.]

In this litigation, the Houston partner is counsel of record for Hutton. As more fully appears hereafter, the New York partner and other members of the New York firm have cooperated with the Houston partner in the preparation and presentation of Hutton's case. Shortly after suit was filed, Brown's present attorney requested the Houston partner and his firm to withdraw from further representation of Hutton in this litigation. The Houston partner refused, whereupon Brown filed the pending motion.

In support of his motion to disqualify, Brown asserts that the New York and Houston partners represented him individually when he appeared at the SEC and bankruptcy hearings and testified about the Hurbrough loan transaction. He asserts that the instant lawsuit may well turn in substantial part on his understanding of that transaction, and contends that counsel's continued representation of Hutton violates their subsisting duty to him as their former client. In opposition, Hutton denies that the partners ever represented Brown individually, and contends that even if they did, Brown is not now entitled to insist on their disqualification. . . .

In this case it is undisputed that Brown's role in the making of the Hurbrough loan was the subject of lengthy questioning at [SEC and bankruptcy] hearings at which he testified. The parties also agree that this issue may become one of the material issues here. These stipulations establish the requisite relationship between the alleged prior representations and the current adverse representation, but three issues presented by the motion to disqualify remain to be resolved:

(1) Whether Brown is a former client; i.e., whether the New York and Houston partners represented him individually, as well as the corporation, at the SEC and bankruptcy hearings.
(2) Whether corporate counsel who have represented a corporate officer individually should be disqualified even though all of the officer's communications with counsel were intended to be conveyed to his corporate employer and were made for the benefit of the corporation.
(3) Whether the requested injunction should issue.

The Court answers the first two of these questions in the affirmative, and will direct present counsel for plaintiff to terminate their representation of plaintiff in this case and to refrain from aiding, consulting or advising new counsel retained by plaintiff, except to the limited extent reasonably necessary to the transfer of their duties to new counsel. The request for an injunction will be denied. . . .

II. Whether Counsel Represented Hutton Only . . .

A. The SEC Hearing

The formal SEC investigation into trading in Westec stock was commenced shortly after trading was suspended. Proceedings were conducted by an investigating officer of the SEC, who examined witnesses under oath. Pursuant to regulation, the hearings were non-public: only the witness, his attorney, and representatives of the Texas State Securities Board and the SEC were allowed in the hearing room. . . .

Early in April 1967, the SEC requested Hutton to produce Brown to testify. Hutton so informed Brown. On the day before the hearing the New York partner and associate flew from New York to Houston. On arrival, they went directly to Brown's office. They and Brown discussed the Westec situation generally, and the Hurbrough loan transaction in particular. Brown was handed copies of the reports the associate had prepared for Hutton after his previous visits to Houston, and asked to study them. Both lawyers urged Brown to give responsive, truthful, and candid answers to all questions the SEC examiner might ask. In the course of the meeting, the partner informed Brown that he would accompany him to the hearing.

The next morning, both lawyers again met briefly with Brown, after which the partner accompanied him to the hearing. There the SEC's examining attorney informed Brown that the hearing was a non-public, formal investigative proceeding conducted jointly by the SEC and the Texas State Securities Board, and recited the SEC's statutory authority for the investigation. He then said to Brown, "I see you are accompanied by (the partner) here this morning. Is he your counsel in this proceeding?" Brown answered, "Yes."

Brown's answer was unexpected, if affidavits filed by the New York partner and the associate are to be believed. In those affidavits, both the partner and the associate claim that during their conference the evening before the hearing, Brown was specifically informed of the New York firm's position as counsel only for Hutton. They also allege that Brown agreed to explain their firm's position to the examining officer if he was asked whether the partner represented him individually.

Brown submitted his supplemental affidavit to deny these allegations. Neither he nor Hutton, however, has offered to present testimony or any other evidence to assist the Court in resolving the conflict between his affidavit and those of counsel. . . .

The official transcript of the SEC hearing states that the New York partner appeared as "Counsel for John D. Brown."

. . .

C. The Bankruptcy Hearing

Shortly after the suspension of trading, Westec experienced severe financial difficulties, and corporate reorganization proceedings were begun under Chapter X of the Bankruptcy Act. Counsel for Westec's court-appointed trustee . . . requested that Hutton produce Brown and two other Hutton employees for examination. This request was reported to Brown and to Hutton's New York office. The latter requested the New York partner to be present in Houston during the examinations. On the day before Brown was due to testify, the New York partner flew to Houston. On arrival, he met briefly with the Houston partner and Brown. The next morning, the New York partner and the Houston partner accompanied Brown to the hearing.

As soon as Brown had been sworn, the Special Master informed him that the SEC was participating, and warned him that the facts developed at the hearing could constitute violations of the securities laws. He then advised Brown of his right to counsel and of his privilege against self-incrimination, and stated that since he could not compel Brown to give incriminating testimony, all of Brown's answers would be deemed voluntary. After Brown had indicated that he understood these warnings, the following colloquy took place:

The Master: "Do I understand correctly that you are represented by counsel of your choice here this morning?"
The Witness: "Yes, sir."
The Master: "Namely (the Houston partner) and (the New York partner)?"
The Witness: "Correct."
The Master: "Thank you, sir."

After this exchange, and following a discussion among counsel concerning documents which counsel for the trustee had subpoenaed from Hutton, counsel for the trustee questioned Brown briefly about his background and experience in the securities field, and then conducted a searching examination with emphasis on the Hurbrough loan transaction.

At the conclusion of the hearing, the New York partner returned to New York and reported to Hutton there with respect to Brown's testimony. Subsequently, when the transcript of Brown's testimony became available, the partner furnished a copy to Hutton in New York. On the transcript, the official court reporter listed the Houston partner and the New York partner as having appeared "on behalf of the witness, John D. Brown."

D. Findings and Conclusions

Brown bases his motion to disqualify chiefly on undisputed record evidence. The official transcript of the SEC hearing reveals that the New York partner entered an appearance as counsel for Brown, not for Hutton. The official transcript of the bankruptcy hearing reveals that both the New York and Houston partners entered appearances for Brown, not for Hutton. At each hearing Brown identified counsel as his counsel, not as Hutton's, and counsel stood mute.

An attorney's appearance in a judicial or semi-judicial proceeding creates a presumption that an attorney-client relationship exists between the attorney and the person with whom he appears. This presumption shifts to Hutton, the party denying the existence of the relationship, the burden of persuasion. When the relationship is also evidenced by the entry of a formal appearance by the attorney on behalf of the person with whom he appears, the presumption becomes almost irrebuttable, for the entry of a formal appearance has quite properly been called "record evidence of the highest character." In this case the Court finds that Hutton's opposition has failed to overcome the presumption that the New York and Houston partners represented Brown when he testified in the SEC and bankruptcy investigations.

Hutton's briefs and affidavits collect and cite a great number of facts to show that counsel represented only Hutton at the SEC and bankruptcy hearings. Several merely evidence Hutton's longstanding relationship with the New York and Houston firms. These are inapposite, for Brown does not assert that counsel did not represent Hutton at the two hearings. His motion is based on the proposition that counsel represented him as well. Hutton and its counsel are in error if they believe that an attorney cannot ever represent two clients with respect to a single matter. Attorneys frequently represent more than one party to a single transaction. Ordinarily there is nothing improper in such a practice so long as the attorney discloses the consequences of the joint representation to all of his clients, and all parties as well as the attorney consent. . . .

The only other event urged by Hutton as establishing that Brown could not have understood counsel's appearances as appearances for him is the conversation alleged by the New York partner and associate to have occurred the evening before the SEC appearance. Counsel allege in their affidavits to have told Brown what to say the next day when he was asked of the attorney appearing with him was his attorney, and that Brown agreed to say that the attorney represented Hutton only. Brown, of course, denies that this discussion occurred.

In pondering this conflict in the affidavits, the Court has discovered that the record in this case provides many more questions than answers. If the conversation occurred as counsel allege, why did Brown not keep his promise when asked the expected question at the hearing? If so, why did the New York partner not cause Brown to clarify his answer, as he caused him to clarify other answers later in the examination? Why did the partner enter an appearance as counsel for Brown, not for Hutton? Why did he not speak to Brown after the hearing or take any steps to correct the transcript, if it was incorrect? Why did he again enter an appearance as counsel for Brown, not for Hutton, when Brown was called four months later to testify in the bankruptcy proceeding? Why did the Houston partner enter an appearance for Brown, not for Hutton, on the same occasion? Why did not the New York and Houston partners explain their firms' position with regard to representing Brown individually immediately before the bankruptcy hearing? Why did they not speak up when Brown described them as his attorneys, not as Hutton's? Why did they fail to correct the transcript of the bankruptcy hearing when it was received, if it was incorrect? Why did Hutton's New York management not correct the transcript on receipt, if it was incorrect? Why did Hutton and its counsel wait until after Brown's present counsel raised the issue — a year after the bankruptcy hearing and sixteen months after the alleged evening conversation — to deny that counsel had represented Brown at the SEC and bankruptcy hearings and to attack the accuracy of Brown's testimony? . . .

III. Whether Counsel Should Be Disqualified

Assuming arguendo that the New York and Houston partners represented Brown individually at the SEC and bankruptcy hearings, Hutton advances three legal arguments against disqualification: (1) Brown is not entitled to move for disqualification because he communicated no information to counsel which was confidential as to Hutton. (2) An order of disqualification in this case would have a distinctly adverse effect on the corporate bar without serving any interest of Brown's, and would therefore violate public policy. (3) Brown has waived whatever right he may once have had to move for disqualification. These contentions may now be considered. . . .

[The opinion rejects each of the arguments against disqualification.]

In this case the Court has found that Brown believed that he, not just Hutton, was the client of counsel and that this created an attorney-client relationship. Once this had occurred, counsel became obligated to exercise an independent professional judgment on behalf of each of their clients, Brown and Hutton. This duty could have been discharged in either of two manners. First, counsel might have elected to make themselves available to represent both Brown and Hutton. Had they done so, their duty to both of their potential clients would have required them to inform each fully. The extent of disclosure necessary would be governed by the reason for requiring counsel to disclose: to enable each potential client to make a reasoned choice. In the context of the two investigatory hearings at which Brown testified, full disclosure would have required counsel to apprise each potential client of the existence of any potential conflict, to advise each of the consequences of a joint representation, to explain to each the serious consequences which could occur to either or both as a result of Brown's testimony at the hearings, and to inform each that either was free to retain independent counsel. Only then would either Hutton or Brown have been in a position to make a knowing waiver of its or his right to retain independent counsel.

Counsel's second option was to inform Brown that when they appeared at the hearings, they would do so solely on Hutton's behalf, and that if Brown had any interest which failed to coincide with some interest of Hutton's his interest would go unprotected unless he employed personal counsel. By so advising Brown, they would have prevented an attorney-client relationship between themselves and him from arising. . . .

The Court emphasizes that not all corporate counsel appearing with corporate officers who are called to testify will risk disqualification. Only those counsel who permit the officer to believe that they represent him individually will disable themselves from appearing in subsequent litigation against him. And it is eminently proper to disqualify these, for they are the persons who are in a position, and have the obligation, to ensure that there is no misunderstanding by the officer. . . .

c. Harder Cases?

KLEMM v. THE SUPERIOR COURT OF FRESNO COUNTY

142 Cal. Rptr. 509 (Cal. Ct. App. 1977)

BROWN (G. A.), P.J.

The ultimate issue herein is to what extent one attorney may represent both husband and wife in a noncontested dissolution proceeding where the written consent of each to such representation has been filed with the court.

Dale Klemm (hereinafter husband) and Gail Klemm (hereinafter wife) were married and are the parents of two minor children. They separated after six years of marriage, and the wife filed a petition for dissolution of the marriage in propria persona. There was no community property, and neither party owned any substantial personal property. Both parties waived spousal support. The husband was a carpenter with part-time employment.

At the dissolution hearing Attorney Catherine Bailey appeared for the wife. It developed that Bailey is a friend of the husband and wife and because they could not afford an attorney she was acting without compensation. The attorney had consulted with both the husband and wife and had worked out an oral agreement whereby the custody of the minor children would be joint, that is, each would have the children for a period of two weeks out of each month, and the wife waived child support.

The trial judge granted an interlocutory decree and awarded joint custody in accord with the agreement. However, because the wife was receiving aid for dependent children payments from the county, he referred the matter of child support to the Family Support Division of the Fresno County District Attorney's office for investigation and report.

The subsequent report from the family support division recommended that the husband be ordered to pay $25 per month per child (total $50) child support and that this amount be paid to the county as reimbursement for past and present A.F.D.C. payments made and being made to the wife. Bailey, on behalf of the wife, filed a written objection to the recommendation that the husband be required to pay child support.

At the hearing on the report and issue of child support on April 25, 1977, Bailey announced she was appearing on behalf of the husband. She said the parties were "in agreement on this matter, so there is in reality no conflict between them." No written consents to joint representation were filed. On questioning by the court the wife evinced uncertainty as to her position in the litigation. The wife said, "She [Bailey] asked me to come here just as a witness, so I don't feel like I'm taking any action against Dale." The judge pointed out that she (the wife) was still a party. When first asked if she wanted Bailey to continue as her attorney she answered "No." Later she said she would consent to Bailey's being relieved as her counsel. She then said she didn't believe she could act as her own attorney but that she consented to Bailey's representing the husband. After this confusing and conflicting testimony and a request for permission to talk to Bailey about it, the judge ordered, over Bailey's objection, that he would not permit Bailey to appear for either the husband or the wife because of a present conflict of interest and ordered the matter continued for one week.

At the continued hearing on May 2, 1977, Bailey appeared by counsel, who filed written consents to joint representation signed by the husband and wife and requested that Bailey be allowed to appear for the husband and wife (who were present in court). The consents, which were identical in form, stated: "I have been advised by my attorney that a potential conflict of interest exists by reason of her advising and representing my ex-spouse as well as myself. I feel this conflict is purely technical and I request Catherine Bailey to represent me." The court denied the motion,[1] and the husband and wife have petitioned this court for a writ of mandate to direct the trial court to permit such representation.

Rule 5-102 of the State Bar Rules of Professional Conduct states:

> (A) A member of the State Bar shall not accept professional employment without first disclosing his relation, if any, with the adverse party, and his interest, if any, in the subject matter of the employment. A member of the State Bar who accepts employment under this rule shall first obtain the client's written consent to such employment.
>
> (B) A member of the State Bar shall not represent conflicting interests, except with the written consent of all parties concerned.

(3BWest's Ann. Bus. & Prof. Code (1974 ed., 1977 cum. supp.) foll. §6076 at p. 65 [Deering's Cal. Codes Ann. Rules (1976 ed.) at p. 614].). . . .

Though an informed consent be obtained, no case we have been able to find sanctions dual representation of conflicting interests if that representation is in conjunction with a trial or hearing where there is an actual, present, existing conflict and the discharge of duty to one client conflicts with the duty to another.

(1) As a matter of law a purported consent to dual representation of litigants with adverse interests at a contested hearing would be neither intelligent nor informed. Such representation would be per se inconsistent with the adversary position of an attorney in litigation, and common sense dictates that it would be unthinkable to permit an attorney to assume a position at a trial or hearing where he could not advocate the interests of one client without adversely injuring those of the other.

---

1. The court grounded its ruling upon the following reasoning:

> [U]nder our canons of ethics and rules of conduct it would be improper for Miss Bailey to appear in this proceeding on behalf of the respondent where there is not in the court's opinion a theoretical conflict, but an actual conflict of interest in this respect: This proceeding is to determine what amount, if any, the respondent will pay on account of child support to the petitioner Gail Klemm. At this point in time the court is advised and at the April 25th hearing that Mrs. Klemm was receiving public assistance, the end result being that whatever amount ordered paid and in fact paid would be paid to the Family Support Division and would not actually be realized by the petitioner in that if such amounts would become a part of the overall monthly grant.
>
> However, there is obviously a potential if not actual point in time when the petitioner may not be receiving public assistance in which case whatever order, if any, is made to her benefit on account of child support in this proceeding would be the amount subject to modification that she would receive on account of child support at least for some period of time.

(2) However, if the conflict is merely potential, there being no existing dispute or contest between the parties represented as to any point in litigation, then with full disclosure to and informed consent of both clients there may be dual representation at a hearing or trial.

(3) In our view the case at bench clearly falls within the latter category. The conflict of interest was strictly potential and not present. The parties had settled their differences by agreement. There was no point of difference to be litigated. The position of each inter se was totally consistent throughout the proceedings. The wife did not want child support from the husband, and the husband did not want to pay support for the children. The actual conflict that existed on the issue of support was between the county on the one hand, which argued that support should be ordered, and the husband and wife on the other who consistently maintained the husband should not be ordered to pay support.

While on the face of the matter it may appear foolhardy for the wife to waive child support, other values could very well have been more important to her than such support — such as maintaining a good relationship between the husband and the children and between the husband and herself despite the marital problems — thus avoiding the backbiting, acrimony and ill will which the Family Relations Act of 1970 was, insofar as possible, designed to eliminate. It could well have been if the wife was forced to choose between A.F.D.C. payments to be reimbursed to the county by the husband and no A.F.D.C. payments she would have made the latter choice.

Of course, if the wife at some future date should change her mind and seek child support and if the husband should desire to avoid the payment of such support, Bailey would be disqualified from representing either in a contested hearing on the issue. . . .

The conclusion we arrive at is particularly congruent with dissolution proceedings under the Family Law Act of 1970, the purpose of which was to discard the concept of fault in dissolution of marriage actions, to minimize the adversary nature of such proceedings and to eliminate conflicts created only to secure a divorce. . . . We hold on the facts of this case, wherein the conflict was only potential, that if the written consents were knowing and informed and given after full disclosure by the attorney, the attorney can appear for both of the parties on issues concerning which they fully agree. . . .

(4) A word as to procedure. Initially, the trial court is entitled to accept properly executed written consents to joint representation at their face value. The judge is entitled to presume the attorney is familiar with the law and code of professional ethics and has complied with the proper standards. However, if the judge has any question regarding whether the proper standards have been observed, it is his duty to either require counsel to inquire further or inquire himself regarding the circumstances of the execution of the written consents and the state of mind of the clients for the purpose of making the necessary factual determination in this regard.

(5) Finally, as a caveat, we hasten to sound a note of warning. Attorneys who undertake to represent parties with divergent interests owe the highest duty to each to make a full disclosure of all facts and circumstances which are necessary to enable the parties to make a fully informed decision regarding the

subject matter of the litigation, including the areas of potential conflict and the possibility and desirability of seeking independent legal advice.

(6) Failing such disclosure, the attorney is civilly liable to the client who suffers loss caused by lack of disclosure. In addition, the lawyer lays himself open to charges, whether well founded or not, of unethical and unprofessional conduct. Moreover, the validity of any agreement negotiated without independent representation of each of the parties is vulnerable to easy attack as having been procured by misrepresentation, fraud and overreaching. It thus behooves counsel to cogitate carefully and proceed cautiously before placing himself/herself in such a position. . . .

It is ordered that a peremptory writ of mandate issue directing the trial court to reconsider Bailey's motion to be allowed to represent both husband and wife, that the court determine if the consent given by each was knowing and informed after a full disclosure by the attorney, and to decide the motion in accordance with the principles set forth in this opinion.

JEDWABNY V. PHILADELPHIA TRANSP. CO.

135 A.2d 252 (Pa. 1957)

Opinion by Mr. Chief Justice JONES

The principal question on these appeals is whether the granting of a new trial because of the trial judge's failure to make certain that one of the litigants had full knowledge of an existing conflict of interest in his attorney's representation of him constituted an abuse of discretion.

Three plaintiffs, one of whom was the owner and driver of an automobile and the other two his guest passengers, sued the Philadelphia Transportation Company for damages for injuries sustained in a collision between the automobile and a street car of the Transportation Company. The defendant joined the automobile owner and driver as an additional defendant.

At trial, the jury by special findings found both the motorman of the street car and the driver of the automobile guilty of proximately causative negligence. Verdicts were accordingly rendered against the defendant and the additional defendant jointly for the sums assessed by the jury, viz., $100 for the one passenger plaintiff and $10,500 for the other. In the case of the automobile owner as plaintiff and the Transportation Company defendant, a verdict was returned for the defendant. The Transportation Company filed motions for a new trial and for judgments n.o.v.; the n.o.v. motions were withdrawn at argument of the new trial motion. Neither the passenger plaintiffs nor the owner and driver of the automobile, all of whom were represented throughout by the same attorney, filed any after-verdict motions although, as already appears, the owner of the automobile stood jointly liable with the Transportation Company for the money verdicts in favor of the passenger plaintiffs.

The court below granted a new trial solely for the reason set forth in the opinion accompanying the order as follows: "We think it was the duty of the trial judge to explain the situation to the additional defendant, a thing that was not done. It is not fatal to a trial that he not be represented, but he should be given the chance to make an informed choice. With a heavy joint verdict against him now, he may not even know his rights relative to a request for a new trial or an appeal."

The instant appeal does not necessarily search the basic ethical question whether a conflict of interest, such as this record presents, serves, as a matter of law, to disqualify an attorney from representing concurrently both of the conflicting interests. The question here is simply whether the trial judge was guilty of a palpable abuse of discretion in awarding a new trial for the reason assigned.

The situation that obtained upon the failure of the attorney to move for the additional defendant's relief from liability for the $10,500 verdict against him in favor of another client of the same attorney, also party to the same record, created in the mind of the trial judge a consciousness that he should have made certain by personal interrogation of the additional defendant at the time of the rendition of the verdicts or, at least, before the time for moving for a new trial had expired that the particular litigant had been fully informed and had an intelligent and complete understanding of his then legal status, and should also have ascertained whether the litigant desired to move for a new trial.

Canon 6 of the Canons of Professional Ethics, adopted by the American Bar Association on September 30, 1937, and by the Pennsylvania Bar Association on January 7, 1938, provides in part that "It is unprofessional to represent conflicting interests, except by express consent of all concerned given after a full disclosure of the facts. Within the meaning of this canon, a lawyer represents conflicting interests when, in behalf of one client, it is his duty to contend for that which duty to another client requires him to oppose." The full disclosure required by this canon contemplates that the possibly adverse effect of the conflict be fully explained by the attorney to the client to be affected and by him thoroughly understood. See opinion No. 160 of the Committee on Professional Ethics of the American Bar Association.

The foregoing canon applies to cases where the circumstances are such that possibly conflicting interests may permissibly be represented by the same attorney. But, manifestly, there are instances where the conflicts of interest are so critically adverse as not to admit of one attorney's representing both sides. Such is the situation which this record presents. No one could conscionably contend that the same attorney may represent both the plaintiff and defendant in an adversary action. Yet, that is what is being done in this case. It was the attorney's duty to protect the $10,500 verdict of his plaintiff client against the additional defendant while it was his duty at the same time to relieve from liability the additional defendant whose representation the attorney had originally undertaken for the purpose of obtaining for him a recovery from the Transportation Company. Obviously, the attorney cannot serve the opposed interests of his two clients fully and faithfully. The ancient rule against one's attempting to serve two masters interposes.

The ethical conception, appropriate to the instant circumstances, was luminously expressed in Bossler v. Wilson, 65 D. & C. 164, 171 (1948), which involved a procedural situation materially akin to the present. It was there said: "Now as to the first stated fact necessitating a new trial as to *both* defendants, namely, the same attorney appearing for both the plaintiff and the additional defendant. It must be borne in mind that the original defendant was a plaintiff as to the additional defendant. No finding rendered under such circumstances can be allowed to stand and to mature into a judgment against the additional defendant, a verdict rendered in a trial wherein the attorney represented the plaintiff in the presentation of her case and the additional defendant in the presentation of his defense to the claims of both plaintiff and original defendant. The interests of these parties were adverse. No attorney can serve two opposing litigants any more so than one man can serve two masters. Upon this point the law of the Commonwealth is in harmony with Holy Writ," citing in a footnote the scriptural references.

The conclusion naturally follows that, in the undisputed situation here present, the action of the learned court below in granting a new trial not only did not constitute an abuse of discretion but was affirmatively proper. As the brief for the appellee reminds us, the additional defendant with a large joint verdict against him, having been awarded a new trial, now asks us on appeal to reverse the action of the court below to the end that the verdict against him may be reinstated and judgment thereon entered against him. The anomaly could hardly be more guarding.

Dissenting Opinion by Mr. Justice BELL:

I disagree with the Court's order and opinion because they are in my judgment both unrealistic and unfair. The Court admits that it is not necessary for a defendant to be represented by an attorney; it is sufficient if he has an opportunity to employ one, and in a case like this, to make "an informed choice." There is no decision, rule, principle or canon that requires the trial Judge under such circumstances to be the informant — only a moron would be unconversant with or ignorant of the situation and the penalty with which the driver of the automobile was and is confronted. Canon 6 of Professional Ethics is wise and salutary if applied as a general rule, but virtually every rule is subject to some exception.

A joint trial of two or several suits arising out of a collision between two or three automobiles or trolleys was designed, not to cause hardship or injustice but to expedite and promote justice. Such trials have frequently raised factual and legal questions and problems which have vexed and perplexed juries, trial courts and appellate Courts alike, and have at times resulted in a miscarriage of justice.

For example, a *poor* man owns and is a passenger in an automobile which is driven by his wife. There is some evidence that it was being driven under his direction although he denies this. A collision occurs with another automobile owned and driven under the same circumstances. Each family engages a lawyer and each is convinced that the other driver is solely at fault. Cross suits are brought and each plaintiff is joined as a defendant in each suit. The suits are tried together and each lawyer explains to his client the legal risks and possibilities. Each family tells their attorney that they cannot afford to employ more than one lawyer. Why should the law or any canon compel each claimant to employ two lawyers — total of six or eight lawyers in this simple case? Isn't such a requirement impractical, unjust and ridiculous?

Notwithstanding the high motive which prompted the lower Court to grant a new trial, I believe that the grant of a new trial was unfair to plaintiffs Jedwabny and Stachowicz (the verdict winners), and for this reason, as well as for the above mentioned reasons, was a manifest abuse of discretion.

Dissenting Opinion by Mr. Justice MUSMANO:

The action of the learned trial Judge in this case, in ordering a new trial when obviously it is not necessary, represents to me either a flagrant usurpation of judicial authority or an incredible indulgence of a despotic whimsicality. In either event it accomplishes an injustice upon two persons who have fairly and squarely won a verdict in a trial which admittedly is free of error, and they should not therefore be compelled to face the shot and shell, worry, expense, suspense and agony of another courtroom battle.

Here are the facts. Leon Jedwabny and Peter Stachowicz were injured in an accident when the automobile in which they were riding as guests of Charles W. Atkinson, collided with a street car on 36th Street in Philadelphia. These persons and Atkinson brought a lawsuit against the Philadelphia Transportation Company, the passengers claiming damages for personal injuries and Atkinson seeking reimbursement for repairs made necessary to his car. The railways company denied liability and charged that Atkinson was either wholly or jointly responsible with the railway company for the happening of the accident. Accordingly it forced Atkinson into the case in the extra role of additional defendant. . . .

In ordering a new trial the trial Judge indicated he was doing this for Atkinson's benefit. But Atkinson does not want a new trial. He had had his day in court. The jury returned a verdict against him and he is willing to let matters rest as they are. There are some people in life who are willing to face realities and they experience no gratification in chasing the evanescent and elusive rainbow. Atkinson apparently finds more peace of mind in accepting the status quo than in making an effort which might result in an even greater loss. Accordingly he is satisfied not to have a new trial. It is for that reason that he did not make a motion for a new trial. It is for that reason that he is today opposed to a new trial. But the trial Judge, in his Olympian wisdom, declares that Atkinson has no right to be satisfied without a new trial and that, therefore, though the Heavens fall, Atkinson shall have a new trial!

But in the meantime what is happening to the innocent bystanders, Jedwabny and Stachowicz? They are entirely content with the result of the trial. They have won their verdict. No one charges them with impropriety. Why should they be subjected to the turmoil, the expense, the loss of time, the worry and the agony which accompany a trial — with the possibility of drowning in a river they have already crossed. . . .

2. ANOTHER AGENCY PROBLEM IN LITIGATION: INSURANCE

a. The Problem Defined

CHARLES SILVER* & KENT SYVERUD,** THE PROFESSIONAL RESPONSIBILITIES OF INSURANCE DEFENSE LAWYERS

45 Duke Law Journal 255 (1995)

Introduction

Law professors are fascinated by civil procedure. Many of us teach the subject and, at most law schools, we emphasize its importance by requiring law students to take our courses in the first year. We write innumerable articles, books, and treatises about procedure. We convene symposia on every topic under the sun. We help judges design procedures for difficult cases. We serve as special masters. We advise judges and legislators on the merits of possible reforms. Few topics in procedure are too small or too arcane to occupy a law professor's time.

It must therefore seem extraordinarily unlikely that legal scholars could have missed any important set of procedural issues. Even so, we have. Law professors have written little about the impact of liability insurance on civil procedure, and if casebooks can serve as a reliable guide, we have taught about the subject even less. The omission is striking because insurance and procedure intersect at many points and in important ways.

In stark contrast to law professors, practicing lawyers understand well the connections between procedure and insurance and make them a primary focus of attention and scholarship. They know that liability insurance explains a great deal of what happens in litigation, including the decision to bring a lawsuit, the decision to plead certain theories of recovery and to omit others, the decision to try a lawsuit instead of settling it, and the decision to settle on particular terms. Practicing lawyers also know that the desire to preserve insurance coverage or to put policy proceeds beyond a claimant's reach accounts for many unusual and even bizarre acts of litigation conduct. Consider a few examples:

- A lawyer representing a female plaintiff denies that a group of male defendants committed intentional misconduct even though the men schemed secretly to videotape the plaintiff having sex.
- Parents whose negligence allegedly caused the death of their 13-year-old son hire a family friend to sue them on behalf of their son's estate.

*Cecil D. Redford Professor, University of Texas School of Law; B.A., University of Florida, 1979; M.A., University of Chicago, 1981; J.D., Yale, 1987.

**Professor, University of Michigan Law School; B.S.F.S., Georgetown University, 1977; J.D., University of Michigan, 1981; M.A., University of Michigan, 1983.

The authors wish to acknowledge the financial support of the International Association of Defense Counsel (IADC) and the Defense Research Institute (DRI). . . .

- A lawyer representing a female victim of sexual exploitation in a civil action argues that the male defendant was innocent of the crime of sexual assault because the victim was sexually promiscuous.
- A lawyer representing a defendant in an automobile accident case subjects his own client to hostile cross-examination and accuses his own client of perjury, all in an effort to show that his client knowingly misdescribed how the accident occurred.
- A lawyer representing an employer facing potential liability for the negligent acts of an employee fails to inform the injured plaintiff that the employee actually worked for someone else.
- A lawyer defending a doctor in a medical malpractice action settles with the plaintiff despite a clear instruction from the doctor to reject the plaintiff's demand.
- A lawyer representing a defendant files a meritorious motion or reply to a motion for (take your pick) summary judgment on the merits, disqualification of opposing counsel, dismissal for defective service of process, or dismissal for lack of capacity to sue, but does so over the defendant's objection.
- A defendant instructs defense counsel to admit liability and damages even though both can properly be contested.
- An insurance company intentionally pays more to settle a claim than the claim is worth.
- An attorney representing an automobile accident victim rescinds a settlement demand at the policy limits on a wholly pretextual ground after the offer was accepted by the defendant's insurance company.

In each instance and in thousands of others equally strange, insurance considerations motivate the conduct described. Experienced litigators would see that immediately, but many fine civil procedure teachers would not. . . .

In this Article, we will examine in great detail one set of issues on the boundary between procedure and insurance. Actually, the issues we will discuss lie at the intersection of three fields: civil procedure, insurance, and professional responsibility/agency law. The focus of our attention will be the rules that govern the conduct of insurance defense lawyers—the lawyers insurance companies hire to defend lawsuits against their insureds. Insurance defense lawyers are integral parts of the engine that drives civil litigation, and the rules that govern their conduct are both extraordinarily vague and often wrong. The rules fail to provide clear and defensible answers to the most basic questions, such as whether an attorney-client relationship exists between the insurance company and the lawyer retained to handle the lawsuit against the insured. Consequently, the rules are almost entirely unhelpful when more complicated questions arise. The obvious danger is that insurance defense lawyers will act improperly, even when they attempt to adhere to the law. The less obvious danger is that the procedural system, broadly understood as encompassing all the rules and forces that influence the progress of litigation, will work less well than it should, driving up insurance costs and distorting insurance contracts. Although we will focus on the microstructure of insurance litigation, our work also has important macroeconomic implications for the procedural system and for the business of insurance. . . .

I. Working Hypotheses About Liability Insurance

Insureds buy liability insurance in the United States to protect against two related but distinct risks of financial loss: the risk of paying the costs of defending a lawsuit and the risk of having to pay money to a plaintiff as a result of a lawsuit. The vast majority of liability insurance policies cover both risks, obligating the insurance company to defend lawsuits against the insured, to pay the costs of defense, and to indemnify the insured for judgments and settlements up to a specified limit. Similarly, the vast majority of policies give the insurance company the right to defend the case, and require the cooperation of the insured in the company's defense of any suits. For the last century, these common insurance arrangements have permitted the company to select counsel to defend an action, to supervise counsel's litigation and settlement strategy, and to settle claims within policy limits at the company's discretion.

There are good economic reasons why both the company and the insured might desire to allocate control over the defense of potential lawsuits to the company. When a loss is fully covered, both parties expect the company to have the predominant financial interest in the outcome of litigation. They expect the company to have a greater incentive than the insured to defend the suit vigorously. Moreover, as a repeat litigant the company is more likely to have substantial judgment and experience in defending claims and managing lawyers. Because of the combined effect of the company's financial incentives and experience, claims costs should be kept lower if the company controls the defense, with a resultant lowering of the cost of liability insurance to all insureds.

The foregoing assumes that, at the time the company and insured execute the typical liability insurance contract, the insured is primarily concerned with the monetary costs of future lawsuits. The policy transfers this financial risk to the company. The company, in turn, can be expected to direct the defense of a particular lawsuit against the insured in a way that minimizes claims costs — usually, by minimizing the amount paid out in judgments, settlements, and litigation expenses. Although it is hazardous to guess at the expectations of the insured and company at the time of contracting, these expectations seem both most common and most reasonable.

Problems arise when the threat of an unknown future claim ripens into a specific lawsuit. When a grocery store buys liability insurance from an insurance carrier, the store may indeed expect that the company will control the defense of any future claims, and it may desire that the company minimize claims costs on all future lawsuits so that premiums can be kept low. But when a customer sues the grocery store for negligence, the specific circumstances of the suit may lead the store and the company to disagree about the handling of the suit. Disagreements may arise for at least four reasons.

First, the company and the insured may disagree about the defense of the lawsuit because the insured no longer bears a risk of paying a judgment or settlement (which is covered by insurance), but does bear other risks related to the lawsuit. These risks include all the manifold side effects of civil litigation. The insured may be concerned about publicity, about its reputation, about a personal or business relationship with the injured plaintiff, or about collateral effects of the lawsuit on other lawsuits and parties. The insured may want the plaintiff to recover as much as possible, perhaps because the plaintiff is related to the insured or because the insured feels compassion or responsibility to the plaintiff. By removing the insured's obligation to pay the judgment or settlement, the policy permits and often encourages the plaintiff to think primarily about these side effects of the lawsuit. And in thinking about these side effects, the insured may prefer a defense strategy different than that employed by the company that will pay the judgment. Second, the company and the insured may disagree about the defense of the lawsuit because the company will bear the costs of the defense and the insured will not. Most often, this fundamental difference will mean that the insured will prefer a more expensive defense effort, particularly where a more expensive effort will benefit the insured. Thus, the insured may value vindication at trial, despite the possibility of a small pretrial settlement, in order to restore a reputation tarnished by a lawsuit.

Third, the company and the insured may disagree about the defense of the lawsuit because the company has an additional stake in the outcome beyond the amount paid to defend or settle it. The company may be anxious to defeat a particular plaintiff's lawyer, to obtain a particular precedent that can benefit it in other cases, or simply to employ a particular defense counsel who has a relationship or tie to the company. The insured, who does not share these concerns, may dissent from defense policies that are driven by them.

Finally, the company and the insured may disagree simply because each can take strategic advantage of the additional stake in the lawsuit possessed by the other. If one party knows that the other values a particular outcome highly (for example, if the company knows that the insured wants to avoid trial at any price because of the fear of reputational consequences), there is room to coerce the other party into bearing a larger fraction of the expense of the lawsuit than called for by the insurance contract (for example, by requesting the insured to contribute to a settlement within policy limits).[32]

Unfortunately, it is defense counsel who often must sort out these disagreements between the company and the insured in particular lawsuits. Generally, the disagreements arise after counsel has been retained by the insurance company (usually without a formal written retainer agreement) to defend the case. Counsel communicates with the insured and the company, and in the course of the defense, is called upon to make decisions about how to handle the litigation. In doing so, counsel often discovers that he is uncertain about the identity of client, the scope of the representation, or the objectives that counsel should seek in the suit.

One simple solution to problems in which counsel perceives a potential conflict of interest between the insured and the company is to require separate counsel for each routinely, with the company paying for both lawyers to

---

32. This behavior by insurance companies, common early in this century, is now considered a per se breach of the insurer's duties to the insured in almost every state. See Syverud, The Duty to Settle, *supra* note 3, at 1153-57.

represent zealously their separate clients' interests. This solution, while admirably removing most ethical dilemmas for defense counsel, imposes significant costs on insureds and insurance companies. A proliferation of lawyers on the defense side substantially increases the expense of lawsuits, and this in turn is reflected in liability insurance premiums. Insureds and companies may well prefer to waive separate counsel except in particular situations, or to provide in advance (in the insurance contract) that separate counsel will be at the expense of the insured rather than the insurer. If one decides not to require separate counsel routinely, the remaining option is to consider conflicts case by case. One must ask defense counsel to assess his professional obligations in potential and actual conflict situations, and one must supply principles, guidelines, and rules that will help counsel decide when a joint representation can proceed and how it should be conducted. It is difficult to craft appropriate principles, guidelines, and rules, however, because insurance law and the law of professional responsibility often seem to be at war. For example, the insurance contract and the prevailing insurance law may give the insurance company the right to control the settlement and the right to accept any settlement within policy limits without the insured's consent. Professional responsibility law may declare that the insured is a client, and that, consequently, the lawyer may not accept any settlement without the insured's consent. The task of a rulemaker is to determine the proper relationship between the two bodies of law and to give defense counsel concrete instruction on how to proceed. To these tasks we now turn. . . .

b. One Solution: Independent Counsel

San Diego Navy Fed. Credit Union v. Cumis Ins. Soc'y, Inc.

208 Cal. Rptr. 494 (Cal. Ct. App. 1984)

* * *

Gamer, J.

Cumis Insurance Society, Inc. (Cumis) appeals a judgment requiring Cumis to pay the San Diego Navy Federal Credit Union (Credit Union), J. W. Jamieson and Larry R. Sharp (insureds) all reasonable past and future expenses of their independent counsel retained for the defense of a lawsuit filed against the insureds by Magdaline S. Eisenmann (Eisenmann action).

The issue presented to this court by the appeal is whether an insurer is required to pay for independent counsel for an insured when the insurer provides its own counsel but reserves its right to assert noncoverage at a later date. We conclude under these circumstances there is a conflict of interest between the insurer and the insured, and therefore the insured has a right to independent counsel paid for by the insurer.

The Eisenmann action against the insureds seeks $750,000 general and $6.5 million punitive damages for tortious wrongful discharge, breach of the covenant of good faith and fair dealing, wrongful interference with and inducing breach of contract, breach of contract and intentional infliction of emotional distress. Under insurance policies issued by Cumis, the insureds tendered the defense of the Eisenmann action to Cumis. Cumis associate counsel Willis E. McAllister reviewed the complaint in the Eisenmann action and concluded Cumis had a duty to provide a defense to the insureds. McAllister selected and retained, at Cumis' expense, the San Diego law firm of Goebel & Monaghan to represent the interests of the insureds in the Eisenmann action. McAllister informed Goebel & Monaghan it was to represent the insureds as to all claims in the Eisenmann action, including the punitive damages claim. He also told Goebel & Monaghan Cumis was reserving its right to deny coverage at a later date and the insurance policies did not cover punitive damages.

McAllister sent Goebel & Monaghan copies of the insurance policies in effect and letters accepting the defense and reserving rights which were delivered to the insureds. McAllister never asked Goebel & Monaghan for an opinion whether coverage existed under the insurance policies, nor did Goebel & Monaghan give any coverage advice to either Cumis or the insureds.

McAllister believed if the Eisenmann action resulted in a finding of willful conduct or an award of punitive damages, the Cumis policies did not provide coverage for those damages. Moreover, his view was if the Eisenmann action resulted in a finding of breach of contract as against any of the insureds, there might be no coverage under the relevant Cumis policies. Accordingly, on behalf of Cumis, McAllister notified each insured by letter Cumis was reserving its rights to disclaim coverage and denying any coverage for punitive damages.[2]

The Credit Union retained the San Diego law firm of Saxon, Alt & Brewer (independent counsel) to provide independent representation to protect the insureds' interests. Independent counsel notified Cumis it was retained to act as co-counsel with Goebel & Monaghan and presented Cumis a claim for its attorneys' fees and costs. McAllister was persuaded California law required Cumis to pay the fees, and he agreed to pay the fees and costs incurred by independent counsel as co-counsel for the insureds. Cumis paid two separate invoices for legal services of independent counsel but additional invoices were not paid. After independent counsel sent a demand letter to Cumis and further

---

2. The reservation of rights letter explained:

Because of the nature of the case and the present lack of factual information relative to the allegations of the plaintiff, it is necessary for CUMIS Insurance Society, Inc. to reserve its rights to disclaim coverage on the ground that the actions complained of by the plaintiff are not covered under the Directors and Officers Endorsement to the CUMIS Discovery Bond, or any other coverage provided by CUMIS to you. CUMIS specifically denies any coverage for punitive damages in the above-mentioned legal action.

On behalf of CUMIS Insurance Society, Inc., we will conduct an investigation of this case, and provide the defense to you under a full reservation of the Society's rights. In addition, if CUMIS settles the above-mentioned legal action, CUMIS reserves its right to seek reimbursement from you for such settlement amount if noncoverage by CUMIS is subsequently established. Such investigation, defense or settlement shall not prejudice the rights of CUMIS Insurance Society, Inc. to disclaim coverage at a later date.

Although CUMIS is not now denying coverage, we are sending this Reservation of Rights letter to you so that we may proceed to investigate the case, defend you or arrange settlement of this suit pending a decision of whether or not the actions complained of by the plaintiff are covered by CUMIS. In the meantime, your rights and interests are being protected as though coverage does extend to the fact situation involved.

discussed the matter with McAllister, McAllister sought a separate opinion on the question from Cumis' home office and asked Goebel & Monaghan if it felt there was a conflict of interest in representing the insureds such that Cumis would be required to pay the expenses of separate counsel. Goebel & Monaghan told McAllister it did not see a conflict of interest. Cumis' home office came to the same conclusion and McAllister notified independent counsel Cumis would pay no further invoices.

In the Eisenmann action settlement conference, the case did not settle after a demand within the Cumis policy limits. Cumis authorized Goebel & Monaghan to make an offer at the settlement conference but in an amount lower than Eisenmann's demand. Goebel & Monaghan did not contact the Credit Union before or during the settlement conference, but informed the Credit Union about the conference afterward.

In this action, the trial court ruled Cumis is required to pay for the insureds' hiring of independent counsel, rejecting Cumis' argument the court was bound by Gray v. Zurich Insurance Co. (1966) 65 Cal. 2d 263, and reasoning:

> 1. *Gray* involved a question of the duty to defend in an assault and battery case rather than the extent and scope of that duty. The reasoning thus used to support Gray is not controlling, especially if it makes little sense.
>
> 2. The reasoning of *Gray*, "[since] . . . the court in the third party suit does not adjudicate the issue of coverage the insurer's argument (as to a conflict of interest) collapses," just does not stand scrutiny. What the defense attorney in the third party case does impacts the coverage case, in that, the questions of coverage depends [sic] on the development of facts in the third party case and their proper development is left to the attorney paid for by the Carrier. *Gray* recognized that a finding in the third party action would [a]ffect the issues of coverage in a subsequent case but analyzed the question from the point of view of the carrier. *Gray* recognized a possible conflict from the point of view of the insured in footnote 18, where it stated: "In rare cases the issue of punitive damages or a special verdict might present a conflict of interest, but such possibility does not outweigh the advantages of the general rule. Even in such cases, however, the insurer will still be bound ethically and legally, to litigate in the interests of the insured." Additionally, *Gray* was looking for a way to avoid a conflict of interest, to hold that it was excluding all other approaches just does not make common sense.

The court further explained its ruling:

> The Carrier is required to hire independent counsel because an attorney in actual trial would be tempted to develop the facts to help his real client, the Carrier Company, as opposed to the Insured, for whom he will never likely work again. In such a case as this, the Insured is placed in an impossible position; on the one hand the Carrier says it will happily defend him and on the other it says it may dispute paying any judgment, but trust us. The dictum in *Gray* flies in the face of the reality of insurance defense work. Insurance companies hire relatively few lawyers and concentrate their business. A lawyer who does not look out for the Carrier's best interest might soon find himself out of work.

In the usual tripartite relationship existing between insurer, insured and counsel, there is a single, common interest shared among them. Dual representation by counsel is beneficial since the shared goal of minimizing or eliminating liability to a third party is the same. A different situation is presented, however, when some or all of the allegations in the complaint do not fall within the scope of coverage under the policy. In such a case, the standard practice of an insurer is to defend under a reservation of rights where the insurer promises to defend but states it may not indemnify the insured if liability is found. In this situation, there may be little commonality of interest. Opposing poles of interest are represented on the one hand in the insurer's desire to establish in the third party suit the insured's "liability rested on intentional conduct" (Gray, supra, 65 Cal. 2d 263, 279), and thus no coverage under the policy, and on the other hand in the insured's desire to "obtain a ruling . . . such liability emanated from the nonintentional conduct within his insurance coverage[.]" Although issues of coverage under the policy are not actually litigated in the third party suit, this does not detract from the force of these opposing interests as they operate on the attorney selected by the insurer, who has a dual agency status.

Here, it is uncontested the basis for liability, if any, might rest on conduct excluded by the terms of the insurance policy. Goebel & Monaghan will have to make certain decisions at the trial of the Eisenmann action which may either benefit or harm the insureds. For example, it will have to seek or oppose special verdicts, the answers to which may benefit the insureds by finding nonexcluded conduct and harm either Cumis' position on coverage or the insureds by finding excluded conduct. These decisions are numerous and varied. Each time one of them must be made, the lawyer is placed in the dilemma of helping one of his clients concerning insurance coverage and harming the other.

The conflict may appear before trial. Goebel & Monaghan represented the insureds in the Eisenmann action settlement conference and the case did not settle although a demand was made within policy limits. Before and during the settlement conference, Goebel & Monaghan was in contact with Cumis but had no contact with the insureds about settlement until after the conference ended. The insureds then wrote a letter to counsel:

> You should know that the Credit Union desires the lawsuit to be settled without trial. Our insurance coverages, duly paid and contracted for, are precisely for such cases and any settlement liability that may arise therefrom. Your confidence in the defensibility of the case is appreciated. Should trial prove you wrong, however, and the jury awards damages, the insurance may no longer cover the Credit Union's possible losses. As you know, such losses would considerably exceed any possible settlement amount. It is clear that trial in lieu of settlement in this case subjects the Credit Union to a considerably additional risk while possibly lowering or eliminating a claim payout by Cumis. Such is not the basic premise upon which we contracted for insurance with Cumis.
>
> I urge you to work for an appropriate settlement before trial in this case so that Cumis will have provided the risk protection for which the Credit Union has contracted.

On the advisability of settlement, Goebel & Monaghan represented clients with conflicting interests. No matter how honest the intentions, counsel cannot discharge inconsistent duties.

The potential problems may develop during pretrial discovery which must go beyond simple preparation for a favorable verdict to develop alternate strategies minimizing exposure. Goebel & Monaghan was bound to investigate all conceivable bases on which liability might attach. These investigations and client communications may provide information relating directly to the coverage issue. Furthermore, counsel may form an opinion about the insureds' credibility. As between counsel's two clients, there is no confidentiality regarding communications intended to promote common goals (Evid. Code, §962). But confidentiality is essential where communication can affect coverage. Thus, the lawyer is forced to walk an ethical tightrope, and not communicate relevant information which is beneficial to one or the other of his clients.

* * *

The standard of care expressed in the ABA canons underscores the existing conflict.

Cumis contends Gray v. Zurich Insurance Co., supra, 65 Cal. 2d 263, is controlling and asserts Cumis fully met its duty to defend when it retained counsel at its expense and instructed counsel to defend the insureds in the underlying action.

Gray dealt with an insurer's duty to defend in the face of a third party complaint against the insured alleging the insured caused intentional injury which by the policy's terms is not within its coverage. . . .

* * *

Gray found the insurer's contractual duty to defend cannot be avoided by creating a conflict of interest. Gray is not controlling here because it does not address whether the scope of the duty to defend includes payment for the insured's independent counsel where a conflict of interest exists.

* * *

Other jurisdictions reach varying conclusions on the issue before us (see Employers' Fire Insurance Company v. Beals, supra, 240 A.2d 397, 404, and works cited).

* * *

We conclude the Canons of Ethics impose upon lawyers hired by the insurer an obligation to explain to the insured and the insurer the full implications of joint representation in situations where the insurer has reserved its rights to deny coverage. If the insured does not give an informed consent to continued representation, counsel must cease to represent both. Moreover, in the absence of such consent, where there are divergent interests of the insured and the insurer brought about by the insurer's reservation of rights based on possible noncoverage under the insurance policy, the insurer must pay the reasonable cost for hiring independent counsel by the insured. The insurer may not compel the insured to surrender control of the litigation. Disregarding the common interests of both insured and insurer in finding total nonliability in the third party action, the remaining interests of the two diverge to such an extent as to create an actual, ethical conflict of interest warranting payment for the insureds' independent counsel.

Judgment affirmed.

CAL. CIV. CODE §2860

(Deering CA Codes, 2009)

(a) If the provisions of a policy of insurance impose a duty to defend upon an insurer and a conflict of interest arises which creates a duty on the part of the insurer to provide independent counsel to the insured, the insurer shall provide independent counsel to represent the insured unless, at the time the insured is informed that a possible conflict may arise or does exist, the insured expressly waives, in writing, the right to independent counsel. An insurance contract may contain a provision which sets forth the method of selecting that counsel consistent with this section.

(b) For purposes of this section, a conflict of interest does not exist as to allegations or facts in the litigation for which the insurer denies coverage; however, when an insurer reserves its rights on a given issue and the outcome of that coverage issue can be controlled by counsel first retained by the insurer for the defense of the claim, a conflict of interest may exist. No conflict of interest shall be deemed to exist as to allegations of punitive damages or be deemed to exist solely because an insured is sued for an amount in excess of the insurance policy limits.

(c) When the insured has selected independent counsel to represent him or her, the insurer may exercise its right to require that the counsel selected by the insured possess certain minimum qualifications which may include that the selected counsel have (1) at least five years of civil litigation practice which includes substantial defense experience in the subject at issue in the litigation, and (2) errors and omissions coverage. The insurer's obligation to pay fees to the independent counsel selected by the insured is limited to the rates which are actually paid by the insurer to attorneys retained by it in the ordinary course of business in the defense of similar actions in the community where the claim arose or is being defended. This subdivision does not invalidate other different or additional policy provisions pertaining to attorney's fees or providing for methods of settlement of disputes concerning those fees. Any dispute concerning attorney's fees not resolved by these methods shall be resolved by final and binding arbitration by a single neutral arbitrator selected by the parties to the dispute.

(d) When independent counsel has been selected by the insured, it shall be the duty of that counsel and the insured to disclose to the insurer all information concerning the action except privileged materials relevant to coverage disputes, and timely to inform and consult with the insurer on all matters relating to the action. Any claim of privilege asserted is subject to in camera review in the appropriate law and motion department of the superior court. Any information disclosed by the insured or by independent counsel is not a waiver of the privilege as to any other party.

(e) The insured may waive its right to select independent counsel by signing the following statement: "I have been advised and informed of my right to select independent counsel to represent me in this lawsuit. I have considered this matter fully and freely waive my right to select independent counsel at this time. I authorize my insurer to select a defense attorney to represent me in this lawsuit."

(f) Where the insured selects independent counsel pursuant to the provisions of this section, both the counsel provided by the insurer and independent counsel selected by the insured shall be allowed to participate in all aspects of the litigation. Counsel shall cooperate fully in the exchange of information that is consistent with each counsel's ethical and legal obligation to the insured. Nothing in this section shall relieve the insured of his or her duty to cooperate with the insurer under the terms of the insurance contract.

c. Variations on the *Cumis* Theme

BLANCHARD v. STATE FARM & CAS. CO.

2 Cal. Rptr. 2d 884 (Cal. Ct. App. 1991)

ASHBY, J.

This is a "bad faith" action by an insured against its insurer for breach of contract and breach of the covenant of good faith and fair dealing. . . . The present action involves respondent's [State Farm's] handling of three previous lawsuits brought against appellant [Blanchard]. Appellant was a general contractor who was insured by respondent under a multiperil insurance policy.

[The underlying action at issue was brought by a homeowners' association against Blanchard for construction defects. State Farm represented Blanchard in this action but subject to a reservation of rights that certain types of damages were not covered under the policy. Blanchard claimed that the reservation of rights created a conflict of interest triggering an obligation for State Farm to provide *Cumis* counsel. Instead, State Farm hired counsel who thereafter settled the action. Blanchard did not contribute money to either the defense or settlement.]

In the present action appellants . . . alleged respondent owed a duty to provide *Cumis* counsel to appellant in the Hyde Park action. The trial court submitted this issue to a jury, which rendered a verdict in favor of respondent.

. . .

II. *Cumis* Counsel

Respondent *accepted* defense of the Hyde Park action but pointed out that certain definitions and exclusions in the insurance policy might limit the extent of damages which respondent would indemnify.

Appellant's broad form property damage endorsement excluded property damage for "that particular part of any property, not on premises owned by or rented to the insured . . . the restoration, repair or replacement of which has been made or is necessary by reason of faulty workmanship thereon by or on behalf of the insured." Thus, the insurance policy was not a performance bond or guarantee of the work of the general contractor or subcontractors. The contractor bears the risk of repairing or replacing faulty workmanship, while the insurer bears the risk of damage to the property of others.

If, for instance, faulty workmanship in the framing or drywall led to rainwater leaking in and damaging a homeowner's furnishings, appellant would be indemnified for the damage to the furnishings, but not for the cost of repairing or replacing the faulty workmanship.

Neither appellant nor appellant's own counsel disputed this interpretation of the damages payable under the policy. Nevertheless, appellant took the position that respondent's reservation of rights as to the extent of damages created a conflict of interest between respondent and appellant, which created a duty for respondent to pay for an additional counsel to act solely on appellant's behalf.

Respondent denied appellant's demand for independent counsel, concluding the reservation of rights did not create a conflict of interest requiring independent counsel. Respondent did, however, defend the Hyde Park action through attorneys selected by respondent at respondent's expense. Respondent settled the Hyde Park case. The expenses of defense and settlement of the Hyde Park case were paid by respondent, and appellant was never asked to contribute to these costs.

Appellants' present action for breach of contract and breach of the covenant of good faith and fair dealing nevertheless asserts appellants are entitled to damages for respondent's failure to appoint independent counsel. We conclude to the contrary that there was no evidence of a conflict of interest of the type requiring appointment of independent counsel.

. . .

Subsequent case law and statutory codification of *Cumis* have made clear . . . that not every reservation of rights creates a conflict of interest requiring appointment of independent counsel. It depends upon the nature of the coverage issue, as it relates to the issues in the underlying case. If the issue on which coverage turns is independent of the issues in the underlying case, *Cumis* counsel is not required. A conflict of interest does not arise unless the outcome of the coverage issue can be controlled by counsel first retained by the insurer for the defense of the underlying claim. (Civ. Code, §2860, subd. (b).) The fact punitive damages are alleged does not itself create a conflict (Civ. Code, §2860, subd. (b) . . .) nor does a conflict exist solely because the insured is sued for an amount in excess of insurance policy limits. (Civ. Code, §2860, subd. (b).)

In the Hyde Park case the attorneys selected by respondent faced no conflict concerning conduct of appellant. The coverage issue involved only damages. Insurance counsel had no incentive to attach liability to appellant. Respondent recognized its liability for certain damages flowing from appellant's liability; thus it was to the advantage of both appellant and respondent to minimize appellant's underlying liability. (Foremost Ins. Co. v. Wilks, supra, 206 Cal. App. 3d 251 [allegations of punitive damages did not create conflict of interest, because insurer was liable for compensatory damages and thus had incentive to defend liability].)

Appellant produced no evidence to show in what specific way the defense attorney could have controlled the outcome of the damage issue to appellant's detriment, or had incentive to do so. Appellant merely urged that there was an unspecified *possibility* of a conflict.

Under these circumstances the trial court should have decided the *Cumis* issue as a matter of law. . . . The *Cumis* opinion was based heavily on the canons of ethics and the possibly conflicting choices confronting an attorney. In the absence of dispute over some underlying fact, the existence of a conflict is a question of law for the trial judge to decide, not a jury question.

V

The judgment is affirmed.

TURNER, P.J., and BOREN, J., concurred.

SCOTTSDALE INS. CO. v. THE HOUSING GROUP

1995 U.S. Dist. LEXIS 8791 (N.D. Cal. 1995)

THELTON E. HENDERSON, C.J.

Order

[T]he Court GRANTS defendants' motion for summary judgment and DENIES plaintiff's motion for summary judgment for the reasons explained below.

I. Factual Background

[Scottsdale Ins. Co. insured The Housing Group ("THG"), a land developer in California under policies covering bodily injury, property damage, and personal injury. The policies limited property damage for losses caused by earth movement.

THG had developed a subdivision called Hidden Hills, and it sold a lot to the Dorrances, who thereafter sued THG. The Dorrances essentially alleged that the home they purchased from THG was defectively constructed, a fact that THG allegedly concealed from them.

THG tendered defense of the Dorrance action to Scottsdale, which took the case under a reservation of rights:]

1. The right to deny coverage for some of the claims asserted, or as to all of the claims in their entirety.
2. The right to withdraw from the defense at a later time, if appropriate.
3. The right to file a declaratory relief action . . . to determine the rights and obligations of Scottsdale and THG.
4. The right to decline to indemnify THG either by contribution to settlement or payment in satisfaction of a judgment for any claimed damage that is not covered by the policies.
5. The right to seek reimbursement from THG for any payments made in settlement or in satisfaction of judgment for any claims and damages that are not covered by the policies.
6. The right to seek reimbursement from THG for any defense fees and/or costs that are attributable or may be allocated to the defense of claims that are not covered by the policies.

[Without consulting THG, Scottsdale retained the Drath law firm to represent the company in the underlying action. THG retained its own attorney because it believed that the reservation of rights created a conflict of interest.]

The issue on these cross-motions for summary judgment is whether Scottsdale is required under California law to provide THG with independent counsel under the circumstances here.

. . .

III. Discussion

[The court excerpts the relevant portions of Cal. Civ. Code §2860(a) and (b).]

The issue in the instant case is whether Scottsdale's reservation of rights in the September 30, 1994 letter created a conflict of interest giving rise to a duty on the part of Scottsdale to provide independent counsel for THG in the defense of the underlying suit.

California courts have explained that "where there are divergent interests of the insured and the insurer brought about by the insurer's reservation of rights based on possible noncoverage under the insurance policy, the insurer must pay the reasonable cost for hiring independent counsel by the insured." San Diego Navy Fed. Credit Union v. Cumis Ins. Soc'y, Inc.[1] However, the courts have emphasized that "not every reservation of rights creates a conflict of interest requiring appointment of independent counsel." *Blanchard v. State Farm Fire & Casualty Co.*

Recently, a California court made clear that the standard set out in *Cumis* and Civil Code §2860 stems from the fundamental obligation of an attorney to provide uncompromised representation to her clients. In Golden Eagle Insurance Co. v. Foremost Insurance Co., 20 Cal. App. 4th 1372 (2d Dist. 1993), the court noted that:

> The governing principle underlying Cumis and section 2860 is the attorney's ethical duty to the clients. Thus, an attorney representing the interests of the insurer and the insured is subject to the rule [that] a "conflict of interest between jointly represented clients occurs whenever their common lawyer's representation of the one is rendered less effective by reason of his representation of the other."

* * *

The *Golden Eagle* court further explained that "the paradigm case requiring independent counsel is one in which the way counsel retained by the insurance company defends the action will affect an underlying coverage dispute between the insurer and the insured."

In light of the rule stated in *Golden Eagle*, the Court finds the question to be resolved here a straightforward one: will the Drath firm's representation of THG be rendered less effective by reason of its retention by Scottsdale? More

---

1. The policy underlying the *Cumis* rule was well explained by the court in State Farm Fire & Casualty Co. v. Superior Court, 216 Cal. App. 3d 1222, 1225 n.1, 265 Cal. Rptr. 372 (4th Dist. 1989) ("When the insurer disputes liability for indemnification but continues to provide a defense for the insured against the claim, a potential conflict of interest arises. Assertions made to defeat the liability of the insurer under the policy may promote the claim of the third party against the insured.").

specifically, will the way in which counsel retained by Scottsdale defends the Dorrance action affect the outcome of the underlying coverage dispute between Scottsdale and THG?[2]

Applying this standard to the undisputed facts in the record in this case, the Court is satisfied that a conflict of interest is created by the Drath firm's representation of THG at the same time that Scottsdale is paying the Drath firm's bills. The defendants argue that the particular reservations of rights made by the plaintiff here create a conflict of interest, citing several specific parts of the reservation of rights letter in support of their claim.

As explained below, the Court finds that the reservations of rights pointed to by THG create a sufficiently definite possibility of conflict to necessitate the provision of independent counsel here. For instance, under the subsidence sublimit contained in the policy at issue, THG is covered only up to $100,000 of bodily injury or property damage "caused by, resulting from, attributable or attributed to, contributed to, or aggravated by" earthquakes and other earth movements. Under the general policy covering damage not caused by such earth movement, THG's general policy damage coverage has an upper limit of $1,000,000 (one million dollars) per occurrence.

THG argues, and the Court agrees, that the resolution at the liability stage of the factual question of whether the damages alleged by the Dorrances were in fact "caused" or "aggravated" by earth movement could have a significant impact on the outcome of the coverage question. If the damage is found to have been caused or aggravated by earth movement, THG is eligible for only up to $100,000 worth of coverage; if the damage was caused by any other source, the coverage limit is $1,000,000. . . .

Plaintiff's response — the assertion that "immutable facts" will determine the outcome of the coverage issues regardless of the Drath firm's conduct — is counterintuitive at best and disingenuous at worst. . . .

As every first-year law student is aware, our adversary legal system rests on the premise that the truth is best uncovered when a zealous advocate for each side interprets the "objective facts" in a manner most favorable to his client's position, leaving the factfinding function to a neutral judge or jury. The Court finds plaintiff's assertion that counsel retained by Scottsdale cannot meaningfully influence the determination of relevant factual issues in the Dorrance action, even as it acknowledges that the coverage issues in this case will

---

2. Relying on Blanchard v. State Farm Fire & Casualty Co., 2 Cal. App. 4th 345 (1991), plaintiff argues in its papers that the applicable rule is that "there is no conflict of interest unless counsel has the potential to control the outcome of the coverage issues." . . . However, even assuming arguendo that the rule stated by plaintiff was once a correct statement of law, the *Golden Eagle* decision explicitly rejected such a narrow construction.

The *Golden Eagle* court explained that, while "attorney control of the outcome of a coverage dispute is written into Civil Code section 2860, subdivision (b) as an example of a conflict of interest which may require appointment of independent counsel," such control is "not . . . the only circumstance in which Cumis counsel may be required." . . . The court acknowledged in a footnote that "there is language in [Blanchard] stating [that] 'A conflict of interest does not arise unless the outcome of the coverage issue can be controlled by counsel first retained by the insurer for the defense of the underlying claim.'" However, the *Golden Eagle* court found that statement to be "mere dictum" because the insured in Blanchard argued that the insurer's reservation of rights per se entitled it to *Cumis* counsel, an argument which was "clearly erroneous" under section 2860(b). Id. In light of the *Golden Eagle* court's explicit disapproval of the Blanchard rule, therefore, the Court is confident that the *Golden Eagle* standard should control here.

"turn on" the development of those facts, to be wholly unpersuasive in light of the realities of the practice of law. For this reason, the Court is persuaded that the manner in which the Drath firm defends the Dorrance action "will affect an underlying coverage dispute between the insurer and the insured" so as to require the appointment of independent counsel. . . .

The situation in the present case is analogous [to *Executive Aviation*]. On a host of damages issues — causation, date of occurrence, and number of occurrences, for example — the factual position favorable to Scottsdale is the precise opposite of the one favorable to THG. Whether or not the Dorrance factfinder will be asked to reach a specific conclusion on these issues in its verdict, plaintiff is correct in acknowledging that the coverage issues "turn on" facts which will be developed in that action. For this reason, requiring THG to rely in the Dorrance action on the pretrial fact gathering and case preparation of attorneys whose clients' interests are served by the establishment of facts detrimental to THG's coverage case clearly runs counter to the principle set out in *Cumis* and *Golden Eagle*. . . .

Without disparaging the competence or honesty of the Drath firm in any way, the Court can state with confidence that the express purpose of Civil Code 2860 and *Cumis* is to ensure that insured parties do not have to settle for a "trust me" offered by counsel retained by an insurer. Because the development of a number of issues in the Dorrance action here will inevitably have an effect on the later resolution of coverage issues, a conflict of interest exists, and Scottsdale must provide independent counsel for THG in that action.

IV. Conclusion

For the foregoing reasons, defendant THG's motion for summary judgment is GRANTED, and plaintiff Scottsdale's motion for same is DENIED.

d. A Different Solution to the Agency Problem: Bad-Faith Liability

STATE FARM V. CAMPBELL

538 U.S. 408 (2003)

Justice KENNEDY delivered the opinion of the Court.

We address once again the measure of punishment, by means of punitive damages, a State may impose upon a defendant in a civil case. The question is whether, in the circumstances we shall recount, an award of $145 million in punitive damages, where full compensatory damages are $1 million, is excessive and in violation of the Due Process Clause of the Fourteenth Amendment to the Constitution of the United States.

I

In 1981, Curtis Campbell (Campbell) was driving with his wife, Inez Preece Campbell, in Cache County, Utah. He decided to pass six vans traveling ahead of them on a two-lane highway. Todd Ospital was driving a small car approaching from the opposite direction. To avoid a head-on collision with Campbell, who by then was driving on the wrong side of the highway and toward oncoming traffic, Ospital swerved onto the shoulder, lost control of his automobile, and collided with a vehicle driven by Robert G. Slusher. Ospital was killed, and Slusher was rendered permanently disabled. The Campbells escaped unscathed.

In the ensuing wrongful death and tort action, Campbell insisted he was not at fault. Early investigations did support differing conclusions as to who caused the accident, but "a consensus was reached early on by the investigators and witnesses that Mr. Campbell's unsafe pass had indeed caused the crash." 2001 UT 89, 65 P.3d 1134, (Utah 2001). Campbell's insurance company, petitioner State Farm Mutual Automobile Insurance Company (State Farm), nonetheless decided to contest liability and declined offers by Slusher and Ospital's estate (Ospital) to settle the claims for the policy limit of $50,000 ($25,000 per claimant). State Farm also ignored the advice of one of its own investigators and took the case to trial, assuring the Campbells that "their assets were safe, that they had no liability for the accident, that [State Farm] would represent their interests, and that they did not need to procure separate counsel." To the contrary, a jury determined that Campbell was 100 percent at fault, and a judgment was returned for $185,849, far more than the amount offered in settlement.

At first State Farm refused to cover the $135,849 in excess liability. Its counsel made this clear to the Campbells: " 'You may want to put for sale signs on your property to get things moving.' " Nor was State Farm willing to post a supersedeas bond to allow Campbell to appeal the judgment against him. Campbell obtained his own counsel to appeal the verdict. During the pendency of the appeal, in late 1984, Slusher, Ospital, and the Campbells reached an agreement whereby Slusher and Ospital agreed not to seek satisfaction of their claims against the Campbells. In exchange the Campbells agreed to pursue a bad faith action against State Farm and to be represented by Slusher's and Ospital's attorneys. The Campbells also agreed that Slusher and Ospital would have a right to play a part in all major decisions concerning the bad faith action. No settlement could be concluded without Slusher's and Ospital's approval, and Slusher and Ospital would receive 90 percent of any verdict against State Farm.

In 1989, the Utah Supreme Court denied Campbell's appeal in the wrongful death and tort actions. Slusher v. Ospital, 777 P.2d 437. State Farm then paid the entire judgment, including the amounts in excess of the policy limits. The Campbells nonetheless filed a complaint against State Farm alleging bad faith, fraud, and intentional infliction of emotional distress. The trial court initially granted State Farm's motion for summary judgment because State Farm had paid the excess verdict, but that ruling was reversed on appeal. On remand State Farm moved in limine to exclude evidence of alleged conduct that occurred in unrelated cases outside of Utah, but the trial court denied the motion. At State Farm's request the trial court bifurcated the trial into two phases conducted before different juries. In the first phase the jury determined that State Farm's decision not to settle was unreasonable because there was a substantial likelihood of an excess verdict. . . .

The jury awarded the Campbells $2.6 million in compensatory damages and $145 million in punitive damages, which the trial court reduced to $1 million and $25 million respectively. Both parties appealed.

[The remainder of the Court's opinion deals with due process limits on the award of punitive damages. In the course of affirming an award of punitive damages but reversing as to the amount, the majority said:]

Turning to the second *Gore* guidepost, we have been reluctant to identify concrete constitutional limits on the ratio between harm, or potential harm, to the plaintiff and the punitive damages award. We decline again to impose a bright-line ratio which a punitive damages award cannot exceed. Our jurisprudence and the principles it has now established demonstrate, however, that, in practice, few awards exceeding a single-digit ratio between punitive and compensatory damages, to a significant degree, will satisfy due process. . . .

Nonetheless, because there are no rigid benchmarks that a punitive damages award may not surpass, ratios greater than those we have previously upheld may comport with due process where "a particularly egregious act has resulted in only a small amount of economic damages."

Justice SCALIA, dissenting.

I adhere to the view expressed in my dissenting opinion in *BMW of North America, Inc.* v. *Gore*, (1996), that the Due Process Clause provides no substantive protections against "excessive" or "'unreasonable'" awards of punitive damages. I am also of the view that the punitive damages jurisprudence which has sprung forth from *BMW* v. *Gore* is insusceptible of principled application; accordingly, I do not feel justified in giving the case *stare decisis* effect. I would affirm the judgment of the Utah Supreme Court.

Justice THOMAS, dissenting.

I would affirm the judgment below because "I continue to believe that the Constitution does not constrain the size of punitive damages awards." Accordingly, I respectfully dissent.

Justice GINSBURG, dissenting.

Not long ago, this Court was hesitant to impose a federal check on state-court judgments awarding punitive damages. . . .

In *Gore*, I stated why I resisted the Court's foray into punitive damages "territory traditionally within the States' domain." It was once recognized that "the laws of the particular State must suffice [to superintend punitive damages awards] until judges or legislators authorized to do so initiate system-wide change." I would adhere to that traditional view. . . .

e. A Different Kind of Agency Problem?

TOM BAKER, BLOOD MONEY, NEW MONEY, AND THE MORAL ECONOMY
OF TORT LAW IN ACTION

35 Law & Society Review 275 (2001)

This article reports the results of a qualitative study of personal injury lawyers in Connecticut. Building on the results of an earlier study of lawyers in Florida, "Transforming Punishment Into Compensation: In the Shadow of Punitive Damages" (Baker 1998), the Connecticut study describes and explores the implications of professional norms and practices that govern tort settlement behavior. In particular, it examines the moral and practical barriers to collecting "blood money" (money from individual defendants, as opposed to liability insurance companies), as well as explanations for victims' apparent ability to partially trump the claims of subrogating workers' compensation and health insurance carriers. The results pose a challenge to the conventional understanding that tort law in action is a simpler, more streamlined version of tort law on the books. In addition, the results suggest that compensation and retribution figure far more prominently in tort law in action than does the deterrence emphasized in much of the theoretical and doctrinal literature.

That personal injury litigation revolves around liability insurance has become almost a truism among tort teachers, scholars, and practitioners alike. As both scholars and practitioners report, personal injury lawyers rarely bring a case unless there is an insured defendant (or a solvent self-insured organization) on the other side. Indeed, tort law analysts are so confident that liability insurance captures the bulk of the personal injury universe that they regularly use liability insurance claims files and liability insurance statistics to document, describe, and otherwise measure the dynamics, cost, and prevalence of personal injury litigation.

At the same time, however, we continue to teach that tort law's claim to corrective justice rests on the moral principle that individuals should provide compensation for harm they wrongly cause others. And, even though we know that tort law in action is in some sense "really" about liability insurance, we also know that many defendants do not have enough liability insurance to compensate the people they injure. Thus, unless all but the well-to-do are judgment proof (a situation that is belied by the ready availability of credit cards, mortgages, and other forms of consumer credit), we might expect that a significant part of the personal injury universe would be financed by "real money" from "real people"; that is, out-of-pocket payments by uninsured or underinsured individual defendants.[1]

This study uses qualitative data from a series of in-depth interviews with personal injury lawyers to examine the place of real money from real people in personal injury litigation. In the process, it begins to map a fascinating, previously unexplored aspect of personal injury practice: the moral code that is implicit in the various kinds of money that are generated and disbursed in personal injury litigation. These kinds of money include the "blood money" and "new money" featured in the title, as well as insurance money, lawyers' fees, collateral sources, doctors' and chiropractors' bills, and a host of different subrogation or lien currencies.

"Blood money" is a term many of my respondents used for what I have been calling real money from real people — money paid directly to plaintiffs by defendants out of their own pockets. As their term reflects, blood money hurts defendants in a way that money paid on behalf of a defendant by a liability

---

1. Of course, "real people" ultimately bear the costs of liability insurance claim payments, but as this study reflects, claimants and lawyers do not subjectively experience insurance money as coming from "real people." For similar findings in connection with first-party insurance, see Baker & McElrath 1996.

insurance company cannot. For that reason, blood money is an entirely different currency than what lawyers refer to as "insurance money."

The blood money story teaches us that the source of money makes a difference in tort litigation. Depending on the context, blood money can be worth much more than insurance money, or much less. Claims to insurance money are closely tied to tort doctrine and statutory entitlements; claims to blood money bear a much looser connection to formal law. Bargaining for insurance money takes place very much in the shadow of law; bargaining for blood money turns more on commonsense morality and practicality. For readers who respond to tactile images, insurance money can be imagined as cold, hard, and flat; blood money as hot, soft, and highly textured.

"New money" is new insurance money, paid on top of old. New money comes into play when a plaintiff has already received health insurance or workers' compensation benefits that must be repaid, or when there are underinsured motorists (UM) benefits available on top of a defendant's inadequate liability insurance. The new money story teaches us that the recipient as well as the source of money makes a difference in tort litigation. When new money is at issue there often are competing claims on a defendant's assets. Not only the plaintiff but also a workers' compensation or health insurance company or a health care provider may expect to be paid. Settlements compromise those claims in predictable ways that do not necessarily track tort doctrine or statutory entitlement. Although claims to new money are more closely tied to doctrine and entitlement than are claims to blood money, plaintiffs' claim on new money often exceeds that which would be granted by formal tort law.

The common denominator among blood money, insurance money, and other forms of money in play in tort litigation is that they have both a moral and, for lack of a better word, practical valence that makes them only imperfect substitutes for one another. As the sociologist Viviana Zelizer has explored in her study of household finance, all money is not the same. In the tort settlement process money is affected both by its source (blood money versus insurance money) and by its recipient (new money versus subrogation money).

Although this study hardly contradicts the claim that liability insurance dominates personal injury litigation, it does suggest that tort analysts have not yet succeeded in wresting all the significance out of that situation. Real money from real people accounts for a very small fraction of tort settlement dollars. Nevertheless, plaintiffs' legal right to exact blood money retains an important role in the tort settlement process. In combination with a strong norm against paying blood money in a negligence case, the plaintiffs' legal claim to blood money motivates all the repeat players in the litigation process to arrive at a settlement within the liability insurance limits.

These and related norms and practices help to explain the paradoxical importance of blood money in tort litigation, despite the fact that so little blood money actually changes hands. In addition, these norms and practices challenge the conventional understanding that tort law in action is a simpler, streamlined, and more administrable version of what the legal realist Roscoe Pound (1910) called the "law on the books." As this study demonstrates, tort law in action sometimes draws moral distinctions that are more finely grained than those drawn by tort doctrine.

This study also corroborates, indirectly, some of the insights described in Kritzer's research on the relationship between contingency fee lawyers and their clients. As his research shows, understanding the ways the interests of client and lawyer converge and diverge requires entering the world of the lawyer. Along these lines, some of the patterns of behavior reported here appear, at first blush, to favor lawyers over clients. But, as I explain, it would be wrong to draw such a simple conclusion from the data.

This article proceeds in four parts. The first part describes the qualitative research methods used in this study and links it to an earlier study that explored other aspects of the relationship between tort law in action and insurance. The second and third parts report findings regarding blood and new money, respectively. Part four summarizes some of the implications of this research for our understanding of tort law in action.

I. Research Method

This report is based on in-depth, semi-structured interviews with thirty-nine personal injury lawyers in Connecticut conducted in 1999. . . .

Eighteen of the respondents currently practice exclusively on the plaintiffs' side in personal injury matters; fifteen of the respondents practice exclusively on the defense side; three of the respondents do both plaintiffs' and defense work; and three of the respondents have a workers' compensation practice focused largely on subrogation (i.e., helping workers' compensation insurance companies to be repaid by the responsible party's liability insurance carrier). All but one of the defense lawyers and most of the plaintiffs' lawyers practice exclusively in the area of personal injury. Two of the plaintiffs' lawyers had practiced on the defense side earlier in their career. Two of the defense lawyers had once practiced on the plaintiffs' side, and one had been an insurance adjuster. . . .

II. Blood Money

"Blood money" is a term that some personal injury lawyers use to describe money that individual defendants pay from their own funds. Here is an example from an interview with a defense attorney:

Q: Do you ever have cases where your defendants are not insured?
A: Those are terrible. Yes, I have. Those are the worst. I did two of those in a row for an attorney, who is now a judge, who had people who for some reason or other forgot to renew their insurance, and was driving the car without insurance. I think they were both like that. Those are terrible. Those are absolutely the worst. Without that umbrella behind you, you don't even want to try. You're petrified. Normally, when you try these cases, even if somebody's only got a twenty policy or fifty policy,[5] if it

---

5. Lawyers refer to insurance policies according to the size of the insurance limits. A "twenty" policy is the Connecticut statutory minimum automobile insurance policy, which pays up to $20,000 per person injured in an accident, up to a total of $40,000 per accident (Conn. Gen. Stat. §§38a- 334-5 and 14-112). If two people are injured, this "20/40" policy would pay up to $20,000 each. If more than two people are injured, the policy would pay no more than $40,000 in total. A "fifty" policy pays up to $50,000 per person and $100,000 per accident.

goes over, the insurance company just pays. But, when there is nothing there, you walk in and they just automatically assume because you're there that there is insurance. I almost want to wear a badge saying, "There is no insurance here." This is what we call blood money, instead of insurance company money. We call it blood money because it is coming out of their pockets.

Insurance money is something that all personal injury lawyers talk about. Blood money is a hidden subject that lawyers have to be pressed to talk about. When they do, most plaintiffs' lawyers claim that they try not to go after blood money, and most defense lawyers back that claim up, as the following excerpts describe:

> We don't do it often. And if you talk to every responsible plaintiffs' lawyer in the state, I'll bet it's rare. (plaintiffs' lawyer)
>
> It's hard to take somebody's house away. I mean, you know, people with kids and mothers and fathers, and they worked their whole lives, probably, to acquire that home. I mean, it's not easy. . . . (plaintiffs' lawyer)
>
> I mean there's a, what we used to call, an unwritten union rule that you take the coverage and you go home. (defense lawyer)
>
> It really doesn't happen too often. Guys will call and say, "What's the policy?" That's it, and then [they] go away. But we do have situations where they go out and put an attachment on the house. You got a heavy case and you find out that there's only a hundred policy[6] and your people don't have any underinsured,[7] and there's nowhere else to go. But there's a lot of money in the house. It's rare, because usually if you got a big house, you got a big policy. Sometimes it happens and they go after the houses, too. Not too often. It's almost like an unwritten code of lawyers that you don't go after those. . . . But there's no rule on that. It's just sort of been something that I think I was taught by my bosses and you see it among the plaintiffs' lawyers. They're the ones. (defense lawyer)

As we will see, there are situations in which the "union rule" or "unwritten code" permits, and perhaps even encourages, collecting blood money, but not in the ordinary negligence case.

My initial reaction was, "What about your clients' interests here?" At least as taught in law school, tort law assumes in the first instance that it is defendants themselves who pay. Of course, we know that typically there is insurance, but insurance is treated as an after-the-fact redistribution of financial responsibility, not as an element of liability. The dramatic exception to that is the risk-spreading logic of strict liability, but true strict liability principles are of limited application in tort law.[8] Tort law asks defendants to pay because they did something wrong and, in the process, injured the plaintiff. Combining tort law's conclusion that the defendant was a wrongdoer with the

---

6. A "hundred" policy has limits of $100,000 per person, $300,000 per accident.

7. "Underinsured" refers to underinsured motorists insurance, which is a form of first-party insurance that pays if the beneficiary is tortiously injured by a person with inadequate liability insurance. A further discussion of underinsured motorists insurance appears in Part III.

8. E.g., at least in the design defect and warning areas, products liability is moving away from strict liability toward a risk-utility approach that is very similar to negligence (see Henderson & Twerski 1992:1530-35).

lawyer's ethical obligation of diligence[9] makes these plaintiffs' lawyers' reluctance to pursue blood money at least potentially problematic:

Q: Now where are the clients on this? I can see — I definitely understand and respect the view — although it's new to me. What about a client who says "I don't care about the doctor. I want my money. Take his house?"

A: Yeah. It's probably a client I wouldn't represent because I'd lay it out right from the beginning, this is not about vengeance and this is not about — in order to take someone's house, you know, the legal hurdles you'd have to jump over are very significant. You got to get the verdict, you've got to get a judgment, you've got to go through an appeal, and it's just on and on and on. And at some point . . . , but my own experience is that in cases that go as far as verdict, that is where they are tried to jury verdict, the client and the lawyer become very close. When you try a medical malpractice case, by the time you're done, you and the client know each other very well. And at least my own experience is that, whether I've won the case or lost the case, I have earned my client's respect. They understand how hard I work for them and for myself. And my experience is that once having been through that crucible of fire, they accept my advice. And they have their day in court and once they've had their day in court, the bitterness tends to leave. They've been vindicated. (plaintiffs' lawyer).

Encapsulated in this response — which is well worth rereading — is much of the essence of the plaintiff personal injury bar's explicitly moralized, complicated, self-serving, and not entirely satisfactory answer to the challenge that lawyers' preferences to avoid blood money places them in conflict with their clients.

One part of the answer to this challenge was to acknowledge that, notwithstanding the lawyer's preference, it is the client who gets to make the decision whether to pursue personal assets. Lawyers don't have to represent clients who want blood money,[10] but if they do, they have to follow those clients' directions. A second — perhaps problematic — part of the answer is the claim that the lawyer can manage the relationship so that the client comes to adopt the "right" view in the end. In this regard, another plaintiffs' lawyer described how he and others feel as follows:

I think there is a predisposition to prefer to take it [money] from an insurance company as opposed to an individual, and there is a certain discomfort level if you are taking it from a person. I mean, that is not to say you don't do it, you have a client that wants you to do it, then you do it, but I

---

9. E.g., Connecticut Rule 1.3, "Diligence," states that "a lawyer shall act with reasonable diligence and promptness in representing a client." The comment to this rule elaborates that "a lawyer should act with . . . zeal in advocacy upon the client's behalf." However, such zeal is not unbounded, and the comment further states that "a lawyer is not bound to press for every advantage that might be realized." The Restatement Third, Law Governing Lawyers §28(d), "Duties of Competence of Diligence," notes that "zealous" representation is aspirational and includes general competence and diligence.

10. E.g., respondent 15 (one of the two who declined to be taped) said that he would turn away a client who wanted to collect more than the insurance money in a negligence case.

think there is probably some sense of trying to dissuade the client from chasing some of the individuals. I mean, unless it's a bad person. (plaintiffs' lawyer)

One implicit aspect of the role of the professional is teaching the client what it means to be a good client, and clients undoubtedly are open to suggestion, consciously or not, in this regard. Good clients, desirable clients, don't want blood money (except in certain circumstances we will explore — note the qualification in the statement above: "unless it's a bad person"). For those who are not able to see the wisdom of this approach, practical considerations are packaged with the moral ones, so that the client, who would like to go after blood money in a morally inappropriate case, is steered away.[11]

The sections that follow explore the main aspects of these answers to my challenge in greater detail: the claim that most plaintiffs don't want blood money; the claim that the preference for avoiding blood money is a moral one; and the claim that, morality aside, it is not in plaintiffs' interest to pursue blood money.

This is a complicated, interesting subject because there is something admirable about the refusal to take real money from a real person except in an "appropriate" case. Indeed, it was refreshing to find that plaintiffs and their lawyers made moral distinctions among kinds of money, particularly because these distinctions contradict the popular image of plaintiffs and their lawyers as "greedy graspers" eager to destroy unlucky people's lives.

A. The Claim That Plaintiffs Usually Don't Want Blood Money

Many respondents began a discussion of blood money by reporting that, even without their interventions, plaintiffs usually prefer not to go after blood money. All but one of the defense lawyers confirmed that was their impression as well. The responses below are typical.

Plaintiffs are not, you know, always the greedy animals that they're . . . , that they are sometimes painted to be. And you know, it is not unusual for a plaintiff to say, "Hey, look. I don't want to take Millie's house." You know, "Take the insurance and that's it. . . ." Even in a classic stranger case. There is a whole lot of clients who don't want to take someone's house. I think there is a level of human kindness. I mean, for most people, money is not the sole motivating force in the world. (plaintiffs' lawyer)

Most clients don't want to take away a doctor's house or attach his pension and so forth. What they're looking for is compensation for what happened to

---

11. This reflects an inevitable power imbalance between attorney and an injured client. The client hires the attorney to solve her particular problem, and looks to the attorney for guidance and advice. After all, the attorney knows the language and ways of the law, and the client does not. Law is a complex language and enterprise, and attorneys often act paternalistically toward their clients, and clients often internalize attitudes of the attorney (Sarat & Felstiner 1995). Even though, under Model Rule 1.2, a client defines the objectives of representation and the attorney defines the tactics or means, under Model Rule 1.4b the attorney must provide the client with sufficient information to make informed decisions about the representation (including the client's goals). If the attorney is disinclined to take "blood money," she will inevitably signal this to the client, and the client may make a decision "informed" by the attorney's disdain for blood money. For a discussion of how attorneys may consciously or unconsciously affect how their clients make decisions, see Wasserstrom, 1975:15-24;. Bok 1978).

them, and if they can't get sufficient compensation, at least they're getting something. We don't want — They're not vindictive. (plaintiffs' lawyer)

I've been practicing law for nineteen years. I can think of [only] a couple of examples. So, I would say most often a plaintiff doesn't want to take the money out of the defendant. Often the plaintiff doesn't want the defendant's money so much as he wants the insurance company's money. (defense lawyer)

Of course, there are situations in which plaintiffs are "after blood," but all but a very few of the respondents reported that this does not happen in an ordinary negligence case — such as a routine auto accident, a doctor who made an understandable mistake, or a "slip and fall."

B. The Morality of Blood Money

All respondents reported that there are different kinds of money, with different moral values, at stake in personal injury litigation. The two poles of personal injury money are blood money and insurance money. Absent fraud, the lawyers report that they never have a moral problem pursuing insurance money in a personal injury case.

> From the moral order, what does insurance do? We attempt to spread the risk in society, underwriting undertakes to determine what the risk is. The carrier is being paid for taking a certain risk, and he's making payment based on his underwriting policies with respect to that risk, and he's still usually making money. That's a little different [from] dipping into someone's everyday bread. That was the purpose of insurance. (defense lawyer)

> It is easier to collect from an insurance company than it is to go against the individual and try to garnish wages, foreclose on a home, as well as other things that most people aren't interested in doing, whereas the insurance companies, they're like a bank. (defense lawyer)

For these lawyers, collecting liability insurance money is what tort litigation is all about. As even defense lawyers emphasized, liability insurance money exists for the purpose of paying claims. . . .

1. Lawyers Who Dispute the Code

During the initial months of the study, all of the plaintiffs' lawyer–respondents reported that they had never collected blood money, and all of the defense lawyers reported that they had never paid blood money, except in a case involving a grievous wrong. Eventually, I found a defense lawyer with a different story. The lawyer agreed to give me the names of lawyers who were "known" for going after blood money.

A: Let me tell you. I can pick up the phonebook right now and dial the guys that don't honor it.

Q: And what characterizes the guys who don't? I mean, what's going on with the people who don't honor it?

A: This thing that you mentioned before. My client. My client. My client is more important than ethics, the profession, our image, or whatever. I'm out there to do a good job for my client. And if my client has been injured, then they're entitled to this money, come hell or high water. I'm gonna get it. And the hell with the bar association, the hell with our image, the hell with ethics, the hell with anything. I'm gonna do it for my client. And I think that's basically it. I don't really think it's a money thing.

With his help, I found two plaintiffs' lawyers who disagreed with the unwritten code against pursuing blood money. A third appeared later in the ordinary course of my snowball recruitment. In addition, I also interviewed one defense lawyer who disagreed with the view that there was anything morally problematic with pursuing personal assets in an ordinary negligence case.

The principled explanation for going after blood money in an ordinary case is the formal one discussed previously. Combining tort law's understanding of fault with the lawyer's ethical obligation of diligence makes pursuing personal assets entirely permissible from the perspective of formal law. Indeed, from that perspective, not the lawyer who goes after blood money, but the lawyer who refuses to pursue blood money, or who discourages her clients from asking her to do that, may be the lawyer who is breaching the code.[13]

The following are excerpts from interviews with plaintiffs' lawyers who disagreed with the common practice of avoiding blood money in an ordinary negligence case:

A: My question is: Are they fulfilling their ethical responsibility to their own client? Then they shouldn't be handling the case. He shouldn't handle the case, then. I mean, I could understand him not wanting — then don't take.

Q: Why? What is it that leads someone not to want to do it?

A: I mean, it's not easy, but you can't — you've got to be detached in that regard because if the injury that was caused by the tortfeasor justifies that amount of money, then, I mean, you know, the tortfeasor's done something wrong. Basically, they've done two things wrong. They caused the injury, number one. And, number two, they didn't have themselves adequately insured. So, should the injured party take responsibility for that or should the tortfeasor? My — listen, my duty is to the client. (plaintiffs' lawyer)

Q: Some people say they won't go after people's assets.

A: That's not my feeling. I mean, I think that's a decision that individuals make. I mean, why should you be able to immunize yourself by not buying insurance? Yeah. It's, you know, "Tell it to the Bankruptcy Court" is what I say. And that's not, it doesn't mean the person is any less hurt.

Q: What about a case where there's, you know, decent insurance, but the accident is just massive? You know, with the auto, someone's got the

---

13. Of course, lawyers may refer "not only to law, but also to other considerations such as moral, economic . . . factors that may be relevant to the client's situation" (Model Rule 2.1). Thus, the true ethical problem here arises only if lawyers do not fully and fairly advise their clients of their legal rights regarding blood money so as to enable the clients to make an informed decision about what money to pursue from third parties (see Connecticut Rules of Professional Conduct, Rule 1.4b).

100/300 or even the 300 policy, and those damages, and that's not enough because the person is badly injured?

A: I've had a lot of those where I've just, if I can get it [the insurance money] with a phone call or two, I generally give it to the person, and if there's no other place to go, that's that. I mean, although it is legal to do, I don't approve of taking the fee. Just personal, my own personal decision.

Q: Right. And suppose the defendant's got a house?

A: I'd take it.

Q: Really?

A: I wouldn't have any second thoughts about it at all. I mean, that's, you know, that's — there are risks in life and that's not something I control. (plaintiffs' lawyer)

Q: Have you actually ever collected from an individual defendant, as opposed to an insurance company or corporation?

A: Oh sure.

Q: What kinds of cases?

A: Oh, silly individuals who don't carry adequate insurance and sometimes who are underinsured and have houses. Yeah, I had a rear-ender where somebody had a 25/50, which was inadequate. My own client was on a comp case; we had to pay back the comp carrier,[14] and she got rear-ended waiting to get on the Merritt [Freeway] and I collected from the tortfeasor over and above his policy. Did I throw him out of his house? No. Would I if he had pushed me to it? Sure. Why not? (plaintiffs' lawyer)

Notwithstanding a willingness to pursue blood money in an ordinary case, each of these lawyers recognized that their willingness to do so breached what others regard as a moral code. Indeed, in a comment that struck me with great force during the interview, one respondent equated his efforts to collect blood money with that of adjusters who delay paying claims of old people because those claims will be worth so much less once they die: "I take the houses. They make people die." This followed a discussion of how "cruel" it is (in his words) for insurance adjusters to delay paying claims of older people.[15]

Thus, although these lawyers disagreed with the others regarding their obligations with respect to blood money, they confirmed the moralized nature

---

14. As will be explained in greater detail in the "new money" discussion, the law in Connecticut and other states grants worker's compensation carriers the right to be repaid out of any tort settlement or verdict for the benefits they provided to an injured worker in connection with the same accident. See *infra* Section III.

15. This remark came in the following context:

> People need the money. And it means much more for them to get this amount of money now than it would to get more money later. So, I'd say that would be the number one factor. Age might play into it, too. If somebody's old, they [insurance adjusters] wait it out for them to die. It's cruel. I take the houses; they make people die. So, but I mean that's a factor. And for somebody who's old, getting the money means a lot.

> My colleague Jim Stark observes that lurking in these responses may be the idea of a reciprocal moral code: "If insurance adjusters would play (and pay) in good faith and in a timely manner, I would forgo blood money. But, to the extent they don't, 'All's fair in love and litigation.'" In that sense these blood money outliers seem to have a more politicized view of the tort/insurance system as a whole; hatred of "the system" — i.e., insurers in most instances — may motivate them as much or more than client zeal. — Ed.

of tort settlement currencies. Significantly, their primary complaint about the other lawyers seemed to be that the others were not tough enough to do what they needed to do.

C. The Claim That Pursuing Blood Money Is Not in Plaintiffs' Financial Interest

The respondents also stressed the practical problems in collecting real money from real people. . . .

What is going on is more complicated than the simple story of "no assets" and "delay" many of the respondents discussed. Often, defendants do not have very many assets that fall outside the statutory exemptions, but they do have some. Yes, there is additional delay involved in collecting blood money, but the delay is attributable in significant part to the moral code against collecting personal assets and, therefore, is not an entirely independent complement to the moral objection to blood money. . . .

2. Sometimes There Are Other, Easier Targets

Perhaps the most persuasive practical explanation for avoiding blood money is the existence of other, easier, targets. In an automobile insurance accident, the plaintiff may have her own underinsured motorists coverage. If so, the plaintiff's own insurance company will pay once the defendant's policy is exhausted. As a result, there is little incentive to collect from the individual defendant (unless, of course, the plaintiff is "out for blood"). As one respondent put it, "That money that you got from the person that's underinsured would be set off against your own policy." Thus, the existence of UM reinforces the no blood money rule. In other cases, particularly medical malpractice, there may be institutional defendants that can be pursued in addition to the underinsured individual defendant.

In addition, there is always the hope that the defendant's liability insurance carrier will negligently refuse to settle within limits, which induces plaintiffs' lawyers to offer to settle within limits, even when they hope that the insurance company will refuse. . . .

3. Does the Blood Money "Union Rule" Favor Plaintiffs' Lawyers at the Expense of Their Clients?

The discussion so far has largely taken the respondents at face value, leaving unanswered a fairly obvious question about the "practical" explanations for the no blood money rule. Why should the fact that the lawyer has to work harder to get blood money be a reason for a plaintiff to be satisfied without it? Settling early for the insurance money would seem to increase plaintiffs' lawyers' effective hourly wage at the expense of their clients, because plaintiffs' lawyers receive contingent fees that do not distinguish between insurance money and blood money.

Yet, that conclusion rests on an assumption that the current contingency fee practice in Connecticut would remain the same if the blood money rule were to change. If more plaintiffs began demanding that their lawyers pursue blood money, plaintiffs' lawyers might adapt their contingent fee arrangements to reflect the higher costs of collecting blood money. Thus it is inappropriate to conclude on the basis of these interviews that the "union rule" necessarily raises lawyers' hourly wage.

It is even more inappropriate to conclude on the basis of this evidence that the no blood money rule benefits lawyers at the expense of plaintiffs. Even assuming plaintiffs would in the long run pay the same contingent fee for blood money as for insurance money, evaluating whether the rule harms plaintiffs would require estimating the amount of the blood money the plaintiff could collect, the time value of the insurance money that is delayed, and the length of the delay — all of which are very difficult to measure. Moreover, if the respondents are accurate, plaintiffs prefer not to pursue blood money in an ordinary negligence case. Therefore, we have to leave in suspense the question of whether plaintiffs' lawyers' resistance to pursuing blood money is against the interests of their clients and must focus instead on the significance of the strong evidence that blood money and insurance money are very different settlement currencies.

D. Some Money Is Less Bloody than Others

As some of the respondents' excerpts have already suggested, personal injury lawyers draw moral distinctions among categories of personal assets. The most "bloody" money is home equity from someone who is not seen as wealthy. . . .

E. It's Not Blood Money if You Chose Not to Buy Enough Insurance

A similar sense of proportion and responsibility explains a related finding: In the moral economy of personal injury practice, pursing personal assets is appropriate when the defendant failed to purchase adequate insurance. This finding reflects a moral judgment that people have a responsibility to purchase insurance. The failure to meet that responsibility is itself a wrongful act, justifying the punishment that is understood to be an inherent part of taking real money from real people. . . .

F. Sometimes, Blood Money Is the Point

All the respondents agreed that there were some circumstances in which collecting blood money was morally appropriate. As with tort doctrine, the blameworthiness implicit in the blood money practice appears to be a product of two factors: the degree to which the defendant's conduct breached social norms and the seriousness of the resulting injury. Nevertheless, these findings regarding blood money provide a significant supplement to the ordinary understanding of the moral economy of tort law. As tort doctrine reflects, a simple mistake makes all the difference whether one victim is entitled to compensation through the tort system and another is not. Nevertheless, tort doctrine alone does not determine whether the person who made the mistake will be held personally responsible for that compensation. Something more than tort doctrine's simple negligence is required.

The respondents reported that rape and other assaults that result in serious harm are the clearest cases that justify pursuing blood money. Drunken driving, however, was the most common example they had encountered in their practice.

> Parents and relatives of people who are killed by drunk[en] drivers want blood. They really want blood. I forgot what question of yours initiated this, but in those cases, the clients themselves have an interest in gouging, to make the point to the person and to have the word get out, usually to other youths, that "Holy shit! Jones's father lost his house." (plaintiffs' lawyer) . . .

IV. Conclusions and Implications: The Moral Economy of Tort Law in Action

The presence of different currencies with different values in the tort settlement process reveals a new facet of law in action. Money has different values according to its source and intended recipient. Liability insurance money is not the same as blood money. Subrogation money is not the same as new money. Money to pay chiropractors' bills is not the same as money to pay doctors' bills. And (although this was not explored in this report) money to pay lawyers' fees is in a category all by itself (Kritzer 1998). Moreover, compensatory damages are valued according to a host of things beyond the harm done to the plaintiff: the size of the defendant's liability insurance policy, the wrongfulness of the defendant's conduct, the presence or absence of subrogation claims, the plaintiff's need for the money, and, in some cases, the amount of the defendant's other assets.

Beyond problematizing the common view that law in action is simpler than law on the books, this study also extends the central conclusion of the earlier Florida study: Insurance systematically shapes tort litigation in a way that goes beyond simply spreading risk (Baker 1998; see also Pryor 1997, 1999; Syverud 1994). As a result of a century's experience with liability insurance, there is a norm among tort practitioners that tort litigation is supposed to be primarily about collecting insurance money, not blood money. Before liability insurance, all tort suits against individual defendants involved real money paid by real people. Surely some of that money might have been termed "blood money," with all the retributive overtones that term suggests, but not all. It is only against the liability insurance norm that tort damages paid by real people are regarded primarily as punishment, and only secondarily as compensation.

The liability insurance norm means that, except for institutional defendants or an outrageous wrong, liability insurance has become a prerequisite for tort liability. It also means that liability insurance limits function as a cap on tort damages and that tort claims are shaped to match the available insurance coverage, with the active participation of both the plaintiff's and the defendant's lawyers. The plaintiff's lawyer shapes the claims to match the coverage because that's the easiest way to get the plaintiff paid (Baker 1998). The defense lawyer cooperates because that's the way to make sure that the defendant does not have to pay blood money.

Although very little blood money is paid, this does not mean that blood money is unimportant to personal injury litigation. A credible claim that a trial could result in a legal obligation to pay blood money provides a significant inducement to settle. It motivates the defendant and the defense lawyer to place pressure on the insurance company to offer the policy limits (Baker 1998:320). Moreover, because the plaintiff and the plaintiff's lawyer ordinarily value blood money less than insurance money, they are very likely to accept any resulting early offer of the policy limits.

This situation appears to benefit all the repeat players in the tort litigation system. Liability insurance companies and plaintiffs' lawyers get quicker settlements, and defense lawyers get fewer dissatisfied clients. Quicker settlements benefit insurance companies by lowering defense costs and clarifying reserves; they benefit plaintiffs' lawyers by reducing the time between client intake and payment and, accordingly, reducing uncertainty. Although defense lawyers as a class earn smaller fees, they face less risk. Because individual defendants in the end are rarely asked to pay blood money, they rarely sue their lawyers for incompetently handling their defense.

Of course, defendants benefit from the no blood money rule as well. Whether plaintiffs benefit is a much more complicated question. There are undoubted advantages to faster settlements, but it is possible that the "union rule" benefits lawyers by increasing their effective hourly wage at the financial expense of plaintiffs. It is important to be clear, however, that the results of this study do not provide a basis for drawing that conclusion, for the pragmatic reasons described earlier. In addition, if plaintiffs in fact do value blood money less than insurance money, they would prefer to leave blood money "on the table."[46] Thus they, too, may benefit from the quicker settlements that result from the "no blood money" dynamic.

As most readers will by now have intuited on their own, the new money and blood money norms are mutually reinforcing. The fact that plaintiffs almost never collect blood money makes them unwilling to settle unless a substantial portion of the liability insurance money is for them — i.e., is "new money." Additionally, the fact that plaintiffs are able to obtain a substantial amount of new money reduces their incentive to pursue blood money.

Note that the new money norms appear to benefit individual plaintiffs at the expense of institutional payers, violating the repeat player bias predicted by Galanter (1974:99-104). Of course, this norm benefits plaintiffs' and defense lawyers by encouraging settlements (thereby exposing them to less risk). It also appears to benefit the perceived interests of judges, who reportedly help the plaintiffs' and defense lawyers in order to avoid cluttering their calendars with extra trials. Thus it may be that the plaintiffs are simply fortuitous beneficiaries of some repeat players (plaintiffs' and defense lawyers and judges) ganging up on others (employers and workers' compensation carriers).

Both the blood money and new money practices treat insurance money differently than money belonging to or targeted for real people, indicating an "extra" redistributive tilt of tort law in action. Since real people ultimately pay insurance money (in the form of increased insurance premiums or prices for goods), the actual tilt is between liability and workers' compensation payers on

---

46. It is important to be clear that this study provides evidence only of what personal injury lawyers report that plaintiffs want, which is, at best, indirect evidence of those preferences.

the one hand and beneficiaries on the other. Of course, liability insurance limits impose significant limits on this redistribution.

These interviews also suggest some tentative conclusions about how personal injury lawyers understand tort law in action in cases involving individual defendants. For practicing lawyers, tort law in such cases appears to be almost entirely about compensation, except in the egregious case. In the egregious case, the lawyers are more likely to describe "going for blood" in retributive terms than they are to discuss deterrence. The one exception is the case in which the "wrong" is the failure to purchase (enough) insurance, and there the deterrence is directed not at unsafe behavior, but at insurance purchasing. Thus, at least according to the practitioners of the art, it seems that tort law in action is less concerned with deterrence than tort doctrine and theory would suggest.

These interviews suggest, moreover, that tort law in practice has only a tenuous link with the corrective justice theories propounded by legal theorists (Weinrib 1995:134-35; Perry 1992b; Coleman 1992). These theorists all stress the importance of tort law's emphasis on the particular defendant's duty to pay for the harm to the particular plaintiff—what Galanter and Luban have felicitously referred to as "poetic justice" (1993:1438). Coleman and Perry are careful to take insurance into account by declaring that corrective justice is not inconsistent with someone else (such as an insurance company) discharging the defendant's duty to pay (Coleman 1992; Perry 1992). Nevertheless, they would be unlikely to conclude that corrective justice is consistent with a defendant unilaterally limiting the extent of her duty to pay (which is what happens when a person purchases an insurance policy with a low limit).

Instead, tort law in action seems more consistent with Coleman's earlier (and apparently now abandoned) "annulment" approach to corrective justice. That approach grounded the morality of tort law in the annulment of wrongful harms and, thus, was indifferent to the defendant's responsibility to pay for the harm. Tort law in action most closely approximates the annulment approach in the case of automobile accidents, in which plaintiffs are entitled to collect the full range of tort damages from their own UM (uninsured or underinsured) policy, as long as the accident was someone else's fault. Indeed, by suggesting that tort law in action embodies an annulment approach to corrective justice, this research supports the expansion of the uninsured motorists concept to other fields (such as, significantly, violence against women [Wriggins 2001]) in which defendants predictably have inadequate liability insurance.

2

FINANCING LITIGATION, FINANCING LAW: BASIC MECHANISMS

INTRODUCTION TO LITIGATION FINANCE

As you have likely already concluded, much of civil litigation turns on the question of who is paying for what. This section explores that question more explicitly. We start with a survey of two related questions: how does civil litigation get financed at the start of the twenty-first century; and how much of that money lands in lawyers' pockets? The underlying assumption is that in a lawyer-driven system, it is difficult to understand litigation finance without understanding how it interacts with the financial models of practice organizations. With that basic knowledge as background, this chapter then explores two widespread models — the large firm and the small firm. The organizing proposition is that both models have strengths and weaknesses. For several decades popular wisdom suggested that the future belonged to the large firm and that small practice organizations were slowly dying. Recent history has dramatically exposed the vulnerabilities of large practice organizations and may highlight some of the strengths of smaller practices.

After examining these two basic practice models, the chapter turns to emerging issues and persistent problems in litigation finance. The emerging issues list includes joint ventures, off-shoring of legal work, fee-shifting statutes, direct lending to lawyers and clients, and the effect of fee caps. Heading the problems list is the question of how, in a market-oriented society, to deliver legal services to poor clients; the chapter explores several solutions, none of which seems entirely adequate. Two questions to bear in mind as you read this chapter are which systems best fill which gaps, and which of the unfilled gaps seems most pressing?

As you explore the materials it may also be helpful to look back on the preceding chapter, asking to what extent is the structure of practice a function of the way litigation is financed? And you might be thinking as well about the question that will dominate the next chapter: how might any given finance mechanism affect decisions to settle?

A. LITIGATION COSTS AND PAYMENT SYSTEMS

1. HOW DO CLIENTS PAY? WHAT DO LAWYERS EARN?

C. W. Brooks, Pettyfoggers and Vipers of the Commonwealth: The "Lower Branch" of the Legal Profession in Early Modern England

233, 236 (Cambridge Univ. Press 1986)

"The only fee to which an attorney was officially entitled for handling a suit at common law (as opposed to fees taken for the drawing of instruments such as writs and pleadings, etc.) was the ancient one of 3 s[hillings] 4 p[ence] per term for each case handled. . . . [T]his basic charge was rarely exceeded.

"Nevertheless, there were a number of other fees which practitioners took for legal work, and which supplemented the basic charge. . . . [T]hese can be divided into four categories: first, those fees for the drawing up of procedural documents such as writs which were an integral part of common law litigation and which the attorneys took or shared with the prothonotaries, filazers, and other court officials; second, those taken by attorneys for giving advice and handling business at assizes [the official court hearing days]; third, those taken in jurisdictions other than King's Bench and Common Pleas; fourth, charges for writing up non-judicial instruments such as conveyances, deeds, bonds, marriage agreements, wills, and so on."

Mike McKee, Ground Wars Grow Ugly

San Francisco Recorder, May 12, 2005, at 1

A few years back, Harold Justman represented a couple who forced a long-time Hillsborough neighbor to tear down a small sitting area — complete with a bird bath and flowers — that he had built atop their mutual property line.

Soon thereafter, the San Mateo solo practitioner says, his clients began finding dead animals in their backyard pool.

"They'd go away and there'd be a squirrel or a cat in their pool when they got back," Justman says. "They ended up selling their house and moving to Carmel."

No one could prove who was responsible for the floating carcasses, he says, but it wasn't hard to put two and two together.

The case — and its nasty aftermath — is a prime example of so-called boundary line disputes, a fast-growing and emotionally charged area of litigation that lawyers and judges say has spread like fire ants, particularly in tightly packed urban areas with soaring housing prices.

"People, because they are paying so much for property, feel like every square foot is gold," says Justman, a real estate lawyer for more than 20 years. "And they want to make an issue out of it."

The Bay Area, where the median price of a single-family home stood at $556,000 in January, is a hotbed for boundary fights, with the cities, towns and burgs of San Mateo County seeming to have more than their fair share.

Mark Watson, a real estate and construction lawyer in Burlingame, says that houses that cost $300,000 only 15 years ago are now often assessed at $1 million. A tiny strip of contested land once worth $15,000 could now be valued at $50,000, he said, convincing neighbors to hire lawyers and duke it out in court rather than resolve their differences over coffee and cake.

Going to court isn't cheap, either. Both Watson and Justman estimate that the average case that goes to trial winds up costing the litigants between $30,000 and $45,000. . . . [emphasis added]

STEPHEN C. YEAZELL, FINANCING LITIGATION

Adapted from Yeazell, Civil Procedure 291-303 (7th ed. 2008)

To understand litigation, one has to understand who is paying for it, how that payment is made, and how the resulting financing affects both sides' strategic decisions.

Some of the expenses — the courtroom, the judge, clerical staff, and bailiffs — are borne by society generally, paid for by taxes. This public subsidy is not trivial; in the early 1990s one state estimated that each "judge-day" of civil litigation cost about $4,000. Cal. Code Civ. Proc. §1775(f) (West 2002). If that figure was accurate in 1990, the same public services would cost about $6,400 a day in 2008.

Other expenses are paid by the parties. Some take the form of fees paid directly either to a court or to nonlawyers who perform some service (e.g., expert witnesses, private investigators, court reporters). But attorneys' fees account for most of the cost of litigation in the United States; those fees are often substantial. Relatively high legal fees result in part from the design of the U.S. legal system, which assigns to parties (and their lawyers) responsibility for conducting the suit: Virtually every step of the lawsuit occurs because the lawyer on one side or the other takes some initiative. In other societies a judge or similar official paid by the state assumes some of these responsibilities; that design results in lower legal fees but higher taxes.

Legal fees shape contemporary litigation. Any fee system in which the parties bear any costs of litigation will cause cases to be brought, abandoned, or settled on bases other than their legal and factual merits. Financing systems will affect not only how many suits are brought but also which ones; for example, the availability of punitive damages in a particular case category, combined with contingent fees, will, all other things being equal, move legal resources toward such cases. Conversely, limitations on damage awards, such as [constitutional limits on punitive damages or fee caps for non-economic damages in medical malpractice cases] will move resources away from such cases. Understanding civil litigation therefore requires comprehending the incentives and barriers to litigation posed by the way in which lawyers are paid. In thinking about fee systems, consider three sorts of incentives: those for the client (when will a prospective litigant be encouraged or discouraged?); those for the lawyer (how will the fee system affect the lawyer's work on the case once it is under way?); and those for the opposing party, who will know or can make educated guesses about financing mechanisms.

1. The "American" & "English" Rules

Who pays for lawyers' work? Essentially there are four candidates: the client, the opposing party, society generally (via subsidies or charity), and the lawyer herself (because she does the work for free). Each of these accounts for a portion of U.S. civil litigation.

The system in which each party pays its own legal fees has come to be known as the *American Rule*. It is so called to distinguish it from the *English Rule*, under which (in its purest form) the losing party pays both its own fees and those of the other side. In practice, to an increasing extent someone other than the client pays U.S. legal fees, and in Great Britain less than the full amount of actual fees is generally taxed to the other side. Thus these two "rules" do not accurately describe present practice in either country; they serve, however, as useful models with which to explore the subject.

The English Rule in its pure form fully compensates the winner: She gets both the damages (or other remedy) *and* the costs of litigation. By contrast, under the pure American Rule, a winning litigant has to subtract from any damages the amount charged by his lawyer, and is to that extent made less than whole. Defenders of the American Rule point out that it permits litigants, typically plaintiffs, with tenable but less-than-certain cases to invoke the legal system without fear of having to bear the expense both of their own and the opposition's attorney. That incentive may be particularly important in a political system in which the courts play a significant role (as they do not in Britain) in protecting the constitutional rights of unpopular groups. One might not wish to burden an unsuccessful effort to protect a constitutional right with the legal fees of the victor.

Rule/Practice	Who Pays Fees?	With What Incentives?
"English"	Loser pays winner's fees	*Encourages* strong but low-damage cases. *Discourages* high-cost "law reform" suits
"American"	Each party pays own fees	*Encourages* "law reform" suits *Discourages* meritorious low-damage suits.

Let us begin to explore the structure of fee arrangements under the American Rule with a common situation—the client who agrees to pay the lawyer's fee. Often, but not always, agreements take the form of a written contract between lawyer and client, sometimes called "a retainer letter" (from the still-occasional practice of requiring a deposit—a retainer—from a client). In some states such written agreements are required in some categories of cases. One common form of agreement calls for the client to pay the lawyer at a specified hourly rate for legal services, plus various costs—travel, telephone calls, and the like.

The hourly fee is probably the single most common financing mechanism for U.S. litigation. Most contract and commercial litigation, which, as you may recall, accounts for the majority of civil filings, is financed this way. In the United States hourly fees range from fifty to hundreds of dollars per hour; one study done at the end of the twentieth century found that the median hourly rate for legal fees was about $100 per hour; this average masks wide variations, with senior lawyers in large urban practices charging up to $1000 per hour and rural solo practitioners charging as little as $75 per hour.

Flat rates mean a lawyer charges a set amount for a particular kind of work: an uncontested divorce, a will, a stock offering, and so on. Some lawyers use such a system or use it in combination with other kinds of compensation. It has the obvious advantage of a predictable, guaranteed fee. Its disadvantages are equally clear. Underestimates are possible: What begins as an uncomplicated conveyance can turn into a nightmare of legal research into the Rule against Perpetuities forcing the lawyers to choose between malpractice and very expensive—and uncompensated—work. Yet if the lawyer tries to allow for such contingencies, she risks charging more than the matter warrants or the market will bear. As a consequence, flat rates are most often used for kinds of work that the lawyer thinks will have predictable investments of time: Wills are probably the most common example. Conversely, most lawyers will not handle contested litigation on a flat-rate basis, though some insurance defense firms who do high volumes of work have entered into per-case agreements with insurance carriers.

2. Insurance and the Contingent Fee

Thus far, the discussion has assumed that the client will pay legal fees directly out of current assets. Often, however, that will not be the case. Consider an everyday occurrence—an automobile accident in which Driver *A* sues Driver *B* for injuries and property damage. In that common source of litigation in the United States it is unlikely that *either* side will pay its own legal expenses directly. Both plaintiff and defendant will probably have their fees paid through schemes that spread the costs among other similarly situated persons.

Take first the defendant. Suppose she has liability insurance (required in some states and by all auto-finance lenders). In that policy the insurer makes two promises: that it will pay damages up to the policy limit; *and* that it will provide a lawyer to defend any lawsuit. Most vehicle owners have thus purchased a form of legal insurance. Homeowners' and tenants' insurance policies typically contain similar provisions for claims arising from household accidents, thereby creating a widespread form of legal insurance for potential defendants.

What about the plaintiff in the automobile accident scenario? Her automobile liability policy will provide a *defense* against any counterclaim the other driver may bring, but it will not finance her claim as a plaintiff. A uniquely American fee arrangement—the contingent fee—will, however, perform a similar function. In the contingent fee system, the lawyer typically agrees to provide legal representation, with the fee to be paid from the proceeds of any settlement or recovery. A standard contingent fee arrangement might provide that the lawyer will receive 20 percent of a settlement reached before filing suit, 25 percent if suit is filed but no further steps taken, 33 percent if the case goes to trial, and perhaps 50 percent if the case goes to appeal. In return for these hefty chunks taken from the plaintiff's recovery, the lawyer agrees to forgo a fee entirely if there is no recovery: The plaintiff thus eliminates the risk of paying legal fees in a losing cause. For the client with limited funds the idea is often inviting—he pays only if he recovers something. No recovery means no fee.

Like other legal fees, contingency fee rates are mostly left to lawyer and client—subject only to the general requirement that they cannot be unreasonable. But a few states have regulated these lawyer-client agreements more closely. For example, New Jersey requires lawyers to explain to their clients the alternative of hourly fee representation. N.J. Gen. Ct. R. 1-21-7(b) (Matthew Bender 2007) (requiring that lawyer raise possible hourly-rate alternative to prospective contingent fee client). Another approach caps contingent fees at some level, *decreasing* the percentage of the recovery or settlement as the absolute amount increases—for example, 33-1/3 percent of damages up to $500,000, 30 percent on the next $500,000, 25 percent on the next, 20 percent on the next, and a fee set by the court on any recovery above $2,000,000. *E.g.*, N.J. Gen. Ct. R. 1:21-7(c) (Matthew Bender 2007); Cal. Bus. & Prof. Code §6146 (Deering 2007) (applying only to medical malpractice actions and with different percentages and "trigger" amounts).

Most individual plaintiffs seeking damages for personal injuries enter into contingent fee arrangements, even when their finances would permit them to hire a lawyer on an hourly basis and even if they are offered alternatives.

People sometimes praise or malign the contingent fee system without understanding it. To do so one must consider several perspectives: that of the individual client, the lawyer's other clients, and the lawyer. The client gains the assurance that he will not suffer out-of-pocket expenses for lawyer's fees, which may make the client more willing to bring a case where recovery is doubtful: He risks no loss and he may gain. Some have criticized and others have praised the system for this characteristic. This assurance (of a risk-free lawsuit) comes at a cost that becomes apparent if one considers the position of the lawyer and the lawyer's other clients. The lawyer, to be sure, does not charge the plaintiff any fees if the case is lost, but the lawyer has incurred expenses on the case—if only such overhead items as rent and secretarial services. Those expenses must be paid, and the only source of payment is the fees generated by clients who have recovered or settled. In setting fees, the lawyer must take the probability of success into account; fees from successful cases must be higher to cover the expenses incurred in unsuccessful cases. To that extent *contingent fees cause the successful clients to bear part of the costs attributable to the unsuccessful clients.* To describe it thus is not to condemn the arrangement; the winners are only going to pay legal fees if in fact they recover something, and the guarantee of no fee if they lose may be an assurance for which they would willingly pay the higher fee if they win. Indeed, the prevalence of such arrangements may suggest that all concerned find them satisfactory. An elaborate study of contingent fee lawyers found that their "effective hourly rate" (their mean hourly earnings including both winning and losing cases) was just a few dollars more than their counterparts in the insurance-retained defense bar. Herbert M. Kritzer, The Wages of Risk: The Returns of Contingency Fee Legal Practice, 47 DePaul L. Rev. 267 (1998).

One can think of the contingent fee in several ways. For medieval and early modern lawyers it was an antisocial practice that stirred up dissension and disserved society.* This view, still prevalent in most of the world today, makes a contingent fee a form of criminal activity.

Alternatively, one can see the contingent fee as a form of insurance. The client buys insurance against losing the case; the "premium" is her agreement that if she wins she'll pay a share of her winnings to the lawyer. Just as all drivers who insure with a given insurance company share risks with their fellow-insureds, each contingent fee client pools his risk with that of the other clients of the same lawyer. So long as the lawyer is a good estimator of risks (or has a sufficiently large inventory of cases), the winners and the losers will balance out.

Contingent Fees and Liability Insurance

Financial Arrangement	Who's in the Risk Pool?	How does the cost get spread?
Liability Insurance	Other policy holders, some of whom will have accidents (or other liability-creating event).	No-accident drivers' premiums subsidize those who have accidents.
Contingent Fees	Other clients of that lawyer, some of whom will not recover damages	Fees recovered from winning cases subsidize costs of losing cases.

One can also think of the contingent fee as a credit system in which the client borrows from the lawyer and repays him only when (and if) there is a recovery. Because repayment is contingent on success, the rate of interest is considerably higher than it would be if the money were borrowed directly.

Theoretically, a meritorious claim could serve as collateral for an ordinary bank loan. In practice, most ordinary bankers would have apoplexy if a client walked into a bank and announced, "I have a perfectly splendid little lawsuit, and I'd like you to lend me some money to pursue it." In fact, that does happen, only indirectly. One reason for the banker's imagined reaction is that bankers are not experts in assessing the merits of legal claims. Lawyers are better at it, and it therefore makes sense for the lawyer to assess the claim. But the lawyer will typically need to pay the rent and support her family while the suit is in progress; to get this working capital she may seek a line of credit from a bank. When the bank lends in such a situation, it is indirectly lending against the expected proceeds, not from a single lawsuit, but from the lawyer's whole inventory of cases. As one banker who writes loans to lawyers put it:

> One thing we do is to look at a firm's collateral base — its receivables, its inventory, how much it makes. . . . With a plaintiffs' firm, there is no asset

---

*There were three common law crimes, each prohibiting a form of litigation finance now common (and legal). *Barratry* was the "stirring up" of litigation (as, for example, by a lawyer who advertised that certain behavior was actionable). *Champerty* was the sharing of earnings from litigation (as in a contingent fee). *Maintenance* was the payment of someone else's litigation expenses (as scores of non-profit affinity groups do today).

base. What they offer is an income stream of several types of cases that will come in over time. So you research their reputation in the marketplace, the size of the organization, the number of cases coming in. . . .

If a lawyer tells you, "I'm going to invest $1 million in this case and it's the only one I have, and I'm sure I'll get paid on June 30," we know that's not how it always works. We are more inclined to lend money to someone who says, "I have seven cases and a business plan that includes a worst-case scenario of what may happen to them."

Michael Grinfeld, Justice on Loan, 19 Calif. Lawyer 39, 40 (1999).

In recent years a small segment of the financial market has done what the typical bank will not: lend money to clients directly on the basis of a single lawsuit. This developing market appears to have two segments. One segment lends directly to clients, allowing them to pay the expenses of daily living while waiting for their case to come to judgment or settlement:

> More than 100 companies nationwide have emerged in the last few years to lend money to people with personal injury lawsuits pending, at rates of 2 percent to 15 percent a month.
>
> At any given time, [an] executive of the loan companies said, the industry has more than $50 million in outstanding loans.
>
> Many legal experts defend the industry. They say these lenders level the playing field between individual plaintiffs and corporate defendants, allowing plaintiffs to outlast their adversaries' delaying tactics and obtain bigger settlements or jury awards.
>
> Other experts say the companies exploit vulnerable people and encourage or prolong litigation in violation of centuries-old but eroding judicial prohibitions against investing in others' lawsuits.

Atam Liptak, Lenders to Those Who Sue Are Challenged on Rates, New York Times, May 19, 2003 at A15. As the headline implies, some of these arrangements have been struck down; others have survived scrutiny. Another segment of this industry lends to lawyers, typically to finance complex, expensive commercial and business litigation. As with lenders to clients, those lending to lawyers face various regulatory challenges; thus far there has not been enough litigation for a pattern to emerge.

Still another way of thinking about the contingent fee is as a partnership entered into by the lawyer and the client. Each brings something to the partnership: The client has a potentially valuable asset — the claim; the lawyer has human capital in the form of her education and experience. They agree ahead of time to divide the proceeds of this mutual investment in a particular way. If there are no proceeds, the two "partners" go their separate ways, sadder but wiser. (Note that this theoretical model of the contingent fee approaches illegality: Some rules of professional ethics make it unlawful for a lawyer to practice law in partnership with a nonlawyer. The contingent fee is saved because the "partnership" is not permanent.)

Finally, consider the contingent fee from the lawyer's perspective. Take first the decision to represent a client. For the hourly-fee lawyer each bill-paying client is a source of income no matter what the merits of her case. Not so for the contingent fee lawyer: for her only the successful cases will yield the contingent fee lawyer any income. Moreover, many cases will require substantial investment by the lawyer — fact investigators, expert witness fees—all of which have to be paid even if there is no recovery. So she may screen her cases differently from the hourly-fee lawyer, turning away clients for whom recovery is unlikely or damages are likely to be low or uncollectible. Many contingent fee lawyers report that one of the most important aspects of their practices involves turning away clients whose cases the lawyer thinks unlikely to succeed—or, in a variation, likely to succeed but to result in a recovery that does not warrant the required investment of time and expenses. Does the effect of this screening offset the greater incentives of contingent fee clients to sue? The question would be very hard to answer with any assurance; at this point it is important for the student to see that this fee system involves complex and offsetting incentives.

Another incentive may affect the lawyer's behavior once she takes the contingent fee case. All lawyers owe their clients the duties of loyalty and competence; financial self-interest sometimes creates a tension with these ethical obligations. Hourly-fee lawyers may be tempted to spend more time on the case than it warrants. At first glance, one might think that the contingent fee would correct this tendency by linking the lawyer's fee to the client's recovery. Recall, however, that the lawyer's economic interest lies not in the maximum absolute fee, but in the maximum profit after subtracting the cost of time and overhead, and, if she has a desk full of work, at the maximum fee per hour of her time. So the contingent fee lawyer faces the temptation to resolve the case in a way that will maximize the lawyer's fee *in relation* to hours (and other costs) expended.

3. Public Subsidies and Professional Charity

Insurance will help only those who have it. Contingent fee systems will help only those who seek to recover money damages (and enough money damages to justify the lawyer's investment of time). That leaves substantial numbers of people who could benefit from legal counsel but who do not seek it. But how substantial is this need? Much depends on how the question is asked. Some would ask how many people would benefit—in the sense of improving their present position—from legal advice or representation but do not think they can spare the money for such assistance. Others would ask how many people handed say, $2,000 (about 20 hours of lawyer's time at about the national median rate), would choose to spend it on legal fees. The response to the first question yields a picture of widespread unmet legal need. The response to the second suggests that the demand is much lower. Much debate occurs over which form of the question is the right one to ask.

However great the need, it's concentrated in pockets. Contingent fee arrangements "cover" people with meritorious claims for significant amounts—providing a market-based form of legal services for plaintiffs seeking money damages. Fee-shifting statutes can help plaintiffs seeking injunctive relief for claims covered by those statutes. Class actions, powered by the common fund theory, can power aggregated small claims—though such actions perform better at deterring defendants (and, some would add, compensating lawyers) than at compensating plaintiffs. What about defendants? In a market economy, people with no insurance and no assets have a grim form of protection against lawsuits: Almost no one intentionally sues a judgment-proof defendant for damages. That leaves two good-sized groups without access to representation: individual plaintiffs with small claims (for whom the legal system has no good answer, regardless of wealth) and persons without liquid assets who are nevertheless sued. These defendants comprise two large subgroups: holdover tenants (their "asset" is the dwelling they are occupying); and spouses and parents sued for divorce and child custody (one cannot legally end a marriage or transfer custody of a child without a court order).

Whatever the measure of need, various local, state, and national efforts address it with varying degrees of success. Some of this representation is done by volunteers operating outside a formal organization—lawyers who donate time either as a professional obligation (some bar associations have established minimum amounts of donated time to be an obligation of membership) or as a personal act of charity. The oldest form of legal assistance to those in need, such professional volunteerism suffers from a certain randomness in the large urban settings where most Americans now live. If a poor citizen has a legal problem, where should he go? It seems unfair to burden the lawyers whose offices happen to be geographically closest to poor areas, and it leaves many lawyers who might wish to participate without a way of linking up with needy prospective clients.

At the opposite pole from these individual acts of charity lie the institutions generically referred to as "legal aid." Funded with a combination of tax dollars from all levels of government and private philanthropic support, legal aid offices typically employ full- or part-time lawyers who deliver assistance directly to clients who seek it. These institutions focus on people of small means who find themselves in the position of defendants faced with eviction or with creditors' suit, or domestic violence. The theory is that for most suits that would yield a money recovery, it is possible to find a lawyer who would take the matter on a contingency basis. Some challenge that assumption—one that often represents a concession to segments of the local bar that opposed the establishment of Legal Aid as unnecessary. Others have argued that such a defensive posture robs Legal Aid of the ability to challenge the conditions that underlie poverty and oppression in the United States. In the past, such programs have mounted challenges to the existing legal and social order. Such challenges have sometimes created opposition, especially when publicly subsidized lawyers question some part of the existing political order. In some instances legislatures have responded by trying to limit the kinds of legal work publicly subsidized lawyers can perform for their clients—for example, by forbidding them to sue state and local governments. Material later in this chapter explores some of those limitations.

If volunteer efforts by individual lawyers mark one end of the spectrum and institutionalized, publicly funded legal aid marks the other, intermediate forms have emerged in recent years that combine features of both systems. In one model private firms pledge support, both of money and professional time, to a small organization that functions as a point of client contact and a referral system, matching clients' needs with available professional services. This enables a relatively small organization to deliver legal services many times greater than its budget. It also enables lawyers and firms to participate in pro bono activities with some assurance that they will get a steady flow of such work and that it will match their legal expertise and capacity. Because such organizations are funded by private donations, they also avoid some of the restrictions on practice that governmentally funded aid encounters.

Still another form of subsidized legal services is that formed around a cause—an ethnic, religious, or political group with an agenda for social change. The hallmark of such groups is that they solicit funds and memberships, using those funds to finance litigation that furthers the group's goals. Such groups have been behind major social impact litigation on a range of issues, on both ends of the political spectrum. The most prominent example is undoubtedly Brown v. Board of Education, 347 U.S. 443 (1954) (striking down racial segregation in public education), financed largely by the Legal Defense Fund of the National Association for the Advancement of Colored People, a pioneer civil rights group. Analogous affinity groups have funded litigation seeking to advance agendas of reproductive rights, environmental causes, and more. In recent decades groups from the right side of the political spectrum have mounted their own litigation challenges, sometimes seeking to undo or roll back earlier impact litigation. Almost 50 years after *Brown* the Supreme Court decided Gratz v. Bollinger, 539 U.S. 244 (2003), striking down a racial preference in admissions for the undergraduate college at the University of Michigan. *Gratz* was financed by the Center for Individual Rights, an organization describing itself as focusing on "defense of individual liberties against the increasingly aggressive and unchecked authority of" government.*

Finally, recall that every lawsuit receives some public subsidy: the amounts necessary to maintain the judicial establishment—everything from judges' salaries to the electricity bill for the courthouse. Each federal district judgeship (including law clerks, secretarial help, and bailiffs) costs in excess of $300,000 annually just in salaries. This amount does not include real estate costs, the central clerks' office, or general overhead. State judgeships, which are less well supported, would typically have lower costs, but even those costs are substantial. No litigant pays for these direct costs of adjudication. Moreover, the amount of the subsidy falls unevenly. For the great majority of litigants who file a complaint, engage in modest procedural maneuvering, and then settle, the subsidy is small. For litigants who proceed to trial, the subsidy is quite large.

2. LAW AS A PROFESSION, LAW AS A BUSINESS

INTRODUCTORY NOTE

If one puts the preceding chapter—exploring forms of practice organization—together with this one, on litigation finance, it becomes clear that there are large areas of overlap between litigation finance and what is sometimes called "the business of practice." There is a large literature on that topic, which this section will not seek to explore. Some of that literature is elegiac and regretful, looking back to some golden era before "law became a business." (Some legal historians would question whether there ever was such a time, but it exists in professional legend.) Another branch focuses instead on how—*if* law is a business—that business should be managed. The following two selections offer first a glimpse into how lawyers' incomes differ by region and second a small sample of the flavor of business advice to lawyers. Note that the first selection draws only on lawyers who are "employees," and thus omits the earnings of those who share the profits of a partnership.

---

*http://www.cir-usa.org/mission_new.html visited November 6, 2007.

MARYANN JONES THOMPSON & STACY LAWRENCE, MAPPING THE MONEY

California Lawyer, September 2004, at 29.

Mapping the Money

A SURVEY OF ATTORNEY SALARIES ACROSS THE NATION PUTS CALIFORNIA ON TOP OF THE LIST AND RANKS SAN JOSE AS THE BEST-PAYING AREA IN THE STATE.

By Maryann Jones Thompson and Stacy Lawrence

Being a lawyer has its downsides, but poverty isn't one of them. In fact, practicing law is the eleventh highest-paid occupation in the country, ahead of podiatrists but behind a host of other medical specialties, chief executives, and airline pilots.

So says the U.S. Department of Labor in its most recent Occupational Employment and Wages report. According to the report, last year California lawyers overtook New Yorkers as the top-earning attorneys in the nation. On average, New York attorney salaries last year edged up one-half of 1 percent, to $125,040, while California's average lawyer salary increased more than 4 percent, to $129,080. Together, California and New York account for more than one-fourth of all dollars paid to lawyers in the United States. But even the attorneys in the lowest-paying states fared well in 2003 compared to people who work in other occupations: Lawyers practicing in North and South Dakota earned roughly half the average annual salaries of

Maryann Jones Thompson and Stacy Lawrence produce data-driven editorial content for publications and businesses. Their work has appeared in Business 2.0, Red Herring, and Wired.

ATTORNEYS RANK 11TH: Top-Paid U.S. Professions

Rank	Profession	Salary
1	Surgeons	
2	Anesthesiologists	
3	Obstetricians/gynecologists	
4	Internists (general)	
5	Pediatricians (general)	
6	Chief executives	
7	Family medicine/general practitioners	
8	Psychiatrists	
9	Dentists	
10	Artho pilots, copilots, and flight engineers	
11	Lawyers	$107,800
12	Podiatrists	
13	Engineering managers	
14	Computer/Information systems managers	
15	Optometrists	
16	Natural sciences managers	
17	Air traffic controllers	
18	Marketing managers	
19	Sales managers	
20	Law teachers (postsecondary)	$91,420
24	Judges and magistrates	$87,540
37	Legal occupations	$78,910

0    $50,000 $100,000 $150,000 $200,000

Salary data excludes annual bounses. SOURCE: U.S. Department of Labor, 2003 their counterparts on the East and West coasts.

Although the U.S. Department of Labor only collected data on salaries and regularly distributed incentives paid to lawyers who practice law for a living and are not self-employed, the government data remains the only nationwide, apples-to-apples comparison of lawyer salaries. Other studies of legal compensation focus on specific regions or examine only the salaries of corporate counsel, first-year associates, or law-firm attorneys.

Of course, that leaves much compensation that the Department of Labor survey doesn't cover. The DOL figures exclude annual bonuses, which often compose a significant portion of the compensation that lawyers earn. For example, in 2003 the nation's in-house counsel earned a median base salary of $114,000 but a median income of $122,000 when cash bonuses and profit sharing were included, according to a survey by Abbott, Langer & Associates, a management-consulting firm based in Illinois. The DOL report also excludes non-cash incentives, such as stock options, which can potentially be worth up to four times an attorney's annual salary, according to a 2004 survey of law department compensation conducted by legal-consulting firm Altman Weil.

ABOUT THE STUDY

The U.S. Department of Labor surveyed 400,000 employers in May 2003 and achieved a 78 percent response rate. The employers reported on their employees' wages for a specific pay period in May. For this reason, year-end bonuses and incentives are not included in the salary estimates. The data on lawyers does not include legal professors, judges, or other law-related professions. Nor does the data include those who are self-employed, those who do not practice law, or those who are primarily in corporate or firm management.

Even without looking at bonuses and other incentives, though, salary data gives a clear picture of the earning potential of lawyers around the country and the factors that affect that potential.

For example, despite the growing number of mega-firms, lawyers who work at smaller law firms have shown greater gains in recent years than those who work at large law firms. According to the 2004 Salary Guide published by legal recruiting firm Robert Half Legal in Menlo Park, salaries for attorneys with three years or less of experience who work in small to midsize law firms (up to 75 attorneys) rose as much as 3.5 percent between 2003 and 2004, while salaries at law firms with more than 75 attorneys held steady or dropped as much as 2.3 percent.

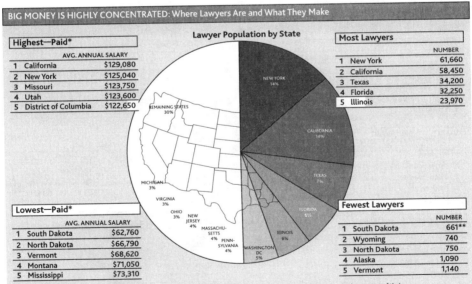

BIG MONEY IS HIGHLY CONCENTRATED: Where Lawyers Are and What They Make

Lawyer Population by State

Highest—Paid*

		AVG. ANNUAL SALARY
1	California	$129,080
2	New York	$125,040
3	Missouri	$123,750
4	Utah	$123,600
5	District of Columbia	$122,650

Most Lawyers

		NUMBER
1	New York	61,660
2	California	58,450
3	Texas	34,200
4	Florida	32,250
5	Illinois	23,970

Lowest—Paid*

		AVG. ANNUAL SALARY
1	South Dakota	$62,760
2	North Dakota	$66,790
3	Vermont	$68,620
4	Montana	$71,050
5	Mississippi	$73,310

Fewest Lawyers

		NUMBER
1	South Dakota	661**
2	Wyoming	740
3	North Dakota	750
4	Alaska	1,090
5	Vermont	1,140

Number of lawyers is rounded to the nearest ten and excludes those who are self-employed and those who do not practice law as part of their primary job function. Total attorney pay is estimated using average annual salary and attorney population figures. *Salary data excludes annual bonuses. **From South Dakota Department of labor, 2000. SOURCE: U.S. Department of Labor, 2003

Not surprisingly, education and experience also drive attorney salaries. The Abbott Langer study found that attorneys who hold a master's degree (MBA, MA, or MS) in addition to a law degree earned a median income of $167,000, compared to $112,000 for those who have only a law degree. Legal recruiters report that among younger associates, possessing a law degree from a top-ranked school remains a primary factor in determining salary.

The Abbott Langer study also found that attorneys with 30 or more years of experience earn an annual median income of $187,000, compared to a median income of $93,600 for lawyers with 5 to 9 years of experience. Within corporate law departments, the Altman Weil survey found that chief legal officers earned an average salary of $278,500 in 2003, while midlevel managing attorneys earned an average salary of nearly $163,000. Corporate lawyers straight out of law school averaged $62,400.

Salaries in different areas of practice also vary dramatically. According to the Department of Labor statistics, the highest-paid lawyers nationally are entertainment agents and attorneys who work for companies in the oil and computer industries. Those positions command upwards of $150,000 a year on average. At the low end of the spectrum are attorneys who work for state and local governments, who earn approximately $70,000 to $75,000 a year. Attorneys in other public sectors—such as waste management, community and family services, and schools—earn annual average salaries ranging from $47,000 to $65,000.

Management responsibilities can also affect a lawyer's income. Attorneys who manage ten or more other attorneys reported a median annual income of $330,000 in the Abbott Langer study, 174 percent higher than those with little or no supervisory duties.

Within California, the Department of Labor found San Jose to be the top-paying metro area, followed closely by San Francisco. One of the likely reasons for this is that many of the in-house and law-firm positions available in these regions require specialization, according to Steve Gomez, division director of Robert Half Legal. "The tendency for certain metro regions to attract certain types of specialized lawyers will drive salaries in that region higher," he says. "For example, intellectual property lawyers at large firms or in-house with a background in hard science can command a premium of up to 30 percent compared to litigation attorneys doing similar work." Although the demand for such lawyers dipped dramatically during the downturn, Gomez says demand today is equal to or exceeds that of 2000. ▨

THE BAY AREA LEADS CALIFORNIA: Attorney Salaries Statewide

Highest-Paid Metro Areas*

		AVG. ANNUAL SALARY
1	San Jose	$155,130
2	San Francisco	$146,540
3	Riverside-San Bernadino	$131,960
4	Los Angeles-Long Beach	$131,290
5	Salinas	$131,020

Lowest-Paid Metro Areas*

		AVG. ANNUAL SALARY
1	Yuba City	$81,520
2	Stockton-Lodi	$81,740
3	Chico-Paradise	$88,320
4	Redding	$89,980
5	Modesto	$95,690

Metro Areas With Fewest Lawyers

		AVG. ANNUAL SALARY
1	Yuba City	80
2	San Luis Obispo-Atascadero-Paso Robles	100
3	Merced	100
4	Chico-Paradise	130
5	Redding	140

Metro Areas With Most Lawyers

		Number
1	Los Angeles- Long Beach	20,360
2	San Fransisco	9,820
3	Orange County	4,390
4	San Diego	4,220
5	Sacramento	4,190

AVERAGE ANNUAL SALARY

- ■ $150,000 or more
- ■ $125,000–$149,999
- ▨ $100,000–$124,999
- □ Less than $100,000

Redding
Chico-Paradise
Yuba City
Vallejo-Fairfiled-Napa
Santa Rosa
Sacramento
Stockton-Lodi
San Francisco
Oakland
Modesto
San Jose
Merced
Fresno
Santa Cruz-Watsonville
Salinas
San Luis Obispo-Atasoa-Paso Robles
Bakersfield
Santa Barbara-Santa Maria-Lompoc
Riverside-San Bernardino
Los Angeles-Long Beach
Orange Country
San Diego

Number of lawyers is rounded to the nearest ten and excludes those who are self employed and those who do not practice law as part of their primary job function. *Salary data excludes annual bonuses. SOURCE: U.S. Department of Labor, 2003

Barbara Lewis & Dan Otto, The Financially Healthy Law Firm

Los Angeles County Bar Update: The Newsletter of the L.A. County Bar
Association, November 2002

As we head into the end of the year, now is a good time to assess your revenues, expenses, and profits for this year and develop your projections for next year. The one-third mantra is the rule of thumb — one-third of revenues goes to overhead, one-third is for salary, and one-third is profit. Although research indicates that average law firm profits are 33 percent prior to partner draw, an efficient and well-run law firm can generate substantially more.

In gauging the health of your firm, the financials are the first place to start. Year-end statistics can give you a benchmark for next year's financial goals. If you have financials from previous years, you can easily ascertain the financial trends in your firm. The four basic areas to analyze are revenues, salaries and other expenses, profit (partner draw), and accounts receivable.

Oftentimes, attorneys pursue revenues only to get caught in a situation where expenses increase and profits sink. That new client who peppers the staff with questions and requires handholding that cannot be recouped through billing eats away at the profits. One hundred small clients who need files opened, database fields filled in, and billing information entered generate less profit margin than one large client with the same total revenues, due to the unbillable administrative tasks.

Another area where attorneys fall victim is increasing expenses. The percentage rise in expenses should be less than the percentage increase in revenue. Yet, when firms grow, they are quick to hire additional people, the largest component of expenses. Rarely do employees tell partners that they don't have enough work, but they are quick to point out when the work increases. The result is that partners hire unnecessary employees when the current ones could have handled more work after implementing some operating efficiencies.

Accounts receivable is a critical barometer for a healthy firm. Calculating the average number of collection days gives you a benchmark for future monitoring. To determine the average number of days it takes you to collect on your invoices, calculate your total outstanding accounts receivable (less current A/R) and divide by current month's billings (or a 12-month average billings), and then multiply that amount by 30.

A high number of collection days indicates that the firm is "loaning" money to its clients who are not paying in a timely manner. Keeping collections under 45 days is healthy. The goal should be to continually drive down this figure. By tracking this amount and using easy-to-view graphs, such as Excel, you can monitor your progress in achieving your goal. If the average collection-day amount is more than 45 days, consider hiring a collection person. Most attorneys don't want to call their clients for monies due, and the result is that collections oftentimes are delayed. Physicians don't dun their patients for fees, and neither should attorneys.

The most important financial metric is profit and profit margin. To calculate the profit margin, subtract expenses from revenues and divide by revenues. This amount is the profit margin percentage. If you are below 33 percent, you need to take a hard look at your operations.

One way to increase profits and margins is to cut expenses. Each line item of expenses should be reviewed to ensure that the expense is a necessary expenditure that cannot be eliminated. Compare your expenses to the average expenses of law firms your size. For example, your rent should be only 10 percent of your expenses for the average law firm. Expenses that may be above average include delivery services, dues and subscriptions, and supplies.

If you haven't already established financial benchmarks, use 2002 statistics as the standard. Then develop revenue and profit projections, and an expense budget with financial goals for 2003. Monitor the goals each month to ensure that the health of your law firm is excellent.

— Submitted by Barbara Lewis, M.B.A., Law Practice Management Section Executive Committee, and Dan Otto, M.B.A.

B. PRACTICE ORGANIZATION AND LITIGATION FINANCE: A CONTEMPORARY TAXONOMY

INTRODUCTORY NOTE

Lawyers provide skilled services. In that respect they are like physicians, engineers, car mechanics, and cabinet-makers. Fifty years ago most lawyers operated solo practices. Today most lawyers operate in practice groups. That is true regardless of whether they are in for-profit, non-profit, or governmental organizations. All those organizations deliver services and incur costs in producing those services. As with all sectors of the service economy, most of those costs are from labor: lawyers, assistants, paralegals, messengers, mailroom and clerical staff, IT specialists, and more. The "market" for those services constitutes one challenge of these organizations: how will they recruit and retain talented, hard-working people? The other challenge comes from lawyers' other "market" — for clients: where will they come from, and what services do they want? Notice that this second market exists even if the legal organization charges its clients nothing: in judging whether to fund a legal aid or government organization, granting agencies, donors, and legislators will be interested in how many clients the organization serves and how well it serves them.

Any practice organization thus has to think about these two markets — for the talent that enables it to deliver legal services and for the clients to whom it will deliver these services. To make matters more complex, these two markets will sometimes pull the organization in opposite directions. To take a crude example, a practice organization can deliver lots of services at low cost if all its lawyers work 80 hours a week. But, whether those lawyers are in a legal aid office or a private firm, they may not be willing to remain in that setting if those hours persist, and potential new lawyers may be unwilling to join if they think such demands will be a constant staple of their professional lives. On the other hand, still remaining in the crude example category, a practice that promised its lawyers they would be compensated in the top 5% of all such professionals but would never have to work more than 20 hours a week, might have little problem attracting talent, but a great deal of difficulty in finding clients willing to pay for such services.

In the reading the materials below, consider how each form of practice — the large and the small — tries to balance these two markets. What are the strengths and weaknesses of each form of practice organization?

1. LARGE FIRM: SCOPE, FLEXIBILITY — AND HIGH EXPENSES

a. The Basic Model: Three Excerpts Taken from Large-Firm Web Sites

KIRKLAND & ELLIS

Compiled from http://www.kirkland.com (last visited February 23, 2009)

Kirkland & Ellis has a 100-year history of providing exceptional service to clients around the world in complex litigation, corporate and tax, intellectual property, restructuring and counseling matters. The groundwork has been established for another century of superior legal work and client service.

Philosophy

Kirkland's principal goals are to provide the highest quality legal services available anywhere; to be an instrumental part of each client's success; and to recruit, retain and advance the brightest legal talent. Our Firm seeks long-term, partnering relationships with clients, to the end of providing the best total solution to the client's legal needs.

Practice Areas

We manage our Firm as an integrated whole. Approximately 1,500 lawyers in varying practice areas work together as multidisciplinary teams to provide the full-service capabilities our clients need for the legal matters they retain Kirkland to handle.

Kirkland's free-market system allows each attorney to choose the practice areas and matters on which they work. This entrepreneurial approach yields higher levels of commitment, morale and results in all of our core practices: [Litigation, Corporate & Tax, Intellectual Property, Restructuring]

Diversity

At Kirkland, we believe that our ability to function at the very highest level of our profession is significantly enhanced by building a team of lawyers who bring us the benefits of a broad range of socioeconomic, racial, ethnic and personal backgrounds. Our commitment to diversity is reflected not only in the Firm's policies, programs and committees, but also through our efforts to build and maintain a culture that values and gathers strength from difference.

The Kirkland Institute

Effective training is critical to the professional development of our lawyers. For this reason, Kirkland emphasizes attorney training that combines a legal practice with a year-round series of development programs including mock exercises, lectures and presentations. From their first days at our Firm, Kirkland lawyers have front-line opportunities to take and defend depositions, draft transaction documents, argue motions in court and draft securities filings. By performing such work under the guidance of senior colleagues, Kirkland lawyers learn through hands-on experience.

Kirkland Institute programs include: Trial Advocacy (KITA); Corporate Practice (KICP); Technology (KTECH); Tax Practice (KITP); Restructuring Training (KIRT); Patent Infringement Litigation (KIPIL); Insolvency Training (KIIT); and the LBO/Private Equity Seminar.

Geographic Reach

Kirkland is a strong and dynamic institution with a strategic network of offices located in major business centers around the globe. In line with our strategy of sensible, organic growth, the Firm has expanded geographically to meet the needs of our clients while maintaining a strong focus on quality control.

Results-Oriented

Kirkland stresses—and clients rightfully expect—good results. To that end, our Firm employs innovative, pragmatic strategies and hard work to ensure that our clients' legal needs are met. We recognize that our success depends on close coordination with our clients, therefore, our lawyers work collaboratively to set objectives, develop budgets and conduct periodic review sessions to measure our progress against those objectives.

Community Service

Our Firm is committed to serving the communities in which we practice and live. Through pro bono work, our lawyers make their skills and talents available to those who cannot afford legal representation. They provide pro bono clients with the same commitment and diligence they show for our traditional clients. The Kirkland & Ellis Foundation provides financial support to charitable and law-related organizations that enhance the quality of life through education, improved community services, cultural awareness, youth programs, healthcare, diversity sensitivity and many other initiatives.

Technology & Support Services

The Firm makes extensive use of legal and administrative personnel to provide the appropriate skill level for the legal services required by our clients. Kirkland keeps pace with today's technology by providing our lawyers, staff and clients with the most advanced technology tools available to facilitate the practice of law.

JONES DAY

Firm Overview: One Firm Worldwide, http://www.jonesday.com/firm/overview
(last visited February 23, 2009)

One Firm Worldwide

Since 1893, Jones Day has grown, in response to our clients' needs, from a small, local practice to a truly global firm with more than 2,400 lawyers in 31 offices around the world. Today, Jones Day is one of the most recognized and respected law firms in the world, and we count more than 250 of the *Fortune* 500 among our clients.

Our Firm's success stems from key strengths:

- Client focus
- Legal skill
- Depth of people, experience and resources
- Team orientation
- A one-Firm organization

Recent Recognition

Jones Day takes pride in these recent achievements:

- "Number One for Client Service," 2002, 2004, and 2005; Top "Market Mover" in 2006, BTI Consulting Group, Inc.
- "International Law Firm of the Year," *Asian Legal Business*, 2005 and 2006
- Second most cited, "Who Represents Corporate America," *Corporate Counsel*, 2006

BAKER & McKENZIE

Our History, http://www.bakernet.com/BakerNet/Firm+Profile/default.htm
(last visited February 23, 2009)

Our History

The history of Baker & McKenzie is a story of imagination, determination and hard work. Over more than half a century, thousands of capable men and women have joined in the great adventure of creating, nurturing and maturing our unique global organization.

Before there was a law firm, there was a man with a dream. Russell Baker grew up in the rugged American Southwest, traveled by cattle car to go to college and started his legal practice years before getting his law degree (a common practice at the time). Follow this link to read more about the Prelude to Baker & McKenzie [hyperlink in original].

In the early years, we embraced the novel idea that qualified lawyers who were not US nationals should be equal partners. We also developed innovative ideas for tax planning that would spur growth across Europe and South America. You can read more about the Early Years here [hyperlink in original].

As we matured, Russell Baker would become one of the oldest lawyers ever to pass the rigorous California bar exam. He took it so that we could open an office in San Francisco. We would be among the first in China as we expanded to Asia Pacific and the Middle East, while growing to become the largest law firm in the world. Learn more about the Middle Years here [hyperlink in original].

By 1987, we would become the first law firm to employ 1,000 lawyers. We also double that number in a decade and triple it by 2001. We were the first to reach US$1 billion in global revenue. To keep up, we focused more than ever on quality and systems to maintain our standards. You can read more about the Recent Years here [hyperlink in original].

A detailed look at the Firm's history is provided in *Pioneering a Global Vision: The Story of Baker & McKenzie* by Jon Bauman. This 327-page book, published by Harcourt Professional Education Group (Chicago), is available for purchase from Amazon.com.

b. Challenges, Adaptations, and the Future of the Large Firm

NATHAN KOPPEL, RECESSION BATTERS LAW FIRMS, TRIGGERING LAYOFFS, CLOSINGS

Wall Street Journal, January 26, 2009, at 1

For years, the law firm Heller Ehrman LLP used a goofy coat of arms inside its offices: a laurel wreath, the scales of justice and a Latin quotation, elvem ipsum etiam vivere. Rough translation: Elvis Lives.

In late September, Heller Ehrman went the way of Elvis. Just two years after its most profitable year ever, the freewheeling San Francisco firm expired, closing its doors after 118 years in business.

After upending a succession of U.S. industries, the recession has arrived for U.S. law firms, which have long seen themselves as partially insulated from economic downturns. In December, Thelen LLP, another large San Francisco firm, also shut down for good, citing recessionary pressures. Later that month, Thacher Proffitt & Wood LLP, a 160-year-old New York firm, announced that it was closing. Dreier LLP of New York is dissolving after its founder was arrested for fraud.

Pay cuts and layoffs are becoming commonplace. This month, Clifford Chance laid off more than 70 lawyers in London; Cooley Godward Kronish LLP fired 50 lawyers and 60 other staffers; and Akin Gump Strauss Hauer & Feld LLP let go of 65 staff members across the U.S.

In November, New York legal giant Cravath, Swaine & Moore LLP announced it was reducing year-end bonuses for junior lawyers, and that it wouldn't raise its billing rates in 2009. Latham LLP, one of the nation's highest-grossing firms, said in December that associates would not get raises in 2009 — a move followed by many other firms.

"More firms are in a fragile condition than I've ever seen," says William Brennan, a law-firm consultant with Altman Weil Inc. and formerly chief financial officer at two large Philadelphia firms.

Profits, on average, were down 8% to 12% across the industry last year, after 15 years of consistent profit growth, says Peter Haugh, managing director for the Legal Specialty Group of Wachovia Wealth Management.

Throughout the industry, business has dropped off in such key practice areas as mergers, public offerings, and corporate finance. Litigation, often counted on to carry firms through downturns, has become less profitable as clients increasingly settle big cases, forgo lawsuits altogether, or pressure firms to discount their fees, lawyers say. Some practice areas, such as bankruptcy, however, are robust. . . .

Many law firms are susceptible to the phenomenon that led to Heller's collapse. Their main assets are their senior lawyers. Job hopping used to be relatively rare among such lawyers. But lawyers with big books of business now commonly shop themselves to more profitable firms that can offer larger compensation packages.

"Law firms are not the kind of companies that do well in adversity," says Jonathan Landers, a partner at Milberg LLP, who has represented banks in law-firm dissolutions. "Their best assets are their most mobile assets. When bad things happen, people get nervous and they start to look around." . . .

"The marketplace is so intensively competitive that when firms encounter financial difficulty, the best and brightest lawyers immediately say, 'I don't want to take a risk with my clients and my compensation,' and they jump quickly to a less risky platform," says Mr. Brennan, the consultant. "Within weeks a firm can go from having financial difficulty to having a run on the bank."

The story of Heller's collapse, pieced together from the accounts of more than two dozen lawyers, underscores the vulnerability of midsize firms specializing in corporate defense work.

Many firms with roughly 200 to 600 lawyers see themselves as susceptible to losing talent to larger, better financed competitors. As a result, they push hard to grow and to increase profits, which can alienate longtime partners who do not share the urge to grow.

Heller, which last year numbered more than 600 lawyers, had been following such a path. Management believed the firm needed to get bigger and more profitable in order to compete against industry-leading firms with more than 1,000 lawyers.

According to Eric Redman, a former Heller lawyer, the stated logic became: "There is room for big firms and tiny firms, but firms in the middle will get crunched. . . . [T]he idea was we had to move in the direction of being a really, really big and profitable firm to survive." . . .

Matthew Larrabee, who became chairman in 2005, pushed hard to beef up the corporate department and to expand Heller's presence abroad. The 53-year-old antitrust lawyer envisioned a firm of 1,000 or so lawyers with a much bigger footprint outside the West Coast. He paid close attention to the firm's profitability—a key to recruiting star lawyers. . . .

The firm ended 2006 on a high note, with its partners earning $1 million, on average, for the first time in its history.

But its financial condition worsened in 2007. That winter and spring, over 45 days, it lost about one-quarter of its litigation business due to settlements, including its defense of Microsoft in the antitrust litigation and Ernst & Young LLP in securities litigation. . . .

Heller's management focused on trying to merge with a bigger, stronger competitor, concluding that it was the only way the firm could stay alive amid continuing lawyer defections. At a shareholder gathering last spring in Colorado Springs, Colo., Heller's chairman, Mr. Larrabee, said the firm had plenty of choices of merger partners, according to lawyers who were there. Last summer, Baker & McKenzie LLP, one of the nation's largest firms, emerged as a serious candidate. But after weeks of negotiations, the deal cratered in August, partly because of business conflicts. Heller lawyers had sued many of Baker's clients. . . .

Heller distributes its income to shareholders at year end. As a result, at the beginning of each year, it has to tap a bank credit line to pay salaries, rent and other expenses. As revenue rolls in, it pays down the credit line. It is usually finished by August.

Last year, however, revenue dropped off so much that it had trouble paying down its loan. By September, its debt hovered around $30 million, according to a lawyer knowledgeable about the finances. The formal departure of the intellectual-property group on Sept. 14 put Heller in breach of a loan covenant that limited the number of shareholders who could depart in a 12-month period.

On Sept. 26, with banks controlling how Heller spent its money, shareholders voted to dissolve the firm. "Employees were crying about it," says Michael Charlson, a former shareholder. "There was an amazingly profound sense of emptiness."

Heller hoped to wind down outside of federal bankruptcy court. But on Dec. 29, after failing to reach agreement with its lenders about terms of repayment, it sought Chapter 11 bankruptcy protection.

Most of Heller's shareholders have landed at other large firms. But as of December, more than 300 former Heller employees, mostly nonlawyers, were still looking for work, according to a report by Heller's dissolution committee.

RENEE DEGER, MODEL BEHAVIOR

San Francisco Recorder, November 13, 2003, at 1

It's called the Legal Model, and it's become a concoction so tempting that lawyers from 160 companies have made the pilgrimage to Wilmington, Del., to test its cost-cutting powers.

Chemical-producing giant DuPont brewed the Model as a way to shrink its legal budget, and Thomas Sager, DuPont's chief litigation counsel, sounds almost like a medicine show pitchman as he hawks the Model's healing powers. It has cured polluted communications, poor-quality work, and most importantly, has saved DuPont $8.8 million in legal bills last year alone.

"There's a groundswell building and over time, you're going to see a shake-out," Sager said. "Until we impose more discipline and rigor on these firms, they're going to continue to charge exorbitant rates to corporate counsel."

The magic behind the Model is simple: Send a portion of your legal work to someone other than attorneys at law firms. In DuPont's case, lawyers from a temporary agency handled relatively simple tasks like initial witness interviews, exhibit collection and document review.

Any formula that slices legal budgets is likely to seduce in-house counsel — particularly when the higher-ups at a company are looking to trim the bottom line. And outsourcing—diverting legal work to companies other than law firms—is exploding in popularity among corporate counsel. Sager says he'd like to see other companies adopt the model to put pressure on firms to change their billing policies.

The trend is two-fold, with companies sending work to agencies in the United States that do discovery, document review and due diligence and pulling in foreign outsourcing companies—particularly in India—to perform tasks like legal transcription and basic patent research.

For law firms, there's an obvious downside: They lose billable hours and training opportunities for young lawyers on less-complicated legal tasks like document review. And all is not rosy for in-house counsel. They give up some control over work assigned to outsourcing agencies, and if an agency is located overseas, confidentiality, security and cultural issues may arise.

Take, for instance, the case of UCSF Medical Center's recent scare over patient medical records. A woman in Pakistan hired to transcribe patient records threatened to reveal patient information if she was not paid money a sub-contractor owed her.

"This is something that's still very much in its formative stages," said Sanjay Prasad, chief patent counsel at Oracle Corp.

The risks, however, aren't posing much of an obstacle to outsourcing's growth. DuPont isn't the only company to see millions of dollars in savings. Cisco Systems Inc. estimates it has saved millions of dollars through outsourcing discovery work. And Sun Microsystems Inc. believes it can save up to $1.5 million by doling out patent work to lawyers who don't punch the clock at a law firm.

"It's catching on," Sager said. "A lot of people don't like to talk about it." He added that law firm partners "are concerned about the quality issues, but the other issue is that law firms don't want to have to admit they have to deal with this."

India Bound

One of the companies aggressively looking to expand its use of outsourcing is Redwood City, Calif.'s Oracle. It's not clear, however, how quickly the company will export work to outsourcing agencies.

Daniel Cooperman, Oracle's general counsel, said he'd like to see more of the company's legal work—especially on patents—done by lawyers located closer to facilities in places like Bangalore, India.

For several years, India has been a hot spot for companies looking to find cheaper labor for tasks from fielding customer service calls to designing software. So why not take it one step further, asks Cooperman, and move some basic legal services there, too? Getting an outsourcing agency to do work in a foreign market is one of the chief ways the practice saves money, Cooperman said.

"I would rather grow in India," he said.

Prasad, the Oracle patent counsel, began researching this summer whether to use lawyers in India to work on patent applications for technology the company develops in the United States or another country. He said he's recommending to move some work on a trial basis to India. But he's not sure if they will be able to handle the work or do it as well as the firms Oracle currently employs, such as Hickman Palermo Truong & Becker in San Jose, Calif.

"It would require a significant amount of training" of lawyers, Prasad said. "It's not clear if you can get work done at the same quality for significantly less money."

Prasad said he favors a conservative approach to using outsourcing overseas. Protecting trade secrets is one issue, he said. He is wary of moving sensitive intellectual property from one part of the world to another, which could expose the company to additional breaches in security.

"It's something you have to watch carefully," Prasad said.

A few law firms have tried to capitalize on the trend toward internationalizing basic legal services. Howrey Simon Arnold & White, for example, is considering ways to take advantage of the increasing movement of legal work from firms to overseas operations, particularly in India. And London's Allen & Overy decided in September to open a document production facility in India.

But many firms see outsourcing as dangerous — and not just to the bottom line. . . .

Model Work

At DuPont, where the Legal Model has been in place for 11 years, a group of nine outside providers is used for a variety of services. The companies range from LRN to Kelly Law Registry, which provides a team of temp lawyers.

Those two companies are part of the growing niche of non-firm legal providers. John Mullenholz of Washington, D.C.-based Staffwise said his company employs a team of lawyers to do document production, review and coding. The attorneys, he said, are generally part-timers who have decided they want flexible schedules to raise families or pursue other careers.

Axiom Legal Solutions Inc., a New York-based network of freelance lawyers, started three years ago with "a handful of big-firm associates," said Mark Harris, the company's CEO. Business has increased by 300 percent since then, he said, and the company has 50 lawyers on assignment.

Outsourcing, Harris said, "is becoming more mainstream."

For Sager, the reliance on outsourcing has allowed him to cut his lawyer headcount from 175 to 127. Sager has been systematically shuffling work to what he calls "the lowest, most appropriate level."

The biggest concern for DuPont's in-house team was convincing the outside law firms that quality wouldn't suffer with the use of outsourcing companies, Sager said. . . .

NOTE ON ORGANIZATIONAL EFFORTS TO CONTROL LEGAL EXPENSES

The DuPont model for reducing legal fees is only one of several approaches to this issue. Other businesses with large legal bills have taken much of their routine work in-house. Others have outsourced it to other nations, with India being a key supplier of legal services. Still others insist on budgets from suppliers of non-routine services, and still others negotiate substantial discounts from regular hourly fees. And still others engage in the "auditing" of legal bills, hiring outside consultants to examine and sometimes to challenge each hour of billing. The next few readings present still more variations.

The common denominator to these approaches is their goal: reduced legal expenses. Lawyers who operate in such environments report that if there ever was a day when lawyers could send out bills "for professional services" rendered and expect a check in return, that day has gone. The only significant exception to that proposition comes in "bet the company" cases, in which the expected size of the damages, were liability proved, would threaten or doom the continued existence of the company. Examples include asbestos litigation, which drove most asbestos producers into bankruptcy, and tobacco litigation, which might have done the same for the tobacco companies had they not struck settlements in these cases. For such cases, clients are prepared to pay premium fees.

ASHBY JONES, MORE LAW FIRMS CHARGE FIXED FEES FOR ROUTINE JOBS

Wall Street Journal, May 2, 2007, at B1

Before Cisco Systems Inc. announced plans to buy WebEx Communications Inc. in March, Cisco's outside lawyers spent several days working around the clock to draw up the papers for the $3.2 billion deal. But the attorneys didn't see the kind of big pay day that often follows work on mergers and acquisitions. They were toiling for a fixed fee.

When it comes to buying legal services, corporations mostly pay lawyers by the hour. But critics say that approach encourages lawyers to be inefficient, leading to wasted time and bloated, unpredictable bills. Now, thanks in part to improved technology for tracking the costs of legal work, companies are increasingly finding ways to avoid the oft-dreaded billable hour.

"Typically, large numbers of associates go off and write memos that get tucked into the lower right-hand side of someone's drawer," says Gordon Davidson, chairman of Fenwick & West LLP of Mountain View, Calif., the firm that represented Cisco Systems in its WebEx purchase. Using a monthly fixed-fee arrangement, he says, Fenwick lawyers have cut down "on stuff that we were doing that was interesting, but not that useful."

Cisco, a leader in the area of so-called alternative billing, now farms out 70% to 75% of its annual legal budget, estimated at $125 million, under fixed-fee arrangements. . . .

General counsels, in charge of their companies' legal matters and budgets, are perpetually under pressure to trim and better manage expenses. But it hasn't been easy to move away from the familiar billable-hour system, in part because neither companies nor law firms typically have a good sense of what a piece of legal work will end up costing. Now, new tools are helping both sides estimate costs up front, giving general counsels more confidence to move ahead with arrangements like fixed fees and "value-based billing," in which the payment a firm gets depends in part on the results it achieves.

The boosts have mostly come from off-the-shelf electronic-billing and "matter-management" software programs. Over time, as data accumulate, general counsels' offices are able to organize cost information on everything from a group of 20 patent filings to a large single task like reviewing three million document pages. . . .

While a growing trend, alternative billing has yet to catch on in a big way, especially with the nation's top law firms, which are generally hugely profitable using the billable-hours system for most of their work. According to a soon-to-be-released study by the General Counsel Roundtable, which is made up of general counsel at large companies, 62% of about 150 respondents said they have used fixed fees "once in a while," up from 54% in a study done in 2002.

Even companies that use alternative billing tend to avoid it for big-ticket items, like a high-stakes merger or a bet-the-company antitrust case. "Right now, fixed fees are most suitable to routine, recurring matters where you have a good estimate of what [a piece of work] should cost," says Craig Glidden, the general counsel at Chevron Phillips Chemical Co.

Among small firms, a handful have worked primarily outside the billable-hour structure for over a decade. Now some regional and boutique firms are using alternative billing as a way to get a toe-hold with blue-chip clients. . . .

For Morgan Lewis, the first two years were a learning exercise. In early 2005, when Mr. Chandler sat down with the firm's litigation heads to discuss renewing the contract, they told him the firm was making 15% less on the deal than it would have under its normal billable-hour approach. Mr. Chandler encouraged the firm to rebid at the same price, and the firm thought hard about it.

Morgan Lewis ultimately decided to sign another two-year deal, says Jami McKeon, the head of the firm's commercial litigation practice. But Cisco agreed to hold frequent meetings with the firm to, in Ms. McKeon's words, "look ahead of the curve, figure out if there's a problem we can head off at the pass."

Both Ms. McKeon and Mr. Davidson at Fenwick say the Cisco arrangements are now profitable, though not hugely so. "You don't want your law firm making a huge profit," says Ms. McKeon, "but you don't want your law firm taking a hit either. They're not going to give you the same level of service."

ARIC PRESS, LEGAL PROFESSIONALS ROLE-PLAY THE FUTURE OF BIG LAW

American Law Daily blog, April 21, 2009, at AmericanLawyer.com

Bill Henderson, the irrepressible Indiana University law professor, had a simple idea. To test the viability of the big firm model—and look for ways to change and rescue it—he and Anthony Kearns, the lead risk manager for the Australian lawyers insurance operation, organized a clever role-playing game, a sort of Dungeons and Dragons for lawyers. FutureFirm, as they called it, is a case study of a hypothetical Am Law 200 law firm in trouble. Teams of law firm partners, clients, law students and consultants would spend a day and a half trying to devise a strategy that would allow the tottering Marbury & Madison LLP to survive for another decade. And in the process, the emerging Power-Points and rump partners meetings would shed light on the current thinking of what firms in peril—and others merely facing the broader economic turmoil—might do to right themselves.

In all, 44 players, 14 judges and assorted hangers-on participated in the game last weekend at Indiana's Maurer School of Law. What emerged from the exercise was a surprising convergence of strategies that gave an outline [of] what a new model might look like. These strategies were not radical, and they attempted to address a variety of much-brooded-about problems among the big firms, including client billing revolts, associate dissatisfaction, peripatetic partners and an unsustainable economic model. What emerged, of course, was governed by the choice of the participants. Included on the roster were members of experimental law firms—both the Summit and Valorem Law Groups—various refugees from big firms, clients with a record of welcoming or demanding different approaches and a variety of agitators for change, most of whom are my friends. But in an era when the heads of major firms talk openly about abandoning the billable hour, and others admit that they've never embraced it, it's getting harder to identify the radicals by their pinstripes.

The competition was more than a game. Hildebrandt, the consulting firm, put up $15,000 in prize money (to be divided among the participating law students) and attached a consultant to each team.

These were the areas of convergence:

- New associates would be paid less, trained more, freed from some or all billable hour requirements, and helped with their law school loan payments. They'd be promoted by achieving a set of "competencies," not seniority. And there'd be fewer of them so leverage would drop. The proposed starting salaries varied from $80,000 to $125,000; bonuses were tied to firm performance. Stepped-up training ran the gamut from nostalgia for the days of "shadowing" senior partners to more efforts to bring associates to deals/depositions/other real-life events that many now only read about. Help with law school debt varied from paying third-year tuition to interest-free loans to experimenting with deferred compensation packages.

  Because of the compressed game schedule, many questions went begging: Who would train; could the firms afford even these reduced pay packages; how would the loan payoffs work; and what would happen to firm structure if the associates, having found an office paradise, chose never to leave?

- Clients would be offered a smorgasbord of alternative fee arrangements, frequently based on the mining of actual billing data. Whenever possible, the firm would offer to share at least a modicum of fee risk as a sign of trust and shared enterprise.

  Clients would be treated to regular evaluation meetings. Their lawyers would learn the intricacies of their business; they'd know their clients even better, as one contestant put it, than "Tom Hagen knew the Corleones." With the proverbial "skin in the game," attorneys would offer "value" and "focus" to their clients, they would build client-friendly wikis to keep them informed, they would monitor retainer-paid help lines to answer questions from line managers, and they would offer client service managers who would, among other things, be the "one throat to choke" in times of crisis or disappointment. And clients all would be offered a flood of secondments.

Questions left open: Might the independent firm become too close to its client to say no; so dependent on a client that it was jeopardized if the client chose to leave; too vulnerable to outsize customer buying power? And what would keep a client loyal, especially if relationship partners left for other firms?

- Partners would have to take an initial compensation hit in the interest of making the rest of the plan work. And partners would not buckle under the pressure of their dissatisfied rainmaking brothers and sisters who threatened to bolt. They would organize into one-tier partnerships; there was no agreement about lockstep or top-bottom salary ratios. To save on overhead, they would move from center city offices to the suburbs or home; they would share secretaries; they would commit to the new order or they could leave.

Unknown: Could the hypothetical firm actually survive the departure of several of its key business generators; when the economy improved and new offers came along, would the glue of "culture" hold or flake?

This is, of necessity, a brief report. Henderson will publish a much more complete discussion and analysis. The value of the exercise is that it gave an organized venue for the airing of grievances and a place for like-minded lawyers to share ideas. We all know that many of these complaints have been sounded for decades. What seems to be different this time is that they are being voiced amid an economic calamity that has called into question whether clients will continue to operate on a business-as-usual basis.

We all know of examples where customers have recently been insistent on changing their arrangements with their law firms; the clients who spoke during the working group sessions at Indiana were not different. They did not speak as supplicants. The existence of this rump agenda is no more powerful than any game; the client demands did not seem like the stuff of fantasy campfires.

To add urgency to this climate, the weekend began with Kearns, the Australian lawyer, offering an amusing but sharply focused description of the American big firm landscape. Here's what he sees:

1. The big firm bubble is about to burst. Choose your pin: angry clients; the exodus of talented people from the practice of law; the competition for associates that firms can't afford; the increased competition for business between and among the firms.
2. The prevalence of bigger and stronger in-house departments.
3. The presence of three generations in the law firm workplace.
4. The global financial crisis, which has broken the old relationships.
5. The utter failure of firms to differentiate themselves to clients or recruits. (And, I might add, to themselves.)

And then he compared this situation to the lot of turkeys. On average, he said, they live 1,000 days. Each day when they wake up, everything seems exactly the same, except that some friends are not around anymore. Everything else seems to be okay. Get to day 1,000, however, and things change, suddenly and with extreme prejudice. He didn't think a lot of firms would die like a slaughtered fowl. Nor did he think that large law firms were going away. But some were in jeopardy, even though they didn't know it. Deaths take a while, and intensive care can prolong all sorts of partnerships.

The question: Is it too late to get healthy?

Or, as the great man wrote, are you busy being born or busy dying?

2. SMALL FIRM: FLEXIBILITY, NIMBLENESS, AND NICHES—AND HOW WILL WE PAY THE RENT THIS MONTH?

a. The Basic Model

HERBERT KRITZER, THE WAGES OF RISK: THE RETURNS OF CONTINGENCY FEE
LEGAL PRACTICE

47 DePaul Law Review 267 (1998)

[Professor Kritzer did both surveys and interviews with a group of Wisconsin lawyers who practiced predominantly using contingent fees. He conducted his survey against the background of news reports of lawyers reaping enormous contingent fees. Kritzer summarized his findings:]

- The returns from contingency fee practice are at best "somewhat" better than what lawyers earn from hourly fee practices. [The article explains that the median hourly compensation for such lawyers was $171; because, of course, contingent fee lawyers don't bill by the hour, Kritzer arrived at this number by dividing fees earned by hours worked.]
- Some, perhaps much of the surplus [over fees earned by hourly rate lawyers] disappears when one takes into account the time and effort contingency fee lawyers devote to screening cases.
- A small segment of cases produces substantial "profits" but few lawyers are able to tap into this segment on a routine basis. ["[T]he top ten percent of the cases . . . tend to produce the significant profits, [but] the typical contingency fee practitioner can expect even the remaining ninety percent of the cases to produce fee premiums amounting to twenty five to thirty percent over what hourly fee work generates. The high proportionality comes from locating a small segment of the cases that produce extremely good returns on the lawyers' investment of time. Some lawyers are able to cherry pick the good cases; others handle large volume of cases in order to find the occasional very profitable case. Relatively few lawyers ever see "the really big one." One of the lawyers observed as part of the study had been doing plaintiffs' contingent fee work for twenty years, had a very successful practice, and had never collected a fee of over $100,000 on a case."]

b. Adaptations

MARK DONALD, JUDGING AMY?

Texas Lawyer, May 3, 2004, at 1

Talking about it seemed easier with Kimberlee Norris—a woman, a lawyer, someone with whom they could entrust their deepest confidences, their fragile psyches.

Norris recounts that the two prospective clients told her strikingly similar stories of betrayal: Both women alleged that, as minors, they were members of the same Jehovah's Witnesses (JW) church when each was sexually assaulted by a different male congregant. After each reported the incident to church elders, as members are instructed to do to help cleanse the church of "sin," these lay ministers initiated an investigation. But these investigations, which applied an Old Testament burden of proof, enabled the same result—the alleged perpetrator was protected, and the victim not believed. In fact, the women said elders told them that if they repeated the allegations to church members or secular authorities, they risked possible "disfellowshipping"—excommunication from the church and God.

Norris found these allegations so "outrageous" she searched the Web site www.silentlambs.org, a group that assists the survivors of alleged JW abuse. She then contacted silentlambs' founder, Bill Bowen, a former church elder. Bowen says that the religion's organizational structure is so intricate, its apocalyptic vision so unconventional, "it takes up to six months to get a lawyer up to speed." In Norris, a self-described "preacher's kid" who had briefly attended Bible study sessions with Jehovah's Witnesses as a teenager, Bowen found someone ahead of the curve.

A partner in the Fort Worth, Texas, firm of Love & Norris, she had some success suing institutions for their negligent supervision of sexually abusive employees. After Bowen began referring prospective clients to her from silentlambs and she enhanced her "Internet presence," Norris was staggered by the number of calls she received from would-be plaintiffs—so many that her practice now is exclusively dedicated to molestation litigation.

"I began evaluating these cases in July 2002 and talked to my 1,500th alleged victim on March 28, 2003," she says. "After I reached 2,000, I stopped counting."

Culling these numbers meant coming up with a rigid profile of what kind of case to take and where.

With a plethora of cases to choose from, Norris and partner Gregory S. Love could afford to be picky. Immediately they "tossed out 80 to 90 percent" of the JW cases, she says, because they did not fall within the "numerical statute of limitations."

In Texas, when conduct involves the sexual assault of a child, §16.0045 of the Civil Practice and Remedies Code requires that a person must bring a suit for personal injuries no later than five years after the victim's 18th birthday, the date of majority.

Love & Norris also decided only to take cases where they could prove the church knew its member was a perpetrator and placed him in a position of authority anyway. "Sexual molestation cases are like dog bite cases," Norris says. "Every dog gets one bite, every perpetrator gets one kid. We only take extreme cases where molestation has been reported to the congregation and the organization gives him its blessing by giving him authority."

The firm has filed 57 suits across the country, including two in Texas, joint venturing the litigation with Houston's Fibich, Hampton & Leebron. One petition often reflects another, alleging that the church structure is so strictly hierarchical, its control over its elders and members so absolute, that each level of the JW organization, from top to bottom, should be treated as the "alter ego of the other."

Pleading causes of action that include vicarious liability and negligence, Love & Norris hopes to prove that the Watchtower Bible and Tract Society, the official name of the New York-based Jehovah's Witnesses organization, negligently performed the duty it had undertaken to investigate reports of child sexual abuse and discipline offenders.

Although Love & Norris filed cases in other states first, a case in Amarillo, Texas, has progressed the fastest. On March 29, Judge Patrick A. Pirtle of the 251st District Court in Potter County allowed Norris & Love's client to partially survive a motion for summary judgment in Amy B. v. Watchtower Bible and Tract Society of New York Inc., et al. (Amy B.'s last name has been protected by the court from disclosure.)

Marvin W. Jones, a shareholder in Amarillo's Sprouse Shrader Smith who represents the Jehovah's Witnesses organization at the congregational (Amarillo-Southwest and Dumas) and national (New York and Pennsylvania) levels, has offered a spirited defense against Amy B.'s suit. Collectively representing all the "Watchtower defendants," he wrote in a motion for summary judgment that his clients owed no duty to protect Amy B. from the crime of a congregant. Besides, he argued, the First Amendment also bars the suit.

Ronald T. Spriggs, an Amarillo solo, represents defendant Larry Kelley, who pleaded guilty to a charge of indecency with a child (Amy B.). In answering Amy B.'s petition, Spriggs filed a general denial on his client's behalf. But before Spriggs began his representation, Kelley filed a pro se answer to Amy B.'s civil suit in which he wrote "there were only two (2) instances of sexual contact" with the plaintiff.

Because Amy B. presents compelling factual, procedural and constitutional questions, its resolution likely will have repercussions in JW molestation litigation across the country. But the Watchtower defendants claim they should not be held liable for doing more than most churches would do under similar circumstances: making good-faith efforts to discipline congregants who succumbed to sin. With so much at stake, each side has, in essence, declared war on the other.

"It's going to be a long, bloody battle," Bowen says. . . .

"We are just at the front end of these cases," Norris says. "And both sides are loaded for bear."

DEBORAH ROSENTHAL, THINKING BIG, STAYING SMALL: EVEN IN TODAY'S
LEGAL MARKET YOU CAN RUN A HIGH-PROFILE PRACTICE WITH
FEWER THAN TEN LAWYERS

California Lawyer, May 2008

With all the attention paid to the AmLaw 100, it may come as a surprise to learn that lawyers can have intellectually challenging — and financially rewarding — careers without joining the faceless ranks of mid-level associates. With a little luck and a lot of ingenuity, it's still possible to think big and stay small.

Todd Noah's career is a good example. Five years out of law school, Noah felt disenchanted with his job as a big-firm intellectual property lawyer in San Francisco. It wasn't the work, Noah says. IP was all he ever wanted to do. What got to him — and to his colleague, Michael Dergosits — were the firm's long hours, layers of bureaucracy, and office politics.

"We started talking to other lawyers around town who were unhappy with their practices," Noah recalls. "We had monthly dinners and discussed starting a new firm, or beefing up someone else's IP department. But they just didn't have the guts to jump. It was too risky for them."

So in 1993, Noah and Dergosits set out on their own, taking a number of their clients with them. One of those clients, a company producing a liquid egg substitute, was engaged as a defendant in patent litigation with competitors over its manufacturing process. That case kept their fledgling practice, Dergosits & Noah, going for two years.

Then came the Internet boom. "We hit it at the right time," Noah says. "We just got swept up." In addition to representing a number of small companies seeking patent applications, the tiny firm landed Netscape Communications as a defense client in a high-profile patent-infringement lawsuit filed in 1997 by Wang Laboratories. Less than a year later, a federal judge dismissed all claims in the case; an appellate court affirmed. By the time of the dot-com bust in 2000, Dergosits & Noah had built a reputation strong enough to generate steady work.

Resourcefulness also is critical to a small firm's ability to compete. David M. Birka-White of San Francisco demonstrates the point. Since 1979, Birka-White has represented homeowners against the manufacturers of allegedly defective building materials. But he found he couldn't continue to represent clients in individual cases and still maintain a viable practice.

"No homeowner can pay an attorney $300 an hour or more to litigate a $10,000 problem," Birka-White says. "And no lawyer can take that case — which may involve an extremely complex product failure — because he's going to get a third of the way into it and discover he's working for free."

Class actions seemed to provide a solution. The trick was finding a way to show the commonality of damages needed to persuade a judge to grant class certification. So, using a bevy of scientific experts with various specialties, Birka-White developed a protocol for identifying defective building materials. Stephen Oroza, an attorney friend and colleague, figured out that the scope and breadth of the damages could be calculated on a classwide basis using sample groups within the class; statisticians could then determine an aggregate award.

The model proved to be a success. Nearly 30 years after Birka-White founded his own firm, he and Oroza now work together representing home-owners in class sizes that typically number in the thousands.

Gradual Growth

Strong small firms can also be built in more traditional ways. Before they hung out a shingle in 1998, Ed Swanson and Mary McNamara of Swanson, McNamara & Haller built their reputations in the white-collar criminal-defense bar, working for the federal public defender's office in San Francisco.

"We wanted to do our work in the public sector representing indigent clients, but neither of us thought we'd be there for an entire career," McNamara says. "We got to know the bench very well, and got to know a lot of other practitioners just from being in court every day" Those relation-ships garnered referrals that later helped their small practice succeed.

Of course, small firms tend to grow when they are successful. In 1991 Clifford Hirsch started a sole practice in Walnut Creek after separating from two other attorneys in a first-party insurance defense firm. The case work, which often ensued from natural disasters such as mudslides and earthquakes, had always been statewide. So in 2004, when Southern California wildfires caused a surge in cases, Hirsch contacted Kellene McMillan, the daughter of a family friend who had worked in his office after being admitted to practice and was then in San Diego. His timing was perfect.

McMillan had grown dissatisfied with her job at a midsize insurance defense boutique. "Most of the people there were big-firm escapees who couldn't really shake the mentality," McMillan says. When Hirsch telephoned to ask if she would open a San Diego office for him, she jumped at the opportunity.

Hirsch says he intended the office to be a one-person branch, but "the minute clients realized we had somebody in San Diego, we attracted more Southern California work." With Hirsch's blessing, McMillan began hiring friends from among former colleagues and staff at her previous firm. "If you know someone who does good work and is a friend of yours, why wouldn't you want that person to work for you?" Hirsch asks.

Biting Off Only What They Can Chew

At the outset, running a small firm as a successful business requires careful appraisal and management of resources. Birka-White says he considers a large number of potential cases but takes relatively few, typically litigating fewer than ten class actions at any time, each ranging in value from a few million dollars to a few hundred million.

"We never file a case without serious investigation and scientific analysis," Birka-White says. "It's not uncommon to spend tens of thousands of dollars to research a product before deciding to take a case. Obviously, if I do that, it's because I think there's a common defect. But if I find there isn't a common defect, I have to be ready to walk away."

Keeping overhead low also is essential, which is why Birka-White has no employees. "We use independent contractors for support," he says. "Over the years, I've developed close working relationships with professionals who can respond immediately to my needs on a full-time basis."

The ability to function with little or no staff is a testament to the effectiveness of law office technology. Says Todd Noah: "It's not like it used to be, when you got a draft, marked it up, and gave it to the word processor to do overnight. With email, scanning, even document production — because Ethel Adobe Acrobat [program] Bates-labels documents for you — it's so easy." Electronic filing, mandatory in the federal courts where Noah files most of his IP cases, also cuts down on the need for clerical services. "You don't even have to serve your adversaries," he says. "It's really streamlined."

Minimal staff also means minimal need for attention to personnel matters. "At this point, we're sort of self-sustaining," says Noah, who serves as his firm's managing partner but estimates he devotes only 10 percent to 15 percent of his time to management duties. "Issues do come up," he concedes. But if a client wants a billing alternative, I just go next door to see Michael. We talk about it and it's done. I don't need a two-thirds majority vote."

McNamara, whose San Francisco criminal-defense practice consists of four attorneys and two support staff, concurs. "The machinery of a large firm dictates that you have to take on bigger and bigger projects and charge higher and higher rates," she says. "And that has an effect on who can afford you and what kind of cases you get."

Equally important to the success of a big-thinking small firm is a realistic understanding of the organization's upper limits. Swanson, McNamara & Haller, for instance, typically represents individual executives or witnesses involved in SEC or U.S. Attorney investigations, leaving institutional clients to the larger firms. . . .

Flexibility and Diversification

Cooperating with big-firm competitors can help small firms stay afloat, but it makes them vulnerable to abrupt changes in the law, the legal market, and the industries they serve. Dergosits & Noah, for example, frequently provides IP expertise to bigger litigation firms. Thus it lost a sizable amount of work in 2005 when Howrey merged with Clements, O'Neill, Pierce, Wilson & Fulkerson, a Houston-based IP boutique.

Kellene McMillan has seen similar effects from consolidation in the insurance industry. "Companies go under all the time, or your friends in the industry might retire or get downsized," she says. On the other hand, when in-house counsel leave one company, they typically go to another, and that can add new business just as quickly for small firms they use for support.

In part, small firms navigate these changes the same way larger firms do: by diversifying. Although 95 percent of the Hirsch firm's work is still first-party insurance cases, Hirsch recently hired an attorney with a product liability defense book of business. The firm now also defends bicycle-helmet manufacturers and automobile dealers who have been sued under California's "lemon law." . . .

Birka-White manages his plaintiffs firm with a similar approach. Even though he and Oroza have worked together for more than two decades, "Steve's not my partner," Birka-White says. "We joint-venture everything. On each case, we have a separate agreement on how we're going to divide up the work and the fees, which means we can divorce each other at any time. We stay together because we want to be together."

At the San Diego office of the Hirsch firm, McMillan—the mother of three sons—says she finds the small-scale flexibility particularly helpful when her husband, a Navy reservist, is away from home. "We work like a team," she says of Hirsch in Walnut Creek. "We're aware of each other's cases. We meet weekly, and our computer system is synced so everyone knows what everyone's doing at all times. We all cover for each other if we feel overwhelmed."

Love What You Do and Who You Work With

Attorneys in small firms usually appreciate the opportunity to wear many hats. "Everybody here has tried at least a couple of cases," Hirsch says. "Not many coverage shops can say that. Being a small office, we didn't have the luxury of segregating duties—and that became a bonus instead of a handicap." . . .

Small Firms, Big Ideas

Firm:	Dergosits & Noah	Birka-White Law Offices	Swanson, McNamara & Haller	Clifford Hirsch
Founded:	1993	1981	1998	1991
Offices:	San Francisco and Santa Rosa	San Francisco	San Francisco	Walnut Creek and San Diego
Attorneys:	9 (including 5 of counsel)	3 (including 1 of counsel)	4	7
Staff:	2	0	2	4
Practice Areas:	IP litigation, patent preparation and prosecution, counseling/opinion work	Defective building materials class actions	White-collar criminal defense, complex civil litigation	Insurance coverage opinions and litigation, landslide litigation, construction defect and product liability defense

3. CONVERGING HEMISPHERES?

NOTE

One of the first readings in these materials—the classic study of Chicago lawyers by Heinz and Lauman (in Chapter 1)—presented a picture of American lawyers not as members of a unified profession but as belonging to two "hemispheres." When one of the authors followed up the 1975 study some 20 years later, he found evidence of some blending of the hemispheres. The next reading presents anecdotal evidence that the trend may be continuing. Consider why that might be so.

TRESA BALDAS, BUSINESS TURNS TO PLAINTIFFS LAWYERS

National Law Journal, July 11, 2005, at col. 4

Though once considered a thorn in the side of corporate America, plaintiffs attorneys say big businesses are hiring them with increasing frequency to help fight their legal battles.

For example, in Florida, personal injury lawyer Jack Scarola was the lead counsel in billionaire Ronald O. Perelman's recent $1.4 billion win in a securities fraud suit against investment bank Morgan Stanley.

In New York, personal injury attorney Bob Clifford of Chicago's Clifford Law Offices is representing General Electric Co.'s insurance arm in the World Trade Center litigation where insurers are suing American Airlines and airport security to recoup costs paid out for damages from Sept. 11.

And in Illinois, asbestos litigator Jeff Cooper's Chicago firm CooperSimmons, which has seen an "explosion of interest from corporations," recently formed a business-to-business, contingency fee-based litigation practice in partnership with New York's Hanly Conroy Bierstein & Sheridan.

"Corporate America is more willing now to dance with the devil — that being your plaintiffs lawyers — in bet-the-company cases to represent them because there is no longer the stigma that there used to be," said Scott Marrs, an intellectual property lawyer with Houston's Beirne Maynard & Parsons who helped a company win a $130 million verdict in a patent case involving a vegetable slicer two years ago.

"You would never, ever find a corporation hiring a plaintiffs lawyer 20 years ago to represent it in litigation," Marrs said. "It's a new phenomenon."

In the past, attorneys note, most business-to-business lawsuits were handled by traditional, full-service law firms that charge by the hour, as well as large defense-oriented firms with strong ties to the business community. Hiring a plaintiffs lawyer, such as a wrongful death or personal injury attorney, was considered taboo.

But that stigma has subsided, they assert, mainly because of two factors: rising legal fees, which have prompted companies to look for less expensive legal options; and tort reform, which has forced plaintiffs attorneys to get more creative with their services.

"I think that in part, this is a response to what we all see as a mounting assault on the tort system and a means by which to begin to build into our practices a safeguard against some draconian tort reform measures," said Scarola, the lead attorney in the Perelman case. "It's not business seeking out the skills of personal injury lawyers, but us going after them as a safeguard."

Scarola, a litigator with West Palm Beach, Fla.'s Searcy Denney Scarola Barnhart & Shipley, said Jenner & Block recruited him in 2001 to assist in Arthur Andersen litigation, and then in the Perelman case, both in Palm Beach, Fla. He said his name came up as someone to consider as local counsel.

Jerold Solovy, chairman of Chicago-based Jenner & Block, recalls bringing Scarola on board. He said that calling on a personal injury litigator to handle a complex business matter didn't concern him.

Instead, he saw Scarola's trial experience as an asset. "What you want is somebody who can try cases. Mr. Scarola knows how to try cases. That's why we picked him," Solovy said.

Ready for the Jury

Scarola said that in recent years he has seen a growing reliance upon lawyers with personal injury skills to present business matters before juries. Of course, he speaks from personal experience.

In the Perelman case, Scarola said he had to simplify complex business concepts before the jury and show how Morgan Stanley covered up the failing finances of Sunbeam Corp. so Perelman would sell his Coleman camping-equipment company to Sunbeam in exchange for cash and Sunbeam shares. Accustomed to explaining complicated medical procedures in his personal injury cases, Scarola said he was prepared for the challenge.

Scarola's tactics worked. The jury in May hit Morgan Stanley with $850 million in punitive damages and $604.3 million in compensatory damages. *Coleman Parent Holdings v. Morgan Stanley*, No. 2003 CA 005045 AI (Palm Beach Co., Fla., Cir. Ct.).

Attorneys for Morgan Stanley include Mark Hansen of Kellogg, Huber, Hansen, Todd, Evans & Figel in Washington and Joseph Ianno of Carlton Fields' West Palm Beach office. Neither was available for comment.

While many attorneys agree that corporations are turning to the plaintiffs bar, they don't agree on why.

Michael Slack, managing partner at Slack & Davis, a personal injury and wrongful death firm in Austin, Texas, said it is not that tort reform is driving plaintiffs lawyers to big companies, as some suggest, but that big businesses are chasing plaintiffs lawyers.

"I think somebody held a business conference somewhere and said, 'You know what, we're not being very smart about shopping for legal services if we're not hiring contingent fee-based plaintiffs lawyers," Slack said. "We were chuckling about it in-house the other day . . . where it seems the inner circles at businesses are now saying, 'The same people that we've been bashing in the tort arena are our new best friends.'"

Slack said that in recent months, his personal injury firm, which deals mainly with aviation accidents and pharmaceutical cases, has been inundated with phone calls from businesses seeking contingent fee-based legal services.

"We've had more inquiries in the last six months than we have had since this firm was established," said Slack, who is planning to hire a top commercial litigator to handle this new demand for litigation services. "All of a sudden, the negative connotations that have been directed to contingent-fee lawyers over the last decade seem to have been overcome."

Then again, some plaintiffs firms find they are not up to the challenge.

Patent attorney Fred Tecce, who specializes in contingency fee-based commercial litigation, said he has seen plaintiffs attorneys cutting in on his turf in recent years.

"From what I've seen and know from talking to some of my clients, they're seeing an uptake in med-mal guys who are worried about tort reform," Tecce said. "A lot of these med-mal guys are trying to fashion themselves and repackage themselves as business-to-business litigants. But I don't mind the competition at all."

Tecce of McShea & Tecce in Philadelphia noted that in the last few years, he's picked up four referrals from plaintiffs law firms that took a shot at commercial contingency fee cases, but found out they couldn't handle them.

"If these guys take these cases, they take one of them. They get burned. And I end up getting referral work," Tecce said.

It's the Big Verdicts

But defense attorney Levi McCathern of McCathern Mooty in Dallas believes corporations are selling themselves out to the plaintiffs bar. He argues that plaintiffs attorneys are winning businesses over because of the lucrative verdicts they get.

Companies are impressed with these big verdicts, he said, so they're willing to hire plaintiffs attorneys to take on their big cases.

"I just think they'd be better served by using the defense bar," McCathern said. "Commercial litigation has long been the work of the defense bar. But not anymore. . . . I've seen it go south."

McCathern also questions plaintiffs attorneys' motives in helping corporate America.

"Sometimes most of the good plaintiffs attorneys are what I call true believers — they really believe that corporations are the evil empire that control the country," McCathern said. "It's interesting to see them get on their side and work these kinds of cases. I certainly think that tort reform has placed them in that position."

There's no denying that, contend several plaintiffs attorneys.

"There's no question that this business model can help firms become tort-reform proof," said Cooper, whose Chicago firm started the business-to-business litigation practice two months ago.

Since then, he said the firm has received more than 200 phone calls from companies of all sizes looking for legal representation. He said the stigma of hiring plaintiffs lawyers appears to be over.

"One CEO we spoke to in his office said, 'Having you guys in my office is like Nixon going to China,'" Cooper said. "We're seeing a loss of that stigma. When we first entered, we thought we'd have to sell a lot harder, and that hasn't been the case."

He said further, "There's a niche in this market that we're able to fill, and I expect other plaintiffs firms to do this."

Despite plaintiffs lawyers' claims that corporations are warming up to them, officials at many companies declined to comment for this story.

Officials at Industrial Risk Insurers, General Electric's insurance arm in the World Trade Center litigation against American Airlines, declined comment on why they picked Clifford as counsel.

C. CHANGES AND CHALLENGES — DEVELOPMENTS IN LITIGATION FINANCE

NOTE ON BAR DEREGULATION AND LITIGATION FINANCE

The readings thus far in this chapter have suggested, first, that recent economic instability has revealed a weakness in the large firm business model and, second, that the modern plaintiffs' bar has reorganized itself in ways that place it on a more even footing with its traditional adversary—the insurance and corporate bar. The next two readings suggest that one factor in this reorganization was the deregulation of the bar, a deregulation that has parallels in other areas of economic life. That deregulation allowed lawyers to experiment with new financing models. As with any deregulation, it's fair to ask what was lost as well as what was gained.

1. THE RECONSTITUTION OF THE PLAINTIFFS' BAR

Mark Ballard, The Little Ad That Changed Everything: 1977 Case Had a Profound Impact on U.S. Law Practice

National Law Journal, September 23, 2002, at A1

Advertisment

DO YOU NEED A LAWYER?

LEGAL SERVICES AT VERY REASONABLE FEES

- Divorce or legal separation--uncontested [both spouses sign papers]
  $175.00 plus $20.00 court filing fee

- Preparation of all court papers and instructions on how to do your own simple uncontested divorce
  $100.00

- Adoption--uncontested severance proceeding
  $225.00 plus approximately $10.00 Duplication cost

- Bankruptcy--non-business, no contested proceedings

  Individual
  $250.00 plus $55.00 court filing fee

  Wife and Husband
  $300.00 plus & 350.00 court filing fee

- Change of Name
  $95.00 plus $20.00 court filing fee

  Information regarding other types of cases furnished on request

Legal Clinic of Bates & O'Steen
617 North 3rd Street
Phoenix, Arizona 85004
Telephone (602) 252-8888

The ad for Bates & O'Steen was designed to help a low-cost clinic become high-volume.

The day after the U.S. Supreme Court rendered its decision 25 years ago that allowed lawyers to advertise, the losers, the Arizona Bar Association, held a news conference in its Phoenix office. The winners weren't invited, but John R. Bates and Van O'Steen showed up anyway.

The media quickly turned away from the bar's hand wringing over the future of the legal profession and grouped around the law partners whose single ad for their low-cost legal clinic had prompted the challenge. Their first question, O'Steen recalls, was how would *Bates v. State Bar of Arizona*, 433 U.S. 350 (1977), change the legal profession.

O'Steen says the answer was easy. "We said we expected that consumer-based law firms would grow much larger thereby opening the legal system to people who otherwise have no access and that growth would be based on advertising," he says. "And that has happened."

What O'Steen did not foresee was a revolution that changed the legal profession to a service-oriented business requiring the same marketing, investment, cost control and production systems as any other profession. The changes spurred by *Bates* have taken hold across the legal community, even in the old-line firms that once tried to get the decision reversed.

"I would have never predicted the extent of advertising among the large corporate firms. It seems almost everybody is advertising now, in one way or another," says O'Steen, whose Phoenix firm became Van O'Steen and Partners after Bates moved to Ohio.

O'Steen and Bates, former attorneys with the Maricopa County Legal Aid Society, opened their legal clinic in March 1974. Their aim was to provide legal services to low- and moderate-income persons who did not qualify for government-funded legal aid. They kept their fees modest by relying on paralegals, standardized procedures and boilerplate forms. Because of the low return, they needed a lot of clients to break even. O'Steen says they realized that only advertising would increase volume.

Using ads would mean challenging the American Bar Association's 1908 ban on lawyer advertising, adopted by the states. They went ahead, ordering up a display ad from the *Arizona Republic*.

Justice William Blackmun, delivering the 5-4 opinion on June 27, 1977, wrote that the State Bar Association of Arizona could not prevent lawyers from advertising for "routine legal services" because such advertising "helped to inform the public and allocate resources in our free enterprise system."

Some lawyers see the case as having changed the course of U.S. law practice.

"Before *Bates*, the legal profession had as its hallmark community service, helping people," says Benjamin H. Hill III, a partner in Hill, Ward & Henderson of Tampa, Fla. "It's now about dollars and cents. We started down that slippery slope with advertising. Clearly, it's a sign of the times, but I would say that *Bates* is the single most important decision in our profession."

For almost 20 years, as president of the Florida Bar Association, and chairman of its special committee on lawyer advertising, Hill spearheaded that state's effort to rein in lawyer advertising through regulation that was challenged and, for the most part, overruled in court.

Bar associations around the country closely monitored the Florida experience and were prepared to follow its example, had the state bar been successful.

The days in which personal injury attorneys sponsor cars in demolition derbies or drive hearses to shill no-frill wills have passed, Hill says, because the marketplace proved that those efforts do not bring in new clients.

But he is still a foe of advertising, which, he says, undermines public confidence in the legal system.

There is evidence that something is undermining it. A Columbia University Law School survey on attitudes toward lawyers, released in April, found that 60% of the respondents said lawyers were overpaid, 39% thought they were dishonest and 41% felt they did not perform a beneficial role.

As public confidence erodes, fewer people may rely on the rule of law to resolve disputes, Hill says. "In terms of the atmosphere, the *Bates* minority had it pegged." Dissenters on the high court predicted that legal ads would soon include uncheckable claims that would erode public confidence in the law.

Hill recalls an ad by Hollywood, Fla., attorney David W. Singer, in which a young boy is nicked while sitting in a barber's chair. The boy whips his head around and tells the barber, "If you do that again, I'll call David Singer."

"That's just the wrong message to convey," Hill says. "That's generating litigation. If people feel like they have a case they'll have no trouble finding a lawyer. But some of these ads suggest that they can make money if they have taken fen-phen or something even if they felt no ill effects and had no bad results."

The settlement fund for the diet drug fen-phen has ballooned from $1 billion to $13 billion. Wyeth, the compound's manufacturer, asserts that it traced the increase to the mass recruitment of new claimants through television and newspaper advertising.

The new claimants have shown no injuries from taking the drug and would not have otherwise been involved in the suit, the company maintains.

Bates "has changed the picture of supply and demand. More lawsuits today are prompted by missives sent out by lawyers than come from people with complaints," says Victor Schwartz, general counsel for the American Tort Reform Association in Washington, D.C. "Advertising gets away from the merits of the claim and goes more to the results possible. It creates a lottery mentality."

The lawyer who had the barbershop ad, however, says humor in his advertisements is an effective way of portraying himself as accessible and willing to "take on the fight of the common man."

Unlike the clientele Hill has targeted through work at charity events and at the country clubs, Singer asserts, low- and moderate-income people usually don't have social connections with lawyers and therefore find the legal system closed to them. They want attorneys they can trust and can view as friends. They don't play golf with lawyers, so they have to rely on advertising, says Singer, of Singer, Farvman & Associates.

"It's so hypocritical," Singer says. "These guys market at the country club but they call marketing on television crass and demeaning to the profession.

You see tasteless advertisements, yeah, maybe for a while, but the marketplace will induce those lawyers to pull those ads because they won't be effective."

Singer and his television ads were the target of ridicule by Hill and his committee during the Florida bar's efforts in the 1980s and early 1990s to overturn or, at least, restrict lawyer advertising. Not only was the established bar seeking to overturn *Bates*, but trial lawyer groups also preached that attorney advertising was bad and must be outlawed again.

"Public confidence, professional credibility, unfilled expectations — these phrases are all stalking horses," says Singer. "This has always been a money issue. Lawyer advertising was taking business away from these firms that used traditional marketing methods.

"The days of fighting lawyer advertising are over. Times have changed. There are younger, newer members on the bar associations and the trial lawyer associations who aren't afraid of competition. The genie is out of the bottle."

Arnie Malham, president of CJ Advertising LLC in Nashville, Tenn., which produces advertising campaigns for 26 personal injury lawyers in 60 markets around the country, points to the 2000 winter convention of the Association of Trial Lawyers of America (ATLA), held in New Orleans, as the time and place that *Bates* won wide acceptance.

"From the moment I got to New Orleans, and throughout my stay, I and the lawyers I represent went from feeling like outsiders to honored guests," Malham says. "Dinners, drinks, lunches, offers of plane rides, promises of riches, and 'good ole boy' lawyers carrying on as if we had all been best friends for years. Handshakes, pats on the back, laughing with us, instead of at us."

The reason was that the lawyers who advertise had shown an ability to bring in new clients, he says. During a July 22 speech at this year's ATLA convention in Atlanta, Malham said that business concerns overshadowed the profession's previous prejudices.

"The 'good ole boys' became known as the 'litigators' and the 'ambulance chasers' became known as the 'marketers' or 'contract fulfillers,'" he said. "Now, in a new era, many of them have teamed together to go after every pharmaceutical with a side effect and every product that ever hurt a hair on your head." In an interview, he says, "I suspect this trend will continue. Litigation firms will continue to court advertising firms in order to generate referrals." . . .

"The *Bates* decision has been far more profound in the development of marketing in large corporate law firms," Hornsby says. With the old-line firms embracing the business model, just as Bates and O'Steen did 25 years ago, the survival of lawyer advertising seems assured, he says.

For two decades, *Bates* was under continual attack. About a dozen appeals to the Supreme Court, from a dozen different angles, attempted to chip at it. All went down to defeat, mostly 5-4.

"The right to commercial free speech by lawyers is a very tenuous one that has always been one vote away," says Hornsby, staff counsel for the American Bar Association Division for Legal Services in Chicago. "That's kind of the nuclear bomb of this issue. It's not out of the question that *Bates* will be repealed if there is a change in the court, but we've grown comfortable with the fact that the bomb hasn't dropped in the last 25 years."

Stephen C. Yeazell, *Brown*, the Civil Rights Movement, and the Silent Litigation Revolution

57 Vanderbilt Law Review 1975 (2004)

[The essay recounts a chain of case law leading from *NAACP v. Button*.[1] In *Button* the U.S. Supreme Court struck down a state bar regulation designed to prevent the NAACP from soliciting clients who wished to challenge racial segregation. *Button* proved important in later cases involving the deregulation of lawyer advertising.]

B. The Reconstitution of the Plaintiffs' Bar

Button and its offspring created a deregulatory opening that allowed the plaintiffs' bar to remake itself. It has taken the opening. Three critical things have changed that bar. First, it has increased its modal organizational size. Second, that bar has recapitalized itself. Third, it has specialized. Each of these changes, sketched below, is important. All were facilitated by the deregulation that, in our history, traces itself to *Button*.

The modal size of the practice organization in which U.S. lawyers operate has increased over the past fifty years. Many have watched with a mixture of awe and horror the much-chronicled emergence of the mega-firm, with hundreds or thousands of lawyers. But most lawyers do not practice in such settings. For my purposes the more important change came at the lower end of the practice spectrum. Until 1960 more than half of all U.S. lawyers practiced alone. Some of these lawyers were excellent, fully justifying their folkloric status; many more were marginal, barely scraping by and doing their clients few favors in the process. Describing the situation of this segment of the bar a few years after *Brown*, Jerome Carlin chronicled their meager professional and economic means. Lacking the intellectual or financial capital to take their cases deep into litigation, they were forced to hope for a quick settlement.

In the closing decades of the twentieth century this segment of the bar reconstituted itself in ways that were facilitated by the deregulation that followed from *Button*. Two basic changes occurred. First, the modal practice group increased in size—not from one to a hundred lawyers but from one to a few. In California, a survey conducted by the State Bar in 2001 found that of the lawyers in private practice—almost 80% of all active lawyers—more than half practiced in firms with between two and twenty lawyers. More precisely, 30% of all lawyers in private practice were in firms of between two and five lawyers; 27% of the same group was in firms of between six and twenty lawyers. Patterns obviously differ among regions, and one would expect, all things being equal, that urban practices would be more likely to contain groups of lawyers than those in rural areas. Nevertheless, the slow national disappearance of the solo practitioner tells us that California is not unrepresentative.

The changes represented by this shift in practice demographics are qualitative rather than quantitative and, together with the modest deregulation of practice, transformative. The shift from a solo practice to a six- or

---

1. 371 U.S. 415 (1963) (the case was originally filed in 1957, but detours through several layers of the Virginia and federal courts delayed its arrival in the U.S. Supreme Court).

ten-lawyer firm was enormous not only in crude statistical terms, though it is worth noticing that such a change dwarfs in percentage terms the growth of many of the highly celebrated or condemned mega-firms. More important than the statistical transformation, however, is the potential for mutually supportive practices. Herbert Kritzer's important work in describing the conditions of life in the plaintiffs' bar in Wisconsin shows us how this effect works out in practice. These small practice groups typically work across a spread of case types: some low-fee, high realization cases like workers' compensation representation; some relatively routine vehicle injury cases on a contingent fee, where careful case selection, good investigation, and experience in dealing with the insurance industry and its lawyers will yield a flow of higher but less certain fees; and a case or two characterized by high risk and high potential recovery (for example, a product liability case with uncertain liability but high damages). This diversification of case "portfolio" may not yield enormous returns — Kritzer reports a number of excellent plaintiffs' lawyers who have never collected a million dollar verdict — but it will enable the lawyers involved to make a decent living, at an imputed hourly rate comparable to that of their defense counterparts. One of Kritzer's most striking findings was that the imputed hourly return to these plaintiffs' lawyers (the total return per hour of lawyer time) was just slightly higher than the hourly rates of the lawyers on the other side, paid by the insurance carriers. This finding is headline news in two respects. At the time *Brown* was decided ordinary plaintiffs' lawyers inhabited economic and professional universes entirely different from those of their defense counterparts. Today, some commentators argue that plaintiffs' lawyers as a group grow fat off the land. For my purposes even the finding of equality with defendants' lawyers is big news.

The growth in modal firm size does more than permit economic stability. In most cases it qualitatively improves the legal product coming from these firms. Again, the reasons are relatively easy but very important to see. Apart from financial stability, a lawyer with five or ten colleagues can do a better job on any given case because she has quick and cheap access to others' expertise and experience. Anyone in a law firm or law faculty knows that a five minute conversation with someone who has dealt with a question before will save twenty hours of research. Just as important, a half hour conversation about basic case strategy will often result in an exponentially stronger approach to the entire matter. One of the many important lessons flowing from the litigation team behind the cases leading to *Brown* is that the discussed case is the better-litigated case. The NAACP provided not only a constitutional landmark but also a model for the effectiveness of a small group of plaintiffs' lawyers with slender financing but a deep grasp of litigation strategies. The change in practice groups was not sufficient to produce higher-quality lawyering, but it was probably necessary.

The reference to *Brown* also, however, highlights an important difference between the ordinary plaintiffs' bar and the NAACP lawyers. Although they suffered from deep disadvantages, the NAACP lawyers, because of their basic strategy, had one very significant advantage over the lawyer representing the traffic accident victim: in lawsuits, law is relatively cheap, but facts are typically expensive. As the Margold report[*] recognized, the NAACP could easily dissipate all its funds by trying to use *Plessy* as a lever, attacking unequal funding on a county by county basis. The frontal assault on segregation flowed as much from litigation budgets as from strategic planning or moral vision: by choosing a strategy in which facts didn't matter much — to the point of stipulating, as they did in some cases, that the funding of the dual school systems was equal — they kept litigation expenses down.

That path will not be open to most plaintiffs' firms, because their cases will, by and large, turn on facts rather than on law. Developing facts, particularly in realms where interpretation of facts requires expert witnesses, is expensive. We have chosen a litigation system that requires — and rewards — extensive pretrial investigation and discovery. Lawyers operating on a contingent fee basis and spending substantial sums on discovery have to be well and stably capitalized. This fundamental capital requirement shapes modern practice. Lawyers who are handling a portfolio of contingent fee cases need both diversification and a steady flow of work to handle the capital requirements of effective representation.

Brown via *Button* and *Bates* indirectly addresses this requirement of capitalization. *Bates* (and cases that followed on — allowing lawyers to solicit clients who had suffered specific kinds of harms, and then to advertise generally) allows lawyers to do mass advertising, creating the possibility of a flow of cases into the office. That flow can then be sorted. Cases can be screened along several dimensions: the size of the potential recovery, the strength of the merits, the estimated investment required, and the area of practice involved. The last two criteria are related. It will cost much more for a lawyer to develop or extend an area of practice than it will for her to take a case in a familiar area. Recent interesting work by Dr. Sara Parikh has documented the vigor and effectiveness of the referral system among Chicago plaintiffs' lawyers. Cases regularly move up and down among members of the bar according to the area of expertise and the size of the investment called for. A big-case firm is likely to refer small cases down the ladder, fully expecting that a smaller firm will refer a large case upwards. Referral fees follow this chain. The combination of advertising and a vigorous referral system has thus created a market in claims representation, in which a plausible claim is quite likely to get into the hands of a competent lawyer who can invest the amount necessary to reach a good result for the client. This situation represents a fundamental change in the conditions of legal representation.

Brown did not create the modern plaintiffs' bar. It was certainly not a sufficient cause, and it may not even have been necessary. One cannot say that we would not have found our way to the same point if desegregation had occurred as a result of legislation or a constitutional amendment, or gradual social change. The years in question saw a number of deregulatory moves in fields far from the legal profession: airline travel, contraception and family planning, trucking fees, federal control over broadcast and telephonic communications,

---

*[An earlier portion of the essay described how the NAACP had, before beginning the desegregation litigation, received a report from a consultant — Margold — recommending that the group attack segregation in principle, rather than attacking the unequal funding of thousands of individual white and black schools.]

and numerous other areas now operate under far less stringent regulatory regimes than they did at the time *Brown* and *Button* were decided. It requires no heroic assumptions to believe that we might well have found ourselves in the same place in regard to the legal profession without *Brown* or *Button*. But it is just as important to note that, in our real, contingent world, our path to the present traveled though *Brown*.

It is important so to note because two separate, roughly parallel paths of intellectual and social history moved out from *Brown*. One was what one might call the cultural aspirations of law students and some lawyers: to use law and litigation as a tool of social change, as the plaintiffs in *Brown* had done. The second was the professional arena in which those cultural aspirations might play out. Through *Button, Brown* allowed the reforming of plaintiffs' practices. Most of those changes did not occur in the name of social change as the *Brown* plaintiffs understood that phrase. The lawyers in question were often looking for a more profitable practice rather than a new vision of social justice. But the two were linked together: the plaintiffs' bar could wrap itself in the mantle of defenders and vindicators of rights, even if those rights were subconstitutional. One can see this heritage in the most homely places; in many U.S. cities, buses carry ads — in several languages — that solicit business for plaintiffs' lawyers, who regularly portray themselves as "defenders" of rights.

By the same token, those attracted to the vindication of rights stance could see litigation as a path to accomplish that goal. And, as the plaintiffs' bar gradually reorganized itself, it amassed both the financial and the intellectual capital to conceive of projects grander than the representation of individuals who had suffered injuries on the job or in auto traffic. This is not the place for histories of the environmental or consumer movements, but both of them can lay claim to *Brown* as at least a distant forebear. Both could plausibly claim that they were seeking to vindicate previously unrecognized rights of large groups. Closer to the civil rights movement, both could also claim to be the litigation extensions of affinity groups: Ralph Nader and Co. served as the analogue to the NAACP for consumers; organizations like the Sierra Club and the Natural Resources Defense Council did so for the environmental movement. For my purposes the important connection is all these groups had strategies that sought social change both through affinity-group organization and through litigation. Even more significant, in both cases the litigation movement had two branches. One, funded by affinity group dues (and, later, partially through fee-shifting statutes) sought change that benefited the public at large. Another branch sought what looked more like individual redress — the suit in which an individual plaintiff sought damages for a violation of consumer or environmental laws, vindicating the values they protected by calling the defendant to account. Such cases formed a bridge between the social reform litigation exemplified by *Brown* and the next generation of social reform litigation, which ambiguously combined strands of self- and public interest.

The bridge between these two generations rested on two pylons, one a theory formed while *Brown* was still a gleam in the eyes of Thurgood Marshall, and the other on statutes enacted in the wake of *Brown*'s success. The theory, elaborated by Harry Kalven and Maurice Rosenfield, enabled those who sought damages to describe themselves as "private attorneys general," vindicating the public interest by allowing regulatory statutes to be uniformly and widely enforced. Kalven & Rosenfield's original article described a new function for the still unusual class action. By vindicating group rights such actions, which the authors imagined as based chiefly on regulatory statutes such as securities laws, would harness self-interest to the common good, supplementing the enforcement actions of governmental officials. This is a powerful and attractive idea. In a market economy, one would like to think that individual rights and the public interest can be joined, that one can do well by doing good, and do good by doing well.

This possibility was reinforced by an important change in the financing of some lawsuits—the fee-shifting statute. When the NAACP and its affiliates filed *Brown* and *Button* the cost of litigation, including attorneys' fees was borne by the groups sponsoring the litigation. Indeed, that fact was one of the motivations behind the southern states' strategy restricting solicitation: not only would they prevent "outsiders" from stirring up trouble, as they saw it, but without access to a funding base, even home-grown litigants would be hard pressed to mount a strong case through the inevitable several layers of appeal. Nor did the Supreme Court cooperate. After some early cases in which lower courts awarded attorneys' fees on a "private attorney general" theory, the U.S. Supreme Court held that it was inappropriate for federal courts to use their common law powers in this way absent Congressional authorization. Congress responded promptly with legislation providing for the award of attorneys' fees "in any action or proceeding to enforce a provision [of specified civil rights statutes]". Moreover, the context of the legislation—designed to support plaintiffs' cases—was sufficiently clear that, in spite of the apparently symmetrical command of the statute—that such fees should be awarded to "the prevailing party"—the Court a few years later interpreted this language to mean that the prevailing *plaintiff*, but not prevailing defendants should get such fees. The Court that so decided was probably correct: the image in the Congressional mind was that of the NAACP plaintiffs, and it was unthinkable that, had they lost *Brown* they would have been liable for the attorneys' fees of half a dozen states.

Given my argument, one cannot imagine the fee-shifting statutes except in the wake of *Brown* and the more general acceptance of litigation as a form of social and political action. But to appreciate the significance of these statutes, it is worth imagining an alternative history. Suppose, in a parallel universe, the U.S. had judicially or legislatively created a fee-shifting arrangement in cases vindicating constitutional rights. Now imagine the strategic choices facing the NAACP in 1930. It would have been financially as well as strategically possible to attack segregation with the levers suggested in *Plessy v. Ferguson*, arguing that the actual facilities, from school buildings to teachers to textbooks were not equal. That path was the one favored by W.E.B. Du Bois, who feared, correctly as it turned out, that the frontal attack on segregation would consume decades and leave a generation of children to suffer the ill effects of segregated education. One cannot know which course the Association would have taken. But it would have been a choice, not a conclusion dictated as much by the economics of litigation as by moral vision and master planning.

As with so many of the collateral effects of the social revolution instigated by *Brown*, the fee-shifting statutes took on a life of their own, independent of the movement for racial justice but very much a part of the transformation of the legal profession. Scores of federal statutes and a couple of thousand state statutes carried such provisions by the middle of the 1980s. Such statutes have a dual effect: on the one hand they testify to legislative acceptance of social change through litigation, and they cast reflected legitimacy on the portion of the bar — typically representing plaintiffs — who conduct such cases. Second, they provide another source of financing for the bar, and make some number of low-value, higher-risk cases economically feasible. Fee-shifting statutes have not proved to be a magic carpet for claimants, even civil rights claimants. For example, the existence of these statutes has not yet produced a robust plaintiffs' bar in employment discrimination. But the existence of these statutes embeds in U.S. law the idea of a plaintiffs' bar engaged in litigation as a means of social change.

Jahna Barry, Wal-Mart Suit Could Be Boon for Plaintiffs Bar

San Francisco Recorder, June 23, 2004, at 1

A federal judge gave a green light to the historic Wal-Mart sex discrimination class action on Tuesday, a decision that could potentially funnel tens of millions of dollars in attorney fees to the lean nonprofit law firms on the plaintiffs' legal team.

But while the plaintiffs' lawyers celebrated U.S. District Judge Martin Jenkins' class certification ruling, they and other experts noted that it would likely face an almost immediate challenge. In a statement, Wal-Mart spokeswoman Mona Williams said the retailer plans to appeal.

On Tuesday, Jenkins issued an 84-page order that made Dukes v. Wal-Mart Stores, 01-02252, the largest gender discrimination class action case in history. The case alleges that the nation's largest employer paid women less and promoted them less often than male workers. The class may include up to 1.6 million former and current employees who worked at Wal-Mart after December 1998.

Jenkins' order didn't weigh the case's merits. However, the judge noted that Dukes' record-breaking scope doesn't give Wal-Mart a free pass when it comes to the 1964 Civil Rights Act.

"This act forbids gender- and race-based discrimination in the American workplace. . . . Insulating our nation's largest employers from allegations that they have engaged in a pattern and practice of gender or racial discrimination — simply because they are large — would seriously undermine these imperatives," Jenkins wrote, noting that his ruling comes during the 50th anniversary of Brown v. Board of Education.

Wal-Mart downplayed the importance of Jenkins' decision. "Let's keep in mind that today's ruling has absolutely nothing to do with the merits of the case. Judge Jenkins is simply saying he thinks it meets the legal requirements necessary to move forward as a class action," spokeswoman Williams said.

The plaintiffs however, were jubilant about the ruling and cautiously optimistic about the future of the case.

"The court said that there is no exception to Title VII for employers," said Jocelyn Larkin, who is litigation counsel for the Impact Fund, one of the nonprofit law firms working on the case.

The legal skirmishes aren't over yet. Under a relatively new rule, Wal-Mart can appeal the certification within 10 days to the 9th U.S. Circuit Court of Appeals. The court then would have discretion over whether to take up the case.

The publicity about the case may prompt the 9th Circuit to take it up, mused Barry Goldstein, a class action expert at Goldstein, Demchak, Baller, Borgen & Dardarian in Oakland, Calif. Any decision made by the 9th Circuit would probably be appealed to the U.S. Supreme Court, he added.

An eventual victory could fund years of public interest litigation. The non-profits on the legal team are Impact Fund, an 11-year-old Berkeley, Calif.-based nonprofit started by ex-Saperstein, Mayeda & Goldstein partner Brad Seligman; Equal Rights Advocates, a 30-year-old San Francisco firm focused on gender discrimination; and Baltimore-based Public Justice Center, a 19-year-old public interest law firm.

The private firm roster includes San Francisco's Davis, Cowell & Bowe; Santa Fe, N.M., firms Merrit Bennett and Tinkler & Firth; and Cohen, Milstein, Hausfeld & Toll, the Washington, D.C., firm that sued Swiss banks on behalf of Holocaust survivors.

While many experts stressed that the plaintiffs still face a long, hard road, that road probably doesn't end in a trial.

Most class actions settle after the class certification. Employers do so because the cost of litigating and the risk of losing are too great, said civil defense attorney Gilmore Diekmann Jr. of Seyfarth Shaw in San Francisco.

Todd Roberts, a Ropers, Majeski, Kohn & Bentley partner who defends employers and has represented carriers who defend employment class action cases, agreed. "There is a substantial amount of money that is invested by both sides," said Roberts. "The cases are extremely costly to get from the pleading stage to the trial stage."

While several experts declined to speculate about the size of potential attorney fees or any settlement award, the plaintiffs' legal team could be poised to reap a huge windfall in attorneys' fees.

Certainly a big cash infusion from the Wal-Mart case would have a major impact on the nonprofits, one observer said.

"I think it would be extraordinary," said Goldstein, a former colleague of Impact Fund founder Seligman and Larkin. He compared the prospective Wal-Mart fee award to when pharmaceutical heiress Ruth Lilly unexpectedly bequeathed $100 million to Poetry Magazine.

"Obviously ERA and the Impact fund have done a lot on a shoestring," Goldstein said.

The nonprofits themselves said it was too early to talk about settlements—key legal battles have not been fought yet. Any money from a settlement or judgment would be plowed back into the organization to fund more litigation and outreach projects.

"That's what public interests groups do," said Irma Herrera, executive director of the Equal Rights Advocates, which has a budget of $1.6 million. "We take attorneys fees and invest them in future cases."

Like Impact Fund and the Public Justice Center, ERA is funded through a combination of attorney fees, contributions, grants and donations.

The Public Justice Center has a budget of "just over $1 million," says legal director Debra Gardner. The Impact Fund's 2003 annual report shows it had $1.6 million in revenue.

One prominent public interest attorney who declined to speak on the record noted that even if the plaintiffs reaped huge fees from the Wal-Mart case, the money might not trickle down to the nonprofits.

When nonprofit law firms staff large legal cases, their work is usually funded by well-heeled firms, foundations or loans. If the nonprofit law firms involved in the Wal-Mart case have to pay back their benefactors first, they may not see much of any fee award, the lawyer said. The lawyer also noted that while most class actions settle, Wal-Mart is known for not settling cases.

2. EMERGING FINANCE TECHNIQUES AND SPECIAL PROBLEMS

a. Outsourcing, Importing, and Foreign Competition

JENNIFER FRIED, OFFSHORING WORK

National Law Journal, May 17, 2004, at S1, col. 2

Cheap foreign labor has long been a frightening specter for some American industries. But these days, garment makers and steelworkers are not the only ones competing with lower-paid counterparts abroad. Spurred by the slow economy, many in-house legal departments are cutting costs by relying less on U.S. outside counsel and more on lawyers in India, New Zealand, South Korea and other countries where professional salaries are lower.

Some corporations and law firms already send copying, accounting and other back-office functions to offshore providers. But bar association rules, among other things, make sending legal work overseas far more complicated.

Nonetheless, law departments have found ways to use foreign employees — sometimes local attorneys, sometimes nonlawyers — to handle such matters as patent prosecution, legal research and contract drafting. While no one expects the American legal profession to be shipped wholesale to the Asia-Pacific region, the result could be less business for U.S. patent and litigation shops and perhaps even large general practice firms. Forrester Research Inc., a Cambridge, Mass.-based market research firm, predicts that more than 489,000 U.S. lawyer jobs, nearly 8 percent of the field, will shift abroad by 2015.

"There are lots of opportunities to use [foreign] lawyers in place of outside counsel or other lawyers at a lower cost structure," says Suzanne Hawkins, senior counsel at General Electric Co. For two GE businesses — GE Plastics and GE Consumer Finance — savings from those lower rates are adding up. GE began adding lawyers and paralegals to its office in Gurgaon, India, in late 2001. It now has eight lawyers and nine paralegals there and has saved more than $2 million in legal fees that would otherwise have been spent on outside counsel, according to Hawkins.

Working at much lower rates than U.S. lawyers, GE's Indian attorneys draft such documents as outsourcing agreements and confidentiality contracts. Like many companies, GE uses senior in-house counsel in the United States to interview, hire and supervise its overseas lawyers. That should alleviate concerns about unauthorized practice of law, says legal ethicist Geoffrey Hazard Jr., a professor at the University of Pennsylvania Law School. "If they're acting under the supervision of U.S. lawyers, I wouldn't think it would make much difference where they are," he says.

It is not just large conglomerates like GE that use foreign lawyers. The Andrew Corp., an Orland Park, Ill., manufacturer of telecom infrastructure equipment, has cut back on its use of American outside counsel by sending some of its patent application work to Baldwin Shelston Waters, a law firm in Wellington, New Zealand. James Petelle, the company's secretary and vice president of law, says that outsourcing to Baldwin Shelston works particularly well because New Zealand's patent rules are similar to those in the United States. "We wouldn't be afraid to send anything to these guys," says Petelle. (A licensed U.S. lawyer or registered patent agent is not needed merely to write a patent application, although only registered agents can deal with the U.S. Patent and Trademark Office.)

At the Chicago-based outsourcing firm Mindcrest Inc. — which has a subsidiary in India that handles legal work — inquiries from U.S. corporations about outsourcing legal work "have easily tripled in the last year," says George Hefferan III, the firm's vice president and general counsel. Hefferan emphasized that Mindcrest's full-time Indian staffers do not practice law. But much of their work, such as drafting research memos and surveying the laws of various jurisdictions, are duties that American lawyers may otherwise have performed.

Despite the proliferation of cheaper offshore alternatives, many Americans remain skeptical about the quality of work done by foreign lawyers. Citing such concerns as language barriers, time zone differences and the fact that foreign workers are often neither trained in U.S. law nor bound to the same ethical obligations as American lawyers, many attorneys in the United States maintain that U.S. lawyers are irreplaceable. Patent lawyer Gregory Maier, a partner at Alexandria, Va.'s Oblon, Spivak, McClelland, Maier & Neustadt, contends that patent prosecution "is something like brain surgery. You really don't want to necessarily have the low bidder. You want it to be done right."

Another patent lawyer, Carl Oppedahl of Dillon, Colo.'s Oppedahl & Larson, acknowledges that foreign workers may be equipped to prosecute patents for basic inventions. But when it comes to more complex creations, he thinks clients will want to stick with lawyers in the United States.

Even so, many expect the amount of U.S. legal work shipped offshore to keep on growing. That could be bad news for U.S. firms specializing in low-margin patent prosecution or contract work. But Hefferan contends that law departments are not the only ones that could benefit from outsourcing: Law firms also stand to profit from inexpensive offshore legal work. Firms that want to focus on complex matters could use offshore lawyers to help "get away from doing the quote-unquote commodity legal work," he says.

Hefferan says foreign outsourcing could benefit large, multiple-office law firms. Much of the work being done by junior associates, for example, could be handled by offshore workers for a fraction of the price. Use of offshore providers, the thinking goes, would allow firms to continue to handle matters profitably and give clients the discounts they demand.

Howrey Simon Arnold & White, a law firm with a large intellectual property practice, does not currently outsource any of its legal work. But Managing Partner Robert Ruyak says he would not rule it out. "I think that the quality or technical capability [of foreign lawyers] may rival or be even better than in the U.S.," says Ruyak. "The reason we haven't at this point is that there are some things we don't know. If you go to a foreign country, there may be technology transfer issues, legal issues, that hamper your ability to do things."

So while it is hard to imagine junior associates losing their jobs to low-wage workers in Calcutta, India, it is clear that American law firms will need to think about how to keep pace with — or even take advantage of — a pool of foreign legal professionals. And for American lawyers who jokingly refer to their firms as sweatshops, the irony in such a notion may soon fade. Additional reporting from Catherine Aman and Susan Hansen

Anthony Lin, Added Visas Could Encourage U.S. Hiring of Aussie Attorneys

New York Law Journal, May 13, 2005, at 1, col. 5

Though few U.S. law firms stock vegemite or serve flat white coffee in their cafeterias, they have embraced Australian lawyers in almost every other way. They may soon embrace many more.

On Wednesday, Congress passed legislation approving a separate visa category for Australian professionals. The E-3 visa program provides the country with 10,500 slots annually, relieving Australians of the need to jockey with other foreigners for H-1B visas, which are currently limited to 65,000 a year.

The new program, widely regarded as a reward for Australia's support of President Bush's policies, opens the door to a vast expansion of the number of Australians working in the United States, only 900 of whom received H-1B visas last year. . . .

Law, banking and accounting are the top industries for Australians in the United States, she said. . . .

Philip Colbran, a partner at Chadbourne & Parke in New York, said his choice to come to the United States rather than the United Kingdom from Australia 20 years ago was influenced by his view that American legal practice is more innovative and exciting.

"I saw the U.K. and the British legal practice as the past," he said. "The U.S. legal practice seemed to be the future." . . .

Despite earning much more than they would back home, where lawyers start at less than $40,000, young Australians abroad often find the high cost of living and the more stressful work environment make them homesick after a few years, he said.

Which may be just fine with the firms. Wallman said that, among firms in London, the perception that Australian lawyers would eventually go home made them attractive to firms worried about managing their other associates' partnership expectations.

"They're seen as well-trained, hard-working lawyers that won't want to make partner," she said.

But Douglas, whose Australian husband is an associate at Simpson, Thacher & Bartlett, said Australians today may be more willing to stick around. Technology, she noted, has collapsed the vast distance between Australia and America.

"You can be living here and still be connected to home," she said.

MARIE-ANNE HOGARTH, COMING TO AMERICA

San Francisco Recorder, May 9, 2005, at 1

When the founders of King & Wood—now the largest law firm in the People's Republic of China—chose that name 11 years ago, it wasn't about ego.

"Actually, we do not have a Mr. King and a Mr. Wood," says Wei Zhang, a Palo Alto-based partner in the firm. Instead, the firm, hoping to appeal to Western clients, named itself with two Chinese characters that, when pronounced, sound like King and Wood. "I think maybe there is a famous Western lawyer named Mr. Wood," adds Zhang.

King & Wood is one of a handful of foreign law firms that have been setting up shop in San Francisco or Silicon Valley as globalizing U.S.-based firms invade their native lands. Though some are more ambitious, most are content to put just a few lawyers on the ground, with the goal of finding and keeping clients and sending some work home.

"It's a model that many American firms have followed overseas," says legal consultant Peter Zeughauser. "They're offices opened to develop relationships with other law firms and search for work."

As American firms learned when venturing overseas, it isn't easy to gain traction and get noticed in a crowded market.

King & Wood sought to open a beach-head in the Bay Area three years ago by merging with a tiny Fremont firm.

But the PRC firm found its new American partners more interested in joining the wave of Chinese-American returnees—dubbed "sea turtles" in China—eager to get in on China's explosive growth.

In March, Zhang showed up with the vision of using the office to market his firm to U.S.-based companies involved in international transactions.

"We have to try," he says. "In China we are very famous. . . . We are [the] top PRC law firm for four consecutive years." . . .

Even Australia's Minter Ellison, the largest firm in the East, took time to become known here.

The 1,400-lawyer firm, which opened first in New York five years ago before settling upon a San Francisco office, also has offices in Bangkok, Hong Kong, Jakarta, Shanghai, Australia, New Zealand and London.

It now has seven lawyers here.

"It's very, very different going from a market where we are a major brand and a significant player to one where the majority of the market isn't very familiar with us," says Darren Gardner, who heads the firm's San Francisco office. . . .

Finding Friends

The Indian firm Nishith Desai Associates staffs its Silicon Valley office with associates who come from Bombay and Bangalore for three- to four-month stints.

The advantage is the lawyers maintain an "India" perspective, says associate Kartik Ganapathy.

Most of the newcomers are from the Pacific Rim. "We're too far for the European firms," says Fenwick's Pais. And few of the newcomers have the size or reach of the top U.S. firms, much less that of the U.K.'s huge Magic Circle firms.

"Most of the Asian firms are not that big and tend to be country specific," said Pais.

That's why relationships with American firms can make all the difference.

King & Wood is now leasing space in Wilson Sonsini Goodrich & Rosati's Palo Alto office. In exchange, Wilson plans on making its home inside King & Wood's Beijing space when it goes to China.

"We have lots of mutual friends," says Wilson partner Lucas Chang. Though they have no formal relationship, Chang says, the firms refer work to each other.

"Most U.S. companies and venture funds prefer to use a U.S. law firm and have them work with a PRC law firm," says Carmen Chang, a partner in Shearman & Sterling's Menlo Park office. Still, she says, "Most of the PRC law firms can stand on their own two feet."

An example is Jun He Law Offices, whose client list includes Fortune 500 companies Motorola, ExxonMobil, General Motors and Wal-Mart. The firm, with a 10-year-old office in New York, handles some matters on its own, others alongside American lawyers.

Many law firms in China, says Jun He partner Xiaolin Zhou, "look like an association of lawyers getting together to practice and share the cost. But we are more like a real structured partnership."

Jun He has stationed one of its lawyers at Fenwick & West, and the firm also lent a lawyer to Wilson Sonsini, back when Carmen Chang worked there.

"So far, Jun He doesn't have a presence in Silicon Valley," says Jie Chen, the Jun He partner at Fenwick. "I hope the people with the companies and the bankers here will know more about Jun He."

Jun He also boasts that more than 30 of its 200 lawyers are U.S.-licensed.

Zhou says other firms may head here from China. But he doesn't expect too much competition. "Law firms are very busy domestically in China. And also to open an office here, it requires a tremendous amount of talent, time and money." . . .

NOTE ON PRACTICE ORGANIZATION AND LITIGATION FINANCE

What connects the reports on the Wal-Mart class action, the offshoring of U.S. legal work, Asian law firms establishing U.S. offices, and Australian lawyers working in the United States? At one level not much — except that all are signs of accelerating change in the legal profession. That itself is a reminder that the profession you are about to enter is not the one that existed a generation ago.

Dig one layer down, however, and consider how each of these examples is either (1) a response to the challenge of financing litigation or (2) a new challenge for the economic model of one or another practice organization.

1. Do a little Internet research and see if you can imagine why the Wal-Mart plaintiffs assembled the group of lawyers that are handling this case. What problems might you expect to arise as the case moves forward?

2. Why might a U.S. firm be interested in employing Indian lawyers? What threats and what benefits would such offshoring present to, say, the associates at a firm using such a strategy?

3. Many large U.S. firms have established overseas offices, with varying degrees of success. Suppose you are a U.S. client with a legal problem in Australia or China. How would you decide whether to hire King & Wood (for your Chinese legal issues) or whether to hire a U.S. firm with Australian lawyers in it (for your Australian legal problem)?

4. As you read the next selection, consider how it figures in the strategy of the Wal-Mart plaintiffs—and in the concerns of Wal-Mart and its lawyers in that case. Be prepared to explain why the statute discussed in the next section is a key part of both sides' strategies in that case.

b. Fee-Shifting Statutes: Possibilities and Constraints

STEPHEN C. YEAZELL, FROM FEE SPREADING TO FEE SHIFTING

Adapted from Yeazell, Civil Procedure 303-306 (7th ed. 2008)

Thus far we have examined means of spreading attorneys' fees, usually the major expense of litigation. Contingent fees and insurance spread fees among particular groups of litigants; public subsidies spread costs among all citizens. There is one more "spreading" device that begins to shade into fee shifting.

a. The Common Fund

Plaintiff brings a lawsuit that benefits him, but in the process also benefits other similarly situated persons. Should those others have an obligation to contribute to the plaintiff's attorneys' fees? Yes, said the U.S. Supreme Court in the late nineteenth century, applying what it took to be a basic principle of equity. Trustees v. Greenough, 105 U.S. 527 (1881). The origin of this theory came in a suit in which a bondholder sued the bond issuer to force payment of the bond. The plaintiff had, by vindicating his interest, helped fellow bondholders to win a valuable legal right. The *Greenough* court held that the original plaintiff could recover part of his attorney's fee from the *fund* that his efforts had created—the sum from which the other bondholders would be paid. Notice that this *common fund* theory requires that the plaintiff's efforts create some fund from which the lawyer's fee can be deducted.

This judicially created doctrine has proved very important in financing class actions, in which one party or a few parties may represent a class of many thousands. If in such a case the class representatives win a judgment or settlement for money damages, they regularly seek a contribution to their fees from the fund created for the benefit of the class. Observe that the common fund theory does not itself shift fees from one party to the other; instead it requires that all who benefit from the recovery share its cost. The common fund theory *shares* fees among similarly situated persons rather than shifting them to the opposing party in a lawsuit.

Because the common fund theory depends on a fund created by a judgment or settlement against the adversary, it straddles the line between fee spreading and fee shifting. We turn now to purer forms of fee shifting, in which the losing party pays the winner's attorneys' fees. When that happens, the so-called American Rule begins to shade into the English Rule. Since the early 1970s, an increasing amount of U.S. litigation has involved the possibility for such fee shifting, a circumstance that has in turn created sublitigation about the conditions and circumstances for such shifting. Notice that such systems fall into two groups. In their purest form, such fee shifts are symmetrical; that is, the loser pays the winner's fees.

b. By Contract

In the contemporary United States, a common form of symmetrical fee shifting arises from contractual agreements. Parties to contracts may provide that if litigation over the contract arises, the loser will pay the winner's legal fees. A lawyer drafting a contract probably commits malpractice if she does not consider such a clause. Such agreements may in theory be asymmetrical (tenant pays landlord's lawyer if evicted; landlord doesn't have to pay tenant's lawyer if effort to evict fails), but courts and legislatures have often required that such asymmetrical clauses be interpreted as symmetrical — loser pays winner's lawyer. Loan agreements and leases often contain such clauses. When a landlord sues a tenant for rent, the tenant may be ordered to pay both the rent and the fee of the landlord's lawyer. The reverse would be true if the tenant sued the landlord for constructive eviction. If the tenant's lease had such a clause, how would it affect her incentives to sue or defend? One often finds such clauses in contracts where the amount in dispute will be relatively small. Do you see the reason for that pattern?

c. By Common Law

Even when the parties have not agreed to shift fees, there are exceptions to the American Rule. A well-established situation in which one side may pay the other's legal fee occurs when a plaintiff has groundlessly brought a suit; in most states one element of damages in a subsequent action for *malicious prosecution* is attorneys' fees for defending the first suit. Beyond any specific statutory authority lies the inherent power of the court to control behavior designed to thwart the just operation of the legal system. Chambers v. NASCO, Inc., 501 U.S. 32 (1991) (upholding imposition of nearly $1 million in fees on party acting in bad faith). In an influential opinion, the U.S. Supreme Court refused to create a generalized common law doctrine shifting fees in "public interest" cases but said that the legislature remained free to do so. Alyeska Pipeline Service v. Wilderness Society, 421 U.S. 240, 257 (1975).

d. By Statute

Over the past several decades legislatures have enthusiastically accepted the invitation in *Alyeska*. Several hundred federal and several thousand state statutes shift attorneys' fees in various categories of cases. Those "exceptions" to the American Rule have now grown so numerous that some have asked whether the rule still exists in the country that supplied its name. That assessment stretches things — in the most common forms of litigation, fees will still not shift — but it properly highlights the importance of such statutes.

In their most general form, such statutes authorize courts to award fees to parties "in any action which has resulted in the enforcement of an important right affecting the public interest." Cal. Code Civ. P. §1021.5 (West 2007). Most legislatures have been less sweeping, enacting fee shifting statutes to cover particular substantive areas. Such statutes cover many topics — mine safety, truth in lending, consumer product safety, endangered species — but among the most important such federal statutes have been those concerning the enforcement of civil rights. The basic provision is contained in 42 U.S.C. §1988(b):

> In any action or proceeding to enforce . . . [various listed civil rights statutes] . . . , the court, in its discretion, may allow the prevailing party, other than the United States, a reasonable attorney's fee as part of the costs.

The quoted statute speaks of a court's having "discretion" to award a "prevailing party" fees. Judicial interpretation has brought forth interpretations of those terms that a casual reader might not suspect. First, the Court has held that courts should ordinarily award such fees unless special circumstances render it unjust. Blanchard v. Bergeron, 489 U.S. 87 (1989). Second, one might think that the statute created a symmetrical entitlement — that an employee who unsuccessfully sued her employer alleging job discrimination would have to pay the defendant's legal fees. Not so, held Christianburg Garment Co. v. Equal Employment Opportunity Commission, 434 U.S. 412 (1978). In light of the legislative history suggesting that Congress wanted to make it easier, not harder, to enforce civil rights, the *Christianburg* court interpreted such statutes to permit routine attorneys' fees awards to prevailing *plaintiffs* but not to defendants. The exception, in which a two-way shift was permissible, occurred only when the plaintiff's claim was "frivolous, unreasonable, or groundless, or that the plaintiff continued to litigate after it clearly became so." *Christianburg* at 422. Combined, *Christianburg* and *Blanchard* mean that one-way fee-shifting occurs in most successful civil rights claim.

c. Direct Lending

ADAM LIPTAK, LENDERS TO THOSE WHO SUE ARE CHALLENGED ON RATES
───

New York Times, May 19, 2003, at A15

Roberta Rancman was having trouble making ends meet after a car accident with a drunken driver sent her to the hospital five years ago. So she borrowed $7,000 for living expenses from two companies that lend money to people whose only asset is a personal injury lawsuit.

The companies charged Ms. Rancman rates that would make a loan shark blush. On the other hand, they agreed that she would have to repay them only if she won or settled her injury suit.

In 2001, an Ohio appeals court declared the contracts that Ms. Rancman had signed void because the interest was so high. It noted that the lowest possible rate on the larger of the two loans, for $6,000, was at least 280 percent. The Ohio Supreme Court will soon decide the companies' appeal.

The case is the first significant legal challenge to the practices of a flourishing new industry. More than 100 companies nationwide have emerged in the last few years to lend money to people with personal injury lawsuits pending, at rates of 2 percent to 15 percent a month.

At any given time, executives of the loan companies said, the industry has more than $50 million in outstanding loans.

Many legal experts defend the industry. They say these lenders level the playing field between individual plaintiffs and corporate defendants, allowing plaintiffs to outlast their adversaries' delaying tactics and obtain bigger settlements or jury awards.

Other experts say the companies exploit vulnerable people and encourage or prolong litigation in violation of centuries-old but eroding judicial prohibitions against investing in others' lawsuits.

Ms. Rancman eventually received a $100,000 settlement from an insurance company in her injury suit. But she had second thoughts about repaying the two companies and sued to cancel the contracts she had signed with them. She declined to comment on her suit. Her lawyer did not return a call seeking comment.

Robert M. Stefancin, a lawyer for the Interim Settlement Funding Corporation, one of the companies that lent money to Ms. Rancman, declined to say whether the fee was justified.

"I don't know, and I can't answer that question," Mr. Stefancin said.

But he said the courts should not interfere with the company's contract. He noted that because Ms. Rancman's injury case was complicated and uncertain, the company had taken a substantial risk that its money would never be repaid. That risk, he said, means the transaction should not be considered a loan for purposes of the usury laws, which prohibit excessive interest, but only when the borrower's obligation to repay is absolute.

Susan Lorde Martin, who teaches business law at Hofstra University, said many objections to such loans were unfounded. Borrowers are seldom exploited, Ms. Martin said, because they are typically represented by lawyers as a consequence of their injury suits. And such loans do not encourage frivolous litigation, because lenders screen out claims that are unlikely to result in recoveries.

"Who doesn't want these firms?" Ms. Martin asked. "Corporate defendants. Without these firms, corporate defendants have these poor consumers just where they want them."

Thirteen finance companies filed a friend-of-the-court brief in the Ohio Supreme Court defending the industry's practices, if not the interest rates at issue in the case, as "individualized tort reform" that "helps plaintiffs resolve their cases solely on the merits, not on the respective financial conditions of the parties."

Some lenders acknowledge that the fees charged in some cases are excessive and that not every firm is perfectly ethical. . . .

Sherry L. Foley, the chief executive of American Asset Finance, a New Jersey firm, said rates had been falling.

"Competition serves to regulate the industry," Ms. Foley said. "Not long ago, 15 percent a month was standard. On the East Coast now, you're looking at 3 percent to 6 percent."

She said those rates were justified. "In some of these cases, you're going to get zero, and you have to allow for that," she said. "Maybe you're making an 18 to 20 percent return after overhead, the cost of money and the cases you lose. It's not the windfall it seems to be."

CARL JONES, LAWSUIT FINANCE INDUSTRY SURVIVES
APPELLATE-LEVEL CHALLENGE

Miami Daily Business Review, September 20, 2005, at p. 1

The controversial lawsuit financing industry has survived its first known appellate-level challenge in Florida. But the state's 2nd District Court of Appeal criticized the business as "one-sided" and called on the Legislature to consider regulating the industry.

Litigation financing companies, many of them run by lawyers, provide money to personal injury plaintiffs. When the plaintiff wins a verdict or settlement, the company collects the principal plus an often hefty fee. If the plaintiff loses, the company generally gets nothing back.

"The court has no authority to regulate these agreements," the 2nd DCA panel said in its unanimous opinion last week in Victoria Fausone v. U.S. Claims Inc., written by Judge Chris Altenbernd. "However, if The Florida Bar is going to allow lawyers to promote and provide such agreements to their clients, it would seem that the Legislature might wish to examine this industry to determine whether Florida's citizens are in need of any statutory protection."

The 2nd DCA opinion upheld the validity of Victoria Fausone's financing deal with Pennsylvania-based U.S. Claims, under which the company collected $50,000. Fausone, who had tried to void the contract, also was ordered to pay the company's legal costs. . . .

Companies that provide such litigation financing say they are providing money for people who need to pay medical bills and living costs while their lawsuits proceed through the courts. But critics, including some plaintiffs lawyers, consider the practice a form of predatory lending, because these financing deals carry charges as high as 200 percent of the amount advanced. The Florida anti-usury statute prohibits loan companies from charging more than 18 percent annually.

The 2nd DCA panel offered its own critique of such financing arrangements. "The purchase agreement in this case is one-sided and designed to prevent a Florida citizen from having access to a local court or another local dispute resolution forum," the panel wrote. "Such agreements create confusion concerning the party who actually owns and controls the lawsuit, and creates risks that the attorney-client privilege will be waived unintentionally."

Fausone originally filed a negligence suit after she was hit by a dump truck while riding her bike in May 2000. In October of that year, Fausone obtained litigation financing from two companies, Advance Settlement Funding Inc. of Silver Springs, Fla., and Advance Legal Funding of Biloxi, Miss.

In 2001, Fausone contacted U.S. Claims for additional litigation financing. The company gave her $18,000, some of which was used to consolidate her previous loans at better rates. Between August 2001 and November 2002, Fausone went back to U.S. Claims, seeking more money. She eventually obtained a total of $30,000 from the company.

In 2003, Fausone settled her personal injury case for more than $200,000. But in a letter to U.S. Claims, her attorney said Fausone had directed him not to pay the $50,397 she owed the company. . . .

As allowed in the financing contract, U.S. Claims began arbitration proceedings in 2004 in Philadelphia. But Fausone challenged that contract in Pasco Circuit Court. She argued that the contract terms were unconscionable, the financing charges were usurious and that she should not be compelled to enter arbitration. . . .

Fausone did not participate in the arbitration proceedings, despite being offered the chance to take part by telephone. . . .

In a March 2002 ethics opinion, the Bar's board of governors said litigation financing is not unethical, but it frowned on the practice. "The Florida Bar discourages the use of nonrecourse advancing funding companies," the 2002 ethics opinion declared. "The terms of the funding agreements offered to clients may not serve the client's best interests in many instances."

Still, the Bar allowed lawyers to dispense information about litigation financing companies to their clients, share information with the financing companies, and disburse settlement funds. That approval, however, came with a number of restrictions, including rules against attorneys recommending a case to a litigation loan company or initiating contact with a company. . . .

In its ruling last week, the 2nd DCA panel noted that a person in Fausone's situation might need extra financial help. . . .

JURIDICA INVESTMENTS, LTD.

Available online at http://www.juridicainvestments.com/investmentob.html

Juridica Investments, Ltd: Strategic Capital for Law Markets

[After explaining that the firm has shares traded on the London Stock Exchange and has raised £80 million (about US$130 million), the Web site goes on to describe investment strategy:]

The Company intends to invest in a wide variety of arbitration and litigation claims. Initially, these investments are expected to be made predominantly in the US and in international arbitration cases through referrals from Timothy Scrantom and Richard Fields' (the "Principals") established network of lawyers and law firms. The investment objective of the Company is to build a diversified portfolio of investments in claims and to provide shareholders with an attractive level of dividends and capital growth through investing directly and indirectly in litigation and arbitration cases, claims and disputes.

The Company will seek to meet its investment and yield objectives through investing in large claims, typically where the total recoveries sought exceed US$2,000,000. Except where specifically approved by the Board, no single investment of the Company will exceed US$10,000,000. The Investment Manager believes that there will be sufficient flow of investment opportunities to fully deploy the net proceeds of the placing between eighteen and twenty-four months from admission to trading on AIM, although there is no obligation on the Company to invest the net proceeds within a certain time period. The Investment Manager anticipates that it will consider or examine several investment opportunities for every investment that is actually funded.

Investment opportunities will be selected using underwriting criteria which were originally established by the Principals. The Investment Manager will seek to achieve diversification of investments by industry, jurisdiction, claim size and expected time-to-return, although most investments will be long-term with an expected return within two to five years of investment.

Investments will be structured as loans when a direct investment by the Company is not possible because, for example, it is not clearly permitted for legal or ethical reasons, in instances where it is not practicable to get all plaintiffs individually to agree to a direct investment, or when the Investment Manager considers that better returns or results could be achieved if a Principal or partner of another law firm takes an active role in the management and strategy of a case under a co-counsel arrangement.

In the medium term, the Company intends to make direct and indirect investments outside the United States, where it has received a reasoned, written legal opinion that such investments are considered to be lawful and permitted under local laws and/or rules on professional ethics. As at the date of Admission, the Company had not made (nor entered into any commitment to make) any direct or indirect investments.

NOTE ON EMERGING TRENDS IN LITIGATION FINANCE

Juridica is one of a number of enterprises whose primary business model involves investing in plaintiffs' claims. Because Juridica is publicly traded (in Britain), it is easier to access information about it than about some of its privately held competitors.

1. What are the most significant differences between entities like the Interim Settlement Funding Corporation and ones like Juridica?

a. To whom do they lend?
b. What kind of claims do they finance?

2. The news accounts describe legal challenges to lenders like Interim Settlement Funding, and the Juridica Web site similarly notes that it will invest

only in claims "considered to be lawful and permitted under local laws and/or rules on professional ethics." What might such challenges look like?

    a. Usury and unconscionability are two possibilities. If one thinks of Interim's investments as ordinary loans, the interest rate may well exceed specific statutory caps (which some states have) or run afoul of the vaguer contractual principle of unconscionability. The lenders would doubtless point out that their "loan" shouldn't be measured by ordinary standards, because, unlike an ordinary lender, they had agreed to forgo repayment entirely if the plaintiff did not prevail. As the articles note, courts have split on such challenges.

    b. For the Juridica model, the questions are a bit more exotic. Juridica has structured its investments to avoid the usury problem. But it might be open to challenge on one of two grounds: (i) engaging in practice with nonlawyers or (ii) champerty.

Take practice with nonlawyers first. Bar regulations in every state prohibit a lawyer from opening a business combining legal representation with, say, investment counseling or auto repair. The concern is that such an arrangement will interfere with the lawyer's duty of undivided loyalty to his client. So a Juridica-style investment would have to be very explicit in establishing that the investor/lender had no control over the legal strategy or tactics of the lawyer.

Champerty is a wild card. Once governing a common law crime, it prohibited any arrangement in which a client divided the proceeds of a lawsuit with others. Taken at its strictest, the doctrine of champerty prohibits the contingent fee (and was so understood in Great Britain until quite recently). Would a Juridica-style direct investment in a claim be champertous (and therefore unenforceable)? In some states champerty seems to be a dead letter, because the courts or legislature have explicitly done away with it. In others it lingers on the books and poses a threat to Juridica's business model.

    3. Lurking behind these questions of doctrine is one of policy. *Should* loans to clients (e.g. Interim Settlement Funding) or loans to lawyers (e.g. Juridica) be lawful? Some argue that anything that finances litigation makes it more likely and is therefore a public evil. Others argue that investors and lenders like these will screen their investments quite carefully and will invest only in *meritorious* litigation—which brings the ideal of the rule of law closer to realization. Stay tuned.

d. Punitive Damages

State Farm Mut. Auto. Ins. Co. v. Campbell

538 U.S. 408 (2003)

Justice KENNEDY delivered the opinion of the Court.

We address once again the measure of punishment, by means of punitive damages, a State may impose upon a defendant in a civil case. The question is whether, in the circumstances we shall recount, an award of $145 million in punitive damages, where full compensatory damages are $1 million, is excessive and in violation of the Due Process Clause of the Fourteenth Amendment to the Constitution of the United States.

I

In 1981, Curtis Campbell (Campbell) was driving with his wife, Inez Preece Campbell, in Cache County, Utah. He decided to pass six vans traveling ahead of them on a two-lane highway. Todd Ospital was driving a small car approaching from the opposite direction. To avoid a head-on collision with Campbell, who by then was driving on the wrong side of the highway and toward oncoming traffic, Ospital swerved onto the shoulder, lost control of his automobile, and collided with a vehicle driven by Robert G. Slusher. Ospital was killed, and Slusher was rendered permanently disabled. The Campbells escaped unscathed.

In the ensuing wrongful death and tort action, Campbell insisted he was not at fault. Early investigations did support differing conclusions as to who caused the accident, but "a consensus was reached early on by the investigators and witnesses that Mr. Campbell's unsafe pass had indeed caused the crash." Campbell's insurance company, petitioner State Farm Mutual Automobile Insurance Company (State Farm), nonetheless decided to contest liability and declined offers by Slusher and Ospital's estate (Ospital) to settle the claims for the policy limit of $50,000 ($25,000 per claimant). State Farm also ignored the advice of one of its own investigators and took the case to trial, assuring the Campbells that "their assets were safe, that they had no liability for the accident, that [State Farm] would represent their interests and that they did not need to procure separate counsel." To the contrary, a jury determined that Campbell was 100 percent at fault, and a judgment was returned for $185,849, far more than the amount offered in settlement.

At first State Farm refused to cover the $135,849 in excess liability. Its counsel made this clear to the Campbells: "'You may want to put for sale signs on your property to get things moving.'" Nor was State Farm willing to post a supersedeas bond to allow Campbell to appeal the judgment against him. Campbell obtained his own counsel to appeal the verdict. During the pendency of the appeal, in late 1984, Slusher, Ospital, and the Campbells reached an agreement whereby Slusher and Ospital agreed not to seek satisfaction of their claims against the Campbells. In exchange the Campbells agreed to pursue a bad faith action against State Farm and to be represented by Slusher's and Ospital's attorneys. The Campbells also agreed that Slusher and Ospital would have a right to play a part in all major decisions concerning the bad faith action. No settlement could be concluded without Slusher's and Ospital's approval, and Slusher and Ospital would receive 90 percent of any verdict against State Farm.

In 1989, the Utah Supreme Court denied Campbell's appeal in the wrongful death and tort actions. State Farm then paid the entire judgment, including the amounts in excess of the policy limits. The Campbells nonetheless filed a complaint against State Farm alleging bad faith, fraud, and intentional infliction of emotional distress. . . .

[The Utah Supreme Court described State Farm's stance in the bad faith case:]

State Farm argued . . . that its decision to take the case to trial was an 'honest mistake' that did not warrant punitive damages. In contrast, the Campbells introduced evidence that State Farm's decision to take the case to trial was a result of a national scheme to meet corporate fiscal goals by capping payouts on claims company-wide. This scheme was referred to as State Farm's "Performance, Planning and Review," or PP&R, policy. To prove the existence of this scheme, the trial court allowed the Campbells to introduce extensive expert testimony regarding fraudulent practices by State Farm in its nation-wide operations. . . .

Evidence pertaining to the PP&R policy concerned State Farm's business practices for over 20 years in numerous States. Most of these practices bore no relation to third-party automobile insurance claims, the type of claim under-lying the Campbells' complaint against the company. The jury awarded the Campbells $2.6 million [later reduced to $1 million] in compensatory damages and $145 million in punitive damages . . .

II

We recognized in Cooper Industries, Inc. v. Leatherman Tool Group, Inc., that in our judicial system compensatory and punitive damages, although usually awarded at the same time by the same decisionmaker, serve different purposes. Compensatory damages "are intended to redress the concrete loss that the plaintiff has suffered by reason of the defendant's wrongful conduct." (citing Restatement (Second) of Torts §903, pp. 453-454 (1979)). By contrast, punitive damages serve a broader function; they are aimed at deterrence and retribution. . . .

Although these awards serve the same purposes as criminal penalties, defendants subjected to punitive damages in civil cases have not been accorded the protections applicable in a criminal proceeding. This increases our concerns over the imprecise manner in which punitive damages systems are administered. . . .

In light of these concerns, in [BMW of North America v.] Gore, we instructed courts reviewing punitive damages to consider three guideposts: (1) the degree of reprehensibility of the defendant's misconduct; (2) the dis-parity between the actual or potential harm suffered by the plaintiff and the punitive damages award; and (3) the difference between the punitive damages awarded by the jury and the civil penalties authorized or imposed in compa-rable cases. We reiterated the importance of these three guideposts in Cooper Industries and mandated appellate courts to conduct de novo review of a trial court's application of them to the jury's award. Exacting appellate review ensures that an award of punitive damages is based upon an "'application of law, rather than a decisionmaker's caprice.'"

III

Under the principles outlined in BMW of North America, Inc. v. Gore, this case is neither close nor difficult. It was error to reinstate the jury's $145 million punitive damages award. We address each guidepost of Gore in some detail.

A

"[T]he most important indicium of the reasonableness of a punitive damages award is the degree of reprehensibility of the defendant's conduct." *Gore*. We have instructed courts to determine the reprehensibility of a defendant by considering whether: the harm caused was physical as opposed to economic; the tortious conduct evinced an indifference to or a reckless disregard of the health or safety of others; the target of the conduct had financial vulnerability; the conduct involved repeated actions or was an isolated incident; and the harm was the result of intentional malice, trickery, or deceit, or mere accident. The existence of any one of these factors weighing in favor of a plaintiff may not be sufficient to sustain a punitive damages award; and the absence of all of them renders any award suspect. It should be presumed a plaintiff has been made whole for his injuries by compensatory damages, so punitive damages should only be awarded if the defendant's culpability, after having paid compensatory damages, is so reprehensible as to warrant the imposition of further sanctions to achieve punishment or deterrence.

Applying these factors in the instant case, we must acknowledge that State Farm's handling of the claims against the Campbells merits no praise. The trial court found that State Farm's employees altered the company's records to make Campbell appear less culpable. State Farm disregarded the overwhelming likelihood of liability and the near-certain probability that, by taking the case to trial, a judgment in excess of the policy limits would be awarded. State Farm amplified the harm by at first assuring the Campbells their assets would be safe from any verdict and by later telling them, post-judgment, to put a for-sale sign on their house. While we do not suggest there was error in awarding punitive damages based upon State Farm's conduct toward the Campbells, a more modest punishment for this reprehensible conduct could have satisfied the State's legitimate objectives, and the Utah courts should have gone no further.

This case, instead, was used as a platform to expose, and punish, the perceived deficiencies of State Farm's operations throughout the country. The Utah Supreme Court's opinion makes explicit that State Farm was being condemned for its nationwide policies rather than for the conduct direct[ed] toward the Campbells. . . .

A State cannot punish a defendant for conduct that may have been lawful where it occurred. *Gore*. . . . Nor, as a general rule, does a State have a legitimate concern in imposing punitive damages to punish a defendant for unlawful acts committed outside of the State's jurisdiction. Any proper adjudication of conduct that occurred outside Utah to other persons would require their inclusion, and, to those parties, the Utah courts, in the usual case, would need to apply the laws of their relevant jurisdiction. *Phillips Petroleum Co. v. Shutts*, (1985). . . .

For a more fundamental reason, however, the Utah courts erred in relying upon this and other evidence: The courts awarded punitive damages to punish and deter conduct that bore no relation to the Campbells' harm. A defendant's dissimilar acts, independent from the acts upon which liability was premised, may not serve as the basis for punitive damages. A defendant should be punished for the conduct that harmed the plaintiff, not for being an unsavory individual or business. Due process does not permit courts, in the calculation of punitive damages, to adjudicate the merits of other parties' hypothetical claims against a defendant under the guise of the reprehensibility analysis, but we have no doubt the Utah Supreme Court did that here. . . .

The Campbells have identified scant evidence of repeated misconduct of the sort that injured them. Nor does our review of the Utah courts' decisions convince us that State Farm was only punished for its actions toward the Campbells. Although evidence of other acts need not be identical to have relevance in the calculation of punitive damages, the Utah court erred here because evidence pertaining to claims that had nothing to do with a third-party lawsuit was introduced at length. Other evidence concerning reprehensibility was even more tangential. For example, the Utah Supreme Court criticized State Farm's investigation into the personal life of one of its employees and, in a broader approach, the manner in which State Farm's policies corrupted its employees. . . .

B

Turning to the second *Gore* guidepost, we have been reluctant to identify concrete constitutional limits on the ratio between harm, or potential harm, to the plaintiff and the punitive damages award. . . . We decline again to impose a bright-line ratio which a punitive damages award cannot exceed. Our jurisprudence and the principles it has now established demonstrate, however, that, in practice, few awards exceeding a single-digit ratio between punitive and compensatory damages, to a significant degree, will satisfy due process. [The Court reviewed its cases, summing up as follows:] They demonstrate what should be obvious: Single-digit multipliers are more likely to comport with due process, while still achieving the State's goals of deterrence and retribution, than awards with ratios in range of 500 to 1 or, in this case, of 145 to 1.

Nonetheless, because there are no rigid benchmarks that a punitive damages award may not surpass, ratios greater than those we have previously upheld may comport with due process where "a particularly egregious act has resulted in only a small amount of economic damages." The converse is also true, however. When compensatory damages are substantial, then a lesser ratio, perhaps only equal to compensatory damages, can reach the outermost limit of the due process guarantee. . . .

In the context of this case, we have no doubt that there is a presumption against an award that has a 145-to-1 ratio. The compensatory award in this case was substantial; the Campbells were awarded $1 million for a year and a half of emotional distress. This was complete compensation. The harm arose from a transaction in the economic realm, not from some physical assault or trauma; there were no physical injuries; and State Farm paid the excess verdict before the complaint was filed, so the Campbells suffered only minor economic injuries for the 18-month period in which State Farm refused to resolve the claim against them. The compensatory damages for the injury suffered here, moreover, likely were based on a component which was duplicated in the punitive award. Much of the distress was caused by the outrage and humiliation the Campbells suffered at the actions of their insurer; and it is a major role of punitive damages to condemn such conduct. . . .

The remaining premises for the Utah Supreme Court's decision bear no relation to the award's reasonableness or proportionality to the harm. . . . The wealth of a defendant cannot justify an otherwise unconstitutional punitive damages award. *Gore* ("The fact that BMW is a large corporation rather than an impecunious individual does not diminish its entitlement to fair notice of the demands that the several States impose on the conduct of its business"); ("[Wealth] provides an open-ended basis for inflating awards when the defendant is wealthy. . . . That does not make its use unlawful or inappropriate; it simply means that this factor cannot make up for the failure of other factors, such as 'reprehensibility,' to constrain significantly an award that purports to punish a defendant's conduct"). The principles set forth in *Gore* must be implemented with care, to ensure both reasonableness and proportionality.

C

The third guidepost in *Gore* is the disparity between the punitive damages award and the "civil penalties authorized or imposed in comparable cases." . . . Here, we need not dwell long on this guidepost. The most relevant civil sanction under Utah state law for the wrong done to the Campbells appears to be a $10,000 fine for an act of fraud, an amount dwarfed by the $145 million punitive damages award. . . .

IV

An application of the *Gore* guideposts to the facts of this case, especially in light of the substantial compensatory damages awarded (a portion of which contained a punitive element), likely would justify a punitive damages award at or near the amount of compensatory damages. The punitive award of $145 million, therefore, was neither reasonable nor proportionate to the wrong committed, and it was an irrational and arbitrary deprivation of the property of the defendant. The proper calculation of punitive damages under the principles we have discussed should be resolved, in the first instance, by the Utah courts.

The judgment of the Utah Supreme Court is reversed, and the case is remanded for proceedings not inconsistent with this opinion.

It is so ordered.

[Justices SCALIA and THOMAS dissented separately on the grounds that neither the due process clause nor the rest of the Constitution provided a basis for controlling states' awards of punitive damages.]

[Justice GINSBURG dissented on two grounds: that it was unwise for the Court to use the Constitution to lay down the kind of rules that were essentially legislative; and that in this case the behavior of State Farm (which included the apparent destruction of materials that had been requested in discovery) warranted the award in question:]

I remain of the view that this Court has no warrant to reform state law governing awards of punitive damages. Even if I were prepared to accept the flexible guides prescribed in *Gore*, I would not join the Court's swift conversion of those guides into instructions that begin to resemble marching orders.

For the reasons stated, I would leave the judgment of the Utah Supreme Court undisturbed.

e. Fee Caps

NOTE ON DAMAGE CAPS

In the nineteenth century it was common for states to limit the amounts recoverable for wrongful death, leading to the often-noted perversity that, so far as liability was concerned, it was "cheaper" negligently to kill someone than to injure him severely. Few such limitations persist today, but in recent decades a number of states have enacted changes to their tort laws that cap some forms of damage in some kinds of cases. California has enacted one such law, the Medical Injuries Compensation Reform Act of 1975, one of whose provisions appears below. Consider how you would expect it to affect the number and kind of medical practice actions brought. Note that the statute, enacted in 1975, does not index the cap amount for inflation; it has not been amended in this respect since its enactment. One can think of damage caps as the litigation opposite of punitive damage awards. Where the prospect of punitive damages will attract representation to cases that might not otherwise warrant large investments of lawyers' time, damage caps will, all other things being equal, drive resources away from the cases to which they apply.

CALIFORNIA CIVIL CODE §3333.2

(Deerings 2009)

Noneconomic Losses in Medical Malpractice Actions

(a) In any action for injury against a health care provider based on professional negligence, the injured plaintiff shall be entitled to recover noneconomic losses to compensate for pain, suffering, inconvenience, physical impairment, disfigurement and other nonpecuniary damage.

(b) In no action shall the amount of damages for noneconomic losses exceed two hundred fifty thousand dollars ($250,000).

(c) For the purposes of this section:

(1) "Health care provider" means any person licensed or certified pursuant to Division 2 (commencing with Section 500) of the Business and Professions Code, or licensed pursuant to the Osteopathic Initiative Act, or the Chiropractic Initiative Act, or licensed pursuant to Chapter 2.5 (commencing with Section 1440) of Division 2 of the Health and Safety Code; and any clinic, health dispensary, or health facility, licensed pursuant to Division 2 (commencing with Section 1200) of the Health and Safety Code. "Health care provider" includes the legal representatives of a health care provider;

(2) "Professional negligence" means a negligent act or omission to act by a health care provider in the rendering of professional services, which act or omission is the proximate cause of a personal injury or wrongful death. . . .

3. WHO'S LEFT OUT IN THE COLD: GAPS IN LITIGATION FINANCE

a. No "Right"

JONATHAN GRONER, MARYLAND MAY BE FIRST
TO APPLY *GIDEON* TO CIVIL TRIALS

Legal Times, October 23, 2003, at 3

Washington—In the 1963 case Gideon v. Wainwright, the U.S. Supreme Court held for the first time that criminal defendants who are too poor to afford a lawyer are entitled to free court-appointed counsel.

But in the 40 years since the Gideon ruling, no U.S. court has ever found that indigent citizens have a constitutional right to an attorney in a civil case—even in a case in which they could lose their job, their home or custody of their child.

That could change soon.

On Oct. 7, Maryland's highest court heard arguments in Frase v. Barnhart, a case in which a team of public interest advocates and pro bono lawyers has asked the court to find that Marylanders have precisely that right. The advocates' rallying cry is that they want to establish a "civil Gideon."

"The heart of the argument is access to justice," says Stephen Sachs, the Wilmer, Cutler & Pickering counsel who is handling the case pro bono on behalf of Deborah Frase, an indigent single mother who lives in Preston, Md. "The guiding hand of counsel is just as relevant to someone who's about to lose a child as to someone who's about to spend 30 days in jail."

But to some observers, it's not that simple. Although liberal public interest lawyers say ensuring a right to a lawyer in civil cases is fundamental to a just society, others say it would amount to an expensive boondoggle that would foster needless litigation without actually helping the poor.

"The idea is almost a formula for a meltdown of the economy," says Philip Howard, a partner in the New York office of Covington & Burling who has written extensively on civil litigation. "Any time anyone gets angry, they will say, 'I want a lawyer.' If a lawyer is available without cost, well, heaven help us."

There is certainly one crucial legal difference between Gideon and Frase.

Gideon, a Supreme Court ruling based on the due process clause of the 14th Amendment to the U.S. Constitution, laid down a national rule that all states had to follow immediately.

But in a 5-4 decision in Lassiter v. Department of Social Services in 1981, the court rejected the contention that the U.S. Constitution guarantees indigents a right to counsel in civil cases.

In light of Lassiter, Sachs, a former Maryland attorney general, tailored his arguments in Frase on provisions of the Maryland Declaration of Rights, a basic law of the state, and not on the federal constitution.

If the Maryland Court of Appeals accepts Sachs' arguments, such a ruling, as an interpretation of state law by the highest court of a state, would not be subject to appeal to the U.S. Supreme Court and would only be binding in Maryland.

Even so, public interest advocates are watching the Maryland matter very closely. No state court anywhere has faced the issue as broadly and directly as it is being posed in this case.

A similar case is percolating in the courts of Washington state. In 2001, the Supreme Court of Indiana held that an Indiana statute grants the right to free counsel, but the state legislature quickly amended the law to say that a judge may appoint a lawyer for an indigent person, but does not have to do so.

"This conversation is taking place in virtually every state," says Jonathan Smith, executive director of the Legal Aid Society of the District of Columbia and one of the chief strategists behind Frase. "If Maryland were to become the first state to find this right, that would be very, very significant on a nationwide basis."

Self-Representation

Deborah Frase, a 32-year-old woman with four children, was locked in a battle for custody of her 3-year-old son with a family that temporarily took care of him while she was in jail awaiting trial on marijuana charges.

Frase was unable to afford a lawyer. She tried to get free help from the legal aid bureau in Caroline County and from other legal services programs, but was told that they were understaffed.

Frase ended up representing herself at trial. She had had a history of alcohol and drug use, but was nonetheless found fit to be a parent and won custody of her child.

But the court attached conditions to its ruling: Frase had to apply to live at a homeless shelter and also allow visitation rights to the other family, which was unrelated to her. Frase found those conditions humiliating and unacceptable—and Sachs says she never would have been subjected to them if she had been represented in court.

Meanwhile, Smith says, a pro bono team of lawyers was already in search of the perfect case in which to establish a civil Gideon. That effort was touched off by Wilmer, Cutler's long-standing pro bono work on the issue and by a grant in 2000 from philanthropist George Soros' Open Society Institute to the Public Justice Center in Baltimore. The justice center, then headed by Smith, used the money to establish an appellate project in poverty law.

Lawyers at the public interest law firm reviewed dozens of cases in which an indigent person had not been represented by a lawyer—until they found Frase's case, whose facts, they thought, presented their arguments in the best possible light.

Frase had filed appeal papers a year ago at the Maryland Court of Appeals, and the pro bono team took over the case in early 2003.

"It was a matter of looking for the proper case," says Smith, who left the Baltimore public interest firm to take over D.C. Legal Aid in 2002. Frase, a mother arguing with limited success for custody of her son but too poor to afford a lawyer, was a natural choice.

In addition to pushing for a right to counsel, Sachs is arguing that the lower courts misapplied U.S. Supreme Court precedent on visitation rights and that a court-appointed master had a conflict of interest because she once represented a party in the case in opposition to Frase. The court could decide the case on those issues without reaching the civil Gideon question.

Timothy Bradford, a partner in Kent, Cizek & Treff in Denton, Md., represents the family seeking custody of Frase's son. He filed a six-page brief in the appeals court, citing Lassiter and also contending that Frase is not ripe for appeal.

"My clients are more concerned about the visitation issue and about the best interests of the child than about the pro bono issue," says Bradford, who himself worked pro bono on the appeal. "At the appellate court, I felt it was one person against a million."

The Maryland attorney general's office did not enter an appearance or file an amicus brief in the case.

English Law

Frase's team spent months researching the Maryland Declaration of Rights and ended up making two basic arguments.

One arcane contention under Article 5 of the declaration is that when Maryland became a state, it adopted all English law that was effective on July 4, 1776. Since the days of Henry VII in the 16th century, England had granted a right to counsel for the indigent in civil cases. This right would then apply up to the present day, the Frase team argued.

Another contention is that Article 19 of the Declaration of Rights guarantees Marylanders access to justice under an "open courts" provision similar to that found in the constitutions of many other states. The Maryland Court of Appeals, Sachs wrote in his brief, "should apply the logic of Gideon in order to fulfill Article 19's unredeemed promise of equal access to the courts."

Julia Gordon, a former senior counsel at the Center for Law and Social Policy who attended the Oct. 7 session, says the judges took these arguments seriously.

"They could have left this aspect of the case on the cutting-room floor," says Gordon, an advocate who has been working on poverty law issues for decades. "It seemed that each one of the judges had spent time thinking about these issues."

Gordon says Chief Judge Robert Bell was particularly active at the argument, posing questions to both sides, indicating his interest in the civil Gideon issue.

Many think the case may have major implications for D.C. law as well.

"I care a lot for Maryland, but I am also trying to pursue solutions to access-to-justice problems in D.C.," says Gordon. "The timing is good for those of us who are looking to solve the dire needs in our own city."

Still, some observers think it may not be a good idea to enshrine a new right in American law, one whose contours may be unclear and one that some say will be very expensive and will bring more lawsuits to an already litigious nation.

"Family law cases, by themselves, will make a good-sized government program, especially if you assume that often, both sides of the case will be indigent," says Walter Olson, a senior fellow and legal scholar at the conservative Manhattan Institute. "Many of those who want a civil Gideon want it simply because it will give Legal Aid a permanent charter and a constitutional status. That helps if you work for Legal Aid and are competing for budget with other programs."

Covington's Howard also says that experts, including many liberals, say family courts worked better many years ago when they were "less adversarial," and that society would benefit from a return to that mode.

The Public Justice Center's Smith says he sees the right as extending not to all civil cases but to those "similar to criminal cases," when a citizen's basic rights or necessities of life are jeopardized.

Sachs' brief pointedly does not deal with the issues of the potential cost to Maryland taxpayers, saying they "are subjects for another day in another place." The point of the case, he writes, is to establish the right to civil counsel, not to figure out who is going to pay for it.

Frase v. Barnhart

840 A.2d 114 (Md. 2003)

Counsel: Argued By Stephen H. Sachs (Wilmer, Cutler & Pickering; Deborah Thompson Eisenberg of Brown, Goldstein & Levy, LLP; Debra Gardner, Wendy N. Hess and Catherine Woolley, Public Justice Center, on brief) all of Baltimore, MD for appellant.

Argued By Timothy A. Bradford (Kent, Cizek and Treff, on brief) of Denton, MD for appellees.

Brief of Amici Curiae in Support of Petitioner Deborah Frase University of Baltimore Family Law Clinic and The Women's Law Center of Maryland: Jane C. Murphy, Esquire, Claire A. Smearman, Esquire, Cheri Wyron Levin, Esquire, University of Baltimore Family Law Clinic, Baltimore, MD, and Tracy Brown, Esquire, The Women's Law Center of Maryland, Towson, MD.

Brief of the Amici Curiae, Legal Services Providers: Hannah E.M. Lieberman, Esquire, Rhonda B. Lipkin, Esquire, Jessica L.C. Rae, Esquire, Baltimore, MD.

Brief of Amicus Curiae Maryland State Bar Association, Inc.: James L. Shea, Esquire, Mitchell Y. Mirviss, Esquire, John B. Howard, Jr., Esquire, Venable, Baetjer and Howard, LLP, Baltimore, MD.

Brief of the Amicus Curiae Maryland Legal Services Corporation: Robert J. Rhudy, Esquire, Maryland Legal Services Corporation, Baltimore, MD.

Wilner, J.

We have before us what began as a custody dispute between Deborah Frase, the mother of three-year-old Brett, and Curtis and Cynthia Barnhart, a couple who, during part of an eight-week period of the mother's incarceration, volunteered to care for Brett and then decided that they wanted custody of the child. The issue at this point is not who should have custody of Brett. The Circuit Court for Caroline County seems to have resolved that in the mother's favor. It is Ms. Frase who complains — that she was not provided free counsel to assist her in defending the action, that the domestic relations master who conducted the evidentiary hearing was conflicted and duty-bound to recuse herself, and that certain conditions that were included as part of the award of custody are impermissible.

There is also a significant procedural issue of whether the appeal is properly before us. That issue arises from two of the conditions attached to the custody determination — conditions that the court refused to strike and that, in effect, put the case in a state of on-going uncertainty. We shall conclude that the appeal, though from an interlocutory order, is properly before us, and we shall hold that the conditions attached to the award of custody are impermissible. That will end this case and therefore make it both unnecessary and inappropriate for us to address the right-to-appointed-counsel issue. . . .

Other Issues

The remaining issues raised by Ms. Frase are whether the court erred in not requiring that the master, who 10 years earlier had represented Ms. Keys in the custody case involving Justin, be recused, and whether Ms. Frase had a common law or State Constitutional right to court-appointed counsel because of her indigency. Because our mandate will direct that the conditions complained of by Ms. Frase be vacated, and that will end this dispute without the need for any further proceedings, both of those issues are moot. There will be no occasion for the master to have any further contact with the current case, and there will be no further proceedings in this case in which Ms. Frase may need or desire counsel.

In this circumstance, it would be especially inappropriate for us to address and rule upon the right-to-appointed-counsel issue. Ms. Frase has argued that she, and any other civil litigant who is unable to afford counsel, has a common law and State Constitutional right to have counsel appointed for her, either by the court or by some State or local agency. The common law right, she says, stems from a statute enacted by the English Parliament in 1494 — 11 Henry VII, ch.12. That statute, among other things, required the judges of the King's Bench, upon the return of any writ that commenced a civil action, to assign to a "poor" plaintiff an attorney, who "shall give their Counsels, nothing taking for the same." Ms. Frase argues that this statute was made part of the common law of Maryland by Article 5 of the Maryland Declaration of Rights and, although it has never been invoked or enforced in any way, has also never been repealed.

She claims, alternatively, that she has a right to a court-appointed attorney under (1) Article 19 of the Maryland Declaration of Rights, which, with the gloss of Article 46 of the Declaration, provides that every person, for any injury done to his/her person or property, "ought to have remedy by the course of the Law of the land, and ought to have justice and right, freely without sale, fully without any denial, and speedily without delay, according to the Law of the land," and (2) Article 24 of the Declaration of Rights, which is the State analogue to the due process clause of the Fourteenth Amendment.

Ms. Frase, as noted, is well represented by counsel in this appeal, and there is no assurance that, should any further litigation be brought by or against Ms. Frase, she would not be represented in that litigation. The evidence in this case documents (and we could take judicial notice in any event) that there are legal service agencies operating in Caroline County, where this case arose, and that lawyers in that county do engage in *pro bono publico* work. Ms. Frase said that she was not supplied with counsel by one of the legal service agencies because of an overload at the time. It would be entirely speculative whether that circumstance would exist should she desire counsel in the future, in some new case.[9] Given that speculative uncertainty, for us, now, to opine on the scope, meaning, and vitality of the ancient 1494 statute or to find the right-to-counsel she posits hidden for 227 years in Article 19 or Article 24 of the Declaration of Rights would be wholly inappropriate.[10]

[Reversed.]

Concurring opinion by CATHELL, J. in which BELL, C.J. and ELDRIDGE, J. join.

I concur with the majority in respect to the general result it reaches. In respect to the appealability issue, however, although I agree that the matters are appealable, I do so on the basis that what occurred here was a change in the conditions of custody and was, therefore, immediately appealable pursuant to the provisions of Courts and Judicial Proceedings Article, Section 12-303(3)(x).

I strongly disagree with the majority's refusal to address the primary issue presented to us — in my view the most certiorari-worthy issue in the case. . . .

The majority declines to address an issue I believe to be properly presented that goes to the very center of the American constitutional, and extra-constitutional promises — equality under the law. I am fully aware that there may be serious concerns as to the reaction of the other branches of government, of the organized Bar (and other members of the profession) and of the people, in respect to any decision this court might reach in addressing this most important question: do the poor receive equal treatment in a matter concerning the most basic of fundamental, and constitutional, rights — the matter of the custody, visitation, and control of children by their parents? Rather than answer, or attempt to answer it, the question is avoided by a majority of the Court. . . .

---

9. We would have to speculate, as well, that none of the five lawyers and three law firms representing Ms. Frase in this appeal would continue to represent her in any further proceeding in the Circuit Court — that, having argued her right to the assistance of counsel, they would then abandon her — and that the Maryland State Bar Association, the University of Baltimore Family Law Clinic, the Women's Law Center of Maryland, the Legal Aid Bureau. Inc., the American Civil Liberties Union of Maryland, the House of Ruth Domestic Violence Legal Clinic, the Maryland Disability Law Center, the Maryland Legal Services Corporation, the Maryland Volunteer Lawyers Service, all of which filed *amicus curiae* briefs in her behalf, would do likewise. We shall not make that assumption.

10. To resolve the issue hinged on the English statute, we would have to determine, among other things, (1) whether that statute, which, to the best of our knowledge, has never been applied in the 379-year history of Maryland as a colony and State, is nonetheless currently a vital part of the Maryland common law, (2) if so, whether it is limited to plaintiffs, as it says, or should be extended by judicial fiat to defendants, like Ms. Frase, as well, (3) at what point the right attaches and how long it continues, and (4) if the right exists and the court is, indeed, required to appoint counsel, what would happen if the lawyer appointed, for one reason or another, refuses to take the case. *See* Mallard v. United States District Court, 490 U.S. 296, 109 S. Ct. 1814, 104 L. Ed. 2d 318 (1989). If the right is to be found under either Article 19 or Article 24 of the Declaration of Rights, either the State or the counties would presumably have to set up a system to appoint and pay the attorneys. Even if we were to leave the fiscal and administrative aspects of such a mandate to the legislative and executive branches, we would at least have to determine in some way the kinds of cases to which the right attached. It is clear that the right asserted by Ms. Frase could never be limited, under the language of either the statute or the Constitutional provisions, solely to defendants in contested custody cases arising in Caroline County. Recognition of the right would carry an enormous fiscal impact and require a substantial administrative structure, yet counsel has given us not a clue, in their briefs or at oral argument, how this right could, in fact, be implemented. In States where this right is recognized, it has been provided for by statute. *See Mallard v. United States District Court, supra.* This is not the case to resolve that issue.

The facts in the present custody related case are not even as egregious as many we see. . . . If a poor person is faced with the prospect of going to jail for a minor theft offense, she is provided counsel. Yet, if the same person is forced into court where she is faced with the prospect of losing a child, or losing partial or full parental rights, to the State or to a third party, she is not provided counsel. . . .

I would leave the consideration of the issue providing representation in respect to other types of civil matters to the cases that bring those issues before the Court.

b. "Unbundling" and Doing It (Almost) Yourself as Solutions

LEONARD POST, LAW FIRMS FIND NEW REVENUE IN "UNBUNDLING"

National Law Journal, July 4, 2005, at 1, col. 1

Rules that allow lawyers to "unbundle" their services—to represent typically cash-strapped clients for parts of their litigation—are spreading across the United States.

In the past six years, nine states—Alaska, California, Colorado, Florida, Maine, Nevada, New Mexico, Washington and Wyoming—have adopted unbundling rules. . . .

Proponents argue that unbundling provides a public service to clients who would not otherwise have any legal representation. They say it is also a potential stream of untapped revenue for law firms.

Critics counter that clients are better served when represented throughout their litigation.

Unbundling allows lawyers to limit their involvement in litigation in the same way that they often have contractually limited their involvement in transactional work for businesses, or have contracted to take a case to trial, but not to do the appeal.

An unbundled lawyer might, for example, advise clients of their rights in a divorce, help clients fill out forms, confine court appearances to child custody issues, and review the judgment. Other than that, clients could be on their own, if they want to proceed that way.

The new rules also facilitate and sanction unbundling for volunteer and legal services attorneys who had long provided unbundled services, called "limited-scope representation."

Plenty of Business

The unbundling of services targets pro se clients whose cases are most often found in family, small claims, housing, traffic and misdemeanor courts. But a 2001 National Center for State Courts study found that 9 percent of defendants who went to trial in contract cases didn't have a lawyer either.

"Some states—such as California, Washington and Florida—have court-house facilitators to assist with detailed procedural information and one-on-one form preparation" for pro se clients, said William Hornsby, staff counsel to the American Bar Association Committee on the Delivery of Legal Services.

In other states, volunteer lawyers play similar roles. Maricopa County, Ariz., has self-help centers where forms and technological tools take individuals through the procedural morass, he said, while many states provide forms through the Internet.

"But for many people that's just not enough," said Hornsby, a specialist in the ethical considerations of unbundling. "They need advice and sometimes more."

Unbundling in Action

Family lawyer Elizabeth Scheffee of Portland, Maine's Givertz, Hambley, Scheffee & Lavoie is an unbundling enthusiast. About 20 percent of her clients use her services on an unbundled basis. These clients' annual income ranges from $75,000 to $225,000, with a few millionaires tossed in, she said.

"It really very well suits a domestic-relations practice," said the former state bar president. "One reason why I really enjoy it is because it allows more legal representation for people of modest means."

She said that if she had to go to her own firm for a lawyer to handle her divorce, "I could not afford myself." She advises her clients of their rights, and helps them fill out legal forms that they can pick up for themselves at the court for $5 a packet.

"Typically, they're going to need a lawyer to draft the divorce judgment so it contains the magic words that are applicable to the client," Scheffee said. "For example, if they own real estate there is a certain way it has to refer to the real estate and allocate it to the parties."

Then there's the division of the pension, "which can be very tricky," Scheffee said. She hasn't "ironed out the wrinkles of appearing in court yet," she said, because she hadn't had much experience doing it for unbundled clients.

Los Angeles solo practitioner Forrest Mosten first championed unbundling in an article in an ABA Section of Family Law journal article in 1991. He has a "no-court rule" in his practice, even when he's doing full-service work, which means he will not make court appearances. In what he described as a very busy mediation-oriented practice, he recommends a variety of lawyers for in-court work.

"Some clients will hire me in an unbundled scope to manage the litigation with the litigator," Mosten said. "Just like an internist will manage the care of a patient who needs surgery."

Mosten represents clients in the same income group as Scheffee. For the working poor, there are few alternatives, at least in Los Angeles. But one nonprofit law firm, Levitt & Quinn, Family Law Center, provides only unbundled legal services, although the firm often sees cases through from beginning to end. Levitt & Quinn clients are charged on a sliding-scale fee basis that supports only half the office's overhead. The other half is raised privately.

"Two days a week we see new clients," said Sharon Hulse, acting director of legal services. "There's a line starting at 7 [a.m.] although the office doesn't open until 8." Full-time attorneys average about 80 cases and are paid on the bottom of the legal-aid scale, she said.

King County, Wash., Superior Court Commissioner Kimberly Prochnau has witnessed unbundling in action.

"Unbundling has increased the pool of volunteer attorneys," said Prochnau. "It has also made it more likely for people to be able to get an attorney at a critical stage of the proceedings," even if they can't afford the kind of retainer that would commit a lawyer through trial.

For example, while in her county, which includes Seattle, only 6.5 percent of family law cases are tried, preliminary hearings held within 14 days of filing often result in orders that affect child custody, child and spousal support, and other significant matters.

Rules Change

The unbundling movement gained momentum after the 1999 Scottsdale, Ariz., Conference on Pro Se Litigation, sponsored by the American Judicature Society, which brought together teams from 49 states. Unbundling was one of the "action plans" that came out of the conference. Soon afterward, the ABA formed Ethics 2000, which recommended revisions to its model rules of professional conduct to facilitate unbundling. Those rules were adopted in 2002.

Unbundling requires revisions of state ethical rules and rules of civil procedure. The most controversial issues, as evidenced by states' diverse procedural and substantive rules, are:

- The scope of an attorney's duty to investigate the facts. Can a lawyer rely on the facts as presented by a client or is an independent investigation required?
- Special appearances by counsel. In addition to contesting jurisdiction, should the rules allow them if a court has written notice of an attorney's limited scope of representation, and should the rules also facilitate an attorney's withdrawal?
- Drafting of pleadings. Does a pro se litigant have to tell a court when a lawyer drafts a pleading?
- Conflicts. Absent knowledge of a conflict, must a volunteer lawyer working under the auspices of a nonprofit organization have to run a conflicts check at his or her firm if the advice a client will get is short-term and limited?

The Critics

The main concerns about unbundling that go beyond rule-making are:

- Clients are better served if they are fully represented.
- Legal service clients need full representation far more than sophisticated clients.
- Clients may not always understand the limits of the representation they have agreed to.

While Legal Services for New York City Executive Director Andrew Scherer doesn't think unbundling is a bad approach for parties of relatively equal bargaining power, when it comes to his clients, he's no fan.

"I think it gets a little more dicey when you have, for example, the government on one side and low-income clients on the other," he said.

That too would apply to situations where private parties who are better equipped to pursue the litigation are on the other side, such as in landlord/tenant disputes, he added.

That said, legal services organizations across the country have long offered limited-scope representation. For example, they have often helped clients fill out pleadings while not appearing with them in court. But that doesn't make it a best practice, Scherer insists.

"Advocacy is a dynamic you can't pick apart," he asserted. "It involves complex and nuanced skills. . . . Our clients are often trying to keep their families together, keep their housing. . . . It's a rare instance where unbundling can resolve those kinds of problems."

New York has not eased its rules on unbundling.

"Home Depot Movement"

Ronald Staudt, a professor at Chicago-Kent College of Law, asserted that unbundling is part of the "self-help Home Depot movement."

"If people can go three-fourths the way down the road by themselves, is there a good reason that we as a profession shouldn't let them?" Staudt said.

"Our profession is client-centric, and if what the client wants is to pay less and only get pieces of service, we should give them what they want as long as it doesn't cause an ethical breach."

With grants from NCSC and others, Staudt directed a team that developed "A2J" — Access to Justice — a computer interface that facilitates the ability of individuals to appear unbundled or pro se. It interviews clients online and, using HotDocs software donated from LexisNexis, helps clients fill out legal forms and pleadings.

But if a client runs into a complication, the program takes them out of the interview and onto a lawyer-referral Web page. Sites could be programmed to include unbundled live chat and teleconferencing services. . . .

STANLEY A. MILLER II, WILLS ON THE WEB ONLINE COVER THE BASICS, BUT ARE NO SUBSTITUTE FOR A LAWYER

Milwaukee Journal Sentinel, June 4, 2002, at 4

Summer vacation is a happy, carefree time when you go off with loved ones for fun, adventure, relaxation or all of the above.

But to prepare for a trip on which all of my immediately family is embarking, I turned to the Internet to set about the grim and sobering task of preparing a will, just in case something horrible happens on our flight.

It's a reaction to the Sept. 11 terrorist attacks and constant warnings from the government that another attack is imminent.

Sure, I have traveled since Sept. 11 — twice for technology trade shows. But the rest of the family was left safely behind, and all of my affairs were in order.

Law-related Web sites are usually quick to point out they are not dispensing legal advice but only providing information or helping visitors fill out forms.

For example, LegalZoom.com, which provides wills and other legal documents over the Internet, says it "provides legal resources and tools to allow individuals to make their own legal decisions." The Los Angeles company promises to "help you prepare reliable legal documents online," and review them for "consistency and completeness."

Visitors begin by filling out an online questionnaire created by attorneys. Besides basic information, you need to select an executor to carry out the wishes in the will, as well as listing any special gifts to specific people.

The questionnaire is interactive—if you say you are single, you are not asked how much you want to leave your spouse. The site also expects an honest answer to the question, "Are you free of any mental illness?"

LegalZoom says the will-writing service performed by an attorney would cost about $366, but it provided the package for $55. An extra $40 gives the option of revising the will at any time for five years.

After visitors have submitted their information, the turnaround time is 48 hours. The site sends the finished product via regular mail, e-mail or express mail for an extra $15. The legal documents are customized to the customer's home state and come with instructions to make sure they are valid.

Before receiving a document from LegalZoom, you are required to acknowledge that "LegalZoom did not provide me with any advice, explanation or representation" about any legal rights, remedies, defenses or options among its wordy disclaimers.

That is because LegalZoom's founders—who include Robert Shapiro, once O.J. Simpson's lawyer—might be charged with practicing law without a license if they did.

And because LegalZoom and its competitors don't give legal advice, they tend to thin out some of the options otherwise enjoyed by having an attorney draft a will from scratch.

For example, I began the Web site's will wizard with the idea that I'd like to leave a sizable amount of money to be held in trust for the education of any children that my best friend and his fiancée might have someday. The site didn't provide that option, so I had to settle on a less sophisticated arrangement.

Local lawyers reviewing my will from LegalZoom criticized it for its sloppy writing and the position of various distribution clauses that could make the document more susceptible to challenges. No one was willing to say the will would be invalid if signed in front of witnesses.

"Anytime you have a complicated legal matter, you really should seek out an attorney," company president Brian Lee said. "We're facilitating so people can prepare their own simple legal documents." It took about 30 minutes to complete the questionnaire—a testament to my meager estate—and the final document arrived about a day later via e-mail.

LegalZoom also offers two varieties of legal help: an online library of information in outline form and access to Tele-Lawyer, which is a $3-per-minute phone service. Sometimes the company tells people—either by e-mail or by phone—to seek legal advice.

The firm has an online referral service in which those with legal needs type in a description of their problem, and the company forwards it to lawyers who bid for the job.

The company has other competitors. Wills for America (www. willsforamerica.com) offers a will for $20. There are also TheWillExpert.com ($19.99) and Willmatic.com ($14.95), which promise wills instantly, but those companies do not claim to review what customers submit.

Ross Kodner, a lawyer and president of Microlaw, a law technology consulting firm in Milwaukee, discouraged people from using an online legal service, stressing that the differing legal requirements between states pose too many potential pitfalls.

"I think it's a recipe for malpractice, and from the consumer side, a recipe for disaster," he said. "A few lawyers are trying to make a quick buck on the Web . . . and make the rest of us look bad. There is a fundamental tension in the mix of Web and legal services, and it ends up being focused on the profit motive instead of a public service motive."

There are compelling reasons to have a lawyer draft a will.

Depending on the size and complexity of the estate, whether a trust is needed and whether there are alternative forms of distribution, a lawyer can write up a will in a matter of hours.

A will isn't effective until it's signed in front of witnesses, and a lawyer's office usually has employees who perform this duty. And despite the millions of jokes, the legal profession's code of conduct is a compelling reason to turn to a real attorney.

LegalZoom's vows "absolute privacy" and says employees breaking the rules risk "termination and other disciplinary measures, up to being criminally prosecuted."

But if lawyers divulge personal information, their clients can file claims with the firms' malpractice carriers if they have them. Disgruntled clients can also file complaints with the disciplinary board for lawyers, sue in civil court for damages and try to get lawyers disbarred.

But the protections and potential punishments of violating attorney-client privilege don't apply to Internet services like LegalZoom because they aren't practicing law.

Michael Bobelian, We The People Pledges to Avoid "Unauthorized Practice of Law"

New York Law Journal, May 12, 2005, at 1, col. 4

We The People, a nationwide legal document preparation service, promised Wednesday in U.S. Bankruptcy Court for the Southern District of New York not to engage in the "unauthorized practice of law."

The promise was part of a stipulation sought by the U.S. Bankruptcy Trustees' Office. It could result in dramatic changes in the way the document firm does business.

We The People offers help to customers in filling out legal documents in various fields, including bankruptcy, divorce and wills. The company states on its Web site that it "serves customers who cannot afford the high cost of attorney fees" from its 170 offices in 32 states, including 34 offices in New York.

Both in New York and nationally, We The People has been accused of providing legal advice without a license. The company, which has franchises offering walk-in services, has denied it provides legal advice.

But Greg Zipes, a Department of Justice attorney who advises the bankruptcy trustees' office, said after Wednesday's hearing that We The People has been "stepping over the line."

Earlier, before Bankruptcy Judge Robert Drain, Zipes said that members of the trustees' office "define legal advice very broadly."

Under the terms of the stipulation, We The People cannot advise customers on when to file for bankruptcy, explain secured versus unsecured debt, or categorize the different types of bankruptcy filings available to a debtor, among other things. Additionally, the center cannot distribute how-to books or guides on filing for bankruptcy to customers.

"They are allowed to be a typing service," Zipes said, in characterizing the stipulation's terms.

Richard Lubetzky of Los Angeles, We The People's lawyer, did not object to the characterization during the hearing, which he attended by phone.

Since its arrival in the New York area last year, We The People has opened dozens of offices and handles a large percentage of personal bankruptcy filings in the region, Zipes said.

The trustees' office took an interest when it saw mistakes in the company's work.

The case before Judge Drain involved Debbie Dallas, a customer of We The People.

Deirdre Martini, the trustee handling the matter, explained that Dallas may lose her house because of faulty advice she received from We The People. The Dallas case provided an opportunity for the trustees' office to curb We The People's practices, Martini explained. . . .

We The People has come under fire in other jurisdictions, including, Florida and Texas, where local bar associations led the attacks.

Martini said that most attorneys in the area charge about $700 for basic bankruptcy advice compared with We The People, which charges about $200. But she added that court clerks will also help potential filers find attorneys willing to do the work on a pro bono basis.

c. Government Aid

LEGAL SERVICES CORPORATION, 2006 APPROPRIATION

LSC's Budget, available online at http://www.lsc.gov/about/budget.php

---

Public Law No: 109-108
119 Stat. 2290
H.R. 2862
November 22, 2005
One Hundred Ninth Congress of the United States of America
AT THE FIRST SESSION

Begun and held at the City of Washington on Tuesday, the fourth day of January, two thousand and five

An Act

Making appropriations for Science, the Departments of State, Justice, and Commerce, and related agencies for the fiscal year ending September 30, 2006, and for other purposes.

Be it enacted by the Senate and House of Representatives of the United States of America in Congress assembled, That the following sums are appropriated, out of any money in the Treasury not otherwise appropriated, for the fiscal year ending September 30, 2006, and for other purposes, namely: Legal Services Corporation

Payment to the Legal Services Corporation

For payment to the Legal Services Corporation to carry out the purposes of the Legal Services Corporation Act of 1974, $330,803,000, of which $312,375,000 is for basic field programs and required independent audits; $2,539,000 is for the Office of Inspector General, of which such amounts as may be necessary may be used to conduct additional audits of recipients; $12,825,000 is for management and administration; $1,255,000 is for client self-help and information technology; and $1,809,000 is for grants to offset losses due to census adjustments.

Administrative Provision — Legal Services Corporation

None of the funds appropriated in this Act to the Legal Services Corporation shall be expended for any purpose prohibited or limited by, or contrary to any of the provisions of, sections 501, 502, 503, 504, 505, and 506 of Public Law 105-119, and all funds appropriated in this Act to the Legal Services Corporation shall be subject to the same terms and conditions set forth in such sections. . . .

LEGAL SERVICES CORPORATION, RESTRICTIONS ON THE USE OF APPROPRIATED FUNDS

LSC Appropriation Acts, available online at
http://www.lsc.gov/laws/appropriations.php

Public Law 104-134, 110 Stat. 1321 (H.R. 3019, 1996) (repeated in subsequent appropriation bills)

Sec. 504. (a) None of the funds appropriated in this Act to the Legal Services Corporation may be used to provide financial assistance to any person or entity (which may be referred to in this section as a "recipient") —

(1) that makes available any funds, personnel, or equipment for use in advocating or opposing any plan or proposal, or represents any party or participates in any other way in litigation, that is intended to or has the effect of altering, revising, or reapportioning a legislative, judicial, or elective district at any level of government, including influencing the timing or manner of the taking of a census;

(2) that attempts to influence the issuance, amendment, or revocation of any executive order, regulation, or other statement of general applicability and future effect by any Federal, State, or local agency;

(3) that attempts to influence any part of any adjudicatory proceeding of any Federal, State, or local agency if such part of the

proceeding is designed for the formulation or modification of any agency policy of general applicability and future effect;

(4) that attempts to influence the passage or defeat of any legislation, constitutional amendment, referendum, initiative, or any similar procedure of the Congress or a State or local legislative body;

(5) that attempts to influence the conduct of oversight proceedings of the Corporation or any person or entity receiving financial assistance provided by the Corporation;

(6) that pays for any personal service, advertisement, telegram, telephone communication, letter, printed or written matter, administrative expense, or related expense, associated with an activity prohibited in this section;

(7) that initiates or participates in a class action suit;

(8) that files a complaint or otherwise initiates or participates in litigation against a defendant, or engages in a precomplaint settlement negotiation with a prospective defendant, unless—

(A) each plaintiff has been specifically identified, by name, in any complaint filed for purposes of such litigation or prior to the precomplaint settlement negotiation; and

(B) a statement or statements of facts written in English and, if necessary, in a language that the plaintiffs understand, that enumerate the particular facts known to the plaintiffs on which the complaint is based, have been signed by the plaintiffs, are kept on file by the recipient, and are made available to any Federal department or agency that is auditing or monitoring the activities of the Corporation or of the recipient, and to any auditor or monitor receiving Federal funds to conduct such auditing or monitoring, including any auditor or monitor of the Corporation. . . .

(9) unless—

(A) prior to the provision of financial assistance—

(i) if the person or entity is a nonprofit organization, the governing board of the person or entity has set specific priorities in writing, pursuant to section 1007(a)(2)(C)(i) of the Legal Services Corporation Act (42 U.S.C. 2996f(a)(2)(C)(i)), of the types of matters and cases to which the staff of the nonprofit organization shall devote time and resources; and

(ii) the staff of such person or entity has signed a written agreement not to undertake cases or matters other than in accordance with the specific priorities set by such governing board, except in emergency situations defined by such board and in accordance with the written procedures of such board for such situations. . . .

(10) that provides legal assistance for or on behalf of any alien, unless the alien is present in the United States and is—

(A) an alien lawfully admitted for permanent residence as defined in section 101(a)(20) of the Immigration and Nationality Act (8 U.S.C. 1101(a)(20));

(B) an alien who—

(i) is married to a United States citizen or is a parent or an unmarried child under the age of 21 years of such a citizen; and

(ii) has filed an application to adjust the status of the alien to the status of a lawful permanent resident under the Immigration and Nationality Act (8 U.S.C. 1101 et seq.), which application has not been rejected;

(C) an alien who is lawfully present in the United States pursuant to an admission under section 207 of the Immigration and Nationality Act (8 U.S.C. 1157) (relating to refugee admission) or who has been granted asylum by the Attorney General under such Act;

(D) an alien who is lawfully present in the United States as a result of withholding of deportation by the Attorney General pursuant to section 243(h) of the Immigration and Nationality Act (8 U.S.C. 1253(h));

(E) an alien to whom section 305 of the Immigration Reform and Control Act of 1986 (8 U.S.C. 1101 note) applies, but only to the extent that the legal assistance provided is the legal assistance described in such section; or

(F) an alien who is lawfully present in the United States as a result of being granted conditional entry to the United States before April 1, 1980, pursuant to section 203(a)(7) of the Immigration and Nationality Act (8 U.S.C. 1153(a)(7)), as in effect on March 31, 1980, because of persecution or fear of persecution on account of race, religion, or political calamity;

(11) that supports or conducts a training program for the purpose of advocating a particular public policy or encouraging a political activity, a labor or antilabor activity, a boycott, picketing, a strike, or a demonstration, including the dissemination of information about such a policy or activity, except that this paragraph shall not be construed to prohibit the provision of training to an attorney or a paralegal to prepare the attorney or paralegal to provide—

(A) adequate legal assistance to eligible clients; or

(B) advice to any eligible client as to the legal rights of the client;

(12) that claims (or whose employee claims), or collects and retains, attorneys' fees pursuant to any Federal or State law permitting or requiring the awarding of such fees;

(13) that participates in any litigation with respect to abortion;

(14) that participates in any litigation on behalf of a person incarcerated in a Federal, State, or local prison;

(15) that initiates legal representation or participates in any other way, in litigation, lobbying, or rulemaking, involving an effort to reform a Federal or State welfare system, except that this paragraph shall not be construed to preclude a recipient from representing an individual eligible client who is seeking specific relief from a welfare

agency if such relief does not involve an effort to amend or otherwise challenge existing law in effect on the date of the initiation of the representation;

[Stricken language to conform with Legal Services Corp. v. Velazquez, 531 U.S. 533 (2001), holding unconstitutional the stricken portion of the statute.]

(16) that defends a person in a proceeding to evict the person from a public housing project if—

(A) the person has been charged with the illegal sale or distribution of a controlled substance; and

(B) the eviction proceeding is brought by a public housing agency because the illegal drug activity of the person threatens the health or safety of another tenant residing in the public housing project or employee of the public housing agency;

(17) unless such person or entity agrees that the person or entity, and the employees of the person or entity, will not accept employment resulting from in-person unsolicited advice to a nonattorney that such nonattorney should obtain counsel or take legal action, and will not refer such nonattorney to another person or entity or an employee of the person or entity, that is receiving financial assistance provided by the Corporation;. . . .

NOTE ON LSC RESTRICTIONS

Practice restrictions like those listed above typically come in appropriations bills, in which Congress blocks funding to any recipient of LSC funding that engages in the forbidden practices, whether or not the forbidden activity is directly supported by the LSC funds. In addition to the restrictions like those above, entities funded by LSC are prohibited from participating in litigation designed to assist clients in obtaining access to euthanasia services and from seeking, in connection with any lawsuit attorney's fees that might otherwise be available under fee-shifting statutes.

Some of the statutory conditions consist of provisions one might find in any government program: requirements that the organization have a mission, that it keep records, and engage in good management practices. Other prohibitions are aimed at preventing LSC-funded organizations from representing certain kinds of clients or from bringing suits seeking certain kinds of relief. For two examples of the first restriction, consider what it means that LSC-funded lawyers are prohibited from (a) representing any client in any case that might generate a fee in the ordinary markets; and (b) from representing tenants facing eviction from public housing if they have been charged with the sale of drugs. For two examples of the second kind of restriction, LSC lawyers may not file class actions, and they may not lobby any legislative body on behalf of their clients. One can get a good sense of the restrictions by visiting the section of the LSC Web site labeled "LSC Regulations," online at http://www.lsc.gov/laws/regulations.php.

In one instance the Supreme Court has struck down, as violating the first amendment, an LSC regulation that forbade lawyers assisting clients claiming welfare benefits from arguing that certain portions of the welfare law violated either federal statutes or the constitution. Legal Services Corp. v. Vasquez, 531 U.S. 533 (2001).

Consider the meaning of the pattern of restrictions that remain, bearing in mind that these have persisted through changes in party control of Congress and the Executive Branch. These restrictions are not, therefore, easily understood as the momentary triumph of one party or dominant set of political values. Why have these restrictions accreted? And how do they shape the practice of Legal Services lawyers?

LEGAL SERVICES CORPORATION, 1999 ANNUAL REPORT

For 25 Years, America's
Partner For Equal Justice

A Special Report to Congress April 30, 2000
Legal Services Corporation
Serving the Civil Legal Needs
Of Low-Income Americans

I. Summary

Legal Services Corporation (LSC) is a private, non-membership, nonprofit corporation in the District of Columbia. The Board of Directors of LSC is composed of eleven voting members who are appointed by the President of the United States with the advice and consent of the Senate. By law, the Board is bipartisan: no more than six members can be of the same political party.

LSC plays a central role in providing low-income Americans with access to legal assistance and information concerning critical civil legal problems. Created in 1974, LSC is charged by Congress "to provide equal access to the system of justice in our Nation for individuals who seek redress of grievances" and "to provide high quality legal assistance to those who would otherwise be unable to afford adequate legal counsel."

For 1999, LSC grantees reported closing 1,038,662 million civil legal cases relating to issues such as domestic violence, child custody and visitation rights, evictions, access to health care, bankruptcy, unemployment and disability claims, and many other issues that millions of low-income Americans face throughout their lives. Without the funding provided by LSC, many of these individuals would have no other source of legal assistance for these problems.

II. The National Legal Services Program

Legal Services Corporation funds local legal services programs to serve clients in every state, county, and congressional district in the United States as well as in Puerto Rico, the Virgin Islands, Guam and Micronesia. In addition, special service areas are funded for two populations with special needs — Native Americans and migrant workers. Eligibility for services is determined on a case-by-case basis pursuant to grantee eligibility criteria established under parameters set forth in LSC regulations. Each grantee establishes a maximum income eligibility level, not to exceed 125 percent of the current official Federal Poverty Income Guidelines.

In 1996, Congress implemented a number of new accountability requirements including competitive bidding for Legal Services Corporation grants. This system of competitive bidding eliminated the right of grantees to a hearing to contest a funding decision awarding a grant to a competitor, ensuring LSC can award grants to the best applicants without unnecessary administrative barriers. Additionally, new compliance monitoring procedures, which use outside auditors to monitor grantee compliance with regulations and to perform comprehensive yearly oversight of grantee activities, were formulated. Another new provision adopted in 1997 prohibits any local program that has been found to engage in a substantial violation of the law or its grant conditions from being considered for an LSC grant in future competitions.

Also in 1996, other new requirements were adopted governing what legal services programs can do and whom they can represent. These new guidelines have refocused the LSC delivery system on serving individual clients with particular legal needs. With the implementation of these restrictions, legal services attorneys are not permitted to initiate or participate in class action lawsuits. They may not challenge or engage in any activity to influence welfare reform. They may not collect court-awarded attorneys' fees. Litigation on behalf of prisoners and representation of undocumented and other categories of aliens is also prohibited. Other new requirements address redistricting, cases involving eviction from public housing of individuals charged with or convicted of drug violations and participation in government rulemaking and solicitation. Unlike past laws restricting the work of legal services, these provisions apply to all the funds of a recipient, with very few specified exceptions.

All local LSC-funded programs are administered by local boards of directors (or other governing bodies, in certain instances), a majority of whose members are appointed by local bar associations, and provide legal assistance to individuals pursuant to locally determined priorities that respond to community conditions and needs. Based on these priorities, local programs hire staff, contact local attorneys, and develop pro bono programs for the direct delivery of legal assistance to eligible clients. LSC requires each legal services program to spend an amount equal to at least 12.5 percent of its annualized grant to encourage participation by private attorneys in the provision of legal assistance to poor individuals.

The legal services delivery system offers a model of efficient resolution of disputes and avoidance of unnecessary litigation. Only a very small percentage

(9% in 1999) of LSC-funded cases are resolved by the decision of a court, and the majority of these are family law cases that require a court determination.

Rather than litigating cases, legal services lawyers consistently find other, more efficient ways to solve problems for their clients. Under tremendous pressure from the demand for their services, they know they must use their limited resources wisely. As in past years, nearly three-fourths of cases in 1999 were resolved through advice, referral, or brief services.

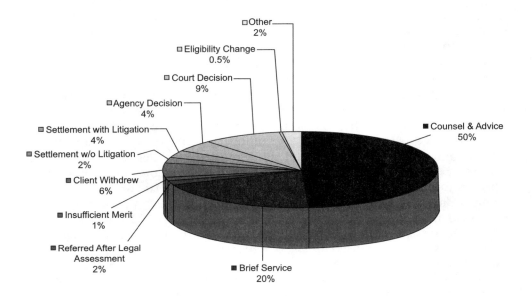

LEGAL SERVICES CORPORATION, 2007 ANNUAL REPORT

Grant Activity Reports 2007

2007 LSC-Eligible
Case Services Summary by Case Type

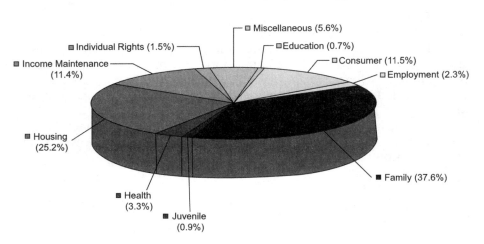

Type of Case	Total Closed Cases	Percent*
Consumer	104,698	11.5%
Education	6,292	0.7%
Employment	20,599	2.3%
Family	340,572	37.6%
Juvenile	8,406	0.9%
Health	30,333	3.3%
Housing	228,029	25.2%
Income Maintenance	103,258	11.4%
Individual Rights	13,925	1.5%
Miscellaneous	50,395	5.6%
Total	906,507	100.00%

LEGAL AID FOUNDATION OF LOS ANGELES

Compiled from http://www.lafla.org, (last visited February 23, 2009)

Sources of Financial Support

The Legal Aid Foundation of Los Angeles receives funding from a wide range of public and private sources: government agencies, law firms, corporations and foundations, attorneys, and public-spirited individuals. Their support in 2007 made it possible for LAFLA to assist more than 55,000 poor and low-income individuals and families who came to one of our six neighborhood offices, three courthouse domestic violence clinics, four courthouse Self Help Legal Access Centers, and numerous off-site clinics and workshops, seeking help with their critical legal needs.

- The federal Legal Services Corporation (LSC), our largest funding source, provided 36% of our operating income in 2007.
- The State Bar of California's Legal Services Trust Fund Program provided 7% of our budget: IOLTA funds accounted for 4%, while the Bar-distributed Equal Access Fund provided an additional 3%.
- The cities of Los Angeles, Santa Monica, Long Beach and West Hollywood together provided 6% of our operating income, funding general legal services to low-income residents of those cities and the Domestic Violence Clinic in the West District Courthouse.
- The County of Los Angeles provided 6% of our budget, funding family law services to victims of domestic violence who are participants in the CalWORKS program.
- Grants from the U.S. Department of Justice, U.S. Department of Health & Human Services, U.S. Department of Housing & Urban Development, Equal Justice Works and from private foundations including the Vera Institute, the United Nations, and Capital Group Companies Foundation provided 6% of our budget, funding specialized projects targeting

---

*Percentages do not total exactly because of rounding.

domestic violence victims, torture survivors and human trafficking victims, low-income consumers, and other vulnerable populations.

- A grant from the United Way of Greater Los Angeles "Pathways Out of Poverty" action plan provided additional unrestricted support for assistance to low-income tenants and victims of domestic violence and for advocacy to increase the financial stability of low-income communities.

[The 2007 Annual Report put total revenues for the Foundation at $21,359,548.]

Frequently Asked Questions
Client Services

q. Who is eligible for LAFLA's client services?

a. LAFLA is only permitted to help people whose incomes are below a level fixed by the federal government and who live in our service area.

q. What kind of eligibility information will I be asked if I apply for services?

a. You will be asked about your income, the property you own, your zip code, family size, age, race, and citizenship or immigrations status.

q. Will my information be kept confidential?

a. Yes. All information you give us is confidential and will not be given to anyone without your permission.

q. Does LAFLA have interpreters for non-English speaking clients?

a. Yes. All of our offices have LAFLA advocates who speak Spanish. We also provide interpretation of several Asian languages through our Asian/Pacific Islander Unit.

q. How can I apply for services?

a. You can either call our Client Intake Number at (800) 399-4529 or click here for an online version of our emergency legal help. Please also see our Contact/Find Us pages for office locations and hotlines.

q. What kind of cases does LAFLA handle?

a. (For detailed information, please visit our Client Services section.)

- Community Economic Development: We help community groups incorporate and maintain nonprofit status, develop business ventures, multi-family residential and commercial developments, and create homeownership opportunities.
- Consumer Law: We handle cases involving consumer fraud, including vocational school fraud, contracts and warranties, loan and installment purchase agreements, unfair sales practices, discriminatory banking practices, debt collection harassment, repossessions, and wage garnishment.
- Employment Law: We handle primarily wage claims and unemployment benefit insurance denials. We help some workers who have been unlawfully terminated.
- Family Law: We provide advice concerning child custody and visitation, child support, and domestic violence. All family law intake is done through two walk-in clinics: Maynard Toll Counseling Center, located in the downtown Superior Courthouse and the Domestic Violence

Project in the Santa Monica Courthouse, and an appointment-only clinic for Santa Monica Residents.

- Government Benefits: We help with problems involving CalWORKS, Social Security Supplemental Income (SSI), Medi-Cal, Medicare, Food Stamps, IHSS, welfare, healthcare, and General Relief.
- Homeownership: We help with foreclosures, problems with home improvement loans, home equity loans, bail bond liens, mechanics liens or other types of loans against your home, faulty home improvement work performed, and legal problems related to a transaction involving your home.
- Housing: The Housing/Eviction Defense Center prepares responses to unlawful detainers and represents some clients in court. We also file lawsuits to get buildings repaired and handle cases involving rent control, unsafe buildings, utility shut-offs, and subsidized or public housing problems. We offer 3/30 day notice and pre-trial clinics.
- Immigration Law: We represent some individuals in deportation proceedings when legal defenses are available, helps immigrants who are victims of domestic violence to become lawful permanent residents, and hold naturalization workshops.
- Victims of Violent Crime: We help residents in the City of LA file claims with the Victims of Violent Crime fund.

q. What cases do you not handle?
a. LAFLA cannot take criminal or fee-generating cases. In addition, there are restrictions on representing prisoners, abortion cases, selective service, and others.

d. Professional Philanthropy: The Rise of Pro Bono

SCOTT CUMMINGS, THE POLITICS OF PRO BONO

52 UCLA Law Review 1 (2004)

Introduction

The dominant narrative of pro bono over the past decade was one of a professional ideal under siege. . . .

Behind the headlines and hand-wringing over decreasing big-firm pro bono, a much more important story was in fact taking shape — one which was transforming the nation's system for delivering free legal services to poor and underserved clients. The defining feature of the 1990s' boom was not that private lawyers were prioritizing profit over pro bono service. This had, to some degree, always been the case. Instead, the real story was the radical change taking place in *how pro bono services were being dispensed.* Whereas pro bono had traditionally been provided *informally* — frequently by solo and small firm practitioners who conferred free services as a matter of individual largesse — by the end of the 1990s pro bono was regimented and organized, distributed through a network of structures designed to facilitate the mass provision of free services by law firm volunteers acting out of professional duty. . . .

[Cummings chronicles the rise of the Legal Aid movement, the federally funded Legal Services Corporation, and the political struggles over achieving adequate funding for either system. He then describes the growth of the large firm in the closing decades of the twentieth century and the growing unease among bar leaders at the unmet need for legal services among the poor.]

The combination of these developments prompted many large firms to augment their pro bono programs as a way to appeal to interested law students, improve their rankings, and facilitate compliance with the Challenge. Firms increased their reliance on pro bono committees, hired full-time coordinators to expand pro bono dockets, formalized pro bono policies, and undertook large-scale pro bono projects. They also cemented relationships with legal services and public interest groups, launched new externship programs, and publicized pro bono achievements on web sites and in annual reports. The end result was striking: Institutionalized pro bono, virtually nonexistent only two decades before, now occupied a central place in the big firm.

II. The New Architecture of Pro Bono

A. Collaboration

"Collaboration" has become the buzzword of the pro bono system, which operates by establishing relationships between private lawyers and the bar-sponsored programs, legal services groups, and public interest organizations that link them with clients. These relationships rely on an infrastructure to connect firms with opportunities, a network of organizations that support and facilitate pro bono programs, and an intrafirm coordinating system to take in and distribute cases to firm lawyers.

1. Connectivity

For this collaborative network to succeed, it is critical that there are organizations external to law firms that operate to connect firm lawyers with pro bono clients. This function is undertaken by two distinct types of pro bono programs: *referral* organizations and *strategic* organizations. The referral organizations tend to be organized in connection with and subsidized by local bar associations, and exist primarily to serve as a conduit between low-income clients and law firm volunteers. Thus, on the community-based side, they set service priorities, make triage decisions, engage in client education and outreach, and conduct initial client screening. On the law firm side, referral organizations establish contacts with firm liaisons, conduct outreach to private lawyers, package cases for volunteers, broker initial meetings between clients and private counsel, provide training to firm lawyers, and troubleshoot difficult lawyer-client relationships. Referral organizations exist in every state, and range in scope from one-person operations to large, multiproject groups.

An example of the large referral organization is Public Counsel, which was established in 1970. Jointly sponsored by the Los Angeles and Beverly Hills Bar

Associations, Public Counsel is now the nation's largest pro bono organization, with twenty-seven attorneys and a significant support staff. Public Counsel is organized into six project areas — child care, homelessness prevention, children's rights, immigration, community development, and consumer law — with staff attorneys and paralegals who prescreen cases, determine whether cases are appropriate for placement with private volunteers, and distribute case listings to firm liaisons. Public Counsel operates a "mixed" program, referring a majority of cases to pro bono volunteers, but also retaining a portion of cases for in-house representation by staff attorneys.[4]

The Volunteer Legal Services Program (VLSP) of the Bar Association of San Francisco is another example of a mixed program, albeit one that moves closer to a pure referral model. Organized in 1982, VLSP coordinates pro bono services in a broad range of areas, including homeless assistance, family law, eviction defense, debt collection defense, guardianships, and home equity fraud. VLSP's homelessness attorneys, who constitute almost half of the staff, regularly represent homeless clients, particularly when emergencies arise or when cases are inappropriate for placement. Outside of the homeless project, however, VLSP lawyers refer almost every case to pro bono volunteers. These core staff attorneys have expertise in different substantive areas and are involved in cases primarily at the level of case selection, volunteer recruitment and training, and case management. For instance, the VLSP family law attorney does not represent any clients, instead providing trainings to pro bono volunteers and acting as a mentor during the representation. She is also responsible for maintaining relationships with client-generating organizations such as battered women's shelters and hospitals, and working with these organizations to assure the quality of service delivery. Other core staff have similar duties and generally do not act as attorneys of record in cases. Similar multi-issue referral projects exist in major cities around the country.

In addition, there are referral programs that are issue-specific. The Harriet Buhai Center for Family Law in Los Angeles is a prime example of this type of group. The Center's mission is to provide legal assistance to low-income clients in the areas of family law and domestic violence through the volunteer efforts of private attorneys, paralegals, and law students. It was opened in 1981 under the auspices of the Women Lawyers Association of Los Angeles, after the Legal Aid Foundation of Los Angeles (LAFLA) closed its family law unit in the wake of the federal cutbacks. It now operates with a small staff that performs client intake, recruits volunteers from the family law bar, and conducts trainings to facilitate pro bono service to over 1000 clients annually. Services are provided primarily through a pro per assistance program, which uses volunteers to train clients to represent themselves in divorce and other family law cases, and a pro bono panel that deploys volunteers to represent clients on more complicated matters.

Referral organizations focused on linking transactional business lawyers with nonprofit and small for-profit organizational clients have gained

---

4. Public Counsel estimates that between 10 and 15 percent of cases are handled by in-house staff attorneys. *See* Telephone Interview with Dan Grunfeld.

increased attention within the pro bono system. This is the result of the convergence of two trends: The expansion of corporate practices within large law firms during the high-tech boom of the 1990s increased the supply of transactional attorneys, who have traditionally done little pro bono work, while the growth of community economic development as an antipoverty field increased the demand for corporate, real estate, and tax law assistance from community-based organizational clients. The Lawyers Alliance for New York, founded in 1969, is the most prominent referral organization linking pro bono business attorneys and community organizations, although others have developed more recently in response to the surge in interest.

Strategic pro bono organizations, in turn, tend to be independent nonprofit groups that have a substantive mandate to pursue a specified advocacy agenda. These organizations have staff attorneys who pursue case representation, leveraging pro bono resources pragmatically to support their advocacy work. This is distinct from the referral organizations, which have as their primary mission the promotion of pro bono volunteerism.

Legal services programs are one type of strategic organization in that their primary mission is direct service. Because of the federal PAI mandate for LSC-funded groups, and frequently out of the need for greater attorney resources, legal services programs rely on a significant base of private-sector volunteers. In Los Angeles, LAFLA is an example of an LSC-funded organization that has begun to develop significant pro bono ties. In the past, LAFLA primarily complied with PAI requirements by paying pro bono organizations, like Public Counsel and the Harriett Buhai Center for Family Law, to facilitate client placements with pro bono attorneys. Recently, LAFLA has started to focus on establishing its own pro bono volunteer network by making efforts to recruit at large firms. It has also devoted more resources internally to identifying, packaging, and marketing cases for pro bono volunteer representation, which has resulted in the expansion of pro bono service. An example in the rural context is Legal Services of Eastern Missouri (LSEM), which has established a Volunteer Lawyers Program, through which "pro bono lawyers can handle their own cases, serve as co-counsel with LSEM staff in cases, participate in outreach programs and make community education presentations."

A notable trend in the legal services area is for faith-based organizations to rely more heavily on volunteer attorneys to serve poor clients. For instance, the Christian Legal Aid Society in Virginia has approximately 700 volunteers who last year provided 4000 individuals and families with free legal services. Baltimore's Jewish Legal Services has approximately 180 volunteers.

Traditional public interest groups constitute the other major type of strategic organization. These range from very large groups with multiple affiliate offices — such as national organizations like the Lawyers' Committee for Civil Rights Under Law (Lawyers' Committee), ACLU, NAACP, and National Resources Defense Counsel (NRDC) — to smaller, single-office agencies — Los Angeles' Asian Pacific American Legal Center (APALC), San Francisco's Equal Rights Advocates, and New York's Brennan Center for Justice being examples. Since these groups, even at their largest, tend to have small staffs and modest budgets, they have developed ways to strategically use an array of pro bono relationships — from active co-counseling to more passive pro bono placement — to lessen the burden of large-scale litigation. These public interest groups tend to be concentrated in large cities — particularly Washington, D.C., New York, Boston, Los Angeles, and San Francisco — and rely significantly on volunteer counsel from these areas.

On one end of the spectrum is the co-counseling model adopted by the Lawyers' Committee, which was established in 1963, and now has a national office in Washington, D.C., and a number of field offices around the country focused on race discrimination lawsuits. Every case the Lawyers' Committee brings is handled in connection with volunteer counsel, a model that is rooted in the organization's original mission of involving the private bar to address racial discrimination during the civil rights era. This means that staff attorneys do not independently handle cases; it also means that pro bono volunteers are not simply handed over the cases and considered counsel of record. Instead, the co-counseling model typically involves one or two staff attorneys who develop a joint litigation plan in connection with law firm volunteers. The volunteers generally take on the bulk of the litigation responsibility, such as discovery and court hearings, although staff attorneys will assist in brief writing and conduct depositions. Staff attorneys are viewed as lending substantive legal and policy expertise, focusing volunteers on the larger picture and ensuring that the positions taken in any given lawsuit are consistent with the Lawyers' Committee's policy goals. In addition, staff attorneys also serve as a bridge between the firms and the clients, who are sometimes skeptical of law firm lawyers. The timing of firm involvement varies: Often, firm lawyers will come in at the beginning of the case and play a critical role in developing litigation strategy; other times, they come in later to perform more defined tasks. All decisions regarding litigation strategy, such as whether to appeal, are made jointly by the firm and staff attorneys.

At the national office, the Lawyers' Committee employs a pro bono coordinator who is responsible for cultivating relationships with law firms, facilitating the placement of cases with volunteer co-counsel, and monitoring ongoing cases. Outreach to firm lawyers is conducted in part through the organization's massive board of directors, which is composed of 244 lawyers who provide access to the country's major firms. The pro bono coordinator at the Lawyers' Committee also develops separate law firm contacts, largely in areas where there is not a Lawyers' Committee local affiliate, by making connections with law firms and keeping lists of other lawyers who have expressed interest in volunteer opportunities. Cases come to the Lawyers' Committee through direct client contacts, as well as referrals from other public interest organizations. Once they are accepted internally, the staff produces a lengthy descriptive memo, which includes a discussion of the case, an evaluation of legal theories, estimates of costs, and a conflicts analysis. This information is condensed into a shorter memo that is then circulated via e-mail to law firm contacts. Once a firm expresses interest and the matter clears conflicts checks, then the full case information is shared. Upon case acceptance, a co-counseling letter is executed that details the allocation of responsibilities, and the case is then assigned within the Lawyers' Committee to a staff attorney to co-counsel with the firm.

Other public interest groups depart from the Lawyers' Committee model, instead adopting a more flexible approach that calibrates pro bono involvement depending on the type of case involved. The ACLU of Southern California is an example of this approach. Most of the cases conducted by the office are handled exclusively by staff attorneys. However, pro bono volunteers are brought in for two different types of cases. One type involves relatively small cases that present discrete issues that the ACLU would like to support but does not have the staff attorney resources to take on. These are referred to pro bono counsel, although the ACLU remains on the briefs as attorney of record. The other type of case is the large-scale class action lawsuit in which the ACLU needs the resources of the firms to carry the discovery load and bring expertise in complex litigation. In these situations, the ACLU actively co-counsels along the lines of the Lawyers' Committee model. To access pro bono volunteers, ACLU lawyers use informal networks, rely on law firms with a proven pro bono record, and recruit new lawyers through firm presentations. In this way, strategic organizations like the ACLU employ processes for pro bono recruitment and case placement that are similar to those used in the referral context, even though their reliance on pro bono is motivated by different organizational goals.

2. Facilitation

Although the pro bono system is not centrally coordinated, it is facilitated and financially supported by a number of important nongovernmental actors. Most significant is the organized bar, which serves as a critical transmission vehicle for pro bono initiatives. The ABA, in particular, is an active participant in the movement to establish formal pro bono policies and structures. . . . State bars are also involved in organizing and supporting pro bono programs. All but six states have established a state-wide pro bono agency, and almost all of these operate with state bar support. These programs are generally involved in recruiting pro bono attorneys, training pro bono volunteers, and connecting clients with volunteer lawyers.

The State Bar of California's pro bono program highlights many of these features. In the late 1970s, the State Bar established an Office of Legal Services, Access & Fairness to promote voluntary pro bono initiatives state-wide. The Office, which staffs and supports the State Bar's Standing Committee on the Delivery of Legal Services, helps "local bar associations, legal services organizations and other groups develop pro bono programs and train lawyers to provide free and low-cost legal services to people who cannot afford to pay for counsel." Specifically, the Office supports local pro bono organizational development and volunteer recruitment, organizes a pro bono awards program to recognize outstanding volunteers, administers an emeritus attorney program that waives the State Bar active membership fee for otherwise retired attorneys to provide pro bono service, and convenes a state-wide conference for legal services and pro bono providers. The State Bar also provides critical funding for pro bono through its IOLTA program, which sets aside 10 percent of each county's IOLTA allocation for organizations that primarily use volunteer attorneys.

. . .

3. Coordination

Although solo and small-firm practitioners play important roles in the pro bono system, the focus is on large law firms, which have been targeted as those in the best position to make significant pro bono investments. As a result, a parallel organizational structure has been built inside big firms that provides the link between nonprofit pro bono programs and law firm lawyers. Two features of pro bono's intrafirm structure stand out: differentiated personnel roles and formalized procedures.

a. Differentiation

* * *

Intrafirm pro bono programs reflect this management structure. For one, rather than adopting a laissez-faire approach to pro bono activities, many firms now have pro bono committees that oversee the intake of pro bono matters, assign cases to lawyers, develop firm-wide policies, and track data on performance. Of the fifty firms on *AmLaw*'s "A-List," which is the list of the nation's most "elite" firms, at least forty have formal committee structures. Committees vary in structure and practice. Some, such as Washington, D.C.-based Dickstein Shapiro Morin & Oshinsky have committees of as few as three attorneys, while others, like Los Angeles' Latham & Watkins, have firm-wide committees of thirty. Some firms have committees composed solely of partners, while others include associates, of counsel, and paralegals. Although some committees have been in existence for many years, there has been a recent surge, triggered in part by the increased pressure to produce higher pro bono numbers brought about by pro bono reporting systems. Moreover, over the past decade, there has been a shift toward broader firm representation on the committees, with many firms now including lawyers from all domestic offices and incorporating a higher proportion of transactional attorneys, who have historically been only marginally involved. . . .

b. Formality

Pro bono, like other firm activities, has also become highly formalized in its procedural implementation. In addition to the codification of billable-hour credit policies, firms have formalized more mundane rules and practices, creating distinct procedural guidelines for case acceptance, conflicts checks, supervision, and closure. There is some convergence in terms of formal policies, although the details are difficult to compare. Most firms now have a written pro bono policy that specifies what constitutes pro bono service, what type of billable credit is given, and how pro bono is evaluated for the purposes of bonuses and promotion. . . .

B. Efficiency

Another key feature of institutionalized pro bono is the emphasis on efficiency. In the pro bono context, efficiency is associated with two primary ideas: transaction cost reduction and carefully targeted resource commitments. . . .

1. Transaction Costs

. . .

a. Menus

In coordinating between clients and volunteers, there arises the problem of interest convergence: Volunteers must be *attracted* to a pro bono opportunity.

This means that it must not only be substantively interesting to the volunteer, but that it also must be feasible in the context of the volunteer's other obligations. In a large firm with differently situated lawyers, the problem is multiplied: Some attorneys will be interested in taking on a large antidiscrimination suit while others will only have time for a smaller engagement, like a legal clinic. For organizations that are seeking to access pro bono resources, it becomes critical to try to match opportunities with the range of possible interests and commitment levels. Organizations have therefore moved in the direction of providing "menus" of cases that span across a range of substantive interests and involve variable time investments. By providing information in a menu format, organizations attempt to more closely coordinate with their volunteer constituency. . . .

d. Signals

Another way that the pro bono system attempts to reduce the costs of information exchange is through signaling. Law firms have multiple demands on their pro bono resources. They receive requests for services from referring pro bono groups, as well as individual client inquiries. It is costly and time-consuming for firms to thoroughly vet these requests, a process which includes ensuring that they are consistent with law firm policy and do not pose any conflicts of interest. One way of minimizing this cost is by relying on the case screening capacity of referring organizations. Some firms thus prefer cases referred from trusted organizations, deeming them "pre-approved" and thereby subject to only a bare conflicts check. Morrison & Foerster, for example, accepts a category of pre-approved cases from designated referral organizations. It also prefers referrals from established legal services groups, which are viewed as better able to screen cases and make triage decisions that comport with firm goals. In a similar vein, the Los Angeles office of Latham & Watkins also as a matter of practice accepts large numbers of cases from trusted pro bono referral organizations, namely Public Counsel and Bet Tzedek Legal Services. Cases referred from these organizations are assumed to be properly vetted such that firm lawyers do not have to overinvest in case evaluation. Referrals from trusted organizations thereby signal important information to firm pro bono liaisons about the acceptability of particular cases, thereby reducing the firm resources expended on close scrutiny. . . .

The D.C. Bar Pro Bono Program has a sophisticated clinic program that developed in the mid-1990s as large Washington, D.C. firms sought to step up their pro bono activity in response to the new *AmLaw* rankings and the Law Firm *Pro Bono* Challenge. At that point, there was a strong pro bono tradition among big D.C. firms, although they tended to engage in large civil rights and death penalty cases, rather than more routine family law or landlord-tenant matters. The concept of the D.C. Bar clinic model was to aggregate a large number of small cases — mostly child custody, landlord-tenant, public benefits, wage-and-hour, consumer, and personal injury matters — to make the scale attractive to firms. The initial goal was to institute one clinic every two weeks, with firms committing to staff two clinics per year. . . .

The D.C. Bar Pro Bono Program underscores the mutual benefits to law firms and pro bono organizations derived from the clinic model. On the law firm side, clinics provide high volume pro bono within a controlled environment. Law firm attorneys carve out well-defined time slots within which to do pro bono cases; gain pro bono credit for minimal advice and referral activities, as well as more traditional case representation on routine matters; and take advantage of extensive training and heavy back-up support. For the pro bono organization, clinics represent a chance to maximize client service by leveraging firm attorneys. Moreover, to the extent that clinics boost pro bono representation, they can also provide financial advantages for pro bono organizations that rely on funding sources that tie contributions to the number of clients served. . . .

2. Calibration

. . .

b. Specialization

While law firms focus on generating efficiencies from scale, they also pursue efficiency gains from specialization. The addition of pro bono coordinators to law firm staff reflects this impulse: By investing in a coordinator position, the pro bono payoff can be high since the coordinator removes many of the institutional impediments that dissuade lawyers from taking on pro bono cases.

Law firms have adopted other pro bono practices as a way of tapping the benefits of specialization. The most notable trend is the increasing use of externships as a means of designating individual attorneys to engage full-time in pro bono work. . . .

c. Accountability

The institutional system of pro bono relies on voluntary participation. Accountability mechanisms are therefore important as a means of ensuring adequate volunteer levels. They are also necessary to target services to low-income clients and underrepresented causes, rather than bar activities or charitable organizations that do not serve the interests of marginalized groups. . . .

III. Pro Bono and the Public Good

In many ways, the system of institutionalized pro bono reflects what is best about the legal profession: Private-sector lawyers marshalling their resources to advance the interests of the poor and underserved. Yet the relationship between pro bono and the public good is more subtle and complex. As a system of multiparty collaborations, the shape of pro bono is influenced by actors with distinct, and sometimes conflicting, interests. Its identity is therefore constantly in flux, contested by the private lawyers, nonprofit staff, bar officials, government bureaucrats, and client groups who constitute its central stakeholders.

Within this fluid system, there are possibilities that actors exploit to advance the public good: Pro bono offers opportunities for pragmatic service provision and flexible advocacy, while providing a mechanism for leveraging private-sector resources. Tensions also arise as ideals of professionalism become explicitly linked to law firm economic interests. And, as with other systems for providing free services, constraints are imposed: corporate client interests limit the range of pro bono cases; law firm practice conditions influence the nature of lawyers' commitments; and financial and organizational demands shape the priorities of pro bono partnerships. . . .

Although there is no hard evidence of the extent to which the economic benefits of pro bono are actually realized by firms, the belief that pro bono can be used to generate a commercial return has nevertheless proven to be an important factor driving its institutionalization. Yet it is precisely the vigor with which this belief is asserted that places strains on traditional conceptions of public service. Indeed, the "business case" for pro bono challenges the ideal of public service by laying bare the nexus between professionalism and the commercial interests of the bar. To the extent that law firms explicitly assimilate pro bono to their bottom line concerns, it begins to look more like pro bono is undertaken for opportunistic rather than legitimate professional reasons. Of course, economic arguments are often used by well-meaning pro bono advocates in order to convince more bottom-line oriented colleagues to embrace pro bono programs. In this sense, the profession might view the economic arguments for pro bono pragmatically — using them to motivate skeptical firm leaders while maintaining a normative commitment to public service. Moreover, as the privatization movement lends credibility to the idea that public goals can be advanced by private actors pursuing private gain, the image of elite lawyers doing pro bono both to serve the public good and to make more money might be viewed as acceptable.

However, the promotion of pro bono as a market strategy also carries risks. Lawyers have always sought to set themselves apart from market pressures, offering their commitment to public service as a way of justifying professional privilege. Embracing the commercial benefits of pro bono may weaken claims to professional status, reinforcing the already low public opinion of lawyers as greedy and dishonest. In addition, law students may come to view pro bono with a jaundiced eye as firms lure them in with rosy promises of pro bono participation that are not matched by reality. Pro bono clients and organizations may also grow frustrated if economic considerations are seen to be impinging too much on firms' willingness to follow through on their volunteer obligations. Law firms are therefore placed in the position of having to carefully manage their pro bono commitments in order to negotiate the competing demands of profitability and professional duty.

C. Constraint

The network of alliances that characterizes institutionalized pro bono pairs commercial law firms with pro bono organizations and matches private lawyers with low-income clients. This network has provided critical sustenance to legal services and public interest groups, which have relied heavily upon pro bono resources to advance their agendas. However, a full accounting of pro bono must consider the tradeoffs made in exchange for this pragmatic alliance. These tradeoffs are a consequence of the dependence of pro bono upon the patronage of private-sector lawyers, particularly those in large commercial firms. This dependence influences the nature of pro bono cases, shapes opportunities for lawyer activism, and defines the content of pro bono partnerships.

1. Cases

Competitive pressures impact both the types of cases law firms undertake and the amount of resources they are willing to invest in pro bono work.

a. Conflicts

The chief consideration for law firms is cultivating their paying client base. Decisions about pro bono are therefore always filtered through the lens of how they will affect the interests of commercial clients. Conflict of interest analyses are of central concern within law firms, where pro bono committees and coordinators are charged with vigilantly monitoring pro bono requests for conflicts problems. As a threshold matter, pro bono requests are subject to the same screening process that applies to fee-generating cases. Under the Model Rules of Professional Conduct, a private lawyer is generally not permitted to take on a pro bono matter that is directly adverse to another client or materially limits the lawyer's ability to represent another client. In specific cases, these conflict rules can operate to preclude pro bono representation, particularly by large firms enmeshed in a complex web of client relations; however, the obstacles imposed by the existence of actual client conflicts can often be circumvented by shopping pro bono cases among a number of different firms.

Even when actual conflicts do not bar pro bono representation, the specter of so-called positional conflicts presents an additional hurdle. Positional conflicts arise when a lawyer advances an argument on behalf of one client that "is directly contrary to, or has a detrimental impact on, the position advanced on behalf of a second client in a different case or matter." Existing ethical rules generally permit representation despite the existence of positional conflicts, stating that a conflict exists only "if there is a significant risk that a lawyer's action on behalf of one client will materially limit the lawyer's effectiveness in representing another client in a different case." This creates a fairly high standard for refusing oppositional work, precluding a lawyer or her firm from asserting antagonistic positions for different clients "when a decision favoring one client will create a precedent likely to seriously weaken the position taken on behalf of the other client." . . .

Although there is no systematic evidence of the impact of positional conflicts, anecdotal accounts are suggestive of the obstacles positional issues impose in the large firm context. The most noticeable effect is to exclude pro bono cases that strike at the heart of corporate client interests, particularly employment, environmental, and consumer cases in which plaintiffs seek pro bono counsel to sue major companies. Thus, pro bono employment discrimination suits, particularly impact cases against major corporate employers, are regularly rejected by big firms. For instance, the pro bono coordinator at Skadden, Arps, Slate, Meagher & Flom indicated that it was difficult to get the firm to take on employment-related civil rights cases because of conflicts with labor clients—in contrast to cases in the voting rights or housing areas that were much easier to place. Similarly, the pro bono coordinator at Kilpatrick Stockton in Atlanta stated that the firm did not sue employers. . . .

c. Market Appeal

On the other side of the coin, big firms are more likely to support pro bono in areas where the potential for positional conflicts is slim and where the firm can expect positive public relations. Thus, firms are attracted to pro bono cases outside the scope of their core practice areas that are politically safe and easy to exit should a conflict arise. Domestic violence, probate, divorce, adoption, and bankruptcy are popular types of pro bono cases precisely because they pose little threat to paying client interests. Immigrant asylum and refugee cases also tend to be favored. When firms do take on employment cases, they are typically claims by individuals seeking to enforce minimum wage and overtime laws against small-scale employers—claims that usually proceed through administrative channels and result in settlements. In addition, firm participation in domestic violence, elder law, homelessness, bankruptcy, and similar types of legal clinics is particularly attractive in that it allows law firm lawyers to spend a discrete amount of time dispensing limited advice without being bound by normal conflicts rules. . . .

d. Comparison

Competitive pressures cause big law firms to strike a balance between different varieties of pro bono cases. Marketing concerns drive firms to take on a manageable number of impact cases, typically against public agencies; training needs are met by smaller direct services cases in areas where the risk of conflicts is low; and pro bono hours are boosted by death penalty cases, legal clinics, and creative measures like rotation programs and fellowships.

That certain cases are privileged while others are marginalized is not a unique feature of pro bono. Legal aid had its own case selection biases shaped by its financial dependence on charities, local businesses, and the bar. Law reform was discouraged while individual case representation was steered toward family disputes and other cases that promised not to challenge local business benefactors or take paying business away from private lawyers. The legal services program has seen its docket influenced by its relationship with the federal government, which has swung from supporting left-leaning law reform to restricting cases within a narrow range of individual service categories. Public interest organizations must take care to bring cases that comport with the goals of philanthropic foundations and other private donors. Private lawyers, in turn, choose pro bono cases based on the business interests of clients. In each context, the economic logic is clear: Patronage shapes case selection.

There are important systemic complementarities. Pro bono reinforces the federal legal services program by providing more attorneys for direct service representation and handling the cases that the program is prohibited from undertaking. Pro bono also augments the public interest sector by contributing firm resources to support large-scale law reform efforts constrained by nonprofit organizational capacities. However, there are also systemic gaps, particularly when it comes to cases involving major challenges to corporate practices, which big-firm pro bono shuns.

Pro Bono: A Postscript

This Article has mapped pro bono's vast institutionalization over the past two decades. Whereas free legal services have historically been dispensed through institutional structures like legal services, supplemented by the occasional act of individual kindness, private-sector lawyers—particularly those in large firms—are now thoroughly integrated into an extensive web of institutions designed to foster pro bono activity. This pro bono infrastructure is striking in its scope, composed of nonprofit pro bono intermediaries, bar-sponsored coordinating groups, philanthropic foundations, law schools, monitoring organizations, and referral web sites. Within law firms, institutionalization appears in centralized pro bono decision-making structures and dedicated pro bono personnel. Pro bono has, as a result, become the dominant means of dispensing free services to the poor and underserved, eclipsing other state-sponsored and nongovernmental mechanisms in importance. . . .

The story of pro bono is still being written. As trends of privatization, volunteerism, and globalization press forward, one can expect pro bono to be a growth industry in the years to come, not simply shaping the American system of free legal services, but informing the discussion about equal access to justice around the world. Questions about pro bono's effectiveness as a model for meeting the legal needs of poor and underserved groups will therefore take center stage. It is important that the advantages of pro bono—its decentralized structure, collaborative relationships, pragmatic alliances, and flexible approaches—receive full attention. Yet these advantages must be carefully weighed against the systemic challenges that pro bono poses: its refusal to take on corporate practice and its dilettantish approach to advancing the interests of marginalized groups. Instead of professional platitudes about the virtues of volunteerism, robust debate is therefore in order—debate that includes a full airing of both the promise and perils of pro bono, and provides a rigorous account of what equal access to justice looks like in practice. To avoid this debate invites the uncritical expansion of pro bono as a stop-gap measure rather than a thoughtful response to the dilemma of unequal legal representation. More fundamentally, the failure to confront pro bono's limitations risks privileging professional interests over concerns of social justice—promoting the image of equal access without the reality.

SUE REISINGER, BREAKING GROUNDS: PAULA BOGGS GIVES A STARBUCKS PRO BONO PROGRAM A DOUBLE ESPRESSO BOOST

Corporate Counsel, March 2, 2004

In 2002 Paula Boggs was one of ten lawyers on Corporate Counsel's short-list of assistant or deputy GCs who we thought had the potential to become a Fortune 500 GC in the next five years. We bet that Boggs—a former army paratrooper, junior staffer on Iran-contra, and partner at Seattle's Preston Gates & Ellis, then working as vice president-legal for products, operations and IT systems at Dell Inc. in Round Rock, Texas—would be in high demand.

We guessed right. That summer Boggs was offered the GC position at Starbucks Corp. The lawyer could have had her pick of jobs, but she chose the Seattle-based company, in large part because of its varied charitable efforts. Boggs was especially interested in expanding a nascent program started by her predecessor and run out of the legal department that helped Seattle's poor make their way through housing court. In the 15 months since she joined the ubiquitous latte purveyor, she has dramatically increased the size of the program, made her department's 30 lawyers and 46 staffers freely available to the project on a regular, ongoing basis — and made expansion of pro bono activity a central part of her department's five-year strategic plan.

The lawyers who regularly participate in pro bono work also get additional points when it comes to bonus time. Boggs says that she asks everyone in the department to note their community service efforts in their annual self-evaluation. But she adds that no one gets penalized if they're too busy to join in.

Starbucks isn't alone in sending its lawyers out to help the needy. Hilton Hotels Corp.'s legal department, along with a few other in-house law departments, participates in annual "adoption days" around the nation, helping orphaned children with medical or emotional problems find parents ["Giving It Away," December 2003].

But the Starbucks program is unique in its year-round time and staff commitment: A rotating group of two lawyers and two support staffers from the legal department spend alternate Tuesdays at Seattle's Kings County Housing Project, representing needy tenants in court disputes with their landlords.

Why is doing good so important to her? Boggs, 44, credits her upbringing and early legal career. "I grew up in the Roman Catholic Church, a faith with a deep history and commitment to social justice issues," she says. Boggs adds that her parents — her late father was a college professor and her mother a teacher and school administrator — "instilled the importance and duty of giving to those less fortunate." Plus, as a onetime federal prosecutor in Seattle, Boggs says she saw "up close and personal the tragic consequences that flow from not having competent counsel in our society." . . .

While the housing program helps the disadvantaged, it gives Boggs' department a benefit, too: It's helping the staff hone their lawyering skills. Esther Lardent, president of the Pro Bono Institute at Georgetown University Law Center, says that, unlike many pro bono legal efforts, the Starbucks program is "litigation-focused, and most corporate lawyers are not litigators."

With a relatively small attorney staff, is Boggs ever frustrated when she goes looking for a lawyer who is spending the day at a housing hearing? "It's never happened," she quickly answers. "Never." The key to making it work, Boggs says, is to ensure that every in-house lawyer is cross-trained in representing a tenant before the court, so the attorneys can provide backup for one another.

Boggs' staffers clearly relish the break from their usual grind. "Our attorneys have managed to keep homes together, and in one case got money back for a wrongfully displaced client," boasts assistant GC Lucy Lee Helm. Other employees share her enthusiasm, including legal secretary Cheryl Storrs, who says she finds it rewarding when "our attorneys go before a judge . . . and present a defense that ends with our client receiving, if nothing else, more time in which to move out." . . .

The department's efforts are clearly paying off. And the clients seem happy with the work. As one housing court defendant told Helm: "Now I have a lawyer just like on TV."

Julie O'Shea, Report Calls for More Pro Bono

San Francisco Recorder, October 3, 2005, at 1

San Jose CA—In response to the high rate of residents who can't afford attorneys, the Santa Clara County Bar Association is encouraging every lawyer in the county to beef up pro bono work to at least 60 hours a year.

But how to go about implementing this goal is still up for debate. The bar association plans to set up a commission early next year to discuss ideas.

It is estimated that more than 70 percent of people who come through the county's family court annually cannot afford a lawyer, and often go without one, according to a SCCBA task force report.

"Access to the legal system for all citizens can only become a reality if the legal profession meets its obligation and responsibilities by a generous commitment," the report stated.

The task force estimated that large Santa Clara County law firms average just 2 percent to 3 percent of pro bono work a year, which is on par with what has been observed nationally.

That comes out to be about 60 hours per firm per year, but SCCBA President Julie Emede, a San Jose family law practitioner, says she would prefer 60 pro bono hours per attorney per year.

"We have an obligation to help people," Emede said. "An hour a week [devoted to pro bono work] doesn't seem onerous to me. It seems achievable." . . .

While there are a lot of willing attorneys, "from [a legal] agency's point of view, it's really hard connecting clients with pro bono work," says Margaret "Peggy" Stevenson, a supervising attorney with the Stanford Community Law Clinic. . . .

The task force's 24-page report, released Thursday, includes a long list of suggestions for the county's lawyers, judges and legal services. . . .

Recommendations include forming a Web site identifying opportunities for free legal aid and training, as well as designating a pro bono liaison in each firm. The report also recommends that attorneys participate in outside activities aimed at improving the legal system, such as court pro tem services. . . .

"Over all, it is probably fair to say that many of the [large] law firms in this community have exhibited [a] strong commitment to pro bono work," the report stated. "However, the hours contributed by a given firm are often reflective of the efforts of a relatively small group of attorneys." . . .

e. Affinity Groups and Litigation Assistance

American Civil Liberties Union

About the ACLU, available online at http://www.aclu.org/about/index.html
(last visited February 27, 2009)

So long as we have enough people in this country willing to fight for their rights, we'll be called a democracy." — *ACLU Founder Roger Baldwin*

The ACLU is our nation's guardian of liberty, working daily in courts, legislatures and communities to defend and preserve the individual rights and liberties that the Constitution and laws of the United States guarantee everyone in this country.

These rights include:

Your First Amendment rights — freedom of speech, association and assembly; freedom of the press, and freedom of religion.

Your right to equal protection under the law — protection against unlawful discrimination.

Your right to due process — fair treatment by the government whenever the loss of your liberty or property is at stake.

Your right to privacy — freedom from unwarranted government intrusion into your personal and private affairs.

The ACLU also works to extend rights to segments of our population that have traditionally been denied their rights, including people of color; women; lesbians, gay men, bisexuals and transgender people; prisoners; and people with disabilities.

If the rights of society's most vulnerable members are denied, everybody's rights are imperiled. Support the ACLU today.

- The ACLU's work is sustained by over 500,000 members and supporters who plan an active role in defending freedom.
- Nearly 200 ACLU staff attorneys and thousands of volunteer attorneys handle countless civil liberties cases every year.
- Our legislative advocates are a constant presence on Capitol Hill and in state legislatures working on civil liberties issue.
- The ACLU has staffed offices in all 50 states, Puerto Rico and Washington, D.C.

Center for Individual Rights

Compiled from http://www.cir-usa.org (last visited January 5, 2005)

Fighting for Individual Rights

The Center for Individual Rights (CIR) is a nonprofit public interest law firm dedicated to the defense of individual liberties. CIR provides free legal representation to deserving clients who cannot otherwise afford or obtain legal counsel and whose individual rights are threatened. CIR strives to make the best use of its limited financial and legal resources. To that end, CIR carefully selects a handful of cases each year that have the greatest potential to protect individual rights.

Because effective legal advocacy requires a high level of specialization, CIR concentrates its resources in those areas where individual rights are most at risk.

A Commitment to Protecting Civil Rights

CIR's civil rights litigation is based on the principle of strict state neutrality: the state must not advantage some or disadvantage others because of their race.

Race, like religion, must be placed beyond the reach of the state. Our objections to racial preferences are legal, moral, and pragmatic. Preferences are almost always unconstitutional when used to achieve an arbitrary racial diversity; they are only legal when narrowly tailored to remedy past discrimination against identifiable individuals. As a moral matter, preferences are dehumanizing and reduce individuals to the color of their skin. And pragmatically, racial preferences almost always add to division and discord in society.

Attacking Affirmative Action in College Admissions

CIR has challenged racial preferences at the University of Michigan, the UM Law School, the University of Washington Law School and the University of Texas Law School.

CIR's decade long campaign to end the use of racial preferences in college admissions took an important step forward in June, 2003, when the Supreme Court issued decisions in Gratz v. Bollinger and Grutter v. Bollinger, CIR's twin challenges to racial preferences at the University of Michigan.

The Court struck down the preference programs in place for the past decade at the University of Michigan's undergraduate college of Literature, Science, and the Arts. This was the first successful Supreme Court challenge of a college racial preference program in over 25 years. The Court ended the wholesale use of mechanical racial preferences favored by many elite schools.

The Court upheld a separate admissions program in place at the University of Michigan's law school. In doing so, the Court placed important new restrictions on the use of race. Schools now may consider race only if they conduct a highly individualized review of each applicant's file. In addition, schools must periodically review the continued need for race preferences in light of race neutral admissions policies now in use in five states that have proven to achieve diversity without discrimination.

Gratz and *Grutter* make the continued use of racial preferences risky for colleges. Schools have a choice. They can try to adopt the UM law school system to other contexts, in which case they face continued scrutiny and possible litigation. Or they can follow the Court's explicit direction to investigate and use the hundreds of race neutral admissions systems now working in five states.

NOTE ON LAW SCHOOL LEGAL SERVICES

One additional source of targeted legal services stands alongside the affinity group: the law school clinic. Every U.S. law school offers clinical courses to its students. Some law school clinics offer training through simulations—trial practice clinics are common example. Other clinics serve "live" clients. In order to get the cooperation of the local bar, the clinics do not charge clients for such services and usually screen their clients for some form of financial need, so they are not competing with for-fee lawyers in private practice. In that respect they resemble legal aid organizations.

Unlike legal aid organizations, which try to serve the entire spectrum of their indigent populations, law school clinics typically specialize—eviction defense, domestic violence, consumer law, immigration, capital appeals, prison law, environmental law, and the like. In that respect they look more like affinity groups, which target a particular area that matches their group's mission. Because law school clinics are typically not funded by the Legal Services Corporation, they operate free from some of its constraints; thus they can, for example, bring class actions or represent convicted prisoners. On the other hand, they are unlikely to sue the organization owned by the school's most generous donor; in that respect they operate under some of the constraints noted in Scott Cummings article on pro bono efforts of private firms. In some cases these clinics have won notable victories as well as providing training for young soon-to-be lawyers.

CHAPTER 3

SETTLEMENT: THE LAW AND STRATEGY OF LITIGATION RISK CONTROL

INTRODUCTORY NOTE

This chapter brings together the themes of the two preceding chapters: professional organization and litigation incidence (Chapter 1) and litigation finance (Chapter 2). This chapter suggests that the forces described in the two preceding chapters have created a litigation dynamic in which both sides struggle to control the risks of litigation while maximizing its potential benefits. Every stage of a lawsuit presents choices and, under the current system of litigation finance, requires investment decisions: How much should be spent on experts; how elaborate should discovery be; how many alternative theories of a claim or defense should be explored? Some of these decisions will be for the client; others will be for the lawyer; and still others will be shared. There is, moreover, no risk-free strategy. Instead the question is which choices entail which risks. Settlement is one of those choices, but settlement has its own risks.

The most obvious choice is that between settlement and trial. In recent decades increasing numbers of parties have chosen settlement. Why? The readings in this chapter offer some possible answers. Another, less obvious risk lies in trying to achieve a settlement that then fails — because the release that lies at the heart of the settlement is overturned. Still another risk lies in choosing the wrong form of settlement, a risk that has increased in recent years as professional creativity has developed multiple paths of settlement. An apparently increasing number of settlements contain a confidentiality clause, forbidding the parties from discussing the lawsuit or its outcome. These agreements — to the extent they are enforceable — control some risks, but perhaps fewer than is commonly supposed. Some of the most challenging problems of settlement occur in multidefendant litigation. For both plaintiff and defendant, choosing the right party with whom to settle and the form that settlement might take require both a deep understanding of the legal requirements and a profound sense of strategic choices. The materials try to give a sense of both. As you encounter these materials, ask yourself what the parties are trying to do and why they are trying to do it.

A. SETTLEMENT AS A CONSEQUENCE OF MODERN PROCEDURE

STEPHEN C. YEAZELL, GETTING WHAT WE ASKED FOR, GETTING WHAT WE PAID FOR, AND NOT LIKING WHAT WE GOT: THE VANISHING CIVIL TRIAL

1 Journal of Empirical Legal Studies 943 (2004)

"But the worst feature of American procedure is the lavish granting of new trials."

Roscoe Pound, The Causes of Popular Dissatisfaction with the Administration of Justice[1]

Introduction

Ninety eight years ago, Roscoe Pound delivered to an American Bar Association meeting an address on the legal system. In that address, which was still being celebrated by professional leaders fifty years later, Pound argued that popular dissatisfaction with the legal system could be cured by procedural reform, and he had a list of reforms in mind.[2] At the top of his list was a concern about trials. But his concern was the mirror image of the image of ours. He identified as the "worst feature" of the American legal system the "lavish granting of new trials" by appellate courts. In the near-century since Pound's pronouncements, we have solved the problem he articulated, solved it so thoroughly that we now hold a Symposium to consider whether trial itself, to say nothing of new trials, is an endangered species, and what to do about it. I bring to this conversation both a word of hope and a word of caution. My principal argument is that we should take both the hope and the caution seriously, lest, at the start of the 22d century, our grandchildren be gathered to consider again how to cope with the deluge of trials that threatens the legal system. . . .

The present state of civil trials results from the convergence of two developments:

- first, what we asked for — a century of procedural reform and changes in the legal profession incorporating the consensus of some very thoughtful people;
- second, what we paid for — a half century of evolution in the demography and economy of the bar.

---

1. Address to the 29th Annual Meeting of the American Bar Association, August 29, 1906; reprinted 29 Report of the Annual Meeting of the American Bar Association 395, 413 (1906).
2. Pound's address was commemorated at the 1964 Convention of the American Bar Association. Proceedings in Commemoration of The Address [sic], 35 F.R.D. 241-291 (1964).

Having got what we asked for and paid for, we are now soberly assessing the results. Such an assessment and any proposals for change will, I argue, be better if we understand more completely why we stand where we do today and, if we don't like the current state of affairs, whether we would like even less changes that might produce a higher trial rate. . . .

II. Getting What We Asked For

The quotation from Roscoe Pound at the top of this paper captured not only his views of trial but in many respects the agenda of thoughtful procedural reformers in the twentieth century. Trials, especially in the common law tradition, are in many respects "wasteful": they produce a victor, but at great cost to both sides and to the public. To quote a pair of more contemporary observers, "a trial is a failure."[8] Moreover, at the start of the twentieth century trials often produced a victor on the basis of incomplete information about the historical facts underlying the dispute. In many respects the procedural agenda of the century just past has sought to change these features — which were flaws in the eyes of the reformers. And we have done so — so completely that we now worry about the results.

Writing fifteen years ago, Samuel Gross and Kent Syverud gracefully summarized the guiding principles of procedural reform in the twentieth century:

> With some notable exceptions [most of whom, the authors noted, were academics], lawyers, judges, and commentators agree that pretrial settlement is almost always cheaper, faster, and better than trial. Much of our civil procedure is justified by the desire to promote settlement and avoid trial.[9]

Procedural reform in the twentieth century reflected this belief. It did so in four ways, all of which incorporate what one might call a Progressive version of procedure: the belief in facts rather than law, the belief in information rather than argument, and the belief in broad rather than narrow focus for disputing, and a belief in agreement rather than adjudicated conflict. The central procedural changes of the twentieth century reflected these beliefs. They diminished the role of pleading, greatly expanded the mechanisms of pretrial discovery and role of expert witnesses, and enabled broad joinder.

Each of these changes the conditions for a reduced trial rate. . . .

Discovery and expert testimony have combined to create a fundamentally new possibility. They permit a properly financed lawyer to bore deeply into an adversary's files, to try out lines of questioning that might turn out to be a dead end, and to inspect documents, objects, while still shaping strategy and without being bound to offer them in evidence. No other legal system has to date attempted these on the scale characteristic of American litigation. The system, though essentially private and adversarial, can marshal facts in a manner that resembles an administrative investigation. I emphasize these points not because they show that modern discovery is a freak or monster, but because it helps us understand the decline in civil trials.

---

8. Samuel Gross & Kent Syverud, Getting to No: A Study of Settlement Negotiations and the Selection of Cases for Trial, 90 Mich. L. Rev. 319, 320 (1991).
   9. Gross & Syverud, *supra* note 8 at 320.

Paradoxically, discovery leads to a decline in trial because it allows litigants to explore, without the constraints of trial theories of liability or defense, factual avenues that would have been practically and tactically impossible at trial. . . .

Third, discovery produces a great deal of information, some about one's own case and almost as much about the other side's case. It is not surprising that such information will sometimes produce converging estimates of the likely outcome of the trial (though Galanter usefully notes how badly even experienced lawyers often make these estimates — a point to which I shall return). On the basis of this information the parties will often settle. That point is important: modern discovery itself *produces* settlements, regardless of the judge's behavior or the availability of devices like early neutral evaluation and settlement conferences. It produces settlements because it produces information that can be introduced at trial and it produces information about what the other side can produce at trial. It enables a lawyer to gain a very good estimate of the information that will come before the trier of fact. In the absence of discovery the only way to gain some of this information was to go to trial. Otherwise put, in the world before 1938 trial was often the only real way to do discovery, and some of the trials in this earlier era can be seen as in-court efforts to seek information.[20] So, all other things being equal, extensive discovery will lower the trial rates because it produces information.

Fourth, discovery and expert testimony substantially increase costs. At one level that point is unbearably obvious. I want, however, to argue the less obvious point that those costs may change both parties' calculations about the desirability of settlement and the risks of trial. U.S. litigation usually requires each side to bear its own litigation costs, including most notably discovery and expert witnesses. . . .

These costs are not just a barrier to litigation — though they are certainly that. They also produce a game of competitive investment. Both parties are trying to "buy" victory by investing in discovery. Discovery may uncover information that will strengthen one's case. Discovery will almost certainly require a symmetrical investment by one's adversary: depositions must be defended; interrogatories must be answered or properly objected to; experts require counter-experts and so on. These discovery and experts' costs mean that as the case progresses, the parties have sunk investments to protect. A loss at trial takes away not only the sum that might have been saved or gained by a victory, but entails as well the loss of the amount already spent in discovery. As a result, a party with tens of thousands invested in experts' fees, depositions, and document discovery will view settlement as a way of limiting the risk of such a total loss. For the plaintiff a settlement may represent a way of salvaging something out of an already expensive enterprise, of achieving a gain smaller than hoped-for, but still a gain. For the defendant it will represent a way of cutting losses, of not sending good money after bad by paying a judgment on top of the costs of litigation, many of which will involve discovery and experts. . . .

---

20. That phenomenon persisted for several decades after 1938, in part because the bar took some time to exploit fully the possibility of discovery and in part because there was a lag of some decades before all the states substantially adopted the "Federal" discovery regime.

III. Getting What We Paid For

The preceding paragraphs, with their emphasis on symmetrical investment by the parties, imply a symmetrical system of litigation finance. Such a system is for many claims and for many parts of the bar now a reality and that symmetry has strong implications for trial rates. If the ability to invest in discovery and experts were systematically asymmetrical, available in practice only to the defense bar, I believe we would have less settlement and higher trial rates — as we did seventy-five years ago. Changes in litigation finance, in practice patterns, and, to a lesser extent, in professional regulation lie at the heart of the phenomenon of the vanishing trial. . . .

Seventy-five years ago the plaintiff's and defense bars were systematically asymmetrical in resources. The plaintiffs' bar, if it could be dignified by such a name, consisted of under-capitalized and sometimes poorly educated lawyers who were widely accused of improperly soliciting clients, suborning perjury, and worse.[28] More to the point of this exploration, they were systematically outgunned by the defense bar, usually retained by insurers. Were there a serious question of investing in litigation — and there usually wasn't because the plaintiff lacked the resources to make such investment necessary — the insured defendant could bring substantial resources to bear, without plaintiff's being able to match them. Under these circumstances one can imagine three outcomes. One would be simple abandonment of the case by the plaintiff, unable to respond even to motions to dismiss; anecdotal evidence suggests such outcomes were common.[29] Another, perhaps more likely would be the acceptance of an offer very heavily discounted by defendant's knowledge that the plaintiff lacked the financing (and perhaps the skill) to bring the case to trial. Again, anecdotes suggest that such outcomes occurred frequently. . . .

Today, the financing, and thus the strategy of trial and investment have changed in ways that render the adversaries more evenly matched. That symmetry allows more equal investments. More equal investment in litigation makes trial riskier for *both* sides. Higher investment, evenly spread among the parties, combined with knowledge about the facts, makes trials scarcer. . . .

This structure creates a climate of rational risk aversion and a slight preference for settlement in most cases. Once upon a time, the plaintiffs' bar had the same characteristics and appetite for risk as the present-day purchasers of lottery tickets: the players knew they had few resources and only a tiny chance of winning, but that chance, represented by trial, was the only chance they had so, if they (and their clients) could hang on that long, they went to trial. Today, this segment of the bar acts more like the manager of a diversified stock fund than like the purchaser of a lottery ticket. They will invest significant amounts in market research (client screening, referral, and pretrial investment), but will generally prefer a "litigation portfolio" with a large number of small gains (settlements) and a much smaller number of cases in which they hope they have accomplished the litigation equivalent of buying Microsoft in 1985.

---

28. Jerold Auerbach, Unequal Justice: Lawyers and Social Change in Modern America (New York, 1976).

29. Jerome Carlin, Lawyers on Their Own: A Study of Individual Practitioners in Chicago (New Brunswick, 1962).

Because they have more to lose and a diversified portfolio, plaintiffs behave like large investors rather than desperate purchasers of lottery tickets. To put the point another way, the plaintiffs' bar, because of its better capitalization, is now in the position to behave like the defendants, to which we now turn.

The defendants' bar has responded to the plaintiffs' side changes in interesting ways. As was the case seventy-five years ago, most of the defense work will be financed by liability insurers (or by self-insured defendants whose size will cause them to behave much like insurers). . . .

These changes have altered the strategy of settlement, and thus contributed to the vanishing of trial. In a world in which the plaintiff's lawyer had made virtually no investment in pretrial investigation or discovery (perhaps because he could not afford any), trial, if he could hang on that long, was a rational choice: there was a very small chance of winning, but there was little chance of winning without it — and there were no sunk costs to consider. In a world of significant pretrial investment — investment made by both sides — settlement looks different.

Some numbers may help. Suppose an auto accident case. The plaintiff has sustained serious injuries in an intersection collision; if permanent, the injuries will require lifetime care, but that diagnosis is uncertain. At the outset of the case plaintiff's lawyer is uncertain about the case for liability: plaintiff and defendant tell different stories, the police report is inconclusive, and there are no known witnesses. The plaintiff's lawyer must make two decisions: whether the case is worthwhile with any level of investment and, if so, whether her practice group can handle it, given their level of capitalization and present case mix. If the answer to the first question is yes and the second no, the lawyer will need to find a referral among her network of appropriate firms. Assuming either that the first firm can handle it or that it has been successfully referred, a series of investments will follow: investigators to uncover potential witnesses; in engineering experts to reconstruct the accident (to replace or bolster the incident witnesses), medical experts to estimate the likelihood of lifetime medical injuries, and actuaries to produce reliable estimates of lost wages and medical expenses. The total investment, exclusive of lawyers' time, is likely to run between $75,000 and $100,000, according to my sources.

Let us now turn to the defendant to see how the dynamics might operate. Suppose that defendant and the carrier conclude there is coverage. At a minimum that means the carrier is obliged to defend. An early question will be whether the policy limits are high enough to pay a substantial settlement. If not, the carrier may well make an early tender of the policy limits, to save itself litigation expenses and, equally important, to protect itself from the prospect of a subsequent suit for bad faith failure to settle — a claim that typically carries both compensatory damages (of the amount of the resulting judgment, even if it is larger than the policy limits) and punitives. Typically a plaintiff will accept such a settlement offer if it's clear that there are no non-insurance assets, and, according to some recent work, even if there are non-insurance assets.[41] But for purposes of exposition let us suppose that either the initial policy or an

---

41. *See* Thomas Baker, Blood Money, New Money and the Moral Economy of Tort Law in Action, 35 Law & Soc'y Rev. 275 (2001).

umbrella policy are large enough, and the initial assessment of liability and damages uncertain enough, that the carrier decides it must defend at least into a deeper stage of the litigation. At that point defendant must essentially match plaintiff's investment decisions, except in the unlikely case it decides that plaintiff is investing foolishly. The defendant must thus make its own symmetrical investments in investigators, experts, and the like. Because the carrier is a bulk purchaser of such professional services, it may be able to obtain them at a slightly lower cost than the plaintiff. But the discount won't be enormous, so let us realistically suppose that the defendant must also make an investment in between $60,000 and $75,000 in experts and the like. At this point, the parties, between them have between $130,000 and $175,000 invested in the case, without regard to lawyers' time. But at this point we cannot ignore lawyers' time, because an expert must, at a minimum, produce a report to be disclosed to the other side (and reviewed by the adversary's lawyer) and submit to a deposition which will enable the adversary (and the proponent) to evaluate the strength and credibility of the expert's testimony. Each such deposition must be prepared and defended, and transcribed or recorded. We are, at this point, approaching the level of $200,000 in joint costs, most of which are *not* in lawyers' time. And recall that those costs have been incurred in a case where the verdict could quite credibly be either $0 or $2,000,000 — given the uncertainty about both liability and damages.

Suppose that plaintiff, an experienced and credible lawyer who is known by the carrier to be able to take cases to trial and to win with some regularity, approaches the carrier relatively early, say after both sides have invested something like $30,000 in the case. From experience the defense lawyer will know that plaintiff's lawyer is prepared and able to invest another $70,000 — and that the carrier will have to match it — before incurring the even higher expenses of trial. The result of trial, of course, could be a ringing defense victory, but even that would end up costing more than $100,000. Or trial could be a disaster, with $2,000,000 in damages to be added to the $100,000 in litigation expenses. A settlement of $150,000 leaves everyone much better off: the carrier has assured that it won't be left with a very large bill, and will pay just $50,000 more than it would pay in litigation expenses even in the even of total defense victory. Considering the possible exposure from a large verdict, this may look very good. To the plaintiff — and his lawyer — the same may be true. Granted that the $30,000 and the lawyer's fee will have to come off the top, they avoid the possibility of a large additional investment followed by a defense victory, which is the most common outcome of a personal injury trial.[43] Under these circumstances, trial has limited attractions and settlement many.

But has this scenario explained too much, suggesting that there should be not just few but no trials? The most common solution to this paradox supposes that it occurs because the parties reach substantially different estimates of the trial outcome. . . . Another possibility, one closer to our investigation, might involve parties who had made little investment in the pretrial stage. Under

---

43. Gross & Syverud report that a slight majority of personal injury cases that go to trial result in a complete defense victory. Samuel Gross & Kent Syverud, Don't Try: Civil Jury Verdicts in a System Geared to Settlement, 44 UCLA L. Rev. 1 (1996).

such conditions, the absence of sunk costs might lead parties to behave differently about trial, since, in the absence of significant investment the defendant will have little incentive to make more than a nuisance offer and the plaintiff will have no sunk costs to protect with a settlement and thus fewer incentives to avoid trial. . . .

IV. Not Liking What We Got?

The title of this symposium is admirably non-judgmental. It neither assumes that a low trial rate represents Nirvana nor that it constitutes a national emergency. That is the right stance to take. But it is also worth examining some of the reasons why one might be concerned about such a trial rate and what one might do if one were. The interesting question is not whether the sky is falling but how best to assess this phenomenon in a thoughtful way, recognizing that trial rates are part of a larger system involving not just trial rules and rates but financing systems, risk pools, the demography of the legal profession, and even the incidence of home and automobile ownership. . . .

JONATHAN D. GLATER, STUDY FINDS SETTLING IS BETTER THAN
GOING TO TRIAL

New York Times, August 8, 2008 available online at http://www.nytimes.com/
2008/08/08/business/08law.html?_r=1&scp=1&sq=study%20finds%
20settling&st=cse

Note to victims of accidents, medical malpractice, broken contracts and the like: When you sue, make a deal.

That is the clear lesson of a soon-to-be-released study of civil lawsuits that has found that most of the plaintiffs who decided to pass up a settlement offer and went to trial ended up getting less money than if they had taken that offer.

"The lesson for plaintiffs is, in the vast majority of cases, they are perceiving the defendant's offer to be half a loaf when in fact it is an entire loaf or more," said Randall L. Kiser, a co-author of the study and principal analyst at DecisionSet, a consulting firm that advises clients on litigation decisions.

Defendants made the wrong decision by proceeding to trial far less often, in 24 percent of cases, according to the study; plaintiffs were wrong in 61 percent of cases. In just 15 percent of cases, both sides were right to go to trial—meaning that the defendant paid less than the plaintiff had wanted but the plaintiff got more than the defendant had offered.

The vast majority of cases do settle—from 80 to 92 percent by some estimates, Mr. Kiser said—and there is no way to know whether either side in those cases could have done better at trial. But the findings, based on a study of 2,054 cases that went to trial from 2002 to 2005, raise provocative questions about how lawyers and clients make decisions, the quality of legal advice and lawyers' motives. . . .

The study, which is to be published in the September issue of the Journal of Empirical Legal Studies, finds that the mistakes were made more often in cases in which lawyers are typically paid a share of whatever is won at trial.

On average, getting it wrong cost plaintiffs at about $43,000; the total could be more because information on legal costs was not available in every case. For defendants, who were less often wrong about going to trial, the cost was much greater: $1.1 million.

"Most of the time, one of the parties has made some kind of miscalculation or mistake," said Jeffrey J. Rachlinski, a law professor at Cornell who has studied how lawyers and clients decide to go to trial and who is co-editor of the journal. "The interesting thing about it is the errors the defendants make are much more costly."

The study's authors have analyzed some data from New York and, after a review of 554 state court trials in 2005, have found parties to lawsuits making the wrong decision at comparable rates.

The findings suggest that lawyers may not be explaining the odds to their clients — or that clients are not listening to their lawyers. . . .

As part of the study, which is the biggest of its kind to date, the authors surveyed trial outcomes over 40 years until 2004. They found that over time, poor decisions to go to trial have actually become more frequent.

"It's peculiar if any field is not improving its performance over a 40-year period," Mr. Kiser said. "That's a troubling finding."

Law schools do not teach how to handicap trials, nor do they help develop the important skill of telling a client that a case is not a winner. Clients do not like to hear such news.

"Most clients think they are completely right," Michael Shepard, a lawyer at Heller Ehrman in San Francisco. A good lawyer has to be able to tell clients that a judge or jury might see them differently, he continued. "Part of it is judgment and part of it is diplomacy."

Several lawyers were dismissive of the study, noting that the statistics mean nothing when contemplating a particular case, with its specific facts and legal issues, before a specific judge. They stressed the importance of a lawyer's experience.

But the study tried to account for that possibility and found that factors like the years of experience, rank of a lawyer's law school and the size of a law firm were less helpful in predicting the decision to go to trial. More significant was the type of case.

For example, poor decisions by plaintiffs to go to trial "are associated with cases in which contingency fee arrangements are common," according to the report. "On the defense side, high error rates are noted in cases where insurance coverage is generally unavailable."

The findings are consistent with research on human behavior and responses to risk, said Martin A. Asher, an economist at the University of Pennsylvania and a co-author. For example, psychologists have found that people are more averse to taking a risk when they are expecting to gain something, and more willing to take a risk when they have something to lose.

"If you approach a class of students and say, I'll either write you a check for $200, or we can flip a coin and I will pay you nothing or $500," most students will take the $200 rather than risk getting nothing, Mr. Asher said.

But reverse the situation, so that students have to write the check, and they will choose to flip the coin, risking a bigger loss because they hope to pay nothing at all, he continued. "They'll take the gamble." . . .

STEPHEN YEAZELL, TRANSPARENCY FOR CIVIL SETTLEMENTS

Rand/University of California–Los Angeles (forthcoming 2009)
(references omitted)

. . . We have a real problem with civil settlement. The bad news is that recent developments have made the problem more apparent. The good news is that the same developments make a solution possible. Right now this problem prevents civil litigation from performing well its primary task — compensating and deterring. . . . The real problem is that we operate a large and important market in civil claims without adequate pricing information. Lacking information about comparable transactions, litigants and their lawyers price in the dark — engaging in transactions for civil claims in a state of ignorance we think intolerable in other similarly important markets. . . .

So what? Parties have been settling claims out of court for millennia with the same lack of information about the settlement value of similar claims. Why should we now worry about it? . . .

The first reason to act now flows from an unusual characteristic of the U.S. economic system. To a greater extent than many of its peers in the developed world the United States relies on civil lawsuits rather than regulatory or social welfare regimes. In the U.S., courts — rather than regulatory agencies or social insurance — assign responsibility and pay compensation in a wide variety of circumstances. Spreading this responsibility among thousands of judges and hundreds of thousands of jurors creates a distinctively decentralized regime of economic and social regulation. Aggregated, the judgments reached in these adjudicated cases guide all of us in realms from daily driving to the design of products. . . .

Settlements form an important part of this regime. If the aggregate of adjudicated outcomes regulate our economic life, then the aggregate of settlement outcomes should occur in the shadow of adjudication. Settlements need not replicate adjudication: one hopes, for example, that the expenses saved by settlement will be reflected in settlement value. If, however, settlement values differed wildly and unpredictably from adjudicated results (and from each other), one would worry that the wheels had come off the regulatory regime. . . .

The Market in Civil Claims

Agreements to settle constitute a market in claims, with defendants "buying" and plaintiffs "selling" the claim in dispute, with the mutual goal of saving the expense and delay of trial. . . .

Market though it is, the market in settlements has one unusual characteristic worth noting at the outset. In this market monopolists dicker with monopsonists. Only the defendant (or his insurer) can buy my claim. Only I can sell it. Unlike markets in used cars or housing, there's not a range of prospective buyers and sellers. . . .

Market Size and Recent Trends

How big is this market in civil settlement? . . . Americans file about seventeen million civil claims annually. Most of those claims seek damages as a remedy. . . . [F]ew of these cases ever reach trial (Galanter, Ostrom et al.), and that proportion has sharply declined since the 1970s. Of those cases not tried, between three-fifths and four-fifths will reach a final resolution by agreement rather than by adjudication (BJS 1992; Yeazell 1992; Sklansky et al. 2006). . . .

How much is this market worth? It is surprisingly difficult to answer this question with accuracy, so I want to expose my very rough calculations. Seventeen million civil claims are filed annually. The most recent figures, based on a large sample suggest that 75% of these claims will settle (BJS 1992). An older, smaller sample arrived at a 50% settlement rate (Trubek, s-23). I propose to split this difference, and assume for calculation purposes that just over 60% of civil claims settle. How should we value them? Of the seventeen million claims, ten million are filed in courts with jurisdictional ceilings below $25,000 (NCSC 2005). Suppose we took a very conservative settlement amount ($1,000 per claim), and applied it to all seventeen million claims. That would yield an annual value of civil settlements of ten and a half billion dollars. That is almost surely too low, if we bear in mind that seven million of the claims sought damages of more than $25,000, the most common lower limit for claims in courts of "general" jurisdiction (NCSC 2005). One could derive a slightly more sophisticated estimate by segregating the settlement value of the limited jurisdiction claims from the others. Such segregation yields six and a half million "limited jurisdiction" settlements, that, in the absence of better data, we could continue to value at $1,000 each. For the larger claims, we have slightly better data. We know values for cases in this category that go to judgment. The median judgment for prevailing plaintiffs hovers in the low $30,000s ($37,000 for tort claims, $28,000 for contract claims) (BJS 2001). If we assume that the median settlement will be substantially lower than the median verdict, a figure of $10,000 for the median settlement seems reasonable. Suppose that the six and a half million limited jurisdiction claims settled for an average of $1,000, and the 4.3 million general jurisdiction cases for an average of $10,000. That calculation yields an annual value just short of fifty billion dollars. That is not a trivial market.

Absence of Good Pricing Information

Good — that is, efficient and trusted — markets require good pricing information. We have recently received a clear reminder of this proposition. During turmoil in the market for sub-prime mortgages, a major European bank suspended redemptions in some of its sponsored funds — because it was unable to get accurate pricing information concerning the value of securitized mortgages (Morgenson). Not only explicit financial markets like those in publicly traded securities, but other markets as well rely on good pricing information. We lack such information for civil settlements; this opacity becomes more striking if one compares it with markets outside the financial arena.

Consider first housing, a market with annual transactions comparable to civil settlements. Two-thirds of U.S. households currently live in owned rather than rental housing, and the U.S. housing market is active and relatively efficient, with about one million new home sales and about six and a half million existing home sales per year (U.S. Census Bureau; National Association of

Realtors). The total, 7.5 million annual home sales, lies in the same order of magnitude as our estimated 10 million annual civil settlements. As the real estate market has grown, so has market information, especially as to residential housing. A buyer or seller today has excellent access to pricing information. For new homes prices are widely advertised: there, may, of course, be hidden costs or unstated willingness to bargain by the seller (Hevesi). But — barring a substantial change in the market as a whole — a buyer is quite unlikely to pay much more than his neighbor or the seller to receive much more or much less than for comparable houses in the same area.

The used housing market is somewhat more complex, but here too the information is much better than for lawsuits. Before buying or selling a house, one can get from a real estate broker a list of sales of similar houses in the area, known in the trade as "comparables." Recently entrepreneurs have taken this market public: several on-line services allow one to punch in basic information about an existing house and get an estimate, based on comparables, of its selling price (Redfin, Zillow, Hagerty). The availability of this information does not assure that buyers won't buy a house with an undisclosed leaky roof or that sellers won't succumb to a low-ball offer because they need cash now. But readily available information will mean that the range of transaction prices will be tighter than it would otherwise be — that the right and left hand tails of the bell curve will be shorter.

The median price of residential housing (ca. $225,000) is substantially more than the median civil judgment (and more than the estimated value of civil settlements). But there are many markets with far lower average transaction levels for which there is much more pricing transparency. Take for example, used cars, whose average value is less than we have assumed for the at least the larger civil settlements. Both print and on-line services quote prices for a great array of used vehicles (Kelley Blue Book). And E-bay has successfully created a gigantic on-line bazaar which enables users to get comparative pricing information on almost any item one can imagine — from carved likenesses of tropical birds to funeral urns, to cite just two examples of prices listed on a recent tour of one on-line system (E-bay). Stepping back, one can say that in the U.S. at the start of the twenty-first century, citizens can get reliable pricing information for almost any lawful transaction.

But not for civil settlements. We can quickly find out the going price of a 10-year old car, of a two-bedroom apartment, or a souvenir of the last Superbowl, but one cannot get a current "market" quote for a broken leg, three weeks of lost work, and a lifetime of residual restricted mobility. Nor for any of the other 7 million large or the additional 10 million smaller civil claims filed annually in the United States. We simply do not know what these are worth. Several gaps in information produce this ignorance.

Gaps in Data Collected

Even for those claims that go to judgment — claims where the outcome is a matter of public record — we lack accurate and complete reporting. Courts keep records on many matters, and most filed documents are accessible to the public, but only by searching paper documents for each case (Eisenberg). Electronic filing and the on-line PACER system may be changing this situation for federal courts, but federal litigation accounts for only 2% of civil filings, and most states have nothing that resembles PACER. Several commercial services purport to record verdicts and judgments systematically, but they have large gaps, missing, according to one study, as many as half the judgments entered (Eisenberg 2002 at 748). In part these gaps appear because the services rely substantially on lawyers' self-reporting. Not surprisingly, few plaintiffs' lawyers are deeply interested in picking up the phone to report that they have just won a verdict well below the median. Nor are defendants' counsel interested in reporting that they have just suffered a $20,000 judgment in a case the plaintiff offered to settle for $10,000. As a consequence, the reported figures are often at the ends of the normal curve-the multi-million dollar wins and the defense verdicts in the face of seven-figure damage claims. The scarcity of good data even as to the subset of cases that go to judgment is reflected in the fact that it required federally funded studies in the last fifteen years to get even basic baseline information (BJS 1992, 1996, 2001).

As scattered and discontinuous as this information is, it far exceeds the information available in the 60-80% of civil cases that end in settlement rather than with a judgment. In the great majority of those cases, we have *no* information about the terms on which the parties resolved the dispute. We know nothing because there is no place where the terms of settlements are officially recorded. Some jurisdictions ask litigants to file a document indicating that there has been a settlement, but those documents reveal nothing about the terms of the settlement. Our lack of information has nothing to do with confidentiality clauses; most settlements lack such clauses, but we nevertheless have no information about their terms. Nor are press accounts of any help in this area. No one bothers to interview the plaintiff who has just settled a run-of-the-mill personal injury case for $20,000 or a contract dispute for $50,000: these items fall into the dog-bites-man news gap, worth no one's while to investigate or report.

One might expect that that one set of parties would have such information: insurers. Insurance companies are in the business of settling claims, and they are in a position to have excellent information about the factors that affect settlements. If they had and used this information regularly, they would also possess a significant advantage over other litigants. To draw on the real estate analogy again, the situation would resemble that in which buyers and their brokers, but not sellers and theirs, knew the prices at which comparable housing had recently changed hands. Such an asymmetry would not inspire confidence in the real estate market, and if a similar informational asymmetry existed in the settlement market, it would give one reason to doubt both its fairness and its effectiveness as a regulator of economic life.

Surprisingly, recent developments suggest that even insurers, whom we might expect to know a good deal about the pattern of settlements, are only beginning to exploit such knowledge and that not very systematically. That inference is fair to draw from the inauguration by a number of insurers of a software system named Colossus. This proprietary software reportedly collects and makes available to the insurer data on settlements of cases resembling the one at stake. According to press sources, twelve of the twenty largest U.S. liability insurers were using Colossus by 2002 (Guidera). Given this information, the insurer can then make a settlement offer within the range of similar settlements. That is, at any rate, the benign version of its use (Bonnett). The plaintiffs' bar and allied organizations have a less benign view of its use (Steele; Guidera). They have taken up arms against the system, and several suits have asserted that it was used in such a way as to prevent the good faith settlement of claims against the insureds (McMurty).

Lost in the furor and the lawsuits about Colossus are the implications of its recency. In business for more than a century, the liability insurers have had data on settlements available to them for decades. That they have systematically begun to gather and disseminate it digitally only in the last few years constitutes startling news. The good news is that the feared asymmetry in litigation information may be much less than one might have suspected. The bad news is that *everyone* seems to be operating largely in the dark.

Unreliability of Expert Estimates

None of this ignorance would be a source of concern if experts could accurately predict settlement value of cases. We would not need real estate comparables if brokers could regularly predict the actual market price within a narrow range of error. In real estate, the prevalence of "comparables" testifies to brokers' doubts that they can intuitively produce reliable estimates. Evidence suggests that legal experts are just as bad — or good — as real estate professionals. Several studies have demonstrated the same point: even experienced handlers of civil claims are not good predictors of claim value. The results are consistent: lawyers, insurance adjusters, and judges all err by very substantial amounts when asked to estimate either the settlement value or predicted trial outcomes (Vidmar & Rice). Indeed, one imagines that the insurers' awareness of the unreliability of adjusters' estimates lay behind the introduction of Colossus.

But the unreliability of estimates of settlement value is not limited to adjusters. Dean Gerald Williams, in an experiment designed to display the value of training lawyers in negotiation, instead discovered almost random variation in estimates:

> The outcomes ranged from a high of $95,000 to a low of $15,000; the average outcome was just over $47,000; and the remainder of the outcomes are scattered almost randomly between the two extremes (Williams).

Dean Williams's findings are consistent both with earlier studies[3] and with more recent, sophisticated work (Saks at 1215-1225). One study reported:

> Sixteen members of the Los Angeles Claims Managers Association were asked to evaluate a hypothetical claim. Nine valued the claim at $50,000 to $150,000; the rest were spread from $6,000 to $750,000. The same variation occurred among claims staff within a single company, and the more experienced the claims adjusters, the wider the variation. Settlements of actual cases show similar degrees of unexplained variations (Saks, summarizing Peterson).

One careful study summarized the anarchic situation in carefully understated academic-speak: "[R]esearch showing greater variability in lawyers'

---

3. Douglas Rosenthal, Lawyer and Client: Who's in Charge 204-205 (1974).

valuations of cases contradicts the assumption that their greater experience increases the stability of their awards" (Vidmar & Rice at 898).

Given these comparisons, one might suspect that this opacity concerning settlements flows from some inherent characteristic of the legal system. It doesn't. Consider the criminal docket. Just as most civil litigation ends in settlement, so do most of the twenty million criminal prosecutions filed in the U.S. (NCSC 2005 at 46; Sklansky & Yeazell). But those who "settle" criminal cases — prosecutors, defendants and their lawyers — do so with far more information than do civil litigants. Even after recent Supreme Court cases have forced changes in present schemes of sentencing, in any given courthouse anywhere in the United States, both sides will have remarkably clear and accurate perceptions of the "going rate" for various criminal offenses: a first offender charged with assault will get a sentence within a known range; a recidivist charged with armed robbery a different and higher, but known, sentence range, and so on. Indeed, the existence of wide inter-judge variations in sentencing patterns was a powerful moral and legal argument behind the move to determinate sentencing laws (Frankel, U.S. Sentencing Commission; Mistretta). Given determinate sentencing laws and local courtroom knowledge, the "rates" for plea bargains are common knowledge. Whether or not one likes the institution of plea bargaining, both sides go into the process knowing how their case compares with comparable ones. The same cannot be said for civil settlements. . . .

B. THE BASIC LAW OF SETTLEMENT

1. SIMPLE RELEASE

RELEASE OF ALL CLAIMS (CALIFORNIA FORM)

CLAIM NO: VV 903924-5, 83-2474.

Know All Men By These Presents:

That the Undersigned, being of lawful age, for sole consideration of $ 2,431.18 TWO THOUSAND FOUR HUNDRED THIRTY ONE AND 18.- 100 DOLLARS to be paid to STEVEN YEAZALL do/does hereby and for my/our/its heirs, executors, administrators, successors and assigns release, acquit and forever discharge

CARYN HARB AND LAUREN HARE and his, her, their, or its agents, principals, servants, successors, heirs, executors, administrators, insurer, insurer's agent and all other persons, firms, corporations, associations or partnerships of and from any and all claims, actions, causes of action, demands, rights, damages, costs, loss of service, expenses and compensation whatsoever, which the undersigned now has/have or which may hereafter accrue on account of or in any way growing out of any and all known and unknown, foreseen and unforeseen bodily and personal injuries and property damage and the consequences thereof resulting or to result from the accident, casualty or event or the handling of any insurance claim or the defense of any legal proceeding arising out of said accident, which occurred on or about the 08TH day of JUNE, 2002 at or near 1ST AT LARCHMONTE, LOS ANGELES CA.

It is understood and agreed that this settlement is the compromise of a doubtful and disputed claim, and that the payment made is not to be construed as an admission of liability on the part of the party or parties hereby released, and that said releasees deny liability therefore and intend merely to avoid litigation and buy their peace.

It is further understood and agreed that all rights under Section 1542 of the Civil Code of California and any similar law of any state or territory of the United States are hereby expressly waived. Said section reads as follows:

"1542. Certain claims not affected by general release. A general release does not extend to claims which the creditor does not know or suspect to exist in his favor at the time of executing the release, which if known by him must have materially affected his settlement with the debtor."

The undersigned hereby declare(s) and represent(s) that the injuries sustained are or may be permanent and progressive and that recovery therefrom is uncertain and indefinite and in making this Release it is understood and agreed, that the undersigned relies/rely wholly upon the undersigned's judgment, belief and knowledge of the nature, extent, effect and duration of said injuries and liability therefore and is made without reliance upon any statement or representation of the party or parties hereby released or their representatives or by any physician or surgeon by them employed.

The undersigned further declare(s) and represent(s) that no promise, inducement or agreement not herein expressed has been made to the undersigned, and that this Release contains the entire agreement between the parties hereto, and that the terms of this Release are contractual and not a mere recital.

FOR YOUR PROTECTION CALIFORNIA LAW REQUIRES THE INFORMATION ON THE REVERSE SIDE TO APPEAR ON THIS FORM:

THE UNDERSIGNED HAS READ THE FOREGOING RELEASE AND FULLY UNDERSTANDS IT.

Signed, sealed and delivered this_____ day of _____, _____

CAUTION: READ BEFORE SIGNING BELOW

STATE OF

COUNTY OF

On the _____ day of _____, before me personally appeared to me known to be the person(s) named herein and who executed the foregoing Release and acknowledged to me that voluntarily executed the same.

NOTARY PUBLIC

My term expires

MELISSA NANN, OK OF SETTLEMENT DENIED IN LEGAL MALPRACTICE SUIT

Legal Intelligencer, March 3, 2004, at 1

A Philadelphia judge Tuesday refused to approve a $4.5 million settlement proposed by the law firm Ballard Spahr Andrews & Ingersoll and limited partners of the Keystone Venture V capital fund in an attempt to resolve a legal malpractice suit alleging that lawyers failed to keep public pension funds in Pennsylvania, Connecticut and Massachusetts from losing money.

Under the proposed settlement, the state workers' pension funds would have recovered $4.5 million — less plaintiff attorney fees and other costs — of

$9 million the limited partners alleged in the complaint was lost when the partnership's principal, Kiernan Dale, wrongfully diverted money to several companies controlled by Michael Liberty, a businessman.

Five limited partners, representing 71 percent of the limited partners, filed the derivative lawsuit, Treasurer of the State of Connecticut v. Ballard Spahr Andrews & Ingersoll, on behalf of Keystone. The complaint and the unopposed stipulation and agreement for settlement were filed on the same day, Dec. 13.

The Pennsylvania State Employees' Retirement System and the city of Philadelphia Board of Pensions and Retirement are two of the plaintiffs.

The limited partners alleged in the complaint that the law firm, while representing Keystone, was told about the misappropriated funds but didn't advise the managing directors who were dealing with the incident to tell the limited partners about Dale's misconduct.

The limited partners also alleged they should have been told that the law firm had negotiated a settlement with Liberty's companies releasing them from legal liability in any claims arising out of the unexplained payments.

The law firm has denied any wrongdoing or liability.

Derivative lawsuits are those brought by shareholders on behalf of a corporation alleging that an action caused the company harm. Under state rules of civil procedure, such lawsuits cannot be dismissed or compromised without the court's OK.

"It is this court's job to determine whether the settlement is fair, reasonable and beneficial to Keystone, its limited partners and the public employees whose money was invested in Keystone and subsequently lost," Common Pleas Judge Gene D. Cohen told lawyers for the parties in City Hall Courtroom 443 Tuesday.

Noting that litigation in the case would undoubtedly be complex, contentious and lengthy, Cohen nevertheless found the proposed settlement was not in the best interest of Keystone.

Cohen said it was "quite possible" that Keystone would be entitled to more than its estimated actual damages, considering that not only Ballard Spahr but also the partnership's managing directors, Liberty's companies and others had apparently caused the damages Keystone suffered.

"The court believes that there is the distinct possibility that Keystone could recover substantially more from Ballard and from the other potential defendants if plaintiffs asserted conspiracy claims against them all," Cohen said. "Therefore, the court finds that the proposed settlement, in which Keystone and the plaintiffs agreed to release all such claims for a mere $4,499,640, is not in Keystone's best interest."

In addition to the possibility the plaintiffs may recover punitive damages on a successful claim for civil conspiracy, Cohen suggested they might recover triple the actual damages on a successful civil claim brought under the federal Racketeering Influenced and Corrupt Organizations Act.

In a footnote, Cohen also suggested that a criminal complaint could have been brought against some or all of the alleged co-conspirators. According to court documents, the Keystone Advisory Board did refer the matter to the U.S. Attorney's Office for the Eastern District of Pennsylvania and the U.S. Securities and Exchange Commission.

However, Cohen said, by the plaintiffs' bringing their claims against each of the possible co-conspirators in "piecemeal fashion," they failed to bring conspiracy claims against all potentially responsible parties.

They had also failed to provide the court with estimates of the best possible recovery and the probability of recovery on these potentially greater claims, Cohen said. . . .

a. Illustrative Law

Cal. Civ. Code §1541: Extinction of Obligations

(West 2004)

OBLIGATION EXTINGUISHED BY RELEASE. An obligation is extinguished by a release therefrom given to the debtor by the creditor, upon a new consideration, or in writing, with or without new consideration.

Cal. Civ. Code §1542: General Release; Extent

(West 2004)

A general release does not extend to claims which the creditor does not know or suspect to exist in his favor at the time of executing the release, which if known by him must have materially affected his settlement with the debtor.

b. Illustrative Cases Interpreting the Risks of Release

INTRODUCTORY NOTE ON THE "SIMPLE" RELEASE

At the heart of every settlement lies a release—a contract in which the releasing party promises not to sue again on the same claim. In return for that promise the plaintiff gets something—usually money, but sometimes the defendant's promise to do or not do something in the future. The next six cases deal with a problem one would think had been solved years ago: what does a release release? Put otherwise, when can a party who has released a claim nevertheless bring a second suit on the same cause of action? As with the rest of this section, it may be helpful to think about the problem in terms of risks. What risks might a defendant think it was taking in paying for this release? What risks might the plaintiff think he was taking in signing the release in return for payment? Do the courts make the right judgments about these risks in the cases below? Do they fall into groups that make sense of their apparently differing outcomes?

CASEY v. PROCTOR

378 P.2d 579 (Cal. 1963)

PETERS, J.

In this action for personal injuries, defendant alleged as a special affirmative defense that plaintiff had signed a release discharging him from all liability, and that the action was barred. Pursuant to Code of Civil Procedure section 597, this issue was tried before the case on its merits. After the introduction of evidence, the trial court, on defendant's motion, directed the jury to find, as a matter of law, that the release "is valid and binding and bars plaintiff from any recovery in this action." Plaintiff appeals from the judgment entered upon this directed verdict.

On April 18, 1959, plaintiff was driving in Los Angeles when traffic in front of him stopped. After plaintiff also stopped, the car owned and driven by defendant ran into the rear of plaintiff's car, pushing it forward into another car. Plaintiff did not see defendant's car prior to the accident and could not have avoided the collision. Defendant's negligence is conceded.

Four days after the accident, Mr. Carrigan, a representative of plaintiff's collision insurer, Motors Insurance Corporation, with whom plaintiff carried a $100 deductible collision policy, met with plaintiff to discuss a claim for the damage to plaintiff's car for which an estimate of $490.90 had been obtained. Carrigan also helped plaintiff fill out a "Report of Accident" which had been sent to plaintiff by defendant's liability insurer, Hardware Mutual Casualty Company. One question on this form was whether plaintiff had been injured in the accident, and "no" was written in answer. Carrigan testified that during the hour long interview plaintiff showed no signs of distress and appeared to be uninjured. No discussion of injuries was had. At the conclusion of the interview, plaintiff assigned to Motors any claim he might have against defendant or Hardware for damage to property insured by Motors, and promised to execute any document necessary to assist Motors in collecting on that claim. In return, Motors was to reimburse plaintiff for the deductible amount of the policy if it were able to collect it from defendant or Hardware.

Six days after the accident the completed "Report of Accident" was received by Hardware. Apart from the notation in this report stating that he had not been injured, plaintiff did not discuss with either defendant or Hardware the question or possibility of personal injuries. Thereafter, plaintiff's car was repaired, Motors paying all but $100 of the cost; plaintiff paying the remainder. Motors then sent a notice of subrogation to Hardware seeking reimbursement for the $490.90 repair bill. Hardware, whose representative testified that he believed his company was liable for all damages suffered by plaintiff in the accident, in turn, sent a release form to Motors for plaintiff's signature. Motors forwarded the release to plaintiff by mail, but plaintiff does not recollect receiving it or returning it. Nor does he remember whether or not he read it. However, he remembers signing it and acknowledges that the signature on it is his. Plaintiff does not remember how long he had the release in his possession, although it appears that he retained it for a period of nine days before returning it. The release provides:

Release of All Claims

FOR AND IN CONSIDERATION of the payment to me . . . of . . . $490.90 . . . I . . . hereby release, acquit and forever discharge . . . [defendant] of and from any and all actions, causes of action, claims, demands, damages, costs, loss of services, expenses and compensation, on account of, or in any way growing out of, any and all known and unknown bodily injuries and property damage resulting or to result from an accident that occurred on or about the 18th of APRIL 1959, at or near 9065 ROSECRANS." Above plaintiff's signature appears the warning: "CAUTION! READ BEFORE SIGNING." The release is dated the 11th of May, 1959, 23 days after the accident.

On receipt of the executed release, Hardware sent a draft for $490.90 to Motors, who forwarded it to plaintiff for his endorsement. Plaintiff endorsed and returned the draft to Motors who later reimbursed him for the $100 he had paid the repair shop.

Plaintiff testified that for ". . . quite a few days after the accident I was completely shook up. . . . My nerves were completely shattered. . . ." He was forced to reduce his work load and could neither read easily nor concentrate. As a result of the accident he was sore and his muscles "hurt," but he thought these complaints would quickly disappear. He did not think that he had been injured. At the time he signed the release, he had not sought medical care. Plaintiff testified categorically that in executing the release he did not intend to release anyone from a claim for personal injuries.

On July 2, 1959, almost two months after he had signed the release, plaintiff, for the first time, sought medical attention. His doctor testified, without contradiction, that as a result of the accident plaintiff suffered a compression fracture of the sixth cervical vertebra resulting in nerve root compression and a ruptured disc between the third and fourth cervical vertebrae. As a result of these injuries, a laminectomy and vertebrae fusion are required. The estimated special damages are $3,000. In addition, plaintiff will have almost continuous pain until the injured portion of the neck can be immobilized.

Thus, there is substantial evidence that plaintiff was seriously injured as a proximate result of defendant's negligence; that the injuries for which compensation is now sought were unknown and unsuspected by the parties at the time the release was executed; that there were no negotiations leading to any settlement; that there were no discussions concerning personal injuries or the possibility of their existence; that plaintiff received no compensation for any personal injuries; and that plaintiff did not intend to execute a release for personal injuries. It should be emphasized that when the release was signed, neither party to it had any reason to believe that personal injuries had been suffered. Four days after the accident plaintiff had reported that he had suffered no injuries, which report was received by Hardware six days after the accident. Later, based on that report or its own investigation, and upon the demand of Motors for property damage only, the release was prepared and sent. The release, however, by its express terms, included a discharge of liability for unknown as well as known injuries.

Plaintiff's initial contention is that he mistakenly believed that the release related only to property damage claims and that its scope should therefore be limited to a discharge of liability for the damage to his car. Alternatively, it is contended that this mistaken belief affords grounds for rescission of the release. Secondly, plaintiff contends that the release is a "general release" within the meaning of Civil Code section 1542, and therefore does not extend to claims for injuries unknown at the time it was executed. Finally, plaintiff contends that he should be allowed to rescind the entire release on the ground of mistake as to existence of any injuries at the time the release was executed.

(2) It has often been held that if the releaser was under a misapprehension, not due to his own neglect, as to the nature or scope of the release, and if this

misapprehension was induced by the misconduct of the releasee, then the release, regardless of how comprehensively worded, is binding only to the extent actually intended by the releaser. Under such circumstances it is unnecessary to effect a rescission of the release, and no question of notice to rescind or of restoration of consideration received arises. (*E.g.*, Garcia v. California Truck Co., 183 Cal. 767, 770 [192 P. 708]; Wetzstein v. Thomasson, *supra*, at p. 560.)

This rule does not here apply. There is no evidence of any fraud, misrepresentation, deception, overreaching, or other unfair conduct on the part of either the defendant or Hardware in obtaining the release. The release was sent through the mail and plaintiff had no personal dealings with either of them.

(3) It is true that even where, as here, there is no evidence of misconduct on the part of the releasee, some courts recognize the rule that one may rescind a release on the basis of a nonnegligent unilateral mistake as to its contents. If it be assumed that this is the rule in California the question is then whether plaintiff's failure to read the release, or, if he did read it, his failure to understand that it extended also to claims for personal injuries was, as a matter of law, the neglect of a legal duty (see Civ. Code, §1577).

Plaintiff contends that he was justified in assuming that the release related only to property damage because he made no claim for personal injuries; because no negotiations were carried out with regard to personal injuries — in fact there were no negotiations at all between plaintiff and the defendant or his insurance carrier; and because the consideration for the release was in the exact amount of the property damage. On the other hand, there is nothing in the record to indicate that at the time he signed the release he was suffering from any disability which would prevent him from giving it his full attention or which would prevent him from exercising his independent judgment. It was signed in his home when he was not subjected to any disabling pressure. Although there is evidence that plaintiff had difficulty reading and concentrating after the accident, there is no contention that he was unable to read, or prevented from reading, the release before signing it. He retained it in his possession for nine days and did not sign it until three weeks after the accident. And, as defendant properly points out, even a cursory reading of the release would indicate that it relates to claims for personal injuries as well as for property damage.

Under these circumstances, the failure of plaintiff to recognize that the release included a discharge of liability for personal injuries has been held to be attributable to his own neglect, both under California authority and in the vast majority of other jurisdictions. It must be concluded, therefore, that plaintiff's mistaken belief that the release related only to claims for property damage does not entitle him to rescind the release under the circumstances of this case.

This leaves for consideration the question of whether section 1542 of the Civil Code is applicable. Plaintiff contends that that section prevents the release from conclusively barring this action because the injuries for which compensation is now sought were unknown and unsuspected at the time the release was executed. This is the basic question presented in this case. Civil Code section 1542 provides that, "A general release does not extend to claims which the creditor does not know or suspect to exist in his favor at the time of executing the release, which if known by him must have materially affected his settlement with the debtor." In the instant case, there is substantial evidence that plaintiff did not know or suspect that he had suffered a broken cervical vertebra and a ruptured disc at the time he signed the release; and since the settlement did not include any payment for personal injuries, it is clear that his lack of knowledge materially affected the terms of the settlement. (4a) Defendant contends, however, that because the release specifically refers to claims for unknown injuries it is a "specific" and not a "general" release within the meaning of section 1542.

The leading California case involving an action to recover for later discovered injuries in the face of a release is O'Meara v. Haiden, 204 Cal. 354. There, after the plaintiff's son had apparently recovered from injuries sustained in an auto accident, plaintiff executed a release for $250 which purported to " '. . . discharge . . . [defendant] from any and all actions, causes of actions . . . by reason of any damage, loss or injury which heretofore have been or which hereafter may be sustained . . . in consequence of . . . [the] accident. . . .' " (204 Cal. at p. 356.) Thereafter, the boy died from a spleen injury suffered in the accident but which was unknown at the time of the execution of the release. A wrongful death action was filed by plaintiff and the release signed by plaintiff was asserted in defense. It was held that the release did not bar the action, the court reasoning that, since it was a general release, Civil Code section 1542 was applicable and an action for the results of an unknown injury had not, therefore, been discharged.

Although the plaintiff in *O'Meara* did serve notice of rescission and offered to return the consideration prior to trial (but after the commencement of the action), it was held that rescission of the release was not a prerequisite to the action. This court stated, "As to the damages sustained by the father for the death of his son due to defendant's negligence we have held that the release did not cover any damages sustained by reason of the boy's death. It only extended to damages for those injuries known to the parties at the time of executing it. The present action was by the instructions of the trial court limited to such damages as the father may have sustained by reason of his son's death. As plaintiff herein has not recovered any damages sustained by him for injuries, which were covered by the release, it was not necessary for him to rescind said release and restore the consideration received therefore before the institution of this action."

If Civil Code section 1542 as interpreted by O'Meara v. Haiden, is here applicable, then the release did not, as a matter of law, bar the instant action, and the timeliness of the notice of rescission and offer of restoration is immaterial. . . .

(5) It therefore appears beyond reasonable doubt that Civil Code section 1542 was intended by its drafters to preclude the application of a release to unknown claims in the absence of a showing, apart from the words of the release of an intent to include such claims. . . .

This interpretation of section 1542 does not prevent all settlements for unknown claims. It was never intended to do so. Rather, its purpose was to prevent the mere recital in the release to that effect from barring a claim for injuries later discovered in the absence of a showing of a conscious understanding that if injuries were suffered which had not yet manifested themselves, they too would be discharged by the release. Certainly a release of "all claims heretofore or hereafter arising" out of an accident is sufficiently broad to include claims for unknown injuries. While the specific inclusion of a discharge of claims for "injuries known and unknown" perhaps adds weight to the argument that such claims were intended to be discharged by the release, it does not add to the scope of the release. The question remains as one of fact whether the releaser actually intended to discharge such claims. If the evidence, independent of the words of the release, indicates that the parties have consciously contracted in reference to unknown claims, the release is, of course, binding.

(4c) Insofar as Berry v. Struble, *supra*, 20 Cal. App. 2d 299, and the cases following it indicate that section 1542 does not preclude a binding settlement for unknown injuries, they are correct. But insofar as those cases make application of section 1542 depend upon the wording of the release, they are incorrect and are disapproved; the distinction drawn between "all claims" and "claims for unknown injuries" was based upon the incorrect assumption that application of section 1542 in the latter case would prevent parties from consciously making such a settlement.

Plaintiff also contends, independently of section 1542, that the existence of unknown injuries at the time the release was executed affords grounds for rescission.

(7) In the absence of statutory provision, the majority of jurisdictions permit a releaser under proper circumstances to avoid a release, regardless of its terms, where it appears that unknown injuries existed at the time it was executed. Prior to Berry v. Struble, *supra*, 20 Cal. App. 2d 299, which also held that the release could not be rescinded on the ground of later discovered injuries, this was apparently the rule in California. Although most of the decisions are couched in terms of "mutual mistake," this rationale does not satisfactorily explain the case holdings. Invariably, the release has been drafted by the releasee in terms sufficiently broad to include a discharge of liability for unknown injuries. While the releasee is ignorant of the existence of injuries, he is also indifferent to their existence. He seeks a discharge of liability in any event, and it cannot be said that he would not have entered into the release had he actually known of them.

There are competing policies involved. On the one hand, the policy of the law is to encourage out-of-court settlements. To further this policy the parties to a dispute should be encouraged to negotiate settlements and to enter into releases. In the absence of unfair conduct on the part of the releasee, the law should extend its protection to the stability of the transaction by holding the parties to the express terms of the release. If later discovered injuries may be asserted, no release would be final and free from attack until the statute of limitations has run. On the other hand, if the releaser is bound by the literal terms of the release, it has been recognized that he is left to suffer personal injuries without compensation, while the releasee, who usually is an insurer, has received a windfall in avoiding liability for a risk it has been paid to assume. Furthermore, the long-term effects of damage to human tissue are extremely difficult to anticipate and the opportunity for error is great. Finally, stress has been laid upon the fact that as between the releaser and the releasee, a large disparity of bargaining power is present; usually the release is a prepared form drafted by experts and presented in a take it or leave it manner, while the releaser is ordinarily an individual without any knowledge of legal documents or assistance from legal counsel. The fact that these considerations warrant special treatment of releases for personal injuries has long been recognized.[5]

The majority of jurisdictions have adopted the sounder doctrine. For that reason, insofar as Berry v. Struble, *supra*, 20 Cal. App. 2d 299, holds that even apart from the application of section 1542 the release cannot be avoided, it and the cases following it on this point are disapproved.

(8) Under the majority rule, however, a release may not ipso facto be avoided upon the ground of later discovered injuries. The essence of the rule is that the wording of the release is not conclusive; it is a question of fact whether the parties to a release actually intended to discharge such liability. As was stated in Denton v. Utley, *supra*, (Mich.) 86 N.W.2d at pages 542-543, "We would not be understood as holding . . . that it is not within one's competence to say 'I may have serious injuries I know nothing about. As to them I will take my chances.' This, one may do. He may, if he wishes, release his rights and assume the risk of future disablement for $1 'and other good and valuable consideration,' or $50, or, indeed, an old beaver hat. In other words, it is possible that a reasonable, intelligent person, in full possession of all his faculties, and with knowledge that he may have serious injuries, will release a tortfeasor from all liability in return for a trifling sum of money. If such has in truth been the intention and the agreement we will not disturb the parties."Whether a release bars an action for later discovered personal injuries is a question of fact and depends upon whether it was "knowingly" made. (Denton v. Utley, *supra*, at p. 541. [86 N.W.2d].) Whether there is substantial evidence that it was not will depend upon the amount of consideration received compared with the risk of the existence of unknown injuries.

(10) If these factors be applied to the instant case, it is clear that under the rule prevailing in the majority of jurisdictions there is substantial evidence to support a holding that plaintiff may avoid the release. Here, no consideration was paid for personal injuries, there were no negotiations leading to the settlement, the risk of the existence of unknown injuries was never discussed, there is substantial evidence that plaintiff's belief that he had not suffered personal injuries was reasonable, and there is little doubt as to defendant's liability.

Since the test of whether the releaser consciously discharged claims for unknown injuries is the same when the release falls within the application of Civil Code section 1542, these factors are equally relevant to a determination of whether there is substantial evidence to support a holding that section 1542

---

5. The peculiar policy considerations relevant to releases for personal injuries have been noted by the legislatures of several states which have enacted statutes permitting a release involving personal injuries to be avoided at the will of the releaser if executed within a specified period after the injury was sustained. North Dakota Century Code Annotated, §9-08-08, for example, provides, "Every settlement or adjustment of any cause of action for damages on account of any personal injuries received, whether death ensues or not to the person injured, and every contract of retainer or employment to prosecute such an action, shall be voidable if made within thirty days after such injury. . . ." For suggested similar legislation in California, see Comment (1949) 1 Stan. L. Rev. 298.

prevents the release in the instant case from barring this action. Therefore, the case should have gone to the jury on the issue of plaintiff's intent. . . .

The judgment based on the directed verdict is reversed.

GIBSON, C. J., TRAYNOR, J., TOBRINER, J., and PEEK, J., concurred.

McCOMB, J. [with whom SCHAUER, J. concurred.]

I dissent.

I would affirm the judgment for the reasons expressed by Mr. Presiding Justice Shinn in the opinion prepared by him for the District Court of Appeal in Casey v. Proctor (Cal. App.) 22 Cal. Rptr. 531.

NOTE ON *CASEY V. PROCTOR*

Consider the possibility that the court makes *Casey* seem too easy. Poor Mr. Casey, who thought he was settling a claim for a broken truck but turns out to have suffered a substantial injury about which he had no inkling when he signed. One of course wants to give him an opportunity to recover for this injury. But are matters this simple?

Because the case does not suggest any over-reaching by the insurance company, the more difficult aspects of the case may appear if one considers matters from the insurer's perspective. Insurers want to settle cases promptly — or know they aren't going to settle so they can begin preparing for litigation. There are financial reasons for doing so: insurers set aside "reserves" for each claim, and the sooner they release these reserves the faster they can reinvest them. There are also legal reasons for doing so: if the case is not going to settle, the insurer wants to gather evidence on liability (not significant in this rear-end collision but critical in other cases) and on extent of injuries (how many rounds of golf did the plaintiff claiming complete immobility play last week?). After the decision in *Casey* what should an insurer do?

1. If it settles as quickly as possible, on the basis of the information supplied by Mr. Casey, it finds itself having to reopen the case with the evidence now stale. By the time the California Supreme Court decided to set aside the release, four years had elapsed since the original accident. That's going to make it very difficult for the insurer to present good evidence on whether Mr. Casey's injuries were entirely caused by the accident or by some pre-existing condition or exacerbated by his failing to seek medical attention as soon as the first symptoms manifested themselves.

2. If it drags things out, waiting for Mr. Casey to be sure he has no latent injuries, it runs two risks:

   a. That Casey will decide he has to hire a lawyer, who will likely increase the cost of eventually settling the case, if only because the insurer will also have to retain counsel.

   b. That it may be liable for bad-faith failure to settle, especially if counsel can present evidence that the insurer regularly delays settlement (as it might if it decided to take such a course of action in all similar cases).

3. Nor would it help if the insurer instructed its adjusters to say something like, "Mr. Casey, I know you've said you're not injured in any way, but my company has a policy of always including a little extra in the settlement to cover the slight chance you may encounter something. So, in addition to the $500 to repair your truck, we're going to add another $250 to cover any possible injuries." Explain why, if you were advising the insurer, you would tell it this was a very bad idea.

4. Assuming none of these approaches will work, what should the insurer do? And if there's nothing the insurer can do to avoid this result, doesn't that cast doubt on the decision in *Casey*?

5. Nor will it help much if the state has enacted a statute like that described in footnote 5. Why not? What fiercely litigated cases would you expect to find in states that had followed North Dakota's pattern?

6. Suppose, as sometimes happens with relatively small claims ($500 wasn't so small in 1959 but would be now), the driver who rear-ended Casey had jumped out of his car, immediately apologized (thus violating the advice a lawyer might have given him, not to make admissions against interest), inquired about whether Casey was injured in any way, and, when Casey said no, immediately offered to pay for the damage to the truck. Further suppose that our driver arranged for all the repairs and asked only that Casey sign a release when the truck was repaired — and Casey had done so. And then Casey had claimed he had suffered the unsuspected injury and brought suit to void the release.

    a. Same result?

    b. If not, is *Casey* best understood not as a case about the effectiveness of releases but as a case about how close calls should go against litigants (here the insurer) who are in business of running calculated risks?

7. The next five cases all present releases that are challenged. The challengers lose in the first three cases and win the last two — including one (*Chubb v. Amax Coal*) in which the defendant apparently has to pay *twice* for the same claim.

    a. Are the cases distinguishable? How?

    b. Are any wrongly decided? Why?

WINET V. PRICE

6 Cal. Rptr. 2d 554 (Cal. Ct. App. 1992)

FROELICH, J.

We are presented in this case with an agreement releasing all claims against a party, including unknown and unsuspected claims, and reinforcing such release by specifically referring to and waiving the benefits of the provisions of Civil Code section 1542. The issue is whether this release can be avoided if the releasor testifies he was unaware of a claim and did not intend to waive the right to pursue that claim. Appellant Robert S. Winet (Winet) argues the answer is yes, while respondent William E. Price (Price) contends the answer is no. The trial court agreed with Price and terminated Winet's attempt to pursue the alleged claim by entering summary judgment based on the release.

We conclude it is possible for a general release to effectively accomplish its primary purpose: to enable parties to end their relationship and permanently terminate their mutual obligations. On the record before us, we conclude the present release accomplishes that goal, and we therefore affirm.

I. Factual Background

A. The Genesis of the Release

The material facts are undisputed. During the period from 1973 to early 1975, Price, an attorney, performed legal services for Winet and Winet's various legal entities. Among the legal services Price performed was the drafting of a partnership agreement for an entity known as Newark Storage Partners, Ltd. (hereinafter referred to as the Newark partnership). Winet was the general partner of the Newark partnership.

A dispute eventually arose between Winet and Price over legal fees owed by Winet. Accordingly, in 1975, Price's law firm, Price & Elster, filed an action to collect its fees from Winet, alleging Winet owed it over $20,000. The matter was eventually settled and a general release signed as part of that settlement. The scope and enforceability of that release concerns us here.

B. The Release

The general release, which named (among others) Price and Winet as releasing parties, provided for a release of "any and all . . . claims, . . . damages and causes of action whatsoever, of whatever kind or nature, *whether known or unknown, or suspected or unsuspected* . . . against any other Party . . ." (Italics added.) The release of all "known or unknown, or suspected or unsuspected" claims also specifically included all claims arising:

"(a) By reason of any matter or thing alleged or referred to, or directly or indirectly or in any way connected with or arising out of or which may hereafter be claimed to arise out of all or any of the matters, facts events or occurrences alleged or referred to in any of the pleadings on file in [the Price v. Winet collection action].

"(b) Arising out of or in any manner connected with the performance of legal services by [Price or his law firms] for [Winet or his entities], or any act or omission by any Party in connection with said legal services or any request for the performance of legal services.

"(c) Arising out of or in any way connected with any loss, damage, or injury whatsoever, known or unknown, suspected or unsuspected, resulting from any act or omission, by or on the part of any Party, committed or omitted prior to the date hereof."

The parties did specifically except from their agreement any claims connected with "any act or omission committed or omitted relating to Canoga Storage Partners, Ltd. . . . ." (Release, [¶] (d)), but made no similar exception for the Newark partnership. The parties then reaffirmed that their agreement included unknown or unsuspected claims, declaring:

"All Parties to this Mutual General Release do hereby further agree as follows:

"(1) There is a risk that subsequent to the execution of this Mutual General Release, one or more Parties will incur or suffer loss, damages or injuries which are in some way caused by the transactions referred to above, but which are unknown and unanticipated at the time this Mutual General Release is signed.

"(2) All Parties do hereby assume the above-mentioned risks and understand that this Mutual General Release Shall Apply to All Unknown or Unanticipated Results of the Transactions and Occurrences Described Above, as Well as Those Known and Anticipated, and upon advice of legal counsel, all Parties do hereby waive any and all rights under California Civil Code §1542, which section has been duly explained and reads as follows: [¶] "A general release does not extend to claims which the creditor does not know or suspect to exist in his favor at the time of executing the release. . . ."

"(4) The advice of legal counsel has been obtained by all Parties prior to signing this Mutual General Release. All Parties execute this Mutual General Release voluntarily, with full knowledge of its significance, and with the express intention of effecting the legal consequences provided by [section 1541], i.e., the extinguishment of all obligations."

Winet was represented by legal counsel during the negotiation of the release.

C. The Present Lawsuit

Nearly 15 years later, some of the limited partners in the Newark partnership sued Winet. The lawsuit sought damages against Winet for breaching his duties as general partner. It also sought declaratory relief and reformation because certain ambiguous language in the Newark partnership agreement did not accurately reflect the agreement or conform to the representations upon which the limited partners relied when they purchased their interests. Winet then cross-complained for contribution and indemnity against Price, alleging that Winet's liability to the plaintiffs, if any, was caused by Price's malpractice in drafting the partnership documents.

Price subsequently moved for summary judgment, arguing that the release was unambiguous and barred any claim by Winet against Price because the claim arose out of the Newark partnership agreement which the general release encompassed. Winet opposed the motion, arguing summary judgment was inappropriate because there was a disputed issue of "fact," i.e., whether the release covered the present claim. In opposition to the summary judgment motion, Winet submitted his own declaration stating, in pertinent part, that when he signed the release he did not intend to waive all possible disputes with Price over Price's legal services, and that he was unaware at the time he signed the release of the possibility of the present action.

The trial court granted summary judgment, concluding that the release was broadly designed to bar all claims of malpractice arising out of Price and Winet's relationship, that it was specifically negotiated with the help of counsel, and that the significance of Winet's waiver of section 1542 was explained and understood by the parties. Winet appeals.

Our independent review of the language of the release convinces us that it does encompass the claims sued upon here, and we therefore affirm. . . .

III. The Language of the General Release Shows the Parties Intended to Encompass All Known and Unknown Claims

Our objective in construction of the language used in the contract is to determine and to effectuate the intention of the parties. It is the outward expression of the agreement, rather than a party's unexpressed intention, which the court will enforce.

It is appropriate to begin this investigation with a review of the literal terminology of the contract. In no fewer than three distinct places the parties declared their intention to release each other from all claims, known or unknown, suspected or unsuspected, arising from either the facts described in the collection lawsuit (which included drafting the partnership agreement Winet now claims was inadequately documented) or any act or omission in connection with the legal services Price rendered to Winet. Moreover, lest this repeated attempt to reinforce their declared intent be deemed inadequate, the parties reiterated that (1) there was a risk they might suffer losses unknown or unanticipated at the time of the release; (2) they were represented by counsel, who advised them of the rights conferred by section 1542; and (3) with knowledge of the risks, and upon advice of counsel, the parties assumed the risks of unknown or unanticipated claims, and agreed ". . . that this Mutual General Release Shall Apply to All Unknown or Unanticipated Results of the Transactions and Occurrences Described Above, as Well as Those Known and Anticipated. . . ."

Despite this strong, clear effort to iterate and reiterate that the release applied to all claims, Winet, citing Vega v. Western Employers Ins. Co. (1985) 170 Cal. App. 3d 922 [216 Cal. Rptr. 592], argues that whether a specific later-discovered claim was intended to be covered by a broad release can always be made a disputable issue of fact. There is a dispute in this case, Winet claims, because his proffered parol evidence indicates an intention contrary to the literal meaning of the words of the release.

We note, first, that the parol evidence tendered by Winet is his uncommunicated subjective intent as to the meaning of the words of the contract. Winet does not suggest that he ever communicated to Price or his attorney his intent to retain the right to sue Price in the future. Further, parol evidence is admissible only to prove a meaning to which the language is "reasonably susceptible" not to flatly contradict the express terms of the agreement. Winet's evidence violates this tenet, because it seeks to prove that a release of unknown or unsuspected claims was not intended to include unknown or unsuspected claims. If an argument such as this were given currency, a release could never effectively encompass unknown claims. A releasor would simply argue that a release of unknown or unsuspected claims applied only to known or suspected claims, making it ineffective as to unknown or unsuspected claims.

Since there is no evidence of the parties' discussions at the time the release was negotiated, there remain only the surrounding circumstances from which to interpret the language of the contract. We are instructed to consider parol evidence of the circumstances which attended the making of the agreement, "'. . . including the object, nature and subject matter of the writing . . . ' so that the court can 'place itself in the same situation in which the parties found themselves at the time of contracting.'" Review of the circumstances confirms our interpretation that the release was designed to extinguish all claims extant among the parties. First, Winet was represented by counsel and was aware at the time he entered into the release of possible malpractice claims against Price relating to certain services Price had rendered to him. With this knowledge and the advice of counsel concerning the language of (and the import of waiving) section 1542, Winet expressly assumed the risk of unknown claims. Second, it is significant that the parties were able to, and did, fashion language memorializing their agreement to preserve identified claims from the operation of the release when such was their intention, specifically, the Canoga Storage Partners, Ltd. malpractice claim exclusion. Finally, Winet was represented by his own counsel, who explained to Winet the import of the release in general and of the waiver of section 1542 in particular. Under these circumstances we may not give credence to a claim that a party did not intend clear and direct language to be effective.

IV. The Authorities Which Permit a Party to Avoid the Terms of a Comprehensive Release Have No Application Here

Winet First Relies on Casey v. Proctor . . .

The factual and legal distinctions render *Casey* inapplicable to the present case. This case does not involve personal injuries; it involves ordinary business relations. Nor does this case involve an unsophisticated claimant who is presented with a form release on a "take it or leave it" basis and signs the release without the benefit of counsel, conferring a windfall on an insurance company. To the contrary, Winet appears to be a sophisticated businessman who, with the benefit of counsel, specifically negotiated the subject release in an arm's-length transaction.

Most importantly, *Casey* is inapplicable because its holding rested principally upon the court's conclusion that the purpose behind section 1542 was to prevent inadvertent waivers of unknown claims by a ". . . mere recital in the release to that effect . . ." but that such waivers would be binding upon a showing the parties consciously understood and agreed such was the effect of their release. Here, unlike *Casey*, Price does not merely seize upon an oblique reference to "all known and unknown" claims to show the parties intended the release to be comprehensive in derogation of section 1542. The release shows Winet consciously understood the benefits conferred by section 1542 and the risks assumed by the release, and, after receiving counsel's advice, consciously waived such benefits and entered the agreement ". . . voluntarily, with full knowledge of its significance, and with the express intention of effecting the legal consequences provided by [section 1541], i.e., the extinguishment of all obligations." In short, the concerns expressed in *Casey* are simply absent here. . . .

V. Conclusion

The law imputes to a person an intention corresponding to the reasonable meaning of his words and acts. It judges of his intention by his outward expressions and excludes all questions in regard to his unexpressed intention. If his words or acts, judged by a reasonable standard, manifest an intention to agree in regard to the matter in question, that agreement is established, and it is immaterial what may be the real but unexpressed state of his mind on that subject. General releases which purport to extinguish unknown and nonmatured claims can no doubt be subject to abusive use. Particularly when the parties are in unequal bargaining positions or other factors make the release doubtful as to whether its terms were actually understood, or its enforcement otherwise inequitable for some reason, judges will seek grounds to avoid literal enforcement. This leads those in the practice of law to conclude, at times, that it is virtually impossible to create a general release that will actually achieve its literal purpose, which is to extinguish all future claims regardless of their then status in terms of either maturity or knowledge. That thought should be rejected. Those engaged in contract law and litigation are in great need of the availability of ironclad and enforceable general releases. We deal in this case with a release that is about as complete, explicit and unambiguous as a general release can be. Our decision to uphold the release and enforce it in accord with its literal terms is in harmony, we believe, with a beneficial principle of contract law: that general releases can be so constructed as to be completely enforceable.

Disposition

The judgment is affirmed.

Work, Acting P. J., and Huffman, J., concurred.

PETRO-VENTURES, INC. v. TAKESSIAN

967 F.2d 1337 (9th Cir. 1992)

LEAVY, Circuit Judge:

We decide the validity of a release of all unknown claims in the context of a settlement of ongoing litigation, where potential violations of federal securities laws were later discovered. The general rule in this circuit is that "[a] release is valid for purposes of a federal securities claim only if [there was] 'actual knowledge' that such claims existed." However, we must decide if the facts of this case warrant an exception to this rule.

In a business venture in May of 1986, Petro-Ventures exchanged certain oil- and gas-producing properties for partnership units in Great American Partners. Two months after the exchange, Great American Partners and its general partner, Great American Resources, Inc. (Great American Resources) filed an action against Petro-Ventures in San Diego Superior Court for breach of contract, fraud, and rescission. The basis of the complaint was that the oil- and gas-producing properties did not yield the monthly revenue that had been represented by Petro-Ventures. The action was removed from San Diego Superior Court to the United States District Court for the Southern District of California.

Petro-Ventures countersued Great American Partners and Great American Resources in the Western District of Oklahoma. The action was transferred to the Southern District of California.

On May 29, 1987, Petro-Ventures, Great American Partners, and Great American Resources settled their dispute. They memorialized the terms in a comprehensive settlement agreement in which California law was selected to govern the terms and conditions. The release provision at issue is in paragraph 9 of the agreement. Paragraph 9 states:

PVI [Petro-Ventures], CUDD [the president of Petro-Ventures], GAP [Great American Partners], GAR [Great American Resources], NEEDCO [a Texas limited partnership], and Takessian hereby release any and all claims demands, damages or causes of action they might have, each against the other, based upon the negotiations for sale and the conveyance of the producing oil and gas properties which were the subject of sale and conveyance from PVI to Needco in May of 1986, regardless of whether or not said claims have been set forth in the litigation referred to in Paragraph B.1. and 2. of this agreement. This release shall be effective as to PVI, CUDD, GAR, GAP, NEEDCO and Takessian and as to their successors, assigns, affiliated entities, directors, officers, employees, agents and attorneys. In further consideration and inducement for the compromise settlement contained herein, the parties expressly waive the benefit of Section 1542 of the California Civil Code which provides:

> "A general release does not extend to claims which a creditor does not know or suspect to exist in his favor at the time of executing this release, which, if known by him must have materially affected his settlement with debtor."

In recognition of the settlement, Petro-Ventures paid $181,000 to Great American Resources and reassigned limited partnership units to them. In turn, certain wells were reassigned to Petro-Ventures.

The mutual parting of ways ended when Petro-Ventures filed an action against Gary Takessian on December 7, 1987, in the Southern District of California, seeking damages for violations of federal and state securities laws. Vrable, Walden, and Hamersly intervened in the action.

Takessian moved to dismiss on the ground that Petro-Ventures' actions were precluded by the release provision. The district court of the Southern District of California dismissed with prejudice. The court found that "the evidence indicates that the parties attempted to draw as broad a release as possible."

Petro-Ventures appeals, contending it did not know the partnership units it obtained in the exchange might not have been registered properly with the Securities and Exchange Commission. Petro-Ventures maintains that the release of securities law claims was not discussed during settlement negotiations and that Takessian represented to its president, B. Keaton Cudd, III, that the units were properly registered. . . .

Petro-Ventures contends that unknown claims pursuant to federal securities law cannot be released under the law of this circuit, even by the execution of a settlement agreement that releases all known or unknown claims.

Discussion

. . .

Whether State or Federal Law Applies

In the settlement agreement, the parties agreed that "[t]he terms and provisions of this Agreement shall be construed according to California law." However, in a non-securities case, we held that "federal law always governs the validity of releases of federal causes of action." . . .

The Release of Federal Securities Claims During Litigation

In dealing with federal securities, the general rule is that unknown or subsequently maturing causes of action may not be waived. The federal anti-waiver provision is found in section 29(a) of the Securities Exchange Act of 1934, 15 U.S.C. §78cc(a), which states:

> Any condition, stipulation, or provision binding any person to waive compliance with any provision of this chapter or of any rule or regulation thereunder, or of any rule of an exchange required thereby shall be void.

We cited this provision without discussion in *Burgess*. See 727 F.2d at 832. . . .

The *Burgess* facts arose in a very different context. When the doctors signed the releases, they were not involved in litigation with Premier. They were still dealing in an exclusively business relationship with Premier. We do not know whether the doctors were represented by counsel at the time the releases were signed. The facts recite only "[w]hen Premier repurchased the cattle herds from the doctors, each doctor filed a document releasing Premier from all claims." When they signed the releases, the doctors were not acting in the adversarial setting that is characteristic of litigation. It was therefore appropriate to apply the general rule. . . .

However, a totally different situation occurs where a plaintiff has affirmatively acted to release another party from any possible liability in connection with a transaction in securities. The parties here, in giving up all claims, "regardless of whether or not said claims have been set forth in this litigation referred to . . . in this agreement" and in "expressly waiv[ing] the benefit of Section 1542 of the California Civil Code" were not so concerned with protecting their rights as investors as they were with establishing a general peace. See C.G.C. Music, Ltd., 804 F.2d at 1463 ("[T]he . . . Release firmly evidences the parties' intent to end their various disputes . . . once and for all."). . . .

The agreement and surrounding facts point to Petro-Ventures' desire to end its litigation with Great American Partners and Great American Resources. To that end, it knowingly gave up all rights to future litigation that might arise out of the transaction. After considering extrinsic evidence, that desire was given effect by the district court. The district court's decision was not clearly erroneous.

AFFIRMED. Each party shall bear its own costs and attorneys' fees.

STROMAN v. W. COAST GROCERY CO.

884 F.2d 458 (9th Cir. 1989)

WIGGINS, Circuit Judge:

West Coast Grocery Company (West Coast) appeals from a judgment entered against it after a bench trial in this action under 42 U.S.C. §2000e brought by appellee Grady Michael Stroman. The district court held that Stroman was denied training for a supervisory position because he was black. The court also held that Stroman was constructively discharged as a result of the actions of several of Stroman's supervisors. The court awarded Stroman $291,445.88 in back and front pay. We reverse the district court's judgment because Stroman's suit was barred by the terms of the release agreement entered into by Stroman and West Coast.

Stroman began working with West Coast as a part time order selector on January 15, 1981. Stroman's job as an order selector consisted of identifying pallets of groceries in West Coast's warehouse and transporting the pallets to different shipping locations throughout the warehouse. He was switched to full time on September 28, 1981.

Beginning in early 1982 Stroman made repeated requests to be trained for a position as a grocery warehouse supervisor in the scheduling office. An employee generally had to be recommended by his supervisors for training in the scheduling office. Stroman's supervisors declined to recommend him for training.

Stroman applied and was interviewed for a supervisor position in the scheduling office in April 1985. He was not selected. As a result of his failure to obtain the position, Stroman filed a discrimination charge with the Washington State Human Rights Commission (WSHRC) and the Equal Employment Opportunity Commission (EEOC) alleging that he was denied the position because of his race. On June 12, 1985, Stroman filed a second discrimination charge alleging retaliation because of the previous charge. In July 1985 Stroman again applied for a supervisor position, but was not selected.

Stroman sought and obtained a voluntary medical leave of absence on August 5, 1985. In late October 1985, Stroman approached his supervisor Willy Mosley regarding the possibility of being put on economic layoff so that he could receive unemployment benefits. Although the economic layoff was meant only for part time employees, West Coast agreed to place Stroman on economic layoff status. In exchange West Coast required Stroman to enter into the following agreement:

> "West Coast Grocery and Grady Michael Stroman agree to the following:"
>
> "1. Mike will leave the Company on an economic lay-off."
> "2. West Coast will not contest the unemployment benefits."
> "3. The employee's record will be cleared and information given out limited to date of hire, rate of pay, and journeyman status."
> "4. The employee will have no recall rights."
> "5. The employee will be entitled to any accrued vacation and his share of Profit Sharing payable as defined by Federal law, and the terms of the Profit Sharing Trust."
> "6. These terms represent a full and final settlement of any and all claims arising out of Mike's employment with West Coast Grocery."

The agreement, dated November 1, 1985, was signed by Stroman, Mosley, and David Hamlin, the Operations Manager for West Coast.

On December 2, 1985, Stroman filed a third discrimination charge alleging that West Coast failed to promote Stroman to the July 1985 supervisor position because of his race. Stroman filed this suit on July 31, 1986, alleging that he was denied training and promotion because of his race. He also stated a claim of retaliation and constructive discharge. During trial, the district court held that the November 1, 1985, agreement was a "termination of work" agreement and not a release of claims against West Coast. . . .

II

A general release of Title VII claims does not ordinarily violate public policy. To the contrary, public policy favors voluntary settlement of employment discrimination claims brought under Title VII."[1] We nevertheless must closely scrutinize a waiver of rights under Title VII because of their remedial nature.

We perceive no public policy that would be harmed by enforcement of the November 1, 1985, agreement.

The interpretation and validity of a release of claims under Title VII is governed by federal law.

The district court's conclusion that the November 1, 1985, agreement did not constitute a release of all claims against West Coast was based primarily on an analysis of the contract provisions. We therefore review the district court's determination de novo. We conclude that the agreement constitutes a clear and unambiguous waiver by Stroman of all legal claims against West Coast. Under the terms of the agreement, West Coast agreed to allow Stroman to leave the company on economic layoff so that he could collect unemployment benefits, clear Stroman's record, and limit the information given to prospective employers to the date of hire, rate of pay, and journeyman status. In exchange, Stroman agreed that the agreement would represent "a full and final settlement of any and all claims" arising out of his employment with West Coast. This language unambiguously indicates that Stroman intended to waive all claims against West Coast, including those then pending before the WSHRC and the EEOC. . . .

Our conclusion that the November 1, 1985, agreement constitutes a release of all Stroman's legal claims does not end the inquiry. We must also determine whether Stroman's release of his discrimination claims was a "voluntary, deliberate and informed" waiver. The district court's findings pertaining to whether Stroman's waiver is valid are reviewed under the clearly erroneous standard.

The determination of whether a waiver of Title VII was "voluntary, deliberate, and informed" is "predicated upon an evaluation of several indicia arising from the circumstances and conditions under which the release was executed." Of primary importance in this calculation is the clarity and lack of ambiguity of the agreement, the plaintiff's education and business experience, the presence of a noncoercive atmosphere for the execution of the release, and whether the employee had the benefit of legal counsel.

Based on his ruling that the agreement was a termination of work agreement, the district court precluded West Coast's counsel from examining either Stroman or Mosley regarding the conditions under which the agreement was signed. The court did, however, permit West Coast's counsel to make an offer of proof incorporating Mosley's affidavit. We conclude that the record as a whole sufficiently establishes the voluntariness of the agreement and no purpose would be served by remanding the case to the district court to reconsider this issue.

---

1. Whether "policies underlying [a federal] statute . . . render [a] waiver unenforceable is a question of federal law." Newton v. Rumery, 480 U.S. 386, 392, 107 S. Ct. 1187, 1192, 94 L. Ed. 2d 405 (1987). "[A] promise is unenforceable if the interest in its enforcement is outweighed in the circumstances by a public policy harmed by enforcement of the agreement." *Id.* (footnote omitted).

We are satisfied that Stroman's release of "all claims" against West Coast under the November 1, 1985, agreement was a deliberate, voluntary, and knowing waiver of his Title VII and related claims. As we have previously indicated, the sixth paragraph of the agreement unambiguously indicates that Stroman intended to waive all legal claims against West Coast. We note that Stroman's work experience and college education were particularly relevant to our determination of a knowing and voluntary waiver. Although Stroman was not a sophisticated businessman, his training in the Army and his business management-related community college degree convince us that Stroman possessed the education and skills necessary to understand that when he signed the agreement he waived all legal claims against West Coast. He was sufficiently intelligent to understand that "all claims" meant all legal claims, including claims brought under Title VII.

Additionally, there is no evidence whatsoever that Stroman was coerced into signing the agreement. To the contrary, it was Stroman who approached Mosley asking to be placed on economic layoff. When the agreement initially was presented to Stroman, he was not coerced into signing it. In fact, Stroman did not sign it until several days later. Although he did not have an attorney read the agreement before signing it, there is no evidence indicating that Stroman was discouraged or precluded from doing so. In fact, Mosley, who was not permitted by the district judge to testify on this issue, indicated in his affidavit that he asked Stroman whether he wished to have an attorney read the agreement before signing and that Stroman responded that he did not. We therefore conclude that the contractual agreement released Stroman's Title VII discrimination claims, and that the release was a deliberate and informed waiver.

III

For the foregoing reasons, we reverse the district court's judgment in favor of Stroman and order that judgment be entered in favor of West Coast and the action dismissed.

REVERSED

TANG, Circuit Judge, dissenting in part:

I agree that the economic layoff agreement was sufficient to waive Stroman's Title VII claims. I dissent, however, from the majority's factual determination that Stroman waived his Title VII rights knowingly and voluntarily.

When an appellate court determines that a lower court made findings based upon an erroneous view of the law, the appellate court may not make contrary findings but must remand for new findings to be made in the light of the correct rule of law. Pullman-Standard v. Swint, 456 U.S. 273 (1982). This is not a game where an incorrect understanding of the law by the fact finder results in automatic granting of relief. Such a rule would require inefficient use of limited resources because the district court would have to make factual determinations in every case regardless of whether they are needed.

The only exception to that rule is if "the record permits only one resolution of the factual issue." *Id.* citing Kelley v. Southern Pacific Co., 419 U.S. 318, 331-332 (1974). The majority presumes that Stroman waived his Title VII rights knowingly and voluntarily but I do not believe that the record permits only one conclusion as to this matter.

I would therefore remand for a determination as to whether the waiver of Title VII rights was made knowingly and voluntarily. It is the fact-finder, not us, who should determine these issues in the first instance.

CHUBB v. AMAX COAL CO.

466 N.E.2d 369 (Ill. App. Ct. 1984)

JONES, Justice:

Plaintiff, Jack Chubb, brought the instant action for disability benefits under a group insurance policy issued to his employer, Amax Coal Company, Inc. (Amax), by Connecticut General Life Insurance Company (Connecticut General). The defendants, Amax and Connecticut General, moved for dismissal of the complaint by reason of a release executed by the plaintiff in settlement of his previous claim for total and permanent disability benefits under the same policy. The trial court granted the motion to dismiss, finding that the release was effective to bar all claims by the plaintiff under the policy in question, including those arising after the execution of the release. On appeal the plaintiff contends that the subject release was limited to claims in existence at the time of its execution and that the court thus erred in dismissing his complaint for benefits for a subsequent unrelated disability.

While the record in the instant case is incomplete due to the summary nature of the proceeding, it appears that the plaintiff had been employed by Amax for a period of time prior to 1981. Early in 1981 he made a claim under group long term disability policy No. 041635, issued by Connecticut General to Amax for the benefit of its employees. He subsequently filed suit in federal court on this claim, which was based upon his alleged total and permanent disability. The suit was settled by the parties, and the plaintiff received a payment of $57,000, representing 80% of the then present value of the policy benefits for total and permanent disability until the age of 65. In consideration for this payment, the plaintiff, on April 6, 1981, executed the release that is involved in this appeal.

Shortly thereafter, on August 31, 1981, the plaintiff returned to work for Amax and continued in this employment through March 31, 1983. During this time Amax deducted $450.12 from the plaintiff's salary, which represented the plaintiff's contributions on premiums to Connecticut General for its group disability coverage. On July 7, 1983, the plaintiff filed the instant complaint in which he alleged that he had suffered a myocardial infarction and was totally disabled as a result. The plaintiff alleged that, pursuant to the terms of the policy provided by Amax through Connecticut General, he was entitled to monthly payments of $1,992 for so long as he remained disabled.

In their motion to dismiss the plaintiff's complaint, the defendants set forth the release that had been executed by the plaintiff on April 6, 1981. This release stated in pertinent part:

> Release
> FOR AND IN CONSIDERATION of the sum of Fifty Seven Thousand Dollars ($57,000.00) . . . Jack L. Chubb executes and agrees to the terms of this Release:
> 1. Jack L. Chubb hereby releases and forever discharges Connecticut General Life Insurance Company . . . from any and all claims, demands, obligations, or

causes of action of any nature whatsoever . . . including, but not limited to, all claims, obligations or causes of action in any way connected with or arising out of:

(a) Group Long Term Disability Policy No. 041635 issued by Connecticut General to Amax Coal Companies, Inc. insuring its employees, . . .

and/or

(b) Civil Action No. 80-4212 filed in the U.S. District Court for the Southern District of Illinois, styled "Jack L. Chubb v. Amax Coal Companies, Inc., and Connecticut General Life Insurance Company, Hartford, Connecticut."

* * *

6. Jack L. Chubb expressly waives and assumes the risk of any and all claims, demands, obligations or causes of action for damages or other relief arising out of any matter described in paragraph 1 which exist as of this date but which he does not know or suspect to exist in his favor, whether through ignorance, oversight, error, negligence or otherwise, and which, if known, would materially affect his decision to enter this Release.

Amax additionally tendered a refund of the plaintiff's premium payments to him, but these payments were placed in escrow pending the outcome of the case.

Pursuant to the defendants' motion the trial court dismissed the plaintiff's complaint with prejudice. The court reasoned that the release executed by the plaintiff barred him from asserting any claim or cause of action under group long-term disability policy No. 041635 and that "[t]his finding of no liability owed by [Connecticut General] pertained[ed] to matters arising after the date of the release, as well as matters arising prior to the date of the release, insofar as any claim . . . would be based upon [policy No. 041635]." While nothing that the condition claimed in the instant case was different from that which was the subject of the release, the court observed, nevertheless, that "the language of said release involve[d] any claims arising out of said policy, and was not limited to the specific condition or injury referred to in paragraph 1(b) of said release." Thus, the court ruled, since the claim set forth in the plaintiff's complaint pertained to policy No. 041635, it had been released by virtue of the release of April 6, 1981.

In considering the plaintiff's appeal from this judgment, we note initially that we are aware of no case that has addressed the situation here presented. The plaintiff contends that the release in question should not be construed to bar his claim for a subsequent unrelated injury that was not within the contemplation of the parties when the release was executed. While, as both the defendants and the trial court have pointed out, the plaintiff's release, by its terms, discharged the defendants of all liability arising under policy No. 041635, we decline to hold that the release was effective to bar new claims, not in existence at the time of the release, that arose after the plaintiff became re-employed by Amax and again came within the coverage of its employees' group disability policy. As will be seen, this result follows from an application of general rules of construction regarding releases as well as from considerations of public policy.

It is well settled that a release, being a contract whereby a party abandons a claim to a person against whom that claim exists, is subject to rules governing the construction of contracts. The intention of the parties, therefore, controls the scope and effect of the release, and this intent is discerned from the language used and the circumstances of the transaction. It is similarly stated that a release, no matter how broad its terms, will not be construed to include claims not within the contemplation of the parties and, where the language of the release is directed to claims then in existence, it will not be extended to cover claims that may arise in the future.

While the plaintiff makes an initial argument that the release in question was a special release limited to the particular injury and cause of action that was the subject of his prior suit, the language contained in paragraph one of the release is plenary in its terms and is not limited by reference to the suit then pending between the parties.

Notwithstanding this express release of claims in existence but unsuspected by the plaintiff, the defendants urge a construction of the release as barring the instant claim that arose after the execution of the release. Here, again, reference must be made to the intention of the parties, as a release ordinarily includes only claims in existence at the time it is executed.

In the instant case there is no indication that the parties considered the possibility of future claims arising under the policy from unrelated causes after the execution of the release.

In the instant case the plaintiff's coverage under policy No. 041635 derived from his employment relationship with Amax. Despite the settlement of his previous claim under that policy, when the plaintiff became re-employed by Amax he again came within the group of employees covered by policy No. 041635. To hold that the plaintiff was precluded from bringing any claim for disability under that policy would render this coverage a nullity and would deprive the plaintiff of any legal recourse on the policy after the parties had again entered into a contract of insurance. Because of the nature of a group insurance policy as a blanket policy covering all employees who come within its eligibility requirements the plaintiff, upon re-employment, should not be denied coverage based upon the fortuitous circumstance that this coverage was provided by the same group policy under which he had released his prior claim. The plaintiff, therefore, will not be presumed to have relinquished his rights under the policy that arose upon his re-employment where such would be contrary to public policy.

Despite our holding, however, that the plaintiff is entitled to make another claim under the policy in question, the fact that he has already received benefits under that policy cannot be disregarded. The plaintiff's benefits are governed by the parties' contract of insurance, and where he has been paid for one total and permanent disability, this would seem to preclude another such recovery under the contract. If, upon remand, then, the plaintiff is found to have been totally and permanently disabled by his present condition, the defendant insurer may be allowed to offset the benefits due under the present policy by the amount already paid to the plaintiff for his previous total and permanent disability.

The result here reached would give the plaintiff the benefit of his renewed contractual relationship with the defendant while preventing a double recovery of amounts due under the policy. We note in passing that the net effect of this approach would be comparable to the situation where, rather than making a lump sum payment of benefits for total and permanent disability, the insurer pays monthly benefits that are terminated upon a showing that the insured has recovered from the disability and resumed employment. (Under insurance policy providing for monthly payments for total and permanent disability, insurer protects itself in case of recovery of insured by policy provision requiring periodic proof of continuance of disability.)

For the reasons stated in this opinion we reverse the judgment of the trial court and remand for further proceedings.

REVERSED AND REMANDED.

WELCH P.J., and KASSEERAN J., concur.

MATSUURA V. ALSTON & BIRD

166 F.3d 1006 (9th Cir. 1998)

PER CURIAM:

After settling their product liability suits against E.I. du Pont de Nemours and Company, Inc. (DuPont), David and Stephen Matsuura allegedly discovered that DuPont had fraudulently induced them to settle for less than the fair value of their claims. They sued DuPont[1] for fraud, but the district court held the suit was barred by general releases in the settlement agreements. We conclude that under Delaware law, which governs, defrauded tort plaintiffs may stand by their settlement agreements and institute an independent action for fraud, which the Matsuura-DuPont releases do not bar. We therefore reverse.

I

The Matsuuras, commercial nurserymen, alleged in their product liability suits that a DuPont fungicide, Benlate, was contaminated with herbicides, which killed their plants. Many similar suits were filed by commercial growers across the nation. In early trials, DuPont falsely represented that soil tests had produced no evidence of contamination. During consolidated discovery proceedings in Hawaii, which included the Matsuuras' suits, DuPont falsely denied withholding evidence of Benlate contamination, and improperly invoked work product protection to resist disclosure of testing data. The Matsuuras allege DuPont took these steps to induce Benlate plaintiffs to settle their cases for less than their fair value.

After the Matsuuras settled, DuPont disclosed its testing data in the Hawaii discovery proceedings. Contrary to DuPont's prior representations, the tests confirmed that Benlate was contaminated. Additional evidence of Benlate contamination was produced in other Benlate litigation. Two district courts held that DuPont had intentionally engaged in fraudulent conduct by withholding this evidence. Although the Eleventh Circuit reversed the Georgia court on the ground that the sanctions were punitive and the court had not followed applicable criminal procedure, the court noted the "serious nature of the allegations" and stated that it assumed the U.S. Attorney would conduct an

---

1. Alston & Bird, a law firm, is also named as a defendant in the fraud action. Because the Matsuuras' claims against DuPont and Alston & Bird are identical insofar as this appeal is concerned, for purposes of simplicity we refer only to the claims against DuPont.

investigation. On remand, the district court asked the United States Attorney to "investigate and prosecute" DuPont for criminal contempt, but the court ultimately approved a civil settlement resolving the matter, which required DuPont and Alston & Bird to make payments totalling $11.25 million.

In their present suit, the Matsuuras allege DuPont committed this fraud to induce them and other Benlate plaintiffs to settle. The district court granted DuPont judgment on the pleadings, ruling the suit was barred by releases signed by the Matsuuras as part of the settlement agreements. The court held the Matsuuras could have rescinded the settlement agreements because of DuPont's fraud, but forfeited that remedy by failing promptly to tender the settlement proceeds. The Matsuuras moved for reconsideration; the court denied the motion. The Matsuuras appeal.

II

Under Delaware law, parties who have been fraudulently induced to enter into a contract have a choice of remedies: they may rescind the contract or they may affirm the contract and sue for fraud. In DiSabatino v. United States Fidelity & Guar. Co., 635 F. Supp. 350 (D. Del. 1986), a federal district court sitting in Delaware held that plaintiffs who have been fraudulently induced to settle tort claims have the same choice of remedies under Delaware law. *DiSabatino's* analysis is persuasive.

DuPont does not argue that *DiSabatino* was wrongly decided, but only that it does not control this case. DuPont claims *DiSabatino* applies only when a tort defendant's insurer fraudulently induces a plaintiff to release claims against its insured. *DiSabatino* cannot be read so narrowly. Its policy and legal analysis apply regardless of who commits the fraud.

DuPont also distinguishes *DiSabatino* because the court did not discuss the effect of the general release included in the *DiSabatino* settlement agreement. The district court agreed, and concluded that the terms of the Matsuura-DuPont releases precluded the Matsuuras from suing for fraud. The Matsuuras argue they may affirm the settlement agreement and sue for fraud without regard to the terms of the release. We need not decide whether the Matsuuras are correct, because we conclude that the Supreme Court of Delaware would not interpret the Matsuura-DuPont releases to bar a claim of fraudulent inducement of the releases themselves.

III

We conclude the Supreme Court of Delaware would not interpret the Matsuura-DuPont releases as barring the Matsuuras' fraud claims, for three reasons.

First, Delaware principles of contract construction preclude DuPont's broad reading of the release. . . .

Second, the Delaware Court is likely to impose a clear statement requirement for release of fraudulent inducement claims. . . .

Third, Delaware courts are reluctant to enforce unintended releases of fraud claims . . .

Permitting the Matsuuras to affirm their settlement agreements and sue DuPont for fraud will further Delaware's policy favoring voluntary settlement of legal disputes. Insistence on the finality of settlements is based on the assumption that the parties have freely bargained to exchange the costs, risks and potential rewards of litigation for the certainty of a settlement that seems fair in light of facts known at the time. Settlements induced by fraud are set aside, however, because the defrauded party has not freely bargained, but has been induced to settle by affirmative misrepresentations by the other party. Enforcing such a settlement would undermine the policy of encouraging voluntary settlement of disputes: if litigants cannot assume the disclosures and representations of the opposing party are made in good faith, they will be reluctant to settle. Assurance of an adversary's good faith is particularly critical when parties are attempting to resolve a dispute amicably. Because DuPont allegedly breached this trust, the Matsuuras could not and did not freely bargain for the settlement. Denying the Matsuuras any further remedy would undermine rather than further Delaware's policy of encouraging voluntary settlement of claims.

Reversed and Remanded.

C. BEYOND THE BASICS: NUANCED RISK-CONTROL

1. CONTROLLING THE RISKS OF COLLATERAL LITIGATION: CONFIDENTIALITY

NOTE ON CONFIDENTIALITY PROVISIONS

To get an orientation to this area, return to the release that appears near the start of this chapter. That settlement occurred before the filing of a suit, but the same one would have been used had a lawsuit been filed. Notice that the release has no confidentiality provision. Why not? A moment's reflection will reveal that there's no need for confidentiality because this is a one-off episode: no one else will be suing as a result of this minor accident, and no one will care how much the defendant's insurer paid to resolve the claim. *Because* no one else will be bringing a suit against this defendant, there is no incentive for her (or her insurance company) to shield information developed in the first case.

Confidentiality provisions arise when that context changes. In our society, some transactions or injuries are replicated hundreds or thousands of times. A mass-produced auto tire with an alleged defect will be on thousands of cars and, if it fails, may injure hundreds of people in different accidents. A multimillion-dollar steam turbine sold to a score of public utilities around the country appears to have serious reliability problems, producing lawsuits from unhappy buyers. Both of these cases will be expensive to prosecute: the plaintiff will have to invest substantial sums in experts and discovery to find out, first, whether there's a good case for liability, and then to demonstrate damages. Some of that discovery may contain information that would make it much easier for a second or tenth plaintiff to bring a similar suit: the first plaintiff would, in effect, have marked a pathway through the thicket of discovery. If later plaintiffs can follow that path, the costs of subsequent suits will be much lower (and therefore more likely to be brought). Some of that discovery may also contain information of great interest to competitors. Other tire companies may be quite interested in the manufacturing and design process, not only because it may enable them to avoid similar defects but also because it may contain clues about how to make manufacturing more efficient. Other turbine makers may similarly want to know what mistakes to avoid or how better to promote the reliability of their competing turbines to public utilities. And the defendants in such cases may wish not to have the amount of settlement be public, lest it become the starting point for negotiations in future lawsuits. Or, to take a different kind of case, suppose an employment suit in which the employer defends a dismissal by alleging that the plaintiff was fired not on account of gender discrimination but because she was dishonest. Under such circumstances the settling plaintiff might well desire not to have such matters part of a public record.

In cases like these, at least one of the settling parties will often want to assure that such information is not easily available to the public. Several devices might achieve this aim. A confidentiality agreement in the release will contractually bind the other side and its lawyer not voluntarily to disclose either the underlying facts or the amount paid to settle the case. Such a clause appears in the next reading. If discovery has occurred and is on file with the court (perhaps as part of a motion for summary judgment, which will usually contain such material), the parties might make a motion under the discovery rules to have such materials "sealed" — that is, to remain part of the record, but a part that will not be available to the public.

Notice what such an agreement or such a confidentiality order will *not* do: it will not prevent a subsequent litigant from gaining the underlying information himself. Thus, to take the case of a defective tire, if another person who is injured when the same model tire fails sues, he can request the same documents, take the same depositions, and uncover the same information. A confidentiality agreement does not prevent access to the underlying information. It may, however, make it more expensive for a subsequent party to uncover that information, because that party cannot simply follow the trial blazed in the first lawsuit. As you read the materials in this subsection, ask yourself what a party is seeking to keep confidential, what means the party is using, why the party wants to maintain confidentiality, and how difficult is it likely to be for a subsequent party to get the underlying information.

a. The Basic Framework

A SAMPLE CONFIDENTIALITY AGREEMENT

How might a settlement agreement be drafted to assure that plaintiff kept the details confidential? Consider one effort:

7. *Return of Documents.* The Plaintiffs agree to return to [Defendant] all originals and copies of all documents and data, obtained from [Defendant], directly or indirectly, at any time, by either Plaintiff, or any agent, attorney, representative, or anyone else acting or purporting to act on his or her behalf. The obligations of this Paragraph 7 are cumulative to other existing obligations that Plaintiffs have as a result of their employment with [Defendant].

8. *Confidentiality.*

8.1 Plaintiffs and their attorneys, and each of them, expressly agree that this Agreement and the terms and conditions of this Settlement are confidential, and agree not to disclose, publicize, or cause to be disclosed or publicized the fact of settlement or any of the terms or conditions of this Agreement, including but not limited to the amounts received pursuant to Paragraph 1 of this Agreement or the amounts paid in connection with the Workers' Compensation Claims, except as required by judicial process, or as otherwise required by law. Notwithstanding the foregoing, it is hereby expressly understood and agreed that the Plaintiffs and their attorneys may need to disseminate certain information concerning the settlement to their accountants, auditors, attorneys, and/or other entities as necessary in the regular course of business. While such disclosures are expressly permitted under the terms of this Agreement, Plaintiffs and their attorneys shall insure that information deemed confidential under this Agreement is treated as confidential by the recipients thereof. Except as required by judicial process, or as otherwise required by law, if any of the Plaintiffs or their attorneys or any recipient of information from Plaintiffs or their attorneys concerning the Settlement is asked about the disposition of the action, such Plaintiff, attorney, or recipient shall state the following in substance: "I am not at liberty to discuss it."

8.2 Each disclosure by Plaintiffs or their attorneys or by any recipient of information from Plaintiffs or their attorneys concerning this Settlement other than a disclosure expressly permitted by subparagraph 8.1 shall be considered a material breach of this Agreement. For each such breach of the confidentiality provision set forth in subparagraph 8.1, the Plaintiff who breaches such confidentiality provision shall be solely liable to [Defendant] for Twenty-Five Thousand Dollars ($25,000.00) in liquidated damages. Plaintiffs, and each of them, agree that said sum represents a reasonable estimate of the actual damages which would be suffered by [Defendant] as a result of a violation of subparagraph 8.1 and that this sum is not punitive in any way. In the event [Defendant] is required to file suit or otherwise seek judicial enforcement of its rights under this paragraph 8, the Plaintiff who breaches such confidentiality provision shall be solely liable for attorneys' fees and costs incurred as a result thereof.

JACK FRIEDENTHAL, SECRECY IN CIVIL LITIGATION: DISCOVERY AND PARTY AGREEMENTS

9 Journal of Law and Policy 67 (2000)

Controversies regarding the extent to which the courts should prohibit free public access to information developed in civil cases are not new. In addition to a number of cases, a series of significant articles have discussed various aspects of the matter and provided reasons both for and against the powers and duties of judges to maintain confidentiality, particularly in situations where the parties themselves agree that information should not be disclosed. One recent article[3] provides an excellent summary of the various views that have

---

3. Dore, [Secrecy by Consent: The Use and Limits of Confidentiality in the Pursuit of Settlement, 74 Notre Dame L. Rev. 283 (1999).]

been advanced. Several states have adopted legislation limiting the enforce-ment of confidentiality agreements,[4] and the matter has arisen in other states[5] as well as before Congress.[6]

The arguments on both sides are on two quite different levels, one involv-ing philosophical concepts of the role of the courts in society and the other concerning the practical effects of disclosure or non-disclosure on parties to disputes and to the public at large. Usually, these considerations are inter-twined. Yet it seems useful at the outset of an analysis to treat them separately because one's ultimate view as to whether broad protection against disclosure is or is not appropriate is rooted in one's belief as to the fundamental nature and purposes of a court system regarding civil disputes.

I. The Role of the Courts

A. The Basic Conflict

Our civil judicial system, in its fundamental concept, exists as an avenue by which one citizen can seek redress from another in an orderly fashion, under a set of logical rules. It is, of course, but one avenue. No one has to file a lawsuit. Parties to contracts can, and often do, agree in advance to other techniques of dispute resolution. And even in the absence of such a provision, or in non-contract cases, litigation in court is hardly the only method of solving problems. There has been an explosion of alternate dispute resolution oppor-tunities and techniques in the recent past, in part reflecting negatively on the efficacy of litigation in the courts.

Courts do not reach out for disputes. They must be brought to the court by one of the parties. Moreover, the mere filing of a case by itself is of little con-sequence. Indeed, that may be true of much of the pre-trial process. The court plays no role in the process unless and until a matter is brought before it for its attention. Furthermore, even when a case is before the court, alternative dis-pute resolution techniques are available. Indeed, they are extolled and sup-ported, and sometimes required, by the courts themselves.[8]

Analytically then, it could be said that the courts exist solely to provide a service to the citizens who need a forum. Courts react to the requests of those who come before them. They have no role other than to provide the service for which they are created, the resolution of disputes of those individuals who are

---

4. *E.g.*, Florida Sunshine in Litigation Act, Fla. Stat. Ann. §69.081 (West 2000); Tex. R. Civ. P. 76a.

5. Rosen, *supra* note 2, at B7 n.5 (listing states that have adopted such legislation).

6. *See* Sunshine in Litigation Act of 1999, S.957, 106th Cong., 1st Sess. (1999). This piece of legislation has been proposed by Senator Kohl of Wisconsin. Members of Congress have proposed similar bills in the past. See Hearing before the Subcommittee on Court and Administrative Practice of the Senate Judiciary Committee on S. 1404, 104th Cong., 2d Sess. (Apr. 20, 1994) [hereinafter Hearings]. It is interesting to note that many years ago, in 1913, Congress enacted the Publicity in Taking Evidence Act of 1913, 15 U.S.C. §30 (1994), which permits public access to depositions taken in civil antitrust actions brought by the government seeking injunctive relief. Recently the Act was applied to permit the New York Times and other news organizations to sit in on depositions in United States v. Microsoft Corp., 165 F.3d 952, 953 (D.C. Cir. 1999), subject to protective orders issued for good cause to prevent public disclosure of trade secrets and other material that the court finds should remain confidential. The case is discussed in the forthcoming edition of the George Washington Law Review.

8. *See* Fed. R. Civ. P. 16(a)(5), 16(c)(9), 26(f).

involved in a particular case. If those parties determine that information concerning their dispute should be kept private and confidential, then the court has no business in interfering.

On the other hand, it can be argued that courts are much more than a service establishment for settling problems of individuals who come before them. Courts are paid for by the citizens of the jurisdiction in which they sit. They exist by virtue of the constitution and laws of those jurisdictions. They are part of the governmental structure and operations, as much as the executive or the legislature. The citizens who pay for the courts are entitled to know what they do and why they do it. Those who enter the court system, voluntarily or by process, are simply not entitled to any rights of privacy and confidentiality. When it comes to judicial decisions, both the procedural and substantive legal rules by which the courts decide cases, in effect, belong to the citizens at large. Citizens need to know those rules to determine if they are improper. If they are, then the citizens can seek legislation to alter them. If a judge ignores or misconstrues existing rules, or otherwise exhibits poor judgment, he or she can be exposed and, in those jurisdictions in which judges must stand for election, can be voted out of office. Under the latter concept, then, it would be fair to say that the courts are government instrumentalities that must operate in the interest of the populous, and every aspect of that operation must be open to public scrutiny.

The above positions are, of course, extremes, and most commentators agree that a balance must be struck to decide when matters are to be kept confidential and when they are to be available to the public. That does not mean, however, that it has been easy to decide where the line is to be drawn and how it is to be administered. . . .

II. Practical Arguments for and Against Confidentiality

Decisions as to confidentiality ought not to be made on abstract theories as to the proper role of the courts in society. On a day-to-day basis courts make decisions that affect citizens, parties and nonparties, in ways that directly involve their lives. Litigants want, and deserve, a system that works, one that operates fairly and efficiently to resolve their disputes whether on their own or by court action.

Protection from disclosure can be sought at different times and in different ways. First, at any stage in the proceeding, parties can enter into a private agreement to ensure confidentiality. If a breach occurs, an aggrieved party can bring a separate action for damages. Second, at the time discovery is sought, a party, acting unilaterally, may seek a protective order to limit the inquiry or to keep the results confidential. Federal Rule of Civil Procedure 26(c), which has been adopted in many states, is the basis for such an order. The rule requires the moving party to show good cause why an order should be granted. Third, a party may unilaterally move for a protective order regarding materials already obtained through discovery or presented to the court in support of a motion or at trial. Fourth, the parties may, at any stage, agree on a protective provision for which they seek court approval. Often, such a confidentiality provision is part of a settlement of the case. If the protective order is sought after the material has been presented to the court, it may take the form of a request to seal the records. The advantage of a protective order lies in the fact that its enforcement does not require a separate lawsuit. The court that issued the order may enforce it directly. . . .

A. The Effect of Existing Rules of Procedure. . . .

This does not mean, of course, that courts should not develop standards for determining when the court should issue a protective order based on a private agreement of confidentiality or when such an agreement should be enforced in a separate action. It does mean that courts should not consider themselves bound by Federal Rule 26(c) in such situations, and, to that extent, should be free to accept party agreements as prima facie valid and to challenge them only if and when contrary considerations are presented. . . .

B. Legislative Solutions, Proposed and Enacted

As noted above, at present the basic rule in most courts regarding protective orders is quite similar to Federal Rule of Civil Procedure 26(c). Perhaps it is because usually there are no other rules than Rule 26(c), in accordance with a "long established legal tradition,"[50] that have often been expanded to apply the requirement of "good cause" to virtually all requested protective orders whether or not as limitations on proposed discovery and even when based on a stipulation of all parties.

Even so, it is not surprising that many federal courts have routinely approved and granted enforcement to confidentiality clauses in settlement agreements without a serious review. As we have seen, Rule 26(c), at least on its face, requires parties to attempt to enter into confidentiality agreements and does not apply if they do so successfully. Thus, it appears to embrace the fundamental notion that a lawsuit is a private matter subject to control by the parties. . . .

To alter this approach and take into account more of the public interest when that is thought to be necessary, a few states, notably Florida,[54] Texas,[55] and Washington[56] have enacted "sunshine" laws that curtail the powers of their courts to issue protective orders in certain situations. The chief focus of each of these provisions are cases involving public health and safety hazards. The Florida statute also deals with matters involving suits against the state or other government entities.[57] The Texas statute includes cases involving the administration of public office or governmental operations.[58]

---

50. Proctor & Gamble Co. v. Bankers Trust Co., 78 F.3d 219, 227 (6th Cir. 1996) (quoting Brown & Williamson Tobacco Corp. v. F.T.C., 710 F.2d 1165, 1177 (6th Cir. 1983)).

54. Fla. Stat. Ann. §69.081 (West 2000) (prohibiting the concealment of public hazards).

55. Tex. R. Civ. P. 76a (prohibiting the concealment of court orders or opinions).

56. Wash. Rev. Code Ann. §§4.24.601, 611 (West Supp. 2000) (prohibiting the concealment of public hazards).

57. Fla. Stat. Ann. §69.081(8) (West 2000).

58. Tex. R. Civ. P. 76a(2)(b).

One of the major arguments against confidentiality agreements involves claims that the public is harmed when health or safety hazards are not revealed. Interestingly, the cited state statutes differ significantly as to when discovery cannot receive protection. The Florida provision simply bars the concealing of a hazard that "has caused and is likely to cause injury." This appears to require a finding that such a hazard indeed exists. The Texas rule, on the other hand, bars protective orders that have "any probably adverse effect upon the general public health or safety," which would seem to require a finding that an adverse effect is likely. The Washington statute goes the furthest, refusing protection for "alleged" hazards. These formulations could not only lead to different results in similar cases, but also to different consequences for the courts regarding the burden placed upon them when deciding whether or not to approve or enforce confidentiality agreements. . . .

C. Arguments Favoring Disclosure of Discovery Materials

There are three basic arguments in favor of a strong policy of disclosure of discovery materials developed during the course of an action. First is the notion, already explored to some extent, that the public is entitled to know what is occurring in cases filed in its courts. . . .

Second, it has been argued that keeping some information confidential, particularly when a case is settled, may result in a continuing hazard to public health and safety. . . .

Professor Arthur Miller has analyzed a number of other similar situations in which protective orders were blamed for harm due to dangerous situations.[83] In each case, the protective order proved to be a scapegoat rather than a cause. . . .

A third argument favoring disclosure is based on the fact that discovery in a case that uncovers important information may be of great significance in subsequent cases based upon closely identical situations. It is the desire for such information that appears to be behind the claims regarding hazards to public health and safety. To attorneys, primarily those who represent plaintiffs in products liability actions, the easier it is to obtain useful information developed in other cases, the better it is. It is much easier, however, to "sell" a proposed statute limiting privacy if public protection appears to be at stake rather than benefits to plaintiffs and their attorneys. Thus, with one notable exception,[90] state provisions that have been enacted,[91] as well as the proposed federal statute,[92] do not deal with the evidence sharing issue.

Nevertheless, the argument for sharing evidence has substantial merit. It is wasteful and inefficient to force parties in subsequent cases to retrace the steps taken in an earlier case, particularly when those steps are costly and time consuming. . . .

---

83. *See* Miller.

90. Va. Code Ann. §8.01-420.01 (Michie 2000). "A protective order issued to prevent disclosure of materials or information related to a personal injury action or action for wrongful death produced in discovery . . . shall not prohibit an attorney from voluntarily sharing such materials or information with an attorney involved in a similar or related matter." *Id.*

91. Fla. Stat. Ann. §69.081 (West 2000); Wash. Rev. Code Ann. §4.24.601, 611 (West Supp. 2000); Tex. R. Civ. P. 76a.

92. S. 957, 106th Cong., 1st Sess., May 4, 1999.

D. Arguments Favoring Limitations

There are a number of fundamental arguments made in favor of permitting confidentiality agreements. First, many believe that individual privacy is valuable in and of itself. . . .

Second, it is claimed that settlement of cases would be inhibited if parties could not include confidentiality clauses in their settlement agreements. . . .

Third, without the ability to arrange a confidentiality agreement that the parties could reasonably expect to be enforced, the scope of discovery itself would likely be affected in a number of cases. . . .

III. Conclusions

The following set of principles should operate with respect to disclosure of information discovered during the course of litigation:

1. Federal Rule of Civil Procedure 26(c), with its "good cause" requirement, should apply only in situations in which a party unilaterally seeks protections prior to or during discovery. It should not apply to subsequent agreements among parties to maintain privacy.

2. As to materials subject to protection in an agreement among parties when those materials have not been used at trial or on motion to obtain a substantive decision, there should be a presumption of nondisclosure. The current situation, whereby some courts routinely approve such provisions, is sensible. Only if an issue is raised as to the justification of such a provision in a particular situation, or if the court itself believes that an inquiry should be made, should the court be required to take the time and energy to make an evaluation and then the burden should be on those who seek disclosure.

3. As to materials subject to a protective agreement among the parties when such materials have been presented at trial or to the court in support of a substantive determination, the presumption should shift, and the court should be required to make a finding that the needs of privacy outweigh the needs for public access. The situation should be treated in the same way as the courts would treat a unilateral motion to seal court records.

4. A special exception to the general rule in conclusion two, above, should obtain upon a showing by or on behalf of a party in a different lawsuit that materials in the present suit contain information significant to the fair resolution of the other lawsuit and that such information is not likely to be discovered without undue cost and effort. Although the presumption should shift in favor of disclosure upon such a showing, the court should nevertheless evaluate the entire situation to make certain that disclosure is not outweighed by reasons for confidentiality, and steps should be taken to restrict the use of the information beyond its need for the other lawsuit.

5. In a case involving the propriety of the actions of a government entity or its employees operating in the scope of their employment, information as to such actions should be open to public scrutiny, except when disclosure is objected to as seriously unfair to non-governmental parties or witnesses.

Hopefully, both federal and state courts can be united in support of such principles. Differences in treatment among courts are not sound. Neither the possibility of protection nor a threat of disclosure should become a motivation for forum shopping.

> **Fed. R. Civ. P. 26**

. . .

(c) Protective Orders. Upon motion by a party or by the person from whom discovery is sought, accompanied by a certification that the movant has in good faith conferred or attempted to confer with other affected parties in an effort to resolve the dispute without court action, and for good cause shown, the court in which the action is pending or alternatively, on matters relating to a deposition, the court in the district where the deposition is to be taken may make any order which justice requires to protect a party or person from annoyance, embarrassment, oppression, or undue burden or expense, including one or more of the following:

(1) that the disclosure or discovery not be had;

(2) that the disclosure or discovery may be had only on specified terms and conditions, including a designation of the time or place;

(3) that the discovery may be had only by a method of discovery other than that selected by the party seeking discovery;

(4) that certain matters not be inquired into, or that the scope of the disclosure or discovery be limited to certain matters;

(5) that discovery be conducted with no one present except persons designated by the court;

(6) that a deposition, after being sealed, be opened only by order of the court;

(7) that a trade secret or other confidential research, development, or commercial information not be revealed or be revealed only in a designated way; and

(8) that the parties simultaneously file specified documents or information enclosed in sealed envelopes to be opened as directed by the court.

If the motion for a protective order is denied in whole or in part, the court may, on such terms and conditions as are just, order that any party or other person provide or permit discovery. The provisions of Rule 37(a)(4) apply to the award of expenses incurred in relation to the motion. . . .

b. Illustrative Statutes

> **Tex. R. Civ. P. 76A: Sealing Court Records**

(West 2004)

1. **Standard for Sealing Court Records.** Court records may not be removed from court files except as permitted by statute or rule. No court order or opinion issued in the adjudication of a case may be sealed. Other court records, as defined in this rule, are presumed to be open to the general public and may be sealed only upon a showing of all of the following:

(a) a specific, serious and substantial interest which clearly outweighs:

(1) this presumption of openness;

(2) any probable adverse effect that sealing will have upon the general public health or safety;

(b) no less restrictive means than sealing records will adequately and effectively protect the specific interest asserted.

2. **Court Records.** For purposes of this rule, court records means:

(a) all documents of any nature filed in connection with any matter before any civil court, except:

(1) documents filed with a court in camera, solely for the purpose of obtaining a ruling on the discoverability of such documents;

(2) documents in court files to which access is otherwise restricted by law;

(3) documents filed in an action originally arising under the Family Code.

(b) settlement agreements not filed of record, excluding all reference to any monetary consideration, that seek to restrict disclosure of information concerning matters that have a probable adverse effect upon the general public health or safety, or the administration of public office, or the operation of government.

(c) discovery, not filed of record, concerning matters that have a probable adverse effect upon the general public health or safety, or the administration of public office, or the operation of government, except discovery in cases originally initiated to preserve bona fide trade secrets or other intangible property rights.

(Added April 24, 1990, eff. Sept. 1, 1990.)

Fla. Stat. §69.081: Sunshine in Litigation; Concealment of Public Hazards Prohibited

---

(West 2005)

(1) This section may be cited as the "Sunshine in Litigation Act."

(2) As used in this section, "public hazard" means an instrumentality, including but not limited to any device, instrument, person, procedure, product, or a condition of a device, instrument, person, procedure or product, that has caused and is likely to cause injury.

(3) Except pursuant to this section, no court shall enter an order or judgment which has the purpose or effect of concealing a public hazard or any information concerning a public hazard, nor shall the court enter an order or judgment which has the purpose or effect of concealing any information which may be useful to members of the public in protecting themselves from injury which may result from the public hazard.

(4) Any portion of an agreement or contract which has the purpose or effect of concealing a public hazard, any information concerning a public hazard, or any information which may be useful to members of the public in protecting themselves from injury which may result from the public hazard, is void, contrary to public policy, and may not be enforced.

(5) Trade secrets as defined in §688.002 which are not pertinent to public hazards shall be protected pursuant to chapter 688.

(6) Any substantially affected person, including but not limited to representatives of news media, has standing to contest an order, judgment, agreement, or contract that violates this section. A person may contest an order, judgment, agreement, or contract that violates this section by motion in the court that entered the order or judgment, or by bringing a declaratory judgment action pursuant to chapter 86.

(7) Upon motion and good cause shown by a party attempting to prevent disclosure of information or materials which have not previously been disclosed, including but not limited to alleged trade secrets, the court shall examine the disputed information or materials in camera. If the court finds that the information or materials or portions thereof consist of information concerning a public hazard or information which may be useful to members of the public in protecting themselves from injury which may result from a public hazard, the court shall allow disclosure of the information or materials. If allowing disclosure, the court shall allow disclosure of only that portion of the information or materials necessary or useful to the public regarding the public hazard.

(8)   (a)Any portion of an agreement or contract which has the purpose or effect of concealing information relating to the settlement or resolution of any claim or action against the state, its agencies, or subdivisions or against any municipality or constitutionally created body or commission is void, contrary to public policy, and may not be enforced. Any person has standing to contest an order, judgment, agreement, or contract that violates this section. A person may contest an order, judgment, agreement, or contract that violates this subsection by motion in the court that entered such order or judgment, or by bringing a declaratory judgment action pursuant to chapter 86.

(b) Any person having custody of any document, record, contract, or agreement relating to any settlement as set forth in this section shall maintain said public records in compliance with chapter 119.

(c) Failure of any custodian to disclose and provide any document, record, contract, or agreement as set forth in this section shall be subject to the sanctions as set forth in chapter 119.

This subsection does not apply to trade secrets protected pursuant to chapter 688, proprietary confidential business information, or other information that is confidential under state or federal law.

(9) A governmental entity, except a municipality or county, that settles a claim in tort which requires the expenditure of public funds in excess of $5,000, shall provide notice, in accordance with the provisions of chapter 50, of such settlement, in the county in which the claim arose, within 60 days of entering into such settlement; provided that no notice shall be required if the settlement has been approved by a court of competent jurisdiction.

Local Civil Rule 5.03: Service and Filing of Pleadings and Other Papers

---

U.S. District Court, District of South Carolina (2005)

Absent a requirement to seal in the governing rule, statute, or order, any party seeking to file documents under seal shall follow the mandatory procedure described below. Failure to obtain prior approval as required by this Rule shall result in summary denial of any request or attempt to seal filed documents. Nothing in this Rule limits the ability of the parties, by agreement, to restrict access to documents which are not filed with the Court. See Local Civil Rule 26.08.

(A) A party seeking to file documents under seal shall file and serve a "Motion to Seal" accompanied by a memorandum, see Local Civil Rule 7.04, and the attachments set forth below in (B) and (C). The memorandum shall: (1) identify, with specificity, the documents or portions thereof for which sealing is requested; (2) state the reasons why sealing is necessary; (3) explain (for each document or group of documents) why less drastic alternatives to sealing will not afford adequate protection; and (4) address the factors governing sealing of documents reflected in controlling case law.

(B) The motion shall be accompanied by (1) a non-confidential descriptive index of the documents at issue and (2) counsel's certification of compliance with this rule.

(C) A separately sealed attachment labeled "Confidential Information to be Submitted to Court in Connection with Motion to Seal" shall be submitted with the motion. The sealed attachment shall contain the documents at issue for the Court's in camera review and shall not be filed. The Court's docket shall reflect that the motion and memorandum were filed and were supported by a sealed attachment submitted for in camera review.

(D) The Clerk shall provide public notice of the Motion to Seal in the manner directed by the Court. Absent direction to the contrary, this may be accomplished by docketing the motion in a manner that discloses its nature as a motion to seal.

(E) No settlement agreement filed with the Court shall be sealed pursuant to the terms of this Rule.

Jill Duman, Settlement Bill Dies Surprising Death on Floor

San Francisco Recorder, June 6, 2005, at 1

Sacramento—In the end, the Assembly floor vote on a bill that sought to ban secret settlements in cases of public danger wasn't even close.

In a mere 7 seconds, 18 abstentions put the vote at 31 to 31—10 shy of what was needed to pass. Outside the state Assembly chamber on Thursday, the halls erupted in cheers, staffers reported.

Seven of those abstaining had promised the bill's author, Assemblywoman Fran Pavley, their support, said Debra Gravert, Pavley's chief of staff.

"This is a blow for consumer safety," said Mary Alexander, former president of the American Trial Lawyers Association. "We always have that with product liability cases — the defense and the argument about proprietary information, but we have to put public health and safety first."

The vote was a solid victory for business lobbyists — in particularly the tech and biomedical industries, which had peppered fence-sitters with phone calls and letters ahead of the floor vote.

"The biotechnology industry stands firm on their opposition to Assembly Bill 1700," read a "floor alert" this week from Biocom, an industry group representing 450 members in the life sciences. "This vote will be used for the production of the state legislative scorecard."

Pavley, a Democrat from Agoura Hills, had spent weeks lobbying moderate Democrat fence-sitters. Just two days before Thursday's votes, she had amended the bill to take out most of the language dealing with the tech and medical industries — two major opponents of the bill. On Tuesday, Gravert predicted AB 1700 had "a solid 36" votes, with 41 needed to move the bill.

But by Thursday, it was clear that the business lobby — headed by the technology and biotech groups that had killed a similar bill in 2001 — had prevailed.

"A lot of people who looked at it decided they didn't want to kill off the tech industry," said Jim Hawley, general counsel for TechNet, a technology industry and lobbying group that also played a huge role in defeating 2001's SB 11 by Sen. Martha Escutia, D-Whittier.

"It was a huge victory," added Barbara Morrow, vice president and general counsel for the California Healthcare Institute, an association representing manufacturers of medical devices, biotech firms and pharmaceuticals.

Industry and business groups — which also included the California Chamber of Commerce and the Civil Justice Association of California — had argued that the bill language pertaining to environmental hazards was too broad. They also insisted that AB 1700 would hurt business by making proprietary information public in the course of the settlement process.

"That argument is so bogus," said Consumer Attorneys of California President Sharon Arkin. "It frustrates me no end."

Pavley and her supporters had argued that the bill only affected defendants in cases involving grave injury or death and that a judge could still step in and keep information confidential.

Bogus or not, the lobbyists' argument clearly swayed moderate Democrats — there are about a dozen who are slow to vote against legislation billed as detrimental to jobs and business. Of the 18 members who abstained on 1700, 10 are considered "mod-squad" Democrats.

"It underscores that legislators are so afraid of pushing for 'job killers' that they miss out on the opportunity to do something good for California," said Ignacio Hernandez, legislative advocate for the Consumer Federation of California.

c. Advanced Issues of Confidentiality

NOTE ON COMPLEX AND FAILED CONFIDENTIALITY AGREEMENTS

With basic issues of confidentiality explored, consider some cases in which attempts at confidentiality fail. Baker v. GM displays the U.S. Supreme

Court seeking to sort out the consequences of embodying a confidentiality agreement in an injunction. Reading the case, see if you can figure out what GM might *justifiably* have expected from its settlement of a lawsuit brought by an unhappy employee. Then explain how GM got considerably more than it might have expected—and how that victory then collapsed. The second case, *Westinghouse Electric* displays a lawyer who seems to have blatantly violated a confidentiality agreement—and gotten way with it. Why? In retrospect is there anything Westinghouse could have done to avoid the outcome? (Reread the confidentiality agreement that begins this section for a clue.)

BAKER v. GEN. MOTORS CORP.

522 U.S. 222 (1998)

Justice GINSBURG delivered the opinion of the Court.

This case concerns the authority of one State's court to order that a witness' testimony shall not be heard in any court of the United States. In settlement of claims and counterclaims precipitated by the discharge of Ronald Elwell, a former General Motors Corporation (GM) engineering analyst, GM paid Elwell an undisclosed sum of money, and the parties agreed to a permanent injunction. As stipulated by GM and Elwell and entered by a Michigan County Court, the injunction prohibited Elwell from "testifying, without the prior written consent of [GM], . . . as . . . a witness of any kind . . . in any litigation already filed, or to be filed in the future, involving [GM] as an owner, seller, manufacturer and/or designer . . ." GM separately agreed, however, that if Elwell were ordered to testify by a court or other tribunal, such testimony would not be actionable as a violation of the Michigan court's injunction or the GM-Elwell agreement.

After entry of the stipulated injunction in Michigan, Elwell was subpoenaed to testify in a product liability action commenced in Missouri by plaintiffs who were not involved in the Michigan case. The question presented is whether the national full faith and credit command bars Elwell's testimony in the Missouri case. We hold that Elwell may testify in the Missouri action without offense to the full faith and credit requirement.

I.

Two lawsuits, initiated by different parties in different states, gave rise to the full faith and credit issue before us. One suit involved a severed employment relationship, the other, a wrongful-death complaint. We describe each controversy in turn.

A.

The Suit Between Elwell and General Motors

Ronald Elwell was a GM employee from 1959 until 1989. For fifteen of those years, beginning in 1971, Elwell was assigned to the Engineering Analysis Group, which studied the performance of GM vehicles, most particularly vehicles involved in product liability litigation. Elwell's studies and research concentrated on vehicular fires. He assisted in improving the performance of GM products by suggesting changes in fuel line designs. During the course of his employment, Elwell frequently aided GM lawyers engaged in defending GM against product liability actions. Beginning in 1987, the Elwell-GM employment relationship soured. GM and Elwell first negotiated an agreement under which Elwell would retire after serving as a GM consultant for two years. When the time came for Elwell to retire, however, disagreement again surfaced and continued into 1991.

In May 1991, plaintiffs in a product liability action pending in Georgia deposed Elwell. The Georgia case involved a GM pickup truck fuel tank that burst into flames just after a collision. During the deposition, and over the objection of counsel for GM, Elwell gave testimony that differed markedly from testimony he had given when serving as an in-house expert witness for GM. Specifically, Elwell had several times defended the safety and crashworthiness of the pickup's fuel system. On deposition in the Georgia action, however, Elwell testified that the GM pickup truck fuel system was inferior in comparison to competing products.

A month later, Elwell sued GM in a Michigan County Court, alleging wrongful discharge and other tort and contract claims. GM counterclaimed, contending that Elwell had breached his fiduciary duty to GM by disclosing privileged and confidential information and misappropriating documents. In response to GM's motion for a preliminary injunction, and after a hearing, the Michigan trial court, on November 22, 1991, enjoined Elwell from "consulting or discussing with or disclosing to any person any of General Motors Corporation's trade secrets[,] confidential information or matters of attorney-client work product relating in any manner to the subject matter of any products liability litigation whether already filed or [to be] filed in the future which Ronald Elwell received, had knowledge of, or was entrusted with during his employments with General Motors Corporation." Elwell v. General Motors Corp., No. 91-115946NZ (Wayne Cty.) (Order Granting in Part, Denying in Part Injunctive Relief, pp. 1-2), App. 9-10.

In August 1992, GM and Elwell entered into a settlement under which Elwell received an undisclosed sum of money. The parties also stipulated to the entry of a permanent injunction and jointly filed with the Michigan court both the stipulation and the agreed-upon injunction. The proposed permanent injunction contained two proscriptions. The first substantially repeated the terms of the preliminary injunction; the second comprehensively enjoined Elwell from "testifying, without the prior written consent of General Motors Corporation, either upon deposition or at trial, as an expert witness, or as a witness of any kind, and from consulting with attorneys or their agents in any litigation already filed, or to be filed in the future, involving General Motors Corporation as an owner, seller, manufacturer and/or designer of the product(s) in issue." Order Dismissing Plaintiff's Complaint and Granting Permanent Injunction (Wayne Cty., p. 2, Aug. 26, 1992), App. 30.

To this encompassing bar, the consent injunction made an exception: "[This provision] shall not operate to *interfere with the jurisdiction of the Court in . . . Georgia* [where the litigation involving the fuel tank was still pending]." Ibid. (emphasis added). No other noninterference provision appears in the stipulated decree. On August 26, 1992, with no further hearing, the Michigan court entered the injunction precisely as tendered by the parties.[1]

Although the stipulated injunction contained an exception only for the Georgia action then pending, Elwell and GM included in their separate settlement agreement a more general limitation. If a court or other tribunal ordered Elwell to testify, his testimony would "in no way" support a GM action for violation of the injunction or the settlement agreement:

> " 'It is agreed that [Elwell's] appearance and testimony, if any, at hearings on Motions to quash subpoena or at deposition or trial or other official proceeding, if the Court or other tribunal so orders, will in no way form a basis for an action in violation of the Permanent Injunction or this Agreement.' "

Settlement Agreement, at 10, as quoted in 86 F.3d 811, 820, n. 11 (C.A.8 1996).

In the six years since the Elwell-GM settlement, Elwell has testified against GM both in Georgia (pursuant to the exception contained in the injunction) and in several other jurisdictions in which Elwell has been subpoenaed to testify.

B.

The Suit Between the Bakers and General Motors

Having described the Elwell-GM employment termination litigation, we next summarize the wrongful-death complaint underlying this case. The decedent, Beverly Garner, was a front-seat passenger in a 1985 Chevrolet S-10 Blazer involved in a February 1990 Missouri highway accident. The Blazer's engine caught fire, and both driver and passenger died. In September 1991, Garner's sons, Kenneth and Steven Baker, commenced a wrongful death product liability action against GM in a Missouri state court. The Bakers alleged that a faulty fuel pump in the 1985 Blazer caused the engine fire that killed their mother. GM removed the case to federal court on the basis of the parties' diverse citizenship. On the merits, GM asserted that the fuel pump was neither faulty nor the cause of the fire, and that collision impact injuries alone caused Garner's death.

The Bakers sought both to depose Elwell and to call him as a witness at trial. GM objected to Elwell's appearance as a deponent or trial witness on the ground that the Michigan injunction barred his testimony. In response, the Bakers urged that the Michigan injunction did not override a Missouri subpoena for Elwell's testimony. The Bakers further noted that, under the Elwell-GM settlement agreement, Elwell could testify if a court so ordered, and such testimony would not be actionable as a violation of the Michigan injunction.

After in camera review of the Michigan injunction and the settlement agreement, the Federal District Court in Missouri allowed the Bakers to depose Elwell and to call him as a witness at trial. Responding to GM's objection, the District Court stated alternative grounds for its ruling: (1) Michigan's injunction need not be enforced because blocking Elwell's testimony would violate

---

1. A judge new to the case, not the judge who conducted a hearing at the preliminary injunction stage, presided at the settlement stage and entered the permanent injunction.

Missouri's "public policy," which shielded from disclosure only privileged or otherwise confidential information; (2) just as the injunction could be modified in Michigan, so a court elsewhere could modify the decree.

At trial, Elwell testified in support of the Bakers' claim that the alleged defect in the fuel pump system contributed to the postcollision fire. In addition, he identified and described a 1973 internal GM memorandum bearing on the risk of fuel-fed engine fires. Following trial, the jury awarded the Bakers $11.3 million in damages, and the District Court entered judgment on the jury's verdict.

The United States Court of Appeals for the Eighth Circuit reversed the District Court's judgment, ruling, inter alia, that Elwell's testimony should not have been admitted. Assuming, arguendo, the existence of a public policy exception to the full faith and credit command, the Court of Appeals concluded that the District Court erroneously relied on Missouri's policy favoring disclosure of relevant, nonprivileged information, for Missouri has an "equally strong public policy in favor of full faith and credit," . . .

* * *

II.

A.

The Constitution's Full Faith and Credit Clause provides:

"Full Faith and Credit shall be given in each State to the public Acts, Records, and judicial Proceedings of every other State. And the Congress may by general Laws prescribe the Manner in which such Acts, Records and Proceedings shall be proved, and the Effect thereof." U.S. Const., Art. IV, §1.

Pursuant to that Clause, Congress has prescribed:

"Such Acts, records and judicial proceedings or copies thereof, so authenticated, shall have the same full faith and credit in every court within the United States and its Territories and Possessions as they have by law or usage in the courts of such State, Territory or Possession from which they are taken." 28 U.S.C. §1738. . . .

* * *

. . . Regarding judgments . . . the full faith and credit obligation is exacting. A final judgment in one State, if rendered by a court with adjudicatory authority over the subject matter and persons governed by the judgment, qualifies for recognition throughout the land. For claim and issue preclusion (res judicata) purposes, in other words, the judgment of the rendering State gains nationwide force. . . .

A court may be guided by the forum State's "public policy" in determining the law applicable to a controversy. See Nevada v. Hall, 440 U.S. 410, 421-424, 99 S. Ct. 1182, 1188-1190, 59 L. Ed. 2d 416 (1979). But our decisions support no roving "public policy exception" to the full faith and credit due judgments. . . .

* * *

Full faith and credit, however, does not mean that States must adopt the practices of other States regarding the time, manner, and mechanisms for enforcing judgments. Enforcement measures do not travel with the sister state judgment as preclusive effects do; such measures remain subject to the even-handed control of forum law. . . .

Orders commanding action or inaction have been denied enforcement in a sister State when they purported to accomplish an official act within the exclusive province of that other State or interfered with litigation over which the ordering State had no authority. Thus, a sister State's decree concerning land ownership in another State has been held ineffective to transfer title. . . .

* * *

B.

With these background principles in view, we turn to the dimensions of the order GM relies upon to stop Elwell's testimony. Specifically, we take up the question: What matters did the Michigan injunction legitimately conclude?

As earlier recounted, the parties before the Michigan County Court, Elwell and GM, submitted an agreed-upon injunction, which the presiding judge signed. While no issue was joined, expressly litigated, and determined in the Michigan proceeding, that order is claim preclusive between Elwell and GM. Elwell's claim for wrongful discharge and his related contract and tort claims have "merged in the judgment," and he cannot sue again to recover more. . . .

Michigan's judgment, however, cannot reach beyond the Elwell-GM controversy to control proceedings against GM brought in other States, by other parties, asserting claims the merits of which Michigan has not considered. Michigan has no power over those parties, and no basis for commanding them to become intervenors in the Elwell-GM dispute. Most essentially, Michigan lacks authority to control courts elsewhere by precluding them, in actions brought by strangers to the Michigan litigation, from determining for themselves what witnesses are competent to testify and what evidence is relevant and admissible in their search for the truth. . . .

* * *

As the District Court recognized, Michigan's decree could operate against Elwell to preclude him from volunteering his testimony. But a Michigan court cannot, by entering the injunction to which Elwell and GM stipulated, dictate to a court in another jurisdiction that evidence relevant in the Bakers' case — a controversy to which Michigan is foreign — shall be inadmissible. This conclusion creates no general exception to the full faith and credit command, and surely does not permit a State to refuse to honor a sister state judgment based on the forum's choice of law or policy preferences. Rather, we simply recognize that, just as the mechanisms for enforcing a judgment do not travel with the judgment itself for purposes of Full Faith and Credit, and just as one State's judgment cannot automatically transfer title to land in another State, similarly the Michigan decree cannot determine evidentiary issues in a lawsuit brought by parties who were not subject to the jurisdiction of the Michigan court. . . .[12]

* * *

---

12. Justice Kennedy inexplicably reads into our decision a sweeping exception to full faith and credit based solely on "the integrity of Missouri's judicial processes." The Michigan judgment is not entitled to full faith and credit, we have endeavored to make plain, because it impermissibly interferes with Missouri's control of litigation brought by parties who were not before the Michigan court. Thus, Justice Kennedy's hypothetical, misses the mark. If the Bakers had been parties to the Michigan proceedings and had actually litigated the privileged character of Elwell's testimony, the Bakers would of course be precluded from relitigating that issue in Missouri. See Cromwell v. County of Sac, 94 U.S. 351, 354, 24 L. Ed. 195 (1876) ("[D]etermination of a question directly involved in one action is conclusive as to that question in a second suit between the same parties. . . .").

In sum, Michigan has no authority to shield a witness from another jurisdiction's subpoena power in a case involving persons and causes outside Michigan's governance. Recognition, under full faith and credit, is owed to dispositions Michigan has authority to order. But a Michigan decree cannot command obedience elsewhere on a matter the Michigan court lacks authority to resolve. See Thomas v. Washington Gas Light Co., 448 U.S. 261, 282-283, (1980) (plurality opinion) ("Full faith and credit must be given to [a] determination that [a State's tribunal] had the authority to make; but by a parity of reasoning, full faith and credit need not be given to determinations that it had no power to make.").

* * *

For the reasons stated, the judgment of the Court of Appeals for the Eighth Circuit is reversed, and the case is remanded for further proceedings consistent with this opinion.

It is so ordered.

Justice SCALIA, concurring in the judgment.

I agree with the Court that enforcement measures do not travel with sister-state judgments as preclusive effects do. It has long been established that "the judgment of a state Court cannot be enforced out of the state by an execution issued within it." McElmoyle ex rel. Bailey v. Cohen, 13 Pet. 312, 325, 10 L. Ed. 177 (1839). To recite that principle is to decide this case. . . .

* * *

Justice KENNEDY, with whom Justices O'CONNOR and THOMAS join, concurring in the judgment.

I concur in the judgment. In my view the case is controlled by well-settled full faith and credit principles which render the majority's extended analysis unnecessary and, with all due respect, problematic in some degree. This separate opinion explains my approach.

I

The majority, of course, is correct to hold that when a judgment is presented to the courts of a second State it may not be denied enforcement based upon some disagreement with the laws of the State of rendition. Full faith and credit forbids the second State from questioning a judgment on these grounds. There can be little doubt of this proposition. We have often recognized the second State's obligation to give effect to another State's judgments even when the law underlying those judgments contravenes the public policy of the second State.

My concern is that the majority, having stated the principle, proceeds to disregard it by announcing two broad exceptions. First, the majority would allow courts outside the issuing State to decline to enforce those judgments "purport[ing] to accomplish an official act within the exclusive province of [a sister] State." Second, the basic rule of full faith and credit is said not to cover injunctions "interfer[ing] with litigation over which the ordering State had no authority." The exceptions the majority recognizes are neither consistent with its rejection of a public policy exception to full faith and credit nor in accord with established rules implementing the Full Faith and Credit Clause. As employed to resolve this case, furthermore, the exceptions to full faith and credit have a potential for disrupting judgments, and this ought to give us considerable pause. . . .

* * *

WESTINGHOUSE ELEC. CORP. v. NEWMAN & HOLTZINGER, P. C.

46 Cal. Rptr. 2d 151 (Cal. Ct. App. 1995)

JOHNSON, J.

Westinghouse Electric Corp. attempts to state causes of action sounding in tort and breach of contract against attorneys who allegedly conspired to disclose documents covered by a secrecy agreement in a previous lawsuit. The trial court held the attempt failed. We agree.

Facts and Proceedings Below

Westinghouse was the defendant in a suit brought by the Southern California Edison Company (SCE) in federal court. The SCE suit alleged Westinghouse made false representations about steam generators it sold to the utility for use in its nuclear power facilities. SCE was represented in the federal court action by Newman & Holtzinger, P. C. (Newman), and Chase, Rotchford, Drukker & Bogust (Chase), defendants in the present action. The other defendant in the present action, Shaw, Pittman, Potts & Trowbridge (Shaw), did not represent a party in the SCE suit but is alleged to have conspired with Newman and Chase to violate the secrecy agreement in that suit.

We summarize the Westinghouse complaint here and discuss it in more detail below.

Essentially the complaint alleges that in the course of the SCE suit Newman and Chase requested production from Westinghouse of certain highly sensitive documents. These documents pertained to evaluations, reviews, and analyses by Westinghouse engineers of actual and potential problems involving the nuclear steam generators Westinghouse manufactured "and the environment in which they operate." Included in these documents were "candid," "rigorous" and "critical self-evaluations" exchanged between the engineers working on these problems. The complaint states that "[a]mong the thoughts expressed . . . in those documents were expressions about the efforts being made by Westinghouse to resolve issues encountered, or said to be encountered, by utilities in operation and to expand upon the state of the art. Wrenched from proper context, portions of those documents were susceptible to contrary meanings."

Westinghouse voluntarily offered to produce the documents on condition SCE and Newman and Chase agree not to disclose them to anyone other than specified parties and not to use the documents for any purpose beyond the SCE suit itself. Newman and Chase orally agreed to these conditions, which were subsequently incorporated into a stipulated protective order in the SCE suit. In reliance on this agreement and the representations of Newman and Chase, SCE produced the documents. Newman and Chase violated their nondisclosure agreement with Westinghouse by filing the restricted documents in the public records of the SCE case and then informing Shaw, which also represented a client in a legal proceeding against Westinghouse, "if it examined the public file in the SCE case it would find Westinghouse documents of which it could make use." Upon receiving this tip, Shaw, knowing the documents were restricted under the agreement, inspected and made copies of the documents and used them in representing its client against Westinghouse. Shaw also disseminated the documents among other utility companies "to generate a united front against Westinghouse."

It is alleged Newman, Chase and Shaw acted in concert for the purpose of disclosing and disseminating the restricted documents to other law firms, particularly Shaw, for use in litigation against Westinghouse and that the defendants made false representations to Westinghouse in an effort to conceal their misuse of the restricted documents.

Westinghouse claims that by reason of the defendants' unlawful disclosure of the documents it was damaged by having to expend "millions of dollars" defending lawsuits based on the information contained in those documents.

Defendants' initial response to the present action was to remove it to federal court. Westinghouse moved for remand to the state court and defendants moved to dismiss. The district court denied the motion to remand and dismissed the action. The Ninth Circuit reversed, holding there was no federal subject matter jurisdiction over the present action and the proper remedy was to remand the matter to the state court. (Westinghouse Elec. v. Newman & Holtzinger, P.C. (9th Cir. 1993) 992 F.2d 932, 933 (Westinghouse I).)

Upon remand to the state court, defendants demurred to the complaint on the ground it failed to state a cause of action under any theory of tort or breach of contract. The trial court sustained the demurrers without leave to amend and ordered the action dismissed. Westinghouse filed a timely appeal from the judgment of dismissal.

For the reasons explained below, we hold the complaint fails to state a cause of action in tort because it fails to allege cognizable tort damages. The complaint fails to state a cause of action for breach of contract because a protective order supersedes any previous secrecy agreement between the parties or their attorneys covering the same documents.

Discussion . . .

II. Inducing a Third Party to Bring Litigation on a Meritorious Claim Cannot Be the Basis for Tort Liability

(1) We first consider whether Westinghouse has alleged facts which give rise to tort liability on the part of the defendants or whether the complaint reasonably could be amended to state a tort cause of action.

The complaint alleges the following facts relevant to tort liability.

In the course of the SCE litigation, Westinghouse voluntarily produced certain sensitive documents to SCE in return for an agreement by SCE's attorneys, Newman and Chase, not to exhibit, deliver or disclose those documents to anyone other than specified parties and not to use those restricted documents for any purpose other than the SCE case itself. "[T]hereafter and pursuant to agreed concert" between Newman, Chase and the Shaw firm, Newman and Chase "filed in the public record in the SCE case the documents produced by Westinghouse and informed [Shaw] that if it examined the public file in the SCE case it would find Westinghouse documents of which it could make use. Thereupon [Shaw], knowing that it could not properly have access to these documents, inspected and made copies of them. Thereafter, [Shaw] hawked them among utility companies to generate a united front against Westinghouse." Shaw also used the documents in representing a client in a legal proceeding against Westinghouse. Newman and Chase placed the restricted documents in the public files with the intent "to disclose and deliver the documents to other law firms, particularly Shaw" for the purpose of encouraging lawsuits against Westinghouse.

At the time Newman and Chase improperly disclosed and delivered the Westinghouse documents to Shaw "Westinghouse was meeting with utilities which had acquired steam generator equipment from it to discuss steam generators and the evolving state of the art and to satisfy customers' concerns on the subject. The documents improperly obtained from the files in the SCE case were published, given widespread dissemination, manipulated and distorted by [Shaw] to divert utilities from continuing to deal on an amicable and commercial basis with Westinghouse as they had done in the past. In disseminating the documents, [Shaw] and those to whom it in turn disseminated them, distorted their meaning as suggesting that Westinghouse had committed fraud upon its customers."

The conduct of Newman and Chase, described above, "was an embezzlement of Westinghouse's files . . . and it inflicted injury and damage upon Westinghouse, and was intended to do so." By receiving and using the documents, Shaw was guilty of receipt of stolen property and liable to Westinghouse for treble damages, attorney fees and costs. (Pen. Code, §496, subds. (a), (d).)

Newman, in concert with Chase and Shaw "affirmatively and falsely represented to Westinghouse in writing on or about July 26, 1988, that neither it nor anyone associated with it had provided to any third party any document produced by Westinghouse pursuant to the protective order."

"As a result of defendants' conduct, Westinghouse has been sued by public utility companies, generally charging Westinghouse with fraud and other misconduct in connection with the sale of steam generator equipment basing the charge on the documents. These lawsuits would not have been commenced or prosecuted but for [defendants'] theft . . . and receipt of Westinghouse's documents as aforesaid, by reason of which Westinghouse has been damaged by the unlawful conduct of defendants as alleged above in an amount exceeding millions of dollars."

Defendants initially contend Westinghouse is attempting to turn violation of a discovery order into a tort — a tactic which courts have uniformly rejected. We reject this characterization of the Westinghouse complaint for the reasons explained below.

The complaint is ambiguous as to whether Westinghouse turned over the documents in reliance on the stipulated protective order entered by the district court, the preexisting agreement with Newman and Chase or both. However, we agree with the Ninth Circuit that reading the complaint in the light most favorable to Westinghouse for purposes of ruling on the demurrer, the alleged tort liability is not premised on a violation of the district court's discovery order. Rather, the complaint suggests Newman and Chase, for themselves and not merely as SCE's representatives, obtained the documents by entering into a nondisclosure agreement with Westinghouse which preceded the stipulated discovery order. As the Ninth Circuit pointed out, the complaint does not say Westinghouse produced the documents solely on the basis of the discovery order; nor does it incorporate the discovery order by reference. In addition, the discovery order only applies to the parties to the litigation and others who agree to be bound by it. The complaint does not allege Newman and Chase ever entered into such an agreement. Thus, it does not appear from the facts pled Newman and Chase would be subject to sanctions for violating the district court's protective order, especially if they acted on their own, without their client's knowledge, in disclosing the documents to Shaw. Shaw, of course, could not be subject to sanctions under the protective order because it was not a party bound by the order. We note SCE, which was subject to the protective order, is not a defendant in this action.

Furthermore, even if the trial court's protective order superseded the secrecy agreement between Westinghouse, Newman and Chase (see discussion in pt. III, post) this would not necessarily bar Westinghouse from bringing a tort suit based on disclosure of the restricted documents. While we agree violation of a discovery order is not in and of itself a tort, we can conceive of situations in which wrongful disclosure of information covered by a protective order could be both a discovery violation and a tort. It could certainly be argued, for example, unlawful disclosure of a trade secret should result in liability for damages regardless of the fact the defendant's disclosure also violated a protective order. Similarly, it would seem disclosure of sensitive or embarrassing facts about a party in violation of a protective order could support an action for invasion of privacy and infliction of emotional distress. In the present case, the Westinghouse complaint appears to allege several theories of tort liability, including interference with contractual relations and prospective business advantage, misappropriation of trade secrets, trade libel and fraud.

However, we do not reach the question whether a separate lawsuit can be maintained for conduct which is both a tort and a discovery violation because Westinghouse's complaint fails to allege compensable tort damages. The only damage alleged to have resulted from defendants' conduct is that "Westinghouse has been sued by public utility companies . . . by reason of which Westinghouse has been damaged . . . in an amount exceeding millions of dollars." Inducing a third party to bring litigation on a meritorious claim cannot be the basis for tort liability.

* * *

III. A Protective Order Issued by the Trial Court Supersedes Any Previous Secrecy Agreement Between the Parties or Their Attorneys Covering the Same Documents

As we explained above, the complaint alleges a secrecy agreement between Westinghouse, Newman and Chase which preceded the district court's protective order. The complaint also alleges the conditions on disclosure of the Westinghouse documents contained in the secrecy agreement were incorporated into the protective order. The question posed by these allegations is whether violation of either the protective order or the preceding agreement will support a cause of action for breach of contract. The answer is no.

A. Violation of a Discovery Order Does Not Give Rise to An Action for Breach of Contract

(2a) At the time the protective order was entered in the SCE case, rule 26(c) of the Federal Rules of Civil Procedure (28 U.S.C.) provided in relevant part: "Upon motion by a party . . . from whom discovery is sought, and for good cause shown, the court in which the action is pending . . . may make any order which justice requires to protect a party or person from annoyance, embarrassment, oppression, or undue burden or expense, including . . . (7) that a trade secret or other confidential research, development, or commercial information not be disclosed or be disclosed only in a designated way."

After such an order is entered, rule 37 of the Federal Rules of Civil Procedure provides the remedies for its violation. These remedies include sanctions against the offending party in the form of costs and attorney fees, evidence preclusion, issue preclusion, striking pleadings, entering a default judgment, and holding the offending party in contempt. (Fed. Rules Civ. Proc., rule 37(b)(2).) The relief afforded for noncompliance with a protective order depends exclusively upon rule 37 of the Federal Rules of Civil Procedure. . . .

B. A Protective Order Supersedes Any Previous Secrecy Agreement Between the Parties or Their Attorneys Covering the Same Documents

(3) It has long been the rule in this state that a preexisting agreement between the parties is extinguished upon its incorporation into a court order. Once the agreement is merged into the court's order, neither party any longer has a right of action based on the agreement because the obligations imposed are not imposed by the agreement but by the order and are enforceable as such through contempt and other sanctions available to the court. . . .

* * *

More importantly, allowing a breach of contract action based on the parties' secrecy agreement would divest the trial court of the power to regulate discovery in the underlying action because the trial court could neither modify the agreement on a showing of "good cause" nor relieve a party from compliance based on a change in circumstances. The court's act of modifying, interpreting or enforcing its order would be entirely ineffectual if a party who disagreed with the court's action could still enforce the preceding agreement. Suppose, for example, on motion of party A the trial court modified the protective order to permit party A to share documents it obtained from party B with attorneys involved in similar litigation against party B. (*See, e.g.,* American Tel. & Tel. Co. v. Grady, *supra*, 594 F.2d at pp. 596-597.) Party A would be subject to both a discovery order permitting disclosure of the documents and a preexisting agreement prohibiting their disclosure. To paraphrase Hough v. Hough, *supra*, 26 Cal. 2d at page 611, instead of the devil of a contempt sanction, party A would face the deep blue sea of a collateral lawsuit.

* * *

(2c) For all of the reasons discussed above, we conclude Westinghouse cannot base a breach of contract action on either the federal court's protective order or the superseded secrecy agreement between the parties; nor can the complaint be amended to state a cause of action. Therefore, the trial court acted correctly in sustaining a demurrer to the contract cause of action without leave to amend.[8]

Disposition

The judgment of dismissal is affirmed.

MIKE McKEE, COURT SLAMS "DECEPTIVE" ARBITRATION DEAL

San Francisco Recorder, October, 5, 2008

San Francisco—Legal blogs were buzzing Tuesday about a California appellate ruling involving a sham arbitration between controversial clothier Dov Charney and a woman who sued him for sexual harassment.

Los Angeles' Second District Court of Appeal revealed in an unpublished ruling Oct. 28 that attorneys for Charney, CEO of American Apparel Inc., a public company known for its racy ads, had conspired with lawyers for former sales manager Mary Nelson. Both sides had agreed, the ruling says, to enter into an arbitration whose outcome was preordained to favor Charney, and agreed to a press release stating that Charney "never sexualized, propositioned or made any sexual advances of any nature whatsoever toward Mary Nelson." Nelson, in turn, would get $1.3 million if she kept the settlement secret, according to the ruling.

The Second District, in an opinion authored by Justice Paul Turner, said that settlement—which never went through—would have raised "considerations of illegality, injustice and fraud." The court also held that the purpose of the proposed press release "was to mislead journalists and the public."

The attempted under-the-table agreement raised some questions about whether JAMS Inc. arbitrator Daniel Weinstein—a retired San Francisco Superior Court judge and co-founder of the 20-year-old JAMS—had gone along with the ruse.

But the appeal court exonerated Weinstein in Nelson v. American Apparel Inc., saying he had "refused to consummate" what the court called a "deceptive procedure." And on Tuesday, JAMS Executive Vice President and General Counsel John "Jay" Welsh fiercely defended Weinstein in a prepared statement. . . .

According to the Second District, Fink [the plaintiff's lawyer] backed out and refused to participate in the arbitration with its preordained settlement facts on Feb. 1 in San Francisco. . . .

---

8. This does not necessarily mean Westinghouse is without a remedy for defendants' alleged violation of the protective order in the SCE action. In the dismissal order reviewed in Westinghouse I, the district court ruled the appropriate remedy was to "seek sanctions for such a violation in the underlying case," i.e., the SCE action. Nothing in the Ninth Circuit's opinion contradicts that ruling. Under facts very similar to those alleged by Westinghouse, the court in Poliquin v. Garden Way, Inc. (D. Me. 1994) 154 F.R.D. 29 ordered sanctions against the plaintiff's attorney for disclosing information and documents covered by a protective order to other counsel for use in a lawsuit against the same defendant. The sanction order was issued after the judgment in the case had become final.

The appellate court, while obviously disturbed by the original arrangement, ordered the case back to JAMS to decide whether Nelson had generally agreed to traditional arbitration.

"There is a public policy in favor of arbitration under federal and state law," Justice Turner wrote. "Any doubts as to whether an arbitration clause applies to a particular dispute should be resolved in favor of ordering the parties to arbitrate."

He — along with Justices Orville Armstrong and Sandy Kriegler — held, however, that their position would have been entirely different if American Apparel had been trying to resurrect sham arbitration under the improper agreement.

"Then there would be considerations of illegality, injustice and fraud," the court held, "which would affect our powers as a court of equity to enforce the 'arbitration.'"

Ethics attorney Diane Karpman, the principal of L.A.'s Karpman & Associates, said that while the sham arbitration pushed the limits, it probably wouldn't lead to State Bar discipline charges.

"Clients have a right to settle on just about any terms," she said. . . . "It's permitted," Karpman added, "because clients are allocated the authority of when to settle. It's their decision, not the lawyers'."

State Bar prosecutors wouldn't comment on the case.

2. CONTROLLING THE RISKS OF COLLATERAL LITIGATION (II): PRACTICE RESTRICTION

NOTE ON PRACTICE RESTRICTIONS

If you've followed the materials on confidentiality thus far you have realized that much of the fiercest fighting is about how difficult it will be for a subsequent party to uncover the information that led to the settlement of the first suit. As a general proposition, the parties cannot by agreement or court order prevent a subsequent party from uncovering the relevant underlying facts. But confidentiality agreements can make the paths of such follow-on suits more expensive than they would otherwise be.

Moreover, you have by now realized that a plaintiffs' lawyer who has settled a lawsuit with a confidentiality agreement has thereby come into a temporarily valuable piece of intellectual property — assuming that there are other similarly situated prospective plaintiffs out there. Such a lawyer knows how to plead the case, knows just which discovery devices yield the critical information at the lowest cost, and knows where the smoking guns are hidden and how to bring them to light. Nothing in the confidentiality agreements you have read thus far would forbid the lawyer from doing just that. And the lawyer might be pleased to do so — might even consider soliciting (within the bounds permitted by professional rules) such business, perhaps explaining that he'd had success in very similar lawsuits.

Can a defendant (or plaintiff, if she's the one interested in confidentiality) prevent this unwelcome prospect? Can a defendant insert into the settlement agreement a clause forbidding the lawyer from representing parties like the plaintiff in subsequent suits? (Notice that such a lawyer, bound to pursue *this* client's interests, might feel bound to enter into such an agreement if it helps the client to achieve an otherwise good settlement.) Read on.

RULES OF PROFESSIONAL CONDUCT OF THE STATE BAR OF CALIFORNIA, RULE 1-500: AGREEMENTS RESTRICTING A MEMBER'S PRACTICE

State Bar of California (2004)

(A) A member shall not be a party to or participate in offering or making an agreement, whether in connection with the settlement of a lawsuit or otherwise, if the agreement restricts the right of a member to practice law, except that this rule shall not prohibit such an agreement which:

(1) Is a part of an employment, shareholders', or partnership agreement among members provided the restrictive agreement does not survive the termination of the employment, shareholder, or partnership relationship; or

(2) Requires payments to a member upon the member's retirement from the practice of law; or

(3) Is authorized by Business & Professions Code sections 6092.5, subdivision (l) or 6093.

(B) A member shall not be a party to or participate in offering or making an agreement which precludes the reporting of a violation of these rules.

ABA MODEL RULES OF PROFESSIONAL CONDUCT R. 5.6: RESTRICTIONS ON RIGHT TO PRACTICE

American Bar Association (2003)

A lawyer shall not participate in offering or making:

(a)   a partnership, shareholders, operating, employment, or other similar type of agreement that restricts the right of a lawyer to practice after termination of the relationship, except an agreement concerning benefits upon retirement; or

(b)   an agreement in which a restriction on the lawyer's right to practice is part of the settlement of a client controversy.

Comment

[1] An agreement restricting the right of lawyers to practice after leaving a firm not only limits their professional autonomy but also limits the freedom of clients to choose a lawyer. Paragraph (a) prohibits such agreements except for restrictions incident to provisions concerning retirement benefits for service with the firm.

[2] Paragraph (b) prohibits a lawyer from agreeing not to represent other persons in connection with settling a claim on behalf of a client.

[3] This Rule does not apply to prohibit restrictions that may be included in the terms of the sale of a law practice pursuant to Rule 1.17.

* * *

ABA MODEL RULES OF PROFESSIONAL CONDUCT R. 5.6:
RESTRICTIONS ON RIGHT TO PRACTICE

American Bar Association (1999)

A lawyer shall not participate in offering or making:

(a) a partnership or employment agreement that restricts the right of a lawyer to practice after termination of the relationship, except an agreement concerning benefits upon retirement; or

(b) an agreement in which a restriction on the lawyer's right to practice is part of the settlement of a controversy between private parties.

ROBERT WEIL & IRA BROWN, CALIFORNIA PRACTICE GUIDE:
CIVIL PROCEDURE BEFORE TRIAL

§§12:996-12:1000, 1002, 1020, 1030-1033, 1042-1043 (2004 ed.)

Chapter 12. Part II Settlement Procedures

H. Professional Responsibility Considerations Re Settlements

[12:996] Various considerations affecting the attorney-client relationship may arise in connection with settlements. For example:

1. [12:997] Attorney's Authority: Absent express authority from the client, the attorney cannot compromise the client's "substantive rights." An attorney has no implied authority to settle the client's claims; nor to stipulate to binding arbitration. [Blanton v. Womancare, Inc. (1985) 38 C3d 396, 404, 212 CR 151, 156, discussed at 1:316]

a. [12:998] Counsel must ascertain each other's authority: In concluding a settlement, counsel cannot simply rely on each other's assertion of authority. The burden is on each counsel to determine at his or her peril whether the opposing party has in fact authorized the settlement. [Blanton v. Womancare, Inc., *supra*, 38 C3d at 406, 212 CR at 156]

→ [12:999] PRACTICE POINTER: To avoid any dispute with your own client re your authority to settle, have your client sign any settlement or other agreement compromising the client's "substantive rights."

And, insist upon the signature of the opposing party individually, in addition to opposing counsel's signature. Otherwise, you may be personally liable to your client for whatever damage results from your relying on an unauthorized stipulation by opposing counsel! (E.g., delays in getting to trial, costs of setting aside dismissals or judgment, etc.)

2. [12:1000] Duty to Communicate Settlement Offers to Client: An attorney is ethically obligated to advise his or her client of any material development in the case; and this includes settlement offers, oral or written. [See ABA Model Rule 1.4(a), and former ABA EC 9-2]

In addition, an attorney is required by the Rules of Professional Conduct and by statute to "promptly communicate" to the client the terms and conditions of any written offer to settle made by the opposing party. [Bus. & Prof. C. §6103.5; CRPC 3-510]

Comment: Although the statute does not require the communication to be in writing, a written transmittal letter would avoid any question of compliance with the statute.

. . .

4. [12:1002] No Communication With Opposing Counsel's Client: A lawyer may not directly or indirectly communicate a settlement offer to an opposing party represented by counsel, or even inquire whether he or she has received an offer delivered to that party's counsel. On the other hand, the parties have the right to discuss settlement without their counsel present. But it is improper for either attorney to "orchestrate" the meeting or negotiations (e.g., by drafting documents). [See Cal. State Bar Form. Opn. 1993-131]

. . .

9. [12:1030] Attorney's Promises to Opposing Party: Attorneys are sometimes asked to make certain promises to the opposing party in connection with a settlement agreement:

a. [12:1031] Promise not to represent other claimants: Defendants may attempt to "buy off" successful plaintiffs' lawyers by conditioning settlement on the lawyers' agreeing not to represent other clients with similar claims against the defendant.

Such agreements may violate applicable rules of professional conduct:

— "A member shall not be a party to or participate in offering or making an agreement, whether in connection with the settlement of a lawsuit or otherwise, if the agreement restricts the right of a member to practice law . . ." [CRPC 1-500(A); see also ABA Model Rule 5.6(b)]

It is equally improper for defense counsel to propose such a provision in a settlement agreement. [See "Discussion" following CRPC 1-500(A)]

→ [12:1032] PRACTICE POINTER: Although plaintiff's lawyer may not agree not to represent other clients with claims against the defendant, there is no bar on the defendant hiring the plaintiff's lawyer (e.g., to counsel it regarding future claims) . . . thereby building in a conflict of interest that would disqualify that lawyer from representing other claimants.

b. [12:1033] Promise not to disclose confidential information ("secrecy clauses"): An attorney may also be asked to promise not to disclose the settlement terms and not to use or share information obtained through discovery or otherwise in the present litigation (e.g., not to disclose damaging evidence regarding the defendant's liability to other lawyers or news media).

The validity of such clauses generally is discussed below (see §12:1040).

To the extent such "secrecy" clauses limit the attorney's disclosure to other clients or future clients of the attorney, they probably violate CRPC 1-500(A) (§12:1031) because they indirectly restrict the attorney's right to practice law. [See American Bar Ass'n Formal Ethics Opn. 00-417] . . .

3. CONTROLLING FINANCIAL RISKS: THE STRUCTURED SETTLEMENT

Barbara Goldberg & Kenneth Mauro, Utilizing
Structured Settlements

658 PLI/Lit 31 (2001)

Introduction

Structured settlements are settlements in which there is typically an immediate lump sum payment, followed by a series of multiple payments over time, rather than a single lump sum cash settlement. Structured settlements can be tailored to the unique needs of an individual claimant, and should be considered in any case where an injured plaintiff has both immediate and long-term needs. They are particularly well-suited to cases involving neurologically impaired infants and other types of catastrophic injuries. Indeed, New York's CPLR §1206, entitled "Disposition of proceeds of claim of infant, judicially declared incompetent or conservatee," specifically provides that in such cases, the court may order that a structured settlement agreement be executed.

In personal injury actions, it is typically the defendant's liability insurance carrier who will pay for and purchase an annuity from a life insurance company. This annuity will provide the injured plaintiff with a stream of income through periodic payments. The amount and timing of these payments, which frequently include such items as medical expenses and lost income, as well as special needs such as wheelchairs or home modifications, are agreed upon as part of the settlement.

Potential Benefits

Using a structured settlement has potentially significant advantages for both sides. These include tax advantages to the recipient; flexibility in creating and defining the schedule of payments; the social benefit of providing lifetime financial security to a plaintiff who might otherwise be likely to squander a cash settlement in a brief period of time; and the ability to reach an agreement between plaintiff and defendant in cases where the parties otherwise appear to be too far apart. Despite the increased complexity which is involved in negotiating and settling a case using a structure, these many advantages may outweigh the difficulties.

Tax Advantages

An important benefit to litigants who have decided to use a structure or an annuity to settle a claim is the tax benefit which the government has provided. Section 104(a)(2) of the Internal Revenue Code provides that gross income does not include "the amount of any damages (other than punitive damages) received (whether by suit or agreement and whether as lump sums or as periodic payments) on account of personal physical injuries or physical sickness." It makes no difference whether the damages compensate the claimant for pecuniary loss, such as lost earnings, or non-economic loss, such as pain and suffering.

The tax-free status for the full amount of periodic payments received by a plaintiff in settlement of a personal injury action was further confirmed by Revenue Ruling 79-220 in 1979. Additionally, the Periodic Payment Settlement Act of 1982 added Section 130 of the Internal Revenue Code, entitled "Certain personal injury liability assignments." This section, which pertains to the assignment of liability for periodic payments in a personal injury action, further clarifies the tax-free status of periodic payments, and confirms that periodic payments are excluded from gross income as provided by Section 104(a)(2).

Another significant tax advantage to a structured settlement is that in the event of the plaintiff's death, any remaining payments which are payable to the plaintiff's estate under the Settlement Agreement are also excluded from income. (Rev. Rul. 79-220).

There are still further tax advantages to the use of a structure. If the plaintiff were to settle for a lump sum, the money received would be tax free. In most cases, however, the plaintiff will not spend all of the money on the first day, but will probably invest a substantial portion of the settlement proceeds in some investment vehicle, even if it is as simple as a Certificate of Deposit. The earnings on any such investment will be subject to taxes, leaving the plaintiff with a reduced net recovery. Had the principal been invested by the defendant, however, the monthly benefits generated would be totally tax free. Ideally, the tax savings on this investment over time could be split between the plaintiff and the defendant, thereby resulting in a savings to both litigants. Or, in other words, for less money the plaintiff could receive a larger benefit. This would benefit both sides!

At the very least, the potential tax savings is a crucial factor supporting the use of a structured settlement. Plaintiff's counsel should explain this distinction between a lump sum settlement and a structure, and indeed probably has an ethical obligation to do so.

Meeting the Injured Plaintiff's Needs

Another significant advantage of a structured settlement is the ability to provide for the plaintiff's long-term needs. By setting up a structure, especially for a plaintiff with a catastrophic injury, the payments can be scheduled to provide up-front cash for immediate needs, and periodic payments to meet such future needs as medical, rehabilitative and custodial care. Structures are very versatile and may also be designed to meet other types of contingencies, including home remodeling or a special vehicle; funding a college education; or providing eventual nursing home care.

In appropriate cases, a structured settlement may also provide for periodic payments to be made into a special or supplemental needs trust. This is defined as a "discretionary trust established for the benefit of a person with a severe and chronic or persistent disability" (EPTL 7-1.12[a]) that is designed to enhance the quality of the disabled individual's life by providing for special needs without duplicating services covered by Medicaid or destroying Medicaid eligibility (Bill Jacket, L. 1993, ch. 433). Under Federal and State Medicaid laws, funds placed in a supplemental needs trust are not considered resources that are "available" to a Medicaid recipient for purposes of assessing the recipient's eligibility for benefits, so long as the trust document conforms to the requirements of the EPTL and grants the State a remainder interest in trust assets remaining at the recipient's death, up to the amount of all public assistance provided. . . .

Protecting the Plaintiff

Such protection for the injured plaintiff is another major advantage of structured settlements. Studies have shown that the vast majority of people who have received lump sum payments, including injured plaintiffs, have squandered all of their money within five years. Indeed, according to insurance industry statistics, as many as 25-30% of all accident victims have completely dissipated their judgments or settlements within two months, and

90% have spent their awards within five years. Thus, notwithstanding a large lump sum settlement, a plaintiff might eventually be unable to meet future medical or economic needs, and might ultimately become dependent on welfare and other social services. As Randy Dyer, the Executive Vice-President of the National Structured Settlement Trade Association put it in a letter to the New York Law Journal:

> Sure, it's easy to suppose . . . that a mythic Jane Doe can take 100 percent of her award and get an annual 9 percent return. But let's go back to reality for a moment: What if Jane Doe has a brother who borrows the money, convinced that he can win a Florida real estate deal—and then loses everything? What if her husband uses the money to start a construction business—that goes bankrupt in a few years? What if they take the money and buy a boat, a couple of cars, and an expensive vacation—and then have little left for the original medical need? Incidentally, these are all real examples (New York Law Journal, October 21, 1999, p. 2, col. 6). . . .

A Structure Could Make a Settlement Possible Between Plaintiff and Defendant

A structured settlement can create possibilities for the injured plaintiff which may not initially have been considered by the parties, and which can be quite attractive. Importantly, the tax-free aspects of the structured settlement may help to close any gap which exists between parties discussing lump sum settlement amounts. These tax benefits provided by the government can serve to make the settlement more attractive to the plaintiff, and may even reduce the defendant's costs while increasing the plaintiff's benefits.

In addition, both the guaranteed payments under a structured settlement, and the anticipated payments over the plaintiff's lifetime, can be significantly higher than a lump sum settlement costing approximately the same amount as the structured settlement. This is demonstrated by an actual case involving a woman in her mid-thirties who had suffered an injury to her leg and buttock, but who was otherwise healthy. In that case, the defendant was willing to offer $1 million in settlement, but the plaintiff initially demanded more. In order to make the proposed settlement more attractive, the defendant obtained quotes indicating that the same $1 million, paid as a structure over twenty years, could have a total payout of $1,955,000, with guaranteed benefits of $1,325,000. The case was eventually settled with a slightly different structure, whereby the plaintiff received a payment of $500,000 up front, together with an annuity certain providing payments of $2,820 a month for twenty years, followed by a final lump sum payment of $500,000 in twenty years. The structure to which the parties agreed had a guaranteed payout of $1,676,800.

A structured settlement was also desirable in this particular case since the plaintiff was a cafeteria worker with a high school education who had never earned more than minimum wage. As such, she probably lacked the financial expertise to manage a large amount of money as a lump sum. . . .

Plaintiff Not Dependent upon Defendant for Payments

Yet a further advantage to a structured settlement is that the defendant is not responsible for the payments under the annuity. This is important for the plaintiff, since a defendant might go bankrupt, or the defendant's liability insurer might go into liquidation. Pursuant to Section 130 of the Internal Revenue Code, either the defendant, or its liability insurance carrier, may assign to a third party assignee its obligation to make future payments to the plaintiff. The assignee then funds the obligation through an annuity which the assignee owns.

The plaintiff's attorney may—and should—insist that the structure be funded by a highly rated life insurance carrier. Ratings are provided by A. M. Best, Standard & Poor's, Moody's and others. In the example discussed above involving the cafeteria worker, the annuity was issued by GE Capital Life Assurance Company of New York, and the obligation to make the payments was assigned to GE Capital Assignment Corporation. . . .

Considerations for Negotiating the Structured Settlement

The "Cost" of the Structure

An important analysis for plaintiff's counsel is to compare the cost of the structured settlement with the verdict potential. This is essentially the same type of analysis which plaintiff's counsel should employ with a lump sum settlement. Since the structured settlement, with its tax free benefits, is more advantageous to the injured plaintiff than a cash settlement, an appropriate discount should be given, but beyond this the usual considerations in evaluating the case for settlement should be applied. These include the potential verdict amount following a trial, the likelihood of winning, consideration for the delay in receiving payment on any potential judgment, consideration for a reduction in the verdict based on comparative negligence or other reductions, the policy limits of insurance, and the rate of return which the plaintiff could receive if the money were placed in reasonable investment vehicles, or in investment vehicles with reasonable risks.

The parties should also make certain that the payments are specifically designed to meet all of the plaintiff's needs. Of course, this may not be the only consideration, since in some instances the verdict potential may be less than what would meet plaintiff's needs.

Defendant Should Negotiate Benefits

For the defendant, it is best to negotiate by offering benefits to the plaintiff rather than agreeing to a specific cost. A discussion of cost may cause the plaintiff to become involved with investment decisions or the yield on the amount invested. Additionally, problems may arise since rates are likely to change during the course of settlement discussions. It is therefore better to discuss benefits and leave the issue of cost or present value until after settlement is reached.

Ascertaining the Life Expectancy of the Plaintiff

If an annuity is designed in such a manner that some or all of the payments cease upon the death of the plaintiff, the annuity company will assess the plaintiff's medical history and present condition in order to make its own determination as to life expectancy. Clearly, payments for medical expenses, therapies or custodial care will not be necessary in the event of the plaintiff's death. The premium charged is based upon the annuity company's evaluation of actual life expectancy, although the annuity company would continue to pay should the plaintiff survive past its predictions.

Thus, for example, a 25-year old plaintiff may be "rated up" to age 75 if it is determined that he only has a few years to live. A child with severe neurological impairments may similarly be "rated" as a much older person. Therefore, even though certain payments may be guaranteed for a lifetime, the cost for such a payout may be relatively inexpensive if it is determined that the plaintiff's life expectancy is considerably less than what would be expected of a healthy person of the same age. This is a key benefit in purchasing annuities and in settling using a structure. Where there is a limited life expectancy, the cost of the annuity will be significantly reduced. . . .

Terms and Conditions of a Structured Settlement

In negotiating a structured settlement, the following aspects of the structure are all negotiable:

1. The amount of an up-front lump sum payment which generally can be used to cover past expenses and immediate needs.
2. The amount and timing of periodic payments which can start immediately and continue for a date certain, for a lifetime, or even beyond the plaintiff's lifetime if the plaintiff has dependents. A combination is possible where some payments would be guaranteed regardless of the life expectancy of the plaintiff.
3. Periodic payments can be made monthly, semi-annually, annually or at any other intervals.
4. The payments may increase over time to account for inflation.
5. Certain "balloon" payments may also be negotiated, to be used for needs above and beyond monthly requirements. Examples include the need to purchase a new wheelchair every several years; the need for a hip replacement in five years; or even the desire to fund a college education for children. Large balloon payments with long deferrals are suggested because they are impressive but comparatively inexpensive.

Since the terms and conditions of the structured settlement are determined when the parties enter into the settlement agreement and cannot be changed at a later date, plaintiff's counsel should obtain expert medical advice in order to determine the plaintiff's future medical needs, as well as other needs which the plaintiff may have. This is especially true in a catastrophic injury case.

A guaranteed minimum payout may also be negotiated. This usually adds very little to the cost of the annuity, and is therefore easy to negotiate. For example, although a plaintiff may be expected to live for 30 years, he could die tomorrow. In the event of such a sudden death, all lifetime benefits would cease. Under such circumstances, it would cost little more in premiums to have guaranteed all payments for a minimum of ten or even twenty years. Since there is a minimal difference in cost between an annuity for life only and an annuity for life with a period certain (where the period certain is less than the plaintiff's life expectancy) plaintiff's counsel has the responsibility to obtain such a benefit for the client. This will maximize the guaranteed benefits of the annuity. . . .

Calculation of Attorney's Fees

Plaintiff's attorney's fees are based on the present value or cost of the annuity; the fees are not based on the total payout to the plaintiff. Since plaintiff and plaintiff's counsel usually agree to a contingency fee, the determination of the present value of the total settlement is necessary and may be calculated in various ways. Of course, the actual cost of the annuity may be utilized; additionally, a present value calculation considering current discount rates, the tax advantages to the plaintiff, and the cost of managing the annuity may be considered in determining the present value.

A defendant may be reluctant to reveal the actual cost of the settlement, but there is no good reason for refusing such disclosure. As indicated above, knowledge of the cost will not jeopardize the plaintiff's tax benefits as was once believed. In addition, once a settlement is reached, there is no longer any negotiating benefit to the defendant in refusing to disclose the cost.

The plaintiff's counsel's fee should follow the settlement and not be discussed in advance. It is considered unethical to agree upon a fee first, and then design the settlement which supports the fee. . . .

Conclusion

In sum, a structured settlement is a potential means of settling a personal injury action which may have significant advantages for both sides. As such, it should be considered in any case where there are substantial injuries, or the plaintiff will have on-going needs into the future. Even where a plaintiff has since recovered from his or her injuries, but a verdict would be likely to result in a substantial award for past damages, a structured settlement should be considered, since it can provide long-term financial security which might not otherwise be available.

Julie Gannon Shoop, Selling Structured Settlements: Boon or Boondoggle for Injury Victims?

Trial, July 1999, at 12

Trial attorneys are accustomed to accepting trade-offs when settling claims for injured clients. In the typical scenario, the client trades a lump sum for a stream of smaller payments spread out over time — the classic structured settlement.

But what happens when the client wants to trade back?

That option is being offered by the emerging "settlement purchase" industry, barely heard of even a few years ago. Companies that started out offering lottery winners lump sums in exchange for the right to collect their future payments have begun offering tort claimants immediate cash in return for all or part of their future income from a structured settlement payer. The trade-off for the client: The lump sum is substantially less than the present value of the payments the claimant agrees to give up. . . .

4. CONTROLLING THE RISKS OF TRIAL: THE HIGH-LOW AGREEMENT

JOHN L. SHANAHAN, THE HIGH-LOW AGREEMENT

33 For the Defense 25 (July 1991)

Lawsuits that present weak arguments for liability but catastrophic damages can be stressful for claims managers and trial lawyers (both plaintiffs' and defense). In a time when there is significant exposure to bad faith actions arising from overage verdicts, the insurance carrier, its claims department, and trial lawyers are wisely reluctant to run the risk of a verdict that may be millions of dollars over the insured's policy limits. The separate possibility of a bad faith action by the insured, seeking punitive damages in addition to the amount of the excess verdict, is another cause for concern. . . .

On the plaintiff's side, there is an attorney pouring endless hours and perhaps hundreds of thousands of dollars into a trial, with a likely prospect of a defense verdict sending all that time and money into a bottomless pit. The plaintiff's attorney desperately wants to settle rather than try the case, but he cannot "give away" the prospect of millions in damages for a mere pittance. The carrier, despite the specter of an excess verdict, cannot ignore the fact that the plaintiff will have great difficulty proving liability. On both sides there is the expenditure of huge amounts of money, with potentially disastrous consequences to the side that makes the wrong call. Consider also the effect of enormous verdicts on the general availability of insurance coverage to the consumer, and the amounts that must be paid in premium. . . .

What Is a High-Low Contract?

A high-low agreement is a unique and relatively novel method designed to address and resolve the problems of both sides in dealing with difficult cases of questionable liability but very high potential damages. The method generally works as follows.

Before the trial, both sides agree upon two figures. First, they select a "high" figure, which is acceptable to the defendant. This often is at or close to the policy limits, since protecting the integrity of that limit is usually the defense's basic consideration that leads to the agreement in the first place. This amount is to be paid if the verdict is for the plaintiff, no matter how much the jury awards over that figure.

The parties then select a "low" figure to be paid to the plaintiff in the event that the jury returns a defense verdict. This generally represents the plaintiff's trial costs, often with a small additional amount to make the offer attractive to the plaintiff. The parties have also been known to select a smaller figure to cover the possibility of a hung jury; this minimal compensation may be enough to convince the plaintiff to avoid the problems and expenses of a retrial.

For example, suppose that the policy has a limit of $100,000, but the potential verdict is one million dollars. The parties may agree to a "high" of $100,000 and a "low" of $25,000. The liability and damages issues, as well as the negotiating skills of the respective parties, will be significant factors in fixing the high and low numbers.

The high-low agreement is then formally put on the record in open court in the same way that one might seek court approval of an infant or incompetent settlement. It is essential that the plaintiffs take the stand and indicate on the record their understanding and acceptance of the terms of the contract. Experience has shown the importance of disclosing the terms in court; with the cachet of a judge's approval, it is far less likely to be subject to later attack. Without such formal proof of the agreement, it may be challenged by the unsuccessful party, and not hold up without some substantiation beyond the testimony of counsel. For example, in Rowe v. Johns-Manville Corp., 1987 Westlaw 12266 (E. D. Pa. 1987), the court, holding an agreement to be an unconditional settlement rather than a high-low, stated:

> I conclude that the settlement entered into by plaintiff and ACF is not a conditional "high-low" settlement, but rather that it is an unconditional settlement of all claims between plaintiff and ACF. All of the documentary evidence surrounding supports this conclusion. If counsel had negotiated an admittedly unusual "high-low" arrangement, they would in all likelihood have created a written record evidencing such a settlement.

See also Rowe v. Johns-Manville Corp., 658 F. Supp. 122 (E. D. Pa. 1987).

It is strongly suggested that the contract include a provision that the agreement applies to any retrial of the case, particularly if the plaintiff's case has gone in particularly well.

With the approval of the high-low agreement, the plaintiff has covered his trial costs and possibly even made a slight profit. The defense has protected itself against any possibility of an overage verdict and any attendant bad faith actions. Admittedly, experience has shown that the defense wins a significant percentage of these matters, but one major overage verdict can easily outweigh many small payments under high-low agreements.

High-Low Agreements in Practice

The origin of high-low agreements is not clear. A 1968 article addressed itself to the "high-low" concept, principally in regard to appeals and matters in arbitration. Coulson, "Negotiating Control Contracts," 52 Judicature 190 (1968). Subsequently, Justice Leonard L. Finz of the Supreme Court of New York wrote an article in which he announced himself as an enthusiastic advocate of the concept. Finz, "The Hi Lo Contract: A Trial by Chance," 49 N.Y.S.B.J. 186 (1976). He wrote (referring to himself, as judge, in the second person):

> You are one who has been involved with the law for nearly 25 years with almost 10 of those years on the Bench. You have tried almost every kind of civil case, running the gamut from the smallest dollar amount to verdicts in the high six figures. In the thousands of cases settled amicably during this period of time, every possible and customary formula and device has been employed in arriving at a sum agreeable to both sides. So that when a unique, innovative settlement approach is presented, you give it serious consideration and a lot of discussion.

The case that inspired Justice Finz's article was a fairly common automobile personal injury matter. The plaintiff had been struck by the defendant's car and sustained substantial injuries. It was a classic situation: liability was tenuous at best, with very severe injuries presenting a potential exposure of several hundred thousand dollars. Besides this all-too-familiar combination, the policy limit in this instance was $100,000, certainly well under the realistic damage exposure faced by the defendant.

The defense counsel advised the court in chambers that his company was prepared to enter into a contract with the plaintiff that would fix the low and high limits of payment, depending upon the jury's verdict as to liability. There was no need to worry about an interim jury figure in that matter since the trial was already bifurcated as to liability and damages. The defendant made the following offer: if the jury returned a verdict for the defendant on liability, the insurance carrier would pay a certain "low" fixed sum despite the verdict. If the plaintiff succeeded on liability, the plaintiff would receive only a certain "high" filed sum. As part of this contract, each party would agree to waive all rights to an appeal concerning the amount of damages, although they would have their rights to appeal on any issues concerning liability.

Negotiations determined the ultimate parameters of the contract. Both sides agreed that the low would be fixed at $25,000 and that the high would be fixed at $75,000. To seal the contract, a complete record was made, with full participation and agreement by the party litigants and their counsel on the record. The case was tried on liability only and the jury, faced with but one question, that of fault, found for the defendant. The plaintiff had lost, but no doubt covered his expenses and had some small recovery to show for his pains. The defendant was spared the risk of an excess verdict and was no doubt quite content at paying only the low figure. Both sides had resolved a difficult situation with reduced exposure and some share of success.

Having seen that the high-low concept could work in such difficult cases, Justice Finz made the following observations (48 N.Y.S.B.J. at 187) [the additional observations, in brackets, are the current author's]:

The "high-low" contract could be employed in those cases in which:

(1) liability is a disputed issue and damages are substantial;
(2) causation and damages are sharp issues;
(3) the damages and possible verdict exposure exceed the insurance policy limits thereby subjecting the insured defendant to deficiency personal liability; [more realistically in today's legal climate, the exposure is most often to the carrier and/or the claims person or attorney personally in various bad faith or malpractice claims]
(4) the defendant is a large public corporation and, as such, a target defendant;
(5) the defendant is part of an unpopular class and, as such, a target defendant; [naturally, this could also simply be a respected class, such as doctors, that are perceived to be either wealthy or obviously insured heavily]
(6) both plaintiff and defendant for reasons best known to themselves do not want to place the entire outcome of the case upon the vicissitudes of a trial.

Clearly, there are many advantages to using the "high-low" contract approach in certain difficult cases. Justice Finz listed some of those advantages:

(1) It limits exposure to what otherwise could result in a huge verdict, thereby benefitting all policy holders whose premiums are determined ultimately on loss ratio computations.

(2) It protects the insured defendant from crushing personal liability beyond the policy limits. [The good Justice's observations, made in 1976, did not really foresee the level to which bad faith rulings have shifted that burden almost entirely to the carrier in most states]

(7) It eliminates compromise [or "quotient"] verdicts with their resulting onerous and unjust impact upon one side or the other. [This is really an important consideration for the defense, particularly when the case is venued in a known "plaintiff' county with a particularly attractive plaintiff or unappealing/target defendant]

(8) It forces jurors to focus on fault, or causation only [obviously this applies only in bifurcated trials such as Justice Finz was accustomed to], leaving the verdict amounts to be determined by experienced attorneys with the assistance of the court — all of whom possess a deep understanding and grasp of the medical and other damage aspects of the case.

(10) It encourages finality to a case without the peripheral expenses of interest and other costs which ultimately are reflected in higher premiums.

(11) It establishes an atmosphere of conciliation and negotiation, thereby furnishing a climate for a "straight" settlement, even where the high-low approach is rejected.

The high-low concept requires the preparation and submission of special jury interrogatories, particularly in those jurisdictions where they are not commonly employed. The parties must know with certainty at least two, and often several other, specific jury findings, viz.:

Question 1: "Was the Defendant [negligent; did he deviate from accepted medical/scientific standards; did he manufacture a defective product; etc.] with respect to the plaintiff?" If the answer is NO, the jury is then instructed to proceed no further and return its verdict. If the answer is YES, the jury would then be instructed to go to question 2.

Question 2: "Was the [negligence/deviation/ product defect, etc.] a proximate cause of any injury suffered by the plaintiff?" If the answer is YES, the plaintiff will have prevailed and would (in a bifurcated trial) be entitled to the high sum agreed by the contract. If the jury's answer is NO, the plaintiff would receive the low agreed sum.

Obviously, in the case of multiple defendants, these questions would be repeated for each defendant.

Generally, in a non-bifurcated trial, the jury interrogatories then go on to issues concerning the proportion of responsibility of each defendant, the contributory negligence of the plaintiff, the total amount of damages, etc.

In any high-low case, it is important to agree whether the plaintiff is to receive any sum falling between the high and low figure. For example, where an agreement is for $25,000 (low) and $150,000 (high), what happens if the jury comes in with a verdict for $65,000? Experience has shown that the most common agreement is one where the plaintiff receives any figure falling between the high and low limits, since the defense's primary interest is usually in preserving the integrity of the policy and by that fulfilling its primary responsibility of protecting its insured. The plaintiff's interest remains primarily in trying its case without the risk of out-of-pocket loss in the event of a defense verdict.

Almost never seen in these contracts is a provisional figure in the event of a hung jury. The defense should try to add a small figure (generally somewhat below the low number, since the plaintiff would be faced with recurring costs in the event of a retrial) to cover this unlikely event. If there is a hung jury figure, the case can go away for a sum smaller than the low and all parties spare themselves and their clients the expense of a retrial. A further provision to consider is that the same high-low agreement be applicable in the event of a retrial necessitated either by a hung jury or a mistrial, regardless of the reason.

Try to bifurcate liability from damages. One defense advantage to the high-low device in a bifurcated trial is that the jury's attention can be focused entirely upon the liability issue. The jury will not be exposed to the highly emotional elements of injury testimony and plaintiff's pain and suffering; such testimony can cloud the jurors' minds and compromise their verdict. When the trials are not bifurcated, the defense is free to concentrate on liability, with minimal trial time devoted to the damage issue (a good procedure to follow in any trial). The argument to the plaintiff for bifurcation is that he in turn is spared the expense of bringing in expensive medical experts, leaving more of the high or the low as profit to him in the event of either a plaintiff's or defense verdict. The downside to this is that you cannot save anything on your high figure.

Considerations in Using High-Low Agreements

There are several important legal issues to be evaluated before the high-low idea can be used freely, particularly where there are multiple defendants.

Mary Carter Agreements

Determine if the high-low is a "Mary Carter" agreement, or a form of it. In most states, Mary Carters are improper or illegal; even if not, provisions of the Mary Carter agreement must be revealed in detail to the jury. See Booth v. Mary Carter Paint Co., 202 So.2d 8 (Fla. App. 1967). This revelation often has such an effect on the jury's perception of the case that one party, generally the plaintiff, cannot afford to enter such a contract.

In Florida, the original home of the Mary Carter agreement, the high-low has been held not to constitute such an agreement. . . .

Federal courts have generally accepted high-low agreements as a viable settlement tool. It has even been approved where it was used as a fall-back agreement to an otherwise improper Mary Carter agreement. . . .

Contribution

The defense must consider the effect that a high-low agreement may have on contribution between codefendants, or the proportional recovery in the event that the jury assigns varying proportions to a number of the codefendants. In Shafer v. Cronk, 220 N.J. Super. 518, 532 A.2d 1131 (Law Div. 1987), a passenger injured in an automobile accident sued the driver and the operator of the other vehicle involved in the accident. The plaintiff entered into a high-low agreement with the driver of the other car, by which the parties agreed to a range of damages regardless of any jury verdict above or below those amounts; the high was $100,000 and the low was $40,000. The jury's verdict was for a total of $500,000; it found that the driver of the other car (the party to the high-low agreement) was 97% at fault, or $485,000. But because of the high-low agreement, the driver was obligated to pay plaintiff only $100,000. Plaintiff then sought to recover the $400,000 from the host driver, an amount which was well above the share set by the jury (3%, or $15,000).

The issue presented in Shafer v. Cronk was whether the plaintiff's high-low agreement with one defendant-tortfeasor, reached prior to verdict, constituted a settlement entitling the other defendant tortfeasor to an offset from the verdict rendered against the settling defendant. The court held that it did constitute a settlement. The plaintiff was precluded from recovering damages from the host driver above the percentage share set by jury. See also Lahocki v. Contee Sand & Gravel Co., 41 Md. App. 579, 398 A.2d 490 (1979).

Liens

There is not a great deal of authority on the effect of third-party liens on high-low agreement recoveries, but it appears that liens are as enforceable as they would be against any other kind of recovery. In City of Tallahassee v. Chambliss, 470 So. 2d 43 (Fla. App. 1985), an alleged third-party tortfeasor was found not liable by the jury. He had previously entered into a high-low agreement whereby the plaintiff would receive $200,000 regardless of the jury's verdict. The plaintiff's employer was held entitled to enforce its workers' compensation lien on the settlement proceeds, with appropriate deduction for attorney's fees and costs.

Primary and Excess Carriers

In United States Fire Insurance Co. v. Royal Insurance Co., 759 F.2d 306 (3d Cir. 1985), the court dealt with the question of whether the primary carrier acted in bad faith by refusing to tender its policy limits in an attempt to achieve a settlement when a high-low settlement approved by both was reached. While the law dealing with the duty of the respective carriers is not germane to this article, it is of interest to note that Royal had a policy of $250,000 and U.S. Fire had an excess policy of $5,000,000. The parties, in a classic poor liability/high damages case, had been unable to achieve settlement by normal negotiations.

In analyzing U.S. Fire v. Royal, it is most interesting to observe that the district court itself recommended a high-low as an alternative settlement arrangement under which plaintiffs would receive $65,000 if they lost the suit, and no more than $750,000 if they won. Royal expressed approval of this arrangement. Plaintiffs were unwilling to accept these figures, but made a counter-offer of $100,000 if they lost and $1,000,000 if they won. Royal, who had allegedly refused to tender its policy limits to a $400,000 settlement demand (which the plaintiff later denied was made or would have been accepted if offered), considered the high-low settlement plan because they felt that the defense had a substantial chance of winning the case. Ultimately, Royal accepted the high-low $1,000,000/$100,000 counteroffer arrangement proposed by the plaintiffs. Fire concurred in this arrangement. Thus, Fire's potential liability was reduced by several strokes of a pen from $5,000,000 to $1,000,000, and if the defense was successful, it would not be required to pay anything. . . .

The jury returned a plaintiff's verdict and the defense paid the high figure. . . .

Conclusion

The "runaway verdict" is the dream of every plaintiffs' attorney and the nightmare of every defense person. It creates additional litigation, unjustly enriches a few at the expense of the many, often destroys careers, skews loss ratios, and affects premium. The publicity attendant upon such often astronomical verdicts creates unwarranted expectations among plaintiffs, and leads to increased demands in settlement negotiations. The high-low agreement is an innovative and first-rate tool for dealing effectively and economically with this problem in certain difficult cases that are, perhaps, otherwise impossible to resolve.

JULIE KAY, DEAL ERASES $159 MILLION FROM JURY AWARD

Miami Daily Business Review, July 25, 2005, at 1

A jury awarded $164 million to a severely brain-damaged Miami man who was hit by a car while walking on the Watson Island bridge when he was 16, but a pretrial agreement will shrink the payment to $5 million.

Jaro Hladik and his family agreed to a "high-low" settlement guaranteeing $5 million regardless of the verdict.

Miami lawyer Arthur Tifford, who tried the case in Miami-Dade Circuit Court with his daughter and law partner, Alexandra Tifford, said he does not regret making the deal with attorneys for Sunrise, Fla.-based Bob's Barricades.

"You had to do that for the protection of the family," Tifford said after the verdict was reached Thursday. He was still pleased with the sizable verdict. "This was twice as much as we had sought. The jury was angry."

Miami attorney James Usich, lead attorney for the state's biggest barricade company, angrily called the verdict "insignificant." He said his company did nothing wrong.

"It's outrageous," he said. "This was not based on facts. It was based on sympathy. This was a tragic accident which should never have happened. But the fault lies entirely with the driver, who was on cocaine and marijuana."

Hladik, then a 16-year-old Homestead, Fla., Senior High School student, was walking his bike on the bridge while heading home from a 60-mile ride in April 1999.

The sidewalk on the bridge linking I-395 and the MacArthur Causeway was closed for construction, so Hladik was in the emergency lane. A car driven by Marie Louise Delgado plowed into Hladik from behind in the breakdown lane, leaving him in a coma for five months. He is now 96 percent disabled, is confined to a wheelchair and has the mind of a 7-year-old, according to Tifford. . . .

Redland and the state settled last year for undisclosed amounts, Tifford said. . . .

The jury deliberated for three hours, awarding Hladik $1.4 million for past medical expenses, $13 million for future medical expenses, $4.2 million for 60 years of lost earnings, $5 million for past pain and suffering and $90 million for future pain and suffering. . . .

5. CONTROLLING THE RISKS OF APPEAL: SETTLEMENT PENDING APPEAL

Brenda Sapino Jeffreys, $1 Billion Fen-Phen Case Settles Before Appellate Arguments

Texas Lawyer, April 16, 2007

Three years ago, when a team of plaintiffs lawyers led by John O'Quinn of Houston tried a fen-phen suit in a Beaumont, Texas, courtroom and won a $1 billion verdict, including $900 million in punitive damages, products liability lawyers on both sides of the docket took notice of the record-setting award.

Defendant pharmaceutical company Wyeth, based in Madison, N.J., appealed the $1.01 billion judgment that 172nd District Judge Donald Floyd of Beaumont had signed in one family's fen-phen case in May 2004. The appeal was noteworthy because of the judgment's astounding size and because the appeal would have tested Texas' statutory cap limiting punitive damages.

But that cap won't be put to the test. Lawyers representing Wyeth and the plaintiffs in Jerry Coffey, et al. v. Wyeth, et al. have negotiated a settlement in the suit.

In a joint motion filed with Beaumont's 9th Court of Appeals on April 5, the parties asked the appeals court to set aside the May 2004 judgment "without regard to the merits" and to remand it to the trial court, where they will ask Floyd to consider a settlement benefiting the minor plaintiffs in the suit and to enter a take-nothing judgment. . . .

But an appellate lawyer for the plaintiffs, David Holman of the Holman Law Firm in Houston, says that in the nearly three years since the verdict in Coffey, no appeals court in Texas has addressed the statutory cap on damages. The cap limits punitive damages to twice compensatory damages plus up to $750,000.

He says a ruling on the statutory cap would have been "huge" and precedent-setting.

D. CONTROLLING RISKS ON MULTIPLE AXES: MULTIPARTY SETTLEMENT

1. A BRIEF REVIEW OF THE GOVERNING LAW

a. Joinder

STEPHEN C. YEAZELL, CIVIL PROCEDURE

731 (Aspen, 6th ed. 2004)

Modern civil procedure in the United States has two distinguishing features. One, discovery, increases the depth of any given lawsuit. The other, broad joinder of claims and parties, increases the breadth of a suit. To achieve this breadth, modern process turned from the single-mindedness of common law procedure and focused on the transaction rather than on the writ or legal theory. This focus permits parties to combine various claims and to add additional parties. A larger litigative "package" confers advantages: It allows a single suit to adjudicate multiple claims against multiple parties and permits litigation to reflect some of life's complexity. Disadvantages can also flow from this freedom: Litigation can become intricate, and considerable procedural skirmishing can occur long before the merits come into view, as parties dispute whether a given effort at joinder is permitted. . . .

b. Federal Rules of Civil Procedure

Rule 18: Joinder of Claims and Remedies

(a) Joinder of Claims. A party asserting a claim to relief as an original claim, counterclaim, cross-claim, or third-party claim, may join, either as independent or as alternate claims, as many claims, legal, equitable, or maritime, as the party has against an opposing party. . . .

Rule 20: Permissive Joinder of Parties

(a) Permissive Joinder. All persons may join in one action as plaintiffs if they assert any right to relief jointly, severally, or in the alternative in respect of or arising out of the same transaction, occurrence, or series of transactions or occurrences and if any question of law or fact common to all these persons will arise in the action. All persons (and any vessel, cargo or other property subject to admiralty process in rem) may be joined in one action as defendants if there is asserted against them jointly, severally, or in the alternative, any right to relief in respect of or arising out of the same transaction, occurrence, or series of transactions or occurrences and if any question of law or fact common to all defendants will arise in the action. A plaintiff or defendant need not be interested in obtaining or defending against all the relief demanded. Judgment may be given for one or more of the plaintiffs according to their respective rights to relief, and against one or more defendants according to their respective liabilities.

(b) Separate Trials. The court may make such orders as will prevent a party from being embarrassed, delayed, or put to expense by the inclusion of a party against whom the party asserts no claim and who asserts no claim against the party, and may order separate trials or make other orders to prevent delay or prejudice.

Rule 13: Counterclaim and Cross-Claim . . .

(g) Cross-Claim Against Co-Party. A pleading may state as a cross-claim any claim by one party against a co-party arising out of the transaction or occurrence that is the subject matter either of the original action or of a counterclaim therein or relating to any property that is the subject matter of the original action. Such cross-claim may include a claim that the party against whom it is asserted is or may be liable to the cross-claimant for all or part of a claim asserted in the action against the cross-claimant.

c. Modern Tort Law

STEPHEN C. YEAZELL, REFINANCING CIVIL LITIGATION

51 De Paul Law Review 183, 190-193 (2001)

B. Changes in Substantive Law

[Following a section summarizing developments in mid-twentieth-century insurance law.] Changes in the incidence of individual insurance coverage produced a greater number of insured owners of houses and cars, but most individual insurance coverages are relatively modest. Before the tort bar could recapitalize itself, additional mechanisms for risk spreading and incentives for deeper investment both had to appear. They did, starting in the late 1950s, as a result of several related developments.

First, products liability laws opened the doors wider. With the California Supreme Court leading the way, manufacturers became liable for a wide variety of injury-producing products. Such liability had long-term consequences for the financing of the plaintiffs' bar. Products liability made deeper investments in specialized knowledge profitable. Automobile accidents might have repetitive patterns, but any given auto accident could injure a fairly limited number of persons. Not so with defective products: one could now attack the design of the bumper, gas tank, or steering wheel as the cause of injuries in hundreds or in thousands of accidents, with the added advantage that a Fortune 500 corporation, not an individual insurance policy, would be the source of damages. Moreover, products liability suits expanded liability into realms that might in an earlier era have seemed to involve self-inflicted injuries: power saws and tools, snow blowers, home heaters and appliances. Mass production and distribution meant that it became increasingly difficult to imagine an injury in which there was not a potentially liable manufacturer. For the bars — plaintiffs' and defendants' — products liability suits required more experts and some knowledge of design and manufacturing processes; a lawyer contemplating a series of such cases might make substantial investments, economic and intellectual, in developing expertise. Others have and will continue to debate the economic and social wisdom of such developments; for my purposes, it is enough to note its existence.

As products liability developed, another previously closed door opened: municipal and charitable immunity crumbled. Hospitals, municipalities, and state and federal governments all began to be subject to something that looked like tort liability. The Federal Tort Claims Act and equivalent state statutes made governments liable for ordinary negligence; their continued immunity existed only for decisions that could be characterized as "discretionary" or intentional and they continued to be immune to punitive damages. Because this lowered liability corresponded with an array of post-war governmental initiatives ranging from the interstate highway system to expanded public education, the tort regime combined with increased governmental activity to produce a broad range of potential lawsuits. The story of charitable institutions was similar: hospitals, orphanages, and similar institutions were now subject to liability, and although their pockets were shallower than those of the product manufacturers or state and federal governments, they were substantial enough to warrant more than an occasional lawsuit. For the many charitable institutions that ran hospitals, the combination of their new exposure to suits with the increasing ability of the plaintiffs' bar to locate physicians willing to testify against a fellow doctor expanded the number of suits in which the plaintiff's lawyer could say, in effect, "I don't know whether this terrible injury was the fault of the doctor or the hospital; I leave that question in the jury's capable hands."

As these events unfolded, a final substantive doctrinal change consolidated their effect: the substitution of comparative fault for the regime of contributory negligence. In its purest form, of course, contributory negligence was a complete defense: any negligence of the plaintiff entirely barred recovery. Anecdotal evidence suggests that juries sometimes declined to apply the comparative negligence rules in their full rigor. Plaintiffs, however, never knew in advance whether juries would thus temper the law, and the formal regime insisted that even a small amount of contributory negligence entirely negated defendant's liability. As a consequence, plaintiff's tort litigation was often a losing, and always a risky game. As courts and legislatures modified contributory negligence into various regimes of comparative negligence, plaintiffs' chances of at least a modest return on a given lawsuit increased. To be sure, comparative negligence could also reduce the plaintiff's recovery by allowing the jury explicitly to recognize his fault. But this feature of comparative negligence only served to emphasize the respects in which both sides to a tort case were engaged in risk management — the plaintiff trying to avoid an investment in excess of recovery, and the defendant seeking to prevent or minimize any recovery.

The expansion of products liability, the fall of municipal and charitable immunities, and the advent of comparative negligence combined to produce the phenomenon that my late colleague Gary Schwartz called "the secondary defendant." In a mass-production society, many injury-producing events will appear to have several legally plausible causes. The immediate moral agent of my injuries is the driver who ran the red light, but the manufacturer of my car (which lacked safety features that could have prevented or contained design features that exacerbated my injuries), the manufacturer of the other car (with a similar list of design defects), the municipality that designed the intersection (failing to light or mark it optimally), the hospital to whose emergency room I was taken (which failed to treat me promptly and properly), and others have some role in bringing about my current state of health. As any lawyer will note, many of these "secondary" defendants have the substantial advantage of possessing deep pockets, so that a liability judgment, even of partial responsibility, has a high likelihood of being collectible. Their attractiveness as plausible defendants is therefore great; I leave to a later section an analysis of the importance of this added attractiveness. . . .

d. Joint and Several Liability: Contribution

LEWIS A. KORNHAUSER & RICHARD L. REVESZ, SETTLEMENTS
UNDER JOINT AND SEVERAL LIABILITY

68 New York University Law Review 427, 435-441 (1993)

* * *

I. Categorizing the Legal Regime

In order to analyze properly the impact of joint and several liability on settlement, one must specify with care each of the components of the competing legal rules. We first categorize such rules by reference to eight elements. We then show why our taxonomy eliminates some of the confusion reflected in judicial decisions.

A. A Taxonomy

For each of the eight elements that we use to define the legal regime governing the litigation of claims involving joint tortfeasors, we discuss the major alternatives. We focus principally on the approaches of the Restatement (Second) of Torts (Restatement), the Uniform Contribution Among Tortfeasors Act (UCATA), and the Uniform Comparative Fault Act (UCFA). In the margin, we consider federal common law rules developed under some important federal statutes.

1. Joint and Several Liability Versus Non-Joint (Several Only) Liability

Under joint and several liability, if the plaintiff litigates against two defendants and prevails against only one, it can recover its full damages from that defendant. In contrast, under non-joint (several only) liability, the plaintiff would only recover the portion of the damages attributable to the actions of the losing defendant.

The Restatement calls for the application of joint and several liability where damages "cannot be apportioned among two or more causes." The comments add that "where two or more causes combine to produce . . . a single result, incapable of division on any logical or reasonable basis, and each is a substantial factor in bringing about the harm, the courts have refused to make an arbitrary apportionment for its own sake, and each of the causes is charged with responsibility for the entire harm." As an example, the Restatement provides the case of two automobiles driven negligently that hit a bystander; the two drivers would be jointly and severally liable to the bystander.

The Restatement has been influential in the development of federal common law. For example, under CERCLA, relying explicitly on the Restatement's provisions, the courts have fashioned a rule of joint and several liability where the harm caused by the presence of hazardous substances at a site is "indivisible."

The remaining elements set forth in this Section are relevant only for joint and several liability. Under non-joint liability, the plaintiff essentially has independent claims against the defendants, and the questions discussed below do not arise.

2. The Right of Contribution

A right of contribution permits a defendant that has paid a disproportionately large share of the plaintiff's liability to obtain compensation from a defendant that has paid a disproportionately small share of this liability. Under the Restatement, there is a right of contribution among defendants found jointly and severally liable for a single harm. Both the UCATA and UCFA also recognize such a right.

The Restatement, the UCATA, and the UCFA thus reject the traditional common law rule, generally traced to Merryweather v. Nixan, barring contribution among defendants found jointly and severally liable for a harm. This common law rule has been rejected by the federal courts under their common law powers, as well as by the vast majority of states.

3. The Nature of the Right of Contribution

Under the UCATA, contribution is determined by reference to pro rata shares of the liability. Contribution is available only to a tortfeasor that has paid more than its pro rata share of the liability. In turn, contribution is not available from a tortfeasor that has paid at least its pro rata share of the liability. Thus, if two defendants are jointly and severally liable, contribution is available only to a defendant that has paid more than half of the liability, and the comparative levels of fault play no role in the determination of whether contribution is available.

In contrast, under the UCFA and the Restatement, contribution is determined by reference to comparative fault. The Restatement further provides that a defendant can avail itself of this right only if it has paid more than its equitable share of the liability. Moreover, no defendant can be required to contribute beyond its equitable share. The comparative fault approach is the rule generally adopted under federal common law and in most state jurisdictions.

4. The Choice of Set-Off Rule

The question of an appropriate set-off rule arises when the plaintiff settles with one defendant and litigates against the other. The UCATA provides that in the event of a settlement with one defendant, the plaintiff's claim against the non-settling defendant is reduced "to the extent of any amount stipulated by the release or the covenant, or in the amount of the consideration paid for it, whichever is greater." This rule is commonly referred to as a pro tanto set-off rule.

In contrast, under the UCFA, the plaintiff's claim is reduced by the settling defendant's "equitable share of the obligation." We refer to this rule as the apportioned share set-off rule. Note that while under the UCFA the apportioned share set-off rule is coupled with contribution by reference to comparative fault, one could have an apportioned share set-off rule in a legal regime in which contribution was determined pro rata. Then, the plaintiff's claim against a non-settling defendant would be reduced by the pro rata share attributable to the settling defendant. In both cases, the plaintiff's claim is reduced by the amount that would have been attributable to the settling defendant if both defendants had litigated and lost. For this reason, we find the term "apportioned share set-off rule" more revealing than the terms "proportional" set-off rule or "comparative fault" set-off rule, which are generally employed by the courts.

The Restatement addresses the issue of set-off rules in two separate places. Section 885(3) provides that "a payment by any person made in compensation of a claim for a harm for which others are liable as tortfeasors diminishes the claim against the tortfeasors, at least to the extent of the payment made." This section thus provides that the set-off would be no less than that provided under the pro tanto set-off rule. The Restatement's comments to section 886A, however, describe both the pro tanto and apportioned share set-off rules, but do not endorse either rule.

As indicated above, the federal courts are deeply divided on the choice between these two set-off rules. This split exists not only across statutory schemes, but also within a single scheme.

The two set-off rules differ in their effect on the plaintiff's recovery when it settles with one defendant and prevails in litigation against the other. Under the pro tanto set-off rule, the plaintiff recovers its full damages regardless of the amount of the settlement. Under the apportioned share set-off rule, if the settlement is for less than the settling defendant's apportioned share of the liability, the plaintiff does not recover its full damages even if it prevails against the other defendant.

Consider an example in which contribution is determined by reference to comparative fault, the two defendants are each equally at fault, and the plaintiff's damages are $100. If the plaintiff settles with one defendant for $20, under the apportioned share set-off rule it can recover only $50 from the other defendant, thus suffering a shortfall of $30. What happens, however, if the settlement is for $70? Can the plaintiff nonetheless recover $50 from the non-settling defendant? Most jurisdictions allow such recovery, as do the federal courts under the securities laws. The reasoning is that because under the apportioned share set-off rule the plaintiff bears the risk of a low settlement, it should obtain the benefit of a high settlement. In contrast, New York follows a constrained version of the apportioned set-off rule — limiting the plaintiff's total recovery to its damages in the event that it settles with one defendant and litigates against the other.

The preceding discussion assumes that there is a right of contribution. In the absence of such a right, there also is a question about how a settlement with one defendant should affect the plaintiff's claim against the non-settling defendant. The most logical approach in that instance is to use a pro tanto set-off rule. Without a right of contribution, if the plaintiff litigates and prevails against both defendants, it can choose to obtain its full damages from one of the defendants, despite the resulting unfairness. It is not clear why one should be more concerned about this unfairness when the plaintiff settles with one defendant and litigates against the other. We are not aware of any jurisdiction that has coupled a rule of no contribution with an apportioned share set-off rule.

5. Contribution Protection for Settling Defendants

Of course, in the absence of a general right of contribution, settling defendants, like all other defendants, are protected from contribution actions. In contrast, regimes that recognize the right of contribution between defendants found jointly and severally liable at trial must answer the further question whether a contribution action can be maintained against a settling defendant.

When one defendant settles, and the other litigates and ultimately loses, the question whether the settling defendant is protected from contribution actions arises only for the pro tanto set-off rule, under which it is possible that the litigating defendant will be liable for more than its equitable share of the liability. Under the apportioned share set-off rule, the litigating defendant never has to pay more than its equitable share of the liability and therefore never has the right to maintain a contribution action.

In contrast, when the plaintiff settles with both defendants, and one of them pays more than its equitable share of the liability while the other pays less than its share, the question whether the former defendant can bring a contribution action against the latter arises under both set-off rules. The resolution depends both on whether settling defendants are protected from contribution actions, which is the focus of this Subsection, and on whether settling defendants have the right to bring contribution actions, to which we turn in the next Subsection.

The Restatement presents examples of legal rules with and without contribution protection for settling defendants, but it does not endorse either option. The UCATA provides that if a settlement is entered in good faith, "it discharges the tortfeasor to whom it is given from all liability for contribution to any other tortfeasor." The UCFA provides that a settlement discharges that defendant "from all liability for contribution." Thus, while the Restatement neither approves nor disapproves of it, both model laws provide for contribution protection, though the UCATA qualifies this protection by limiting it to settlements entered in good faith.

2. LITIGANT REPONSES

a. The *Mary Carter* Agreement

J. D. BOOTH v. MARY CARTER PAINT CO.

202 So. 2d 8 (Fla. Dist. Ct. App. 1967)

PER CURIAM

Appellant, J. D. Booth, in his complaint charged the defendants with the negligent operation of their motor vehicles which resulted in the death of his wife. Defendants' answer denied the charge of negligence. Trial was had and the jury returned a verdict in the amount of $15,000 for the plaintiff. The trial court denied appellant's motion for a new trial and he brings this appeal seeking a new trial primarily on the question of damages only.

This action at law was previously before this Court in the case styled Booth v. Mary Carter Paint Company, reported in 182 So. 2d 292. The facts reported in the opinion of that case should be reviewed in order to more fully understand the facts established in the trial of the case sub judice. . . .

An agreement between William T. Keen of the firm of Shackleford, Farrior, Stallings, Glos & Evans, as counsel of record for the defendants, B. C. Willoughby and Harry Lee Sutton, and Mark R. Hawes, of the firm of Hawes and Hadden, counsel of record for the plaintiff, J. D. Booth, provides:

> 1. That the maximum liability, exposure or financial contribution of the defendants, B. C. Willoughby and Harry Lee Sutton, shall be $12,500.00.

The agreement further provides:

> Second, that in the event of a joint verdict against Willoughby and the Mary Carter Paint Company exceeding $37,500.00, that the plaintiff will satisfy said judgment against Mary Carter Paint Company entirely, with no contribution from Willoughby and Sutton. Provided, however, that if the Mary Carter Paint Company is not financially responsible to the extent of $37,500.00, the defendant Willoughby will contribute an amount of money between Mary Carter Paint Company's actual responsibility and the figure of $37,500.00, but not to exceed $12,500.00.
>
> Third, Willoughby and Sutton agreed that in the event of a verdict for all the defendants, they would pay the plaintiff $12,500.00; and in the event of a verdict against Mary Carter Paint Company less than $37,500.00, that Willoughby and Sutton would contribute the sum of $12,500.00.
>
> Fourth, Willoughby and Sutton shall continue as active defendants in the active defense of said litigation until all questions of liability and damages are resolved between the plaintiff and the other defendants.
>
> Fifth, that should the conditions laid down in the agreement result in any financial responsibility on the part of Willoughby and Sutton, they will pay the plaintiff within five days after the questions of liability and damages between the plaintiff and the other defendants are settled or concluded.

In paragraph 6 we again find the provision that the financial responsibility, exposure or liability of Willoughby and Sutton shall not exceed the sum of $12,500.00.

Seventh, it is stated:

> It is the intention of the parties hereto that this agreement shall be construed as a conditional agreement between them as to financial responsibility only, and that it shall in no wise constitute, or be construed to constitute, a release, settlement, admission of liability, or otherwise, and shall have no effect upon the trial of this case as to liability or extent of damages, nor shall said agreement be revealed to the jury trying said case.

Eighth, it was agreed that the contents of this agreement would be furnished to no one, unless so ordered by the court, and

Ninth, that the terms and conditions specified in the agreement, which are dependent upon a jury verdict, should be equally applicable to and binding on the parties in the event plaintiff Booth amicably settles the issues of liability and damages with Mary Carter Paint Company.

This instrument was signed by Mark R. Hawes of Hawes and Hadden, attorneys for the plaintiff Booth, and William T. Farrior of Shackleford, Farrior, Stallings, Glos & Evans, attorneys for B. C. Willoughby and Harry Lee Sutton.

The appellees, Mary Carter Paint Company, Hancock and Tompkins, in their brief state a Fourth Point as follows:

> Whether or not the trial court erred in failing to construe the Agreement between William T. Keen as counsel of record for the Defendants Willoughby and Sutton, and Mark R. Hawes as counsel of record for the Plaintiff Booth, as a release, and in denying the ore tenus motion of Defendants Mary Carter Paint Company, Hancock and Tompkins to offset the $12,500.00 consideration being paid by Defendants Willoughby and Sutton to Plaintiff Booth under the terms of said Agreement, as provided by Section 54.28, Florida Statutes?

We hold that the instrument hereinabove discussed was not a release and that the lower court did not err in denying the ore tenus motion of defendants Mary Carter Paint Company, Tompkins and Hancock to offset the $12,500.00 consideration being paid by the defendants Willoughby and Sutton to be plaintiff Booth under the terms of said agreement, as provided by Section 54,28. Fla. Stats., F.S.A.

No cases on point were cited by the appellees and we have failed to find any. We think the instrument is what it purports to be, an agreement that would limit the liability of defendants Willoughby and Sutton to pay a sum not exceeding $12,500.00 and which would guarantee the plaintiff the sum of $12,500.00 if any verdict was secured for less than $37,500.00.

We do not think the errors raised by the parties need be discussed and we specifically deny each of the same and affirm the lower court.

Affirmed.

b. *Mary Carter* Attacked and Defended

DOSDOURIAN V. CARSTEN

624 So. 2d 241 (Fla. 1993)

GRIMES, Judge.

We review Dosdourian v. Carsten, 580 So. 2d 869 (Fla. 4th DCA 1991), in which the court certified the following question as being of great public importance:

> Is a non-settling defendant entitled to have the jury informed of a settlement agreement between the plaintiff and another defendant whereby the settling defendant's obligation is fixed but the settling defendant is required to continue in the law suit?

Id. at 872. We have jurisdiction under article V, section 3(b)(4) of the Florida Constitution.

Richard Paul Carsten brought suit against Patricia Dosdourian and Christine DeMario alleging that each of them had negligently operated their automobiles in such a manner as to cause him serious personal injuries. Shortly before trial, Carsten filed a motion in limine seeking to prevent disclosure to the jury that he had entered into an agreement under which he settled all claims against DeMario in return for payment of her insurance policy limits of $100,000 and her continued participation in the litigation through trial and judgment. The trial judge granted Carsten's motion by ruling that the agreement would not be disclosed to the jury unless the live testimony of DeMario was presented at trial. In that event, the matter could be addressed on cross-examination. Further, the judge ruled that Dosdourian could not raise matters pertaining to the agreement if it was Dosdourian who called DeMario as a witness during trial. In the face of this ruling, Dosdourian moved that DeMario be dismissed from the litigation. This motion was denied.

At the trial, Carsten introduced DeMario's deposition, which had been taken before the settlement was reached. Because DeMario did not personally testify at the trial, the jury was not made aware of the settlement agreement between Carsten and DeMario. . . .

In deciding this case, it became necessary for us to consider in depth the ramifications of *Mary Carter* agreements and the effect such agreements have on the trial process. As a consequence, this Court asked the parties to submit supplemental briefs with respect to the continuing viability of *Mary Carter* agreements and permitted the filing of amicus curiae briefs on the subject. We now conclude that the time has come to do away with *Mary Carter* agreements.

Unique to the scheme of *Mary Carter* agreements, settling defendants retain their influence upon the outcome of the lawsuit from which they settled: so-called settling defendants continue "defending" their case. Defendants who have allegedly settled remain parties throughout the negligence suit, even through trial. As a consequence, these defendants remain able to participate in jury selection. They present witnesses and cross-examine the witnesses of the plaintiff by leading questions. They argue to the trial court the merits and demerits of motions and evidentiary objections. Most significantly, the party status of settling defendants permits them to have their counsel argue points of influence before the jury.

In many instances, *Mary Carter* defendants may exert influences upon the adversarial process before a trial as well. They may, for example, share with a plaintiff work product previously (or subsequently, if the agreement remains secret) disclosed to them by a nonsettling defendant. The plaintiff and the settling defendant can combine their combatant energies far in advance and coerce nonsettling defendants, out of fear that they will be subject to an unfair trial, to settle for sums in excess of that which would otherwise be proportional to those defendants' fair shares of the burden.

By virtue of a *Mary Carter* agreement, settling defendants often acquire a substantial financial interest in a trial's outcome should the jury rule favorably for the plaintiff. For example, a settling defendant may agree to settle at some ceiling figure upon the condition that if the jury awards the plaintiff a judgment against the nonsettling defendant in excess of a certain amount, the settling defendant's settlement money is returned proportionately or perhaps entirely. In these instances, *Mary Carter* defendants desire to remain parties to the suit so that their counsel may influence the jury's verdict in favor of the plaintiff and against the nonsettling defendant.

Rather than cooperating with their codefendants to minimize the culpability of all defendants and to minimize the jury's assessment of plaintiff's damages, *Mary Carter* defendants offer to the plaintiff their counsel's services for the purpose of persuading the jury to apportion to nonsettling defendants the greatest percentage of fault and to award the full amount of damages the plaintiff has requested. Even possible collusion between the plaintiff and the settling defendant creates an inherently unfair trial setting that could lead to an inequitable attribution of guilt and damages to the nonsettling defendant.

In addition, *Mary Carter* agreements, by their very nature, promote unethical practices by Florida attorneys. If a case goes to trial, the judge and jury are clearly presuming that the plaintiff and the settling defendant are adversaries and that the plaintiff is truly seeking a judgment for money damages against both defendants. In order to skillfully and successfully carry out the objectives of the *Mary Carter* agreement, the lawyer for the settling parties must necessarily make misrepresentations to the court and to the jury in order to maintain the charade of an adversarial relationship. These actions fly in the face of the attorney's promise to employ "means only as are consistent with truth and honor and [to] never seek to mislead the Judge or Jury by any artifice or false statement of fact or law." Oath of Admission to the Florida Bar, Florida Rules of Court 977 (West 1993). The Arizona State Bar Committee on Rules of Professional Conduct has expressly concluded that certain types of *Mary Carter* agreements contravene the canons of professional ethics concerned with representing conflicting interests, ensuring candor and fairness, taking technical advantage of opposing counsel, and pursuing unjustified litigation. Op. No. 70-18, Ariz. State Bar Committee on Rules of Prof. Conduct (1970). Some courts have even held that a *Mary Carter* agreement in which the settling defendant retains a financial interest in the plaintiff's success against the nonsettling defendant is champertous in character.

. . .

Some courts have done exactly what Professor Entman recommends by declaring *Mary Carter* agreements void as against public policy. . . .

The main argument in favor of *Mary Carter* agreements is that they promote settlement. However, while it is true that a *Mary Carter* agreement accomplishes a settlement with one of the defendants, the intent of the agreement is to proceed with the trial against the other. Some agreements even give the settling defendant veto authority over a prospective settlement with the other defendant. Therefore, the existence of *Mary Carter* agreements may result in an increased number of trials, and they certainly increase the likelihood of posttrial attacks on verdicts alleged to have been unfairly obtained as a result of such agreements. Of course, if the existence of the agreement is known, it is possible that the other defendant may feel compelled to also reach a settlement. However, in that event the remaining defendant may have been unfairly coerced into settling for more than his fair share of liability. . . .

We are convinced that the only effective way to eliminate the sinister influence of *Mary Carter* agreements is to outlaw their use. We include within our prohibition any agreement which requires the settling defendant to remain in the litigation, regardless of whether there is a specified financial incentive to do so.

We recognize that until this opinion *Mary Carter* agreements were legal in Florida, and we are loath to penalize those who have entered into such agreements. In some instances it might even be impossible to restore the parties to the status quo if such agreements were set aside. Therefore, our holding shall be prospective only and shall not affect the legality of any such agreements that have been entered into prior to the date of this opinion. Accordingly, we must decide the instant case upon the premise that the settlement agreement was legal.

It is so ordered.

Lisa Bernstein & Daniel Klerman, An Economic Analysis of Mary Carter Settlement Agreements

83 Georgetown Law Journal 2215 (1995)

This paper explores the social desirability of *Mary Carter* agreements, a type of settlement agreement used most commonly in suits against multiple tortfeasors. Under a typical *Mary Carter* agreement ("MCA") one defendant either guarantees the plaintiff a minimum recovery or extends him a loan that need only be repaid if, and to the extent that, the plaintiff recovers from the other defendants. Under such agreements, the settling defendant (the "*Mary Carter* defendant") often remains a party to the suit and is generally given the right to veto any settlement between the plaintiff and the other defendants.

Mary Carter agreements have been described as "settlement virus[es]," "unholy alliance[s]," and "contractual monstrosit[ies]." They have been prohibited in four jurisdictions, most recently in Texas and Florida, and are viewed with suspicion even in jurisdictions that permit them. Some courts and numerous commentators from both academia and the practicing bar have suggested that MCAs are against public policy because they encourage perjury, discourage settlement, and result in an unfair allocation of liability and damages among tortfeasors. They have also been criticized on the grounds that they are unethical and amount to champerty, barratry, and maintenance.

This article argues that contrary to the view of some courts and most commentators the use and availability of MCAs may have socially desirable effects in a variety of circumstances. It suggests that these agreements may increase the amount of information revealed during discovery and trial, may enable plaintiffs to finance meritorious suits that might not otherwise have been brought, and may allocate some of the risk of trial to those best able to bear it. It concludes that while MCAs do create some of the problems suggested by their critics, these problems have been overstated and it is important to recognize that such agreements may have offsetting benefits. As the analysis presented here suggests, in some circumstances MCAs may further the compensatory and deterrent functions of tort law without adversely affecting the settlement rate, distorting the fair allocation of liability among defendants, or compromising adjudicative accuracy.

* * *

I. *Mary Carter* Agreements

There are two basic types of MCAs. Under one type of MCA, the *Mary Carter* defendant extends a loan to the plaintiff that is only repayable if, and to the extent that, the plaintiff recovers from the nonsettling defendants. Under another type of MCA, the *Mary Carter* defendant guarantees the plaintiff a minimum recovery. The agreements are often structured as combinations of regular settlements and either guarantees or *Mary Carter* loans; when they are structured in this way they are referred to as hybrid MCAs. The guaranteed amount, or the extent of the loan repayment obligation, sometimes depends on whether the *Mary Carter* defendant and/or the nonsettling defendants are found liable. It is often linked to the amount of the plaintiff's recovery from the nonsettling defendants in complex ways. Some MCAs make the amount of the guaranty or the loan repayment obligation contingent on whether the case goes to trial or is settled. Others give the *Mary Carter* defendant a specified percentage of each dollar the plaintiff recovers up to the amount of the loan or guaranty. Under most MCAs, the *Mary Carter* defendant remains a defendant in the case. She is sometimes given the right to veto some or all settlements between the plaintiff and the other defendants.

Many early MCAs had provisions requiring the agreements to be kept secret. However, as MCAs came under greater judicial scrutiny, most courts held that they are both discoverable and at least partially admissible. As a result, secrecy provisions are no longer found in MCAs. . . .

II. Legitimate Reasons MCAs Are Used

Most courts and commentators maintain that parties enter into MCAs primarily to gain improper tactical advantages at trial. However, there are also a variety of legitimate reasons that parties might find it desirable to enter into such agreements. This Part explores three explanations for the use of MCAs—the information hypothesis, the financing hypothesis, and the risk allocation hypothesis.

A. Information Hypothesis

The use and availability of MCAs may enable plaintiffs to obtain recovery-enhancing information that would otherwise have remained hidden at the time of settlement or judgment. In a typical lawsuit, defendants have no incentive to voluntarily reveal information that would strengthen the plaintiff's case. Defendants generally have an incentive to withhold damaging evidence for as long as possible in the hope that they will be able to take advantage of this informational asymmetry to negotiate a favorable settlement or that they will succeed in concealing the information until after a trial judgment is entered. Adverse information is ordinarily disclosed only in response to narrowly tailored discovery requests or when a defendant or his attorney fears that not revealing the information will lead to the imposition of sanctions. A recent study of the discovery process found that attempts to conceal information are often successful. The study reported that in 39 percent of settled cases, defendants' lawyers "believed they still knew something significant about the case that opposing counsel had not discovered." It also found that even in cases that went to trial, defendants' lawyers thought they "knew something of consequence," that had not been revealed in 32 percent of their cases.

The use and availability of MCAs can increase the amount of information revealed in multidefendant lawsuits. As the examples below illustrate, entering into an MCA gives a defendant a way to reduce his own expected liability by revealing information that will increase the plaintiff's chance of prevailing. As a consequence, it is likely that defendants will reveal more adverse information if MCAs are available than they would if MCAs were unavailable. In this regard, an MCA is similar to a plea bargain in which the prosecutor promises to drop certain charges or to request a more lenient sentence if a defendant cooperates by providing information or testimony that will help to convict a codefendant.

Example

Consider a medical malpractice suit against a surgeon and an anesthesiologist. The issue, upon which liability turns, is whether the doctors followed the sponge count procedures in the hospital's surgical manual. These procedures require the surgeon to call out the number of each sponge inserted and extracted and for the anesthesiologist to say "check." Assume that the jurisdiction apportions liability according to relative fault, applies the proportionate share set-off rule, and that the plaintiff's damages are stipulated to be $10,000. Further assume that if the plaintiff prevails, the surgeon and anesthesiologist will each be apportioned 50% of the liability.

Suppose that the doctors failed to follow the procedures in the manual, but nevertheless plan to collude and testify that they followed the manual's procedures. If they testify as planned, the plaintiff's probability of prevailing would be only 25. . . .

In such a situation, if the plaintiff could enter into an enforceable agreement with one of the doctors, for example the surgeon, whereby the surgeon promised to testify truthfully at trial and the plaintiff promised to release his claim against her, both parties would be better off than they would have been in the absence of the agreement. The plaintiff's expected recovery would increase from $2,500 to $3,750, and the surgeon's expected liability would decrease from $1,250 to zero. The anesthesiologist's expected liability would be $3,750, exactly what it would have been had he testified truthfully at trial.

* * *

In such a situation, an MCA can be used to solve the negotiator's dilemma. As the example below illustrates, entering into an MCA gives the surgeon a way to credibly bind herself to testify as promised, while ensuring that her testimony will not be used to increase her expected liability. . . .

* * *

In the example presented above, once the MCA is entered into, the *Mary Carter* defendant's expected liability if she does not testify as promised will be even higher than it would have been had she never entered into the agreement. By entering into the MCA, she has, in effect, posted a performance bond. When the amount of the *Mary Carter* loan is set in the mutually beneficial loan range, even if the *Mary Carter* defendant decided to forgo the bond and withhold the promised information or testimony, the plaintiff's expected recovery would be greater than it would have been in the absence of the agreement. At a minimum, the plaintiff will be entitled to keep the *Mary Carter* loan even if he does not prevail. The agreement makes it rational for the plaintiff to release the *Mary Carter* defendant even before she has testified or been deposed. It solves the negotiator's dilemma by functioning as a combination of a performance bond and a guaranty.

* * *

2. Agency Costs

Agency costs are another reason that the *Mary Carter* loan amount may not be negotiated up to the top of the mutually advantageous loan range or bid up to its theoretical maximum in an auction. As the loan amount increases, the plaintiff's incentive to prevail at trial becomes weaker, and the interests of the *Mary Carter* defendant (principal) and the plaintiff (agent) become increasingly divergent.

Several common features of MCAs can be understood as partial solutions to this agency problem. Most agreements give the *Mary Carter* defendant the right to veto any settlement or any settlement below a specified amount between the plaintiff and the nonsettling defendant. The veto prevents the plaintiff from accepting a small settlement from the remaining defendant when litigation costs exceed the expected benefit of going to trial. It is also common for the agreements to include a provision requiring or permitting the *Mary Carter* defendant to remain in the case as a defendant. When the *Mary Carter* defendant remains in the case she can closely monitor the plaintiff's lawyer's management of the litigation and can introduce arguments and/or evidence at trial if the plaintiff's lawyer fails to do so.

A number of variations on the structure of the repayment clause also provide a partial solution to this agency problem. Some repayment clauses (known as "incentive clauses") specify that the plaintiff and the *Mary Carter* defendant are to share each dollar recovered in a fixed proportion. Others vary the proportion of each dollar recovered that each party receives depending on the size of the total recovery. By giving the plaintiff a share of each dollar recovered, these clauses help align the incentives of the plaintiff and the *Mary Carter* defendant.

* * *

3. Conclusion

Although courts and commentators have recognized that MCAs may induce the *Mary Carter* defendant to reveal information to the plaintiff, they view this as undesirable since they assume that the type of information the *Mary Carter* defendant will reveal is most likely to be perjured testimony or the work product of a codefendant's attorney.[59] However, as the examples presented here suggest, MCAs can also provide incentives for a defendant not to perjure herself or improperly withhold evidence in a situation where she would otherwise have had an incentive to do so. They may therefore have a beneficial effect on the amount of truthful information revealed. In addition, while critics of MCAs often argue that certain common features of MCAs — such as veto provisions, clauses requiring or permitting the *Mary Carter*

---

59. The information-revealing effect of MCAs was explicitly recognized by the Florida Supreme Court. *See* Dosdourian v. Cartsen, 624 So. 2d 241, 246 (Fla. 1993) (noting that MCAs "pressure the 'settling' defendant to alter the character of the suit by contributing discovery material"). The effect of MCAs on the aggregate amount of perjury is discussed in Part IIID *infra*.

defendant to remain in the case, and incentive clauses — can only be understood as attempts to gain improper tactical advantage at trial, the discussion presented here has suggested that these provisions can also be understood as sensible responses to the agency problems created by the agreements themselves.

V. Conclusion

This article has argued that, contrary to the view of most commentators and even those courts that permit their use, MCAs may be entered into for legitimate reasons. It has also suggested that while MCAs may have some of the undesirable effects identified by their critics, the use and availability of these agreements may also create off-setting benefits that should be taken into account in evaluating the social desirability of MCAs.

The analysis presented here also suggests that discussions of suit and settlement need to recognize that a simple monetary payment from one defendant to the plaintiff in exchange for release of the claim is only one of many forms that a settlement can take, and that the existence of MCAs, as well as other types of explicit agreements and implicit understandings between the plaintiff and less than all of the defendants, or among the defendants themselves, can have an important impact on the ways that legal rules affect parties' litigation decisions.

c. *Mary Carter* Refined

> ## Cal. Civ. Proc. Code §§877, 877.5, 877.6

(West 2004)

§877. Release of One or More Joint Tortfeasors or Co-Obligors; Effect upon Liability of Others

Where a release, dismissal with or without prejudice, or a covenant not to sue or not to enforce judgment is given in good faith before verdict or judgment to one or more of a number of tortfeasors claimed to be liable for the same tort, or to one or more other co-obligors mutually subject to contribution rights, it shall have the following effect:

(a) It shall not discharge any other such party from liability unless its terms so provide, but it shall reduce the claims against the others in the amount stipulated by the release, the dismissal or the covenant, or in the amount of the consideration paid for it whichever is the greater.

(b) It shall discharge the party to whom it is given from all liability for any contribution to any other parties.

(c) This section shall not apply to co-obligors who have expressly agreed in writing to an apportionment of liability for losses or claims among themselves.

(d) This section shall not apply to a release, dismissal with or without prejudice, or a covenant not to sue or not to enforce judgment given to a co-obligor on an alleged contract debt where the contract was made prior to January 1, 1988.

§877.5. Sliding Scale Recovery Agreement; Disclosure to Court and Jury; Service of Notice of Intent to Enter

(a) Where an agreement or covenant is made which provides for a sliding scale recovery agreement between one or more, but not all, alleged defendant tortfeasors and the plaintiff or plaintiffs:

(1) The parties entering into any such agreement or covenant shall promptly inform the court in which the action is pending of the existence of the agreement or covenant and its terms and provisions.

(2) If the action is tried before a jury, and a defendant party to the agreement is called as a witness at trial, the court shall, upon motion of a party, disclose to the jury the existence and content of the agreement or covenant, unless the court finds that this disclosure will create substantial danger of undue prejudice, of confusing the issues, or of misleading the jury.

The jury disclosure herein required shall be no more than necessary to inform the jury of the possibility that the agreement may bias the testimony of the witness.

(b) As used in this section, a "sliding scale recovery agreement" means an agreement or covenant between a plaintiff or plaintiffs and one or more, but not all, alleged tortfeasor defendants, which limits the liability of the agreeing tortfeasor defendants to an amount which is dependent upon the amount of recovery which the plaintiff is able to recover from the nonagreeing defendant or defendants. This includes, but is not limited to, agreements within the scope of Section 877, and agreements in the form of a loan from the agreeing tortfeasor defendant or defendants to the plaintiff or plaintiffs which is repayable in whole or in part from the recovery against the nonagreeing tortfeasor defendant or defendants.

(c) No sliding scale recovery agreement is effective unless, at least 72 hours prior to entering into the agreement, a notice of intent to enter into an agreement has been served on all nonsignatory alleged defendant tortfeasors. However, upon a showing of good cause, the court or a judge thereof may allow a shorter time. The failure to comply with the notice requirements of this subdivision shall not constitute good cause to delay commencement of trial.

§877.6. Determination of Good Faith of Settlement with One or More Tortfeasors or Co-Obligors; Review by Writ of Mandate; Tolling of Time Limitations

(a)(1) Any party to an action in which it is alleged that two or more parties are joint tortfeasors or co-obligors on a contract debt shall be entitled to a hearing on the issue of the good faith of a settlement entered into by the plaintiff or other claimant and one or more alleged tortfeasors or co-obligors, upon giving notice in the manner provided in subdivision (b) of Section 1005. Upon a showing of good cause, the court may shorten the time for giving the required notice to permit the determination of the issue to be made before the commencement of the trial of the action, or before the verdict or judgment if settlement is made after the trial has commenced.

(2) In the alternative, a settling party may give notice of settlement to all parties and to the court, together with an application for determination of good faith settlement and a proposed order. The application shall indicate the settling parties, and the basis, terms, and amount of the settlement. The notice, application, and proposed order shall be given by certified mail, return receipt requested. Proof of service shall be filed with the court. Within 25 days of the mailing of the notice, application, and proposed order, or within 20 days of personal service, a nonsettling party may file a notice of motion to contest the good faith of the settlement. If none of the nonsettling parties files a motion within 25 days of mailing of the notice, application, and proposed order, or within 20 days of personal service, the court may approve the settlement. The notice by a nonsettling party shall be given in the manner provided in subdivision (b) of Section 1005. However, this paragraph shall not apply to settlements in which a confidentiality agreement has been entered into regarding the case or the terms of the settlement.

(b) The issue of the good faith of a settlement may be determined by the court on the basis of affidavits served with the notice of hearing, and any counteraffidavits filed in response, or the court may, in its discretion, receive other evidence at the hearing.

(c) A determination by the court that the settlement was made in good faith shall bar any other joint tortfeasor or co-obligor from any further claims against the settling tortfeasor or co-obligor for equitable comparative contribution, or partial or comparative indemnity, based on comparative negligence or comparative fault.

(d) The party asserting the lack of good faith shall have the burden of proof on that issue.

(e) When a determination of the good faith or lack of good faith of a settlement is made, any party aggrieved by the determination may petition the proper court to review the determination by writ of mandate. The petition for writ of mandate shall be filed within 20 days after service of written notice of the determination, or within any additional time not exceeding 20 days as the trial court may allow.

(1) The court shall, within 30 days of the receipt of all materials to be filed by the parties, determine whether or not the court will hear the writ and notify the parties of its determination.

(2) If the court grants a hearing on the writ, the hearing shall be given special precedence over all other civil matters on the calendar of the court except those matters to which equal or greater precedence on the calendar is granted by law.

(3) The running of any period of time after which an action would be subject to dismissal pursuant to the applicable provisions of Chapter 1.5 (commencing with Section 583.110) of Title 8 of Part 2 shall be tolled during the period of review of a determination pursuant to this subdivision.

SUGGESTED FORMS:

West's Cal. Code Forms, Civ. Pro. §877.6—Form 5 (5TH ED).
NOTICE OF MOTION CONTESTING GOOD FAITH SETTLEMENT
[TITLE OF COURT AND CASE]

TO: _____, PLAINTIFF [DEFENDANT], AND TO _____, HIS/HER
ATTORNEY: YOU AND EACH OF YOU WILL PLEASE TAKE NOTICE THAT AT
THE ABOVE-STATED DATE, TIME AND LOCATION PLAINTIFF [DEFENDANT]
WILL MOVE THE COURT TO CONDUCT A HEARING TO DETERMINE
WHETHER A SETTLEMENT WAS ENTERED INTO IN GOOD FAITH. THIS
MOTION WILL BE MADE ON THE GROUND THAT _____, WILL BE
BASED UPON THE PROVISIONS OF CALIFORNIA CODE OF CIVIL PRO-
CEDURE SECTION 877.6, UPON THE AFFIDAVIT [OR DECLARATION]
OF _____, AND ALL PAPERS, RECORDS AND DOCUMENTS ON FILE HEREIN
AND UPON EVIDENCE, ORAL AND DOCUMENTARY, TO BE PRESENTED AT
THE HEARING OF THIS MOTION.

DATED: _____
ATTORNEY FOR PLAINTIFF [DEFENDANT]
West's Cal. Code Forms, Civ. Pro. §877.6—Form 3 (5TH ED).
RELEASE—FINDING OF GOOD FAITH SETTLEMENT

[TITLE OF COURT AND CASE]

The hearing on the good faith of a settlement in the above-entitled action
having come on regularly before the undersigned on _____ *[Date]*,
upon notice duly and regularly given, _____ appearing as Attorney
for Plaintiff and _____ appearing as Attorney for Defendant, and
documentary and oral evidence having been received and the matter having
been submitted, and good cause appearing therefor,

IT IS THE FINDING of this Court that the settlement between
_____, Plaintiff, and _____, Defendant, was and is made
in good faith.

Dated: _____
Judge of the Superior Court

ABBOTT FORD, INC. v. THE SUPERIOR COURT OF LOS ANGELES COUNTY

741 P.2d 124 (Cal. 1987)

PANELLI, J.

The issue presented here is whether a "sliding scale recovery agreement,"[1]
entered into by plaintiffs and one of several defendants in a personal injury
action, represents a "good faith" settlement within the meaning of sections

---

1. [Citation to] Section 877.5, subdivision (b) of the Code of Civil Procedure . . .

As noted below, in the legal literature and in other jurisdictions such agreements are commonly known as "Mary Carter" agreements. (See fn. 9, post.) For convenience, we shall generally
refer to such agreements simply as sliding scale agreements.

877 and 877.6 of the Code of Civil Procedure,[2] so as to relieve the settling defendant of any liability for contribution or equitable comparative indemnity to other defendants in the action. The trial court concluded that the agreement in question was not a good faith settlement and denied the settling defendant's motion to bar cross-complaints by the remaining defendants. The settling defendant then sought review by writ of mandate, and ultimately the Court of Appeal—after remand by this court—concluded that while the "good faith" of such a sliding scale agreement must properly be measured by the standard set forth in our recent decision in Tech-Bilt, Inc. v. Woodward-Clyde & Associates (1985) 38 Cal. 3d 488 [213 Cal. Rptr. 256, 698 P.2d 159], the agreement at issue here satisfied that standard as a matter of law. We granted review to consider the question of the appropriate application of the statutory "good faith" requirement in the context of sliding scale agreements.

I.

To place the issue in perspective, we review the facts and the litigation background as revealed by the declarations and other materials that were presented to the trial court in connection with its hearing on the good faith settlement question.

The underlying personal injury action in this case arose out of a somewhat unusual automobile accident that occurred on September 10, 1981. At the time of the accident, Ramsey Sneed was driving a used 1979 Ford Econoline van that he had purchased from Abbott Ford, Inc. (Abbott). As Sneed was driving, the left rear wheel came off the van and crashed into the windshield of an on-coming car, a 1965 Mercury station wagon driven by Phyllis Smith. The windshield shattered and Smith suffered serious injuries, including the loss of sight in both eyes and the loss of her sense of smell.

Thereafter, Smith and her husband (hereafter plaintiffs) filed the underlying lawsuit against four defendants—(1) Sneed, (2) Abbott, (3) Ford Motor Company (Ford) and (4) Sears, Roebuck & Co. (Sears)—seeking recovery on a variety of theories. Plaintiffs' mandatory settlement conference statement—prepared after considerable discovery—summarized the case against each defendant as follows:

(1) With regard to Sneed, plaintiffs claimed that he had been negligent in the maintenance and operation of his van, and had continued to drive the vehicle after hearing sounds indicating that there might be some difficulty with the wheels.

(2) With regard to Abbott—a car dealer which had purchased the van used, had "customized" it by replacing the original wheels and tires with "deep dish mag wheels" and oversized tires, and had then resold it to Sneed—plaintiffs sought recovery on both negligence and strict liability theories. With regard to the negligence claim, discovery revealed that Ford, the manufacturer of the van, had provided a warning in its owner's manual—which Abbott received—cautioning against the installation of "aftermarket

---

2. Unless otherwise noted, all section references are to the Code of Civil Procedure.

wheel assemblies," like the "deep dish mag wheels," on the van. Despite the warning, Abbott had installed the customized wheel assembly, had failed to give the owner's manual or provide any other warning to Sneed, and had failed to advise Sneed of the need to retighten the lug nuts on the wheel assembly periodically because of their tendency to become loose.

(3) With regard to Ford—which had manufactured both the van and the station wagon involved in the accident—plaintiffs claimed that liability could be posited on the basis of Ford's relationship with each vehicle. With respect to the van, plaintiffs relied on both strict liability and negligence theories, suggesting that, notwithstanding the warning provided in its owner's manual, Ford should have reasonably foreseen that potentially dangerous aftermarket wheel assemblies would be installed and should have taken further steps— such as attaching a warning against such installation to the vehicle itself—to minimize the problem. With respect to the station wagon, plaintiffs alleged that a defect in the design of the windshield led it to shatter on impact by the wheel and tire, aggravating plaintiffs' injuries.

(4) Finally, with regard to Sears—which had serviced the van three months before the accident—plaintiffs claimed that while Sears' service records indicated that Sneed had neither requested nor been charged for a brake check, Sneed had in fact requested such a check and Sears' employees had either negligently replaced the wheels on the van or had negligently failed to conduct an inspection which would have revealed the looseness of the lug nuts. . . .

With the case in this posture, a mandatory settlement conference was set for March 26, 1984. In anticipation of that conference, representatives of Abbott, Ford and Sears met on March 14, 1984.[4] At that meeting, Abbott's counsel stated that he believed a reasonable settlement value for the case was $2.5 million and that Abbott was willing to contribute 70 percent of that sum.[5] Counsel for Ford and Sears, however, maintained that their clients had only minimal, if any, responsibility for the accident and were unwilling to bear 30 percent—$750,000—of such a settlement.

At about the same time, plaintiffs offered to settle with Ford or Sears if they would enter into a sliding scale agreement guaranteeing plaintiffs $1.5 million. Both Ford and Sears declined the offer.

On March 23, 1984, three days before the settlement conference, plaintiffs filed their "mandatory settlement conference statement" setting forth the facts of the case, their theories of liability against all parties, and their expected recovery. With respect to liability, the statement concluded: "The liability of Abbott Ford in this case is clear on either a products liability theory or on a negligence theory because Abbott Ford modified the van with unsafe, defective after-market wheels and tires notwithstanding Ford's warning to the contrary. Ford's and Sears' liability is not as clear as Abbott Ford's, but it is for the jury to decide whether they should be held accountable for this accident. The liability of Sneed is also clear because he had the last opportunity to avoid the accident." With respect to damages, the statement declared that—on the basis of a

---

4. There was no objection at the good faith hearing to the court's consideration of evidence relating to the settlement negotiations of the parties.

5. Abbott's liability insurance policy provided coverage of $3.25 million.

detailed review of damage awards in numerous cases involving similar injuries—"[p]laintiffs expect a favorable verdict in this case in an amount not less than $3,000,000."

Three days later, at the mandatory settlement conference, Abbott's insurer announced that it had agreed in principle to enter into a sliding scale agreement with plaintiffs, guaranteeing plaintiffs a recovery of $3 million. Several months later, plaintiffs and Abbott's insurer formally entered into the sliding scale agreement that is the focus of the present proceeding.

The agreement—which took the form of two separate contracts, one with each plaintiff, twenty-two and twenty pages in length respectively—contained three key and interrelated elements: (1) Abbott's insurer guaranteed Phyllis Smith an ultimate recovery of $2.9 million, and her husband an ultimate recovery of $100,000; if, at the conclusion of the lawsuit, plaintiffs had not collected the guaranteed amounts from the remaining defendants, Abbott's insurer would pay the balance up to the guaranteed sum. Thus, if plaintiffs recovered $3 million or more from Ford and Sears, Abbott would not bear any ultimate liability to plaintiffs; if plaintiffs recovered less than $3 million from Ford and Sears, Abbott would be obligated to pay plaintiffs the difference. In return for these guaranties, plaintiffs agreed (a) to dismiss all of their actions against Abbott and (b) to continue to prosecute their action against Ford and Sears[6] in the same way that they would have in the absence of the agreement—through appeal, if necessary—"except that [plaintiffs] shall not settle all or any portion of this litigation with defendants Ford and Sears Roebuck for less than the amount of [their] guaranty, without the express written consent of" Abbott's insurer.

(2) In addition to providing the guaranties, Abbott's insurer agreed to make substantial, periodic no-interest loans to plaintiffs and their attorneys during the course of the litigation. Under the agreement, a total of $390,000 in interest-free loans had been made to plaintiffs and their attorneys by January 1986, and Abbott's insurer was obligated to pay plaintiffs and attorneys the full $3 million—in the form of a loan—by July 1, 1987, if plaintiffs' action had not been terminated by then. The agreement provided that the loan payments would serve as credits for the insurer's obligations under the guaranty provision; if plaintiffs collected $3 million or more from Ford and Sears, plaintiffs were obligated to repay the loans in full—but without interest—to Abbott's insurer.

(3) Finally, the agreement contained an additional provision under which the insurer agreed to pay plaintiffs the full $3 million outright if the agreements were found to be invalid or not in good faith.

On August 30, 1984, a few months after the sliding scale agreement was signed, Abbott moved in the trial court pursuant to section 877.6 for an order declaring the agreement to be in good faith and dismissing all claims against Abbott for contribution or comparative indemnity. Both Ford and Sears opposed the motion, arguing, inter alia, (1) that sliding scale agreements, by their nature, cannot constitute good faith settlements within the meaning of

---

6. The settlement agreements disclose that plaintiffs had previously settled their case against Sneed for $25,000, the amount of Sneed's liability insurance.

the relevant statutes, and (2) that, in any event, the settlement agreement at issue here was not a good faith settlement because "the settlement price is potentially grossly disproportionate to Abbott Ford's fair share of the damages."

On September 10, 1984, the trial court held a hearing on Abbott's section 877.6 motion. At the conclusion of the hearing, the court entered a minute order denying Abbott's request to have the agreement declared a good faith settlement so as to bar Ford's and Sears' indemnity cross-complaints against it. The court's order stated that its determination was based "on the fact that Abbott Ford has not paid any amount in settlement and that the guarantee agreement does not constitute a settlement, but rather constitutes a gambling transaction."

Abbott thereafter sought review of the trial court's order in the present writ proceeding, as authorized by section 877.6, subdivision (e). The Court of Appeal issued an alternative writ and, relying on a line of Court of Appeal decisions which had interpreted the "good faith" standard of sections 877 and 877.6 to require simply that settling parties refrain from "tortious or other wrongful conduct" (*see, e.g.,* Dompeling v. Superior Court (1981) 117 Cal. App. 3d 798, 809-810), concluded that the agreement in this case was a good faith settlement as a matter of law. Thereafter, we granted a hearing and retained the matter while we considered the general question of the appropriate interpretation of the "good faith" settlement standard. In Tech-Bilt, Inc. v. Woodward-Clyde & Associates, *supra,* 38 Cal. 3d 488 (hereafter *Tech-Bilt*), we disapproved the lines of cases that had been relied on by the Court of Appeal in its earlier decision in this case, finding that those cases had adopted an improperly narrow view of "good faith." We concluded that "[a] more appropriate definition of 'good faith,' in keeping with the policies of American Motorcycle [Assn. v. Superior Court (1978) 20 Cal. 3d 578 (146 Cal. Rptr. 182, 578 P.2d 899)] and the statute, would enable the trial court to inquire, among other things, whether the amount of the settlement is within the reasonable range of the settling tortfeasor's proportional share of comparative liability for the plaintiff's injuries." (38 Cal. 3d at p. 499.) Thereafter, we remanded this matter to the Court of Appeal, directing the court to consider "whether and to what extent the principles enunciated in *Tech-Bilt* . . . may be applicable to an agreement of [the] type [involved in this case.]"

On remand, the Court of Appeal concluded that the "good faith" standard embodied in *Tech-Bilt* does apply to sliding scale agreements. Nonetheless, the court found that even under the *Tech-Bilt* standard the agreement at issue here constituted a good faith settlement as a matter of law. We again granted review to consider the important and difficult issues presented by the case.

II.

(2) As Ford and Sears point out, sliding scale — or, as they are more commonly known throughout the country, "Mary Carter" — agreements have engendered a considerable body of academic commentary, much quite critical of this genre of settlement agreements.[10]

---

10. The titles of many of the law review articles make this quite clear. (See, *e.g.,* [citing thirteen articles with such titles as "The Expected Demise of 'Mary Carter': She Never Was Well," suggesting disapproval of the concept].)

The majority of out-of-state decisions have, however, declined either to condemn or condone such agreements and, for a number of reasons, we believe such a cautious approach to the problems posed by sliding scale agreements is appropriate. First, an enormous variety of contractual arrangements fall within the general rubric of sliding scale or Mary Carter agreements. Although in all such agreements the settling defendant's ultimate liability to the plaintiff is dependent, at least in part, on the amount of money which the plaintiff recovers from the nonsettling defendants, there are a virtually unlimited number of additional provisions that may be included in such agreements—for example, provisions which mandate secrecy, restrict settlement with the remaining defendants, or provide various forms of financing for the plaintiff's action—that will often substantially affect the operation and validity of the agreements.[11] These differences caution against hasty overgeneralization of the merits or demerits of sliding scale agreements as a class.

Second, in addition to the variety of provisions that may supplement the sliding scale or "guaranty" clause of such agreements, the content and effect of the sliding scale provision itself and the factual background against which the agreement is negotiated frequently vary significantly from case to case. In some cases, like this one, the sliding scale clause may be structured so that the settling party may ultimately bear no liability to the plaintiff; in other cases, the settling party may make a substantial noncontingent payment to the plaintiff, and the sliding scale element may simply provide a supplemental guaranty of some additional recovery.[12] In some cases, again like this one, the guaranty figure may be for an amount equal or close to the plaintiff's total damages; in others, the guaranty figure may represent only a relatively small share of the plaintiff's damages. In some cases, the settling defendant who may potentially be relieved of all liability by virtue of the agreement may be clearly the most culpable of all of the defendants, while in other cases a sliding scale agreement may be entered into by only peripherally involved defendants in order to obtain an escape from a potentially lengthy and costly suit. Finally, in some cases a sliding scale agreement may be obtained by one defendant in the early stages of negotiation without regard to the willingness of other defendants to engage in settlement negotiations in good faith, while in others such an agreement may be resorted to only as a last resort, after one or more defendants unreasonably refuse to make any settlement offer that may be commensurate with their fair share of responsibility for the plaintiff's damages, thwarting a fair and complete settlement of the litigation. These differences too may have a significant bearing on the fairness and propriety of a particular agreement.

Third, and finally, a broad ruling on the inherent validity or invalidity of sliding scale agreements "in general" is inappropriate because such agreements

---

11. As one court observed: "[T]he number of variations of the so-called 'Mary Carter Agreement' is limited only by the ingenuity of counsel and the willingness of the parties to sign." (Maule Industries, Inc. v. Rountree, *supra*, 264 So. 2d 445, 447).

12. In *Dompeling*, the settling defendant made a noncontingent payment of $100,000—the limits of his insurance policy—and guaranteed plaintiff up to an additional $10,000 under a sliding scale arrangement. In *Torres*, the settling defendant made a noncontingent payment of $50,000 and provided an additional $150,000 guaranty on a sliding scale basis.

may have a variety of effects at different stages of the litigation process — discovery, settlement, trial or appeal. The potential problems posed by a particular provision in such an agreement may call for one remedy — e.g., disclosure of the agreement to the nonagreeing parties or to the jury — in one context, and another remedy — e.g., invalidation of a specific provision, or the agreement as a whole — in a different context. Thus, analysis requires close attention to the specific provisions of the agreement itself, the factual setting in which the agreement is entered into, and the agreement's effect on the particular aspect of the judicial process at issue.

In the present case, the question before us is not the broad one of the validity of sliding scale agreements in general, but the more limited question of whether the sliding scale agreement at issue here should properly be considered a "good faith" settlement under the relevant statutory provisions so as to absolve Abbott from any liability for contribution or indemnity to the remaining codefendants, Ford and Sears. As we shall see, that issue in itself raises a number of complex questions.

III.

As we explained in our recent decision in *Tech-Bilt*, the provisions of sections 877 and 877.6 — governing the effect that a settlement agreement has on a settling defendant's potential liability to other defendants for contribution or comparative indemnity — have two major goals: the equitable sharing of costs among the parties at fault and the encouragement of settlements.[15] The provisions of section 877 make it quite clear that the two goals are inextricably linked. Section 877 establishes that a good faith settlement bars other defendants from seeking contribution from the settling defendant (§877, subd. (b)), but at the same time provides that the plaintiff's claims against the other defendants are to be reduced by "the amount of consideration paid for" the settlement (§877, subd. (a)). Thus, while a good faith settlement cuts off the right of other defendants to seek contribution or comparative indemnity from the settling defendant, the nonsettling defendants obtain in return a reduction in their ultimate liability to the plaintiff.

Tech-Bilt recognized that the "good faith" requirement of sections 877 and 877.6 is the key to the harmonization of the twin statutory objectives. "The good faith provision of section 877 mandates that the courts review

---

15. Although several Court of Appeal opinions have suggested that there is an established "hierarchy" or "priority" to the various public policy objectives in this area that can be applied in all contexts, our decisions have never embraced any such mechanical hierarchical approach. Instead, we have generally attempted to harmonize the competing public policies, taking into account the specific context in which the potential conflict between the various policies appears. Accordingly, the fact that we have determined, in one setting, that a particular goal should properly give way to another objective, does not mean that the goal that prevailed should always "trump" the competing objective when a conflict arises between the two in a different setting. For example, while we determined in American Motorcycle Assn. v. Superior Court, *supra*, 20 Cal. 3d 578, that the long-established joint-and-several-liability doctrine should be preserved in part because it furthered the state interest in ensuring that an injured plaintiff is adequately compensated for his loss (*see* 20 Cal. 3d at p. 590), in that same decision we also held the injured party's interest in "maximizing" his recovery could not justify preserving the plaintiff's control over litigation by prohibiting a defendant from joining other tortfeasors who were also responsible for damages. (*See* 20 Cal. 3d at p. 606).

agreements purportedly made under its aegis to insure that such settlements appropriately balance the contribution statute's dual objectives." At the same time, we explained that the "good faith" concept cannot be captured in a simple formula. "'Lack of good faith encompasses many kinds of behavior. It may characterize one or both sides to a settlement. When profit is involved, the ingenuity of man spawns limitless varieties of unfairness. Thus, formulation of a precise definition of good faith is neither possible nor practicable. The Legislature has here incorporated by reference the general equitable principle of contribution law which frowns on unfair settlements, including those which are so poorly related to the value of the case as to impose a potentially disproportionate cost on the defendant ultimately selected for suit.'"

Rejecting the line of cases — beginning with Dompeling v. Superior Court, *supra*, 117 Cal. App. 3d 798 — which had indicated that settling parties were free "to further their respective interests without regard to the effect of their settlement upon other defendants" (*id.*, at pp. 809-810) so long as they refrained "from tortious or other wrongful conduct" (*ibid.*), we concluded in *Tech-Bilt* that "[a] more appropriate definition of 'good faith,' in keeping with the policies of American Motorcycle Assn. v. Superior Court and the statute, would enable the trial court to inquire, among other things, whether the amount of the settlement is within the reasonable range of the settling tortfeasor's proportional share of comparative liability for the plaintiff's injuries."[16] Elaborating on the parameters of the good faith concept, we observed that "the intent and policies underlying section 877.6 require that a number of factors be taken into account including a rough approximation of plaintiffs' total recovery and the settlor's proportionate liability, the amount paid in settlement, the allocation of settlement proceeds among plaintiffs, and a recognition that a settlor should pay less in settlement than he would if he were found liable after a trial. Other relevant considerations include the financial conditions and insurance policy limits of settling defendants, as well as the existence of collusion, fraud or tortious conduct aimed to injure the interests of nonsettling defendants. Finally, practical considerations obviously require that the evaluation be made on the basis of information available at the time of settlement. '[A] defendant's settlement figure must not be grossly disproportionate to what a reasonable person, at the time of the settlement, would estimate the settling defendant's liability to be.' (Torres v. Union Pacific R.R. Co. (1984) 157 Cal. App. 3d 499, 509 [203 Cal. Rptr 825].) The party asserting the lack of good faith, who has the burden of proof on that issue, should be permitted to demonstrate, if he can, that the settlement is so far 'out of the ballpark' in relation to these factors as to be inconsistent with the equitable objectives of the statute. Such a demonstration would establish that the proposed settlement was not a 'settlement made in good faith' within the terms of section 877.6." (*Id.*, at pp. 499-500, italics added, fn. omitted.)

---

16. The dissent takes issue with our interpretation of the term "good faith" as it is used in section 877. According to the dissent, "good faith" under section 877 "simply requires noncollusive conduct" on the part of the settling parties. However, as noted above, we considered and rejected that very contention in our recent decision in Tech-Bilt, Inc. v. Woodward-Clyde & Associates (1985) 38 Cal. 3d 488 [213 Cal. Rptr. 256, 698 P.2d 159]. We find no compelling reason to reexamine or overturn the conclusions reached in *Tech-Bilt*.

By requiring a settling defendant to settle "in the ballpark" in order to gain immunity from contribution or comparative indemnity, the good faith requirement of sections 877 and 877.6 assures that—by virtue of the "set-off" embodied in section 877, subdivision (a)—the nonsettling defendants' liability to the plaintiff will be reduced by a sum that is not "grossly disproportionate" to the settling defendant's share of liability, thus providing at least some rough measure of fair apportionment of loss between the settling and nonsettling defendants.

As *Tech-Bilt* emphasizes, of course, a "good faith" settlement does not call for perfect or even nearly perfect apportionment of liability. In order to encourage settlement, it is quite proper for a settling defendant to pay less than his proportionate share of the anticipated damages. What is required is simply that the settlement not be grossly disproportionate to the settlor's fair share. As the Court of Appeal observed in Torres v. Union Pacific R.R. Co., *supra*, 157 Cal. App. 3d 499, 507: "If [a settling] codefendant wishes to enjoy the section 877 bar against indemnity, he must make some attempt to place the price of his settlement within a reasonable range of his relative share of the liability."

As noted above, the Court of Appeal—after remand from this court—concluded that the "good faith" standard articulated in *Tech-Bilt* applies to sliding scale agreements. Abbott has not challenged that conclusion here and, in any event, we agree with the Court of Appeal's conclusion on this point. Neither section 877 nor section 877.6 exempts sliding scale agreements from its "good faith" requirement, and nothing in section 877.5—a provision which was enacted to protect against the unfair consequences that may flow from undisclosed sliding scale agreements—indicates that such agreements need not meet the generally applicable good faith standard. Indeed, the legislative history of section 877.5 suggests that the Legislature contemplated . . . a broad good faith standard . . .

The crucial question presented by this case is how *Tech-Bilt*'s good faith standard should apply to sliding scale agreements. Ford and Sears claim broadly that sliding scale agreements can never satisfy the good faith standard of *Tech-Bilt*'s, asserting that such agreements, by their very nature, irreconcilably conflict with both goals—fair apportionment of loss and encouragement of settlement—sought to be advanced by the statutory scheme. In addition, they argue that even if some sliding scale agreements may properly be found to be good faith settlements, the agreements at issue here clearly cannot. We first consider the claims with respect to apportionment of loss.

A.

Ford and Sears argue initially that sliding scale agreements inevitably thwart the goal of a fair apportionment of loss among responsible tortfeasors. Because, by definition, such an agreement is one in which the settling defendant's final out-of-pocket payment to the plaintiff is dependent on the amount which the plaintiff ultimately recovers from the remaining defendants, Ford and Sears insist that such an agreement always has the effect of improperly shifting the settling defendant's share of liability onto the nonsettling defendants, thus undermining equitable apportionment. To support their claim, Ford and Sears note that under the sliding scale agreement at issue here, if a jury were to assess plaintiffs' damages from the accident at $3 million or more and to find that Ford or Sears was in any degree responsible for the injury, Ford or Sears would ostensibly be required to bear all of the damages, and Abbott — the party who, by all appearances, is the most culpable tortfeasor[20] — would escape any ultimate out-of-pocket loss whatsoever. Ford and Sears argue that such a result cannot be squared with the statutory goal of fairly apportioning loss among the responsible tortfeasors.

Although the scenario outlined by Ford and Sears does seem difficult to reconcile with the fair apportionment objective, a review of the facts of other cases suggests that Ford and Sears have overstated the argument in claiming that sliding scale agreements invariably conflict with a fair apportionment of loss. The sliding scale agreement in Dompeling v. Superior Court, *supra*, 117 Cal. App. 3d 798, for example, required the settling defendant to pay $100,000 outright and included an additional $10,000 sliding scale guaranty; though the settling defendant's ultimate payment was thus dependent, to some extent, on the plaintiff's recovery from the nonsettling defendant, the nonsettling defendant received an offset for the $100,000 noncontingent payment and thus the agreement as a whole did not necessarily undermine a fair apportionment of loss. Similarly, although the sliding scale agreement in Rogers & Wells v. Superior Court, *supra*, 175 Cal. App. 3d 545, provided for no noncontingent payment by the settling defendants and therefore could result in no ultimate out-of-pocket cost on their behalf, because the settling defendants in that case apparently bore only minimal, if any, responsibility for the plaintiffs' injuries, the Rogers & Wells court concluded that the agreement was not at odds with the fair apportionment objective.

These diverse situations reveal that the fact that a settlement agreement involves some sort of sliding scale or guaranty provision is not alone sufficient to demonstrate that the agreement is irreconcilable with the fair-apportionment-of-loss objective. Although sliding scale agreements may frequently present problems in this regard, we must proceed beyond the simple presence of a sliding scale provision and delve into the specifics of both the particular agreement and the factual background to properly assess the question.

In analyzing the apportionment problem, it is important to keep in mind that, under the terms of section 877, a settlement — if found to be in "good faith" — has two interrelated consequences: (1) it discharges the settling tortfeasor from all liability to other defendants for contribution or indemnity, and (2) it reduces the plaintiff's claims against the other defendants by "the amount of consideration paid for it." Although past cases have often overlooked the interrelationship of these two features in our view the ultimate analysis of the effect of the sliding scale agreement resolves itself to a consideration of fairness to the nonsettling defendants. If a court finds that a settling defendant, by entering into a sliding scale agreement, has realistically paid a "consideration" that is within its *Tech-Bilt* "ballpark," and if the nonsettling defendants obtain a reduction in the plaintiff's claims against them in an

---

20. During settlement negotiations, it will be recalled, Abbott agreed to bear 70 percent of its proposed $2.5 million settlement, and plaintiffs' settlement conference memorandum clearly designated Abbott as the principal tortfeasor.

amount equal to that consideration, the statutory fair apportionment objective should be satisfied. Accordingly, the analysis of whether a sliding scale agreement conflicts with the fair apportionment objective lies in "the amount of consideration" which is attributed to the settling defendant as the "payment" for his release from liability by entering into the sliding scale agreement. Since the sliding scale agreement is given by the settling defendant in exchange for the plaintiff's release and the immunity from contribution or indemnity from the claims of the nonsettling cotortfeasors, we should assume the exchange is of equivalents. If we focus, then, not on what the settling defendant gave up, but rather what he received, then we have a simple application of *Tech-Bilt* rules. This is so because one of the principal difficulties in this area has been the attempt to arrive at an accurate evaluation of the "price" or "consideration" which has been paid by a settling defendant who enters into a sliding scale arrangement.

Unlike an ordinary settlement agreement in which the amount the settling defendant has paid — and correspondingly the amount to be deducted from the plaintiff's claims against the remaining defendants — is typically easy to identify, the contingent nature of a sliding scale obligation has created considerable confusion as to the proper valuation of such an agreement.

The parties are in sharp disagreement on this point. Ford and Sears argue that the "consideration paid" should be calculated solely by reference to the amount of any noncontingent payment which the settling defendant has made to the plaintiff under the agreement; in this case, where Abbott has made no noncontingent payment, they suggest that the "consideration" or cost paid by Abbott should be valued at zero. Abbott, on the other hand, points to the fact that it has guaranteed plaintiffs a $3 million recovery, and argues the consideration which it has paid should be fixed at its possible maximum payment, $3 million.

The economic reality, we believe, lies between these two extreme positions. Contrary to the arguments of Ford and Sears, a guaranty agreement, even if totally contingent, is not completely cost-free from the point of view of the guarantor. At the same time and contrary to the position of Abbott, however, the "cost" or "price" of such an agreement is not equal to the maximum amount that the guarantor may possibly be required to pay under the agreement. Accordingly, given the nature of sliding scale agreements, we believe the court should not be burdened with the obligation to determine the actual value of such an agreement by the use of actuarial or other valuation methods. Rather, the parties to such an agreement, since they are in the best position to place a monetary figure on its value, should have the burden of establishing the monetary value of the sliding scale agreement.

In many cases, negotiations between the parties will have included a traditional "straight" settlement as an alternative to the sliding scale agreement, and this background will give the settling parties a vantage point in declaring the agreement's value. In addition, since the plaintiff and the settling defendant are likely to have somewhat different, and somewhat conflicting interests in placing a value on the agreement — the plaintiff would prefer the value to be on the low side to reduce the amount that its claims against other defendants will be reduced; the settling defendant will want the value to be high enough to assure that the agreement is found to be within its *Tech-Bilt* "ballpark" so as to relieve it of liability for comparative indemnity or contribution — requiring a joint valuation by the plaintiff and the settling defendant should generally produce a reasonable valuation.

Once the parties to the agreement have declared its value, a nonsettling defendant either (1) can accept that value and attempt to show that the settlement is not in good faith because the assigned value is not within the settling defendant's *Tech-Bilt* ballpark, or (2) can attempt to prove that the parties' assigned value is too low and that a greater reduction in plaintiff's claims against the remaining defendants is actually warranted.

In the present case, of course, the settling parties placed no value on the sliding scale agreement. Accordingly, if the case had not been settled, we would have ordered the Court of Appeal to remand the matter to the trial court for further consideration of this issue.

B.

In addition to the fair apportionment issue, Ford and Sears contend that sliding scale agreements in general, and the agreement in this case in particular, should be found not in "good faith" because such agreements improperly impede the full settlement of the case. We pointed out in *Tech-Bilt* that "from the standpoint of the public interest and the legal process, a prime value in encouraging settlement lies in 'remov[ing] [the case] from the judicial system, and this occurs only when all claims relating to the loss are settled.'" Ford and Sears maintain that while the availability of the sliding scale agreement mechanism may induce the plaintiff to settle with one or perhaps a number of defendants, such an agreement effectively prevents the remaining defendants from thereafter settling with the plaintiff without a trial. Abbott responds that the availability of a sliding scale agreement often has exactly the opposite effect, and is frequently used as an incentive to persuade an otherwise recalcitrant defendant to engage in settlement negotiations in good faith and to participate with other defendants in contributing its fair share to a settlement pool that will secure the full settlement of the case. Abbott suggests that if one defendant stubbornly refuses to participate in good faith in such settlement negotiations, a sliding scale agreement may be the only means available to the other defendants to escape from the litigation without paying the portion of the plaintiff's damages that should appropriately be borne by the unyielding defendant.

Although it is somewhat paradoxical, we think there is considerable merit in both of the parties' arguments on this point. In some circumstances, the availability of sliding scale agreements can facilitate the settlement process; at the same time, particular sliding scale agreements may operate to thwart or impair the full settlement of the case. Our task is to attempt to identify the different situations, and to regulate the use of sliding scale agreements so as to further the state interest in fostering the full settlement of litigation.

1.

As Abbott suggests, in some instances sliding scale agreements have been entered into only as a matter of last resort, when one defendant in a multidefendant action refuses to participate in settlement negotiations or to make a good faith offer commensurate with its fair share of responsibility for plaintiff's damages. In such a setting, the recalcitrant defendant's unyielding position may threaten to make it impossible for any of the defendants to settle the litigation with the plaintiff, because the plaintiff may be unwilling to release any of the joint-and-severally liable defendants without an assurance that he will at least recover a minimum sum which he feels is necessary to compensate him for his injuries. . . .

At the same time, however, we think that there must properly be limits on the consequences that may be visited on a defendant who is found to have been unreasonably recalcitrant in settlement negotiations. Because it may be difficult to distinguish between defendants who unreasonably or in bad faith refuse to make a fair contribution to a settlement fund and defendants who in good faith honestly and reasonably believe that they bear no liability for a plaintiff's injury, a rule which permits settling defendants to thrust the entire economic responsibility for an injury on a single defendant through a sliding scale agreement is likely to have an unduly coercive effect on defendants who may be acting in good faith, unfairly compelling them to settle to avoid a financial disaster whenever there is any risk that their conduct might later be viewed as unreasonable. . . .

[W]e think that the trial court's "ballpark" determination may also appropriately be adjusted to take into account any unreasonable or bad faith conduct of a nonsettling party which may have impeded the settlement process. If the court finds that the party challenging the settlement engaged in such conduct, it may reduce the lower threshold of the "ballpark" cutoff, and find a settlement in good faith even if the "consideration" paid for, i.e., the "value" of, the sliding scale agreement is somewhat lower than the court would otherwise have found acceptable. Through this approach, a nonsettling defendant who unreasonably impedes settlement can be saddled with a greater portion of economic responsibility than it would otherwise have borne; the sanction, however, should not be so out of proportion to the hold-out defendant's conduct as to be unduly coercive. In this way, a court can give recognition to the positive role sliding scale agreements may have in deterring unreasonable nonparticipation in settlement negotiations.

2.

Ford and Sears contend, however, that even if the potential availability of a sliding scale agreement may be a valuable tool for encouraging settlement in some instances, once a sliding scale agreement is actually entered into, the agreement invariably interferes with the ability of the nonparticipating defendants to settle the remainder of the litigation. Ford and Sears argue that because sliding scale agreements necessarily have this antisettlement effect, we should find that such agreements are not compatible with the purposes of sections 877 and 877.6 and should never be accorded "good faith" settlement status under those provisions. As we explain, while the potential antisettlement effect of a consummated sliding scale agreement is a legitimate cause for inquiry and concern, we believe that the problem can be met by a remedy less sweeping than the condemnation of all sliding scale agreements.

As Ford and Sears point out, the most obvious conflict between sliding scale agreements and a subsequent settlement of the balance of the lawsuit is posed by explicit provisions contained in most sliding scale agreements which purport to grant the settling defendant a "veto power" over any subsequent settlement which would affect the settling defendant's ultimate out-of-pocket costs under the guaranty agreement. The provision contained in the agreement in the present case is fairly typical in this regard, providing that "[plaintiffs] shall not settle all or any portion of this litigation with defendants Ford and Sears Roebuck for less than the amount of [their] guarant[eed recovery], *without the express written consent of* [Abbott's insurer]." (Italics added.)

The reason for the inclusion of some such "veto" provision in a sliding scale agreement is, of course, readily apparent. Because the settling defendant has agreed to guarantee that the plaintiff ultimately recovers some minimum amount, it "has an obvious and legitimate interest in ensuring that the plaintiff diligently prosecutes its claims against the remaining defendants." As Judge Pollak points out, however, the authority afforded by such contractual veto provisions frequently exceeds the settling defendant's "legitimate" interest. While it may be reasonable for the earlier settling defendant to reserve the right to veto subsequent settlements which are unfairly low and which would result in its bearing an ultimate out-of-pocket cost higher than its fair share of the plaintiff's damages, there is no similar compelling justification for permitting that defendant to bar the remaining defendants from settling with the plaintiff for an amount that is sufficiently high that it would not have such an unfair effect. An open-ended veto provision conflicts with the public policy which favors the full settlement of litigation and may frequently result in unnecessary trials. Accordingly, we conclude that to be valid and enforceable, such a veto provision must, by its terms, be confined only to those subsequent settlements that will require the earlier settling defendant to bear more than its fair "ballpark" share of damages.

IV.

As discussed above, Abbott maintains that the sliding scale agreement in this case is not disproportionate to its fair share of liability and does not improperly impair full settlement of the action. It also apparently contends, however, that even if the agreement were found to be flawed in those respects, the agreement should nonetheless be found to be a good faith settlement within the meaning of sections 877 and 877.6 because of two additional considerations. We discuss each in turn.

A.

We agree that affording an injured person prompt payment of funds for his losses serves a very important state interest. But nothing we have said above is inconsistent with that purpose. We have not suggested that it is improper for a settlement agreement to take the form of a noninterest loan from the settling defendant to the plaintiff, repayable out of the proceeds of any recovery;[26] rather, we simply note that the value of such a loan will realistically be considered by the parties to the agreement in arriving at the agreement's value. Of course, if a plaintiff chooses to release his or her claims against a defendant for less than that defendant's "ballpark" figure, the plaintiff remains free to do so; if, however, the settling defendant wishes to obtain immunity from potential claims for comparative indemnity or contribution under sections 877 and 877.6, (1) the "consideration" paid by it must not be grossly disproportionate to its fair share of responsibility and (2) the remaining defendants are entitled to have the plaintiff's claims against them reduced by the amount of the consideration paid. Although plaintiffs may be less willing to enter into such agreements once they recognize that their claims against the nonsettling defendants will be reduced by the value of the agreement,[27] we do not believe that consequence can itself justify a contrary result. Offsets have been routinely required in normal settlement agreements since the inception of section 877, and we can find no justification for exempting the more questionable sliding scale agreements from similar treatment. . . .

V.

In sum, we conclude: (1) that *Tech-Bilt*'s good faith standard applies to sliding scale agreements, (2) that to satisfy the statutory objective of a fair apportionment of loss (i) the "consideration" paid by a defendant who enters into a sliding scale agreement must fall within the *Tech-Bilt* "ballpark" and (ii) the plaintiffs' claims against the remaining defendants must be reduced by the amount of the "consideration paid" by the settling defendant, (3) that any unreasonable or bad faith conduct of the nonsettling defendants which impeded the settlement process and led to the sliding scale agreement may be taken into account in determining whether the agreement satisfies the "ballpark" standard, and (4) that any provision which purports to give a settling defendant a "veto" over subsequent settlements is valid only if it is limited to settlements which would leave the earlier settling defendant to bear more than its fair share of liability for the plaintiff's damages. . . .

---

26. Some out-of-state decisions have found such loan agreements invalid as violative of the common law doctrines of champerty and maintenance, which generally preclude a "stranger" to a lawsuit from financing the litigation in return for a portion of any recovery. (*See*, e.g., Lum v. Stinnett, *supra*, 87 Nev. 402 [488 P.2d 347].) California, however, has never adopted the common law doctrines of champerty and maintenance (*see, e.g.*, Estate of Cohen (1944) 66 Cal. App. 2d 450, 458 [152 P.2d 485]; Cain v. Burns (1955) 131 Cal. App. 2d 439, 443 [280 P.2d 888]; Muller v. Muller (1962) 206 Cal. App. 2d 731, 733 [23 Cal. Rptr. 900]), and thus the fact that a settlement takes the form of such a loan does not in itself render the settlement invalid.

27. The rapid increase in the attractiveness of such agreements to plaintiffs in recent years may have been based, in large part, on the fact that prior decisions have permitted plaintiffs to receive the substantial benefits of sliding scale agreements without any corresponding reduction in their claims against the remaining defendants.

Moreover, as a result of our resolution of the issues presented in this case, defendants may also find such agreements less attractive in the future. The result of the offset requirement will be a reduction in the amount of exposure of a nonsettling defendant to the plaintiff by the amount of the settling parties' declaration of value, thereby increasing the odds that the settling defendant will be obligated to perform under its guaranty agreement with plaintiff. Thus, after trial, the obligation of the settling defendant to the plaintiff under the sliding scale agreement will now be the difference, if any, between the amount of total damages awarded against a nonsettling defendant, reduced by the valuation of the sliding scale agreement, and the guaranteed amount.

LUCAS, C. J., ARGUELLES, J., EAGLESON, J., and KAUFMAN, J., concurred.

BROUSSARD, J.

I concur in the majority opinion. I write separately to express one substantial reservation.

The majority opinion concludes: "Once the parties to the agreement have declared its value, a nonsettling defendant either (1) can accept that value and attempt to show that the settlement is not in good faith because the assigned value is not within the settling defendant's *Tech-Bilt* ballpark, or (2) can attempt to prove that the parties' assigned value is too low and that a greater reduction in plaintiff's claim against the remaining defendants is actually warranted."

I would prefer to delete the second alternative for several reasons. As the majority recognized in its footnote to the above quotation, the evaluation of a sliding scale agreement is a complex matter with the court able to do no more than make its best estimate. The second alternative provides a substantial danger that efforts to establish the proper value will require a minitrial with actuaries and economists testifying at length. And ordinarily the evaluation will not serve any legitimate purpose of the nonsettling defendant but will only result in delays. . . .

MOSK, J.

I dissent.

The majority opinion's central holding is as follows: The "good faith" required by Code of Civil Procedure section 877 (hereafter section 877) to relieve a defendant, settling under a sliding scale recovery agreement, from liability for contribution or comparative equitable indemnity demands that the settling defendant pay an amount within the reasonable range of his proportional share of comparative liability for the plaintiff's injury. As I shall explain, this holding is fundamentally unsound. Section 877 requires nothing more than that the plaintiff and the settling defendant simply refrain from collusive conduct intended to prejudice the interests of the nonsettling defendants. Accordingly, I would affirm the judgment of the Court of Appeal which correctly found such "good faith" as a matter of law on the facts of this case.

At the threshold I approve the majority's conclusion that sliding scale recovery agreements are subject to the "good faith" requirement. I also approve the conclusion that such agreements are not invalid as against public policy. There, however, my approval ends. I am of the opinion that both the language of section 877 and its history establish that the phrase "good faith" simply requires noncollusive conduct. . . .

NOTE ON *ABBOTT FORD*

Consider this case as an example of modern tort litigation — with the addition of some behind-the-scenes information gleaned from one of the lawyers who represented plaintiff. The plaintiff was obviously seriously injured and could not be said to have contributed to the accident in any way, so potential damages were quite high — if plaintiff could identify a solvent defendant responsible for the harm. The other driver—Sneed—was an obvious defendant (one doesn't need a deep knowledge of torts to realize that if a tire flies off my car and blinds another driver, I'm liable). But, like many drivers of used vans, Sneed was unlikely to have substantial insurance coverage or any other assets—and he did not, in fact. So the question was whether there was another defendant who was partly responsible for the accident and who, under California's law of joint and several liability (see the next section) was responsible—and solvent.

The plaintiffs' lawyers' first theory focused on Abbott Ford, which modified the van wheels (in contravention of Ford's instructions) to make it more attractive to prospective buyers. The difficult with that straightforward theory of liability was that it didn't seem to bear up factually. The plaintiffs had hired an engineering expert from a local university, and he subjected the van to a series of increasingly stressful drops (the idea being that the after-market wheel had come off when the van hit a pothole). The problem was that the wheel just wouldn't come off, so the theory of liability didn't seem promising.

Almost as a precaution, the plaintiffs had also joined Sears and Ford as defendants, but the case for liability against them seemed thin. Sears asserted it hadn't been asked to touch the wheels during its service, and it seemed a stretch to hold them liable for not having performed an inspection that no one had asked them to do. Ford had cautioned the dealers against the modification that Abbott had nevertheless performed, and protested that it couldn't expect them to post a guard at every dealership to prevent dealers from ignoring its bulletins.

Then, as luck would have it, the engineer who was dropping the van from ever-greater heights without jarring the wheels loose happened to have conversation with a former classmate, also an engineer now retired from Ford. That classmate, not in any way involved in the case, mentioned his frustration that Ford, during the years he was active there, had rejected a recommendation for a modified windshield design. The modification would have layered a thin sheet of plastic between two layers of windshield glass—a change that would have prevented exactly the kind of shattering that blinded Phyllis Smith. (Such a design is now standard in cars and trucks but was not at the time the van was manufactured.) The classmate also complained that the cost would have been relatively low. Bingo! The plaintiff's lawyers now had a classical modern product liability suit—now against Ford, which could pay any imaginable damage judgment.

But such a case against Ford would be expensive to mount. Even with the new information, plaintiffs would have to hire another set of experts—this time in windshields—and conduct extensive discovery against Ford, which could be expected to resist strenuously, since this was now a theory that might apply to many vehicles. And the plaintiff's lawyers, from a reasonably well capitalized small firm, were not in a position to invest hundreds of thousands of dollars in discovery and experts' fees—unless they could find bridge financing. Enter the sliding scale agreement. Abbott's liability insurance policy was for $3.25 million, the opinion tells us. By entering into a sliding scale agreement with a $3 million cap the insurer "saved" $250,000 even if it had to pay the full amount. The insurer was willing to pay this much because the deal opened up the possibility that ultimate payment would be much smaller — if the plaintiffs recovered substantial amounts against Ford or Sears. And, both Abbott and plaintiff had some concerns that this deal, as good as it was for them, might be struck down by the California Supreme Court or held to be in "bad faith."

With this background look back at the case, noticing, first, that almost none of this strategizing surfaces in the opinion. Some of it would be unknown to the judges. Other parts they might surmise but would not be legally relevant. What does the opinion mean for future parties in this situation? Is it the right decision?

d. An Anatomy of Multiparty Settlement Issues: Torts Meet Procedure

LEWIS A. KORNHAUSER & RICHARD L. REVESZ, SETTLEMENTS
UNDER JOINT AND SEVERAL LIABILITY

68 New York University Law Review 427, 430-434, 442-444 (1993)
(footnotes omitted without indication)

Introduction . . .

In many . . . contexts . . . common law courts are choosing among alternative rules governing the litigation of claims involving multiple defendants based on the courts' views about the relative settlement-inducing properties of these rules. . . .

The purpose of this Article is to guide the choice of an appropriate legal regime — at both the federal and state levels — to govern litigation involving joint tortfeasors. Our analysis focuses solely on the impact of the competing legal rules on the choice between settlement and litigation: the plaintiff has already suffered the harm, and the question is whether it will have to litigate in order to recover. We do not consider which rules are better from the perspective of inducing the socially desirable amount of deterrence. . . .

Part I categorizes legal rules in this area by reference to eight relevant elements: (1) whether there is joint and several liability; (2) whether there is a right of contribution; (3) whether the right of contribution is pro rata or by reference to comparative fault; (4) whether, when the plaintiff settles with one defendant and litigates against the other, its claim against the non-settling defendant is reduced by the amount of the settlement (a pro tanto set-off rule), or, instead, by the settling defendant's share of the liability (an apportioned share set-off rule); (5) whether settling defendants are protected from contribution actions; (6) whether settling defendants have a right to bring contribution actions; (7) whether there is judicial supervision of the substantive adequacy of settlements; and (8) whether the claims involving all the joint tortfeasors are joined together in a single proceeding. This scheme, rather than the truncated taxonomy generally used by the courts, significantly aids the analysis of the relative merits of the competing rules. . . .

Because the correlation of the plaintiff's probabilities of success plays such a central role in our analysis and yet has been overlooked in the prior works, it is important at this point to elucidate the concept. These probabilities are independent if the outcome of the plaintiff's claim against one defendant does not depend upon whether the plaintiff prevails against, loses to, or settles with the other defendant. For example, suppose that the plaintiff seeks to recover the costs of cleaning up a hazardous waste site, and each of two unrelated defendants argues that it did not send hazardous substances to the site. The outcome of the plaintiff's case against one defendant is then independent of the outcome of its case against the other. Or, consider a "hub and spoke" conspiracy in which several parties are alleged to have conspired with the "hub." The fact that one party did so says nothing about whether others did so as well; thus the plaintiff's probabilities of prevailing against the various "spokes" are independent.

In contrast, the plaintiff's probabilities are perfectly correlated if, when the plaintiff litigates against both defendants, it either prevails against both or loses to both. In the previous example, suppose that the defendants argue, instead, that the plaintiff's cleanup was inappropriately expensive; there is then no scenario under which one would prevail if the other does not. The plaintiff's probabilities of success are also perfectly correlated in a case in which only two defendants are alleged to have engaged in a conspiracy; because it is not possible for a party to conspire with itself, if one defendant prevails, the other will do so as well. Respondeat superior cases in which the agent's authority is conceded also have this feature.

Part II establishes that if the plaintiff's probabilities of success are independent, the plaintiff litigates against both defendants unless the costs of litigation are sufficiently high; this result also holds if the probabilities are sufficiently, though not wholly, independent. In contrast, if these probabilities are perfectly correlated, the plaintiff settles with at least one defendant regardless of the magnitude of the litigation costs; this result also holds if the probabilities are sufficiently, though not perfectly, correlated. Part II concludes with an analysis of the relevance of the model's assumptions.

Part III studies the settlement-inducing properties of some alternative legal rules. It reaches three principal conclusions. First, the pro tanto set-off rule generally promotes more settlements than the apportioned share set-off rule when the costs of litigation are low, but can promote fewer settlements when these costs are high. Second, a regime with no right of contribution has identical effects on the choice between settlement and litigation as one with contribution. Third, joint and several liability discourages settlement when the plaintiff's probabilities of success are independent; in contrast, when these probabilities are perfectly correlated, joint and several liability generally promotes settlement when it is coupled with the pro tanto set-off rule, and has no effect on settlement when it is coupled with the apportioned share set-off rule. . . .

7. The Nature of "Good Faith" Hearings on the Adequacy of Settlements

Under the pro tanto set-off rule, if the plaintiff enters into an inadequately low settlement with one defendant and that defendant obtains contribution protection as a result of the settlement, the other defendant is responsible for the shortfall if it litigates and loses. To protect the interests of non-settling defendants, courts typically require "good faith" or "fairness" hearings on the adequacy of settlements.

The Restatement, UCATA, and UCFA are all silent on the nature of good faith hearings. The courts are divided on whether this hearing should involve only a procedural inquiry about the absence of collusion between the plaintiff and the settling defendant, or whether it should also scrutinize the substantive adequacy of the settlement. This split is well illustrated by Tech-Bilt, Inc. v. Woodward-Clyde & Associates. In *Tech-Bilt*, the California Supreme Court held that the good faith inquiry "would enable the trial court to inquire, among other things, whether the amount of the settlement is within the reasonable range of the settling tortfeasor's proportional share of comparative liability for the plaintiff's injuries." In a strong dissent, Chief Justice Bird argued that "a settlement satisfies the good faith requirement if it is free of corrupt intent, that is, free of intent to injure the interests of the nonsettling tortfeasors. A settlement is made in bad faith only if it is collusive, fraudulent, dishonest, or involves tortious conduct." Under her approach the inquiry is solely procedural; she would not inquire into the substantive adequacy of the settlement.

The preceding discussion was limited to regimes of contribution, contribution protection, and pro tanto set-off. There is no reason to have good faith hearings in the absence of a right of contribution. If the plaintiff can collect its damages in any way that it wants when it litigates and prevails against both defendants, it is not logical to be concerned about fairness when the plaintiff settles with one defendant and litigates against the other. Also, there is no reason for such hearings under contribution regimes that do not provide contribution protection to a settling defendant. Then, the remedy for a non-settling defendant that pays more than its apportioned share of the liability is to seek contribution from the settling defendant. Finally, good faith hearings are not necessary under the apportioned share set-off rule because there the plaintiff, rather than the non-settling defendant, suffers the loss from a low settlement.

8. Joinder Rules

If the plaintiff joins all the joint tortfeasors in a single suit, its claims against all of them will be adjudicated in the same proceeding. If the plaintiff chooses not to join all the tortfeasors as defendants, the question arises whether a named defendant can join another tortfeasor as a third-party defendant. Otherwise, the named defendant would have to file a separate action for contribution after the adjudication of its liability to the plaintiff.

Both the Restatement and the UCATA state in their comments that this matter is governed by the procedural rules of the state in which the action is brought. The UCFA states that the right of contribution "may be enforced either in the original action or in a separate action brought for that purpose," but does not specify how this determination should be made.

In federal court, this question is determined by reference to Rules 14(a) and 42 of the Federal Rules of Civil Procedure, which govern third-party practice. Rule 14(a) provides that a defendant, acting as a third-party plaintiff, may bring an action for contribution, as of right within ten days of the filing of its answer, and with leave of the court thereafter. Rule 42 gives the court discretion either to order a single trial or to sever the actions for separate trial. In general, courts have been reluctant to sever contribution or indemnification claims from the primary action. . . .

Cal. Civ. Code §§1431 et seq. ("Proposition 51")

(West 2004)

§1431.1. Findings and Declaration of Purpose

The People of the State of California find and declare as follows:

(a) The legal doctrine of joint and several liability, also known as "the deep pocket rule," has resulted in a system of inequity and injustice that has threatened financial bankruptcy of local governments, other public agencies, private individuals and businesses and has resulted in higher prices for goods and services to the public and in higher taxes to the taxpayers.

(b) Some governmental and private defendants are perceived to have substantial financial resources or insurance coverage and have thus been included in lawsuits even though there was little or no basis for finding them at fault. Under joint and several liability, if they are found to share even a fraction of the fault, they often are held financially liable for all the damage. The People — taxpayers and consumers alike — ultimately pay for these lawsuits in the form of higher taxes, higher prices and higher insurance premiums.

(c) Local governments have been forced to curtail some essential police, fire and other protections because of the soaring costs of lawsuits and insurance premiums.

Therefore, the People of the State of California declare that to remedy these inequities, defendants in tort actions shall be held financially liable in closer proportion to their degree of fault. To treat them differently is unfair and inequitable.

The People of the State of California further declare that reforms in the liability laws in tort actions are necessary and proper to avoid catastrophic economic consequences for state and local governmental bodies as well as private individuals and businesses.

Added by initiative measure (Prop. 51), adopted June 3, 1986.

§1431.2. Several Liability for Non-economic Damages

(a) In any action for personal injury, property damage, or wrongful death, based upon principles of comparative fault, the liability of each defendant for non-economic damages shall be several only and shall not be joint. Each defendant shall be liable only for the amount of non-economic damages allocated to that defendant in direct proportion to that defendant's percentage of fault, and a separate judgment shall be rendered against that defendant for that amount.

(b)

(1) For purposes of this section, the term "economic damages" means objectively verifiable monetary losses including

medical expenses, loss of earnings, burial costs, loss of use of property, costs of repair or replacement, costs of obtaining substitute domestic services, loss of employment and loss of business or employment opportunities.

(2) For the purposes of this section, the term "non-economic damages" means subjective, non-monetary losses including, but not limited to, pain, suffering, inconvenience, mental suffering, emotional distress, loss of society and companionship, loss of consortium, injury to reputation and humiliation.

Shannon P. Duffy, Last-to-Settle Defendant Gets Credit for Earlier Agreements

Legal Intelligencer, November 13, 2006

When a federal judge handed down a $28 million verdict in August in a trio of lawsuits stemming from Tropical Storm Allison's flooding of several corporate offices, the court battle was hardly over.

Soon after the verdict, a dispute erupted over how the court should treat the $20 million in settlements that were reached with two defendants — one before trial began and a second reached during the interim between the liability and penalty phases of the trial.

Lawyers for the plaintiffs argued that judgment against the nonsettling defendants should be increased by nearly $4 million in delay damages.

But defense lawyers cried foul and insisted that the court should first "mold" the verdict to delete the full $20 million in settlements before calculating the delay damages.

In their brief, attorneys Edward M. Koch, William J. Schmidt and Wayne Partenheimer of White & Williams argued that the proper delay damages were about $1.1 million.

In response, the plaintiffs argued that the two settlements — worth $4 million and $16 million — were significantly different due to the nature of the releases they generated.

For the $4 million settlement, the plaintiffs said, the release was "pro tanto," but for the $16 million settlement, the release was "pro rata."

As a result, lead plaintiff attorneys Thomas J. Duffy and Patrick J. Keenan of Duffy & Keenan argued that the court should reduce the judgment against the non-settling defendant by $4 million for the pro tanto settlement, but that the pro rata release triggered a much smaller reduction equal to the 2 percent liability the jury had assigned to that defendant.

Now Eastern District of Pennsylvania Judge Gene E. K. Pratter has sided with the defense, finding that the plaintiffs were attempting to "justify a recovery far in excess of the total awarded damages."

In her 11-page opinion in St. Paul Fire & Marine Insurance Co. v. Nolen Group Inc., Pratter wrote: "The court will not countenance plaintiffs' effort to avoid an equitable adjustment here." . . .

"Plaintiffs and their very able counsel have labored mightily to craft settlement documents that would maximize the amount of damages recoverable against Baringer. Not surprisingly, plaintiffs hoped to escape having to credit the $16 million settlement monies," Pratter wrote.

But Pratter found that Baringer was "a stranger to the two settlement agreements," and therefore "cannot be assigned obligations under those agreements."

Both "logic and reality," Pratter said, "lead the court to evaluate the obvious intent and import of the Nolen settlement agreement, i.e., to secure $20 million for plaintiffs from multiple sources, all emanating from or through Nolen, and to underscore that evaluation by the obvious mathematical certainty that under no circumstances would $16 million bear any sensible relationship to Brubacher's jury-assessed 2 percent liability responsibility while, in contrast, fitting so neatly into the gap left between the $20 million Nolen settlement liability and the $4 million Erie payment on Nolen's account."

Pratter said it was obvious that the plaintiffs believed that Baringer was being stubborn in refusing to settle, and therefore "endeavored to exert maximum economic pressure on Baringer and its insurer" by drafting a pro tanto release and then a pro rata release.

"However, in shooting for maximum pressure, they in fact overshot as they now try to justify a recovery far in excess of the total awarded damages from a defendant, i.e. Baringer, against whom the jury deliberately assessed only nominal liability," Pratter wrote.

Pratter instead concluded that "regardless of what name plaintiffs may want to give . . . it does not matter what these agreements are called or what they promote. The court holds that in operation they result in a full $20 million molding of the damages award."

In an order attached to her opinion, Pratter said the lawyers should confer and see if they can agree on the proper amount of delay damages to be assessed.

E. SETTLEMENT PRACTICES AS TORTS

1. IS THERE A DUTY TO SETTLE?

KENT SYVERUD, THE DUTY TO SETTLE

76 Virginia Law Review 1113 (1990)

Introduction

Litigation and liability insurance are symbiotic institutions. They are dissimilar organisms intimately associated in a mutually beneficial relationship. Without tort litigation, liability insurance and the profit it generates for insurance companies would largely disappear. Without liability insurance, most tort suits would be significantly less attractive to plaintiffs and their attorneys, and a large fraction of the lawsuits and the tort law bar would fade away. The insurance industry and the trial lawyers may take potshots at each other in attempts to reform aspects of the relationship, but they cannot afford to shoot to kill.

Despite the symbiosis, liability insurance is often ignored in the study of tort litigation. To the extent we do acknowledge the relationship, we tend to place insurance in the reactive role: tort litigation expands, liability insurance adjusts; courts create a new type of tort, insurance companies respond with a new type of policy; juries award larger verdicts, insurance companies raise their premiums. We look to changes in tort law and civil procedure for the causes of changes in liability insurance. Tort litigation, not liability insurance, dominates the relationship.

Or does it? Watching a plaintiff's lawyer for a day makes one wonder. Who gets sued often depends on who has insurance. The complaint is often amended, and the discovery and trial strategy accordingly altered, to conform to what the insurance policy covers and what it does not. The value of the case, which we so often assume to be a function of the substantive tort law and costs of civil process, may be just as much a function of how much insurance coverage the defendant has purchased.

It even may be that insurance precedes tort liability in the sequence — that insurance institutions cause some forms of tort litigation to come into existence, rather than the other way around. There are some indications, for example, that the first "clergy malpractice" policies, which cover a minister or rabbi's liability for injuries caused by professional counseling, were created and marketed before any plaintiff's lawyer creatively drafted a complaint seeking damages for such injuries. It is certainly possible that some forms of tort litigation might never have developed had not some insurance broker first paved the way by creating awareness of the liability risk and an insurance policy to cover the judgment.

I believe liability insurance and tort litigation evolve together, with each institution acting upon, reacting to, and supporting the other. If this is true, then just as we must look to tort litigation to understand any clause of a liability insurance contract, we must also look to liability insurance to understand and explain any aspect of tort litigation. In this Article, I examine one aspect of tort litigation — settlement — in which the influence of liability insurance has rarely been acknowledged. I address a reality that is obvious from liability insurance contracts but ignored in almost all recent scholarship on settlement: in a wide array of tort suits, even where there is a single defendant, the potential liability is fractured, with the defendant, the insurance company, and sometimes reinsurance companies and excess insurance companies holding shares. Control over settlement may also be divided among these parties, but not necessarily in the same patterns as ownership of liability. Efforts to explain the settlement process, or to encourage settlement, must take into account the diverse incentives of those who hold the liability and those who control the settlement.

In order to explore how liability insurance influences the settlement of tort litigation, I look to the body of tort and contract law that regulates liability insurance companies. For seventy-five years, courts have invoked a doctrine known as "the duty to settle" to impose liability on insurance companies who fail to settle lawsuits against the people they insure. The classic and still most common fact pattern arises when a plaintiff sues an insured for damages in excess of the limits of insurance company liability specified in an insurance policy. In this situation, which most torts students encounter in Crisci v. Security Insurance Co., the insurance company and the insured each hold a share of the potential liability, but the insurance company by contract controls the defense of the lawsuit. Conflicts arise when the plaintiff proposes to settle for amounts close to the policy limits, because the policy holder has a greater exposure to additional liability than the insurance company if the proposal is rejected and the case tried. Employing a variety of legal standards, courts often sanction insurance companies for going to trial in such circumstances. Typically, when courts find the company's conduct in refusing the proposal to be unreasonable or in bad faith, the company is held liable to the insured for the entire judgment, including any portion in excess of the policy limits.

In the last twenty years, duty-to-settle doctrine has spread well beyond this classic scenario. As a result, reported duty-to-settle decisions open a window from which we can view how insureds and insurance companies order their relationships to provide for settlement. This Article shows how the arrangements affect settlements of tort litigation. In Part I, I describe the typical duty-to-settle suit and the insurance arrangements that produce it. In this context, the duty-to-settle problem is a product of shared liability between insurer and insured coupled with exclusive insurer responsibility for defense and settlement. Part II analyzes the settlement conflicts that arise when potential liability and settlement control are allocated in this fashion. The analysis of the sources of conflict helps both to explain the complexity of duty-to-settle doctrine and to identify some ways in which the doctrine should be reformed. Part III looks more globally at the costs and benefits of judicial efforts to prescribe reasonable settlements, and proposes a modified form of strict liability for failure to settle. Finally, Part IV addresses settlement behavior pursuant to the more complex allocations of potential liability and control of settlement found in many professional and commercial liability insurance policies.

I conclude that settlement behavior in tort cases is a product of the interaction between liability insurance and the law and procedure of tort litigation. The different allocations of control over settlement in various types of tort litigation affect which cases are settled and which are tried, and they do so in ways that should concern anyone interested in the justice, frequency, or timing of settlements.

I. An Overview of a Duty-to-Settle Suit

Duty-to-settle doctrine, like much of liability insurance law, is an unwieldy blend of insurance economics with the law of contracts, torts, and civil procedure. It is difficult to analyze any part of the problem without simultaneously addressing all its aspects. Perhaps the least misleading place to start is with a description of the typical duty-to-settle suit in a state court. The paradigmatic duty-to-settle case arises out of the most common form of tort suit: a personal injury claim filed against the owner of real property or an automobile. For example, a car strikes a pedestrian, a shopper slips in the supermarket, or a child dives into a swimming pool and hits the bottom. The injured party files a claim, and eventually a lawsuit, against the owner of the car or property (or perhaps against the operator or maintainer of the car or premises). The complaint seeks damages for the defendant's alleged negligence.

The defendant has purchased liability insurance against just such an eventuality. More precisely, she has purchased insurance against two related but distinct risks of financial loss: the risk that she will have to pay the costs of defending a lawsuit, and the risk that, as a result of the suit, she will have to pay money to the plaintiff. The defendant's liability insurance covers the first loss by requiring the insurance company to defend the suit, and to pay the cost of the defense. The policy covers the second loss by requiring the company to indemnify the insured for judgments or settlements, but only up to a specified liability limit.[7] In cases where the claim exceeds the limit, the potential liability is therefore broken into two pieces, with the liability limit determining which piece of the damage claim is held by the insurance company and which by the insured defendant. The company's piece is the first that will be paid in any trial or settlement; the insured's piece is paid only when the company's piece is first exhausted.

Typically, the same part of the liability insurance contract that requires the company to defend the suit also gives the company control over the settlement decision. . . .

At some point in the litigation, it becomes apparent that the potential liability in the case exceeds the liability limit in the policy. The complaint itself may so indicate, or, in states where complaints do not specify the amount of damages sought, the insurer may discover the possibility of excess liability through discovery, its own independent investigations, or discussions with the plaintiff's representatives.

The insurance company chooses to let the case go to trial. In the vast majority of cases, it does so after rejecting one or more "demands" from the plaintiff—proposals to settle the litigation for a fixed sum of money.[12] The demands often fall within the policy limits. At trial, the insured defendant loses, and a jury awards damages in excess of the policy limits. The insurance company insists that the plaintiff must look to the insured defendant's personal assets to pay the excess. The insurance company is thereupon sued for failing to settle the case. In almost every state, the insured defendant can sue; in many states the insured defendant can and frequently does assign her claim against the insurance company to the plaintiff; in a few states the plaintiff may by statute be able to sue the company even in the absence of an assignment. The suit against the insurance company invariably seeks damages at least in the amount of the excess liability. In some states attorneys' fees may be recovered; in three states damages for emotional distress may also be awarded.

The trial of the case against the insurance company will focus on the behavior of the company, and, in particular, the behavior of the claims personnel and defense attorney during the settlement negotiations. No state

---

7. Automobile and property owner's liability insurance policies rarely have a single provision limiting insurer liability. Instead, policies often impose a limit on coverage for each person injured as well as a limit on coverage for each accident or occurrence, regardless of how many people are injured. Commercial liability policies often also impose an "aggregate limit"—a ceiling on the total amount the insurer will pay on multiple claims covered by the policy. Hence, the plural term "policy limits" in referring to a single insurance contract.

12. Among personal injury lawyers and liability claims adjustors, settlement proposals from plaintiffs are generally referred to as "demands," whereas settlement proposals from defendants are known as "offers." This Article follows this convention. Scholars and judges tend to lump both offers and demands together under the term "offers." Economic models of litigation often refer to demands as "asks."

holds the insurance company strictly liable for the excess judgment when it rejects a settlement demand within the policy limits. Instead, the insurance company is liable only if its behavior in failing to settle departs from some norm by a margin a jury can fairly label "negligent," "bad faith" (a standard purportedly more onerous than negligence), or some combination of the two. Both the norm and the margin for error have been the subject of disagreement among the courts.

The norm specifying ideal insurance company behavior in settlement negotiations has varied greatly. What degree of deference should an insurance company give to the interests of the insured when considering settlement demands? The earliest cases seemed to give insurance companies complete discretion whether and when to settle, and required no deference whatsoever to the interests of the insured. The majority of states today require the insurance company to give "equal consideration" to the interests of the insured and the company in evaluating settlements. In applying this standard to actual cases, courts in sixteen states profess to accept Robert Keeton's 1954 suggestion that the insurance company should disregard the policy limits in evaluating settlement demands: "With respect to the decision whether to settle or try the case, the insurance company must . . . view the situation as it would if there were no policy limit applicable to the claim."

The practical distinction between a negligent failure to settle and a bad faith failure to settle remains elusive, as scholars have long pointed out, and reference to jury instructions in "bad faith" states will show. Michigan, for example, tells its juries that bad faith cannot be based upon negligence or poor judgment, but can exist where the insurer acts with a selfish purpose. In deciding whether an insurance company acted with bad faith, Michigan juries weigh the following factors, among others: failure to make a proper investigation of the claim prior to refusing a demand within the policy limits; failure to solicit a reasonable settlement demand or to initiate settlement discussions when warranted by the circumstances; failure to accept a reasonable demand within the limits; undue delay in accepting a reasonable demand "where the verdict potential is high"; failure to keep the insured fully informed of developments in the suit that could reasonably affect the interests of the insured; disregarding the advice of an adjustor or defense attorney with respect to settlement; and "serious and recurrent negligence by the insurer." This list of factors gives a jury many ways to interpret "unreasonable" conduct as bad faith, and more significantly, it shows that liability in "bad faith" states, as in "negligence" states, often turns on whether a particular settlement demand was reasonable.

When is a proposed settlement reasonable? Lawyers, legal scholars, and philosophers have found that question vexing. Nevertheless, juries in duty-to-settle cases answer the question on a regular basis. . . . By the time the jury retires to deliberate, it has been presented with a thorough description of how attorneys and claims adjustors evaluate the value of a lawsuit. . . .

II. The Sources of Settlement Conflicts Between Insurance Companies and Their Insureds

Scholars of settlement have long appreciated that Americans sue and are sued largely through their attorneys, and that rules governing attorney compensation may therefore affect the trial and settlement of tort litigation. Several studies have addressed the situations in which the interests of attorneys in litigation will conflict with the interests of their clients, and how these conflicts affect whether and when cases settle.[38] The settlement conflicts between insureds and their insurance companies have attracted less attention, perhaps in part because there are so many more ways for incentives to diverge. Duty-to-settle cases focus primarily on liability limits as a source of conflict, and therefore seek to neutralize the effect of liability limits by requiring insurers to ignore them in evaluating settlements. The cases also reflect four other sources of conflict: the allocation of defense costs; differences in the levels of risk aversion of insurers and insureds; strategic bargaining by the insurance company; and the additional stakes, beyond the amount of the settlement or judgment, which the insured or the company may have in the outcome. . . .

* * *

B. Allocation of Defense Costs

Defense costs, like liability limits, may cause insureds and their insurance companies to disagree about whether to accept a settlement demand. When a demand is rejected, the insurance company, and not the insured, pays the defendant's attorneys' fees and court costs associated with a trial. In comparing a proposed settlement to the expected loss from trial, the insurance company will rationally add in these defense costs, whereas the insured will not. All other things being equal, this would increase the insurance company's incentives to settle relative to the insured, and would ameliorate some of the settlement conflicts arising from liability limits. The higher the litigation costs, the less likely the insurance company will reject a demand within the policy limits, and the more likely it will accede to the insured's preference to accept all such demands.

For settlement demands in excess of the policy limits, the allocation of defense costs may actually flip the typical preferences of insured and insurer with respect to settlement: it may cause the insured to prefer trial while the insurer would prefer settlement. The insurance company accepting such a settlement saves defense costs; the insured may have to contribute more to such a settlement than the excess judgment that the insured expects will result from trial.

To illustrate this latter conflict, assume that a plaintiff who is suing for $200,000 proposes to settle for $120,000, and that the defendant has $100,000 in liability insurance. Assume further that both the insurance company and the defendant expect that the judgment should the case be tried will be $105,000, and that the insurance company estimates it will cost $16,000 to try the case. Should the $120,000 demand be accepted? A rational defendant holding the entire liability would save $1,000 by accepting the demand, because the sum of the expected judgment and the defense costs is $121,000. The insurance company will save $16,000 by accepting the demand: if the demand is accepted it will pay its $100,000 liability limit, whereas if it is rejected it expects to pay both the liability limit and

---

38. *See* Coffee, Understanding the Plaintiff's Attorney: The Implications of Economic Theory for Private Enforcement of Law Through Class and Derivative Actions, 86 Colum. L. Rev. 669 (1986); Kritzer, Fee Arrangements and Negotiation, 21 L. & Soc'y Rev. 341 (1987); Miller, Some Agency Problems in Settlement, 16 J. Legal Stud. 189 (1987); Rowe, Predicting the Effects of Attorney Fee Shifting, 47 Law & Contemp. Probs. 139 (1984).

$16,000 in defense costs. The insured, however, will lose $15,000 if the demand is accepted: she will have to contribute $20,000 to the settlement, but only $5,000 to the expected judgment. The result is that the insurance company and a holder of the entire liability would accept the demand, while the insured would reject it. Slight tinkering with the amount of the defense costs can also produce situations where only the insurance company would accept the demand, and both the insured and the holder of the entire liability would reject it.

* * *

C. Risk Aversion

An individual who compares a potential judgment to a settlement proposal is comparing an uncertain prospect to a sure thing. The more risk-averse the individual — for example, the higher the premium the individual is willing to pay to trade the uncertain prospect for a sure thing of equal expected value — the more likely the individual is to favor settlement over the uncertainties of trial. If an insured and an insurance company have different levels of risk aversion, there will be a set of demands that one would rationally accept and the other reject.

Normally, we assume insureds are more risk-averse than insurance companies. The greater risk aversion of insureds makes insurance possible. When insureds are willing to pay more in premiums than their expected losses, insurers can profit by assuming the risks of a large group of similarly situated insureds. As the size of the group increases, the actual loss for the group approaches the expected loss for the group, and the premium each insured pays above the expected loss is left over for the insurer.

It is not much of a leap beyond this analysis to assume that insureds are usually more risk-averse with respect to the decision to go to trial than are insurance companies. If true, this would mean that, for some significant set of proposed settlements, the insurance company will prefer to go to trial and the insured will prefer to settle. Because the insurance company controls the settlement of the typical personal injury suit, more cases will be tried than would be the case if the insured controlled the settlement. . . .

D. Strategic Bargaining by the Insurer

* * *

2. Strategic Bargaining with the Insured

Early in this century, the first qualifications to what had been unlimited insurer discretion to settle tort litigation came in situations where the insurance company bargained strategically with its insured. Courts had long been comfortable with the notion that insurance companies need consider only their own interests, and not the interests of insureds, in responding to settlement demands. But during World War I, a few courts became troubled to discover that insurance companies might even reject demands that appeared to be in the interests of a selfish insurance company. The situation they confronted was insurance companies who used the risk of excess liability to coerce an insured to contribute to a settlement within the liability limits and below the expected judgment. . . .

Current duty-to-settle doctrine accordingly places insurers in a delicate situation. There is some chance they may be liable if they fail to notify insureds that a contribution could effectuate a settlement. But an insurer's "insistence upon a contribution as the price of settlement" will almost certainly be considered evidence of bad faith in any subsequent action for excess liability. Judges and juries make the largely subjective judgment whether a suggestion that an insured contribute to a settlement is merely "notice" or instead a threat not to settle absent a contribution. . . .

V. Conclusion

In the grand scheme of tort and insurance law, duty-to-settle doctrine is a small, interesting, and increasingly overlitigated wrinkle. . . .

More important than duty-to-settle doctrine itself is the insight duty-to-settle cases afford into the settlement behavior of defendants in tort litigation, and into the relationship between tort litigation and liability insurance. At least in the context of settlement, tort litigation and liability insurance often become intertwined. Insureds and insurers have an array of conflicting and combining interests in the disposition of most tort suits, and courts protect those interests in ways that vary across different types of tort litigation. No explanation of how a particular type of tort litigation settles is complete if it ignores the insurance policy provisions that allocate potential liability and settlement control. . . .

Even when the defendant is an insurance company, it turns out, tort litigation and liability insurance evolve together, adjusting to changes in the environment. Our understanding of both institutions will improve as we come to regard them as inextricably linked, as symbiotic organisms whose response to any stimulus—including a settlement demand—is ultimately the product of their interaction.

NOTE ON BAD FAITH AND *MORADI-SHALAL*

Bad-faith liability is an insurer's nightmare and the underinsured plaintiff's friend. Faced with many claims, some of which it suspects are bogus or perhaps just not as strong as the allegations suggest, insurers will want to investigate and settle selectively. But if they fail to settle a claim that—with the advantage of hindsight now appears strong—they find themselves liable not only for an amount in excess of policy limits but also for punitive damages. Because insurers know this, plaintiffs have a powerful bargaining tool—the prospect of a bad-faith suit. Insurers, of course, battle back in various ways. They have instituted procedures designed to assure that claims get prompt and accurate review and that they can justify offers of settlement with reference to previous claims. And they have—with some success—convinced the U.S. Supreme Court to place limits on punitive damages. *Campbell v. State Farm*, which you encountered in the section on litigation finance, resulted from a challenge to the amount of a bad-faith award. The plaintiffs' bar, no less resourceful, has sought to preserve and extend the concept of bad-faith liability. The next case displays one phase of this battle in one state. To understand its significance pay careful attention to what the court held in the case being overruled: under the regime of *Royal Globe* (the case being overruled) what could a plaintiff do? Why might the insurers have thought the *Royal Globe* regime outrageous? And why might the plaintiffs' bar have mourned the decision in *Moradi-Shalal*?

Moradi-Shalal v. Fireman's Fund Ins. Cos.

758 P.2d 58 (Cal. 1988)

Lucas, C.J. (with Panelli, Arguelles, Eagleson and Kaufman, J.J., concurring.)

We initially granted review in this case to attempt to resolve some of the widespread confusion that has arisen regarding the application of our opinion in Royal Globe Ins. Co. v. Superior Court (1979) 23 Cal. 3d 880. In *Royal Globe*, the court held that Insurance Code section 790.03, subdivision (h) (a provision of the Unfair Practices Act, Ins. Code, §790 et seq.), created a private cause of action against insurers who commit the unfair practices enumerated in that provision. (All further statutory references are to the Insurance Code unless otherwise indicated.) Among the issues raised and argued by counsel and amici curiae, however, is the more basic question whether we should reconsider our holding in *Royal Globe*.

In light of certain developments occurring subsequent to *Royal Globe* which call into question its continued validity, we have found it appropriate to reexamine that decision. As will appear, we have concluded that the *Royal Globe* court incorrectly evaluated the legislative intent underlying the passage of section 790.03, subdivision (h), and that accordingly *Royal Globe* should be overruled. We also have concluded, however, that our holding in that regard should be prospective only, that is, applicable only to cases filed after the date our opinion herein becomes final. As for cases pending prior to that time, including the present case, the *Royal Globe* rule shall apply, as construed in part VI of this opinion.

I. The Facts

In this case, plaintiff settled her personal injury suit for damages against defendant's insured, and that suit was dismissed with prejudice. Her subsequent complaint against defendant insurer for violations of section 790.03, subdivisions (h)(2), (3), and (5),[2] alleged the following facts:

---

2. Section 790.03 reads in relevant part: "The following are hereby defined as unfair methods of competition and unfair and deceptive acts or practices in the business of insurance.

"...

"(h) Knowingly committing or performing with such frequency as to indicate a general business practice any of the following unfair claims settlement practices:

"...

"(2) Failing to acknowledge and act reasonably promptly upon communications with respect to claims arising under insurance policies.

"(3) Failing to adopt and implement reasonable standards for the prompt investigation and processing of claims arising under insurance policies.

"...

"(5) Not attempting in good faith to effectuate prompt, fair, and equitable settlements of claims in which liability has become reasonably clear."

In July 1983, plaintiff was injured in an automobile accident in which a vehicle driven negligently by defendant's insured struck her vehicle. In April 1984, plaintiff's attorneys wrote to defendant, submitting evidence of damages incurred by plaintiff as a result of the accident, and requesting settlement of the claim against its insured. On June 6, 1984, having received no acknowledgement or response to their letter, plaintiff's attorneys again wrote defendant requesting settlement of the claim and notifying it that plaintiff was reserving her rights of action against defendant under *Royal Globe*. Plaintiff sued the insured on June 21, 1984. In September, five months after her first communication to defendant, plaintiff settled the action against the insured. (According to the representations of counsel at oral argument, the settlement amount was $1,800 less than plaintiff's original demand.) Plaintiff's action against the insured was dismissed with prejudice.

Thereafter, plaintiff brought suit against defendant under *Royal Globe*, based on its alleged refusal to promptly and fairly settle her claim against the insured. In her first amended complaint against defendant, plaintiff alleged defendant "did not acknowledge or act upon [her attorneys'] communication, did not promptly investigate or process the claim, and did not attempt in good faith to effectuate a prompt, fair, and equitable settlement of the claim, in which liability was reasonably clear." She sought compensatory damages according to proof and $750,000 in punitive damages. The trial court sustained defendant's general demurrer without leave to amend, based on its conclusion that the absence of a final judgment in the underlying action precluded a *Royal Globe* action against defendant.

The Court of Appeal reversed, holding that settlement coupled with a dismissal with prejudice was a sufficient conclusion of the underlying action to support a subsequent *Royal Globe* action against defendant. In part VI hereof, we review the correctness of that holding within the constraints of *Royal Globe*. First, however, we reconsider the validity of the *Royal Globe* holding itself.

II. The Royal Globe Decision

In *Royal Globe*, a bare majority of the court held that under section 790.03, subdivisions (h)(5) and (14), a private litigant could bring an action to impose civil liability on an insurer for engaging in unfair claims settlement practices. The court further held that such an action could be brought against the insurer by either the insured or a third party claimant, that is, "an individual who is injured by the alleged negligence of an insured." . . .

In addition, the *Royal Globe* court interpreted the foregoing provisions as conferring on the injured claimant a cause of action arising from a *single instance* of unfair conduct, so that a plaintiff did not have to prove that the insurer committed the acts prohibited by the statute as a general business practice. . . .

The *Royal Globe* court concluded by holding that the plaintiff may not sue both the insured and the insurer in the same action, and that the suit against the insurer must be "postponed until the liability of the insured is first determined." . . .

* * *

IV. Subsequent Developments

A. *Rejection by Other State Courts*—We decided *Royal Globe* in 1979. Since then, the courts of other states have largely declined to follow our *Royal Globe* analysis. . . .

B. *Scholarly Criticism*—Commentary on *Royal Globe* has been generally critical of that decision. . . .

E. *Adverse Consequences*—Although we are not in a position to verify the accuracy of each of their observations, the commentators who have focused on *Royal Globe* suggest our holding has had several adverse social and economic consequences.

Confirming Justice Richardson's prediction in his *Royal Globe* dissent, several commentators have observed that the rule in that case promotes multiple litigation, because its holding contemplates, indeed encourages, two lawsuits by the injured claimant: an initial suit against the insured, followed by a second suit against the insurer for bad faith refusal to settle. . . .

V. Royal Globe Should Be Overruled

The points raised by the dissent in *Royal Globe*, as reflected in the cases from other states, the adverse scholarly comment, and the available legislative history, seem irrefutable. Neither section 790.03 nor section 790.09 was intended to create a private civil cause of action against an insurer that commits one of the various acts listed in section 790.03, subdivision (h). The contrary *Royal Globe* holding reportedly has resulted in multiple litigation or coerced settlements, and has generated confusion and uncertainty regarding its application. For all the foregoing reasons, we have concluded *Royal Globe, supra*, 23 Cal. 3d 880, should be overruled. . . .

VI. Requirement of a Prior Determination of Liability

In *Royal Globe* we did not discuss the procedural prerequisites of a third party's section 790.03 claim against the insurer, except to hold that such a claim "may not be brought until the action between the injured party and the insured is concluded." We did not explicitly consider what would constitute a sufficient "conclusion" of the action. For purposes of the present case and other pending *Royal Globe* actions which are not affected by the decision here, we must now decide whether settlement of the third party's underlying claim against the insured "concludes" the action within the meaning of *Royal Globe*, so that after settling the underlying claim a claimant can bring a subsequent suit against the insurer under section 790.03, subdivision (h). We will hold, for these pending cases, that settlement is an insufficient conclusion of the underlying action: there must be a conclusive judicial determination of the insured's liability before the third party can succeed in an action against the insurer under section 790.03. . . .

The judgment of the Court of Appeal is reversed, and the cause remanded for further proceedings consistent with this opinion.

MOSK, J. (with BROUSSARD, J., concurring.)
I dissent.

Royal Globe (1979-1988), may it Rest in Peace. During its life it served the people of California well, particularly the victims of unfair and deceptive practices. The majority have now replaced *Royal Globe* with a "Royal Bonanza" for insurance carriers, i.e., total immunity for unfair and deceptive practices committed on innocent claimants. They have exalted principal over principle. It will be interesting to observe whether this judicial largesse causes insurance premiums to decrease or insurance profits to increase. . . .

LOCKWOOD INT'L V. VOLM BAG CO.

273 F.3d 741 (7th Cir. 2001)

POSNER, Circuit Judge.

This diversity suit, based on Wisconsin law, presents a novel but potentially quite important issue of insurance law: whether a liability insurer, asked to defend (or pay the defense costs in) a suit against its insured that contains some claims that are covered by the insurance policy and others that are not, can limit its responsibility to defend by paying the plaintiff in the liability suit to replead the covered claims as uncovered claims.

For simplicity we treat the case as a three-cornered dispute among a single plaintiff, Lockwood; a single intervenor, North River, the insurance company; and a single defendant, Volm. It began with Lockwood, a foreign manufacturer of machines for weighing and bagging produce, suing Volm, which Lockwood had appointed to be its exclusive North American distributor. Lockwood's complaint charged that Volm had secretly formed and funded a new company, Munter, staffed by former employees of Lockwood that Volm had lured to work for Munter. Having done so, the complaint continued, Volm stole Lockwood's intellectual property and manufactured machines that copied Lockwood's. To complete its infamy, Volm then — by disparaging Lockwood and its products (even spreading false rumors about Lockwood's financial solidity), by soliciting purchases of Lockwood products and then substituting knock-offs of them manufactured by Munter, and by warning customers that Lockwood machines infringed a Volm patent (acquired by fraud, the complaint alleged) — had induced customers for weighing and bagging machines to switch their orders from Lockwood's machines to Munter's. The complaint charged that these acts constituted breach of fiduciary duty, tortious interference with contract, unfair competition, and conspiracy. The suit is still pending.

North River had issued a commercial general liability (CGL) policy to Lockwood. Under the heading "personal injury," the policy covers product and producer disparagement. Under the heading of "advertising injury," it covers (so far as bears on this case and does not duplicate "personal injury") misappropriation of "advertising ideas or style of doing business" or "infringement of copyright," provided the misappropriation or infringement occurs "in the course of advertising" the insured's products. Since the complaint expressly charged disparagement of Lockwood and its products, and strongly implied (especially in the bait and switch allegation) that Volm had appropriated Lockwood's "advertising ideas or style of doing business," North River agreed to handle Volm's defense. Had the case gone through to judgment or settlement in the usual way, North River would probably have borne the entire expense of conducting Volm's defense, although its duty of indemnifying Volm for any damages that it was determined through judgment or settlement to owe Lockwood would have been limited to so much of the judgment or settlement as was fairly allocable to the claims in Lockwood's suit that were covered by the policy. The difference reflects the greater difficulty of apportioning defense costs than damages. But the rationale of a rule often limits its scope, and does here: if defense costs are readily apportionable between the covered and the uncovered claims, the insurance company need pay only for the former.

Four years into Lockwood's suit, North River paid Lockwood $1.5 million to file an amended complaint that would delete the covered claims. Lockwood agreed to credit that amount against any judgment it might obtain against Volm. Since the policy limit was only $1 million, the agreement (to which Volm was not a party) protected Volm up to the policy limit against having to pay any covered claims. With the agreement in hand, North River, which had already intervened in the litigation to obtain a declaration of its duties to the insured, asked the district court to rule that it had no further duty to defend or indemnify Volm, since the effect of the amended complaint was to eliminate any possible liability of Volm to pay the covered claims in Lockwood's original complaint. The district judge agreed and entered a partial final judgment against Volm, which was immediately appealable because it resolved the claim of one of the parties, namely North River. Fed. R. Civ. P. 54(b). Volm then appealed. It asks us to rule that North River must continue to pay its defense costs notwithstanding the settlement between North River and Lockwood.

North River's lawyer acknowledged at argument—what is anyway obvious—that either he or other counsel for North River had gone over the amended complaint with Lockwood's counsel line by line to make sure that all insured claims had been deleted. In other words, the insurance company sat down with its insured's adversary to contrive a complaint that would eliminate any remaining contractual obligation of the insurance company to defend the insured. (We limit our attention to defense costs, ignoring indemnity, in view of the fact that North River's settlement agreement with Lockwood gave Volm more than the policy limit; thus only defense costs are at issue in this appeal.) It did this without consulting the insured or obtaining the latter's agreement. We have difficulty imagining a more conspicuous betrayal of the insurer's fiduciary duty to its insured than for its lawyers to plot with the insured's adversary a repleading that will enable the adversary to maximize his recovery of uninsured damages from the insured while stripping the insured of its right to a defense by the insurance company. The limits of coverage, whether limits on the amount to be indemnified under the policy or, as in the present case, on the type of claims covered by the policy, create a conflict of interest between insurer and insured. The insurer yielded to the conflict, in effect paying its insured's adversary to eliminate the insured's remaining insurance coverage.

It is true as North River points out that if in the course of litigation the covered claims fall out of the case through settlement or otherwise, the insurer's duty to defend his insured ceases. That is the easiest case for readily apportioning defense costs between covered and uncovered claims. Nor can the insured prevent the insurer from settling covered claims for an amount that protects the assured from having to pay anything on those claims out of his own pocket, merely because the settlement, by giving the insured all that he contracted for, will terminate the insurer's duty to defend the entire suit. But North River did not merely settle covered claims; as part of the settlement it paid Lockwood to convert some of the covered claims to uncovered claims. That was not dealing in good faith with its insured.

An example may help make this clear. Suppose that a suit against the insured makes two claims, both covered by the defendant's liability insurance policy. The insurer could settle one claim for $1 million and both for $2 million, but $2 million is too high. Instead it says to the plaintiff, "I'll give you $1.5 million to settle the first claim if you'll agree to redraft the second so that it's an uncovered claim, which you can of course continue to press against my insured." The only purpose of such a deal would be to spare the insurance company the expense of defending against the second claim, even though it was a covered claim when filed and would have continued to be a covered claim had it not been for the insurer's bribe of the plaintiff.

The duty of good faith is read into every insurance contract, in order to prevent opportunistic behavior by the contracting party that has the whip hand. That was North River, which neither needed nor sought its insured's permission to settle with Lockwood and by doing so expose the insured to having to bear its own defense costs for the remainder of the litigation.

North River's maneuver is also defeated by the principle that the duty to defend depends on the facts alleged rather than on the pleader's legal theory. If Lockwood was alleging what was in fact personal injury or advertising injury within the meaning of the policy, the fact that, whether at North River's urging or otherwise, it redrafted its complaint to change the name of the tort it was charging Volm with, but retained the same factual allegations that had triggered North River's initial duty to defend, would be ineffective to terminate that duty.

North River and Lockwood were apparently mindful of this principle. Their agreement not only requires Lockwood to delete the specific claims in the original complaint that are covered by the insurance policy that North River had issued to Volm, such as disparagement, defamation, misappropriation of advertising ideas or style of doing business, and copyright infringement, plus several of the theories of liability asserted in its original complaint (the ones most likely to involve disparagement or solicitation), such as tortious interference and unfair competition, and thus likely to be covered by the policy that North River had issued to Volm; it also forbids Lockwood to "undertake to prove" at trial a number of specific allegations, such as that Volm caused Lockwood's customers to believe that Lockwood products infringed Volm's patent. This effort to get around the principle that the insurer's duties to the insured are determined not by legal theories but by facts portends unbearable awkwardness in the forthcoming trial. Suppose that in an effort to prove its remaining theories of liability, such as breach of fiduciary duty, which disparagement and other excluded charges would bolster (especially since Lockwood is seeking punitive damages), Lockwood presents evidence in support of these charges at trial. Volm will be delighted, because the introduction of such evidence will trigger North River's duty of indemnity and defense. North River will therefore have to have a lawyer in the courtroom to object whenever Lockwood crosses the line into forbidden territory. Either that (and what will the jury make of it?) or North River will sit out the trial but later sue Lockwood for breach of the settlement agreement if by crossing the line Lockwood resurrects Volm's rights under North River's policy.

No case that has been cited to us or that our own research has uncovered authorizes so convoluted a mode of proceeding. To recapitulate: North River had every right to settle the claims that gave rise to its duty to defend in the first place — the covered claims and the potentially covered claims in Lockwood's suit — in order to avoid having to defend the claims in the same suit that were not actually or potentially covered. But that is not what North River did. The duty to defend turns on the facts alleged rather than on the theories pleaded; and even after its deal with North River, Lockwood was alleging facts that could well, depending on the course of trial, describe a covered claim. Thus North River did not leave behind only clearly uncovered claims when it tried to shuck off its contractual responsibility to pay for its insured's defense.

It is irrelevant that the trial may show that Lockwood's only meritorious claims against Volm are ones that are not within the scope of the policy. The duty to defend (and hence to reimburse for defense costs when the insurance company doesn't provide the lawyer for the insured) is broader than the duty to indemnify. The reason goes beyond the practical difficulties, noted earlier, involved in apportioning defense costs between covered and uncovered claims. The duty is broader because it "is triggered by arguable, as opposed to actual, coverage." General Casualty Co. of Wisconsin v. Hills, 209 Wis. 2d 167, 561 N.W.2d 718, 722 n. 11 (Wis. 1997). The insured needs a defense before he knows whether the claim that has been made against him is covered by the policy, assuming there is doubt on the question. If the duty to defend were no broader than the duty to indemnify, there would be the paradox that an insured exonerated after trial would have no claim against the insurance company for his defense costs, since the company would have no duty to indemnify him for a loss resulting from a judgment or settlement in the suit against the insured. The duty to defend must therefore be broader than the duty to indemnify, and so the fact that North River paid the policy's limit on indemnification does not exonerate it.

The judgment is reversed and the case remanded for further proceedings consistent with this opinion.

Reversed and Remanded.

ASHER HAWKINS, JUDGE AWARDS $8.5 MILLION VERDICT IN BAD FAITH ACTION

Legal Intelligencer, February 8, 2007

Following a bench trial in a bad faith action, a Delaware County, Pa., judge has slapped insurer Penn National with a $6 million punitive damages finding in a verdict that also included nearly $2.5 million in compensatory damages.

Johnson v. Pennsylvania National Mutual Casualty Insurance Co. stems from the April 2001 shooting death on the Chester, Pa., street of Sami Toler during a scuffle with Duane Johnson, a married father of three who was insured by a Penn National homeowner's policy, according to court documents in the case.

Although he ultimately pleaded guilty to voluntary manslaughter as part of a plea bargain that carried a five-to-10-year sentence, Johnson always maintained that he had fought with Toler only after a gun-toting Toler had assaulted Johnson and his uncle, and that he would never harm anyone intentionally. Johnson said he agreed to the plea bargain reluctantly out of fear of the possibility of a life sentence if he went to trial.

When Toler's survivors filed a negligence action against Johnson in civil court in the wake of his plea bargain, Penn National declined to defend him, arguing that the existence of his voluntary manslaughter guilty plea triggered an "intentional act" clause in Johnson's homeowner's insurance policy. . . .

In a 27-page ruling filed last week, Delaware County Common Pleas Judge Charles B. Burr II suggested that Penn National had incorrectly jumped to the conclusion that Johnson's guilty plea to his criminal charges served to absolve it of its duty to defend him in Toler's survivors' negligence action.

"In the instant case, the character of Penn National's actions were at best offensive, but at worst repulsive," Burr wrote. "In addition to exhibiting virtually total disregard of the standards and practices of the insurance industry, Penn National continually and willfully ignored its fiduciary responsibilities to its insured."

Burr—who noted that Penn National had ignored an offer from the administrator of Toler's estate to settle the negligence action for Johnson's $100,000 policy limits—found that $6 million was an appropriate punitive damages award based on the insurer's wealth and "the likelihood that this amount will punish and deter Penn National and deter other insurers in the same position from acting in a similar fashion in the future." . . .

Media, Pa., solo practitioner Robert Ewing—who represents in the action Toler's survivors, to whom Johnson has assigned his right to pursue damages against his insurer—said he will be filing for more than $700,000 in delay damages and a maximum of $2.8 million in attorney fees. . . .

2. CREATIVE SETTLEMENTS, WRONGFUL SETTLEMENT?

EVANS v. JEFF D.

475 U.S. 717 (1986)

Justice STEVENS delivered the opinion of the Court.

The Civil Rights Attorney's Fees Awards Act of 1976 (Fees Act) provides that "the court, in its discretion, may allow the prevailing party . . . a reasonable attorney's fee" in enumerated civil rights actions. 42 U.S.C. §1988(b).

. . . In this case, we consider the question whether attorney's fees must be assessed when the case has been settled by a consent decree granting prospective relief to the plaintiff class but providing that the defendants shall not pay any part of the prevailing party's fees or costs. We hold that the District Court has the power, in its sound discretion, to refuse to award fees. . . .

I

[The plaintiff class of emotionally and mentally handicapped children sued the State of Idaho seeking injunctive relief that would improve the treatment of institutionalized class members. Johnson, the class's attorney, was employed by the Idaho Legal Aid Society; his representation agreement with the class representatives contained no provision covering legal fees.]

[O]ne week before trial, petitioners presented respondents with a new settlement proposal . . . "offer[ing] virtually all of the injunctive relief . . . sought in the[] complaint[,]" [but] includ[ing] a provision for a waiver by respondents of any claim to fees or costs. Originally, this waiver was unacceptable to the Idaho Legal Aid Society, which had instructed Johnson to reject any settlement offer conditioned upon a waiver of fees, but Johnson ultimately determined that his ethical obligation to his clients . . . "forced," [him] by an offer giving his clients "the best result [they] could have gotten in this court or any other court," to waive his attorney's fees.[6] The District Court, however, evaluated the waiver in the context of the entire settlement and rejected the ethical underpinnings of Johnson's argument. . . .

. . . Rule 23(e) wisely requires court approval of the terms of any settlement of a class action, but the power to approve or reject a settlement negotiated by the parties before trial does not authorize the court to require the parties to accept a settlement to which they have not agreed. . . . The question we must decide, therefore, is whether the District Court had a duty to reject the proposed settlement because it included a waiver of statutorily authorized attorney's fees.

That duty, whether it takes the form of a general prophylactic rule or arises out of the special circumstances of this case, derives ultimately from the Fees Act rather than from the strictures of professional ethics. Although respondents contend that Johnson, as counsel for the class, was faced with an "ethical dilemma" when petitioners offered him relief greater than that which he could reasonably have expected to obtain for his clients at trial (if only he would stipulate to a waiver of the statutory fee award), and although we recognize Johnson's conflicting interests between pursuing relief for the class and a fee for the Idaho Legal Aid Society, we do not believe that the "dilemma" was an "ethical" one in the sense that Johnson had to choose between conflicting duties under the prevailing norms of professional conduct. Plainly, Johnson had no ethical obligation to seek a statutory fee award. His ethical duty was to

---

6. Johnson's oral presentation to the District Court reads in full as follows:

In other words, an attorney like myself can be put in the position of either negotiating for his client or negotiating for his attorney's fees, and I think that is pretty much the situation that occurred in this instance. I was forced, because of what I perceived to be a result favorable to the plaintiff class, a result that I didn't want to see jeopardized by a trial or by any other possible problems that might have occurred. And the result is the best result I could have gotten in this court or any other court and it is really a fair and just result in any instance and what should have occurred years earlier and which in fact should have been the case all along. That result I didn't want to see disturbed on the basis that my attorney's fees would cause a problem and cause that result to be jeopardized.

serve his clients loyally and competently.[14] Since the proposal to settle the merits was more favorable than the probable outcome of the trial, Johnson's decision to recommend acceptance was consistent with the highest standards of our profession. The District Court, therefore, correctly concluded that approval of the settlement involved no breach of ethics in this case.

The defect, if any, in the negotiated fee waiver must be traced not to the rules of ethics but to the Fees Act. Following this tack, respondents argue that the statute must be construed to forbid a fee waiver that is the product of "coercion." They submit that a "coercive waiver" results when the defendant in a civil rights action (1) offers a settlement on the merits of equal or greater value than that which plaintiffs could reasonably expect to achieve at trial but (2) conditions the offer on a waiver of plaintiffs' statutory eligibility for attorney's fees. Such an offer, they claim, exploits the ethical obligation of plaintiffs' counsel to recommend settlement in order to avoid defendant's statutory liability for its opponents' fees and costs. . . .

III

The text of the Fees Act provides no support for the proposition that Congress intended to ban all fee waivers offered in connection with substantial relief on the merits. On the contrary, the language of the Act, as well as its legislative history, indicates that Congress bestowed on the "prevailing party" (generally plaintiffs) a statutory eligibility for a discretionary award of attorney's fees in specified civil rights actions. It did not prevent the party from waiving this eligibility anymore than it legislated against assignment of this right to an attorney, such as effectively occurred here. . . . The statute and its legislative history nowhere suggest that Congress intended to forbid all waivers of attorney's fees — even those insisted upon by a civil rights plaintiff in exchange for some other relief to which he is indisputably not entitled[20] — anymore than it intended to bar a concession on damages to secure broader injunctive relief. . . .

---

14. Generally speaking, a lawyer is under an ethical obligation to exercise independent professional judgment on behalf of his client; he must not allow his own interests, financial or otherwise, to influence his professional advice. ABA, Model Code of Professional Responsibility EC 5-1, 5-2 (as amended 1980); ABA, Model Rules of Professional Conduct 1.7(b), 2.1 (as amended 1984). Accordingly, it is argued that an attorney is required to evaluate a settlement offer on the basis of his client's interest, without considering his own interest in obtaining a fee; upon recommending settlement, he must abide by the client's decision whether or not to accept the offer, see Model Code of Professional Responsibility EC 7-7 to EC 7-9; Model Rules of Professional Conduct 1.2(a).

20. Judge Wald has described the use of attorney's fees as a "bargaining chip" useful to plaintiffs as well as defendants. In her opinion concurring in the judgment in Moore v. National Assn. of Security Dealers, Inc., she wrote:

On the other hand, the *Jeff D.* approach probably means that a defendant who is willing to grant immediate prospective relief to a plaintiff case, but would rather gamble on the outcome at trial than pay attorneys' fees and costs up front, will never settle. In short, removing attorneys' fees as a "bargaining chip" cuts both ways. It prevents defendants, who in Title VII cases are likely to have greater economic power than plaintiffs, from exploiting that power in a particularly objectionable way; but it also deprives plaintiffs of the use of that chip, even when without it settlement may be impossible and the prospect of winning at trial may be very doubtful.

762 F.2d, at 1112.

In fact, we believe that a general proscription against negotiated waiver of attorney's fees in exchange for a settlement on the merits would itself impede vindication of civil rights, at least in some cases, by reducing the attractiveness of settlement. [As we said in] Marek v. Chesney, 473 U.S. 1 (1985) . . . [:]

> . . . Some plaintiffs will receive compensation in settlement where, on trial, they might not have recovered, or would have recovered less than what was offered. And, even for those who would prevail at trial, settlement will provide them with compensation at an earlier date without the burdens, stress, and time of litigation. In short, settlements rather than litigation will serve the interests of plaintiffs as well as defendants.

. . . We conclude, therefore, that it is not necessary to construe the Fees Act as embodying a general rule prohibiting settlements conditioned on the waiver of fees in order to be faithful to the purposes of that Act.

IV

The question remains whether the District Court abused its discretion in this case by approving a settlement which included a complete fee waiver. As noted earlier, Rule 23(e) wisely requires court approval of the terms of any settlement of a class action. The potential conflict among members of the class — in this case, for example, the possible conflict between children primarily interested in better educational programs and those primarily interested in improved health care — fully justifies the requirement of court approval.

The Court of Appeals, respondents, and various amici supporting their position, however, suggest that the court's authority to pass on settlements, typically invoked to ensure fair treatment of class members, must be exercised in accordance with the Fees Act to promote the availability of attorneys in civil rights cases. . . .

[The court rejected this proposition, holding that the question was instead the overall fairness of the settlement agreement; in deciding whether to approve such a settlement, the court could consider the demand for a fee waiver.]

Remarkably, there seems little disagreement on these points. . . . The Solicitor General, for example, has suggested that a fee waiver need not be approved when the defendant had "no realistic defense on the merits," or if the waiver was part of a "vindictive effort . . . to teach counsel that they had better not bring such cases." . . .

[The court found no such evidence.]

In light of the record, respondents must — to sustain the judgment in their favor — confront the District Court's finding that the extensive structural relief they obtained constituted an adequate quid pro quo for their waiver of attorney's fees. . . .

What the outcome of this settlement illustrates is that the Fees Act has given the victims of civil rights violations a powerful weapon that improves their ability to employ counsel, to obtain access to the courts, and thereafter to vindicate their rights by means of settlement or trial. For aught that appears, it was the "coercive" effect of respondents' statutory right to seek a fee award that motivated petitioners' exceptionally generous offer. Whether this weapon might be even more powerful if fee waivers were prohibited in cases like this is another question,[34] but it is in any event a question that Congress is best equipped to answer. Thus far, the Legislature has not commanded that fees be paid whenever a case is settled. Unless it issues such a command, we shall rely primarily on the sound discretion of the district courts to appraise the reasonableness of particular class-action settlements on a case-by-case basis, in the light of all the relevant circumstances. In this case, the District Court did not abuse its discretion in upholding a fee waiver which secured broad injunctive relief, relief greater than that which plaintiffs could reasonably have expected to achieve at trial. . . .

[Justice Brennan's dissent is omitted.]

NOTE ON EVANS v. JEFF D.

In 1996 Congress, in the bill appropriating the funding for the Legal Services Corporation (LSC), forbade any agency delivering services funded by the LSC — a provision that includes most significant legal services organizations in the United States — from seeking attorneys' fees in any of its cases. This restriction, which has persisted in subsequent appropriations, now appears in a regulation promulgated by the LSC. Code of Federal Regulations 45 Part 1642 (1997). So, if Evans v. Jeff D. arose today, there would have been no question concerning Johnson's seeking fees from Idaho: the regulation would prohibit it. Congress might have just been trying to thwart the work of agencies funded by the LSC; consider, however, what other considerations may have been behind this legislation.

ALEX BERENSON, ANALYSTS SEE MERCK VICTORY IN VIOXX DEAL

New York Times, November 10, 2007

For the drug maker Merck to pay almost $5 billion to settle lawsuits from people who contended that the painkiller Vioxx caused their heart attacks and strokes may not seem like a corporate victory.

But it is, according to lawyers and drug industry analysts who have followed the Vioxx litigation since Merck stopped selling the drug in September 2004, after a clinical trial showed it raised the risk of strokes and heart attacks.

At a fraction of the price that analysts initially estimated it would pay, Merck, one of the largest American drug makers, hopes to put one of the most troubling episodes in its history behind it.

---

34. We are cognizant of the possibility that decisions by individual clients to bargain away fee awards may, in the aggregate and in the long run, diminish lawyers' expectations of statutory fees in civil rights cases. If this occurred, the pool of lawyers willing to represent plaintiffs in such cases might shrink, constricting the "effective access to the judicial process" for persons with civil rights grievances which the Fees Act was intended to provide. H.R. Rep. No. 94-1558, p. 1 (1976). That the "tyranny of small decisions" may operate in this fashion is not to say that there is any reason or documentation to support such a concern at the present time. Comment on this issue is therefore premature at this juncture. We believe, however, that as a practical matter the likelihood of this circumstance arising is remote.

The settlement amount it announced yesterday, $4.85 billion, represents only about nine months of profit for Merck, whose stock rose 2.3 percent on news of the agreement, even as the broader stock market was sharply lower. Two years ago, some analysts estimated that Merck would have to pay as much as $25 billion to settle Vioxx claims.

The success of Merck's strategy—fighting every claim against it in court for several years and only then agreeing to a blanket settlement—could encourage other pharmaceutical companies to take the same route in other lawsuits, independent legal experts say. Merck has won most of the cases to reach juries, as plaintiffs' lawyers have struggled to convince jurors that Vioxx caused the heart problems their clients suffered.

Clinical trials prove that Vioxx raises the risk of heart attacks, but linking its use to any one person's problems is difficult, especially when the person had other risk factors like smoking.

More broadly, the case shows that after years of aggressively lobbying against trial lawyers, corporate America has regained substantial leverage against plaintiffs and their lawyers—whose lawsuits bankrupted Dow Corning and the asbestos industry in the 1990s. In many states, changes governing lawsuits have made claims tougher to bring and win, while much public opinion has turned against plaintiffs.

"The law governing class-actions has grown decidedly less favorable than it was," said Peter Schuck, a professor at Yale Law School who specializes in complex litigation.

Merck said it was agreeing to a settlement now because the judges overseeing the cases had encouraged both sides to come to terms and because it wanted to stop spending $600 million a year on its defense.

Of course, what is good news for Merck may be less so for the patients who suffered heart attacks or strokes after taking Vioxx. Depending on how many claims are filed to the settlement fund, those people will receive payments averaging about $120,000 each before legal fees and expenses, which could swallow about 40 percent of their payments.

Plaintiffs are not required to accept the settlement. But under terms of the agreement their lawyers must encourage them to do so—and would not be allowed to represent those clients if they insisted on bringing their cases to court.

Besides Merck, the biggest winner in the case may be the plaintiffs' lawyers. They will split nearly $2 billion in fees and expenses, although that figure is far lower than they initially hoped.

Dr. Eric Topol, a cardiologist who in 2001 was co-author of a paper in the Journal of the American Medical Association warning of the risks of Vioxx, said he believed that the payment amounted to little more than a slap on the wrist for Merck. "I think they've gotten off quite easily, frankly, for the problems that they've engendered," Dr. Topol said. If Dr. Topol's view is correct, Merck's lawyers deserve much of the credit. In 2005, as it faced a public relations nightmare, Congressional hearings, angry doctors, a plunging stock price and tens of thousands of lawsuits, Merck could have opted to empty its corporate coffers for a quick settlement. Instead, said Benjamin Zipursky, a professor at Fordham Law School who has closely followed the case, the company chose to fight, despite the short-term public relations hit.

"They decided they would deal with it by taking a 'no-holds-barred, we're going to fight every case' strategy." Mr. Zipursky said, "What it looks like today is that's a good strategy when you get in that situation."

. . .

NOTE ON THE VIOXX SETTLEMENT

Some background will make both the creativity and the tenuousness of the Vioxx™ agreement more apparent. From defendants' standpoint, such lawsuits are potential company-killers: a widely distributed product alleged to be responsible for a number of deaths carries with it the potential for bankruptcy, as manufacturers of asbestos discovered a few decades ago when every one of them was driven into insolvency by the burden of judgments resulting from their long concealment of the perils of asbestos. The defendants in such circumstances are willing to go to great lengths to avoid this result. But they are willing to go to great lengths only if they can thereby achieve "total peace"— an end to all similar suits. If they cannot achieve this goal, settlement with one or even scores of defendants does little, because there are scores or hundreds more waiting in line. Indeed, partial settlements make matters worse, as defendants see things, because the fees generated by such settlements allow the plaintiffs' lawyers (the same lawyers, having gained expertise in the area, may be representing hundreds or even thousands of plaintiffs) to improve financing for those suits waiting in line.

For several decades defendants have been looking for ways to achieve such settlements. An initial gambit involved the "settlement class action." Briefly, such suits sought to bundle into a class all those who had not yet sued but who had been exposed to whatever hazard was alleged, and then to arrive at a global settlement that included them as well as those who had active suits. Had a court embodied the settlement in a judgment, all future suits would be barred by claim preclusion. The problem, said the U.S. Supreme Court, was that the same lawyers were representing both the "active" and the "futures" classes, and the inherently conflicting positions of these two groups made it impossible for the same lawyers to represent both. Exit the settlement class.

But the problem—as defendants saw it—still remained. Was there a way in which a defendant could achieve a global solution to such lawsuits? The agreement below represents a new effort. It eschews the class action, relying instead on the plaintiffs' lawyers to recruit plaintiffs and to encourage them to settle on the terms offered. The "carrot" is that the plaintiffs get to collect a settlement without proving liability. The "stick" is that Merck can walk away from the settlement if plaintiffs' lawyers fail to enroll 85% of the plaintiffs. The agreement doesn't formally bar the plaintiffs' lawyers from representing other plaintiffs (nor could it, as you now understand), but it certainly discourages them from doing so; notice how. Finally, it apparently binds the plaintiffs' lawyers to "recommend" the settlement to their clients. Notice that the amended agreement tries to back away from this provision. Do you understand why? Some have praised this settlement for its creative solution of an otherwise difficult problem; others have attacked it as a betrayal of legal ethics. See if you can understand what the sides are disagreeing about.

Excerpts from Original Vioxx Settlement Agreement
and Amendments

November 9, 2007

Settlement Agreement

SETTLEMENT AGREEMENT, dated as of November 9, 2007 (the "Execution Date"), between (i) Merck & Co., Inc., a New Jersey corporation (together with its successors and assigns, "Merck"), and (ii) the counsel listed in the signature pages hereto under the heading "Negotiating Plaintiffs' Counsel" (collectively, the "NPC"; the NPC and Merck, each a "Party" and collectively the "Parties").

Certain terms used in this *Agreement* are defined in Article 17. These terms are italicized the first time that they appear in the text of this Agreement.

Preamble

This is an agreement between (i) Merck and (ii) the NPC, which includes all counsel appointed to the Executive Committee of the Plaintiffs' Steering Committee in In re VIOXX Products Liability Litigation, MDL No. 1657, a federal multi-district litigation which is venued in the United States District Court for the Eastern District of Louisiana (such court, the "MDL Court," and such steering committee, the "PSC") and representatives of plaintiffs' counsel in the *Coordinated Proceedings* in the state courts of New Jersey, California, and Texas. This Agreement establishes a program to resolve the actions, disputes and claims that these, and other, plaintiffs' counsel have asserted against Merck on behalf of their clients related to their clients' alleged use of VIOXX.

Recitals

A. Merck voluntarily withdrew VIOXX from the market on September 30, 2004.

B. As of October 1, 2007, there were approximately 26,000 active VIOXX personal-injury actions filed against Merck nationwide, representing approximately 47,000 claimant groups.

C. Approximately 14,500 additional claimants asserted direct claims against Merck but agreed to refrain from filing suit while their claims were tolled. Approximately 13,250 of those agreements remain in effect.

D. More than 95% of the active plaintiffs are presently coordinated in one of the following four "Coordinated Proceedings":

    a. In re VIOXX Products Liability Litigation, Federal MDL No. 1657, venued in the MDL Court;

    b. In re VIOXX Coordinated Cases, JCCP No. 4247, venued in the Superior Court of California, County of Los Angeles;

    c. In re VIOXX Litigation, Cases No. 619 and 273, venued in the Superior Court of New Jersey, Law Division, Atlantic County; and

    d. In re Texas State VIOXX Litigation, Master Docket No. 2005-59499, yenned in the District Court of Harris County, Texas, 157th Judicial District.

E. The NPC and Merck have agreed to establish a pre-funded, structured private settlement program, as set forth herein, to resolve pending or tolled (and certain previously tolled) VIOXX claims against Merck involving heart attacks, ischemic strokes and sudden cardiac deaths for an overall amount of $4,850,000,000 (the "Program").

F. The Program is intended to resolve, in lieu of further litigation, the claims of all *Eligible Claimants* (including both Eligible Claimants within the Coordinated Proceedings and Eligible Claimants with pending lawsuits against Merck in any District of Columbia court, any Puerto Rico court or any court or tribunal of the United States outside the Coordinated Proceedings) who participate in the Program (except only as otherwise set forth in Section 2.7.3.1).

G. A key objective of the Program is that, with respect to any counsel with an *Interest* in the claims of any *Enrolled Program Claimant*, all other Eligible Claimants in which such counsel has an Interest shall be enrolled in the Program.

H. No claims brought against Merck after the date of this Agreement will be eligible to participate in the Program or receive any payment under the Program.

I. The Program will not be construed as evidence of, or as an admission by, Merck or any *Released Party* of any fault, *Liability*, wrongdoing or damages whatsoever or as admission by any Enrolled Program Claimant of any lack of merit in their claims.

Merck and the NPC hereby agree as follows. . . .

* * *

1.2.6. Enrolling Counsel may submit Enrollment Forms for Eligible Claimants on a rolling basis. However, without limitation of Section 1.2.5, at any time on or prior to the 60th day after service of the Certification of Final Enrollment included in the "Enrollment Materials" included in the Enrollment Form, Merck in its sole and absolute discretion may reject any or all Enrollment Forms submitted by an Enrolling Counsel, in relation to any or all of the Program Claimants covered thereby, for the following reasons:

1.2.6.1. Such Enrolling Counsel has failed to file a Registration Affidavit complying with the Registration Order; or

1.2.6.2. Such Enrolling Counsel has been determined pursuant to Section 1.2.9 to have failed in any respect to comply with the requirements of Section 1.2.8.1, 1.2.8.2 or 1.2.8.3;

1.2.6.3. Such Enrolling Counsel has since the Execution Date received compensation (or entered into any agreement or arrangement to receive or potentially to receive compensation) for relinquishing his or her Interest in any Claim Connected With VIOXX of any Eligible Claimant who has not enrolled in the Program as of the date of service of the Certification of Final Enrollment (or, if earlier, June 30, 2008).

1.2.7. The parties agree that a key objective of the Program is that, with respect to any counsel with an Interest in the claims of any Enrolled

Program Claimant, all other Eligible Claimants in which such counsel has an Interest shall be enrolled in the Program.

1.2.8. While nothing in this Agreement is intended to operate as a "restriction" on the right of any Claimant's counsel to practice law within the meaning of the equivalent to Rule 5.6(b) of the ABA Model Rules of Professional Conduct in any jurisdictions in which Claimant's Counsel practices or whose rules may otherwise apply, it is agreed that (except to the extent waived by Merck in its sole discretion in any instance):

1.2.8.1. By submitting an Enrollment Form, the Enrolling Counsel affirms that he has recommended, or (if such Enrollment Form is submitted prior to February 28, 2008) will recommend by no later than the earlier of the date of service of the Certification of Final Enrollment and February 28, 2008, to 100% of the Eligible Claimants represented by such Enrolling Counsel that such Eligible Claimants enroll in the Program.

1.2.8.2. If any such Eligible Claimant disregards such recommendation, or for any other reason fails (or has failed) to submit a non-deficient and non-defective Enrollment Form on or before the earlier of the date of service of the Certification of Final Enrollment and June 30, 2008, such Enrolling Counsel shall, on or before the earlier of June 30, 2008 and the 30th day after the date of service of the Certification of Final Enrollment (or, if such Enrolling Counsel first becomes an Enrolling Counsel after June 30, 2008, shall have, by the date such Enrolling Counsel so first became an Enrolling Counsel), to the extent permitted by the equivalents to Rules 1.16 and 5.6 of the ABA Model Rules of Professional Conduct in the relevant jurisdiction(s), (i) take (or have taken, as the case may be) all necessary steps to disengage and withdraw from the representation of such Eligible Claimant and to forego any Interest in such Eligible Claimant and (ii) cause (or have caused, as the case may be) each other Enrolling Counsel, and each other counsel with an Interest in any Enrolled Program Claimant, which has an Interest in such Eligible Claimant to do the same.

1.2.8.3. Each Enrolling Counsel, by submitting an Enrollment Form, agrees to abide by Section 1.2.8.2 in relation to any Eligible Claimant in which such Enrolling Counsel is an "other Enrolling Counsel" referenced in clause (ii) of said Section 1.2.8.2 (and to do so in the same time frame as is applicable to the Enrolling Counsel who represents such Eligible Claimant).

1.2.9. Upon request from Merck at any time, the Chief Administrator will determine whether an Enrolling Counsel has failed to comply with the requirements of Section 1.2.8.1, 1.2.8.2 or 1.2.8.3 in any respect. The Chief Administrator's decision on this matter shall be final, binding and Non-Appealable. . . .

1.2.10. Without limitation, for purposes of Sections 1.2.6, 1.2.7, 1.2.8, 1.2.9, 2.5.3.1, 3.2.1.1 and Section 11.1.5, (i) any Person that would be considered to be an "Eligible Claimant" based on the information set forth in such Person's (or such Person's *Product User's*) complaint, *Profile*

Form and/or PME Records shall be considered to constitute an "Eligible Claimant" and (ii) a lawyer or law firm shall be considered to have an Interest in each Person in which such lawyer or law firm claims to have, or have had, an Interest in a Registration Affidavit.

* * *

Article 11
Walk Away Rights and Termination of the Agreement

Section 11.1. Walk Away Rights and Termination of the Agreement

Merck shall have the option, in its sole discretion, to terminate the Program and this Agreement under any of the following circumstances (such option, the "Walk Away Right"):

11.1.1. if:

11.1.1.1. the number of *MI Eligible Claimants* (constituting Registered Eligible Claimants) who deliver Enrollment Forms to the Claims Administrator by the Walk Away Enrollment Deadline Date, and whose Enrollment Forms are not rejected (in relation to such MI Eligible Claimants) by the Claims Administrator or Merck prior to the 30th day after the Walk Away Enrollment Deadline Date, is less than

11.1.1.2. 85% of the greater of (x) the aggregate number of Registered Eligible Claimants constituting (according solely to the respective Registration Affidavits) MI Eligible Claimants, and (y) 28,500;

11.1.2. if:

11.1.2.1. the number of *IS Eligible Claimants* (constituting Registered Eligible Claimants) who deliver Enrollment Forms to the Claims Administrator by the Walk Away Enrollment Deadline Date, and whose Enrollment Forms are not rejected (in relation to such IS Eligible Claimants) by the Claims Administrator or Merck prior to the 30th day after the Walk Away Enrollment Deadline Date, is less than

11.1.2.2. 85% of the greater of (x) the aggregate number of Registered Eligible Claimants constituting (according solely to the respective Registration Affidavits) IS Eligible Claimants, and (y) 17,000;

11.1.3. if:

11.1.3.1. the number of Registered Eligible Claimants who (i) are alleging (according solely to the respective Registration Affidavits) use of VIOXX prior to the respective *Related Eligible Events* for more than 12 months and (ii) deliver Enrollment Forms to the Claims Administrator by the Walk Away Enrollment Deadline Date, and whose Enrollment Forms are not rejected (in relation to such Registered Eligible Claimants) by the Claims Administrator or Merck prior to the 30th day after the Walk Away Enrollment Deadline Date, is less than

11.1.3.2. 85% of the aggregate number of Registered Eligible Claimants alleging (according solely to the respective Registration Affidavits) use of VIOXX prior to the respective *Related Eligible Events* for more than 12 months; or

11.1.4. if:

11.1.4.1. the number of Registered Eligible Claimants who (i) are alleging (according solely to the respective Registration Affidavits) death as an injury and (ii) deliver Enrollment Forms to the Claims Administrator by the Walk Away Enrollment Deadline Date, and whose Enrollment Forms are not rejected (in relation to such Registered Eligible Claimants) by the Claims Administrator or Merck prior to the 30th day after the Walk Away Enrollment Deadline Date, is less than

11.1.4.2. 85% of the aggregate number of Registered Eligible Claimants alleging (according solely to the respective Registration Affidavits) death as an injury; or

11.1.5. if any member of the PSC, any member of the steering committee in the Texas Coordinated Proceeding, any member of the steering committee in the California Coordinated Proceeding, any counsel who served in any capacity as trial counsel in any case in the Coordinated Proceedings, or any counsel who as of the Execution Date has entered an appearance in any case in or outside the Coordinated Proceedings that has a trial date (or any law firm of or with which any such individual lawyer is a partner, associate or otherwise affiliated) (a "Section 11.1.5 Counsel"), either (i) is the subject of a determination of non-compliance pursuant to Section 1.2.9 with respect to the requirements of Section 1.2.8.1, 1.2.8.2 or 1.2.8.3 or (ii) is the subject of a determination of non-compliance pursuant to Section 11.1.5.1 with respect to the requirements of Section 1.2.8.1, 1.2.8.2 or 1.2.8.3 applied solely for this purpose as if such Section 11.1.5 Counsel submitted an Enrollment Form and a Certification of Final Enrollment on December 31, 2007 and on such date continued to represent 100% of the Eligible Claimants in which such Section 11.1.5 Counsel bad an Interest as of the Execution Date; . . .

For the avoidance of doubt, for the purpose of Merck's Walk Away Right and termination of this Agreement under this Article, all Legal Representatives of a decedent, which decedent and/or any of whose Legal Representatives is an "Eligible Claimant," are counted as a (single) "Registered Eligible Claimant" (so long as data for such decedent is provided in a properly completed, and submitted, Registration Affidavit). (For the purpose of Settlement Payments, a Legal Representative of a decedent is entitled to no payment before a court of competent jurisdiction approves the distribution.)

Section 11.2. Time to Exercise Walk Away Right

11.2.1. Merck may exercise its Walk Away Right in relation to Section 11.1.1, 11.1.2, 11.1.3, 11.1.4, 11.1.5 or 11.1.6 at any time until forty-five (45) days after the Walk Away Enrollment Deadline Date. . . .

Amendment to Settle Agreement

AMENDMENT TO SETTLEMENT AGREEMENT, dated as of January 17, 2008 (this "Amendment"), between Merck & Co., Inc., a New Jersey corporation (together with its successors and assigns, "Merck"), and the counsel listed in the signature pages hereto under the heading "Negotiating Plaintiffs' Counsel" (collectively, the "NPC"; the NPC and Merck, each a "Party" and collectively the "Parties").

Recitals

A. The Parties are parties to that certain Settlement Agreement, dated November 9, 2007 (the *"Settlement Agreement"*).
B. In the course of explaining the Settlement Agreement to counsel for potential participants, it has become apparent that the original document could have more clearly reflected the intent of the Parties in certain respects and the Parties have concluded that it would be desirable to underscore their original intent in these respects.
C. The Parties therefore wish to make certain technical and clarifying amendments to the Settlement Agreement pursuant to Section 16.10 thereof, as further provided herein, to ensure that the document accurately and clearly reflects the Parties' original intent.
D. The Parties are making this one and only set of necessary modifications in this single document at this time, so that the Settlement Agreement will be finalized in a readily accessible form in advance of full commencement of the Resolution Program enrollment process.

Merck and the NPC hereby agree as follows:

Section 1.1. *Certain Terms.* Capitalized terms used but not defined in this Amendment shall have the meanings ascribed to such terms in the Settlement Agreement.

Section 1.2. *Amendments.* The Settlement Agreement is hereby amended as follows:

1.2.1. All references in the Settlement Agreement to "Chief Administrator" are hereby amended to say "Honorable Eldon E. Fallon."

1.2.2. Section 1.2.8.1 of the Settlement Agreement is hereby amended and restated as follows: "Each Enrolling Counsel is expected to exercise his or her independent judgment in the best interest of each client individually before determining whether to recommend enrollment in the Program. By submitting an Enrollment Form, the Enrolling Counsel affirms that he or she has exercised such independent judgment and either (1) has recommended to 100% of the Eligible Claimants represented by such Enrolling Counsel that such Eligible Claimants enroll in the Program or (2) (if such Enrollment Form is submitted prior to February 28, 2008 and is not accompanied by a Certification of Final Enrollment) will recommend by no later than February 28, 2008, to 100% of the Eligible Claimants represented by such Enrolling Counsel that such Eligible Claimants enroll in the Program." . . .

1.2.6. Section 6.1.1 of the Settlement Agreement is hereby amended and restated as follows: "This is a private agreement. At the joint request of the Parties, the Honorable Judge Eldon E. Fallon has agreed to preside over the Program in the capacities specified herein." . . .

F. SETTLEMENT STRATEGY

NOTE ON *ZIEGLER* AND *EXXON VALDEZ*

You are now in a position to appreciate the evaluations that lawyers for both sides must make as they consider settlement. The next two cases display lawyers stretching existing law to achieve settlements—settlements that were then attacked as violating rules of professional responsibility or other rules. As you read these two cases, put yourself successively in the shoes of each of the participants in these two cases: the parties and the judge.

For the parties

a. Consider what each thought it might gain from settling or not settling: what risks was it eliminating; what new risks might the settlement itself create?

b. What other forms of settlement might it have chosen? What did it think was to be gained by the specific type of settlement it actually entered into?

c. What guesses do you have about the other parties' reaction to the settlement?

d. What guess do you have about the judge's reaction to the settlement?

For the judge

a. First consider how and why the judge became involved in these settlements at all, bearing in mind that most settlements require neither judicial participation nor approval.

b. What role did the trial judge play in these two settlements?

c. Why does the appellate court respond as it does?

ZIEGLER V. WENDEL POULTRY SERVS., INC.

615 N.E.2d 1022 (Ohio 1993)

* * *

On September 28, 1988, plaintiff-appellant/cross-appellee, Bonnie K. Ziegler, administrator of the estate of Michael S. Ziegler, filed a wrongful death action in the Crawford County Court of Common Pleas against defendant-appellee/cross-appellant, Wynford Local School District Board of Education ("Wynford"), and defendants-appellants/cross-appellees, Wendel Poultry Services, Inc. and its employee, Terry E. Hummel (collectively "Wendel"). In the complaint, Ziegler alleged that June Scott, a school bus driver for Wynford, and Hummel, a semi driver for Wendel, negligently caused a motor vehicle accident on February 18, 1988 on U.S. Route 30 in Wyandot County, which resulted in the death of Michael S. Ziegler.

A three-week jury trial commenced on February 13, 1990. The parties stipulated that Michael Ziegler was free from negligence in operating his vehicle. The evidence showed that at approximately 8:00 a.m. on the day in question, Scott, the bus driver, encountered heavy fog as she traveled west on Route 30 approaching Township Road 132, an area known as the "Mini-Farms." Scott turned onto Township Road 132, picked up five children, turned around in the cul-de-sac, and headed back towards Route 30, where she planned to turn left.

Scott testified that when she stopped at the stop sign at the intersection of Route 30, she found herself in the second worst fog she had ever encountered in her twenty-two years of driving school buses. As Scott sat at the stop sign, she observed an eastbound semi pass by on Route 30 at approximately thirty-five m.p.h. At one point, she stated she observed this semi for approximately the distance from the witness stand to the brass rail in the courtroom (a distance later measured at twenty-three feet), before it disappeared in the fog, although she later stated it was a larger distance.

Before attempting to turn left onto Route 30, Scott pulled the bus right to the edge of Route 30, turned off the bus engine, and opened the door and a window. She stated she took these precautions so she could listen and look for any oncoming traffic. Unable to hear or see any approaching vehicles, Scott started the bus and "took off" "as fast as it would go," intending to reach a speed of thirty-five m.p.h., the speed she estimated the semi had been traveling.

At approximately the same time, Hummel was driving a semitrailer loaded with eggs east on Route 30. Hummel testified that he had been traveling at the posted speed of fifty-five m.p.h. until he ran into heavy fog. He downshifted into eighth gear, slowing his truck to approximately forty-five m.p.h., knowing there was traffic behind him.

Hummel testified he was "two, three, four car lengths away from it at the most" when he saw the school bus. He stated that the bus was one-half to three-quarters of the way through its turn and that it was not quite straight on the road. Hummel immediately applied the brakes; however, he was unable to stop in time and hit the rear of the bus. Hummel went left of center, striking Michael Ziegler's pickup and killing him immediately. The semi eventually ended up in a ditch on the side of the road. Scott was able to steer the bus onto the right shoulder. Expert testimony established that Scott was traveling approximately twenty-two m.p.h. at the time of the impact. Expert testimony about Hummel's speed ranged from thirty-four to forty-eight m.p.h.

The jury awarded the Ziegler estate $1,607,735 in damages, attributing one hundred percent of the liability to Wynford and zero percent to Wendel. Ziegler filed a motion for prejudgment interest, which was granted by the trial court.

Wynford filed a timely appeal with the Court of Appeals for Crawford County. The appellate court reversed the trial court's judgment, concluding primarily that the court should have granted Wynford's motion for directed verdict against Hummel and Wendel, since Hummel was negligent per se for violating the assured-clear-distance statute, and that the trial court erred in failing to submit Wynford's proposed interrogatories to the jury. Ziegler and Wendel filed an appeal to this court from the court of appeals' decision, and Wynford filed a cross-appeal.

KOEHLER, Acting Chief Justice.

The parties have raised numerous propositions of law, which are set forth in their entirety in the appendix to this opinion. We will consider the issues raised by subject matter. We find that two of Ziegler's and Wendel's arguments have merit, and we therefore reverse the decision of the court of appeals. . . .

* * *

III

"High-Low" Agreement

On the first day of trial, counsel for Ziegler and Wendel informed the trial court that they had reached a settlement. Under the terms of the unwritten agreement, which was read into the record prior to voir dire of the jurors, in exchange for a covenant not to execute on judgment, Wendel's insurance company guaranteed the Ziegler estate payment of $325,000 regardless of the jury verdict and payment of up to $450,000 if the jury determined that Wendel was liable to that extent. Over Wynford's objection, the trial court approved the so-called "high-low" agreement and held that it would not be disclosed to the jury.

Wynford contends this agreement constituted a Mary Carter agreement. See Booth v. Mary Carter Paint Co. (Fla. App. 1967), 202 So. 2d 8. It urges this court to declare Mary Carter agreements void as against public policy as some states have done, see Elbaor v. Smith (Tex.1992), 845 S.W.2d 240; and to hold that Wendel should not have participated in the trial. In the alternative, Wynford asks us to hold that the Mary Carter agreement must be disclosed to the jury. The court of appeals concluded that the high-low agreement in the present case is not a Mary Carter agreement as that term has been defined in Ohio and that the trial court did not err in allowing Wendel to participate in the trial or by failing to disclose the agreement to the jury. We agree.

In Vogel v. Wells (1991), 57 Ohio St. 3d 91, 93, 566 N.E.2d 154, 156, this court defined a "Mary Carter agreement" as "a contract between a plaintiff and one defendant allying them against another defendant at trial." We further stated:

> " 'Mary Carter agreements may incorporate any variety of terms, but are generally characterized by three basic provisions. First, the settling defendant guarantees the plaintiff a minimum payment, regardless of the court's judgment. Second, the plaintiff agrees not to enforce the court's judgment against the settling defendant. Third, the settling defendant remains a party in the trial, but his exposure is reduced in proportion to any increase in the liability of his codefendants over an agreed amount. Some Mary Carter agreements include a fourth element: that the agreement be kept secret between the settling parties.' "

Id. at 93, 566 N.E.2d at 157, fn. 1, quoting Note, It's a Mistake to Tolerate the Mary Carter Agreement (1987), 87 Colum. L. Rev. 368, 369-370.

We conclude that the agreement in the present case is not a "Mary Carter agreement" as that term is defined in Vogel. Wendel's exposure to liability was not reduced in proportion to any increase in liability of Wynford over an agreed amount. The amount of damages assessed against Wynford had no impact on the amount Wendel would pay to Ziegler. There was no built-in incentive on Wendel's part to increase Ziegler's damages.

One of the major dangers of Mary Carter agreements lies in the distortion of the relationship between the settling defendant and the plaintiff, which allows the settling defendant to remain nominally a defendant to the action while secretly conspiring to aid the plaintiff's case. That concern is not present here. Wendel still had an incentive to keep the amount of damages down, since a higher verdict could result in Wendel paying up to $125,000 more should the jury's verdict have been over $325,000. As stated by the court of appeals, "[t]he fact that Wendel Poultry remained at risk of liability in a significant amount is indicative of a lack of collusive purpose in executing the agreement." Further, our review of the record does not support Wynford's allegation that Wendel was allied with Ziegler, but instead shows that their positions remained adversarial and that Wendel presented its case with vigor.

Accordingly, the trial court did not err by approving the agreement or by allowing Wendel to participate in the trial. Likewise, the trial court did not err in refusing to disclose the agreement to the jury. The law favors prevention of litigation by compromise and settlement. "So long as there is no evidence of collusion, in bad faith, to the detriment of other, non-settling parties, the settlement of litigation will be encouraged and upheld." Krischbaum v. Dillon (1991), 58 Ohio St. 3d 58, 69-70, 567 N.E.2d 1291, 1307.

Despite its conclusion that the high-low agreement was valid, the appellate court also concluded that the trial court erred in overruling Wynford's motion to set off the $325,000 Wendel paid to Ziegler pursuant to the agreement against the verdict under the Ohio Contribution Among Joint Tortfeasors Act. We agree. R.C. 2307.32(F) provides:

> "When a release or a covenant not to sue or not to enforce judgment is given in good faith to one of two or more persons liable in tort for the same injury or loss to person or property or the same wrongful death, the following apply:
> "(1) The release or covenant does not discharge any of the other tortfeasors from liability for the injury, loss, or wrongful death unless its terms otherwise provide, but it reduces the claim against the other tortfeasors to the extent of any amount stipulated by the release or the covenant, or in the amount of the consideration paid for it, whichever is the greater[.]"

Ziegler argues that this statute does not apply, because Wendel and Hummel were not found to be liable by the jury and therefore they are not joint tortfeasors, an argument we view as an overly technical interpretation of the statute. Courts have concluded that there does not have to be a judicial determination of liability for a settling defendant to be considered a tortfeasor within the meaning of contribution statutes.

This case presents a somewhat unusual situation. Usually the settling defendant will not participate in the trial and there would be no jury determination of that defendant's liability. Even though in this case Wendel did participate in the trial, we think the setoff provision is still applicable. The settlement agreement between Wendel and Ziegler was clearly executed in contemplation of Wendel's being found jointly and severally liable for Michael Ziegler's death. We believe that the situation at the time of the settlement should be controlling. To hold otherwise would be to permit the plaintiff to obtain a double recovery, something the statute was clearly designed to prevent. The jury determined that Ziegler was entitled to total damages of $1,607,735; she is not entitled to recovery above that amount. We conclude, therefore, that the appellate court's decision that the $325,000 payment from Wendel to Ziegler should be set off against the total verdict is proper.

IV

Prejudgment Interest

The trial judge assessed prejudgment interest against Wynford because it failed to make a good faith effort to settle the case pursuant to R.C. 1343.03(C). The court of appeals affirmed. Wynford now argues that that award is neither legally nor factually justified. . . .

Wynford . . . argues that the evidence does not support the trial court's conclusion that it failed to make a good faith effort to settle. It claims that it had a good faith, objectively reasonable belief that it had no liability and therefore was not obligated to make a settlement offer.

R.C. 1343.03(C) provides:

> Interest on a judgment, decree, or order for the payment of money rendered in a civil action based on tortious conduct and not settled by agreement of the parties, shall be computed from the date the cause of action accrued to the date on which the money is paid, if, upon motion of any party to the action, the court determines at a hearing held subsequent to the verdict or decision in the action that the party required to pay the money failed to make a good faith effort to settle the case and that the party to whom the money is to be paid did not fail to make a good faith effort to settle the case.

In Kalain v. Smith (1986), 25 Ohio St. 3d 157, 495 N.E.2d 572, syllabus, we held:

> A party has not "failed to make a good faith effort to settle" under R.C. 1343.03(C) if he has (1) fully cooperated in discovery proceedings, (2) rationally evaluated his risks and potential liability, (3) not attempted to unnecessarily delay any of the proceedings, and (4) made a good faith monetary settlement offer or responded in good faith to an offer from the other party. If a party has a good faith, objectively reasonable belief that he has no liability, he need not make a monetary settlement offer.

The decision whether a party's settlement efforts indicate good faith is within the discretion of the trial court. This court will not disturb the trial court's findings absent an abuse of discretion.

The evidence shows that Wynford's insurance company, Personal Service Insurance Corporation ("PSI"), consistently maintained it had no liability at all, based on Hummel's alleged violation of the assured-clear-distance statute. Even though Wynford's policy limits were $250,000, PSI had reserves of only $30,000, which its representatives acknowledged were to cover litigation expenses. The rest of the funds were in the hands of its reinsurer, whom PSI did not involve until after the jury verdict. Five days before trial, PSI offered $25,000 and told Ziegler's counsel he should take the offer because PSI planned an appeal to the court of appeals and to the Supreme Court and it would be a long time before Ziegler received any money. After trial began, and Ziegler and Wendel had reached an agreement, PSI offered to pay $100,000 and would not go over that amount, despite a request by Wynford's counsel to settle for policy limits.

The trial court concluded that PSI did not have an objectively reasonable belief that it had no liability at all, based upon the undisputed fact that Scott pulled out onto a heavily traveled highway in the fog with little or no visibility. The trial court also concluded that Ziegler bargained in good faith despite her failure to supply a "settlement package" (that is, a report of plaintiff's attorney's investigations and analysis supporting his settlement demand), and that PSI did not respond in good faith to Ziegler's settlement offers, forcing plaintiff to "bid against [herself]." These findings of facts are supported by competent, credible evidence. Accordingly, we cannot find that the trial court's decision to award prejudgment interest is so arbitrary, unreasonable, or unconscionable as to connote an abuse of discretion.

VII
Summary

The judgment of the court of appeals is affirmed in part and reversed in part. The jury verdict against Wynford in favor of Ziegler is reinstated, but shall be reduced by the appropriate setoffs for the $325,000 paid by Wendel and the $10,336.60 paid by Grange. The award of prejudgment interest is affirmed.

Judgment affirmed in part and reversed in part.

NOTE ON *ZIEGLER*

Think about the case as an evolving story about risk: the initial risks taken by the various parties, then the lawyers' and parties' evaluation of other risks as the case proceeded into litigation. The case has three parties: the plaintiff, Bonnie Ziegler; and two defendants, the school district and the poultry transport company. Two of these parties have insurers who hired the defense lawyers and evaluated whether to make or accept settlement offers. Draw on your knowledge of the material thus far to engage in educated speculation about the parties' strategies.

1. Why do you suppose Wendel decided to make a settlement offer? And how do you think it came up with the numbers in the offer?

2. Why do you suppose Ziegler and her lawyer decided to accept Wendel's offer rather than to continue to litigate?

3. Why do you suppose the Wendel settlement took the form it did? And what additional risks were the parties running by having it take this form?

4. Turning the question around, why did the school district *not* make a settlement offer? Speculate on its calculations, remembering who was making those calculations.

5. Reading the case quickly, it looks like a very big loss for the school district, a $1.3 million dollar verdict affirmed ($1.6 minus the $325,000 setoff) *plus* pre-judgment interest, most of that uninsured. Suppose the Wynford superintendent, gloomily contemplating cuts in next year's teaching staff and sports programs to cover the uninsured portion of the judgment, consults his lawyer. That lawyer says she's just reread Part IV of the opinion carefully

and believes that the superintendent won't need to cut anything. Explain what the school district's lawyer will recommend and why she's confident it will be successful.

INTRODUCTORY NOTE ON *EXXON VALDEZ*

As in *Ziegler*, the *Exxon* litigation involved constantly evolving assessments of the risks by the parties. A little background may make those evaluations easier to grasp. First, as you might imagine, the oil spill was an economic and social disaster for the entire state of Alaska. Not only were fisheries and wildlife harmed, but because Alaska funds most of its governmental programs with oil royalties (residents pay no income taxes and in some years receive payments from royalty income in excess of government expenses), this revenue stream was also threatened. The ensuing lawsuit created front-page news: not just the initial filing and eventual trial but virtually every pretrial ruling and hearing was the lead item in every news outlet in the state. Lawyers representing the plaintiffs and defendants established branch or new offices in the state, and both sides were prepared to invest massive sums in the litigation.

A second piece of relevant background: the law was unsettled concerning proximate causation in such cases. A commercial fisher who fished exclusively in waters fouled by the oil spill could pretty clearly recover for his lost income. But a school cafeteria in Georgia that had to pay higher prices for frozen fish sticks because of the loss of the Alaskan fishery could not recover. Some of the plaintiffs stood between these two polar examples: plaintiffs in one such group were Seattle-based fish canneries, who relied substantially on the Alaskan catch to supply their product. They could not confidently predict whether they would be within the zone of proximate cause (and thus able to collect damages) or outside it (like the hypothetical Georgia school cafeteria).

Finally, be clear that there were in effect two cases proceeding in parallel: the compensatory damages case, in which Exxon had conceded liability, leaving "only" causation and damages to try; and a parallel punitive damages class action, in which all the compensatory damage claimants were members of the plaintiff class.

IN RE THE EXXON VALDEZ

229 F.3d 790 (9th Cir. 2000)

SCHROEDER, Circuit Judge:[1]

This appeal represents a small part of the massive litigation generated by the 1989 Exxon Valdez oil spill into the waters of Prince William Sound, Alaska. The dispute we consider here arises from the punitive damages claims filed against Exxon[2] by private parties injured by the spill and consolidated into a single mandatory class action in federal court. Aligned on one side in this

---

1. Judge Schroeder was drawn to replace Judge Wiggins. She has read the briefs, reviewed the record and listened to the tape of oral argument held on May 3, 1999.

2. We follow the practice of other panels of this court who have decided cases involving the Exxon Valdez, and use "Exxon" to refer to Exxon Corporation, Exxon Shipping Company, Exxon Transportation Company, and any other related entity.

appeal are Exxon and a group of plaintiff seafood processors known as the Seattle Seven. The Seattle Seven reached a $64 million settlement agreement with Exxon in the immediate aftermath of the Valdez spill. On the other side are the remaining class plaintiffs, referred to in this opinion as "plaintiffs."

The critical factual element is the settlement agreement between Exxon and the Seattle Seven. The Seattle Seven, who process seafood caught in Prince William Sound, sued Exxon for compensatory and punitive damages after the spill forced their operations to shut down for significant periods of time. The settlement agreement they reached with Exxon did not include a release and therefore did not formally terminate the Seattle Seven's claims against Exxon. The Seattle Seven agreed, however, that they would not execute on any compensatory damages award entered in their favor and also would pay or "cede" back to Exxon any punitive damages they might recover. The agreement was subsequently modified to permit the Seattle Seven to retain a portion of the punitive damages award received.

Although both the district court and the plaintiffs knew that there had been a settlement agreement between Exxon and the Seattle Seven, neither knew of the existence of the cede back provision. Acting in its own best interest, Exxon chose not to inform the punitive damages jury either. On September 16, 1994, the jury assessed punitive damages against Exxon in the amount of $5 billion. The plan of allocation the plaintiffs eventually proposed for this award, and that the district court approved, did not include the Seattle Seven.

The central issue for us to decide is whether the jury should have been told of the cede back provision during the last phase of the punitive damages trial. The district court, agreeing with the class plaintiffs, held that Exxon's failure to affirmatively disclose this information to the jury merited exclusion of the Seattle Seven from the plan of allocation. Exxon and the Seattle Seven appeal this ruling.

Exxon's liability for any punitive damages, and the amount of punitives the jury imposed are challenged in related appeals. We here assume without deciding, for purposes of this appeal, the validity of the judgment against Exxon. We do not intimate what the result of that appeal will be.

Background

The oil tanker Exxon Valdez ran aground on the Bligh Reef in Prince William Sound, Alaska on the evening of March 23, 1989. Damage to the Valdez's cargo holds caused it to spill 11 million gallons of oil into the Sound, resulting in a great environmental disaster. The spill grievously injured both the environment and the economic livelihood of those individuals who relied on the theretofore abundant marine life of the region for their livelihood.

The State of Alaska and the United States brought actions against Exxon for the injury to the environment. Those cases were resolved by entry of a consent decree on October 8, 1991, under the terms of which Exxon agreed to pay at least $900 million to restore damaged natural resources. See Eyak Native Village v. Exxon Corp., 25 F.3d 773, 775 (9th Cir. 1994).

The hundreds of private civil actions filed in federal court were consolidated before Judge H. Russel Holland of the District of Alaska. First the plaintiffs, and then Exxon moved the district court to certify a mandatory punitive damages class. Judge Holland granted Exxon's motion on April 19, 1994. Alaska's state courts agreed to recognize the class action as the only avenue through which any plaintiff, whether in state or federal court, could recover punitive damages from Exxon. See Chenega Corp. v. Exxon Corp., 991 P.2d 769, 775 (Alaska 1999).

The Seattle Seven, the largest of the region's seafood processors, sued Exxon in 1989. Exxon sought to reach a settlement as quickly as possible, but its negotiations with the Seattle Seven and other plaintiffs revealed a roadblock posed by the increasing likelihood that a mandatory punitive damages class would be certified. Claims for compensatory damages could be easily disposed of by exchanging payment for releases, but a plaintiff's release of its slice of the future lump-sum punitive damages award merely reduced the number of claimants sharing the punitive damages pie, not the size of the pie itself. Exxon thus actually faced a financial disincentive to settle, because any amount of money it paid to persuade a plaintiff to forgo its slice would nevertheless be included in the amount of the eventual award.

On January 8, 1991, the Seattle Seven and Exxon settled the Seattle Seven's claims for the 1989 and 1990 fishing seasons in exchange for a payment of $63.75 million. To avoid the punitive damages dilemma, the parties included in the agreement a "cede back" provision. The provision stated that the Seattle Seven would not release their punitive damages claims against Exxon but would instead remain parties to the litigation in order to receive their share of an eventual punitive damages award, which they would then cede back to Exxon. The existence of a settlement agreement was made known to the rest of the subsequent punitive damages class, but its terms were kept confidential.

The mandatory punitive damages class action was tried to a jury in three phases in 1994. The first determined that Captain Joseph Hazelwood's behavior had been reckless, a necessary prerequisite for an award of punitive damages. The second phase assessed the amount of compensatory damages attributable to the spill to give the jury guidance in fixing the appropriate amount of punitive damages. For purposes of this appeal, we need not question the determinations during those phases. The third phase fixed the amount of punitive damages.

Before the third phase began, the parties entered into an Impact Stipulation. This described the harm the Valdez spill had caused private parties and quantified part of it by referring to the total amount already paid by Exxon to private parties in compensation (approximately $300 million). This figure included the approximately $64 million paid to the Seattle Seven under the 1991 settlement agreement.

In the third phase of the punitive damages proceedings, the plaintiffs emphasized to the jury the magnitude of the harm and the resulting need for punishment and deterrence. Exxon, for its part, sought to demonstrate that it had already accepted corporate responsibility by pointing to the fact that in many cases, it had paid money to injured parties without requiring anything in return but a receipt and without requiring releases. Exxon's president testified that Exxon had paid "over $300 million" receiving only receipts in return, and thus, that it had received nothing of value in return for its payments. Exxon's counsel reiterated this in his closing argument. In fact, however, because the $300 million figure included amounts paid to parties such as the Seattle Seven, who did agree to settle their claims, these statements were inaccurate. The amount paid in return for nothing but receipts was actually somewhere around $168 million.

Exxon's apparent strategy to maximize to the jury what Exxon had already paid in order to minimize punitive damages did not work well. On September 16, 1994, the jury awarded punitive damages in the sum of $5 billion, at that time the largest award of its kind in history.

The next step was to allocate those damages among the plaintiffs in a manner proportionate to their injury. The original plan of allocation, drawn up by the non-settling plaintiffs, did not include the Seattle Seven because the Seven's lack of a financial interest in the recovery meant that they also lacked motivation to pursue a stake in the award. In order to create a financial incentive for the Seattle Seven, in 1996 Exxon negotiated a modification to the 1991 settlement agreement with the Seattle Seven. The modification permitted the Seattle Seven to retain $12.4 million of their punitive damage allocation rather than ceding it all back to Exxon.

The Seattle Seven then filed an objection to the proposed allocation with the district court, contesting their exclusion from the plan. At this point, the reason for the requested modification, the cede back provision, became known both to the district court and to the plaintiffs. The plaintiffs began vigorously to oppose inclusion of the Seattle Seven in the plan of allocation.

The district court agreed with the plaintiffs, originally taking the position that the cede back provision itself was unlawful as against public policy. The Seattle Seven and Exxon moved for reconsideration, supporting their motion with declarations of numerous legal luminaries, including former U.S. Attorneys General, judges of various U.S. Courts of Appeal, law professors, and an Alaska Supreme Court Justice, all to the effect that cede back agreements are ethical, enforceable, and necessary for the orderly administration of justice in mass tort cases.

Upon reconsideration, the district court agreed that the cede back agreement was not in and of itself unethical, but held that the Seattle Seven were nonetheless barred from participating in the allocation of damages because the jury was not told of the agreement's existence. The court's order stated that the problem was Exxon's failure to tell the jury "the whole story" regarding the agreements. The court emphasized its belief that the jury should have been entitled to determine how much Exxon should actually pay in punitive damages, out of its own pocket, stating: "Punitive damages are imposed to punish the conduct which juries determine to be reckless. The court has no doubt that the Exxon Valdez jury would be outraged if Exxon, through the Seattle Seven settlement agreement, rather than the claimants, were to wind up with almost 15% of the punitive damages award."

In this appeal, appellants Seattle Seven and Exxon contend both that cede back agreements are lawful and that for their proper administration, they must not be disclosed to juries. Otherwise, appellants argue, the jury in order to compensate for them or to prevent the defendant from paying less than what the jury believes is appropriate punishment will inflate the punitive damages award.

The appellee plaintiffs defend the district court's reasoning, arguing that such agreements are unethical and unenforceable unless juries are told of them. They also contend that even if juries should ordinarily not be told, disclosure in this particular case was warranted by Exxon's exaggerated statements to the jury regarding the amount paid to claimants without releases in return. We review approval of the plan of allocation for abuse of discretion and any necessary legal questions de novo. See In re Mego Financial Corp. Sec. Litig., 213 F.3d 454, 460 (9th Cir. 2000).

There are accordingly three principal issues that we must consider in the disposition of this appeal: (1) the lawfulness and enforceability of cede back agreements like the one in this case; (2) whether, if lawful and enforceable, they should generally, as a matter of law, be kept from the jury; and (3) if they should ordinarily be kept secret, whether there were circumstances present in this case that should have required Exxon to tell the jury about the existence of this particular agreement. We hold that cede back agreements are enforceable; that in accordance with the general principle that indemnification arrangements should not be allowed to affect a jury's determination of damages, cede back agreements should not be disclosed to the jury; and, finally, that there are no circumstances in this case that would have warranted disclosing the terms of this cede back provision to the jury. We therefore conclude that the district court abused its discretion in approving a plan of allocation that denied enforceability of the settlement agreement between Exxon and the Seattle Seven and that barred the Seattle Seven from receiving any allocation of punitive damages.

I. Enforceability of the Cede Back Provision

In recent years, federal courts have become all too familiar with the peculiar problems posed by mass tort litigation. Such litigation clogs dockets for decades, creating burdens on the judicial system and delaying relief for injured parties. As a result, the general policy of federal courts to promote settlement before trial is even stronger in the context of large-scale class actions. See Franklin v. Kaypro Corp., 884 F.2d 1222, 1229 (9th Cir. 1989) (stating that the fact that "there is an overriding public interest in settling and quieting litigation . . . is particularly true in class action suits."). It is unfortunately also true, however, that such settlements are difficult to reach. "[O]btaining a settlement in multi-party litigation may be quite complex." It will frequently be very close to impossible for a mass tort defendant to achieve a settlement with every potential plaintiff. The resulting presence of non-settling defendants, non-settling plaintiffs, or both, may seriously affect the parties' incentives to settle in the first place.

In addition to encouraging individual settlements, courts have encouraged the use of mandatory class actions to handle punitive damages claims in mass tort cases. Mandatory class actions avoid the unfairness that results when a few plaintiffs — those who win the race to the courthouse — bankrupt a defendant early in the litigation process. They also avoid the possible unfairness of punishing a defendant over and over again for the same tortious conduct. As a result, mandatory classes have been endorsed by many courts and commentators. . . .

One drawback to the mandatory class action, however, is that it makes it even more difficult to settle the claims of any individual plaintiff. Because punitive damages in a mandatory class action are awarded in one lump sum, a defendant has a serious disincentive to settle with any plaintiff unless it can negotiate a settlement with them all, a staggering feat if not a practical impossibility. Partial settlement merely reduces the number of plaintiffs who share an eventual award. It does not reduce the award's amount. Because a defendant like Exxon would presumably be indifferent as to whether it paid 10,000 plaintiffs $500,000 each or 500,000 plaintiffs $10,000 each, the creation of mandatory punitive damages classes cuts against the strong judicial policy of encouraging settlement in class actions.

We deal here with multiple plaintiffs suing one defendant, but an analogous problem frequently occurs in the more typical situation of a single plaintiff with claims against multiple defendants. When a plaintiff is able to settle with fewer than all of the defendants, the question becomes how to determine what share of a jury's total assessment of damages a non-settling defendant should pay. Courts agree that the non-settling defendant does not have to pay the entirety of any eventual damages award. They diverge, however, on the issue of apportionment, taking three distinct approaches.

Under the first approach, the non-settling defendant pays the entire amount of the award less the actual amount the plaintiff has already received from the settling defendant, even if this total turns out to be in excess of the non-settling defendant's share of the fault as determined by the jury. The non-settling defendant then retains the right to seek contribution from the settling defendant in order to bring total payments in line with allocation of fault. This is called the "pro tanto with contribution" approach, and it creates little incentive for any defendant to settle.

The second approach is known as "pro tanto without contribution." Under this approach, the non-settling defendant pays the entire amount of the award less the amount of the settlement and does not retain the right to seek contribution. This helps ensure that the plaintiff receives the full amount of damages and maintains incentives to settle, but can result in the non-settling defendant paying more than its share of fault.

Finally, under the "proportionate share" approach, the non-settling defendant pays only the amount of the award that is allocable to its share of the fault, as determined by the jury. The proportionate share approach is the law in the Ninth Circuit, has been adopted by the Supreme Court for use in maritime actions, and is the approach recommended by the American Law Institute.

The main advantage of the proportionate share approach is that it is the only one of the three that combines fairness to all parties with an appropriate balance of individual incentives to settle. The effect of proportionate share apportionment, however, is that the actual amount of damages the plaintiff receives will deviate from the amount awarded by the jury, unless the amount of the settlement exactly matches the settling defendant's share of fault as subsequently determined by the jury. If the jury later determines that the settling defendant's share of fault is less than the amount paid in settlement, this will result in a windfall to the plaintiff. If the jury's allocation is higher, this will result in a shortfall.

This case differs from the typical situation in that we do not have a single plaintiff seeking to recover a single award from multiple defendants. The Exxon Valdez punitive damages class involves multiple plaintiffs seeking to recover a single award from a single defendant. Neither our court nor leading authorities have addressed this situation. The potential distortion of settlement incentives that occurs when some parties settle and some do not is the same, however, as with the multiple defendant situation. If Exxon could have been sure that the district court would eventually adopt a form of the proportionate share approach, permitting non-settling plaintiffs to recover damages only in proportion to their allocation of harm and allowing the remaining punitives to go uncollected, settlement incentives would have been preserved and the cede back provision would not have been necessary. Exxon had no such certainty, though (and indeed, the district court eventually refused to adopt such a method). Exxon therefore sought to achieve a proportionate share result without the court's assistance by adding the cede back provision to its settlement agreement with the Seattle Seven.

An analogous type of cede back agreement has been used in the multiple-defendant context and is called a *Pierringer* release, after the leading case to consider it, Pierringer v. Hoger, 124 N.W.2d 106 (Wis. 1963). *Pierringer* releases have been approved in Wisconsin and Minnesota. See *id.*; Frey v. Snelgrove, 269 N.W.2d 918, 922 (Minn. 1978).

Pierringer releases have the effect of reaching a proportionate share result and have principally been used in jurisdictions that adhere to the "pro tanto with contribution" approach. A plaintiff who settles with one of multiple defendants agrees to indemnify that defendant for any eventual contribution action brought by the non-settling defendants after the entry of judgment. . . .

What Exxon and the Seattle Seven did, therefore, was use a *Pierringer* device to obtain the functional equivalent of a proportionate share allocation of damages. Since both the Ninth Circuit and the Supreme Court have endorsed the proportionate share approach because of its superiority in blending fairness to the parties with incentives to settle, we cannot hold such an agreement unenforceable as a matter of public policy. Far from being unethical, cede back agreements make it easier to administer mandatory class actions for the assessment of punitive damages and encourage settlement in mass tort cases. As a result, such agreements should typically be enforced.

II. Whether Cede Back Agreements Should Generally Be Disclosed to the Jury

The district court in this case held that cede back agreements, though ethical, should be disclosed to the jury because the jury should be able to take them into account in assessing punitive damages. Exxon and the Seattle Seven contend, however, that juries should never be told. They argue persuasively that the salutary purposes of such agreements would be frustrated if the jury knew about the terms of the agreement and were permitted to offset them by increasing damages. We agree.

If a jury was told that the defendant would eventually get back a portion of the punitive damages assessed, the jury would likely compensate by imposing more damages, thereby assuring that the defendant would pay the entire amount deemed appropriate by the jury. This is exactly what the district court believed the jury should have been permitted to do in this case. Yet if that were to be the result of the settlement agreement, from the defendant's perspective there would be no point in settling in the first place. The defendant would still have to pay the full amount assessed by the jury, in addition to the amount paid in settlement.

This is what we have recognized elsewhere in our law: that a jury should assess damages but not determine how much defendants should "actually" pay or how much plaintiffs should "actually" receive. In Larez v. Holcomb, 16 F.3d 1513 (9th Cir. 1994), we held that it was prejudicial error to inform a jury deliberating on an award of punitive damages that the defendant would be indemnified by his employer for any such award. We stated that a jury's task is to arrive at a "dispassionate" determination of the proper award, and that evidence of indemnification might have tempted the jury to inflate the award out of sympathy for the plaintiff. See *id.* at 1519. Similarly, we held in Brooks v. Cook, 938 F.2d 1048 (9th Cir. 1991), that juries should not be told about the availability of attorneys' fees when fixing an award for a prevailing plaintiff. We explained that "the fear is that a jury, informed of plaintiff's right to additional funds, will view the money as a windfall and take steps to offset it."

These principles are not unique to this circuit. It is uniformly held that absent exceptional circumstances, a jury deliberating on the amount of a damages award is not to consider where the funds that constitute that award will come from, or where they will end up. For example, the states of Georgia and Oregon both have enacted tort reform measures that provide that large portions of punitive damages awards (75 percent in Georgia and 50 percent in Oregon) go to the state or state-designated charities rather than the prevailing plaintiff. Both states have held that it is prejudicial error to inform the jury of this ultimate outcome, because of the temptation for the jury to inflate the award in order to more fully compensate the plaintiff. . . .

In cases involving settling and non-settling defendants, several states provide by statute that in allocating fault, the jury cannot be told of a settlement or its terms. The reason for this is the danger that the jury will adjust its award of damages according to the amount of the settlement. If the jury perceives that the settlement amount is low, for example, it might be tempted to increase the amount of fault allocable to the non-settling defendants in order to maximize the plaintiff's recovery.

In Minnesota, a state that has recognized the validity of agreements similar to the cede back provision in this case, the Supreme Court has held that the existence of a *Pierringer* release may be admissible for limited purposes such as to show witness bias. The court must exercise its discretion, however, as to what details of the agreement should be provided to the jury, and "as a general rule the amount paid in settlement should never be submitted." Thus, the existence of an agreement between the parties is clearly relevant should the settling defendant attempt to testify at trial in a manner favorable to the plaintiff. The details of the agreement should not be disclosed, though, and the evidence admitted should be limited to avoid distorting the jury's deliberations on damages. . . .

Therefore, it is clear that cede back agreements should generally not be revealed to juries deliberating on punitive damages. The only remaining question is whether any particular circumstances in this case warranted an exception from this general rule.

III. Special Circumstances

The plaintiffs argue that even if evidence of a cede back agreement would ordinarily be kept from a jury, Exxon should have volunteered it in this case to correct the false impression Exxon created when it announced that it had paid out $300 million in compensation requiring only receipts in return when the correct figure was approximately $168 million. They further argue that the fact that the exaggeration went uncorrected justifies the district court's decision to exclude the Seattle Seven from the plan of allocation and render the cede back provision completely unenforceable.

The plaintiffs rely on Lawson v. Trowbridge, 153 F.3d 368 (7th Cir. 1998). Lawson holds that otherwise inadmissible evidence of indemnification may be admitted on cross-examination to impeach a testifying defendant who intimates to the jury that he will be financially ruined by a large damages award. See *id.* at 379. *Lawson* does not concern the enforceability of the underlying indemnification agreement.

We will not extend *Lawson* beyond its holding to justify the district court's exclusion of the Seattle Seven from the plan of allocation on the basis of Exxon's trial conduct. Denying the Seattle Seven recovery on the basis of Exxon's actions would be manifestly unfair.

As for Exxon itself, we do not condone its conduct. The exaggerations it made at trial, however, have little, if anything, to do with the cede back provision. Exxon stated that it had paid out $300 million requiring only receipts in return; the only correction necessary was the alteration of that figure to $168 million. There would have been no need to mention the cede back provision, and thus no need to disturb the general rule that such agreements should be ordinarily be kept from the jury. Furthermore, the only conceivable prejudice the plaintiffs could have suffered when Exxon overstated its corporate benevolence would have been a downward adjustment by the jury of the damages award, and the proper remedy for such prejudice would be a new trial on punitive damages. The plaintiffs have never claimed that $5 billion was too low an award, however, nor have they ever sought a new trial. Refusing to enforce the cede back provision is not a remedy that relates to the error complained of.

IV. Other Arguments

The plaintiffs raise on appeal two alternative arguments in support of the district court's decision to exclude the Seattle Seven from the plan of allocation. First, the plaintiffs claim that because the Seattle Seven "settled" their claims against Exxon, they have no right to claim a share of punitive damages regardless of the existence of the cede back provision. It is clear, however, that the settlement agreement did not contain a release of any claims; it merely "settled" the matter of what would happen to the claims once the claims were finally adjudicated. Second, the plaintiffs argue that public policy precludes any agreement that diminishes the deterrent effect of a punitive damages award. This argument runs contrary to the law of this circuit, which permits indemnification agreements and the settlement and release of punitive damages claims. As exemplified by *Larez*, it is not up to the jury to decide how much a defendant must actually pay at the end of the day, or how much a plaintiff will actually receive. We therefore reject both of the plaintiffs' alternative arguments.

Conclusion

We hold that the district court abused its discretion in approving the plan of allocation over the Seattle Seven's objection. Cede back agreements are lawful and enforceable, and generally should not be disclosed to the jury. No special circumstances in this case justify the district court's refusal to enforce the cede back agreement between Exxon and the Seattle Seven. As a result, the existence of the cede back agreement cannot justify exclusion of the Seattle Seven from the plan of allocation.

The approval of the Allocation Plan is Vacated and the matter is Remanded.

NOTE ON *EXXON VALDEZ*

1. Why did the Seattle canneries decide to settle with Exxon for what was likely a fraction of their lost profits? The answer likely lies not in procedure but in uncertainty about tort law. As noted in the introduction to *Exxon Valdez*, the law of proximate cause for such marine catastrophes was unsettled, and it was entirely possible that a court would decide that the canneries were outside the "zone" of proximately caused injuries and that they would recover nothing. (Subsequent decisions in maritime law suggest this was a real risk—that the canneries would likely have lost had the question of proximate cause been litigated.)

2. Why did Exxon want to include the "cede-back" agreement in the settlement with the Seattle canneries? Why would it not have worked for these plaintiffs simply to have "settled" their punitive damage claims at the same time as their compensatory claims?

3. Finally, consider how Exxon might have arrived at its decision to conceal the cede-back agreement from the trial judge. It could make a very good guess that the judge would be annoyed. (In fact his first reaction was to remove all of Exxon's lawyers from the case and to recommend that they be subjected to disciplinary actions by their various state bars; only after extensive testimony from experts on legal ethics was he persuaded to allow them to continue representing Exxon at all—and only after voiding the cede-back agreement.) Assume for a moment that Exxon's lawyers anticipated something like this reaction. Why might they have nevertheless have decided to run the risk?

4. In subsequent litigation, the permissibility, the amount, and the procedure for awarding punitive damages under the precedential effect of cases decided in the last decade continued to be litigated. *See* In re Exxon Valdez, 270 F.3d 1215 (9th Cir. 2002). In 2008 the U.S. Supreme Court heard the case and — as a matter of federal maritime common law — reduced the most recent punitive damage award to an amount equal to the compensatory damage award — $507.5 million. Exxon Shipping Co. v. Baker, 128 S. Ct. 2605 (2008).

G. ASSISTED SETTLEMENT, COERCED SETTLEMENT

NOTE ON THIRD-PARTY PARTICIPATION IN SETTLEMENT

"Classical" settlement negotiations involve two parties. But, as you have already seen, even simple litigation often involves additional actors, such as insurers, whose consent is necessary to effect a settlement. And even when there are only two parties, litigants and lawyers can get themselves locked into positions in which they cannot reach a settlement that, seen from an outsider's perspective, seems obvious and mutually advantageous. Under such circumstances the parties sometimes bring in a third party — a mediator — to explore solutions and to help them reach agreement. The next selection comes from the Web site of a for-profit organization that offers such mediation for a fee. As you read it consider which of the settlement situations in this chapter might have benefitted from such intervention.

Sometimes the third party involved in settlement negotiations is not selected by the parties but is rather the judge in the case. Some judges pride themselves in helping, or maybe even pushing, parties toward settlement. The last reading in this chapter displays a judge who appears deeply invested in helping the parties toward settlement, to the point where some might ask whether he had crossed the line into coercion.

JAMS, MEDIATION

Compiled from the JAMS Web site, online at http://www.jamsadr.com
(last visited July 7, 2005)

Nature of the Process

Mediation is a process wherein the parties meet with a mutually selected impartial and neutral person who assists them in the negotiation of their differences.

Role of the Mediator

Mediation leaves the decision power totally and strictly with the parties. The mediator does not decide what is "fair" or "right," does not assess blame nor render an opinion on the merits or chances of success if the case were litigated. Rather, the mediator acts as a catalyst between opposing interests attempting to bring them together by defining issues and eliminating obstacles to communication, while moderating and guiding the process to avoid confrontation and ill will. The mediator will, however, see concessions from each side during the mediation process.

Forbearance from Litigation During Mediation and Confidentiality of Proceedings

At the outset of a mediation process, the mediator may well seek agreement from the parties to forbear from litigation during the mediation process and to hold everything that is said in the various sessions confidential and not deemed an admission or used against any party in any other proceeding if mediation fails.

Procedures: Joint Session Followed by Private Caucuses

Mediation generally begins with a joint session to set an agenda, define the issues and ascertain the position and/or concerns of the parties. This allows the parties to attack the resolution process either on an issue-by-issue or group-by-group basis.

The joint session is then followed by a separate caucus between the mediator and each individual party or their counsel. This allows each side to explain and enlarge upon their position and mediation goals in confidence. It also gives the mediator an opportunity to ask questions which may well serve to create doubt in an advocate's mind over the validity of a particular position.

Confidential Listener

One form of mediation is known as "confidential listening" where each side agrees to reveal their settlement positions to the mediator in a private caucus so that it can be ascertained if there is any overlap or common ground upon which to reach a settlement. The ground rules must be agreed upon up front and the mediator, of course, does not reveal the information given in the private caucus. The only thing revealed is whether or not it appears to the mediator that the parties are within a zone of settlement.

The Mediation

What actually happens in mediation? The following information is provided to demystify the process and assist you in your preparations. The procedures discussed herein are those normally followed in a dispute that is mediated through the auspices of JAMS.

Mediation can be described as an assisted negotiation. The mediator is neutral and has no bias against any of the parties or their positions. He/she is the facilitator who assists the parties in reaching an agreement that is acceptable to them. The agreement is not imposed upon the parties; it is reached through the facilitated negotiation process typical of a mediation proceeding. Judges and arbitrators make decisions that are imposed on the parties. Mediators may be requested during the course of a mediation to provide their evaluation of the probable outcome of a dispute were it to be litigated or arbitrated. If there is such an evaluation, it is done at the request of the parties but is not binding upon them unless they request and agree to it. Binding mediation is not true mediation because, like a court or arbitration decision, it is imposed upon the parties and is not a product of their own negotiation. The formal procedures found in court or arbitration proceedings are not present in mediation proceedings. There are no rules of evidence or set procedures for the presentation of facts or positions. Before mediation commences, the parties and the mediator agree upon the procedures that will be followed. It is the party's proceeding; they can fashion it in any way that makes sense to them and the mediator. This absence of formality provides for open discussion of the issues and allows the free interchange of ideas. Thus, it becomes easier to determine the interests of the parties and to fashion a solution that satisfies those interests.

The Mediators

The mediator is an invaluable neutral resource to all participants in the mediation process. Lawyers, insurance professionals and their clients use the knowledge and skills of a neutral mediator to plan negotiation strategies and develop options for settlement. The mediator keeps the process focused and moving forward.

[The site describes the qualifications and training of its mediators.]

The Preliminary Meeting

In most cases, the mediator will meet with the parties and/or their representatives prior to the joint mediation session. Sometimes, for the sake of convenience, a conference call substitutes for the initial meeting.

This initial meeting or conference call provides:

- An introduction to the participants and the mediation process.
- An opportunity to discuss issues affecting settlement which are important for the mediator to know in advance.
- An opportunity to determine what information would be helpful for the mediator to have at or in advance of the mediation.
- An appropriate time to discuss any concerns a party might have about the mediation and his/her role in the process.

The Joint Meeting

When all of the procedures have been agreed to and a mediation agreement has been signed, the mediation session or sessions are scheduled. The mediation normally commences with a joint conference among all of the parties and their counsel. The joint session provides an opportunity for each participant, either directly or through counsel, to express their view of the case to the other participants and how they would like to approach settlement. The opening statements are intended to begin the settlement process, not to be adversarial or a restatement of positions. This session may last anywhere from a few minutes to many hours depending on the number of participants and the complexity of the issues. The mediator will let you know in advance how to prepare for this session.

The Individual Sessions

After the initial joint meeting, the parties break up into separate groups and "shuttle diplomacy" commences. The mediator has a number of private and confidential meetings or caucuses with each of the parties and their representatives to explore interests and settlement possibilities. He/she shuttles back and forth between the parties, carrying various settlement proposals and communicating the interests and needs of each participant to the other participants. The mediator keeps information from the private sessions confidential unless he/she is authorized to disclose it.

The mediator will often act as "devil's advocate" in these sessions to explore how realistic the positions of the participants are and what is possible considering the no agreement alternative. The mediator often assists parties to prioritize interests and options for settlement and to assess the relative strengths and weaknesses of positions.

Once settlement is achieved, the mediator will record it for signature immediately to prevent second thoughts from destroying a good agreement.

Evaluation by the Mediator

Most mediations commence with the mediator as a facilitator not an evaluator. An early evaluation by a mediator often destroys his/her effectiveness to act as a neutral. When appropriate, and in consultation with the participants, mediators will provide a formal or informal evaluation and analysis of the case, to focus on strengths and weaknesses, likely outcome at trial, and value of the case. Quite often, risk analysis tools are used in the evaluative process. A mediator's evaluation is simply that and nothing more; it is not binding upon the parties unless the parties agree to the contrary.

Follow Up

In some cases, telephone conferences occur following mediation sessions if no agreement has yet been reached. Sometimes, further information is required for the process to continue or additional people may need to be involved in the decision making process.

Agreement

The mediator will work with counsel to finalize a settlement agreement and determine the procedures necessary for implementation. The mediator is available to provide assistance throughout the process.

LOCKHART V. PATEL

115 F.R.D. 44 (E.D. Ky. 1987)

BERTELSMAN, District Judge:

Unfortunately, the court finds it necessary in this case to discuss the question of its authority to order parties and their insurers to attend settlement conferences. Also involved is the propriety of sanctions for failure to attend.

This is a medical malpractice action in which the plaintiff, a teenager, lost the sight of one eye, allegedly due to the defendant doctor's negligence. In a summary jury trial[*] an advisory jury awarded the plaintiff $200,000.

---

*[Editor's Note: A summary jury trial is, essentially an advisory jury which is used as a settlement device. The judge calls "jurors" (who can include real jurors, various court personnel, and anyone else), the lawyers present their cases in very abbreviated form (usually by summarizing what witnesses are expected to say, rather than by calling witnesses) and the jury then renders a "verdict." That verdict has no binding effect; its value is that it reveals to the parties how a real jury might respond to their cases. The hope is that the parties, given this information, will now be able to settle the case.]

Following the summary jury trial, the court held several formal and informal pretrial and settlement conferences, both in person and by telephone. In a telephone conference on October 30, 1986, the attorney for the defendant doctor's liability insurance carrier, St. Paul Fire & Marine Insurance Company, advised the court that he had been authorized by that company's home office to offer $125,000 and no more and not to negotiate any further. At this time, the plaintiff's demand was $175,000.

Having had some success with settlement conferences in the past, the court directed the defense attorney to attend a settlement conference on November 3, 1986, and to bring with him the representative of the insurance company from the home office who had issued these instructions, or one with equal authority. The court specifically and formally admonished defense counsel: "Tell them not to send some flunky who has no authority to negotiate. I want someone who can enter into a settlement in this range without having to call anyone else."

November 3 arrived, and so did the defense attorney. But the representative from St. Paul's home office did not. Instead, an adjuster from the local office appeared. She advised the court that her instructions from the officials at the home office were to reiterate the offer previously made and not to bother to call them back if it were not accepted.

When asked by the court whether there was some misunderstanding that it had stated a representative from the home office was required to attend, the adjuster replied, "I doubt if anyone from the home office would have come down even if in fact this is what you said."

Measures in response to such clearly improper conduct seemed called for. At this point, the court made the appropriate oral findings, promptly followed by a written order, that "St. Paul had deliberately refused to obey the order of the court" and that "such disobedience was deliberately contemptuous, contumacious and purposely demonstrated disrespect and disregard for the authority of the court."

Accordingly, the court forthwith struck the pleadings of the defendant and declared him in default. The court further ordered that the trial set for the next day would be limited to damages only and that a hearing to show cause why St. Paul should not be punished for criminal contempt be held on December 12, 1986. Later that day, St. Paul settled with the plaintiff for $175,000.

December 12 arrived, and this time so did not one but several representatives from St. Paul's home office. The home office representatives through their counsel assured the court that it had all been a misunderstanding, not their fault indeed, but that of the local lawyer and adjuster. The court accepted these assurances at face value and permitted St. Paul to purge itself of contempt by providing a letter of apology from its Chief Executive Officer, assuring the court that it was not company policy to refuse to attend settlement conferences or take it on itself to disregard court orders. The letter was forthcoming and is attached hereto as an appendix.

This opinion is written, therefore, solely to discuss the authority of the court to hold meaningful settlement conferences and the propriety of the civil sanction imposed in this instance.

The authority of a federal court to order attendance of attorneys, parties, and insurers at settlement conferences and to impose sanctions for disregard of the court's orders is so well established as to be beyond doubt. 6 Wright & Miller, *Federal Practices & Procedure*, §1526 (1971); Moore's *Federal Practice*, para.16.16.1, 16.22. F.R. Civ. P. 16(f) specifically provides:

> (f) Sanctions. If a party or party's attorney fails to obey a scheduling or pretrial order, or if no appearance is made on behalf of a party at a scheduling or pretrial conference, or if a party or party's attorney is *substantially unprepared to participate* in the conference, or if a party or party's attorney fails to participate in good faith, *the judge, upon motion or his own initiative, may make such orders with regard thereto as are just, and among others any of the orders provided in Rule 37(b)(2)(B), (C), (D).* In lieu of or in addition to any other sanctions, the judge shall require the party or the attorney representing him or both to pay the reasonable expenses incurred because of noncompliance with this rule, including attorney's fees, unless the judge finds that the noncompliance was substantially justified or that other circumstances make an award of expenses unjust." (Emphasis added)

Rule 16(f) was added to original Rule 16, along with several other amendments in 1983. Although the rule refers to "parties," it clearly would be meaningless if it did not also apply to a party's liability insurer.

The Advisory Committee Note to the Amendment states that the purpose of the addition of this subrule was to "reflect that existing practice, and to obviate dependence upon Rule 41(b) or the court's inherent power" to compel respect for the court's pretrial orders. The Committee Note cites several cases illustrating practice prior to the subrule's adoption.

"Furthermore," the Advisory Committee continues, "explicit reference to sanctions reinforces the rule's intention to encourage forceful judicial management."

The Note also makes clear that the striking of a party's pleadings is an appropriate sanction, as under F.R. Civ. P. 37. Further, the rule itself makes it clear that sanctions may be imposed on the court's own motion. . . .

. . . The normal caseload of a United States District Judge is now considered to be 400 civil cases. At this time, every judge in this district has half again that many, because of the extended illness of one of our judges. Although some of these cases are simple, many are complex. And in addition to this civil caseload the court is also expected to deal with the criminal docket, which for this court averages about 40 cases per judge per year, some taking several weeks to try.

The drafters of amended Rule 16 knew of the docket pressures to which our courts are subject, and knew that to process 400 cases you have to settle at least 350. That is why they encouraged "forceful judicial management," which is the only means of settling a high percentage of cases.

As I have observed in another place, the exigencies of modern dockets demand the adoption of novel and imaginative means lest the courts, inundated by a tidal wave of cases, fail in their duty to provide a just and speedy disposition of every case. These means may take the form of compulsory arbitration, summary jury trials, imposing reasonable limits on trial time, or, as here, the relatively innocuous device of requiring a settlement conference attended by the clients as well as the attorneys.

Of course, the court cannot require any party to settle a case, whether the court thinks that party's position is reasonable or not, but it can require it to make reasonable efforts, including attending a settlement conference with an open mind.

The court hopes that the sanctions imposed here will be sufficient to convince St. Paul and other similarly minded companies and individuals of this fact and prevent similar occurrences in the future.

WILLIAM O. BERTELSMAN, JUDGE

Appendix

December 29, 1986
Hon. William O. Bertelsman
United States District Court
Eastern District of Kentucky
Covington, Kentucky 41011

RE: Roger Daniel Lockhart, et al. v. Ramon Patel, M.D., et al.
Civil Action No. 84-224

Dear Judge Bertelsman:

As Chief Executive Officer of St. Paul Fire & Marine Insurance Company, I am writing this letter in response to the court's order dated December 12, 1986. St. Paul Fire & Marine Insurance Company publicly apologizes to the court for the events set forth in the record of Lockhart, et al, v. Patel, et al. and in particular for the misunderstanding which occurred at the settlement conference held on Monday, November 3, 1986. It has never been, is not now, nor will it be in the future, the policy of St. Paul Fire & Marine Insurance Company to ignore the orders of this court or any other court of law. To the contrary, it is the established policy of St. Paul Fire & Marine Insurance Company to respect the orders of this court and other courts concerning the attendance of its employees at settlement conferences.

It is the company's policy that its employees attend all settlement conferences when ordered to do so by a court of competent jurisdiction. This requirement is known to all claim handlers.

Once again, St. Paul Fire & Marine Insurance Company apologizes to the court for the events of November 3, 1986. St. Paul Fire & Marine Insurance Company wishes the court and its staff a happy, healthy and prosperous 1987.

Sincerely,
/s/ signature
Chairman
RJH/mb

NOTE ON *LOCKHART*

1. *Lockhart* obviously looks backwards at this chapter on settlement. In this guise the case reveals the fervor with which some judges pursue settlement. Note that Judge Bertelsman devoted substantial judicial time to a summary jury trial and then to a settlement conference.

    a. One could see such efforts as admirable, given the judge's view that the parties were not far apart in their valuation of the case and that a settlement would save scarce judicial time. Those favoring this view often explain how judicial participation in settlements helps parties face reality and, in some cases, to back away from their lawyers' excessively optimistic view of the case.

    b. One could see such efforts as an abrogation of the judge's proper role, which, from this perspective, is to hear and decide controversies, not to push the parties toward a settlement that one of them obviously did not want. Those favoring this view point out that, unlike the National Labor Relations Act, which requires employers and unions to "bargain in good faith," there is no such requirement for litigants. Some would add that even the most stubbornly unreasonable litigant has a due process right to a trial.

    c. Still a third perspective might take no position about the ideal judicial role, but ask instead whether the judge's repeated efforts to settle the case in fact wasted time. Most federal civil trials take three or fewer days. We're not told how long the "several" pretrial conferences and summary jury trial and contempt hearing took; if they lasted longer than the average trial, one might think that, paradoxically, the efforts to save trial time took more time than a trial would have taken. The most elaborate study of various judicial efforts to manage litigation suggested that the only technique that consistently reduced both the length and the expense of litigation was the setting and adherence to firm trial dates. James S. Kakalik et al., *An Evaluation of Judicial Case Management Under the Civil Justice Reform Act* (Rand Institute for Civil Justice 1996).

2. Beyond these matters of principle lie questions of technique. Even lawyers who value a judge's role in facilitating settlement often express discomfort when the same judge who will preside at trial also seeks to facilitate settlement. Their concern flows from the circumstance that a judge may form an unfavorable opinion about the reasonableness of the parties' refusal to settle (as Judge Bertelsman apparently did), and that bad opinion is likely to carry over into trial rulings on such matters as evidence and instructions. Some judicial systems honor this view by ensuring that different judges conduct the settlement conference and any ensuing trial. Rule 16 — the federal provision — is silent on this question.

3. *Lockhart* also looks forward to the next chapter, on judicial selection, recusal, and discipline. As a transition consider the following: Although the *Lockhart* opinion asserts that the judge's authority to take these actions was clearly established, several authorities on procedure disagreed, believing that it was at best tenuous and perhaps simply unauthorized. Suppose these authorities are correct.

   a. Further suppose that in spite of its letter of apology—almost certainly drafted by its general counsel—St. Paul's Insurance thinks that Judge Bertelsman acted outrageously in this case. How would it raise that complaint and what would be likely to happen if it did? The next chapter provides an answer to that question.

   b. Alternatively, suppose the insurer bites its corporate tongue and does nothing. Then, the next month, another medical malpractice claim is filed against one of its insureds in Kentucky, and, by random assignment, the case goes to Judge Bertelsman, whom St. Paul's believes may still be simmering in resentment about what he says was its contemptuous behavior. Can St. Paul's get Judge Bertelsman removed from this new case? Stay tuned.

CHAPTER 4

JUDGES

INTRODUCTORY NOTE ON JUDGES

In the preceding chapters the parties and their lawyers have occupied the center of our attention. But every lawsuit has another actor—an actor who will determine its outcome if the parties do not prevent that by settling. That actor is, of course, the judge. The judge plays an obvious and important role at trial. But in contemporary civil litigation most cases don't reach trial. Does the judge matter in these cases?

Absolutely. Indeed one can argue that the judge matters *more* in the majority of cases that settle before trial than in those cases that go to trial. At trial the judge may well share power with a jury, and even the judge who presides without a jury will be subject to appeal in any case that goes to judgment. Neither control exists in cases that settle. The judge matters because he or she will make numerous pretrial rulings—on the pleadings, on discovery matters, perhaps on summary judgment motions. Further, because many of these motions will not result in a final judgment and because in the United States typically only final judgments are appealable, an erroneous ruling will never be appealed—the parties will be stuck with it. The following sections survey the selection (sometimes involving election) of judges, the recusal of judges, and the disciplinary mechanisms that try to weed out bad apples. As you read them, consider how this information reflects back on earlier chapters. Does knowing how the judge got there and whether she can be removed from this case (or from all cases) explain why lawyers might behave as they do? Does this knowledge explain why cases settle?

A. OVERVIEW—WHY JUDGES MATTER, WHAT THEY DO

1. WHO, WHERE, AND WHAT?

Lynn Langton & Thomas Cohen, Bureau of Justice Statistics
Special Report: State Court Organization 1987-2004

October 2007, available online at http://www.ojp.usdoj.gov/ bjs/pub/pdf/sco8704.pdf

From 1987 to 2004, state courts nationwide experienced a variety of structural and staffing changes, ranging from increased judicial staffing levels to consolidated court administration. These changes can be partially attributed to growing caseload pressures at the trial and appellate court levels. Over the 18-year period, total non-traffic case filings in state appellate and trial courts increased by almost 45%, from approximately 31.3 million in 1987 to 45.2 million in 2004.

In addition to caseload pressures, growing numbers of state courts sought to consolidate and professionalize court systems that were highly fragmented. In terms of organization and structure, many state court systems traditionally had multiple trial courts which evolved as local institutions at the county or municipal level. Administratively, funding and rulemaking authority were either split between state and local governments or fully assumed at the local level.

The court reform movement, initiated early in the Twentieth Century, was aimed at reducing the fragmentation and disparity inherent in many state court systems. The movement focused on consolidating state trial courts, creating state-centralized court administrations for budgetary and regulatory purposes, and increasing professionalism among court judicial, clerical, and administrative staff.

These efforts produced gradual and modest changes in state courts nationwide. By 2004, 10 states had consolidated their court systems by merging general and limited jurisdiction trial courts. Some of the responsibility for trial court expenses was also shifted from the county to the state.

Since 1987 state courts have also become increasingly professionalized. Over half of all states have mandated that their trial court judges hold law degrees and take judicial education classes during their time of service on the bench. Some states have sought to professionalize the judicial selection process by moving away from party-driven elections. By 2004 four states at the appellate level and three states at the trial court level were no longer using partisan elections to retain judges. . . .

Despite increases, the number of state court judges has not kept up with population growth. From 1987 to 2004, the ratio of trial judges to the population nationwide decreased slightly from 10 to 9 judges per 100,000 persons. . . .

Table 2. State Court Judges and Clerks by Jurisdictional Level of Court, 1987-2004

Level of Court	Number of Court Staff			
	1987	1993	1998	2004
Courts of last resort				
Total judges	338	340	340	340
Total law clerks	657	744	769	837
Average number law clerks per—				
Chief justice[a]	2.1	2.2	2.4	2.6
Associate justice[a]	1.8	2.0	2.1	2.3
Intermediate appellate courts				
Total judges	769	857	922	964
Total law clerks	1,269	1,552	1,727	1,963
Average law clerks per—				
Chief justice[b]	2.0	2.2	2.3	2.4
Associate justice[c]	1.6	2.0	2.1	2.2
Trial courts				
Total judges[d]	23,913	24,418	25,678	26,557
Number of trial judges per 100,000 persons	9.9	9.5	9.5	9.1

Note: Staffing figures include courts from all 50 states unless otherwise noted. Law clerk refers to an individual who has passed the bar exam and works under a judge, assisting with case research and analysis.

[a]Data were not available for Pennsylvania (1987, 1993, 1998).
[b]Data were not available for Ohio (1987) and Texas (1993, 1998).
[c]Data were not available for Ohio (1987), Texas (1993, 1998), and Oklahoma (1993, 1998, 2004).
[d]Includes general and limited jurisdiction trial court judges.

* * *

Increasing professionalism in state courts is illustrated by the greater percentage of trial courts that required judges to hold a law degree in 2004 compared to 1987. The increase in the percentage of trial courts requiring all judges to have graduated law school and passed the state bar exam was most pronounced in the limited jurisdiction trial courts. In 1987, 44% of these courts required judges to have a law degree compared to 52% in 2004.

Level of trial court	1987	2004
General jurisdiction		
Number reporting	62	67
Percent requiring judges to have a law degree	87%	88%
Limited jurisdiction		
Number reporting	126	125
Percent requiring judges to have a law degree	44%	52%

Note: Includes courts in all 50 states for which law degree requirement data were available. Data were available for 93% of general jurisdiction and 91% of limited jurisdiction trial courts in 2004. Court types that varied the requirements from jurisdiction to jurisdiction were counted as not requiring a law degree for all judges.

Judicial Pre-bench and Continuing Education Requirements More Common in 2004

An increasing number of states established pre-bench and continuing education requirements for appellate and trial court judges. These requirements refer to any training courses, beyond general state bar membership requirements, that are specifically mandated for judges before taking office (pre-bench) or during their tenure (continuing education). Judicial training typically covers topics such as rules of evidence, criminal law and procedure, ethics, judicial responsibilities, and court and trial management.

From 1993 to 2004, the number of states that instituted pre-bench education requirements for appellate judges rose from five to nine. For trial court judges, six additional states at the limited jurisdiction level and seven at the general jurisdiction level established pre-bench education requirements during the 12-year period. The largest increase in continuing education requirements was among the appellate courts where 10 additional states began mandating periodic training for judges already serving on the bench.

NOTE ON THE FEDERAL JUDICIARY

There currently 674 authorized district court judgeships in the federal courts; given normal attrition rates from retirement, resignation, and death, not all of these positions are filled at any given time. In 2006 these judges had an average caseload of 464 cases, with civil filings dominating the dockets; as you may recall from the first chapter, federal courts see about 250,000 civil filings per year. This average conceals large regional disparities. In 2008 the district of Alaska had 200 cases per judge; the Eastern District of California 1,077. In 2008 those judges conducted 6,754 trials that ended in a verdict or judgment, divided almost equally between civil and criminal. Of the 3,244 civil trials, 1,888 lasted three days or less, and only 21 took more than twenty days.

2. UNDERSTANDING THE NUMBERS

Stephen C. Yeazell, The Misunderstood Consequences of Modern Civil Process

1994 Wisconsin Law Review 531 (1994)

Without realizing it, we have rearranged the power relationships of civil litigation in the past seventy-five years. We did so by redesigning the process of litigation in courts of the first instance while holding mostly constant the principles of appellate review. By changing just part of a larger system, we have encountered the law of unintended or at least misunderstood consequences. As an intended and widely understood consequence of procedural reform, trial judges and lawyers now have available a greatly expanded menu of pretrial processes. As a possibly intended but less widely understood result, the proportion of trials to filed civil cases has declined by four-fifths over the past half century. As a result, trial courts enjoy effective insulation from appellate review for a greater proportion of their decisions than was the case fifty years ago. The resulting realignment of power affects the outcome of cases and the level of authority at which that outcome is decided. If one remembers that courts are instruments of government, it is not too much to call it both a change in the location of government power and the passage to private hands of some of what was once governmental power. . . .

I. A New Shape for Civil Process

A. The Decline of the Trial, the Rise of the Motion

Civil process based on the Federal Rules of Civil Procedure has largely replaced trials with motions. One sees this change if one examines the proportion of filed civil cases going to trial over a span of just over fifty years. The Federal Rules became effective in 1938. In the fiscal year ending two months before the Rules took effect, about one in five federal civil cases ended in a judgment rendered at trial. In 1940 (two years after the Federal Rules were adopted), the Administrative Office of the United States Courts issued its first statistical report. The trial rate had already dropped by a fifth, to 15.4% of the federal civil cases filed. Fifty years later, in 1990, only 4.3% of the filed civil cases resulted in trials, a proportional decline of almost four-fifths from the pre-Rules world. . . .

What, then, has happened? One can put the question structurally by asking what has become of the civil trial, or provocatively by asking what federal judges are doing with their time if they have stopped trying civil cases. The answers begin to emerge if one looks not just at trials but at all "adjudicated dispositions." Federal courts have almost gone out of the business of trying civil cases, but they have not stopped adjudicating them. Instead of trials, judges are making rulings on other dispositive motions: dismissals on the pleadings, summary judgments, and similar rulings that end a case.

Unlike trials, the proportion of such adjudications has remained quite constant over fifty years at about one-third of all federal civil cases. The change has come in the nature of the dispositive adjudication; where once such events came at trial, now they occur beforehand, in other procedural contexts. . . .

The picture emerging from these statistics suggests that today's federal judges have moved their focus away from trial to earlier stages of litigation. The figures reflect the new focus of activity. In 1940, pretrial motions, including dismissals for lack of jurisdiction, comprised about 42% of adjudicated dispositions; in 1990, the corresponding figure was 75%, two-thirds of these by pretrial motions.

These pretrial motions consist, however, of two quite different forms of activity. On one hand, judges are finally disposing of about a third of their civil cases. On the other hand, they are engaging in a wide range of activity that does not result in disposition of the cases. This non-dispositive decision-making has grown substantially over the past fifty years, necessitated and created by changes in the rules of procedure. Examples of such non-dispositive judicial tasks and a rough measure of their extent appear in statistics describing an increasingly important group of subjudicial officers, the U.S. magistrate judges, whose work focuses on the pretrial stage. In 1990, magistrate judges heard 119,372 civil matters, ranging from discovery motions to pretrial conferences to evidentiary hearings and social security appeals. If one compares these matters to the total number of filed cases, it appears that magistrates conducted some formal proceeding in just over 50% of all civil cases in 1990. Because of limitations on the jurisdiction of magistrate judges, we know that few of these motions resulted in the adjudicated disposition of the cases in question. Instead, the magistrate judges' activity is concentrated in matters that do not result in a tried or adjudicated case. Their work thus consists of an exaggerated version of the civil tasks of a district judge. They are almost entirely out of the business of trying cases, whereas for federal district judges, trial continues to be part of the job description, no matter how infrequent its actual occurrence. . . .

One sees the result of such pretrial activity in cases that end without any adjudication, as most still do: fewer cases are abandoned, more "managed," and more settled. . . . Federal district judges (and their magistrate judge colleagues) in 1990 are thus not underworked by comparison to their predecessors. Rather, they are devoting less of their time to trials and more to earlier phases of the civil litigation process. They are vigorously presiding, sometimes as managers, sometimes as judges. Other phases of litigation now consume time that once went into presiding at trials, and these phases yield a different kind of typical resolution. . . .

III. The Relocation of Power

In the last seventy-five years, we have redesigned process in civil courts of first instance. This redesign has fundamentally changed the relationship between trial and appellate courts, and between courts and lawyers. This change has come as a result of a redesigned procedure, which interposed numerous procedural steps before trial, but did not correspondingly alter the principles of appellate review. We have altered one variable in a two-variable system. The results have been striking.

During the age of trial, the final judgment rule resulted in rapid and searching review of procedure. The system kept a tight rein on trial judges, who in turn immediately scrutinized most procedural decisions of lawyers. Today, in the dawning age of litigation, the final judgment rule results in late and little review. . . . The combination of these two developments means that control of litigation has moved further down the legal food chain—from appellate to trial courts, and from trial courts to lawyers. . . .

The adoption of the Federal Rules of Civil Procedure in 1938 diminished the significance of pleading and trial, a lawsuit's first and last phases. . . .

B. The Consequences for Trial Court Power . . .

In contrast to most continental systems of judgment, the common law world adopted the principle that appellate review was available only when the final decision had been entered by the court of first instance. . . . During eras in which a substantial proportion of trial court rulings produced judgments, the rule yielded prompt appellate review and tight appellate control. . . .

Given this structure, the Rules worked their major change by not changing anything in the scheme of appellate review. Keeping the final judgment rule in place as the Rules provided for several new stages of pretrial proceedings, the Rules created a new procedural layer that extended the length of a lawsuit while creating the opportunity for important judicial rulings. The result was a set of lower court rulings that, while often significant, were as likely as not to be unreviewable. Creating such a set of rulings while holding appellate review constant effectively allocated more power to trial courts. Because many of the

Rules' innovations were adaptations of equity practice, one can speculate how the world might look if, together with these practices, the federal courts had borrowed equity's easy access to interlocutory review. Or, to put matters another way, it was the adoption of equity's pretrial processes without equity's interlocutory review that reallocated powers to the trial courts. . . .

IV. Thinking About Procedural Change

The argument thus far has suggested that the past century, particularly the last fifty years, has seen a significant change in the location of final authority in civil lawsuits. One could put the matter briefly by saying that we designed the appellate rules for "trial court" rulings, but the lower courts are no longer "trial" courts.

At the start of the period trials lay at the center of litigation, and appellate courts could control the outcome of trials. Neither proposition holds true today. "Litigation," usually meaning discovery, summary judgment, settlement negotiations, alternatives to judicial process, sanctions for lawyer misbehavior, and similar pretrial matters, lies at the center of judges' and lawyers' attention. Trials are an endangered species. Appellate courts, while now more active than ever, no longer control the outcome of a high proportion of cases. Because appellate control over outcomes has loosened, the center of power has moved down the judicial hierarchy, from appellate to lower courts, and from courts to lawyers operating outside the scrutiny of any court. The system has decentralized; trial judges rather than appellate judges have the last word in a higher proportion of cases than was the case a century ago. . . .

LOS ANGELES COUNTY BAR ASSOCIATION, "JUDGE IN A FLASH"

E-mail message received by members of the Los Angeles County
Bar Association, December 16, 2008

Powered by the LACBA Searchable Superior Court Civil Register, the Judge in a Flash (JIF) is the best way for practitioners to get detailed information about judges very quickly. These details are also organized in a way that will allow quick analysis of a particular judge's case background.

How JIF Works

JIF is a special tool built into a standard USB flash drive. Simply insert your JIF flash drive into a computer with a USB port and an Internet connection. Within seconds, you can access four unique features to analyze a judge:

1. Enter a single judge name and get a statistical chart on selected case activity since 1997;
2. Enter up to three judge names, and get that statistical chart comparing case activity for all three judges;
3. Click on any of the 21 activity categories in a judge's chart, and instantly the most recent five cases for that category display—including the attorneys and parties that recently appeared in front of that judge for that category; and
4. Click on any of those five most recent cases, and immediately jump to the LA Superior Court website display of that particular "Case Summary"—showing all attorneys and parties involved, "documents filed" and "proceedings held" in that case according to Court records.

This data is updated at least weekly, so the information is always current.

JIF Information

Statistical profiles include peremptory challenges filed against a judge, demurrers sustained with or without leave to amend, motions for summary judgment granted and denied, days spent in trial, attorneys' fees awarded, injunctions granted and denied, motions for new trials granted and denied, class actions certified, arbitration awards vacated and continuances granted and denied.

No serious civil litigator should be without this inexpensive "Inside info tool." Get the factual information you want about judges at an unbeatable price of just $59* for members and $89* for non-members, a perfect inexpensive yet valued gift for the colleagues, associates or partner that you want to recognize.

Purchase the 2009 JIF online for yourself or for a colleague today or call LACBA Member Services to purchase a JIF over the phone by dialing (213) 896-6560.

For more information about the LACBA JIF, visit the JIF FAQ.

*Only $5 for shipping.

NOTE ON JUDICIAL POWER

1. Explain why Yeazell might think that his argument about the power of trial judges would lead one to expect brisk sales of the "Judge in a Flash" device.

2. If it's true that, in practice, most of a trial judge's rulings will be insulated from effective judicial review, one might predict growing interest in judicial selection and in judicial disciplinary systems, which deal with judges who either slipped through cracks in the selection process or "went bad" after taking the bench. The next two sections deal with the selection (or election) of judges and with the disciplinary systems that address inappropriate behavior by judges.

B. SELECTING JUDGES

1. FEDERAL JUDGES

U.S. Const., art. II, §2

The President . . . shall nominate, and by and with the advice and consent of the Senate, shall appoint ambassadors, other public ministers and consuls, judges of the Supreme Court, and all other officers of the United States, whose appointments are not herein otherwise provided for, and which shall be established by law. . . .

ALEX KOZINSKI, SO YOU WANT TO BECOME A FEDERAL JUDGE BY 35?

National Law Journal, August 19, 1996, at C6

You're daydreaming in your office "procrastiwriting" a brief, when the phone rings.

"John [or Jane]," a deep voice at the other end says, "this is the president. I've been looking for a distinguished lawyer to fill that judgeship in your circuit, and everyone I ask mentions your name. I have the nomination papers all drawn up. You'll be doing me a big favor if you accept."

"Well, Mr. President, this is certainly unexpected," you lie. "I've never even imagined that I deserve to wear the robe. May I have a few days to talk it over with my domestic partner?"

"Why, of course John [or Jane]," the president replies, "but don't take too long. I'm counting on you — and so is your country."

Hasn't happened yet? Well, it could, but only if you follow the directions below to the letter. Don't improvise.

1. Decide early. This, the most obvious step of all, is too often overlooked. You'll surely flounder if you're not willing to admit — at least to yourself — that you have judicial ambitions. Go ahead, lock yourself in the bathroom, look in the mirror and say: "I'm honored to be in the presence of such a distinguished jurist." If these words send a chill down your spine, go to step two.

2. Get into politics. Judging is not a partisan political process, but being fitted for the robe definitely is. Pick a party or candidate and lend your support when it matters.

And don't be too finicky about the kind of work you're willing to do. If there's a job serving coffee, don't hold out for senior policy adviser. All organizations — and political campaigns in particular — are overrun by incompetents. If you keep the coffee fresh and hot, you'll quickly earn a can-do reputation; in no time, you'll be promoted to speechwriter or special confidant.

3. Never back a loser. Campaigning for the Spotted Owl Party in the middle of lumberjack country may soothe the soul but won't get you a robe. Of course, you shouldn't campaign for a candidate whose views you despise, but within the realm of what you can tolerate, let ambition, not idealism, guide you.

4. Get a job in Washington. If you want to become a federal judge, you might as well peddle your wares in the federal judgeship bazaar. Sure, a lot of judges are appointed from the provinces, but your odds improve if you share an area code with the people who pick judges. While you're there, you'll want to . . .

5. Get to know your senators. You won't get a federal judgeship if a senator from your state objects, particularly if the senator belongs to the same party as the president.

If your senators don't sun themselves at your pool on weekends, at least have lunch with members of their staff. A good word from an aide can turn an ambivalent senator into an ally.

6. Make friends on both sides of the aisle. If you get into political trouble, it's always good to have open channels to those who oppose you. You might be able to blunt, if not repel, their attacks.

7. Ask a lot of people for favors. This is very important, so pay close attention. Most people believe that the way to get ahead in politics is to do a lot of favors for others so they'll owe you favors when you need help. In fact, people hate to pay back favors — it makes them feel cheap; anyway, they always think the favor you're cashing in is worth much less than the one you're asking in return. So, they promise to help you but don't. Or, they pretend to help but damn you with faint praise.

The way to get ahead in politics, in fact, works just the opposite; call it Kozinski's Axiom: Get people to do you small favors and next time they'll owe you big favors. Once people have a stake in your career they start to take pride in your success. Unless you turn out to be an ingrate (See No. 8 below) or a dizzard (See No. 9 below), they'll be pleased to learn you've made the most of the help they gave you. Your success becomes their success and next time they'll be willing to do a little more.

8. Give credit where it's due — and especially where it's not. When you do achieve a measure of success — perhaps your first political appointment — be sure to thank all those who helped. And by all means go overboard; give everyone full credit. Even if you suspect someone didn't help very much, or that the help given didn't do much good — no matter. Your goal is to give as many people as possible a stake in your success because — well, remember No. 7 above.

9. Do your level best at whatever job is entrusted to you. Political assignments are not merely stepping stones; they are important jobs in themselves. People in politics have very long memories. If you disappoint someone who has helped you, don't expect that person's help again.

10. Don't be daunted. People will look at you as if you're nuts the first time you mention your ambition, and it may take friends and family a while to get used to the idea. But the second time you mention it they won't seem quite so

surprised and, by the third time, you may find out they've already taken steps to help you.

There's a fine line between being persistent and being a pest; don't cross it, but do get very close to it.

Will it work? If you follow these simple rules—and have a modicum of intelligence and common sense—you'll have a very good shot. And if you don't make it, don't worry: You're now 35, so you're all set to run for President (See Nos. 1-10 above).

Judge Kozinski was appointed to the Ninth Circuit when he was 35.

NOTE ON SCREENING JUDGES

As Judge Kozinski's piece says, federal judges are nominated by the president of the United States, but long-standing custom—not law—dictates that the senators of the state where the judges will sit have a say in the process. If the same party controls both the White House and the Senate, the senators may play an especially prominent role in nominations. Custom further says that senators will often initiate appointments for district courts, with the executive branch playing an approving and monitoring role. In the case of an appointment to the court of appeals, the roles are reversed: the executive branch typically suggests a nominee, and the senators approve. If the executive branch and the Senate are in the hands of different parties, the dance is more complicated. In such instances the president does the nominating, but long-standing traditions of senatorial "courtesy" dictate that the nomination will not proceed to a vote unless both senators from the state in question "pass" the nominee. In practice, this means that sometimes the White House staff will negotiate such nominations in advance with the senators. In deciding whether to recommend that a federal district judge be nominated or to approve a nomination by the president, a senator wants to know who this person is. In a few states with very small population, it's possible that a senator would know most of the plausible candidates personally. But that won't usually be the case, certainly not in populous states. In such circumstances the senator will want to know quite a bit about the nominee in order to reach a decision. Many senators have developed screening mechanisms to allow their staffs to sort candidates. One step in such a screening mechanism—a substantial questionnaire used by California's senior senator—appears below. Senator Dianne Feinstein's questionnaire resembles those used by many of her colleagues. Read the application over and think about what a senator is interested in knowing. Why?

SENATOR DIANNE FEINSTEIN PERSONAL DATA QUESTIONNAIRE
JUDICIAL APPOINTMENTS

1. Name: _____
2. Specific Judicial Position(s) Sought: _____

   If you have previously applied for consideration for the Federal District Court, please specify year and district. _____

3. Office Address: _____
   Phone: _____ Fax: _____
   Home Address: _____
   Phone: _____ Fax: _____
   Driver's License Number: _____

4. Date of Birth: _____ Age: _____

5. Date of Admission to California Bar: _____
   State Bar Number: _____

6. Dates of Admission to Federal Court (*Please List Courts*):
   _____
   _____

7. Educational History:
   _____
   _____
   _____

   Colleges and Law Schools Attended From _____ To _____
   Degree Received _____

8. Professional Work History: _____
   Employer   Position   City   From   To   Present

9. If you are currently sitting as a judge or magistrate, were you:
   Appointed: _____ Date: _____
   Elected: _____ Date: _____

10. Are you a registered voter? Yes _____ No _____
    County _____
    If yes, what is your party affiliation? _____

    Please answer the remaining questions sequentially on plain, letter size paper. Re-type each question before the corresponding response. Answers should be typed and single spaced.

    Senator Dianne Feinstein

    Name _____

PERSONAL DATA QUESTIONNAIRE
JUDICIAL APPOINTMENTS

11. List your residences for the past ten years, or the three most recent, whichever is fewer.

12. Give the place of your birth.

13. If you are a naturalized citizen, please give the date and place of your naturalization.

14. Indicate your marital status; if married, your maiden name or the maiden name of your wife; and the names of your children.

15. Indicate the periods of your military service, if applicable, including the dates, and the branch in which you served, your rank or rate, and your serial number.

16. List all courts in which you are presently admitted to practice, including the dates of admission in each case. Give the same information for administrative bodies having special admission requirements.

17. What is the general nature of your practice? Indicate the nature of your typical clients and mention any legal specialties you possess. If the nature of your practice has been substantially different at any time in the past, give the details, including the nature of such and the periods involved.

18. (a) Do you regularly appear in court?
    (b) What percentage of your appearances in the last five years was in:
       (1) federal courts?
       (2) state courts of record?
       (3) other courts of administrative tribunals or agencies?
    (c) What percentage of your litigation in the last five years was:
       (1) civil? (2) criminal?
    (d) What percentage of your trials in the last five years was:
       (1) jury? (2) non-jury?
    (e) Describe ten of the more significant litigated matters which you have handled and give the citations if the cases were reported. Please list the judges and your opposing counsel in each case.

19. Summarize your experience in court prior to the last five years. If during any prior period you appeared in court with greater frequency than during the last five years, indicate the periods during which this was so and give for such prior periods the same data which was represented in question 18.

20. Have you ever been engaged in any occupation, business, or profession other than the practice of law? If so, please give the details, including dates.

21. If you are now an officer or director of any business organization or otherwise engaged in the management of any business enterprise, please give details, including the name of the enterprise, the nature of the business, the title of your position, the nature of your duties, and the term of your service. If you do not intend to resign such positions and give up any other participation in the management of any of the foregoing enterprises, please so state, giving reasons.

22. Have you ever held judicial office, or have you ever been a candidate for such an office? If so, give the details, including the courts involved, whether elected or appointed, and the periods of service.

23. Have you ever held public office other than a judicial office, or have you ever been a candidate for such an office? If so, give the details, including the offices involved, whether elected or appointed, and the length of your service.

24. Have you ever been convicted of a violation of any federal law, state law, county, or municipal law, regulation, or ordinance? If so, please give details. Do not include traffic violations for which a fine of $50.00 or less was imposed.

25. Have you ever used any controlled substance? If so, when, where and how much of the controlled substance did you take? Please be specific.

26. Have you always paid the necessary taxes for any employee, including household and domestic workers? If not, please be specific.

27. Have you ever been sued by a client? If so, please give particulars.

28. Have you ever been a party of or otherwise involved in any other legal proceedings? If so, give the particulars. Do not list proceedings in which you were merely a guardian ad litem or stakeholder. Include all legal proceedings in which you were a party in interest, a material witness, were named as a co-conspirator or co-respondent, and any grand jury investigation in which you figured as a subject, or in which you appeared as a witness.

29. Have you ever been disciplined or cited for a breach of ethics or unprofessional conduct by, or been the subject of a complaint to, any court, administrative agency, bar association, disciplinary committee, or other professional group? If so, please give the particulars. (Please list any complaint even if it was dismissed or did not result in disciplinary action.)

30. (a) What is the present state of your health?

    (b) Have you in the last ten years (i) been hospitalized due to injury or illness or (ii) been prevented form working due to injury or illness or otherwise incapacitated for a period in excess of ten days? If so, give the particulars, including the causes, the dates, the places of confinement, and the present status of the conditions which caused the confinement or incapacitation. Also furnish a medical report about any connection between the previous incapacitating condition and your present capacity for judicial work.

    (c) Do you suffer from any impairment of eyesight or hearing or any other physical handicap? If so, give details.

    (d) When did you have your most recent general physical examination, and who was the supervising physician? Attach a current medical report focusing on any health restrictions affecting the performance of judicial duties.

    (e) Are you currently under treatment for an illness or physical condition? If so give details.

(f) Have you ever been treated for or had any problem with alcoholism or any related condition associated with consumption of alcoholic beverages or any other form of drug-addiction or dependency? If so, give details.

(g) The name, address and telephone number of your personal physician. Do you object if your physician is consulted about your health?

31. Please list and provide copies of all publications, speeches and new articles of any kind in which you have been featured. This should also include newspaper and magazine articles, legal articles, books, etc. If you cannot locate a copy of the document, please list the specific dates when publications appeared and describe the content of your comments.

32. Have you published any legal books or articles? If so, please list them, giving the citations and dates. Please submit all writings with your application.

33. List any honors, prizes, awards, or other forms of recognition which you have received.

34. List all bar associations and professional societies of which you are a member and give the titles and dates of any offices which you have held in such groups. List also chairmanships of any committees in bar associations and professional societies, and memberships on any committees in bar associations and professional societies, and memberships on any committees which you have believe to be of particular significance (e.g. judicial selection committee, committee of censors, grievance committee).

35. Have you, to your knowledge, ever been under federal, state or local investigation for possible violation of a criminal statute? If so, give particulars.

36. Has a tax lien or other collection procedure ever been instituted against you by federal, state, or local authorities? If so, give particulars.

37. Describe the nature and extent of any free legal services you have provided to nonprofit organizations, indigent individuals, and others, including the names and addresses of such organizations and/or individuals where appropriate.

38. Describe the nature and extent of your service, if any, as an arbitrator, either privately or through the judicial arbitration program. Describe the more significant cases and identify the counsel involved.

39. Describe the nature and extent of the non-professional efforts you have made in this regard.

40. What role can an attorney or a judge play in making our society a better place? Relate any personal or professional efforts you may have made in this regard.

41. If allegations have ever been printed or broadcast or otherwise been made public concerning you or your activities or statements

(irrespective of the factual accuracy of such allegations) which reflect adversely on your character or job performance, please so state and explain fully.

42. Describe any aspects of your personal, business or professional conduct which may reflect positively or adversely on you or which you believe should be disclosed prior to further consideration of you for appointment to judicial office.

43. Why do you want to be a judge? Why do you believe you are qualified? What would you seek to accomplish if appointed?

44. Are you a member of a club, organization or association that by policy or practice prohibits or limits its membership on the basis of race, color, religion, sexual orientation, gender, disability or national origin?

45. Have you ever, knowingly or not, employed an illegal alien?

46. Memberships or participation in organizations:

    (a) Please list all organizations you have been a member of since 1970. Please note the years you were a member of the organization and if you held any leadership posts.

    (b) Please list any other groups, organizations and committees that you have been affiliated with in any way since 1970. This should include all groups that have participated in or attended meeting for during this timeframe. There is no need to list groups already identified in the first part of this question.

PAMELA MacLEAN, NEW REPORT TRACKS BUSH JUDICIAL NOMINEES' CAMPAIGN CONTRIBUTIONS

National Law Journal, November 17, 2006

An investigative report of campaign contributions by President George W. Bush's judicial nominees showed that 45 appointees to appellate and district courts have made political donations while under official consideration for judgeships.

Although currently no ethical rules prohibit campaign contributions by candidates to the federal bench, proposed changes to the American Bar Association's Model Code of Judicial Conduct would ban the practice. Currently, federal judges are prohibited from making political contributions only after they are confirmed to the bench.

The final code revisions, which recommend a wide range of judicial ethics reforms aimed at state judicial elections but also affecting federal judges, were scheduled to be set for release on Nov. 15 and will be voted on by ABA delegates during the Miami convention in February 2007.

Under the proposed ethics canon, once an attorney is clearly a candidate for a federal judgeship, he or she "definitely cannot contribute to politicians," said William Hodes, a professor emeritus at Indiana University School of Law. He is co-reporter on the ABA Joint Commission to Evaluate Model Code of Judicial Conduct. When a private citizen starts talking to senators about the desire to be a federal judge, he or she would fall under engaging in solicitation of support in Canon 4, Hodes said. That person "would be a candidate and would have to stop giving contributions," he said.

A report released on Oct. 31 by the Center for Investigative Journalism examined political contributions by nominees to federal judgeships under Bush. It found that 11 of 47 appellate judges and 34 of 202 district judges gave campaign contributions to the senators that recommended them or to Bush or the Republican Party while under consideration.

Among the judges cited in the report was Judge Deborah Cook of the 6th U.S. Circuit Court of Appeals, who, along with her husband, Robert Linton, gave $11,000 in donations to Ohio Republican Sens. Michael DeWine and George Voinovich and Ohio Gov. Bob Taft after her May 9, 2001, nomination to the bench.

Following her confirmation on May 5, 2003, an $800 contribution identified as from Deborah Linton, U.S. District Judge, in December 2005, was made to DeWine. He refunded the check three weeks later, the report states.

The report also found that U.S. District Judge Dean Pregerson of Los Angeles, appointed by President Bill Clinton in July 1996, had contributions recorded in his name to a Republican candidate for Mississippi secretary of state, a Montana Democrat running for Senate in 2000, and to Sen. Joseph Biden, D-Del.

Neither Cook nor Pregerson returned calls seeking comment. The center report indicates Pregerson told them any contributions made were through his wife and their joint checking account.

NOTE ON MONEY, POLITICS, AND JUDICIAL APPOINTMENTS

Although the short article above applies only to one president and only to federal judges, the picture it paints is consistent with what we broadly know about state judgeships as well. Appointing authorities — state and federal — are above all interested in judges who won't embarrass them. So they want probity and competence. And they want at least broad resonance between their views of the world and those of their nominees and appointees. If they can find a party stalwart who has all these qualities, so much the better. But except in very unusual situations, a judgeship isn't the way to reward large political donors, if only because only a very few lawyers will be able or willing to contribute the kind of very large money that drives contemporary political contests.

That's not to say that money never matters. But when it does, it is likely to run in the opposite direction — not from the prospective judicial nominee to a political campaign of a president or governor, but instead from those who hold a political or economic or social view *toward* the judicial nominee. And that happens primarily in situations in which the state chooses its judges by elections. The next section explores state judicial selection and election processes, including the role that money plays in those processes. Put more simply, the data suggest that few judges "buy" their judicial offices, but some claim that other people's money can buy an election for a judge. Keep reading.

2. STATE JUDGES

a. Surveying Judicial Selection Methods

DANIEL DEJA, HOW JUDGES ARE SELECTED: A SURVEY OF THE JUDICIAL
SELECTION PROCESS IN THE UNITED STATES[1]

75 Michigan Business Journal 904 (1996)

Several judges from various jurisdictions across the country are sitting around a table at the National Judicial College in Reno. The judges all experience similar problems with case volumes and types. They are all trying to perfect their skill in the science of judging. Pervasive violent crime and drugs dominate the conversations, but occasionally, the conversation turns to other issues, such as how judges are selected.

The judge from South Carolina was elected by the state Legislature. Not surprisingly, he is a former legislator himself, as are many of the South Carolina judges. A second judge was appointed by the governor of New Jersey. That judge indicates that half of the judicial appointments must be from the Republican Party and half from the Democratic Party.[2] After an initial seven-year term, a formal evaluation is prepared and submitted to the Legislature; if acceptable, the judge is appointed for life to age 70.[3] A less formal evaluation is conducted by the Supreme Court after the first three years of the judge's term.[4]

The Arkansas judge is concerned about the effects of changing from a partisan to a nonpartisan selection process. She is predicting much doom and gloom. Under the current partisan elections an early primary system settles nearly all judicial races by early summer in the largely Democratic state. A nonpartisan election for judges would require that candidates campaign until the general election in November. The two judges from Indiana are both elected, but because one is in a county that was the subject of special legislation, he is elected on a nonpartisan ballot, the other is elected on a partisan ballot as are the majority of Indiana judges.[5] The Michigan judge was appointed by the governor to fill an unexpired term, and since then was elected on the familiar nonpartisan ballot.

Somehow, in each state, the system works. Judges are seated and justice dispensed, all with a surprising amount of uniformity and sincerity. Any re-examination of how we select our judges should be with the knowledge

---

1. The bulk of the information for this article came from David B. Rottman, Carol R. Flango & R. Shedine Lockley, *State Court Organization, 1993,* U.S. Department of Justice, Bureau of Justice Statistics (Washington, D.C. USGPO 1995). The information in that publication was updated by the author for inclusion herein. A portion of the information was obtained by the author from discussions with judges and court administrators across the country. Unless otherwise noted, the statistical information contained in this article was obtained from the Rottman, Flango, and Lockley work.

2. N.J. Const., art. 6, §6(1) provides for the appointment of judges, but makes no mention of a requirement that an equal number of judges be selected from each of the two major political parties.

3. *Id.*

4. This information was obtained by the author from conversations with a judge from New Jersey.

5. This information was obtained by the author from two Indiana judges from different counties in a conversation as described.

of how judges are selected elsewhere. This article is intended to supply that type of background information for the current discussions on the best method of judicial selection for Michigan.

Methods of Selection

This discussion focuses primarily on general jurisdiction trial courts, but a look at some of the methods used for certain limited jurisdiction courts is interesting and adds perspective. Predictably, 50 different selection methods are not in use. Disregarding the local modifications, only a handful of judicial selection processes are in use in the various states. Somewhat surprising, however, is the fact that more than one process may be used for the same court in the same state, depending on the location within the state.

Four primary methods are used to select judges in the United States: gubernatorial appointment, gubernatorial appointment with retention election, partisan election and nonpartisan election. Three states select judges by legislative appointment or election. Three states fill unexpired terms by Supreme Court appointment.[6]

The gubernatorial appointment without a retention election most closely emulates the federal system of judicial selection. U.S. District Court judges are appointed by the executive (the president), with consent of the Senate, for life.[7] Nine states plus Puerto Rico select judges by gubernatorial appointment but do not have subsequent retention elections. Only three of those, Massachusetts, New Hampshire and Rhode Island, appoint for life (to 70 years of age in Massachusetts and New Hampshire). The remaining employ some type of reappointment process. Vermont judges submit to an election by the Legislature every six years after the initial gubernatorial appointment.

Delaware, Maine, Maryland, New Jersey and Puerto Rico use the same process to reappoint as for the initial appointment: gubernatorial appointment with the consent of the Senate. As noted earlier, New Jersey's reappointment after the initial seven-year term becomes appointment until age 70. Delaware has 12-year terms, Maine seven, and Maryland 15. Hawaii has 10-year terms and reappointment is done by that state's judicial nominating commission.[8] Gubernatorial appointments without a retention election are characterized by significantly longer terms, if any, than all other methods.

The very nature of periodic elections is to give the electorate an opportunity to directly either select or reject judges. Gubernatorial appointment without a retention election removes the electorate from directly influencing the judicial selection process. Judicial selection becomes a function of elected representatives of the people.

The legislative election of judges peculiar to Connecticut, Virginia and South Carolina has the same effect of removing the judicial selection process one step away from the electorate. In these states, the Legislature reappoints after regular terms; eight years in Connecticut and Virginia, six years in South Carolina.

---

6. Rottman, Flango, & Lockley *supra*, n. 1.
7. U.S. Const., arts. II and III.
8. Called the Judicial Selection Commission, it is established by the Constitution in Hawaii. Rottman, Flango & Lockley, *supra*, n. 1.

Thirty-nine of the states allow some direct input by the electorate in the judicial selection process. These states either allow the electorate to reject previously appointed judges or allow the electorate to select judges in a partisan or nonpartisan election.

Ten states select judges by gubernatorial appointment followed (after a term of years) by a retention election in which the judicial candidate runs on her or his own performance record. The electorate votes to retain or not to retain the judge for an additional term. There are no opposition candidates, partisan or nonpartisan. This is often referred to as the "Missouri Plan."[9]

Curiously, Missouri uses this method of judicial selection in only five metropolitan circuits. The remaining 40 circuits select judges in partisan elections. Neighboring Kansas has a similar breakdown: gubernatorial appointment with retention election in 17 districts, partisan election in 14 districts. In Arizona, Maricopa County (Phoenix) and Pima County (Tucson) select judges by gubernatorial appointment with subsequent retention election. The remainder of the state (13 counties) elects judges in nonpartisan elections.

The remaining seven states, Alaska, Colorado, Iowa, Nebraska, Tennessee,[10] Utah, and Wyoming, use the Missouri Plan in all judicial election districts. Tennessee has changed, since 1993, from a system of partisan elections to the Missouri Plan. This was the only significant change in the judicial selection process noted in any state since 1993.[11]

Partisan election of judges is a fairly common method of judicial selection, particularly in the southern states. Fourteen states select judges in this manner. Terms range from four to eight years, four or six being most common. New York has 14-year terms for the Supreme Court (its general jurisdiction trial court) and Pennsylvania has 10-year terms.[12] Pennsylvania has a partisan election for the first full term only. Subsequent elections for additional terms are retention elections, similar to those held in the Missouri Plan jurisdictions. This system of a retention election following a partisan election for the first full term is also used in Illinois, Indiana and New Mexico.

The balance of the states, 17, select judges in nonpartisan elections for both the initial full term and for subsequent terms.[13] Michigan, of course, is included in this group. Except for South Dakota and Kentucky, which have

---

9. Common parlance among most judges, the "Missouri Plan" is described briefly by Rottman, Flango and Lockley at page 29 of their work. The system dates to a 1940 constitutional amendment in Missouri. Rottman, Flango & Lockley, *supra*, n. 1, at 29.

10. Telephone contact with the Tennessee office of the Administrative Director of the Courts indicates that this procedure is now used in Tennessee rather than the partisan election process formerly used there.

11. As noted above, the Rottman, Flango and Lockley work, *supra*, n. 1, was updated by the author in preparing this article. The court administrative agency of each state was contacted to either verify the Rottman, Flango and Lockley data or supply any changes in that information from the 1993 date. The changes in the Tennessee system were received in this manner.

12. County court judges in New York, also general jurisdiction trial court judges, have 10-year terms instead of 14-year terms. Rottman, Flango & Lockley, *supra*, n. 1.

13. These are: California, Florida, Georgia, Idaho, Kentucky, Louisiana, Michigan, Minnesota, Montana, Nevada, North Dakota, Ohio, Oklahoma, Oregon, South Dakota, Washington, and Wisconsin. Rottman, Flango & Lockley, *supra*, n. 1.

eight-year terms, these states have judicial terms of four years (four states) or six years (11 states).[14]

The above discussion describes the selection of judges to fill full terms and the method of retaining judges once selected. The manner in which unexpired terms are filled is important to the discussion of the judicial selection process, since a very large number of judges are first selected in this manner. That number in Michigan is so large that, coupled with other factors, such as the judicial designation on the ballot, serious consideration needs to be given to whether the method for filling a full term can fairly be different from the method of filling an unexpired term.[15]

Forty-four states fill unexpired terms by gubernatorial appointment. Three states, Connecticut, Virginia, and South Carolina, fill vacancies by legislative appointment. That is the same manner in which these states select judges for full terms. Illinois, Indiana, and Louisiana fill unexpired terms by appointment of the Supreme Court. Full terms in those states are filled by partisan or nonpartisan elections.

There are some very logical and practical reasons for using the gubernatorial appointment method to fill unexpired terms. Where that is the method of judicial selection for full terms, it is a logical and natural extension of the process. In states where judges are elected, there are other practical considerations. Judicial vacancies do not occur at regular intervals coinciding with other judicial elections. Judges die or resign from office on schedules that are determined by factors other than the dates of general elections. The cost and time needed to schedule special elections is generally prohibitive. The presumption is that gubernatorial appointment is a more expedient and cost-efficient means of filling judicial vacancies.

In states where judges are elected for full terms, the number of judges who are initially appointed as compared to the number of judges who are initially elected becomes important for analysis. It may be that election is not as significant a judicial selection process as it was designed to be, particularly in Michigan, where incumbent judges are so designated on the nonpartisan ballot, whether they were first appointed or first elected. In effect, there are two approximately equal methods of judicial selection in Michigan. Of the 617 judges currently sitting in all Michigan courts, 280 (45 percent) were initially appointed.[16] It could be argued that the incumbency designation on the ballot has the practical effect of making the periodic election process a retention election. Only when vacancies occur at the expiration of a term, does the electorate truly choose between two candidates. . . .

The Legislature and the Judicial Selection Process

The Legislature actually appoints judges in three states: Connecticut, South Carolina and Virginia. In addition, 10 states plus Puerto Rico require Senate

---

14. Washington, Oklahoma, Idaho, and Georgia have four-year terms. Rottman, Flango & Lockley, *supra*, n. 1.

15. The Michigan State Court Administrative Office's *Court List of Judges Showing Appointed/ Elected Dates*, prepared 1/22/96, shows that 280 of the 617 judges in all courts of Michigan were initially appointed to their seat.

16. *Id.*

approval of all appointments for full terms and to fill unexpired terms. This is just over half of the 19 states (plus Puerto Rico) that use a gubernatorial appointment selection process with or without a retention election. In addition, three states that elect judges for full terms, but use gubernatorial appointment to fill unexpired terms, require Senate approval of those appointments: New York, Pennsylvania, and Texas. Sixteen states (plus Puerto Rico) either have the Legislature directly appoint judges or require Senate approval of gubernatorial appointments. Vermont retains judges by legislative election every six years.

As discussed at the outset, federal judges are appointed by the president and confirmed by the Senate. It is interesting that fewer than one-third of the states follow this pattern in any respect. Six appoint with the consent of the Senate and only one, Rhode Island, can be said to follow the federal model of appointment by the executive for life with the consent of the Senate. The states generally have favored popular election of judges over the federal model, and if an appointment process is used, it is followed by a retention election. Thirty-nine states incorporate the electorate in the judicial selection process in some fashion. The executive branch is involved in appointing judges to full terms or to fill unexpired terms in 44 states, yet only 17 states involve the Legislature to any extent in the judicial selection process.

The Judicial Nominating Commission

In addition to the process of gubernatorial appointment and retention election, a significant part of the Missouri Plan is the judicial nominating commission. In Missouri, this originally consisted of a judge, lawyers representing the state bar association, and several nonlawyers appointed by the governor.[19] The purpose of the nominating commission in Missouri is to screen all applicants for judicial appointment and select three from which the governor must make her or his selection. Many states have adopted this model in some form. The purpose of nominating commissions is to minimize the political patronage in judicial appointments and maximize the quality of those appointments.

Thirty-three states have a form of judicial nominating commission for various levels of judicial appointments. This discussion, like the prior discussion, focuses on the judicial selection process for general jurisdiction trial courts, concentrating on the involvement of judicial nominating commissions in the selection process and not on the make-up, origin, or authority of each commission. Generally, the make-up of these commissions is broad, similar to the original Missouri commission described above. Their function is also similar: to select from the applicants for judicial appointment a qualified group from which the appointing authority must choose.

With the exception of Maine, New Hampshire, New Jersey, Rhode Island, and Puerto Rico, all states that use gubernatorial appointment as the means of selecting judges (whether retention is by retention election or otherwise) appoint from judicial nominating commissions.[20] Among these 16 states are

---

19. Rottman, Flango & Lockley, *supra*, n. 1, at p. 29.
20. Alaska, Colorado, Delaware, Hawaii, Iowa, Maryland, Massachusetts, Nebraska, Tennessee, Utah, Vermont, Wyoming, Arizona, Kansas, and Missouri all use judicial nominating commissions in the judicial selection process. Rottman, Flango & Lockley, *supra*, n. 1.

Missouri, Kansas and Arizona, where judicial selection by gubernatorial appointment occurs in less than all election districts of those states, but even in those districts, unexpired terms are filled by gubernatorial appointment from nominating commissions. It is interesting to note that the states that select judges by gubernatorial appointment but not from nominating commissions are all in the East. As with the frequency of partisan elections in the South, this is another example of regional similarities in the judicial selection processes.

In states selecting judges by partisan election, only Mississippi and Pennsylvania use judicial nominating commissions for gubernatorial appointments to fill unexpired terms. In states selecting judges by nonpartisan election, Florida, Georgia, Idaho, Kentucky, Minnesota, Montana, Nevada, North Dakota, Oklahoma and South Dakota use judicial nominating commissions for gubernatorial appointments to fill unexpired terms. Wisconsin, Washington, Oregon, Ohio, Louisiana, California and Michigan do not have judicial nominating commissions as part of their appointment process for unexpired terms. Wisconsin has a Governor's Advisory Committee on Judicial Selection and Michigan uses the State Bar of Michigan's Judicial Qualifications Committee to assist in appointments for unexpired terms. In Michigan, the State Bar's committee on judicial qualifications makes advisory ratings of all candidates for judicial appointment, but the governor may appoint any applicant, regardless of the rating that may have been given.

None of the three states selecting judges by legislative appointment use judicial nominating commissions in the process.

Conclusion

The process of selecting judges in the United States is diverse, with local variations further complicating the area and making analysis very difficult. At first blush, judicial selection seems to be somewhat of a free-for-all where the prevailing politics of the state and, in many instances, a locality within the state, dictate the method of selecting judges. Several philosophical threads run through this field, however, that this article has attempted to highlight. Four basic methods of judicial selection have been identified. Intermixed within those methods are issues concerning the degree of involvement of the electorate in the process, the extent to which the Legislature participates, if at all, and whether the field of judicial aspirants should first be qualified by an independent body representing a cross section of the judiciary's constituents.

It is difficult to identify any sort of "trend" in the field of judicial selection. Only one state has changed its process between 1993 and the present. Tennessee changed from partisan elections to a Missouri Plan system, specifically, gubernatorial appointments from a judicial nominating commission, for a specific term of years, followed by a retention election. Similar discussions have been occurring in other states. Alabama has had recent discussions in which certain factions support changing that system from partisan elections to the Missouri Plan.[21] The Missouri Plan has been promoted in South Carolina to

---

21. Some of this history was obtained through conversations with the office of the Administrative Director of the Courts, in Montgomery, Alabama.

replace their system of legislative appointment.[22] Arkansas has discussed changing from partisan to nonpartisan elections.[23]

As Michigan launches into this debate, it is best to do so with an understanding of the methods currently in use and their philosophical underpinnings. The objective should always be to select a system that will provide the citizens of Michigan with the best judges, selected in a manner that will instill confidence in the judiciary and allow the citizens an appropriate voice in the selection process; all without impinging on the independence necessary for judges to make impartial, well-reasoned decisions. In discussing these issues, factors such as how many judges are initially appointed as opposed to initially elected and the percentage of ballots cast in any election that indicate preferences on the nonpartisan portion of the ballot must be analyzed. Such analyses will help to determine how judges are actually selected in Michigan and by whom. If change is to occur in the judicial selection process, it must be change that reflects a philosophy for judicial selection held by the public both in the form of the design as well as its effect in practice.

Note. Hon. Daniel R. Deja is a 5th District Court judge, Berrien County. He received his B.S. from Michigan State University, his J.D. from the New England School of Law magna cum laude and has completed course work on his master's degree from the University of Nevada/National Judicial College. He was appointed by the Michigan Supreme Court to serve on the Michigan Justice Project Planning Committee on Court Reorganization, has assisted in the planning and presenting of several seminars with the Michigan Judicial Institute and is currently one of 11 judges in the Berrien County Trial Court Demonstration Project.

NOTE ON STATE JUDICIAL SELECTION

Stand back from the apparently bewildering variety of state judicial selection processes to focus on just one sentence in Judge Deja's survey: "Forty-four states fill unexpired terms by gubernatorial appointment." Consider what that means: only those judgeships in which the vacancy exactly coincides with the end of the judge's term will be filled by the variety of methods described in the article. For other vacancies, the governor will fill the vacancy "temporarily" until the term of judicial office expires. Such "temporary" appointments, however, usually become permanent; in most of the states where the governor fills the unexpired term, the now-incumbent will have an enormous leg up in being reappointed or re-elected. This individual now carries the "judge" title on her resume or on the ballot. And unless she has managed to draw large amounts of negative attention or has the very bad luck to attract a well-financed opponent, she will be elected to a term of her own. That common scenario puts enormous weight on the governor's office. The next section describes some relatively typical state-level appointing processes — the first

---

22. From discussions of the judicial selection process with a South Carolina judge.

23. From discussions of the judicial selection process with an Arkansas judge. This particular judge was inquiring how the nonpartisan system worked in Michigan.

simply by describing California's process, the second by allowing a governor of Michigan to say how the process looked from his chair.

b. Appointing Judges

So You Want to be a [California] Judge? Here's How

California Bar Journal, April 2007

If you want to become a judge, here's how it works. Any lawyer in good standing with 10 years of practice may submit an application to the governor's office.

The 10-page application forms for the superior and appellate courts are available at his Web site, and contain 61 questions, ranging from the number of years of civil litigation or criminal practice experience, to community service, to number of languages spoken. [Editor's note: the California questionnaire is very similar to Senator Feinstein's that appeared in the previous section.] Sitting judges wishing to be elevated to the appellate bench answer different questions and submit a different form.

The governor has local vetting committees in many counties that do their own screening. Their proceedings are secret.

The governor then sends the application to the Commission on Judicial Nominees Evaluation (JNE), a group of up to 38 people, who evaluate each applicant. The commission is an agency of the State Bar, created by statute. The evaluation process, described by one commissioner as daunting, is different for the trial and appellate courts, but applicants are asked to submit names of 75 people who know them well, as well as everyone they've litigated with or before or against.

The commission independently seeks input from district attorneys, public defenders, judges and attorneys in the same practice area. If the county is small, every lawyer who practices in the county is asked for input. The goal is to receive a minimum of 50 random responses.

Local bar associations also evaluate judicial candidates.

The comment form asks about the candidate's professional ability, experience and reputation, judicial temperament, work ethic and bias.

A team of two evaluates candidates for the superior court; teams of four do the vetting for the appellate bench. Each candidate is interviewed by one team.

Anyone who submits a negative comment receives a phone call for corroboration and the candidate has an opportunity to respond.

After 90 days, the entire commission submits a summary report to the governor, with one of four ratings: exceptionally well qualified, well qualified, qualified or not qualified. Any candidate found not qualified has the right to appeal.

All JNE proceedings are confidential and commissioners do not make public the ratings or the basis for the ratings for the trial courts.

Helen Zukin, a former chair, said JNE balances two interests — those of the candidate and those of the people of the state who are entitled to a qualified judiciary. "We want to be very, very careful so there isn't an error and someone is foreclosed" from a judgeship, she said.

The ultimate appointment power rests with the governor.

John Engler & Lucille Taylor, Judicial Selection: A View from the Governor's Perspective

75 Michigan Bar Journal 910 (1996)

There is a lot of truth in the axiom "where you stand depends on where you sit," and where I sit predisposes me to espouse the virtues of an appointed judiciary. Since becoming governor in January 1991, I have made approximately 85 appointments to fill vacancies in the state judiciary. While this is a small number in comparison to the total number of judgeships in the state — 579 — statistics indicate that one-half of all judges initially reach the bench through appointment. Gubernatorial appointments remain in effect until January 1 following the next general election, at which time the appointed judge is required to run to secure either the balance of the term or a subsequent full term.

I have made multiple appointments to all courts in Michigan, with the notable exception of the Supreme Court. I consider this constitutional appointment authority one of the most important obligations of my office. I hope that the citizens of Michigan will recognize the manner in which I have discharged this responsibility as one of the significant legacies of my administration. I recognize this responsibility as an opportunity to demonstrate the efficacy of gubernatorial appointment as a desirable alternative to an elected judiciary. Finally, I like making judicial appointments, not only because this process allows me to acknowledge the accomplishments of the successful candidate, but also because it permits me to identify other capable attorneys and recruit them to serve on one of the numerous — state boards or commissions which a governor also appoints.

Given the importance of these appointments to the citizens of the state, it is significant that, historically, Michigan constitutions have granted a governor sole authority to appoint as a judge any person who meets the constitutional qualifications. These require a person to be licensed to practice law in this state and to be under the age of 70 years. This authority is unique in that it does not require advice and consent oversight. In virtually all other cases, whether appointing a department director, agency head, paid or volunteer boards and commissions,[1] the governor's appointment is subject to senate advice and consent. While this could lead a governor to believe that he has unlimited license, to me it means unlimited responsibility.

The state's original 1835 Constitution provided for gubernatorial appointment of the Supreme Court, subject to senate advice and consent. Circuit and probate judgeships were secured by election. By the 1850 Constitution, all judicial offices were secured by election. Gubernatorial appointment to fill judicial vacancies existed in the 1850 and 1908 Constitutions, but was intentionally omitted from the 1963 Constitution "in order to maintain the idea that this state should have an 'elected judiciary.'" This determination, having proved itself unworkable or undesirable, was altered by the 1967 amendments to the judicial article restoring the status quo ante of gubernatorial appointment to fill interim vacancies.

---

1. The other exception is Const. 1963, art. 6, §5, civil service commission, on which political balance is required.

I have developed a process for filling all judicial vacancies, which evolved during my first six months in office. This process has produced judges of exceptional quality and ability, with whom I am very well satisfied. It is carried out by my legal division and operates in the following manner. Upon receiving notification of a vacancy, a timetable of several weeks is set for receiving applications. A self-nomination system applies for all trial court positions; however, I have instituted a recruitment process for appellate court vacancies. Notice of the time for submitting applications is transmitted through the county bar president and, in larger counties, through special membership bar organizations as well.

I have also adopted a special condition of appointment. To receive consideration, a candidate must have been admitted to practice law at least five years. I was pleased by the Legislature's action adopting SJR D by a two-thirds vote. This resolution will place an additional constitutional qualification for election or appointment to judicial office — that the candidate shall have been admitted to the practice of law for at least five years — on the November 1996 general election ballot for voter approval. I enthusiastically endorse this ballot proposal.

At the conclusion of the application period, the list of all applicants meeting the age, licensure, practice and residence requirements is forwarded to the Judicial Qualifications Committee of the State Bar of Michigan for background investigation, interview and rating.[6] The understanding I have with the committee is that a candidate must receive a "qualified" or higher rating in order to receive an appointment. The committee's activities are very important to this process and offset additional administrative tasks and costs my office would incur absent their participation.

The bar process requires candidates to provide comprehensive education, experience, character and reference information. Each candidate is assigned to a committee member for reviewing and reporting on required writing submissions and the results of a series of local interviews with the applicant's peers. In addition, an attorney grievance committee representative provides a grievance/tenure report and interviews local judges about the candidates' qualifications. All information given to and reported by committee members, as well as the rating of each candidate, is absolutely confidential. A personal interview before the entire committee, at which legal counsel from my office is always present, completes the rating process.

Possible ratings are: EWQ (exceptionally well qualified); WQ (well qualified); Q (qualified); NQLE (not qualified, lacks experience), and NQ (not qualified). After personally reviewing the ratings and additional candidate information that comes into my office by way of letters or calls, credit and police background checks, the number of candidates for final consideration is reduced to two or three. A second interview, conducted by my counsel and deputy counsel, discusses personal, family, civic, philosophical, and electibility issues.

---

6. An exception to this practice occurs when the number of applicants exceeds 15, which only occurs with 3rd Circuit (Wayne County), 36th District (City of Detroit) or Recorder's Court (City of Detroit) vacancies. The bar's evaluation process works most effectively when rating this number of candidates or less. Where this number is exceeded, my counsel make preliminary inquiries about all applicants with the local bench and bar to reduce the list submitted to a manageable size.

The entire process takes from six to eight weeks. We are most successful in assisting a local court to make an orderly transition if the outgoing judge notifies me of an intent to resign or retire three months in advance of the actual effective date.

This process is both broad and deep in its inquiry. My goal in this process is not to read anything in the press about an appointee that we have not known or explored in either the personal or professional interview processes. While there is a political component in any gubernatorial appointment process, I can state emphatically that I have never considered judicial appointments as political patronage. On several occasions, this has aroused outright anger and often dismay from local political activists. My judicial appointments are merit selections in which political participation is the icing on the cake. As I travel the state I am proud of the compliments I continually receive for the quality and caliber of these appointments.

A final but important point that cannot be overlooked when comparing the appointment and election routes to the state judiciary — each has special advantages for particular kinds of candidates. In the current electoral arena, gender, ethnic surname, prior electoral status or general notoriety provide advantages wholly independent of criteria that prevail in the appointment arena where professional reputation, philosophy, diligence, temperament, and integrity concerns predominate. The appointment process also affords the opportunity to promote to the judicial ranks those traditionally excluded either from the profession or the judiciary. I am especially proud of the women and African Americans I have appointed, many to courts or in communities where neither have served either by election or appointment.

When I am no longer governor of Michigan, I will look back with gratitude on the opportunity I had to impact the judiciary of this state through the appointment process and look forward to the many years of service those men and women will continue to provide to the citizens of this state long after I am gone.

Note. Michigan's 46th Governor John Engler earned a bachelor's degree from Michigan State University and his law degree from Thomas M. Cooley Law School. He is chair of the Republican Governors Association, the Council of Great Lakes Governors and the National Education Goals Panel. Lucille Taylor has been Legal Counsel to Governor John Engler since 1991. She earned her L.L.B. (now J.D.) from George Washington University Law School and has been a member of the State Bar of Michigan since 1972.

Jill Duman, Schwarzenegger's Judges

San Francisco Recorder, July 29, 2005

Sacramento — Observers say Gov. Arnold Schwarzenegger's bench appointments — under the direction of former Gov. Pete Wilson's judge-picker John Davies — are deja vu all over again.

Relying on multiple screenings by local community and advisory boards, Davies helped Wilson select mostly moderate judicial candidates. He seems to be bringing the same flavor to the current governor's picks.

"The sense I have is that they have been pretty middle-of-road, nonpartisan appointments," said John Van de Kamp, outgoing president of the State Bar of California. "[Davies] said that was what he was going to be doing, and it looks like that has been the case."

Of the 73 Schwarzenegger appointments made as of Monday, Davies — with the assistance of Schwarzenegger's legal secretary Peter Siggins — has selected 17 prosecutors (25 percent of the total appointments), 23 private practice attorneys (34 percent), and 18 court commissioners (roughly 27 percent).

The appointments have also been fairly evenly split between avowed Democrats (27, nearly 37 percent) and Republicans (35, roughly 48 percent). Nine appointees declined to state a party affiliation. . . .

The governors' appointments have also been short on attorneys traditionally under-represented on the bench.

To date, just 21 of Schwarzenegger's judicial appointments have been women — 29 percent. According to figures compiled by the California Women Lawyers, 35 percent of Gray Davis' judicial appointees were women, as were 24.4 percent of Wilson appointees, 16.4 percent of Jerry Brown appointees and 15.7 percent of Gov. George Deukmejian's appointees.

The California Association of Black Lawyers says Schwarzenegger has appointed just one African-American judge during his tenure — a difficult statistic to track since most nominees don't indicate their race on materials released to the public. Schwarzenegger's appointments of judges of color include Ricciardulli, a Latino, and Third District Court of Appeal Justice Tani Cantil-Sakauye, an Asian American.

California State Bar statistics published in 2001 indicated that members of color constituted 17 percent of the total bar, and women made up 32 percent of membership. . . .

c. Electing Judges

NOTE ON JUDICIAL ELECTIONS

As you have already gathered, most states allow electoral participation in judicial selection at some stage; the devil lies in the details. Sometimes voters participate through electoral "confirmation," in which after a judge has served for a term, she has to face the voters for a new term. Sometimes such elections occur only if an opponent files "against" the judge; if no opponent files, the judge is reappointed without a vote having occurred — and without having to campaign or raise funds. In other systems the judge appears on a ballot giving the voters a yes/no choice: no competitive candidate appears; again only in rare cases will opponents raise funds and campaign against such judges. (However, it has happened: in the mid-1980s three California Supreme Court justices were "unelected" after a well-financed campaign against them.) Both these forms of election differ substantially from that faced by candidates for other offices, in which even "safe seats" actually appear on a ballot and face at least token opposition. Such forms of judicial election have not stirred much controversy.

The form that has created much heat occurs in those states that choose judicial candidates for at least some offices through contested elections, sometimes partisan, sometimes nonpartisan. The next two selections describe the position of a "good government" group, the American Judicature Society, on such elections; its primary concern is the financing of such campaigns, and the worry that those who contribute heavily may receive (or be perceived as receiving) favorable treatment when they appear as litigants.

Following these two descriptions is a case that confronts another aspect of judicial elections. In elections for legislative and executive offices, voters expect and get a lot of information about candidates' positions and sometimes promises about what they will do in office. How might candidates for judicial offices present their positions? Would we want them to tell us how they would rule on various matters coming before them? Could we forbid them from telling us how they would rule? And what might the First Amendment have to say about these questions?

AMERICAN JUDICATURE SOCIETY, JUDICIAL SELECTION IN TEXAS: AN INTRODUCTION

Available online at http://www.ajs.org/js/TX.htm (last visited July 6, 2005)

Texas is one of only two states with two courts of last resort — the supreme court, which hears only civil matters, and the court of criminal appeals. The court of appeals is the state's intermediate appellate court, and the district court is the trial court of general jurisdiction. Courts of limited jurisdiction include county, probate, municipal, and justice of the peace courts. When Texas became a state in 1845, judges were appointed by the governor with senate consent, but since 1876, judges at all levels of courts have been elected by the people in partisan elections.

In 1980, Texas became the first state in which the cost of a judicial race exceeded $1 million. Between 1980 and 1986, campaign contributions to candidates in contested appellate court races increased by 250%. The 1988 supreme court elections were the most expensive in Texas history, with twelve candidates for six seats raising $12 million. Between 1992 and 1997, the seven winning candidates for the Texas Supreme Court raised nearly $9.2 million dollars. Of this $9.2 million, more than 40% was contributed by parties or lawyers with cases before the court or by contributors linked to those parties.

To address the perceived impropriety of judges soliciting and accepting large campaign contributions from attorneys and parties who appear before them, the Texas legislature passed the Judicial Campaign Fairness Act in 1995. Under the act, limits on individual contributions to candidates in statewide races range from $5,000 from individual donors to $30,000 from law firms. While some commentators believe the law has been successful in curbing the excesses of the late 1980s and early 1990s, others assert that the contribution limits are too generous to have a meaningful effect.

Support for an elected judiciary in Texas has declined in recent years. A 1990 poll revealed that 71% of Texans supported electing judges; by 1997 that figure had dropped to 52%.

AMERICAN JUDICATURE SOCIETY, JUDICIAL SELECTION IN MISSISSIPPI: AN INTRODUCTION

Available online at http://www.ajs.org/js/MS.htm (last visited July 6, 2005)

The Mississippi judiciary consists of the supreme court, the court of appeals, and various trial courts. The chancery court and the circuit court are trial courts of general jurisdiction. Trial courts of limited jurisdiction include county courts, justice courts, and municipal courts. Except for judges of the justice courts and municipal courts, Mississippi judges are chosen in nonpartisan elections.

Throughout its history, Mississippi has experimented with all methods of judicial selection. The state's original constitution of 1817 left the selection of judges to the legislature. In 1832, Mississippi became the first state in the nation to establish popular elections for all judges, and in 1868, it became one of the first elective states to move away from the election of judges when it adopted gubernatorial appointment with senate confirmation. Popular elections were reinstated in 1910 and 1914 and have been maintained ever since. In 1994, the legislature passed the Nonpartisan Judicial Election Act, which changed the elections for most judicial offices from partisan to nonpartisan contests.

The 2000 and 2002 judicial elections in Mississippi gained national attention because of the large amounts of money spent by both candidates and special interest groups. In 2000, nine candidates for four seats raised nearly $3.4 million. The 2002 election saw the most expensive campaign in the state's history for a single seat on the Mississippi Supreme Court, with three candidates raising nearly $1.7 million. In 2000, the U.S. Chamber of Commerce spent nearly $1 million on television advertising favoring four Mississippi Supreme Court candidates. Expenditures by trial lawyer groups brought the total in "soft" money in the 2000 judicial elections to an estimated $1.5 million. In the 2002 elections, the Chamber itself did not sponsor any advertisements, but some commentators speculate that it financed the more than $500,000 worth of television ads presented by a group called the Law Enforcement Alliance of America.

In recent years, both the legislature and the supreme court have enacted various reforms aimed at improving the tone and conduct of judicial elections. In 1999, the legislature imposed limits on contributions to judicial candidates and strengthened disclosure requirements, and it amended the Nonpartisan Judicial Election Act to bar political parties from contributing to or endorsing judicial candidates. This provision of the legislation was struck down by a federal court in 2002 as a violation of the First Amendment. In 2002, the supreme court amended the Mississippi Code of Judicial Conduct to allow litigants to file a motion to recuse a judge when an opposing party or attorney is a major donor to the judge's election campaign. The amendments to the code also limit the period during which campaign contributions can be accepted and create a special committee on judicial election campaign intervention to address allegations of campaign misconduct. A 2002 proposed constitutional amendment that would have lengthened the terms of chancery and circuit court judges from four to six years was rejected by voters.

Republican Party of Minnesota v. White

536 U.S. 765 (2002)

Justice Scalia delivered the opinion of the Court.

The question presented in this case is whether the First Amendment permits the Minnesota Supreme Court to prohibit candidates for judicial election in that State from announcing their views on disputed legal and political issues.

I

Since Minnesota's admission to the Union in 1858, the State's Constitution has provided for the selection of all state judges by popular election. Minn. Const., Art. VI, §7. Since 1912, those elections have been nonpartisan. Act of June 19, ch. 2, 1912 Minn. Laws Special Sess., pp. 4-6. Since 1974, they have been subject to a legal restriction which states that a "candidate for a judicial office, including an incumbent judge," shall not "announce his or her views on disputed legal or political issues." Minn. Code of Judicial Conduct, Canon 5(A)(3)(d)(i) (2000). This prohibition, promulgated by the Minnesota Supreme Court and based on Canon 7(B) of the 1972 American Bar Association (ABA) Model Code of Judicial Conduct, is known as the "announce clause." Incumbent judges who violate it are subject to discipline, including removal, censure, civil penalties, and suspension without pay. Minn. Rules of Board on Judicial Standards 4(a)(6), 11(d) (2002). Lawyers who run for judicial office also must comply with the announce clause. Minn. Rule of Professional Conduct 8.2(b) (2002) ("A lawyer who is a candidate for judicial office shall comply with the applicable provisions of the Code of Judicial Conduct"). Those who violate it are subject to, *inter alia*, disbarment, suspension, and probation. Rule 8.4(a); Minn. Rules on Lawyers Professional Responsibility 8-14, 15(a) (2002).

In 1996, one of the petitioners, Gregory Wersal, ran for associate justice of the Minnesota Supreme Court. In the course of the campaign, he distributed literature criticizing several Minnesota Supreme Court decisions on issues such as crime, welfare, and abortion. A complaint against Wersal challenging, among other things, the propriety of this literature was filed with the Office of Lawyers Professional Responsibility, the agency which, under the direction of the Minnesota Lawyers Professional Responsibility Board,[1] investigates and prosecutes ethical violations of lawyer candidates for judicial office. The Lawyers Board dismissed the complaint; with regard to the charges that his campaign materials violated the announce clause, it expressed doubt whether the clause could constitutionally be enforced. Nonetheless, fearing that further ethical complaints would jeopardize his ability to practice law, Wersal withdrew from the election. In 1998, Wersal ran again for the same office. Early in that race, he sought an advisory opinion from the Lawyers Board with regard to whether it planned to enforce the announce clause. The Lawyers Board responded equivocally, stating that, although it had significant doubts about the constitutionality of the provision, it was unable to answer his

---

1. The Eighth Circuit did not parse out the separate functions of these two entities in the case at hand, referring to the two of them collectively as the "Lawyers Board." We take the same approach.

question because he had not submitted a list of the announcements he wished to make.[2]

Shortly thereafter, Wersal filed this lawsuit in Federal District Court against respondents,[3] seeking, *inter alia*, a declaration that the announce clause violates the First Amendment and an injunction against its enforcement. Wersal alleged that he was forced to refrain from announcing his views on disputed issues during the 1998 campaign, to the point where he declined response to questions put to him by the press and public, out of concern that he might run afoul of the announce clause. . . .

II

Before considering the constitutionality of the announce clause, we must be clear about its meaning. Its text says that a candidate for judicial office shall not "announce his or her views on disputed legal or political issues." Minn. Code of Judicial Conduct, Canon 5(A)(3)(d)(i) (2002).

We know that "announc[ing] . . . views" on an issue covers much more than *promising* to decide an issue a particular way. The prohibition extends to the candidate's mere statement of his current position, even if he does not bind himself to maintain that position after election. All the parties agree this is the case, because the Minnesota Code contains a so-called "pledges or promises" clause, which *separately* prohibits judicial candidates from making "pledges or promises of conduct in office other than the faithful and impartial performance of the duties of the office," —a prohibition that is not challenged here and on which we express no view.

There are, however, some limitations that the Minnesota Supreme Court has placed upon the scope of the announce clause that are not (to put it politely) immediately apparent from its text. The statements that formed the basis of the complaint against Wersal in 1996 included criticism of past decisions of the Minnesota Supreme Court. One piece of campaign literature stated that "[t]he Minnesota Supreme Court has issued decisions which are marked by their disregard for the Legislature and a lack of common sense." It went on to criticize a decision excluding from evidence confessions by criminal defendants that were not tape-recorded, asking "[s]hould we conclude that because the Supreme Court does not trust police, it allows confessed criminals to go free?" It criticized a decision striking down a state law restricting welfare benefits, asserting that "[i]t's the Legislature which should set our spending policies." And it criticized a decision requiring public financing of abortions for poor women as "unprecedented" and a "pro-abortion stance."

---

2. Nor did Wersal have any success receiving answers from the Lawyers Board when he included "concrete examples," *post*, at 2547, n. 2 (STEVENS, J., dissenting), in his request for an advisory opinion on other subjects a month later:

> "As you are well aware, there is pending litigation over the constitutionality of certain portions of Canon 5. You are a plaintiff in this action and you have sued, among others, me as Director of the Office of Lawyers Professional Responsibility and Charles Lundberg as the Chair of the Board of Lawyers Professional Responsibility. Due to this pending litigation, I will not be answering your request for an advisory opinion at this time." App. 153.

3. Respondents are officers of the Lawyers Board and of the Minnesota Board on Judicial Standards (Judicial Board), which enforces the ethical rules applicable to judges.

Although one would think that all of these statements touched on disputed legal or political issues, they did not (or at least do not now) fall within the scope of the announce clause. The Judicial Board issued an opinion stating that judicial candidates may criticize past decisions, and the Lawyers Board refused to discipline Wersal for the foregoing statements because, in part, it thought they did not violate the announce clause. The Eighth Circuit relied on the Judicial Board's opinion in upholding the announce clause, and the Minnesota Supreme Court recently embraced the Eighth Circuit's interpretation, In re Code of Judicial Conduct, 639 N.W.2d 55 (Minn.2002).

There are yet further limitations upon the apparent plain meaning of the announce clause: In light of the constitutional concerns, the District Court construed the clause to reach only disputed issues that are likely to come before the candidate if he is elected judge. The Eighth Circuit accepted this limiting interpretation by the District Court, and in addition construed the clause to allow general discussions of case law and judicial philosophy. The Supreme Court of Minnesota adopted these interpretations as well when it ordered enforcement of the announce clause in accordance with the Eighth Circuit's opinion.

It seems to us, however, that — like the text of the announce clause itself — these limitations upon the text of the announce clause are not all that they appear to be. First, respondents acknowledged at oral argument that statements critical of past judicial decisions are *not* permissible if the candidate also states that he is against *stare decisis*. Thus, candidates must choose between stating their views critical of past decisions and stating their views in opposition to *stare decisis*. Or, to look at it more concretely, they may state their view that prior decisions were erroneous only if they do not assert that they, if elected, have any power to eliminate erroneous decisions. Second, limiting the scope of the clause to issues likely to come before a court is not much of a limitation at all. One would hardly expect the "disputed legal or political issues" raised in the course of a state judicial election to include such matters as whether the Federal Government should end the embargo of Cuba. Quite obviously, they will be those legal or political disputes that are the proper (or by past decisions have been made the improper) business of the state courts. And within that relevant category, "[t]here is almost no legal or political issue that is unlikely to come before a judge of an American court, state or federal, of general jurisdiction." Buckley v. Illinois Judicial Inquiry Bd., 997 F.2d 224, 229 (C.A.7 1993). Third, construing the clause to allow "general" discussions of case law and judicial philosophy turns out to be of little help in an election campaign. At oral argument, respondents gave, as an example of this exception, that a candidate is free to assert that he is a " 'strict constructionist.' " But that, like most other philosophical generalities, has little meaningful content for the electorate unless it is exemplified by application to a particular issue of construction likely to come before a court — for example, whether a particular statute runs afoul of any provision of the Constitution. Respondents conceded that the announce clause would prohibit the candidate from exemplifying his philosophy in this fashion. Without such application to real-life issues, all candidates can claim to be "strict constructionists" with equal (and unhelpful) plausibility.

In any event, it is clear that the announce clause prohibits a judicial candidate from stating his views on any specific nonfanciful legal question within the province of the court for which he is running, except in the context of discussing past decisions — and in the latter context as well, if he expresses the view that he is not bound by *stare decisis*.[5]

Respondents contend that this still leaves plenty of topics for discussion on the campaign trail. These include a candidate's "character," "education," "work habits," and "how [he] would handle administrative duties if elected." Indeed, the Judicial Board has printed a list of preapproved questions which judicial candidates are allowed to answer. These include how the candidate feels about cameras in the courtroom, how he would go about reducing the caseload, how the costs of judicial administration can be reduced, and how he proposes to ensure that minorities and women are treated more fairly by the court system. Whether this list of preapproved subjects, and other topics not prohibited by the announce clause, adequately fulfill the First Amendment's guarantee of freedom of speech is the question to which we now turn.

III

As the Court of Appeals recognized, the announce clause both prohibits speech on the basis of its content and burdens a category of speech that is "at the core of our First Amendment freedoms" — speech about the qualifications of candidates for public office. The Court of Appeals concluded that the proper test to be applied to determine the constitutionality of such a restriction is what our cases have called strict scrutiny; the parties do not dispute that this is correct. Under the strict-scrutiny test, respondents have the burden to prove that the announce clause is (1) narrowly tailored, to serve (2) a compelling state interest. In order for respondents to show that the announce clause is narrowly tailored, they must demonstrate that it does not "unnecessarily circumscrib[e] protected expression."

The Court of Appeals concluded that respondents had established two interests as sufficiently compelling to justify the announce clause: preserving the impartiality of the state judiciary and preserving the appearance of the impartiality of the state judiciary. Respondents reassert these two interests before us, arguing that the first is compelling because it protects the due

---

5. In 1990, in response to concerns that its 1972 Model Canon — which was the basis for Minnesota's announce clause — violated the First Amendment, see L. Milord, The Development of the ABA Judicial Code 50 (1992), the ABA replaced that canon with a provision that prohibits a judicial candidate from making "statements that commit or appear to commit the candidate with respect to cases, controversies or issues that are likely to come before the court." ABA Model Code of Judicial Conduct, Canon 5(A)(3)(d)(ii) (2000). At oral argument, respondents argued that the limiting constructions placed upon Minnesota's announce clause by the Eighth Circuit, and adopted by the Minnesota Supreme Court, render the scope of the clause no broader than the ABA's 1990 canon. Tr. of Oral Arg. 38. This argument is somewhat curious because, based on the same constitutional concerns that had motivated the ABA, the Minnesota Supreme Court was urged to replace the announce clause with the new ABA language, but, unlike other jurisdictions, declined. Final Report of the Advisory Committee to Review the ABA Model Code of Judicial Conduct and the Rules of the Minnesota Board on Judicial Standards 5-6 (June 29, 1994), reprinted at App. 367-368. The ABA, however, agrees with respondents' position, Brief for ABA as *Amicus Curiae* 5. We do not know whether the announce clause (as interpreted by state authorities) and the 1990 ABA canon are one and the same. No aspect of our constitutional analysis turns on this question.

process rights of litigants, and that the second is compelling because it preserves public confidence in the judiciary. Respondents are rather vague, however, about what they mean by "impartiality." Indeed, although the term is used throughout the Eighth Circuit's opinion, the briefs, the Minnesota Code of Judicial Conduct, and the ABA Codes of Judicial Conduct, none of these sources bothers to define it. Clarity on this point is essential before we can decide whether impartiality is indeed a compelling state interest, and, if so, whether the announce clause is narrowly tailored to achieve it.

A

One meaning of "impartiality" in the judicial context — and of course its root meaning — is the lack of bias for or against either *party* to the proceeding. Impartiality in this sense assures equal application of the law. That is, it guarantees a party that the judge who hears his case will apply the law to him in the same way he applies it to any other party. . . .

We think it plain that the announce clause is not narrowly tailored to serve impartiality (or the appearance of impartiality) in this sense. Indeed, the clause is barely tailored to serve that interest *at all*, inasmuch as it does not restrict speech for or against particular *parties*, but rather speech for or against particular *issues*. To be sure, when a case arises that turns on a legal issue on which the judge (as a candidate) had taken a particular stand, the party taking the opposite stand is likely to lose. But not because of any bias against that party, or favoritism toward the other party. *Any* party taking that position is just as likely to lose. The judge is applying the law (as he sees it) evenhandedly.[7]

B

It is perhaps possible to use the term "impartiality" in the judicial context (though this is certainly not a common usage) to mean lack of preconception in favor of or against a particular *legal view*. This sort of impartiality would be concerned, not with guaranteeing litigants equal application of the law, but rather with guaranteeing them an equal chance to persuade the court on the legal points in their case. Impartiality in this sense may well be an interest served by the announce clause, but it is not a *compelling* state interest, as strict scrutiny requires. A judge's lack of predisposition regarding the relevant legal issues in a case has never been thought a necessary component of equal justice, and with good reason. For one thing, it is virtually impossible to find a judge who does not have preconceptions about the law. As then-Justice Rehnquist observed of our own Court: "Since most Justices come to this bench no earlier than their middle years, it would be unusual if they had not by that time formulated at least some tentative notions that would influence them in their interpretation of the sweeping clauses of the Constitution and their

---

7. Justice Stevens asserts that the announce clause "serves the State's interest in maintaining both the appearance of this form of impartiality and its actuality." We do not disagree. Some of the speech prohibited by the announce clause may well exhibit a bias against parties — including Justice Stevens' example of an election speech stressing the candidate's unbroken record of affirming convictions for rape, *ibid.* That is why we are careful to say that the announce clause is "*barely* tailored to serve that interest," *supra*, at 2535 (emphasis added). The question under our strict scrutiny test, however, is not whether the announce clause serves this interest *at all*, but whether it is *narrowly tailored* to serve this interest. It is not.

interaction with one another. It would be not merely unusual, but extraordinary, if they had not at least given opinions as to constitutional issues in their previous legal careers." *Laird v. Tatum*, (1972) (memorandum opinion). Indeed, even if it were possible to select judges who did not have preconceived views on legal issues, it would hardly be desirable to do so. "Proof that a Justice's mind at the time he joined the Court was a complete *tabula rasa* in the area of constitutional adjudication would be evidence of lack of qualification, not lack of bias.". . . .

C

A third possible meaning of "impartiality" (again not a common one) might be described as open-mindedness. This quality in a judge demands, not that he have no preconceptions on legal issues, but that he be willing to consider views that oppose his preconceptions, and remain open to persuasion, when the issues arise in a pending case. This sort of impartiality seeks to guarantee each litigant, not an *equal* chance to win the legal points in the case, but at least *some* chance of doing so. It may well be that impartiality in this sense, and the appearance of it, are desirable in the judiciary, but we need not pursue that inquiry, since we do not believe the Minnesota Supreme Court adopted the announce clause for that purpose. . . .

The short of the matter is this: In Minnesota, a candidate for judicial office may not say "I think it is constitutional for the legislature to prohibit same-sex marriages." He may say the very same thing, however, up until the very day before he declares himself a candidate, and may say it repeatedly (until litigation is pending) after he is elected. As a means of pursuing the objective of open-mindedness that respondents now articulate, the announce clause is so woefully underinclusive as to render belief in that purpose a challenge to the credulous. . . .

IV

To sustain the announce clause, the Eighth Circuit relied heavily on the fact that a pervasive practice of prohibiting judicial candidates from discussing disputed legal and political issues developed during the last half of the 20th century. It is true that a "universal and long-established" tradition of prohibiting certain conduct creates "a strong presumption" that the prohibition is constitutional: . . . The practice of prohibiting speech by judicial candidates on disputed issues, however, is neither long nor universal.

We know of no restrictions upon statements that could be made by judicial candidates (including judges) throughout the 19th and the first quarter of the 20th century. Indeed, judicial elections were generally partisan during this period, the movement toward nonpartisan judicial elections not even beginning until the 1870's. . . . Thus, not only were judicial candidates (including judges) discussing disputed legal and political issues on the campaign trail, but they were touting party affiliations and angling for party nominations all the while.

The first code regulating judicial conduct was adopted by the ABA in 1924. 48 ABA Reports 74 (1923) (report of Chief Justice Taft); P. McFadden, Electing Justice: The Law and Ethics of Judicial Campaigns 86 (1990). It contained a provision akin to the announce clause: "A candidate for judicial position . . . should not announce in advance his conclusions of law on disputed issues to secure class support. . . ." ABA Canon of Judicial Ethics 30 (1924). The States were slow to adopt the canons, however. "By the end of World War II, the canons . . . were binding by the bar associations or supreme courts of only eleven states." J. MacKenzie, The Appearance of Justice 191 (1974). Even today, although a majority of States have adopted either the announce clause or its 1990 ABA successor, adoption is not unanimous. . . .

* * *

There is an obvious tension between the article of Minnesota's popularly approved Constitution which provides that judges shall be elected, and the Minnesota Supreme Court's announce clause which places most subjects of interest to the voters off limits. (The candidate-speech restrictions of all the other States that have them are also the product of judicial fiat.[15]) The disparity is perhaps unsurprising, since the ABA, which originated the announce clause, has long been an opponent of judicial elections. . . . That opposition may be well taken (it certainly had the support of the Founders of the Federal Government), but the First Amendment does not permit it to achieve its goal by leaving the principle of elections in place while preventing candidates from discussing what the elections are about. . . .

The Minnesota Supreme Court's canon of judicial conduct prohibiting candidates for judicial election from announcing their views on disputed legal and political issues violates the First Amendment. Accordingly, we reverse the grant of summary judgment to respondents and remand the case for proceedings consistent with this opinion.

It is so ordered.

Justice O'CONNOR, concurring.

I join the opinion of the Court but write separately to express my concerns about judicial elections generally. Respondents claim that "[t]he Announce Clause is necessary . . . to protect the State's compelling governmental interes[t] in an actual and perceived . . . impartial judiciary." I am concerned that, even aside from what judicial candidates may say while campaigning, the very practice of electing judges undermines this interest.

We of course want judges to be impartial, in the sense of being free from any personal stake in the outcome of the cases to which they are assigned. But if judges are subject to regular elections they are likely to feel that they have at least some personal stake in the outcome of every publicized case. Elected judges cannot help being aware that if the public is not satisfied with the outcome of a particular case, it could hurt their reelection prospects. See Eule, Crocodiles in the Bathtub: State Courts, Voter Initiatives and the Threat of Electoral Reprisal, 65 U. Colo. L. Rev. 733, 739 (1994) (quoting former

---

15. These restrictions are all contained in these states' codes of judicial conduct, App. to Brief for ABA as *Amicus Curiae.* "In every state, the highest court promulgates the Code of Judicial Conduct, either by express constitutional provision, statutory authorization, broad constitutional grant, or inherent power." In the Supreme Court of Texas: Per Curiam Opinion Concerning Amendments to Canons 5 and 6 of the Code of Judicial Conduct, 61 Tex. B.J. 64, 66 (1998) (collecting provisions).

California Supreme Court Justice Otto Kaus' statement that ignoring the political consequences of visible decisions is " 'like ignoring a crocodile in your bathtub' "). . . .

Moreover, contested elections generally entail campaigning. And campaigning for a judicial post today can require substantial funds. Unless the pool of judicial candidates is limited to those wealthy enough to independently fund their campaigns, a limitation unrelated to judicial skill, the cost of campaigning requires judicial candidates to engage in fundraising. Yet relying on campaign donations may leave judges feeling indebted to certain parties or interest groups. . . .

Despite these significant problems, 39 States currently employ some form of judicial elections for their appellate courts, general jurisdiction trial courts . . .

Minnesota has chosen to select its judges through contested popular elections instead of through an appointment system or a combined appointment and retention election system along the lines of the Missouri Plan. In doing so the State has voluntarily taken on the risks to judicial bias described above. As a result, the State's claim that it needs to significantly restrict judges' speech in order to protect judicial impartiality is particularly troubling. If the State has a problem with judicial impartiality, it is largely one the State brought upon itself by continuing the practice of popularly electing judges.

Justice KENNEDY, concurring.

I agree with the Court that Minnesota's prohibition on judicial candidates' announcing their legal views is an unconstitutional abridgment of the freedom of speech. There is authority for the Court to apply strict scrutiny analysis to resolve some First Amendment cases, see, *e.g.*, Simon & Schuster, Inc. v. Members of N.Y. State Crime Victims Bd., 502 U.S. 105 (1991), and the Court explains in clear and forceful terms why the Minnesota regulatory scheme fails that test. So I join its opinion. . . .

The citizen's respect for judgments depends in turn upon the issuing court's absolute probity. Judicial integrity is, in consequence, a state interest of the highest order.

Articulated standards of judicial conduct may advance this interest. To comprehend, then to codify, the essence of judicial integrity is a hard task, however. . . . To strive for judicial integrity is the work of a lifetime. That should not dissuade the profession. The difficulty of the undertaking does not mean we should refrain from the attempt. Explicit standards of judicial conduct provide essential guidance for judges in the proper discharge of their duties and the honorable conduct of their office. The legislative bodies, judicial committees, and professional associations that promulgate those standards perform a vital public service. . . .

Justice STEVENS, with whom Justice SOUTER, Justice GINSBERG, and Justice BREYER join, dissenting.

In her dissenting opinion, Justice Ginsberg has cogently explained why the Court's holding is unsound. I therefore join her opinion without reservation. I add these comments to emphasize the force of her arguments and to explain why I find the Court's reasoning even more troubling than its holding. The limits of the Court's holding are evident: Even if the Minnesota Lawyers Professional Responsibility Board (Board) may not sanction a judicial candidate for announcing his views on issues likely to come before him, it may surely advise the electorate that such announcements demonstrate the speaker's unfitness for judicial office. If the solution to harmful speech must be more speech, so be it. The Court's reasoning, however, will unfortunately endure beyond the next election cycle. By obscuring the fundamental distinction between campaigns for the judiciary and the political branches, and by failing to recognize the difference between statements made in articles or opinions and those made on the campaign trail, the Court defies any sensible notion of the judicial office and the importance of impartiality in that context.

The Court's disposition rests on two seriously flawed premises — an inaccurate appraisal of the importance of judicial independence and impartiality, and an assumption that judicial candidates should have the same freedom " 'to express themselves on matters of current public importance' " as do all other elected officials. . . .

Justice GINSBURG, with whom Justice STEVENS, Justice SOUTER, and Justice BREYER join, dissenting.

Whether state or federal, elected or appointed, judges perform a function fundamentally different from that of the people's elected representatives. Legislative and executive officials act on behalf of the voters who placed them in office; "judge[s] represen[t] the Law." Unlike their counterparts in the political branches, judges are expected to refrain from catering to particular constituencies or committing themselves on controversial issues in advance of adversarial presentation. Their mission is to decide "individual cases and controversies" on individual records, neutrally applying legal principles, and, when necessary, "stand[ing] up to what is generally supreme in a democracy: the popular will," Scalia, The Rule of Law as a Law of Rules, 56 U. Chi. L. Rev. 1175, 1180 (1989). . . .

The ability of the judiciary to discharge its unique role rests to a large degree on the manner in which judges are selected. The Framers of the Federal Constitution sought to advance the judicial function through the structural protections of Article III, which provide for the selection of judges by the President on the advice and consent of the Senate, generally for lifetime terms. Through its own Constitution, Minnesota, in common with most other States, has decided to allow its citizens to choose judges directly in periodic elections. But Minnesota has not thereby opted to install a corps of political actors on the bench; rather, it has endeavored to preserve the integrity of its judiciary by other means. Recognizing that the influence of political parties is incompatible with the judge's role, for example, Minnesota has designated all judicial elections nonpartisan. And it has adopted a provision, here called the Announce Clause, designed to prevent candidates for judicial office from "publicly making known how they would decide issues likely to come before them as judges." . . .

The question this case presents is whether the First Amendment stops Minnesota from furthering its interest in judicial integrity through this precisely targeted speech restriction. . . .

I

The speech restriction must fail, in the Court's view, because an electoral process is at stake; if Minnesota opts to elect its judges, the Court asserts, the State may not rein in what candidates may say.

I do not agree with this unilocular, "an election is an election," approach. Instead, I would differentiate elections for political offices, in which the First Amendment holds full sway, from elections designed to select those whose office it is to administer justice without respect to persons. Minnesota's choice to elect its judges, I am persuaded, does not preclude the State from installing an election process geared to the judicial office. . . .

Thus, the rationale underlying unconstrained speech in elections for political office — that representative government depends on the public's ability to choose agents who will act at its behest — does not carry over to campaigns for the bench. . . .

* * *

This Court has recognized in the past, as Justice O'Connor does today, a "fundamental tension between the ideal character of the judicial office and the real world of electoral politics." We have no warrant to resolve that tension, however, by forcing States to choose one pole or the other. Judges are not politicians, and the First Amendment does not require that they be treated as politicians simply because they are chosen by popular vote. Nor does the First Amendment command States who wish to promote the integrity of their judges in fact and appearance to abandon systems of judicial selection that the people, in the exercise of their sovereign prerogatives, have devised.

For more than three-quarters of a century, States like Minnesota have endeavored, through experiment tested by experience, to balance the constitutional interests in judicial integrity and free expression within the unique setting of an elected judiciary. I would uphold it as an essential component in Minnesota's accommodation of the complex and competing concerns in this sensitive area. Accordingly, I would affirm the judgment of the Court of Appeals for the Eighth Circuit.

ADAM LIPTAK, JUDICIAL RACES IN SEVERAL STATES BECOME PARTISAN BATTLEGROUNDS

New York Times, October 24, 2004, at 1

Judicial elections, which used to be staid and decorous affairs, have been transformed this year into loud and vicious fights, fueled by money, venom and television.

Campaign spending has skyrocketed. In one Illinois race, two vying candidates have raised $5 million. In West Virginia, a group financed by business interests is spending $2.5 million to defeat a sitting State Supreme Court justice. About a third of the total spending nationwide comes from interest groups, much of it from the independent but partisan organizations known as 527's. Their main contributors are business interests and plaintiffs' lawyers, and their agenda is most often the election of judges who could help — or the defeat of judges who could hinder — efforts to impose limits on lawsuits seeking damages for injuries.

Voters in eight states are seeing television advertisements in judicial races for the first time. And the ads are as pointed as those used in races for legislative and executive positions. One charge, leveled in separate advertisements against sitting judges in two states, is that they released dangerous sexual predators.

When judges are not attacking their opponents, they are telling voters their views on the legal and political issues of the day, something they had avoided until a 2002 decision by the United States Supreme Court. Statements by judges on issues they might be called upon to decide were generally thought to violate codes of judicial ethics before that decision.

All these developments, many lawyers and legal scholars warn, threaten the reputation, independence and integrity of the judiciary in the 38 states that elect at least some of their judges. Even the people involved in some of the nastiest campaigns are critical of their own work, saying it is the upshot of an unfortunate but inevitable political arms race.

"This is the year the dam is bursting," said Bert Brandenburg, the acting executive director of Justice at Stake Campaign, a judicial reform organization.

About 40 supreme court seats in 20 states are in play. State high courts decide thousands of cases each year, compared with the 80 or so rulings issued annually by the United States Supreme Court. They are the last word on issues of state law, which governs most injury and contract cases.

Most state high courts have five or seven judges, as opposed to the nine who sit on the federal Supreme Court, and they are often closely divided, meaning that a shift in a single seat can have enormous significance.

The sums of money being spent to capture those seats is growing exponentially. . . .

AMANDA BREONSTAD, SPECIAL INTEREST CASH HITS A WALL
IN JUDICIAL ELECTIONS

National Law Journal, November 17, 2006

Special interest groups gave millions of dollars to judicial candidates in the month before last week's elections, but failed to defeat their opponents in some of the tightest races in the country.

In the most expensive race, various business groups were unable to win the retention of the incumbent chief justice of the Alabama Supreme Court. A former appellate judge defeated the Republican candidate to become the sole Democrat on the state high court.

In Georgia, an affiliate of the National Association of Manufacturers bank-rolled a series of last-ditch television ads for a state Supreme Court candidate who lost after being accused of threatening to kill his sister.

In Illinois, special interest groups sparked one of the most expensive appellate court races in U.S. history. And a Supreme Court race in Kentucky pitting an anti-abortion candidate against a self-declared impartial judge dealt a setback for judicial First Amendment advocates.

"Business groups continue to spend a lot of money in a number of these campaigns," said Jesse Rutledge, communications director of the Justice at Stake Campaign, a bipartisan group in Washington that tracks judicial elections. But unlike in past election cycles, "this year, their investments, it appears, did not pay off."

Cash Competition

Among the five Alabama Supreme Court races, Sue Bell Cobb, the challenger for chief justice, was the only Democrat to win. Campaigning as a churchgoing mother, Cobb raised more than $1.85 million in cash contributions from several political action committees (PACs) and the state Democratic Executive Committee. Chief Justice Drayton Nabers Jr., who boasted an anti-abortion stance in TV ads, raised $3.9 million in cash contributions from state tort reform PACs. The American Taxpayers Alliance, a group that has received funds from the U.S. Chamber of Commerce, paid for Nabers' ads in the primaries.

Although Nabers outspent her, Cobb acknowledged how much she raised in contributions. "We were very cognizant of the fact that we had to have sufficient resources to prevail," she said. "Do I think that's an attractive part of the process? No, I do not. Do I want that to change? Yes, I do." . . .

While not the most expensive, the race for a Kentucky Supreme Court seat exemplified the debate over whether judicial candidates should make political or legal statements. Pledging impartiality, Circuit Judge Bill Cunningham defeated Rick Johnson, a Court of Appeals judge who campaigned against abortion.

"The candidates who take a more aggressive First Amendment approach are consistently meeting with failure at the ballot box," Rutledge said.

MEGAN GARVEY AND JESSICA GARRISON, JUDGE'S LOSS STUNS EXPERTS; ELECTION SYSTEM AND THE JURIST'S LATVIAN NAME ARE CITED. WINNER IS A LAWYER AND SHOPKEEPER

Los Angeles Times, June 8, 2006, at B 1

The rare defeat of a highly regarded sitting judge ousted from the bench Tuesday by a bagel store owner who'd barely practiced law in the last decade sent a jolt through Los Angeles County legal circles, leading some to question whether the system to select judges needs overhauling.

When the ballots were counted it wasn't even close: Judge Dzintra Janavs, a 20-year veteran of the bench, lost by almost 8 percentage points to Lynn Diane Olson, a Hermosa Beach resident and business owner who only late last year reactivated her state bar membership.

Rare in judicial contests, the race had drawn preelection attention because of speculation by political consultants and court observers that Janavs could be particularly vulnerable—and even may have been targeted—because of her unusual name.

The morning after the vote, Janavs went back to work in the Writs and Receivers Court, where she is the assistant presiding judge. Olson, mother of a 5-month-old daughter, kept a long-scheduled appointment with the dentist.

"I am thrilled. I am humbled. I am energized. I don't even know what to say," Olson said.

In the legal community, a different mood prevailed: shock.

"Judges are devastated by the loss of an esteemed colleague," said Judge Terry Friedman, president of the California Judges Assn. He said he could recall only two other times in 30 years when a sitting judge was voted out of office.

Janavs, whose accent still has a trace of her native Latvia, said she had been inundated with calls from lawyers and judges.

"All I hear is 'outraged,' 'disgusted,' 'appalled,'" Janavs said. "I'm not a person that uses those kinds of adjectives."

When asked what words she would use, Janavs said: "Let me put it this way, my reaction is: Money can buy anything. That's my reaction. My name probably didn't help. But had she not spent a fortune on these slates, I don't think my name alone would have helped her."

Olson, who was rated "not qualified" by the Los Angeles County Bar Assn., outspent Janavs by more than 2 to 1, giving about $100,000 of her own money compared with about $42,000 in contributions reported by May 20 by the judge.

Janavs is valued by court administrators for her analytical skills and ability to handle what many consider to be one of the toughest judicial assignments: fast-paced decisions involving cases that include injunctions and restraining orders being sought by governments, electoral candidates, businesses, environmental groups and media outlets.

Superior Court Presiding Judge William McLaughlin called Janavs "an American success story" and said she would be deeply missed. A Republican, Janavs fled Latvia with her parents during World War II. . . . Her parents were lawyers in Latvia but worked as a gardener and a housekeeper in this country, Janavs' campaign consultant said.

Although Olson beat Janavs, she will not take her exact position on the bench. As with all new judges, Olson is likely to be assigned to a traffic or arraignment court to learn the ropes, court officials said.

She is a graduate of the University of Illinois law school and practiced commercial litigation law for four years before leaving to open Manhattan Bread & Bagel in Manhattan Beach with her husband in 1992. A recent remodel gave the store on busy Sepulveda Boulevard a chic modern facade, and patrons say the shop is known for its ginger snaps.

On the ballot in the nonpartisan race, Olson's profession was listed as "attorney at law." Janavs appeared as "Judge of the Superior Court." . . .

Janavs was one of only two judicial candidates of 28 in the county rated "exceptionally well qualified" by the Los Angeles County Bar Assn. "But she has an odd name. And she is thrown out by someone who is not even practicing law," said Loyola Law School professor Laurie Levenson. "It makes me very troubled by our whole judicial election process. This is the poster child for how really messed up things are."

Olson and her husband, Michael Keegan, a Hermosa Beach councilman, said they did not target Janavs because of her name, but rather because she was Republican.

"I targeted Janavs because of her political affiliation, time on the bench and what I hear about her from people in the legal community," Olson said, referring to Janavs' reputation for courtroom gruffness.

Thousands of campaign mailers funded by Olson, as well as about 50,000 e-mails directed at registered Democrats, emphasized the candidate's endorsement by the Los Angeles County Democratic Party.

NOTE ON THE STATE OF PLAY IN JUDICIAL ELECTIONS

The materials above reflect a good deal of concern about several aspects of judicial elections: What can candidates, newly empowered by the interpretation of the First Amendment in Republican Party of Minnesota v. White, say during campaigns? Will their taking public positions close their minds to litigants? Does money buy votes? Will certain forms of election create an irresistible pressure to raise large amounts of money — which in turn will distort (or be seen as distorting) judicial impartiality?

Hovering in the background of such questions is consistent polling data which indicate that the electorate strongly favors some form of electoral participation either in the selection of judges or in their reappointment. Such polls appear to take off the table changes that would convert the states to a lifetime appointment system like that of the federal government: if the polling data is accurate, no state electorate would support such a change.

The question, then, is what to make of the current situation. The gloomy view, which one sees reflected in several of the readings above, suggests a perfect storm of money and politics leading to the election of bad judges and the defeat of good ones. Other readings suggest a more optimistic view: voters don't like it when judges start announcing how they will vote — and punish candidates who do so — and that really big money often fails to buy elections for the chosen candidates. What information would one want in order to decide which view is the more accurate assessment? And how might the current state of play bear on the design of judicial disciplinary systems — the topic of the next section?

C. DISCIPLINING JUDGES

1. SOME EXAMPLES AND A SURVEY

Joel Stashenko, Caseload, Marital Problems Raised as Factors in Judge's Tirade over Courtroom Cell Phone

New York Law Journal, April 8, 2008

Marital problems and a heavy caseload helped create the "perfect psychological storm" for a city court judge who began jailing defendants for not taking responsibility for a ringing cell phone in his courtroom one day in 2005, his attorney told New York state's highest court Tuesday. . . .

Restaino failed to recognize the "stressors" in his life that led to his outburst on March 11, 2005, when the judge ordered 46 defendants in a Domestic Violence Court detained because no one would own up to having the cell phone, Connors [the judge's attorney] said. Fourteen defendants were eventually sent to the Niagara County Jail because they could not make bail. All the defendants were released by the end of the day.

Connors cited Restaino's heavy caseload as one of his major stressors. The judge typically handled between 100 and 125 cases a day in court and from 1996 to 2006 he was responsible for some 90,000 cases, his attorney said. . . .

Connors told the Court of Appeals that Restaino's case presents them with an opportunity to address an issue the Court has never written about: "judicial burnout and stress." . . .

Chief Judge Judith S. Kaye and Judges Robert S. Smith and Susan P. Read all noted Tuesday that heavy dockets are the norm for state court judges. Read observed that if Restaino is returned to the bench, "I don't suppose that his caseload is going to get any lighter."

"We've got to deal with a judge, a very hard-working judge with an excellent record," Smith said. "Well, we have a lot of very hard-working judges with excellent records. He [Restaino] went completely off the rails. He victimized several dozen harmless, innocent people, or at least innocent of anything that would have justified his conduct. How can we say to the community, 'Well, we understand why he did it and he's not going to do it again?'" . . .

The commission voted for removal by a 9-1 margin, finding that Restaino's behavior "transcended poor judgment" and brought the judiciary into "disrepute." The former chairman of the commission, Raoul Felder, disagreed in what he called the most difficult decision in his four years on the panel. . . .

Restaino was appointed to a part-time city judgeship in Niagara Falls in 1996 and elected to a 10-year full-time term in 2001. He has been suspended with pay since December as he challenged the commission's removal recommendation before the Court of Appeals.

Since the inception of the commission in 1983, the Court of Appeals has upheld 63 of the panel's 72 removal recommendations. The other nine were reduced to censure. . . .

[On June 6, 2008, New York's highest court handed down an opinion upholding the recommended removal of Judge Restaino:

City Court Judge Robert M. Restaino of Niagara Falls has "irretrievably lost" the confidence of the public in his community due to his actions on March 11, 2005, a 6-0 Court of Appeals concluded in *Matter of Restaino*, 82.

"By indiscriminately committing into custody 46 defendants, petitioner deprived them of their liberty without due process, exhibited insensitivity, indifference and a callousness so reproachable that his continued presence on the Bench cannot be tolerated," the court held in a per curiam ruling.]

SHERI QUALTERS, SUSPENSION, FINE RECOMMENDED FOR BOSTON JUDGE WHO SENT IMPROPER LETTERS TO NEWSPAPER

National Law Journal, April 2, 2008

The Massachusetts Commission on Judicial Conduct recommended a $25,000 fine, a 30-day suspension without pay and a public censure for state court Judge Ernest B. Murphy for sending improper letters to Boston Herald publisher Patrick J. Purcell that demanded settlement of Murphy's libel lawsuit against the newspaper.

The commission made its recommendations to the Massachusetts Supreme Judicial Court, which makes final rulings on judicial disciplinary cases.

The commission concluded that Murphy's conduct was willful and that he attempted to both intimidate Purcell and persuade the Herald to pay him more than the courts had awarded him at that point in the case.

In a statement, Purcell said he was "appreciative" of the commission's approach and "very pleased with its findings and recommendations." Murphy's Feb. 20, 2005 letter, which was on court stationary, warned Purcell that it would be a "mistake. In fact, a BIG mistake" to show the letter to anyone except "the gentleman whose authorized signature will be affixed to the check in question." Murphy's second letter said Purcell had "ZERO" chance of winning an appeal.

Murphy sued the Herald for libel over stories quoting "several courthouse sources" that allegedly heard Murphy say a teenage rape victim should "get over it."

Murphy said the stories sparked virulent public criticism and nationwide attention that caused significant emotional strain for him and his family.

A jury awarded Murphy $2.09 million in February 2005. The amount was reduced to $2.01 million, but the Herald paid Murphy $3.4 million including interest after Murphy won an appeal in May 2007.

Murphy did not return a message left at Suffolk Superior Court. . . .

YVETTE BEGUE & CANDICE GOLDSTEIN, HOW JUDGES GET INTO TROUBLE: WHAT THEY NEED TO KNOW ABOUT DEVELOPMENTS IN THE LAW OF JUDICIAL DISCIPLINE

26 Judges' Journal 8 (1987)

Defining judicial misconduct, and developing procedures to deal with it, are problems that are still being worked out today in recent cases and rulings from judicial conduct commissions. The difficulty this presents becomes even greater, because as a society we make the independence of the judge paramount but also insist on accountability. Judges are held to a stricter code of conduct than other people because their role demands that there be not even a hint of impropriety. This extends to off-the-bench conduct.

Before modern judicial conduct commission systems were developed, the traditional methods of dealing with serious misconduct by judges were impeachment, address and recall. Since these procedures were cumbersome, they were rarely invoked; additionally, they only provided for removal, which was not appropriate in most cases of misconduct. In 1960, the first state judicial conduct commission was established, followed by many others, until today all 50 states, the District of Columbia and the federal circuits have some mechanism for receiving, investigating, and adjudicating complaints against judges.

Since 1972, when the ABA Model Code of Judicial Conduct was approved, 47 states and the District of Columbia have adopted it in one form or another. The Code consists of statements of norms for judicial behavior in the form of canons, with an accompanying text that delineates specific rules, which are followed by commentaries. (The three noncode states are Montana, Rhode Island and Wisconsin.) The constitutional and statutory provisions that define judicial misconduct also establish judicial conduct commissions.

Misconduct that is punishable often involves violations of the Code of Judicial Conduct, persistent failure to perform the duties of office, habitual intemperance, and conduct prejudicial to the administration of justice. Typical sanctions include admonition, censure, suspension and removal from office. Removal from office is the most severe, because it may have additional serious consequences, such as loss of retirement benefits, ineligibility to hold future judicial office, and loss of license to practice law.

This article discusses some of the recent decisions of judicial conduct commissions and courts that discipline judges, focusing on those decisions that suggest trends or define misconduct in particular areas. It is important to keep in mind how young the field of judicial discipline is — only 25 years-old — and consequently, how important the development of a comprehensive body of law is to commissions, judges and the public.

On-Bench Conduct

Bias and Appearance of Partiality

Bias and appearance of partiality cases often refer to violations of Canons 1, 2 and 3 of the Code of Judicial Conduct. Canon 1 requires that judges uphold the integrity and independence of the judiciary; Canon 2 calls upon judges to avoid impropriety and the appearance of impropriety in all activities; and Canon 3 requires judges to perform the duties of their office impartially and diligently.

Bias is one of the most common complaints lodged against judges. Apart from the obvious, such as hearing cases involving family members, bias is often difficult to determine. Even more troublesome is the question of the appearance of partiality—where the judge's conduct simply looks bad. In actual bias, the harm is to the individual litigant. In appearance of partiality situations, the emphasis is on the damage done to public confidence in the judiciary.

In studying bias cases, it is helpful to keep in mind that the issue may be raised in a variety of legal contexts, such as routine motions to disqualify, complaints filed with a judicial conduct organization or, less often, challenges based on constitutional grounds. For example, in Gardiner v. A.H. Robins Co., a 1984 federal case, Judge Lord refused to accept a settlement in the Dalkon shield litigation without the presence of three corporate officers in the courtroom. When they appeared, Judge Lord accused the officers of permitting women to wear a "deadly depth charge in their wombs" and of "violating every ethical precept." On appeal, the corporate officers claimed Judge Lord had violated their due process rights, including denying them an opportunity to be heard by an impartial tribunal. The court of appeals rejected Judge Lord's defense that because the comments were made in a judicial setting, they did not show bias and ordered the statements stricken from the record. Judge Lord's statements were made without the benefit of a trial and without hearing all the evidence.

In In re Eads, a 1985 Iowa case, a judge who was friendly with two lawyers became disturbed at what he believed to be the unethical manner in which one lawyer handled the divorce action of the other lawyer's wife. When the attorney refused to change his course of conduct, and his firm supported his manner of representation, the judge began a two-year campaign of harassment against the lawyer and his firm, including warning him that judges rate lawyers for Martindale-Hubbell, and behaving in such a hostile manner that the firm was obliged to advise its clients to seek other representation when their cases were assigned before the judge. The Iowa Supreme Court issued a public reprimand and ordered the judge suspended from office for 60 days.

A second issue in the bias cases is the showing necessary to establish misconduct. For example, in U.S. v. Murphy, the criminal defendant discovered after his conviction that the judge and prosecutor were close friends and had, with their families, vacationed together twice, the second time after the trial. In a post-conviction motion, the defendant unsuccessfully moved to have the judge recused. On appeal the court interpreted this motion as an attempt to have the conviction set aside, which was properly denied because a showing of actual partiality is required to have prior judicial acts set aside.

In contrast, the In re Wait decision held that actual favoritism need not be shown where a judge heard six cases involving his relatives. The mere appearance of partiality here was enough to justify removal from office.

When a determination of bias is made, the commission or court must decide whether the litigants' rights have been damaged sufficiently to interfere in the actual litigation. In Judicial Qualifications v. Schirado, a judge heard two cases in which he had previously been involved as an attorney. The court not only censured the judge but also had copies of the order of censure sent to the litigants in anticipation of possible motions to vacate. In *Aetna*, the decision was vacated and remanded. In both cases, actual partiality was involved and the courts fashioned remedies tailored to the individual litigants. In contrast, the *Murphy* court, while acknowledging the possible harm to public confidence in the judiciary, did not set aside the defendant's conviction where the appearance of partiality was at issue. In *Murphy*, however, the court was probably influenced by the fact that the defendant's attorney knew of the friendship between the judge and prosecutor because he also was a close friend of the two.

Legal Error vs. Abuse of Judicial Authority

Another type of on-bench misconduct is abuse of judicial authority, including improper use of the contempt power. In reviewing these cases, courts and commissions must separate legal error from misconduct. The Code of Judicial Conduct and state discipline mechanisms were never intended to correct judicial error; judicial error is left to the appeals process. But a pattern of denying litigants their rights — or even a single, particularly egregious error — violates, Canons 1,[1] 2A,[2] and 3A(1)[3] of the Code of Judicial Conduct and is conduct prejudicial to the administration of justice.

Some cases illustrate a pattern of judges repeatedly denying important rights to litigants. These judges ordered unrepresented defendants to jail in civil cases in lieu of fine or for failure to complete public service work that had not been court ordered; sent debtors to jail without providing a hearing on ability to pay; employed improper methods to obtain payment for public defender services from indigent criminal defendants; failed to advise litigants of their right to remain silent and to have a blood-grouping test in paternity cases; and threatened a defendant with a harsher sentence in order to discourage the defendant from requesting a public defender. In response to this behavior, courts imposed censure, suspension and/or removal from judicial office. . . .

Two recent cases involving judicial reaction to criticism highlight the tension between legal error and abuse of judicial authority. These judges responded to their critics by threatening them with contempt. In one case, a Georgia judge agreed to a 30-day suspension from office without pay after admitting he had threatened a critic with contempt. The critic had written derogatory letters about the judge to a newspaper. . . .

The Alabama Supreme Court found that Judge Sheffield violated the Code of Judicial Conduct by commenting on the case to a newspaper reporter and failing to recuse himself from the case. However, the court held that initiating the contempt charge did not violate the Code, since clear and convincing evidence did not show that Judge Sheffield acted in bad faith in issuing his show cause order. . . .

In contrast to the Alabama court's ruling that only bad faith errors are disciplinable, the California Supreme Court determined that a judge's good faith though improper use of the contempt power constituted conduct prejudicial to the administration of justice. . . .

Language Used to Address Lawyers and Litigants. Racist comments by judges violate the obligation to maintain the appearance of impartiality required by Canon 2A. The In re Agrestai decision from New York is typical of the serious attention racist remarks receive from discipline authorities. While presiding over the sentencing hearing of a defendant who was black, Judge Agrestai attempted to elicit information about a black person whom the

---

1. "A Judge Should Uphold the Integrity and Independence of the Judiciary. An independent and honorable judiciary is indispensable to justice in our society. A judge should participate in establishing, maintaining, and enforcing, and should himself observe, high standards of conduct so that the integrity and independence of the judiciary may be preserved. The provisions of this Code should be construed and applied to further that objective." Canon 1, ABA Model Code of Jud. Conduct (1973).

2. "A Judge Should Avoid Impropriety and the Appearance of Impropriety in All His Activities
A. A judge should respect and comply with the law and should conduct himself at all times in a manner that promotes public confidence in the integrity and impartiality of the judiciary." Canon 2A, ABA Model Code of Jud. Conduct (1973).

3. "A Judge Should Perform the Duties of His office Impartially and Diligently. The judicial duties of a judge take precedence over all his other activities. His judicial duties include all the duties of his office prescribed by law. In the performance of these duties, the following standards apply:
A. Adjudicative Responsibilities
(1) A judge should be faithful to the law and maintain professional competence in it. He should be unswayed by partisan interests, public clamor, or fear of criticism." Canon 3A(l), ABA Model Code of Jud. Conduct (1973).

judge referred to as the "real culprit." He asked in open court: "I know that there is another nigger in the woodpile, I want that person out, is that clear?" The New York Court of Appeals, the state's highest court, affirmed the discipline commission's censure of the judge.

Two recent cases indicate that belittling comments to women are also subject to discipline. In one case, a judge referred to a woman attorney as "lawyerette" and asked her why she wasn't wearing a tie. . . .

In New York, a district court judge was admonished for commenting on the figures of women lawyers. In some instances, the judge suggested that the women could obtain what they were asking of the court because of their physical appearance. The comments occurred in the course of the judge's official duties but not within the hearing of the general public. The discipline commission considered in mitigation the judge's good reputation and his acknowledgment that his comments were inappropriate. Further, the commission remarked that had the comments been made within the hearing of the public, a more severe sanction might have been warranted.

Off-Bench Conduct
Abuse of Position — Ticket-Fixing

In this section, three types of off-bench conduct will be examined: abuse of position, personal improprieties and campaign improprieties. One interesting point to note in the area of ticket-fixing is that in several New York cases the judges were removed from office. . . .

Abuse of Position — Prestige of Office

Abusing the prestige of the office is usually a more subtle problem than ticket-fixing or receiving favors. One definition of this type of misconduct is the attempt to obtain special treatment for oneself simply on the basis that one is a judge. For example, in In re Tschirhart, a judge became upset at a bank's efforts to collect on a loan he had guaranteed for his son. The judge visited the bank, identified himself as a judge and demanded special treatment. He further threatened to withdraw court funds on deposit with the bank. After the bank filed suit, he called the bank's counsel and told him that as a judge he was "not insignificant." For this and other conduct, he was censured.

In In re Muszinski, a judge, angry at being disturbed while having lunch at a restaurant, ordered a police officer to turn off his radio despite the officer's explanation that he was prohibited from doing so by police regulations. He later summoned the officer to this courtroom by letter on official stationery and threatened him with contempt. Censure was also imposed in this case. . . .

Abuse of Position — Political Activities

In In re Staples, a 1986 Washington decision, a judge became actively involved in a campaign to have the county seat transferred. Judge Staples organized a committee, made campaign speeches and circulated petitions. The commission recommended that Judge Staples be admonished for violating Canon 7A(4), which prohibits political activity unrelated to the administration of justice. The commission argued that this referred to such issues as court procedure. The court disagreed, taking a broader view of Canon 7A(4). Judge Staples' activities had not been shown to impair the performance of his judicial duties. Because his activities were nonpartisan in nature, fears of bias were unfounded. The court concluded that judges should not lose their rights as citizens by assuming the bench. The court felt that excluding judges from legal reform processes would deprive citizens of a wealth of expertise. The opposite argument, of course, is that the appearance of partiality would cause loss of public confidence in the judiciary.

Personal Improprieties

The underlying issue in the personal improprieties cases is whether personal, off-bench conduct should be regulated, and if so, how to evaluate that conduct in a manner fair to judges. Various standards have been suggested, ranging from applying criminal law standards to using a " 'community morality' " test. A significant factor in the caselaw appears to be whether the conduct becomes public.

For example, in In re Tschirhart, a 1985 Michigan case, a judge was arrested and acquitted of defrauding a taxi driver of his fare on a visit to a legal brothel in Nevada. The judge later discussed the visit with a reporter, stating that he had enjoyed his visit and would do it again. The Michigan Supreme Court censured him, not for the actual visit to the brothel, but rather for making inflammatory remarks to the press. In the Commission Decision and Recommendation, one commissioner argued in a concurrence that the judge should also be disciplined for visiting the brothel, because houses of prostitution were illegal in Michigan and Judge Tschirhart should be evaluated according to Michigan Laws.

In In re Hyland, a 1985 New Jersey case, a judge became the subject of public scrutiny when his secretary claimed sexual harassment and wrongful discharge. Judge Hyland admitted to having sexual relations with her and exchanging sexually-related literature and gifts with her in chambers. While the secretary's charges of sexual harassment and wrongful discharge were not proven, Judge Hyland was nonetheless publicly reprimanded for his indiscreet conduct. The court noted that such a relationship was suspect because (1) as her employer, the voluntariness of the relationship was questionable and (2) the liaison could lead to the impression that the judicial office had been compromised.

In both cases, the personal, off-bench conduct became public and as such, may have deserved investigation. But it is also worth noting that the conduct happened to involve the sexual activities of the judges.

Canon 3B(3)

Canon 3B(3),[4] often known as the "Squeal Rule," requires judges to report unethical conduct on the part of other judges or lawyers. Until recently, courts rarely invoked this section of the Code in determining whether or not

---

4. "A judge should take or initiate appropriate disciplinary procedures against a judge or lawyer for unprofessional conduct of which the judge may become aware." Canon 3B(3) ABA Model Code of Jud. Conduct (1973).

misconduct had occurred. Since the cases applying Canon 3B(3) thus far have involved other misconduct, it is not clear whether a court would sanction a judge simply for not reporting misconduct by others. However, the trend seems to be that failure to report misconduct will at the very least be considered in determining the severity of the other misconduct.

Campaign Improprieties

Campaign conduct cases often evaluate what constitutes permissible speech. . . . [Text deleted because it discusses cases decided before Republican Party of Minnesota v. White.]

Defenses and Mitigating Circumstances

Mootness, Prior Misconduct, Overlapping Misconduct

A common occurrence in judicial disciplinary proceedings is for a judge to resign and then raise the defense that the complaint is moot because the judge has resigned or the judge's term has expired. Court commissions have various policies to respond. Some courts are not permitted to remove a judge from office if the judge has already resigned, . . . Other states take the policy view that judges must not be permitted to escape disciplinary proceedings by means of resignation, even if the judge's term has expired.[5] Finally, one court took a more pragmatic stance, holding that judges must be formally removed from office even after resignation in order to prevent reappointment or service as a reserve judge.[6]

Sometimes, commissions will consider prior misconduct by a judge in evaluating current misconduct. Judges typically argue in defense that the prior conduct is moot and should not be considered. However, in In re Whitaker, the Louisiana high court held that conduct prior to assuming office was relevant to the probability that the conduct continued once the judge took office, and was also relevant in determining the appropriate sanction. . . .

Policy

When accused of misconduct, judges often raise the defense that they were merely following court policy, or the orders of their chief judges. The following three cases are interesting because the courts arrived at different sanction for rather similar offenses.

In re Greene, a West Virginia 1984 case, involved a magistrate, who while following the instructions of the chief magistrate, refused to issue a complaint form to a defendant who wished to file a cross-warrant against his accuser. The court excused the judge because he relied in good faith on existing court policy and had no intention to prejudice the rights of the parties.

The following year, in In re Wharton, also from West Virginia, the court publicly censured a magistrate, who, acting pursuant to court policy, contacted the prosecutor's office prior to issuing an arrest warrant to determine whether the warrant should be issued for a police officer on a non-support charge. By this conduct, the magistrate had failed to act neutral, detached

---

5. *See e.g.*, W. Va. Jud. Hearing Bd. v. Romanello, 336 S.E. 2d 540 (W. Va. 1985).
6. In re Sterlinske, 365 N.W. 2d 876 (Wis. 1985).

and independent of the prosecutor. The court noted that magistrates must act as checks on the police power.

Finally, in In re Walter, a 1985 Illinois case, a judge was censured for accepting fees for performing marriages outside of court on his own time. He was not found guilty of willful misconduct because his chief judge had referred the parties to him, thus giving the impression he condoned the practice.

The three cases are difficult to reconcile. The judge who refused to permit a criminal defendant to issue a complaint for a cross-warrant was excused although his conduct was seemingly as serious a violation of the law as accepting money for performing marriages or checking with the prosecutor's office before issuing a warrant.

Overburdened Court

Several judges have recently raised the defense of an overburdened court. Although courts in two jurisdictions rejected the defense in cases involving courtroom courtesy, the California Supreme Court indicated that, under certain circumstances, the defense would shield a judge from charges of untimely decision-making.

In Mardikian v. Commission on Judicial Performance, a superior court judge failed to promptly decide 14 cases between 1980 and 1983, seven of which remained undecided in excess of the state's statutory and constitutional 90 day time period. Instead of deciding the cases, Judge Mardikian entered orders "resubmitting" the cases without the consent of the parties.

The supreme court affirmed the commission's finding that, although the superior court system was extremely overburdened, and Judge Mardikian hardworking, the judge engaged in conduct prejudicial to the administration of justice. According to the court, when a heavy caseload makes prompt decision-making impossible for even the conscientious judge, no discipline will be imposed. However, trial judges are obliged to minimize the impact of the delay by assigning priorities based on the time necessary to decide the case and the effect of the delay on the parties. Since Judge Mardikian failed to assign a high priority to divorce cases involving child custody issues, and made no effort to give precedence to resubmitted cases over newer ones, he engaged in misconduct. The court ordered a public censure. . . .

Substance Abuse

The Michigan discipline authorities took a rehabilitative approach towards a judge suffering from alcoholism who had undertaken a course of treatment by the time the court heard the matter. Rather than remove a judge from office for alcohol-related conduct, the court suspended her from office for two months, followed by a six-month period of supervision. . . .

Commission Authority and Procedure

Scope of Commission Powers — Investigation; Subpoena Powers

Two issues appear in the caselaw involving investigative and subpoena powers — the personal privacy rights of individual judges, and the institutional integrity or privacy rights of organizations such as bar associations or grand juries.

In re Agerter, a 1984 Minnesota case, highlights the personal privacy issue. The court upheld a subpoena issued by the Board on Judicial Standards to the extent that it required the judge to appear and answer questions concerning an alleged drinking problem but quashed the subpoena in regard to an alleged sexual relationship. There was a sufficient state interest in the information to justify questioning the judge on his drinking habits. Further, the information would be elicited in a confidential setting. . . .

In re Judicial Inquiry Board's Petition of Hayward, a 1984 decision, confronted the issue of institutional integrity. Here, an Illinois appellate court upheld the quashing of a subpoena issued by the Judicial Inquiry Board against a local bar association seeking production of documents used in evaluating judges for retention election. The bar association had promised confidentiality to the lawyers and judges interviewed in order to obtain the information. The board asked for information on the judges not recommended for retention and any documents showing misconduct generally.

The court found that confidentiality was essential to the bar association's evaluations. While recognizing that the board and the bar association shared the same goal of ensuring the integrity of the judiciary, the public interest was best served by allowing the bar records to remain confidential and thus preserving the bar association's service to the public. The court rejected the argument that the board was entitled to greater deference because it was created by constitutional amendment, noting that since the state constitution also requires judges be elected by the public, it would be foolish to do damage to an important source of information about the quality of judges. The court, however, failed to address the question of how the board is to do its job if it can't get information about judicial misconduct, and did not take into account that the board also promises limited confidentiality to its witnesses.

Confidentiality

Confidentiality provisions have come under considerable challenge in the past two years, raising such issues as who should be protected by confidentiality and to what extent disciplinary proceedings should be confidential.

First, some important procedural aspects of confidentiality have been addressed recently. In Gubler v Commission on Judicial Performance, a judge successfully challenged the commission practice of issuing press releases upon filing recommendations for discipline with the high court, arguing that the public could be misled into believing that the commission findings were final, when in fact judges have 30 days to file a petition for modification or rejection before the decision is final. The court reasoned that the commission's original practice unnecessarily jeopardized public confidence in the integrity of sitting judges and, therefore, the judicial process.

In contrast, In re Alvino rejected a similar argument by a judge who requested an opportunity to persuade the New Jersey Supreme Court that a private reprimand or dismissal was appropriate instead of the judicial conduct committee's recommendation becoming public. The court reasoned that the potential for public cynicism was great where judges have the responsibility of disciplining other judges. Public confidence in the system was maintained by informing the public whenever the committee, composed of laypersons, lawyers and retired judges, recommended discipline regardless of whether the supreme court thereafter agreed or disagreed. . . .

Issues of Court Administration

Handling Court Funds. All of the recent decisions—with a single exception—order removal from office, for judges who commingle or otherwise mishandle court funds. . . .

The Judges

It is not uncommon for discipline authorities to apply an objective standard to evaluate whether a particular behavior by a judge violated Code. . . .

Federal Judicial Discipline

There is a small but growing body of law on the subject of federal judicial discipline. The Judicial Council Reform and Judicial Conduct and Disability Act of 1980[7] came into being only six years ago and its interpretation is still undergoing much revision. At present, perhaps the most interesting and relevant question being debated is the constitutionality of the act itself.

Following his acquittal on bribery charges, Judge Hastings became the subject of a complaint filed against him under the act.[8] In response, Judge Hastings filed several lawsuits, alleging, *inter alia*, that the act was unconstitutional, principally on due process grounds. In 1985, the D.C. Circuit Court of Appeals held that a determination of the validity of the act was premature because the investigation had not proceeded sufficiently. Further, Judge Hastings had the right to appeal to the Judicial Conference should he eventually be sanctioned.

However, the Eleventh Circuit Court of Appeals more recently held that, at least insofar as the investigation had proceeded, the act is constitutionally valid.[9] The court noted the D.C. Circuit decision, but stated that its holding was in fact consistent with the other circuit, because the D.C. court withheld judgment on the validity of the act since nothing had at that time taken place under the ostensible authority of the act. In contrast, the Eleventh Circuit had been asked to rule on the validity of subpoenas issued by the investigating committee against members of Judge Hastings' staff and, therefore, could extend its ruling to the constitutional validity of the act to the extent that the act had been invoked. Thus, the court held that the act did not violate the separation of power doctrine, nor did it impermissibly intrude upon the independence of judges or invade the House's exclusive authority to remove judges through impeachment proceedings.

* * *

Commissions are now proceeding against conduct that may not have been perceived as wrongful 25 years ago when the discipline apparatus was put into

---

7. 28 U.S.C. §331, 332, 372(c), 604 (1982).
8. Hastings v. Jud. Conf of U.S., 770 F.2d. 1093,1096-7 (D.C. Cir. 1985).
9. In re Certain Complaints v. Mercer, 783 F.2d 1488 (11th Cir. 1986).

place. Belittling comments to women, for example, increasingly have come under fire as part of a larger program against gender bias in the courts. It is essential, however, that the general public and members of the legal community in particular become familiar with the important decisional law being carved out in the area of judicial discipline. Lawyers must keep abreast of changes in judicial conduct law in order to better protect both themselves and their clients. Judges must stay informed in order to uphold public confidence in the judiciary.

Yvette Begue is a staff attorney with the Center for Judicial Conduct Organizations of the American Judicature Society. Candice Goldstein is Assistant Research Director of the Defense Research Institute in Chicago.

CYNTHIA GRAY, JUDICIAL DISCIPLINE IN 2003

87 Judicature 193 (2004)

In 2003, as a result of state judicial discipline proceedings, 12 judges (or former judges) were removed from office, 20 resigned or retired in lieu of discipline pursuant to agreements with judicial commissions that were made public, and one judge resigned pursuant to an agreement that also included a public reprimand. (Two more removal decisions were pending on appeal at the end of the year.) Eighty-one additional judges (or former judges in 10 cases) were publicly sanctioned in 2003. In 51 of those cases, the discipline was imposed pursuant to the consent of the judge or former judge or based on stipulated facts. Ten of these cases involved former judges, and in five of those cases, the former judge either agreed not to serve as a judge again or was barred from doing so.

There were 15 suspensions without pay with the length of the suspensions ranging from one month to one year. (Four of the suspensions also included a censure, one required the judge to have his disability adequately treated before returning to judicial duties, one was followed by a one-year probation, one required the judge to complete 20 continuing legal education credit hours on ethics, and one provided that the judge not be allowed to resume judicial duties until he completes a course for judges of limited jurisdiction courts). One additional suspension was stayed pending the judge's compliance with several conditions and will be dismissed if the conditions are timely completed. There were 21 public censures, 14 public admonishments (one admonishment also included an order of additional education), 27 public reprimands (one reprimand also included a $50,000 fine), and three public warnings (one of the warnings also included an order of additional education).

The AJS Center for Judicial Ethics reports on discipline cases and other developments in judicial ethics and discipline in the Judicial Ethics News portion of its web-site, a weekly feature at www.ajs.org/ethics/.

NOTE ON STATE JUDICIAL DISCIPLINE

The readings above give you a flavor of state judicial discipline. Focus on three aspects: who's administering the system; what penalties they have at their disposal; and the degree of transparency of the mechanism. As to the first aspect, the precise design varies widely—recall a similar variation in the methods for appointing judges. But most state systems involve persons other than the judiciary: the variation is in the proportion of non-judges and the stages at which they participate. Second, the great majority of state systems allow the removal of the judge from office as the most serious of the penalties available. And, finally, as the reports above suggest, at least the final phases of the state systems are transparent—one knows which judges have been accused of what and what the outcome of the case was. Consider how these elements play out as we look more closely at one state's experience with such a system. Conversations with the subjects of California's system—the state's judges—suggest that some find it harsh, and believe it sometimes punishes for actions that others might consider "good judging." Consider whether you think the readings bear out this assessment.

2. THE CALIFORNIA EXPERIENCE

Cal. Code of Judicial Ethics

(Sup. Ct. of Cal. 2003) (extensive commentary deleted)

CANON 1: A judge shall uphold the integrity and independence of the judiciary.

CANON 2: A judge shall avoid impropriety and the appearance of impropriety in all of the judge's activities.

CANON 3: A judge shall perform the duties of judicial office impartially and diligently.

CANON 4: A judge shall so conduct the judge's quasi-judicial and extrajudicial activities as to minimize the risk of conflict with judicial obligations

CANON 5: A judge or judicial candidate shall refrain from inappropriate political activity.

STATE OF CALIFORNIA COMMISSION ON JUDICIAL PERFORMANCE

Available online at http://cjp.ca.gov/(last visited March 20, 2006)

The Commission on Judicial Performance is the independent state agency in California responsible for investigating complaints of judicial misconduct and judicial incapacity and for disciplining judges, pursuant to article VI, section 18 of the California Constitution.

The commission's jurisdiction includes all active California state court judges. The commission also has authority to impose certain discipline on former judges and has shared authority with local courts over court commissioners and referees. The commission does not have authority over federal judges, judges pro tem or private judges.

The commission acts on complaints it receives. Anyone may submit a complaint.

TWO RECENT CALIFORNIA DISCIPLINARY CASES

Compiled from California Commission on Judicial Performance, online at
http://cjp.ca.gov/(last visited March 20, 2006)

Order of Removal of Judge Michael E. Platt, August 5, 2002

Judge Michael E. Platt of the San Joaquin County Superior Court was
ordered removed from office by the Commission on August 5, 2002, for willful
misconduct in office and conduct prejudicial to the administration of justice
that brings the judicial office into disrepute. The Commission's action concluded formal proceedings, during which there was a hearing before special
masters and an appearance before the Commission. On February 19, 2003, the
California Supreme Court denied the judge's petition for review.

The Commission determined that Judge Platt improperly ordered dismissal of three traffic tickets based on his personal relationship with a man
from whom he had borrowed $3,500, a debt that had been discharged in bank-
ruptcy. The judge dismissed a traffic ticket issued to the man and a ticket issued
to the man's niece. The judge also attempted to dismiss a ticket issued to the
man's wife. All of the judge's actions were taken after ex parte communications
from the man's wife. The Commission adopted the special masters' finding
that "ticket fixing is a quintessential bad act of a judge," and is "an abuse of
power that citizens unquestionably understand and are suspicious about." The
Commission adopted the masters' finding that when Judge Platt ordered dismissal of the tickets, he knew that his actions were wrong, although he acted
out of a desire to help others. The Commission concluded that the judge's
actions were willful misconduct.

The Commission determined that Judge Platt also improperly ordered dismissal of a traffic ticket issued to the minor son of a reserve deputy sheriff. After
ex parte communications with his courtroom bailiff about the matter, Judge
Platt initiated an ex parte communication with the California Highway Patrol
officer who had issued the ticket. Thereafter, Judge Platt caused the ticket to be
dismissed. The Commission adopted the masters' findings that the judge had
the ticket dismissed to help the son of an acquaintance, and knew when he
took the action that it was wrong. His actions were willful misconduct.

The Commission found that Judge Platt telephoned a court commissioner
and said that an individual, whom he identified by name and as the judge's
godfather, had received a traffic ticket. He also said that the man was active in
the community. The Commission found that conveying this information was
an attempt to influence the commissioner and was prejudicial misconduct.

In another instance, the Commission found that Judge Platt visited the
arraignment judge and asked him to grant an "own recognizance" release to
the defendant in a case. Judge Platt told the other judge that the defendant was
an acquaintance or family member of an acquaintance of Judge Platt's. The
Commission found that Judge Platt was attempting to use the prestige of his
office to advance the personal interests of an acquaintance; his actions constituted willful misconduct.

In another matter, the Commission found that Judge Platt telephoned
another judge about a juvenile dependency matter that was before that

judge. The case involved a parent who had been a client of Judge Platt's when he practiced law. Judge Platt told the judge about a communication he had received from one of the parents in the case. The Commission found that Judge Platt's conveyance of substantive information about the parties and the case constituted improper action.

In determining that removal was the appropriate sanction, the Commission pointed out that Judge Platt had received a private admonishment from the Commission in 1997 for soliciting attorneys who appeared before him to purchase raffle tickets for a church fundraiser and tickets to a fundraiser for a childcare center, and for selling candy bars at court to benefit his children's parochial school. The judge had been cautioned by colleagues against such activities before being admonished. The Commission noted that Judge Platt, in accepting the private admonishment, had stated in a letter that he would conduct himself and his affairs in compliance with the Code of Judicial Ethics in all areas. The Commission also stressed that Judge Platt's responses to the allegations raised concerns about his truthfulness, noting in particular that his testimony that he did not recognize an ethical problem with dismissing the tickets at the time he dismissed them was not credible. The Commission concluded that despite some factors in mitigation, removal was necessary for protection of the public, enforcement of rigorous standards of judicial conduct, and maintenance of public confidence in the integrity and independence of the judicial system.

In a separate statement of dissent setting forth her position that Judge Platt should be publicly censured, Commission member Ms. Ramona Ripston expressed the view that, in light of Judge Platt's motivations, personal history, and record as a judge, as well as his public and private apologies, unequivocal acceptance of responsibility, and effort to improve future performance, public censure would be adequate discipline.

Commission members Judge Risë Jones Pichon, Justice Vance W. Raye, Ms. Lara Bergthold, Judge Madeleine I. Flier, Mr. Marshall B. Grossman, Mr. Michael A. Kahn, Mrs. Crystal Lui, Ms. Barbara Schraeger, and Dr. Betty L. Wyman voted in favor of all the findings and conclusions, and in the removal of Judge Platt from office. Commission member Ms. Ramona Ripston voted in favor of all the findings and conclusions, but voted to publicly censure Judge Platt. One public member position was vacant at the time of the decision.

Decision and Order Imposing Public Admonishment on Judge Joseph W. O'Flaherty, September 29, 2004

By its Notice of Formal Proceedings, the Commission on Judicial Performance (the Commission) has charged Placer County Superior Court Judge Joseph W. O'Flaherty with two counts each of willful misconduct in office, conduct prejudicial to the administration of justice that brings the judicial office into disrepute, and improper action within the meaning of article VI, section 18 of the California Constitution.

In December 1999, Judge O'Flaherty presided over a jury trial in the case of People v. Joy Ann Mello (Placer County Superior Court case No. 62-7093). Ms. Mello, an African-American, was charged with second degree robbery and false imprisonment. [T]he prospective jurors were sworn to tell the truth during voir dire concerning their qualifications and competency. As a resident of Placer County for 23 years, Judge O'Flaherty has become familiar with the demographics of the county. According to the judge, the jury venire panels in 1999 were almost entirely Caucasian.

His recollection is that during voir dire in the Mello case, the jury panel was overwhelmingly Caucasian, and Ms. Mello was the only African-American in the courtroom. Concerned that racial bias could impact the verdict, Judge O'Flaherty instructed the panel:

> "Now, a touchy subject. Some of these voir dire issues are kind of touchy here. If you feel that an issue is so sensitive that you'd rather not answer it in front of all these people, we can arrange so that it would be the Court, myself, the two attorneys, the defendant and the court reporter, but some of these questions do need to be asked.
>
> "All right. Here's a sensitive one. The defendant is African American. Okay. Almost everybody in this courtroom is white, Caucasian.
>
> "Now, race simply does not — I don't want any racism in my court, which most of you know by now, but I go a little further than that.
>
> "I recognize that most people in today's age don't want to raise their hand and say I am a bigot or I'm a racist. So what I'm going to do, if any of you have the slightest doubt that you might not, for racial reasons, be able to give this defendant a fair trial, I'm going to give you permission to lie.
>
> "I want you to tell me — there's plenty of other reasons, which you as intelligent people know that you can dream up, how you will not — you can get out of sitting here.
>
> "Okay. I want you to come up with something so that you can get out of sitting here. I don't want that issue to raise its head in this courtroom. All right. Can everybody assure me of that?"

Judge O'Flaherty decided to give this instruction either on the morning of the trial or on the previous day. This was the first time he had given such an instruction. Although Judge O'Flaherty has previously presided over at least 10 jury trials involving minority defendants he had no direct evidence that jurors had lied during voir dire to cover up their racial prejudice. He was, however, still concerned that some jurors might not acknowledge racial animus, and he wanted to give them a way to get off the jury. . . . Judge O'Flaherty testified that when he gave this instruction, he was looking for any kind of false excuse that would get the person with racial animus off the jury. Typical excuses jurors might give would be that they had a business to attend to or that the type of crime would engender prejudice on their part. Judge O'Flaherty gave a number of reasons for instructing the jurors to lie. One rationale for the instruction related to a prior case involving a minority defendant, in which a prospective juror admitted during voir dire that he did not think he could be fair " 'because the defendant is Mexican.' " . . . Finally, the judge explained that he had had conversations with criminal defense attorneys who complained that jurors in Placer County were not giving minority defendants a "fair shake."

Judge O'Flaherty thought that the Mello trial was a " 'perfect storm' " for the problem of a jury finding the defendant guilty due to his race. According to the judge, there were three elements which made the case a " 'perfect storm' ": (1) the defendant was of a different race than the jury; (2) the facts of the case were inflammatory; and (3) there was a perception in Placer County that criminals were invading the county to commit crimes. . . .

[The opinion went on to recount a similar statement to prospective jurors in the Abbaszadeh case:]

> "Now, you probably all know that race and nationality have no place in this courtroom. The very integrity of the system that has developed in the last several generations depends on that we keep this social problem at least out of the courtroom.
>
> "Now, obviously being labeled a bigot or a racist, this sort of thing, is insulting to most people. And so it's entirely possible that if you harbor these types of feelings that you may not want to raise your hand and basically put a sign on yourself saying: I am a racist, etcetera.
>
> "I don't want somebody who harbors those types of feelings sitting on this jury, for obvious reasons.
>
> "So I would ask that you do whatever you have to do to get off the jury. And it's much more important, in my opinion, that you get off the jury, even if, you know, you have to answer my questions in such a way that you get off in some other way, then do it.
>
> "Does everybody understand that? . . .

Judge O'Flaherty acknowledged at the hearing that it was a "mistake to do it" (give the instructions) and "I feel real badly about it." Judge O'Flaherty submitted the declarations of five Abbaszadeh jurors and two Mello jurors. In general, the jurors found Judge O'Flaherty to be a fair judge who conducted the trial in an appropriate manner. Several jurors commented that Judge O'Flaherty was sensitive to racial issues and emphasized that individuals with racial animus should not serve on the jury. . . .

Having considered all the evidence, the Special Masters find there is clear and convincing proof that Judge O'Flaherty's actions in instructing potential jurors to (1) lie during voir dire in Mello, and (2) violate their oath in Abbaszadeh, constitute conduct prejudicial to the administration of justice that brings the judicial office into disrepute, as alleged in counts one and two. We further find that the Commission has failed to prove by clear and convincing evidence that Judge O'Flaherty committed willful misconduct. The Commission has asserted that Judge O'Flaherty acted with knowledge that his actions were beyond lawful judicial power and/or that he acted with a conscious disregard for the limits of his judicial authority. We do not agree. We accept Judge O'Flaherty's explanation that he believed in good faith that he was acting within his lawful judicial authority, without a conscious disregard for the limits of his judicial power. . . .

Judge's O'Flaherty's conduct would appear to an objective observer to be prejudicial to public esteem for the judicial office. It is uncontroverted that the jurors were sworn to tell the truth in the presence of Judge O'Flaherty. He thereafter directed and encouraged them to ignore and violate that oath. Such action on its face cannot be reconciled by any objective observer to be anything but prejudicial to public esteem for the judicial office. The public expects and embraces the concept that a judge shall be faithful to the law. This is so fundamental to a system of justice that it serves as a basic cornerstone of public confidence.

In addition, such conduct casts doubt upon whether the jury selected in each case was truly fair and impartial. Rather than providing a probing examination by the court and counsel to determine if racial bias existed, Judge O'Flaherty's actions allowed jurors to create excuses to avoid jury service thereby depriving the defendants of a jury drawn from a fair and representative cross-section of the community. . . .

Judge O'Flaherty asserts that his instructions should not subject him to discipline because he was condoning lying only in limited or narrowly-defined circumstances. We could not disagree more. Lying of any kind is never appropriate in a court of law, the very existence of which is the ascertainment of the truth. White lies, limited lying, carefully-defined permissible lying are at the edge of a slippery slope that we decline to even approach. We cannot conceive that any judicial complicity in any lying in any courtroom ever could be proper, no matter how laudable any other goal the lying may be thought to advance. . . .

STATE OF CALIFORNIA COMMISSION ON JUDICIAL PERFORMANCE, SUMMARY OF DISCIPLINE STATISTICS, 1990-1999

Available online at http://www.cjp.ca.gov/Miscellaneous/Web%20Version.rtf (last visited March 20, 2006)

This report summarizes statistics concerning cases in which discipline was imposed by the Commission on Judicial Performance, or imposed by the California Supreme Court on recommendation by the Commission,[10] during the years 1990 through 1999. . . .

Tables 2-A, 2-B, 2-C: Age Comparison

As noted above, for purposes of this study, the age of the judges disciplined was calculated as of the earliest occurrence of the misconduct in the case.

Table 2-A sets forth disciplinary rates according to the judges' ages for each year as well as ten-year average rates. Although the size of each subgroup varies, the use of rates standardizes the subgroups to permit comparisons, as discussed on page 3. The ten-year average disciplinary rates are as follows:

Age	Disciplinary Rate [Per Thousand Judges]
30 through 39 years	42.2
40 through 49 years	31.8
50 through 59 years	32.0
60 years and over	28.9
Entire judiciary	**31.4**

* * *

---

10. Prior to the amendment of the California Constitution in 1995, the California Supreme Court was responsible for imposing censures and ordering judges removed from office. Since 1995, that responsibility has been vested in the Commission, subject to discretionary review by the Supreme Court upon the judge's petition.

Tables 3-A, 3-B, 3-C: Initially Appointed Versus Initially Elected Comparison

For purposes of this study, each judge's status was determined according to whether the judge *initially* assumed office by appointment or election. Subsequent elevations and retention elections were not considered.

Table 3-A sets forth disciplinary rates according to whether the judges were initially appointed or elected to office for each year as well as ten-year averages. Although the size of each subgroup varies, the use of rates standardizes the subgroups to permit comparisons, as discussed on page 3. The ten-year average disciplinary rates are as follows:

Initially Assumed Office	Disciplinary Rate [Per Thousand Judges]
Appointed	29.8
Elected	43.6
Entire judiciary	**31.4**

* * *

Trial Court Size	Disciplinary Rate [Per Thousand Judges]
Counties with 1-2 authorized positions	56.7
Counties with 3-9 authorized positions	52.5
Counties with 10-42 authorized positions	39.8
Counties with 43-428 authorized positions	29.1
All trial courts	**33.8**

* * *

Type of Misconduct	Percentage of Total Discipline
Demeanor/decorum	13.4%
Bias/appearance of bias (not toward a particular class)	9.8%
Disqualification/disclosure and related retaliation	9.3%
On-bench abuse of authority—in performance of judicial duties	7.9%
Ex parte communications	7.6%
Decisional delay/tardiness/attendance/other dereliction of duty	6.9%
Failure to ensure rights	6.8%
Off-bench abuse of office	6.8%
Abuse of contempt/sanctions	6.2%

3. THE FEDERAL SYSTEM OF DISCIPLINE

NOTE ON COMPARING STATE AND FEDERAL JUDICIAL DISCIPLINE SYSTEMS

Just as the states and the federal systems select judges differently, so they operate divergent systems of judicial discipline. In the not-too-distant past there was no system of federal judicial discipline short of impeachment. Some argued that it was unnecessary because federal judges went through a more rigorous selection process. Others argued that such a system would violate Article III. Congress has disagreed with these propositions, and has in occasional hearings and by statute pressured the federal judiciary to exercise more oversight over its members — and to be more transparent about its efforts to do so. The statute below is the most recent and most elaborate provision for such sub-impeachment discipline. Following the statute are several press accounts of behavior calling forth discipline, and a case in which a federal district judge inconclusively challenged the disciplinary apparatus. As you read the accounts, consider what might have happened to a judge in, say, California who had displayed the same behavior.

---

28 U.S.C. Chapter 16, Complaints Against Judges and Judicial Discipline

---

§351. Complaints; judge defined

(a) Filing of complaint by any person. Any person alleging that a judge has engaged in conduct prejudicial to the effective and expeditious administration of the business of the courts, or alleging that such judge is unable to discharge all the duties of office by reason of mental or physical disability, may file with the clerk of the court of appeals for the circuit a written complaint containing a brief statement of the facts constituting such conduct.

(b) Identifying complaint by chief judge. In the interests of the effective and expeditious administration of the business of the courts and on the basis of information available to the chief judge of the circuit, the chief judge may, by written order stating reasons therefor, identify a complaint for purposes of this chapter and thereby dispense with filing of a written complaint. . . .

§352. Review of complaint by chief judge

(a) Expeditious review; limited inquiry. The chief judge shall expeditiously review any complaint received under section 351(a) or identified under section 351(b). In determining what action to take, the chief judge may conduct a limited inquiry for the purpose of determining —

(1) whether appropriate corrective action has been or can be taken without the necessity for a formal investigation; and

(2) whether the facts stated in the complaint are either plainly untrue or are incapable of being established through investigation.

For this purpose, the chief judge may request the judge whose conduct is complained of to file a written response to the complaint. Such response shall not be made available to the complainant unless authorized by the judge filing the response. The chief judge or his or her designee may also communicate orally or in writing with the complainant, the judge whose conduct is complained of, and any other person who may have knowledge of the matter, and may review any transcripts or other relevant documents. The chief judge shall not undertake to make findings of fact about any matter that is reasonably in dispute.

(b) Action by chief judge following review. After expeditiously reviewing a complaint under subsection (a), the chief judge, by written order stating his or her reasons, may —

(1) dismiss the complaint —

(A) if the chief judge finds the complaint to be —

(i) not in conformity with section 351(a);

(ii) directly related to the merits of a decision or procedural ruling; or

(iii) frivolous, lacking sufficient evidence to raise an inference that misconduct has occurred, or containing allegations which are incapable of being established through investigation; or

(B) when a limited inquiry conducted under subsection (a) demonstrates that the allegations in the complaint lack any factual foundation or are conclusively refuted by objective evidence; or

(2) conclude the proceeding if the chief judge finds that appropriate corrective action has been taken or that action on the complaint is no longer necessary because of intervening events.

The chief judge shall transmit copies of the written order to the complainant and to the judge whose conduct is the subject of the complaint.

(c) Review of orders of chief judge. A complainant or judge aggrieved by a final order of the chief judge under this section may petition the judicial council of the circuit for review thereof. The denial of a petition for review of the chief judge's order shall be final and conclusive and shall not be judicially reviewable on appeal or otherwise.

(d) Referral of petitions for review to panels of the judicial council. Each judicial council may, pursuant to rules prescribed under section 358, refer a petition for review filed under subsection (c) to a panel of no fewer than 5 members of the council, at least 2 of whom shall be district judges.

§353. Special committees

(a) Appointment. If the chief judge does not enter an order under section 352(b), the chief judge shall promptly —

(1) appoint himself or herself and equal numbers of circuit and district judges of the circuit to a special committee to investigate the facts and allegations contained in the complaint;

(2) certify the complaint and any other documents pertaining thereto to each member of such committee; and

(3) provide written notice to the complainant and the judge whose conduct is the subject of the complaint of the action taken under this subsection. . . .

(c) Investigation by special committee. Each committee appointed under subsection (a) shall conduct an investigation as extensive as it considers necessary, and shall expeditiously file a comprehensive written report thereon with the judicial council of the circuit. Such report shall present both the findings of the investigation and the committee's recommendations for necessary and appropriate action by the judicial council of the circuit.

§354. Action by judicial council

(a) Actions upon receipt of report.

(1) Actions. The judicial council of a circuit, upon receipt of a report filed under section 353(c) —

(A) may conduct any additional investigation which it considers to be necessary;

(B) may dismiss the complaint; and

(C) if the complaint is not dismissed, shall take such action as is appropriate to assure the effective and expeditious administration of the business of the courts within the circuit.

(2) Description of possible actions if complaint not dismissed.

(A) In general. Action by the judicial council under paragraph (1)(C) may include —

(i) ordering that, on a temporary basis for a time certain, no further cases be assigned to the judge whose conduct is the subject of a complaint;

(ii) censuring or reprimanding such judge by means of private communication; and

(iii) censuring or reprimanding such judge by means of public announcement.

(B) For Article III judges. If the conduct of a judge appointed to hold office during good behavior is the subject of the complaint, action by the judicial council under paragraph (1)(C) may include —

(i) certifying disability of the judge pursuant to the procedures and standards provided under section 372(b); and

(ii) requesting that the judge voluntarily retire, with the provision that the length of service requirements under section 371 of this title shall not apply. . . .

(3) Limitations on judicial council regarding removals.

(A) Article III judges. Under no circumstances may the judicial council order removal from office of any judge appointed to hold office during good behavior. . . .

(b) Referral to judicial conference.

(1) In general. In addition to the authority granted under subsection (a), the judicial council may, in its discretion, refer any complaint under section 351, together with the record of any associated proceedings and its recommendations for appropriate action, to the Judicial Conference of the United States.

(2) Special circumstances. In any case in which the judicial council determines, on the basis of a complaint and an investigation under this chapter, or on the basis of information otherwise available to the judicial council, that a judge appointed to hold office during good behavior may have engaged in conduct —

(A) which might constitute one or more grounds for impeachment under article II of the Constitution, or

(B) which, in the interest of justice, is not amenable to resolution by the judicial council,

the judicial council shall promptly certify such determination, together with any complaint and a record of any associated proceedings, to the Judicial Conference of the United States. . . .

§355. Action by judicial conference

(a) In general. Upon referral or certification of any matter under section 354(b), the Judicial Conference, after consideration of the prior proceedings and such additional investigation as it considers appropriate, shall by majority vote take such action, as described in section 354(a)(1)(C) and (2), as it considers appropriate.

(b) If impeachment warranted.

(1) In general. If the Judicial Conference concurs in the determination of the judicial council, or makes its own determination, that consideration of impeachment may be warranted, it shall so certify and transmit the determination and the record of proceedings to the House of Representatives for whatever action the House of Representatives considers to be necessary. Upon receipt of the determination and record of proceedings in the House of Representatives, the Clerk of the House of Representatives shall make available to the public the determination and any reasons for the determination.

(2) In case of felony conviction. If a judge has been convicted of a felony under State or Federal law and has exhausted all means of obtaining direct review of the conviction, or the time for seeking further direct review of the conviction has passed and no such review has been sought, the Judicial Conference may, by majority vote and without referral or certification under section 354(b), transmit to the House of Representatives a determination that consideration of impeachment may be warranted, together with appropriate court records, for whatever action the House of Representatives considers to be necessary.

§357. Review of orders and actions

(a) Review of action of judicial council. A complainant or judge aggrieved by an action of the judicial council under section 354 may petition the Judicial Conference of the United States for review thereof.

(b) Action of Judicial Conference. The Judicial Conference, or the standing committee established under section 331, may grant a petition filed by a complainant or judge under subsection (a).

(c) No judicial review. Except as expressly provided in this section and section 352(c), all orders and determinations, including denials of petitions for review, shall be final and conclusive and shall not be judicially reviewable on appeal or otherwise. . . .

§360. Disclosure of information

(a) Confidentiality of proceedings. Except as provided in section 355, all papers, documents, and records of proceedings related to investigations conducted under this chapter shall be confidential and shall not be disclosed by any person in any proceeding except to the extent that—

(1) the judicial council of the circuit in its discretion releases a copy of a report of a special committee under section 353(c) to the complainant whose complaint initiated the investigation by that special committee and to the judge whose conduct is the subject of the complaint;

(2) the judicial council of the circuit, the Judicial Conference of the United States, or the Senate or the House of Representatives by resolution, releases any such material which is believed necessary to an impeachment investigation or trial of a judge under article I of the Constitution; or

(3) such disclosure is authorized in writing by the judge who is the subject of the complaint and by the chief judge of the circuit, the Chief Justice, or the chairman of the standing committee established under section 33.

(b) Public availability of written orders. Each written order to implement any action under section 354(a)(1)(C), which is issued by a judicial council, the Judicial Conference, or the standing committee established under section 331, shall be made available to the public through the appropriate clerk's office of the court of appeals for the circuit. Unless contrary to the interests of justice, each such order shall be accompanied by written reasons therefor.

§361. Reimbursement of expenses

Upon the request of a judge whose conduct is the subject of a complaint under this chapter, the judicial council may, if the complaint has been finally dismissed under section 354(a)(1)(B), recommend that the Director of the Administrative Office of the United States Courts award reimbursement, from funds appropriated to the Federal judiciary, for those reasonable expenses, including attorneys' fees, incurred by that judge during the investigation which would not have been incurred but for the requirements of this chapter.

John Council, Panel Sends McBryde Stinging Rebuke: In Unprecedented Move, Group Suspends Judge's New Case Assignments

Texas Lawyer, September 28, 1998, at 1

In an unprecedented ruling, a national judicial panel has affirmed a decision stopping the assignment of new cases to U.S. District Judge John McBryde of Fort Worth for one year.

The Sept. 18 decision by the Judicial Conference of the United States marks the only time a federal judge's case assignments have been temporarily suspended for disciplinary reasons since the Judicial Misconduct and Disability

Act was passed by Congress in 1980. It is one of the harshest punishments possible, save an impeachment recommendation. Only Congress can impeach a federal judge.

In federal circles, the decision is considered a landmark because it directly addresses for the first time the question of how far federal judges can go in policing their own behavior.

McBryde will continue to preside over hundreds of cases that are still on his docket, but will stop receiving new cases as of the date the order was issued. He cannot appeal the decision.

"As you could imagine, he's disappointed," says David Broiles, a partner in Fort Worth's Kirkley Schmidt & Cotten, who represents McBryde. "I'm disappointed and hope that there's a way that we can see this through and possibly remedy it. But we'll see."

McBryde declines to comment.

Up until the Judicial Conference's decision was released two weeks ago, none of the primary documents used to support the disciplinary action against McBryde had been made public. The recent decision sheds some light on the extraordinary action by the 5th U.S. Circuit Court of Appeals' Judicial Council late last year, which had grown weary of McBryde's intemperate behavior and "abusive" treatment of lawyers and decided to suspend his new case assignments. The Judicial Conference is an oversight body for the federal judiciary. It acts as an appellate court concerning administrative actions taken against federal judges.

The Judicial Conference's decision, In re: Complaints of Judicial Misconduct or Disability, No. 98-372-001, seeks to give McBryde a period of "deep reflection" and even offers to lift the penalty early if he corrects his behavior. But it also presents a question as to whether such a punishment violates the U.S. Constitution by infringing on the independence of a federal judge.

The Decisions

The 5th Circuit's Judicial Council began investigating McBryde in 1995 after an attorney filed a complaint alleging that the judge had been "obstructive, abusive and hostile" during a trial.

On Dec. 31, 1997 the Judicial Council issued its order and reprimand stopping the flow of new cases into McBryde's court after two years of investigations and closed-door hearings in which dozens of lawyers testified about the judge's actions—hearings McBryde attended. In its own precedent-setting ruling, the council minced no words about its displeasure with McBryde.

Quoting from the Judicial Council's decision, the Judicial Conference wrote: "Judge McBryde's intemperate, abusive and intimidating treatment of lawyers, fellow judges, and others has detrimentally affected the effective administration of justice and the business of the courts in the Northern District of Texas. Judge McBryde has abused judicial power, imposed unwarranted sanctions on lawyers, and repeatedly and unjustifiably attacked individual lawyers and groups of lawyers and court personnel."

But the council suspended the implementation of the sanction, giving McBryde the opportunity to appeal the action to the Judicial Conference, which he did.

In its decision, a conference committee — a body of five federal judges — did not reveal the specific supporting evidence presented to the 5th Circuit's Judicial Council. That information remains confidential. McBryde had wanted the proceedings to be public, but his request was denied by 5th Circuit Chief Judge Henry A. Politz.

The conference's decision, written by Judge William J. Bauer, an Illinois judge on the 7th U.S. Circuit Court of Appeals, clearly stated that the action was not being taken because of rulings by McBryde. "The sanctions are not based upon the legal merits of the judge's orders and rulings on the bench, but on the pattern of conduct that is evidenced by those orders and rulings," Bauer wrote.

The punishment fits within the guidelines of the Judicial Conduct and Disability Act of 1980, 28 U.S.C. §372, the opinion stated. The act authorizes the suspension of a federal judge's caseload for various reasons, including if the jurist is suffering from a disability or is a defendant in a criminal action.

The decision made it clear that the suspension was meant to be remedial instead of punitive and compares the suspension to one given to a judge who has a substance abuse problem.

"The purpose of this suspension of new case assignments, therefore, is the same as in the case of a remedial suspension of new cases for a judge with a substance abuse problem, or with some other physical or mental problem, who refuses to take steps to confront the problem," Bauer wrote.

The opinion noted that McBryde has refused to acknowledge the impropriety of his actions and has not given any indication that he has a problem. If he becomes more contrite in the future, the sanction could be lifted before the one-year suspension has elapsed, Bauer wrote.

"In keeping with the purely remedial nature of the suspension, however, the suspension should not continue once it has fairly achieved its remedial purpose," Bauer wrote.

Constitutional?

There is no doubt that the Judicial Conference embarked into uncharted legal waters with its decision, lawyers say.

Because such a penalty has never been issued, it raises a constitutional question that is central to McBryde's defense: Does such an action violate the independence of the judiciary? . . .

Reaction

In Fort Worth, where courts and lawyers enjoy a friendly, laid-back reputation, news of the punishment of the town's most feared jurist was not met with glee.

Even some lawyers who have been on the receiving end of McBryde's barbs seemed sad that the disciplinary action had to go as far as it did.

"I don't think anyone will applaud it," says Mike Heiskell, a Fort Worth federal criminal-defense attorney. "I think it's regrettable that it came to this. It could have been avoided but Judge McBryde chose to do things his way."

About 20 North Texas lawyers who testified during McBryde's disciplinary proceedings, including Heiskell, have had all of their cases removed from

McBryde's court and reassigned to other courts by a 5th Circuit ruling earlier this year. That ruling promises that none of their future cases will be assigned to McBryde for a period of three years. The Judicial Conference also affirmed that decision.

Still, that's of little comfort to outspoken lawyers like Art Brender, who testified during McBryde's disciplinary hearings and has openly criticized the judge. Brender has a federal civil practice in Fort Worth.

"Some of us are kind of concerned that at the end of the three years that he's really going to come down on us," Brender says. "I'm just going to be concerned that Judge McBryde has not given up on that sort of thinking that prompted all of this."

Brender and other Fort Worth attorneys say that McBryde is no doubt a brilliant jurist. But his actions, like freely sanctioning lawyers, sending them to remedial reading courses for misinterpreting his orders and examining witnesses when he disapproves of attorneys' lines of questioning, [are] too much to bear. Some lawyers even charge clients more if they have to appear in McBryde's courtroom.

In the meantime, the Northern District of Texas will partially lose one of its most efficient judges in McBryde by taking him out of the new case loop. As of March 31, McBryde and Lubbock's Samuel R. Cummings were the only district judges in the Northern District with no civil cases on their dockets that were older than three years. . . .

As for McBryde, some observers wonder whether the finality of the decision will have any impact on him.

"It has elements of both rehabilitation and punishment," says James W. Paulsen, an associate professor at South Texas College of Law affiliated with Texas A&M University. "For a person with the prestige of a federal judge, the shame of shutting down their court for a year is extremely substantial. And if indeed the cause of the problems is overwork and pressure, then it may well have a good effect."

But telling a grown man that he has to behave may not get the desired results, says David Keltner, a Fort Worth civil appellate lawyer and former 2nd Court of Appeals judge. That's especially true for McBryde, who is extremely independent and has fought the disciplinary action every step of the way. . . .

The Honorable John H. McBryde v. Comm. to Review Circuit Council Conduct & Disability Orders of the Judicial Conference of the United States

264 F.3d 52 (D.C. Cir. 2001)

Williams, Circuit Judge:

On December 31, 1997 the Judicial Council of the Fifth Circuit (the "Judicial Council" or "Council"), acting under the Judicial Conduct and Disability Act of 1980, 28 U.S.C. §372(c) (the "Act"), imposed sanctions on the Honorable John H. McBryde, United States District Judge for the Northern District of Texas. The sanctions followed a two-year investigation by a Special Committee of the Judicial Council ("Special Committee"), including nine days of hearings. The Committee took evidence relating to incidents spanning the entirety of

Judge McBryde's judicial career and involving encounters with judges and lawyers both inside and outside his courtroom. (We will consider an example from the exhaustive record when we address Judge McBryde's argument that the Council illegally considered the merits of his judicial decisions.)

The investigation culminated in a 159-page report in which the Special Committee concluded that "Judge McBryde had engaged for a number of years in a pattern of abusive behavior" that was "'prejudicial to the effective and expeditious administration of the business of the courts.'" The Report also recommended a variety of sanctions based on the provisions of §372(c)(6)(B):

- that Judge McBryde receive a public reprimand, pursuant to subsection (v);
- that no new cases be assigned to him for a year, pursuant to subsection (iv);
- and that he not be allowed for three years to preside over cases involving any of 23 lawyers who had participated in the investigation, pursuant to subsection (vii) (providing for "other action" considered appropriate in light of circumstances).

The Judicial Council endorsed the recommendations and issued an order imposing the recommended sanctions. The lawyer-related disqualification became effective on February 6, 1998, but the Council stayed the reprimand and the one-year suspension pending review by the Committee to Review Circuit Council Conduct and Disability Orders of the Judicial Conference of the United States (the "Review Committee"). On September 18, 1998 the Review Committee substantially affirmed the Council's action and lifted the stay.

Soon thereafter Judge McBryde brought suit in district court, claiming that the Act, both facially and as applied, violated the due process clause and the Constitution's separation of powers doctrine. He also claimed that the initiation and conduct of the investigation against him exceeded the authority granted by the statute. Finally, he posed a First Amendment challenge to the Act's restrictions on disclosing the record of the proceedings. On cross motions for summary judgment, the district court agreed with Judge McBryde's First Amendment argument, but rejected the rest. Only Judge McBryde appealed; here he repeats the essence of his remaining arguments.

Judge McBryde's claims are moot insofar as they distinctively relate to the one-year suspension, which expired on September 18, 1999, and the three-year disqualification, which expired on February 6, 2001. Certain of the non-moot claims are barred by the Act's preclusion of judicial review, 28 U.S.C. §372(c)(10), namely the "as applied" and statutory challenges; the district court was therefore without jurisdiction to hear them. We vacate the district court's judgment insofar as it addressed the moot or precluded issues. Judge McBryde's remaining constitutional challenges fail on their merits; we therefore affirm the district court's ruling. We address first mootness, then preclusion, and finally the merits. . . .

* * *

[Mootness]

The one-year and three-year bans have expired. No relief sought in this case would return to Judge McBryde the cases he was not assigned or otherwise improve his current situation. These claims will therefore be moot. . . .

The dispute over the public reprimand, however, remains alive. Any thought that the reprimand is a past and irreversible harm is belied by the fact that it continues to be posted on the web site of the Fifth Circuit Court of Appeals, link on the home page alongside items for current use such as the court's calendar and opinions. Even absent that use of modern technology it would be a part of the historical record. Were Judge McBryde to prevail on the merits it would be within our power to declare unlawful the defendants' issuance of stigmatizing reports and thereby to relieve Judge McBryde of much of the resulting injury. . . .

Although the injury to Judge McBryde's reputation preserves the public reprimand from mootness and affords standing, yet another question remains about our jurisdiction. The statute enabling the Judicial Council and Review Committee to consider Judge McBryde's conduct sets out the avenues through which a judge may challenge actions taken against him. 28 U.S.C. §372(c)(10). It allows a petition to the Judicial Conference for review of a decision of the judicial council taken under §372(c)(6). It then appears to preclude alternative avenues of review:

> Except as expressly provided in this paragraph, all orders and determinations, including denials of petitions for review, shall be final and conclusive and shall not be judicially reviewable on appeal or otherwise.

28 U.S.C. §372(c)(10). Twice in the past this provision has appeared before us, but on neither occasion did we need to resolve its meaning. [citations omitted]

There are some claims that this section definitely does *not* preclude. The statutory language closely parallels that construed in Johnson v. Robison, 415 U.S. 361 (1974), where Congress provided that "decisions" of the Veterans Administration "on any question of law or fact" under certain laws "shall be final and conclusive," and expressly withheld jurisdiction from any court to review "any such decision." The Court held that §211(a) had no application to challenges to the constitutionality of the statutes in question, i.e., challenges to the decisions of Congress, not the Veterans Administration. This interpretation allowed the Court to avoid the " 'serious constitutional question' " that would be posed "if a federal statute were construed to deny any judicial forum for a colorable constitutional claim." Webster v. Doe, 486 U.S. 592 (1988). Similarly, the wording of §372(c)(10) does not withhold jurisdiction over Judge McBryde's claims that the *Act* unconstitutionally impairs judicial independence and violates separation of powers.

This leaves four claims in addition to the facial constitutional challenges. Two of these four also invoke the Constitution, challenging the actions of the defendants in applying the Act to Judge McBryde. The first claim is that the defendants inflicted their sanction without providing him due process. This claim principally involves an assertion that the whole project arose out of a conflict between himself and then-Chief Judge Politz, whose actions furthering the investigation Judge McBryde regards as "retaliation" and who, he claims, combined "investigative, charging, prosecutorial and adjudicative functions." Judge McBryde argues, in effect, that he was denied due process because Judge Politz refused to recuse himself. The second constitutional claim is somewhat obscure. He argues, in essence, that the *methods* used by the Judicial Council and Judicial Conference in imposing the sanction, were particularly invasive and therefore violated judicial independence. He cites two examples. When the Review Committee amended the Judicial Council's order so as to permit reinstatement if the council found that Judge McBryde had "seized the opportunity for self-appraisal and deep reflection in good faith," Judicial Conference Report at 24, it engaged (he says) in forbidden "judicial behavior modification." And the Judicial Council's use of psychiatrists for advice on Judge McBryde's mental health, and on the possible causes of his conduct, was "fundamentally destructive of judicial independence."

. . . We conclude that §372(c)(10) bars all four challenges.

[The statute satisfied due process because, as the D.C. Circuit read the legislative history, it permitted constitutional review by the Judicial Conference of the United States; that conclusion put the D.C. Circuit at odds with the Judicial Conference, which had disavowed any powers of appellate review over such orders:]

We note that the Judicial Conference committee has disclaimed authority to rule on as applied, as well as facial, constitutional challenges:

> We have no competence to adjudicate the facial constitutionality of the statute or its constitutional application to the speech of an accused judge, however inappropriate or offensive his words may be. We are not a court. Our decisions are not subject to review by the Supreme Court of the United States. We sit in review of the action of the Circuit Council. The courts of the United States are open for the adjudication of such questions.

Judicial Conference Report at 21, quoting its decision in No. 84-372-001. The committee offered no reason for this position. While we apply deference under Chevron, U.S.A., Inc. v. NRDC, 467 U.S. 837 (1984), to agencies' jurisdictional decisions, the statutory mandate to the committee appears to contain no language justifying a decision to disregard claims that a circuit judicial council has violated a judge's constitutional rights in application of the Act. To be sure, agencies ordinarily lack jurisdiction to " 'adjudicate . . . the constitutionality of congressional enactments.' " . . . But agencies do have "an obligation to address properly presented constitutional claims which . . . do not challenge agency actions mandated by Congress." We can see neither any reason why Congress would have withdrawn that power and obligation from a reviewing "agency" composed exclusively of Article III judges nor any indication that it has done so.

[After a long review of the legislative history, the opinion concluded that the Conference was wrong in taking this view of the matter:]

It seems fair to suppose that both houses of Congress realistically expected that the Judicial Conference would hear all *serious* claims. Indeed, explaining its rejection of the Senate proposal for a new court, the House Judiciary Committee only expressed concern that its formal character would unduly invite complaints *against* judges and thereby threaten judicial independence. . . .

In short, we find the evidence clear and convincing that Congress intended §372(c)(10) to preclude review in the courts for as-applied constitutional claims. Members of Congress were aware of *Robison* and more generally of doctrines presuming access to Article III review of decisions impinging on important interests. Put ultimately to a choice between review by an Article III "Court" and review by a committee of Article III judges chosen by and from the Judicial Conference, they chose the latter. They did so in order to protect judges from the "chilling" effects of unnecessary complaints, not with any expectation that the Judicial Conference would scant judges' rights . . .

* * *

Judge McBryde makes two related facial constitutional challenges that survive both mootness and preclusion. First, he reads the clause vesting the impeachment power in Congress as precluding *all* other methods of disciplining judges; on this theory, the Act violates separation of powers doctrine. Second, he says that the principle of judicial independence implicit in Article III bars discipline of judges for actions *in any way* connected to his actions while on the bench.

[The court rejected both challenges, saying about the second:]

It may help put Judge McBryde's theory in perspective to look at one of the many episodes that led to the present sanctions. In 1992, Judge McBryde sanctioned a lawyer appearing before him for failing to have her client attend a settlement conference in violation of Judge McBryde's standard pretrial order, which required all principals to attend the conferences. Counsel represented a corporation and its employee, defendants in a suit in which plaintiffs, a woman and her 10-year old daughter, had alleged sexual harassment. One of the allegations was that the individual defendant "had terrorized the 10-year old . . . by popping out his glass eye and putting it in his mouth in front of her." The lawyer thought the presence of the individual defendant would be counter-productive to settlement efforts; the individual had no assets and had given her full authority to settle.

After chastising the lawyer, Judge McBryde required that she attend a reading comprehension course and submit an affidavit swearing to her compliance. The attorney submitted an affidavit attesting to the fact that she found a course and attended for three hours a week for five weeks. Judge McBryde challenged her veracity and required that she submit a supplemental affidavit "listing 'each day that she was in personal attendance at a reading comprehension course in compliance with [the] court's order; the place where she was in attendance on each date; the course title of each course; how long she was in attendance on each day; and the name of a person who can verify her attendance for each day listed.'" She complied. The Special Committee characterized this incident as reflecting a "gross abuse of power and a complete lack of empathy." Judge McBryde tells us that the defendants unconstitutionally impugn judicial independence when they express a formal, institutional condemnation of this sort.

We assume arguendo that the procedures of the Act may not constitutionally be used as a substitute for appeal. But Judge McBryde's theory plainly goes well beyond judicial acts realistically susceptible of correction through the avenues of appeal, mandamus, etc. Appeal is a most improbable avenue of redress for someone like the hapless counsel bludgeoned into taking reading comprehension courses and into filing demeaning affidavits, all completely marginal to the case on which she was working. Possibly she could have secured review by defying his orders, risking contempt and prison. But we are all at a loss to see why those should be the only remedies, why the Constitution, in the name of "judicial independence," can be seen as condemning the judiciary to silence in the face of such conduct. Counsel punched out by the judge could not even pursue a remedy by risking contempt, of course, since the punch involves no judicial order that he could disobey.

* * *

The process of construing §372(c)(10) led us to raise and answer the question whether the Review Committee was authorized to entertain Judge McBryde's constitutional as-applied challenges, and we concluded that it was. The Committee, as we noted, has given a contrary answer. As we read §372(c)(10) to deny us the authority to review any aspect of the decisions about Judge McBryde other than the facial constitutional claims, we have no authority to mandate the Committee's consideration of the as applied claims. We believe, nonetheless, that the Review Committee should reconsider its view in light of our opinion and we therefore request it to do so.

* * *

Accordingly, the judgment of the district court as to the one-year and three-year suspensions is *vacated* and the judgment as to the reprimand is *affirmed*.

So ordered.

TATEL, Circuit Judge, concurring in part and dissenting in part:

I agree with the court in many respects: that Judge McBryde's challenge to the reprimand is not moot; that the Judicial Councils Reform and Judicial Conduct and Disability Act of 1980 is not facially unconstitutional; and that the Act bars us from reviewing Judge McBryde's statutory claims. I do not agree, however, that the Act precludes us from reviewing Judge McBryde's as-applied constitutional claims. I would therefore have reached those claims and, because I think one claim has merit, reversed the district court and directed that the matter be remanded to the Fifth Circuit Judicial Council for further proceedings. Although the Council's Report finds that Judge McBryde engaged in some clearly egregious and sanctionable conduct, the Report also describes judicial conduct that was either less clearly abusive or apparently quite appropriate, and the Report never adequately explains how—or even in some instances whether—such behavior rises to the level of a clear abuse of judicial power. The Report thus leaves open the possibility that Judge McBryde was sanctioned in part for behavior that was not at all abusive. In addition, because the Report is imprecise and leaves much conduct unexplained, using the Report as a basis for sanctions risks chilling other district judges' ability to manage their courtrooms effectively. I thus believe that the Council's actions amounted to an unconstitutional infringement of judicial independence. . . .

Mark Hamblett, Council Finds Judge's Apology Fulfills Sanction

New York Law Journal, April 13, 2005, at 1, col. 3

An admonition from the chief judge of the 2nd U.S. Circuit Court of Appeals and a public apology by 2nd Circuit Judge Guido Calabresi were found to be an appropriate sanction for a speech given by Calabresi in which he made an "academic" analogy between Bush v. Gore and the use of legitimate institutions by fascist leaders to cement their rise to power.

Acting on a report filed by a special committee charged with investigating complaints about Calabresi for his comments last year at an American Constitutional Society event, the circuit's Judicial Council concluded that his apology—coupled with his public admonition by Chief Judge John M. Walker—was an appropriate sanction for violating the proscription in the Canons of Judicial Ethics against political behavior by judges.

Complaints filed against the judge alleged that his speech advocated the defeat of President George W. Bush in November's election; compared Bush to Adolph Hitler and Benito Mussolini; evidenced political "bigotry" or bias; and demonstrated incompetence by disagreeing with the U.S. Supreme Court's decision in Bush v. Gore.

Following the recusal of Judge Walker because of the admonition, 2nd Circuit Judge Dennis Jacobs became acting chief and chaired a committee that included 2nd Circuit Judge Joseph McLaughlin and Eastern District Judge Carol B. Amon. Michael Zachary, a supervisory staff attorney for the Court of Appeals, was named as counsel to the committee.

Calabresi made his remarks, which he said were intended to address the "deeper structural issue that is at stake in this election," from the floor at a June 19 panel discussion on the implications of the 2000 presidential election.

Bush, he said, "came to power as a result of the illegitimate acts of a legitimate institution."

He continued, "That is what the Supreme Court did in Bush v. Gore. It put somebody in power. Now, he might have won anyway, he might not have, but what happened was that an illegitimate act by an institution that had the legitimate right to put somebody in power [sic]. The reason I emphasize that is because that is exactly what happened when Mussolini was put in by the king of Italy, that is, the king of Italy had the right to put Mussolini in though he had not won an election and make him prime minister. That is what happened when Hindenburg put Hitler in.

"I'm not suggesting for a moment that Bush is Hitler. I want to be clear on that, but it is a situation which is extremely unusual. When somebody has come in that way they sometimes have tried not to exercise much power. In this case, like Mussolini, he has exercised extraordinary power. He has exercised power, claimed power for himself that has not occurred since Franklin Roosevelt, who after all was elected big and who did some of the same things with respect to assertions of power in time of crisis that this president is doing.

"It seems to me that one of the things that is at stake is the assertion by the democracy that when that has happened it is important to put that person out, regardless of anything else, as a statement that the democracy reasserts its power over somebody who has come in and then has used the office to . . . build himself up.

"That is what happened after 1876 when Hayes could not even run again. That is not what happened in Italy because, in fact, the person who was put in there was able to say 'I have done all sorts of things and therefore deserve to win the next election.' That's got nothing to do with the politics of it. It's got to do with the structural reassertion of democracy."

One week later, the circuit released a letter from Calabresi to Walker in which he expressed his "profound regret" for his comments. Calabresi said he understood how his remarks "too easily" could be interpreted as taking a partisan position and that he strongly deplored the "politicization of the judiciary."

Calabresi said he was merely trying to make "a rather complicated academic argument about the nature of reelections after highly contested original elections."

Walker responded with a memo of his own saying that, while the remarks were meant to make "an academic point with various historical analogies," the issue was whether Calabresi could have been understood as making partisan comments, which are violations of the conduct code.

After reviewing the committee's report on the complaints, docketed under In re Charges of Judicial Misconduct, 04-8547, the council found Calabresi had violated only Canon 7, which instructs that judges should "refrain from political activity" and "should not . . . publicly endorse or oppose a candidate for public office."

Certain factors, the council said, militated in favor of sanctions — that it was a "clear and serious" violation of Canon 7; the remarks were made before a large public audience; and were widely reported by the media.

"On the other hand," the council said, Calabresi "conceded his remarks could reasonably be understood as violating Canon 7;" he said the remarks were not planned; and he had not intended to "veer" into remarks that could be construed as partisan advocacy. Moreover, the council said, the judge apologized, promised there would be no recurrence, and there was widespread coverage of both the apology and Walker's admonition. . . .

LYNNE MAREK, AN ALL-POINTS BULLETIN: BE ON THE LOOKOUT FOR AGING, CRANKY JUDGES

National Law Journal, May 21, 2008

Chief Judge Frank Easterbrook, who presides over the 7th U.S. Circuit Court of Appeals, asked lawyers and judges to be on the lookout for aging, cranky, deteriorating judges who might need a call from the top judicial officer in the circuit.

"I urge all of you — judges and lawyers alike — to keep in mind that you are the chief judge's eyes and ears in dealing with any issues that may develop," Easterbrook told some 400 lawyers and judges attending a lunch at the 7th Circuit Bar Association's annual meeting this week in Chicago.

"Judges are not immune from the risks of aging. When a judge slows down, or becomes cranky, or shows signs of losing a step mentally, I need to know."

Easterbrook made the plea as he delivered the report on the state of the circuit at the meeting, noting that often "a simple intervention" can solve the problem. Anyone can make a complaint about judges under the Judicial Conduct and Disability Act of 1980 and chief judges of a federal appellate court have the authority to remove judges if necessary.

Easterbrook gave his listeners a variety of ways to report on federal judges who might not be keeping pace. Ring up Easterbrook himself, talk to the executive of the circuit, Collins Fitzpatrick, or, for those that are more wary and want a bit of anonymity, they can share their insights with the Bar association, which will pass along the information to the chief judge.

"The more I know about how well the courts of this circuit are functioning, the better we can administer justice," Easterbrook said.

Dan Levine, Despite Discipline Panel's Harsh Words, Federal Judge Beats the Rap

San Francisco Recorder, December 16, 2008

Judges on a federal discipline panel vindicated Judge Manuel Real on Friday, but they did it through clenched teeth.

The Judicial Council of the 9th Circuit dismissed two misconduct complaints accusing Real of failing to state the reasons for his rulings. The complaints had previously led the council to privately reprimand Real. But a U.S. Judicial Conference committee sent the matter back to the circuit earlier this year, with instructions to probe the element of willfulness.

The conference required "clear and convincing evidence of a judge's arbitrary and intentional departure from prevailing law," a special 9th Circuit committee explained Friday. Real's conduct just didn't meet that standard, it found.

Still, the Judicial Council had words for Real.

"Judge Real's acts and omissions have resulted in needless appeals and unnecessary cost to litigants in both money and time, and have tended to undermine the public's confidence in the judiciary," it wrote. "The occurrences here are more than anecdotal or occasional."

The council concluded: "That such conduct was not found to be 'virtually habitual' or to have occurred in a 'substantial number' of similar cases in no way lessens the importance of and the need to give reasons for a decision when required by law." . . .

In the same order, remanding these complaints to the 9th Circuit, the U.S. Judicial Conference upheld a public censure against Real for improperly intervening in a bankruptcy case. With Friday's dismissal, Real's public disciplinary troubles are, for the moment, concluded.

"The question now, since he has been vindicated to this extent, is, will he take senior [status]?" said Professor Arthur Hellman of the University of Pittsburgh School of Law. Real will turn 85 next month. . . .

Applying the clear and convincing standard for willfulness, the committee found that Supreme Court case law was too vague to justify misconduct for many of Real's cases, especially in the sentencing realm. Other lapses can be attributed to "an attitude that can best be characterized as inattentive or negligently indifferent" to the legal standard. . . .

Patricia MacLean, Federal Bench Reforms Fall Short

National Law Journal, March 3, 2008

Cardinals' papal conclave may be the only earthly body more secretive than the disciplinary system of the federal judiciary.

Complaints against judges are secret, although the subject judge immediately sees who complained. Any subsequent investigation by the circuit is secret. The resulting report is secret. A decision to dismiss the claim or punish the judge rarely discloses the name of the errant judge, and appeals by either side remain secret.

Just how cloaked in confidentiality judge discipline has become can be seen in a new batch of reforms under review by the judiciary's policy arm, the Judicial Conference of the United States.

The 29 draft rules went out for public comment last year — but all public responses remain confidential. . . .

Under the draft changes, the Judicial Conference's Conduct Committee, which reviews circuit discipline actions, would expand its oversight authority.

It would be empowered to see every complaint filed, although a last-minute change in the draft plan made on Feb. 24 eliminated the requirement that a copy of each complaint filed must also go to the committee. The new version now says circuits must "provide access" to complaints for committee "auditing purposes." . . .

In addition, the changes would provide limited review power to the Conduct Committee, such as determining whether a chief circuit judge's summary dismissal was made too quickly, which would require a further investigation by a specially appointed investigative committee. . . .

A Few Steps Back

But the final version of the proposals also retreats in at least one important area. The original version of the draft rules required chief judges — who are aware of alleged misconduct — to initiate complaints. But the final draft rolled back to the existing standard of allowing chief judges to file complaints only if "clear and convincing" evidence of misconduct is present.

In high-visibility cases, the chief judge would be allowed to confirm the existence of a complaint, but not discuss the merits.

In addition, the Conduct Committee would have no ability to impose punishment on misbehaving judges and would be limited to telling circuits to reconsider such actions as dismissal of a complaint. It would be allowed, in "extraordinary circumstances," to conduct additional investigation under the proposal's Rule 21.

"We're trying to set up procedures to allow real misconduct to be brought to our attention," said Judge Ralph K. Winter of the 2d U.S. Circuit Court of Appeals, who heads the Conduct Committee, the group that produced the discipline reform proposals. . . .

He added that the Conduct Committee left the possibility of requiring more public disclosure to potential future reforms.

Falling Short?

Some observers — including the American Judicature Society, a national group dedicated to improving the justice system — suggest that the potential reforms do not go far enough and may create legal uncertainty that could lead to litigation in future misconduct cases.

"I remain unconvinced that the major problem is procedural," said Charles Geyh, professor at Indiana University School of Law — Bloomington and expert on judicial ethics. "When the only language you're dealing with is whether misconduct is 'conduct that is prejudicial to the administration of justice,' that is largely an empty phrase. [Judges] don't find a problem unless people say they have a problem."

Geyh added, "[I]f they confront a problem they largely do it privately and no one will hear about it. They only deal with it if the press starts screaming or Congress is screaming."

"I think they are more protective than necessary," said Steven Lubet, co-author of *Judicial Conduct and Ethics*, and professor at Northwestern University School of Law, of the lack of transparency in the proposals. "It goes too far to protect confidentiality. There is a public interest in knowing about these proceedings," he said of judicial discipline. . . .

Supporters counter that the proposed changes mark this as the first set of national discipline standards for federal judges, with better guidance for circuits on how to implement the Judicial Conduct and Disability Act of 1980. . . .

Escalating hostility from some in Congress in recent years over controversial court decisions prompted calls by Senator Charles Grassley, R-Iowa, and Representative James Sensenbrenner, R-Wis., to propose separately the creation of an inspector general as a congressional watchdog over the bench. There were also calls to impeach a half-dozen judges for controversial rulings.

Those moves were widely seen as an effort to intimidate judges and a threat to judicial independence.

But it also prompted the late Chief Justice of the United States William H. Rehnquist in 2004 to appoint the Breyer Commission, headed by Justice Stephen G. Breyer, to investigate enforcement of the Judicial Conduct and Disability Act.

The federal judiciary is on the verge of enacting the first discipline reforms to the 1980 act since minor revisions in 1990 and 2002, based on the 2006 recommendations of the Breyer Commission. The current reforms were widely viewed as an effort to forestall Congress from getting into the judge discipline business.

Congress has backed off the inspector general bills. Currently, a measure to curtail judges from attending all-expenses-paid educational junkets has been added to a judicial pay raise bill by senators Russell Feingold, D-Wis., and Jon Kyl, R.-Ariz.

Sharp Disagreements

Whether the proposals do more than nibble at the edges of reform remains to be seen.

Mark I. Harrison, an attorney at Osborn Maledon in Phoenix who chaired the American Bar Association commission evaluating the Model Code of Judicial Conduct, noted that "every time the process is opened up, it functions with more efficacy. And the concerns about secrecy go down the drain. . . .

"Virtually all state discipline systems are far more open and transparent than the federal system," Harrison said. . . .

Committee Power Contested

The extent of the Conduct Committee's power became an issue in the 2006 investigation of U.S. District Judge Manuel Real in Los Angeles over allegations that he interfered in a bankruptcy case to aid a woman under his supervision on probation.

In the committee's 2006 ruling, a 3-2 majority held it had no jurisdiction to overrule the 9th Circuit's decision to dismiss the complaint against Real. In re Opinion of Judicial Conference Committee to Review Circuit Council Conduct and Disability Orders, 449 F.3d 106 (2006).

The language of the statute, 28 U.S.C. 352(c) states that any circuit council's dismissal of a complaint "shall be final and conclusive and not judicially reviewable on appeal."

But under the current reform proposal, the Conduct Committee has reversed its position on jurisdiction over cases such as Real's.

The committee, with new membership, now says it would have authority to overturn a circuit's summary dismissal of a complaint, and order the circuit to impanel a special investigative panel to reconsider the complaint.

That appears to fly in the face of the statute, according to Arthur Hellman, a professor at the University of Pittsburgh School of Law who filed a critique of some rule changes. . . .

On Jan. 18, in an appeal of a previously undisclosed 2004 misconduct case involving Real, the Conduct Committee issued a precedent-setting decision. Real had been accused of abuse of power by refusing to follow appellate orders and failing to state reasons for decisions, with at least 23 cases identified as remanded multiple times or reassigned to a new judge on remand.

The 9th Circuit issued a private reprimand, which was appealed by an unidentified complainant as too lax, sending it up to the Conduct Committee separately from the earlier bankruptcy case.

The Conduct Committee decision establishes for the first time that judges may be disciplined if they "willfully" ignore legal standards or the directions of appeals courts. . . .

The American Judicature Society (AJS) weighed in on the reform proposals, applauding the committee's "impressive work," but warned that several rules may not go far enough. . . .

Since 2002, Congress has encouraged the courts to post final discipline orders online, but so far only the 7th and 9th circuits have begun posting routine orders. The 7th Circuit has posted 68 orders and the 9th Circuit posted 10 in 2008. . . .

D. RECUSING JUDGES

NOTE ON RECUSAL, APPOINTMENT, AND DISCIPLINE

Conceptually, recusal is directed to problems quite different from appointment and discipline. Elementary fairness suggests that a judge could not sit in a case in which she was a party. One branch of recusal prevents such miscarriages of justice. The problem cases are, of course, far more subtle than this obvious one, as you'll see below. Another aspect of recusal looks back on the processes of selection and discipline. Could a judge who had taken the invitation presented by Republican Party of Minnesota v. White to announce in her election campaign material that she thought all tort plaintiffs (or all insurance companies) were the scum of the earth then preside in cases involving such parties? Or would a party have grounds for recusal? As you read the federal recusal statute (which closely resembles those of most states), consider under which provision such a judge might be challenged. Consider as well a second relationship: in states in which judicial elections play an important role, should there be special recusal provisions aimed at judges to whom certain parties have contributed substantial amounts? Or does recusal fail to address the underlying issues?

1. STATUTORY FRAMEWORK: TWO APPROACHES TO RECUSAL

a. Recusal for Cause: The Federal Framework

28 U.S.C. §455: Disqualification of Justice, Judge, or Magistrate

(2004)

(a) Any justice, judge, or magistrate of the United States shall disqualify himself in any proceeding in which his impartiality might reasonably be questioned.

(b) He shall also disqualify himself in the following circumstances:

(1) Where he has a personal bias or prejudice concerning a party, or personal knowledge of disputed evidentiary facts concerning the proceeding;

(2) Where in private practice he served as lawyer in the matter in controversy, or a lawyer with whom he previously practiced law served during such association as a lawyer concerning the matter, or the judge or such lawyer has been a material witness concerning it;

(3) Where he has served in governmental employment and in such capacity participated as counsel, adviser or material witness concerning the proceeding or expressed an opinion concerning the merits of the particular case in controversy;

(4) He knows that he, individually or as a fiduciary, or his spouse or minor child residing in his household, has a financial interest in the subject matter in controversy or in a party to the proceeding, or any other interest that could be substantially affected by the outcome of the proceeding;

(5) He or his spouse, or a person within the third degree of relationship to either of them, or the spouse of such a person:

(i) Is a party to the proceeding, or an officer, director, or trustee of a party;

(ii) Is acting as a lawyer in the proceeding;

(iii) Is known by the judge to have an interest that could be substantially affected by the outcome of the proceeding;

(iv) Is to the judge's knowledge likely to be a material witness in the proceeding.

(c) A judge should inform himself about his personal and fiduciary financial interests, and make a reasonable effort to inform himself about the personal financial interests of his spouse and minor children residing in his household.

(d) For the purposes of this section the following words or phrases shall have the meaning indicated:

(1) "proceeding" includes pretrial, trial, appellate review, or other stages of litigation;

(2) the degree of relationship is calculated according to the civil law system;

(3) "fiduciary" includes such relationships as executor, administrator, trustee, and guardian;

(4) "financial interest" means ownership of a legal or equitable interest, however small, or a relationship as director, adviser, or other active participant in the affairs of a party, except that:

(i) Ownership in a mutual or common investment fund that holds securities is not a "financial interest" in such securities unless the judge participates in the management of the fund;

(ii) An office in an educational, religious, charitable, fraternal, or civic organization is not a "financial interest" in securities held by the organization;

(iii) The proprietary interest of a policyholder in a mutual insurance company, of a depositor in a mutual savings association, or a similar proprietary interest, is a "financial interest" in the organization only if the outcome of the proceeding could substantially affect the value of the interest;

(iv) Ownership of government securities is a "financial interest" in the issuer only if the outcome of the proceeding could substantially affect the value of the securities.

(e) No justice, judge, or magistrate shall accept from the parties to the proceeding a waiver of any ground for disqualification enumerated in subsection (b). Where the ground for disqualification arises only under subsection (a), waiver may be accepted provided it is preceded by a full disclosure on the record of the basis for disqualification.

(f) Notwithstanding the preceding provisions of this section, if any justice, judge, magistrate, or bankruptcy judge to whom a matter has been assigned would be disqualified, after substantial judicial time has been devoted to the matter, because of the appearance or discovery, after the matter was assigned to him or her, that he or she individually or as a fiduciary, or his or her spouse or minor child residing in his or her household, has a financial interest in a party (other than an interest that could be substantially affected by the outcome), disqualification is not required if the justice, judge, magistrate, bankruptcy judge, spouse or minor child, as the case may be, divests himself or herself of the interest that provides the grounds for the disqualification.

b. Recusal Without Cause: A State Variation on the Theme

Cal. Civ. Proc. Code §170.6

(Deering 2008)

§170.6. Motion to disqualify
    (a)
        (1) No judge, court commissioner, or referee of any superior court of the State of California shall try any civil or criminal action or special proceeding of any kind or character nor hear any matter therein that involves a contested issue of law or fact when it shall be established as hereinafter provided that the judge or court commissioner is prejudiced against any party or attorney or the interest of any party or attorney appearing in the action or proceeding.
        (2) Any party to or any attorney appearing in any action or proceeding may establish this prejudice by an oral or written motion without notice supported by affidavit or declaration under penalty of perjury or an oral statement under oath that the judge, court commissioner, or referee before whom the action or proceeding is pending or to whom it is assigned is prejudiced against any party or attorney or the interest of the party or attorney so that the party or attorney cannot or believes that he or she cannot have a fair and impartial trial or hearing before the judge, court commissioner, or referee. Where the judge, other than a judge assigned to the case for all purposes, court commissioner, or referee assigned to or who is scheduled to try the cause or hear the matter is known at least 10 days before the date set for trial or hearing, the motion shall be made at least 5 days before that date. If directed to the trial of a cause where there is a master calendar, the motion shall be made to the judge supervising the master calendar not later than the time the cause is assigned for trial. If directed to the trial of a cause that has been assigned to a judge for all purposes, the motion shall be made to the assigned judge or to the presiding judge by a party within 10 days after notice of the all purpose assignment, or if the party has not yet appeared in the action, then within 10 days after the appearance.

If the court in which the action is pending is authorized to have no more than one judge and the motion claims that the duly elected or appointed judge of that court is prejudiced, the motion shall be made before the expiration of 30 days from the date of the first appearance in the action of the party who is making the motion or whose attorney is making the motion. In no event shall any judge, court commissioner, or referee entertain the motion if it be made after the drawing of the name of the first juror, or if there be no jury, after the making of an opening statement by counsel for plaintiff, or if there is no opening statement by counsel for plaintiff, then after swearing in the first witness or the giving of any evidence or after trial of the cause has otherwise commenced. If the motion is directed to a hearing (other than the trial of a cause), the motion shall be made not later than the commencement of the hearing. In the case of trials or hearings not herein specifically provided for, the procedure herein specified shall be followed as nearly as may be. The fact that a judge, court commissioner, or referee has presided at or acted in connection with a pretrial conference or other hearing, proceeding, or motion prior to trial and not involving a determination of contested fact issues relating to the merits shall not preclude the later making of the motion provided for herein at the time and in the manner hereinbefore provided.

A motion under this paragraph may be made following reversal on appeal of a trial court's decision, or following reversal on appeal of a trial court's final judgment, if the trial judge in the prior proceeding is assigned to conduct a new trial on the matter. Notwithstanding paragraph (3), the party who filed the appeal that resulted in the reversal of a final judgment of a trial court may make a motion under this section regardless of whether that party or side has previously done so. The motion shall be made within 60 days after the party or the party's attorney has been notified of the assignment.

(3) If the motion is duly presented and the affidavit or declaration under penalty of perjury is duly filed or an oral statement under oath is duly made, thereupon and without any further act or proof, the judge supervising the master calendar, if any, shall assign some other judge, court commissioner, or referee to try the cause or hear the matter. In other cases, the trial of the cause or the hearing of the matter shall be assigned or transferred to another judge, court commissioner, or referee of the court in which the trial or matter is pending or, if there is no other judge, court commissioner, or referee of the court in which the trial or matter is pending, the Chair of the Judicial Council shall assign some other judge, court commissioner, or referee to try the cause or hear the matter as promptly as possible. Except as provided in this section, no party or attorney shall be permitted to make more than one such motion in any one action or special proceeding pursuant to this section; and in actions or special proceedings where there may be more than one plaintiff or similar party or more than one defendant or similar party appearing in the

action or special proceeding, only one motion for each side may be made in any one action or special proceeding.

(4) Unless required for the convenience of the court or unless good cause is shown, a continuance of the trial or hearing shall not be granted by reason of the making of a motion under this section. If a continuance is granted, the cause or matter shall be continued from day to day or for other limited periods upon the trial or other calendar and shall be reassigned or transferred for trial or hearing as promptly as possible.

(5) Any affidavit filed pursuant to this section shall be in substantially the following form:

[Case caption]   PEREMPTORY CHALLENGE

_____, being duly sworn, deposes and says: That he or she is a party (or attorney for a party) to the within action (or special proceeding). That the judge, court commissioner, or referee before whom the trial of the (or a hearing in the) aforesaid action (or special proceeding) is pending (or to whom it is assigned) is prejudiced against the party (or his or her attorney) or the interest of the party (or his or her attorney) so that affiant cannot or believes that he or she cannot have a fair and impartial trial or hearing before the judge, court commissioner, or referee.

Subscribed and sworn to before me this

_____day of _____, 20_____.

(Clerk or notary public or other officer administering oath)

(6) Any oral statement under oath or declaration under penalty of perjury made pursuant to this section shall include substantially the same contents as the affidavit above.

(b) Nothing in this section shall affect or limit Section 170 or Title 4 (commencing with Section 392) of Part 2, and this section shall be construed as cumulative thereto.

(c) If any provision of this section or the application to any person or circumstance is held invalid, that invalidity shall not affect other provisions or applications of the section that can be given effect without the invalid provision or application and to this end the provisions of this section are declared to be severable.

NOTE ON RECUSAL PROCEDURE

Notice several aspects of the contrast between federal recusal procedure and the California statute above. First, the federal system operates *only* for cause; if there is cause, as defined in §455 the judge must recuse herself. Second, the federal statute allows (but does not require) a judge at whom a recusal motion is aimed to decide it herself—as did Justice Scalia in the case below. Some federal judges routinely ask that such motions be decided by other judges, but the statute does not require such reassignments.

Second, notice that the California statute reproduced above makes the affidavit of bias uncontestable: the judge at whom such a peremptory recusal is aimed *must* recuse himself; there will be no particularized weighing of the grounds for bias: recusal under this statute is automatic. California, like other states, also has its own version of a "for-cause" statute which functions in addition to the peremptory challenge statute above. So, a litigant could "paper" (as local parlance calls the peremptory challenge) one judge, and then challenge a second judge to whom the case was assigned for cause, if, for example, she had a financial interest in one of the parties.

2. THE FOR-CAUSE SYSTEM AT WORK

SELECTED NOTES ON THE INTERPRETATION OF 28 U.S.C. §455

Available online at http://w3.lexis.com/lawschoolreg/

Judicial rulings alone almost never constitute valid basis for bias or partiality motion, as judicial rulings (1) cannot possibly show reliance upon extrajudicial source, (2) can only in rarest circumstances evidence required degree of favoritism or antagonism when no extrajudicial source is involved, and (3) almost invariably, are proper grounds for appeal, not for recusal; opinions formed by judge on basis of facts introduced or evidence occurring in course of current proceedings or of prior proceedings do not constitute basis for bias or partiality motion unless such opinions display deep-seated favoritism or antagonism that would make fair judgment impossible; thus, judicial remarks during course of trial that are critical or disapproving of, or even hostile to, counsel, parties, or their cases, ordinarily do not support bias or partiality challenge, but such remarks (1) may do so if they reveal opinion that derives from extrajudicial source, and (2) will do so if they reveal such high degree of favoritism or antagonism as to make fair judgment impossible. Liteky v United States 510 US 540 (1994).

Alleged procedural errors judge made during trial did not warrant recusal since they were not based upon knowledge acquired outside proceedings nor did they display deep-seated and unequivocal antagonism that would render fair judgment impossible; judges are known to make procedural errors on occasion, which would be basis for reversal, not recusal. F.J. Hanshaw Enters. v. Emerald River Dev., Inc. 244 F.3d 1128 (9th Cir. 2001).

NOTE ON "INTRA-CASE" RECUSAL

The stance described in the note above is universally embraced: judges do not recuse themselves when the only evidence of bias is adverse rulings or comments made in the course of those rulings. To do otherwise would be to permit the loser of such rulings or the lawyer who had "earned" such adverse comments to remove the judge from the case. Nevertheless, parties sometimes argue that something so unusual has happened that recusal is necessary.

Consider the following report and decide whether you think recusal is warranted. And in the case that follows, Cheney v. U.S. District Court, decide (a) whether you think Justice Scalia's declining to recuse himself is warranted and (b) whatever you think of his decision on recusal, whether you think the practice of explaining a refusal to recuse is a good one.

MATHEW HIRSCH, TOYOTA WANTS CALIFORNIA JUDGE OFF THE CASE

San Francisco Recorder, April 7, 2008

A few years ago, Toyota Motor Corp. briefly had cause for celebration when it won a wrongful death jury trial in San Francisco Superior Court. Then Judge James McBride granted a new trial and slapped the automaker with $138,984 in discovery sanctions.

Now, facing a motion for terminating sanctions that would automatically find Toyota liable during the retrial, the company is hoping to bring in a new judge.

In court papers, Toyota doesn't dispute the factual basis for the 2005 sanctions by McBride. Nonetheless, the company argues that he should be disqualified from presiding over future proceedings, including the retrial, because McBride has "expressed comments" about Toyota's integrity, raising doubts about his impartiality.

The case was recently transferred to Alameda County Superior Court Judge Frank Roesch, who will rule on the disqualification motion. . . .

"Generally speaking, it's pretty hard to disqualify a judge. And litigators are usually loath to try," said Sean SeLegue, a partner in Howard, Rice, Nemerovski, Canady, Falk & Rabkin's litigation department, who is not involved in the Toyota case. "Having tried to disqualify a judge and failed, one would assume you have succeeded at alienating the judge."

St. John v. Toyota Industrial Equipment Manufacturing, 407101, arose from a fatal accident that occurred seven years ago during renovations at San Francisco's Ferry Building.

According to court papers, as a construction worker tried using a Toyota-brand forklift to move lumber, the forklift tipped forward. Hilary St. John, a safety foreman at the site, ran to the back of the forklift and tried to stabilize the vehicle but failed. More than 5,200 pounds of lumber slid off the forks, and the back of the forklift fell to the ground, on top of St. John, who died on site. . . .

After eight weeks of trial, where Toyota was represented by San Jose-based lawyers at Bowman and Brooke, the jury sided with the automaker and returned a defense verdict.

But before and during the initial trial, McBride had twice found that the defense had failed to produce forklift design documents.

Among the penalties, he told jurors that Toyota had failed to produce documents in violation of a court order and that they could infer those documents were unfavorable to Toyota. And then, in a post-trial order, he imposed sanctions of $138,984.33 and wrote that Toyota had "intentionally concealed" documents.

He also granted the plaintiffs' motion for a new trial. Carcione, the plaintiffs' lawyer, said this week that his request had been based on the discovery incidents and juror misconduct.

A 1st District Court of Appeal panel affirmed McBride's monetary sanction and granting of a new trial last year.

In a motion filed last month, an attorney with Oakland, Calif.'s Lombardi, Loper & Conant asked to disqualify McBride from retrying the case or presiding over any other proceedings, including a plaintiffs' motion for terminating sanctions that had been filed one week earlier.

"Because Judge McBride has previously expressed comments regarding the integrity and veracity of defendants, an average person on the street might reasonably entertain a doubt that the judge would be able to be impartial," Lombardi's John Ranucci wrote in the disqualification motion.

Ranucci also wrote that normally a judge is not disqualified merely for saying in court that a party obfuscated the truth, but the circumstances are different when the party is facing a retrial: "It is irrelevant that the judge's earlier statements about willful misconduct are founded in evidence. . . . All further proceedings are infected by the perception of bias." . . .

In McBride's signed answer to the disqualification motion last month, he said the sanctions against Toyota "did not occur as a result of any antipathy, bias or prejudice against them, but instead occurred as an effort to control the courtroom proceedings and to ensure a fair trial."

McBride's lawyer, Deputy Attorney General Troy Overton, also argued in reply papers that to disqualify a judge, a party must show proof of bias, or the presumption is that none existed. . . .

CHENEY v. UNITED STATES DIST. COURT

514 U.S. 913 (2004)

Background: Public interest law firm and environmental group sued National Energy Policy Development Group (NEPDG) and individual members thereof, including Vice President of the United States . . . claiming violations of Federal Advisory Committee Act (FACA), Freedom of Information Act (FOIA), and Administrative Procedures Act (APA). Vice President filed interlocutory appeal from orders of the United States District Court for the District of Columbia. The Court of Appeals dismissed petition and interlocutory appeal. Following the United States Supreme Court's grant of petition for writ of certiorari, environmental group moved to recuse Justice Scalia.

Alan B. Morrison, Counsel of Record, Scott Nelson, Public Citizen Litigation Group, Washington D.C., David Bookbinder, Sierra Club Environmental Law Program, Washington, D.C., Patrick Gallagher, Alex Levinson, Sanjay Narayan, Sierra Club Environmental Law Program, San Francisco, CA, Attorneys for Respondent Sierra Club.

Theodore B. Olson, Solicitor General, Counsel of Record, Peter D. Keisler, Assistant Attorney General, Paul D. Clement, Deputy Solicitor General, Gregory G. Katsas, Shannen W. Coffin, Deputy Assistant Attorneys General, David B. Salmons, Assistant to the Solicitor General, Mark B. Stern, Michael S. Raab,

Douglas Hallward-Driemeier, Attorneys Department of Justice, Washington, D.C., for the Petitioners.

Paul J. Orfanedes, Denotes Counsel of Record, James F. Peterson, Michael J. Hurley, Judicial Watch, Inc., Washington, DC, Counsel for Respondent Judicial Watch, Inc.

Memorandum of Justice Scalia.

I have before me a motion to recuse in these cases consolidated below. The motion is filed on behalf of respondent Sierra Club. The other private respondent, Judicial Watch, Inc., does not join the motion and has publicly stated that it "does not believe the presently-known facts about the hunting trip satisfy the legal standards requiring recusal." Judicial Watch Statement 2 (Feb. 13, 2004) (available in Clerk of Court's case file). (The District Court, a nominal party in this mandamus action, has of course made no appearance.) Since the cases have been consolidated, however, recusal in the one would entail recusal in the other.

I

The decision whether a judge's impartiality can " 'reasonably be questioned' " is to be made in light of the facts as they existed, and not as they were surmised or reported.

For five years or so, I have been going to Louisiana during the Court's long December-January recess, to the duck-hunting camp of a friend whom I met through two hunting companions from Baton Rouge, one a dentist and the other a worker in the field of handicapped rehabilitation. The last three years, I have been accompanied on this trip by a son-in-law who lives near me. Our friend and host, Wallace Carline, has never, as far as I know, had business before this Court. He is not, as some reports have described him, an "energy industry executive" in the sense that summons up boardrooms of ExxonMobil or Con Edison. He runs his own company that provides services and equipment rental to oil rigs in the Gulf of Mexico.

During my December 2002 visit, I learned that Mr. Carline was an admirer of Vice President Cheney. Knowing that the Vice President, with whom I am well acquainted (from our years serving together in the Ford administration), is an enthusiastic duck-hunter, I asked whether Mr. Carline would like to invite him to our next year's hunt. The answer was yes; I conveyed the invitation (with my own warm recommendation) in the spring of 2003 and received an acceptance (subject, of course, to any superseding demands on the Vice President's time) in the summer. The Vice President said that if he did go, I would be welcome to fly down to Louisiana with him. (Because of national security requirements, of course, he must fly in a Government plane.) That invitation was later extended—if space was available—to my son-in-law and to a son who was joining the hunt for the first time; they accepted. The trip was set long before the Court granted certiorari in the present case, and indeed before the petition for certiorari had even been filed.

We departed from Andrews Air Force Base at about 10 a.m. on Monday, January 5, flying in a Gulfstream jet owned by the Government. We landed in Patterson, Louisiana, and went by car to a dock where Mr. Carline met us, to take us on the 20-minute boat trip to his hunting camp. We arrived at about 2 p.m., the 5 of us joining about 8 other hunters, making about 13 hunters in all; also present during our time there were about 3 members of Mr. Carline's staff, and, of course, the Vice President's staff and security detail. It was not an intimate setting. The group hunted that afternoon and Tuesday and Wednesday mornings; it fished (in two boats) Tuesday afternoon. All meals were in common. Sleeping was in rooms of two or three, except for the Vice President, who had his own quarters. Hunting was in two- or three-man blinds. As it turned out, I never hunted in the same blind with the Vice President. Nor was I alone with him at any time during the trip, except, perhaps, for instances so brief and unintentional that I would not recall them — walking to or from a boat, perhaps, or going to or from dinner. Of course we said not a word about the present case. The Vice President left the camp Wednesday afternoon, about two days after our arrival. I stayed on to hunt (with my son and son-in-law) until late Friday morning, when the three of us returned to Washington on a commercial flight from New Orleans.

II

Let me respond, at the outset, to Sierra Club's suggestion that I should "resolve any doubts in favor of recusal." Motion to Recuse 8. That might be sound advice if I were sitting on a Court of Appeals. There, my place would be taken by another judge, and the case would proceed normally. On the Supreme Court, however, the consequence is different: The Court proceeds with eight Justices, raising the possibility that, by reason of a tie vote, it will find itself unable to resolve the significant legal issue presented by the case. Thus, as Justices stated in their 1993 Statement of Recusal Policy: "[W]e do not think it would serve the public interest to go beyond the requirements of the statute, and to recuse ourselves, out of an excess of caution, whenever a relative is a partner in the firm before us or acted as a lawyer at an earlier stage. Even one unnecessary recusal impairs the functioning of the Court." (Available in Clerk of Court's case file.) Moreover, granting the motion is (insofar as the outcome of the particular case is concerned) effectively the same as casting a vote against the petitioner. The petitioner needs five votes to overturn the judgment below, and it makes no difference whether the needed fifth vote is missing because it has been cast for the other side, or because it has not been cast at all.

Even so, recusal is the course I must take — and will take — when, on the basis of established principles and practices, I have said or done something which requires that course. I have recused for such a reason this very Term. See Elk Grove Unified School District v. Newdow, 540 U.S. — , 124 S. Ct. 384 (cert. granted, Oct. 14, 2003). I believe, however, that established principles and practices do not require (and thus do not permit) recusal in the present case.

A

My recusal is required if, by reason of the actions described above, my "impartiality might reasonably be questioned." 28 U.S.C. §455(a). Why would that result follow from my being in a sizable group of persons, in a hunting camp with the Vice President, where I never hunted with him in the same blind or had other opportunity for private conversation? The only possibility is that it would suggest I am a friend of his. But while friendship is a ground for recusal of a Justice where the personal fortune or the personal freedom of the friend is at issue, it has traditionally *not* been a ground for recusal where *official action* is at issue, no matter how important the official action was to the ambitions or the reputation of the Government officer.

A rule that required Members of this Court to remove themselves from cases in which the official actions of friends were at issue would be utterly disabling. Many Justices have reached this Court precisely because they were friends of the incumbent President or other senior officials—and from the earliest days down to modern times Justices have had close personal relationships with the President and other officers of the Executive. John Quincy Adams hosted dinner parties featuring such luminaries as Chief Justice Marshall, Justices Johnson, Story, and Todd, Attorney General Wirt, and Daniel Webster. 5 Memoirs of John Quincy Adams 322-323 (C. Adams ed. 1969) (Diary Entry of Mar. 8, 1821). Justice Harlan and his wife often " 'stopped in' " at the White House to see the Hayes family and pass a Sunday evening in a small group, visiting and singing hymns. M. Harlan, Some Memories of a Long Life, 1854-1911, p. 99 (2001). Justice Stone tossed around a medicine ball with members of the Hoover administration mornings outside the White House. 2 Memoirs of Herbert Hoover 327 (1952). Justice Douglas was a regular at President Franklin Roosevelt's poker parties; Chief Justice Vinson played poker with President Truman. J. Simon, Independent Journey: The Life of William O. Douglas 220-221 (1980); D. McCullough, Truman 511 (1992). A no-friends rule would have disqualified much of the Court in Youngstown Sheet & Tube Co. v. Sawyer, 343 U.S. 579 (1952), the case that challenged President Truman's seizure of the steel mills. Most of the Justices knew Truman well, and four had been appointed by him. A no-friends rule would surely have required Justice Holmes's recusal in Northern Securities Co. v. United States, 193 U.S. 197 (1904), the case that challenged President Theodore Roosevelt's trust-busting initiative. See S. Novick, Honorable Justice: The Life of Oliver Wendell Holmes 264 (1989) ("Holmes and Fanny dined at the White House every week or two . . .").

It is said, however, that this case is different because the federal officer (Vice President Cheney) is actually a *named party*. That is by no means a rarity. . . .

Richard Cheney's name appears in this suit only because he was the head of a Government committee that allegedly did not comply with the Federal Advisory Committee Act (FACA), 5 U.S.C. App. §2, p. 1, and because he may, by reason of his office, have custody of some or all of the Government documents that the plaintiffs seek. If some other person were to become head of that committee or to obtain custody of those documents, the plaintiffs would name that person and Cheney would be dismissed. . . .

The recusal motion, however, asserts the following:

> Critical to the issue of Justice Scalia's recusal is understanding that this is not a run-of-the-mill legal dispute about an administrative decision. . . . Because his own conduct is central to this case, the Vice President's "reputation and his integrity are on the line." (Chicago Tribune.)

Motion to Recuse 9.

I think not. . . .

IV

While Sierra Club was apparently unable to summon forth a single example of a Justice's recusal (or even motion for a Justice's recusal) under circumstances similar to those here, I have been able to accomplish the seemingly more difficult task of finding a couple of examples establishing the negative: that recusal or motion for recusal did *not* occur under circumstances similar to those here.

[Justice Scalia reviewed several instances of close association between Supreme Court Justices and various high governmental officials, in which the justice involved had not recused himself.]

Justice White and Robert Kennedy . . .

Justice Jackson and Franklin Roosevelt . . .

I see nothing wrong about Justice White's and Justice Jackson's socializing — including vacationing and accepting rides — with their friends. Nor, seemingly, did anyone else at the time. (The Denver Post, which has been critical of me, reported the White-Kennedy-McNamara skiing vacation with nothing but enthusiasm.) If friendship is basis for recusal (as it assuredly is when friends are sued personally) then activity which suggests close friendship must be avoided. But if friendship is *no* basis for recusal (as it is not in official-capacity suits) social contacts that do no more than evidence that friendship suggest no impropriety whatever.

Of course it can be claimed (as some editorials have claimed) that "times have changed," and what was once considered proper — even as recently as Byron White's day — is no longer so. That may be true with regard to the earlier rare phenomenon of a Supreme Court Justice's serving as advisor and confidant to the President — though that activity, so incompatible with the separation of powers, was not widely known when it was occurring, and can hardly be said to have been generally approved before it was properly abandoned. But the well-known and constant practice of Justices' enjoying friendship and social intercourse with Members of Congress and officers of the Executive Branch has *not* been abandoned, and ought not to be.

V

Since I do not believe my impartiality can reasonably be questioned, I do not think it would be proper for me to recuse. . . .

My recusal would also encourage so-called investigative journalists to suggest improprieties, and demand recusals, for other inappropriate (and increasingly silly) reasons. . . .

* * *

As I noted at the outset, one of the private respondents in this case has not called for my recusal, and has expressed confidence that I will rule impartially, as indeed I will. Counsel for the other private respondent seek to impose, it seems to me, a standard regarding friendship, the appearance of friendship, and the acceptance of social favors, that is more stringent than what they themselves observe. Two days before the brief in opposition to the petition in this case was filed, lead counsel for Sierra Club, a friend, wrote me a warm note inviting me to come to Stanford Law School to speak to one of his classes.

(Available in Clerk of Court's case file.) (Judges teaching classes at law schools normally have their transportation and expenses paid.) I saw nothing amiss in that friendly letter and invitation. I surely would have thought otherwise if I had applied the standards urged in the present motion. . . .

Denied.

3. A PROPOSAL TO CHANGE RECUSAL STANDARDS

James Sample, David Pozen & Michael Young, Fair Courts: Setting Recusal Standards

Brennan Center for Justice, 2008

Foreword

An impartial and independent tribunal is the *sine qua non* of our nation's promise of equal justice under law. The rule of law is imperiled if justice is not done and if it is not seen to be done. As Chief Justice Harlan Fiske Stone said simply, "The law itself is on trial in every case."

One method to help litigants secure a fair judge for their disputes is the motion for disqualification or recusal, available in some form in every American jurisdiction. But recusal has traditionally been a difficult, cumbersome process, seldom considered and even less often actually used.

In earlier times, throwing up roadblocks to discourage frequent recusal motions made some sense, as cumbersome communication and slow travel made replacing a judge a difficult and expensive matter. The doctrine of necessity, by which even a presumptively biased judge could decide a case when no substitute was available, made legal and practical sense. But now, no judicial system should accept a process which leaves a litigant acting in good faith saddled with a judge whose fairness can be reasonably questioned.

In recent years, the need for viable judicial recusal systems has been exacerbated by the increasing politicization of both federal and state judicial selection. Appointing authorities are under unprecedented public pressure from political parties and special interest groups to select "reliable" judges. As a result, many judges come to the bench with a "label" that seemingly predisposes them to one side or the other in many cases. In elective systems, the new pressures are even worse. As the Brennan Center, the National Institute on Money in State Politics, and the Justice at Stake Campaign have documented in a series of reports, record-breaking campaign contributions, frequently unreported special interest expenditures, and misleading advertising campaigns threaten to undermine public confidence in the entire judicial branch. Perhaps most significantly, the states' most effective checks on unseemly judicial campaign behavior, the Codes of Judicial Conduct, have been seriously undermined in the wake of the Supreme Court's 2002 decision in Republican Party of Minnesota v. White. Although the *White* decision itself was fairly unremarkable, several federal circuit and district court opinions have applied its rationale to strike down, on free speech grounds, state restrictions on judges making pledges or promises about or committing to future performance in office. In some of these cases, the complainants have also challenged the applicable state code's recusal provision. These challenges have almost invariably failed. In fact, in his concurrence to the *White* opinion, Justice Kennedy even suggested that "more rigorous" recusal standards are the proper response to concerns that unfettered judicial speech may undermine the real and perceived fairness of the courts.

Thus, now as never before, reinvigorating recusal is truly necessary to preserve the court system that Chief Justice Rehnquist called the "crown jewel" of our American experiment. In many jurisdictions, judges still decide their own disqualification challenges, with little prospect of meaningful review. There is no obligation for judges to give reasons for their recusal decisions, and they rarely do. The cumulative result of these policies, along with other incentives, the authors show, is that "disqualification provisions may be systematically underused and underenforced in many states relative to Model Code expectations."

The Brennan Center's recusal report provides a roadmap to achieving meaningful reform. Judges, legislators, and citizens who care about the integrity of America's state courts will want to consult its ten proposals. As the authors recognize, certain of these proposals, such as adopting the ABA's contribution-based recusal provision or moving towards independent adjudication of disqualification motions, represent difficult but potentially promising steps. Others, like expanded commentary in the canons, may have only limited effect. Different jurisdictions will come to different conclusions as to whether and how to implement such reforms. No state will likely adopt all the suggestions, but every state should adopt some of them.

As the authors acknowledge, threats to judicial impartiality and the appearance of impartiality will persist no matter how perfectly a state structures its recusal process. As political pressures on the judiciary mount, most states should consider more fundamental changes to their systems of judicial selection. But until that day, improved recusal procedures are among the most promising incremental reforms. Hopefully, the Brennan Center's report will be a significant contribution to achieving those changes.

The Honorable Thomas R. Phillips
Retired Chief Justice, The Supreme Court of Texas

Thomas R. Phillips was appointed Chief Justice of the Supreme Court of Texas by Governor William P. Clements in 1988. He was elected and reelected to that office in 1988, 1990, 1996 and 2002. He resigned in 2004, and is now a partner in the Austin office of Baker Botts LLP.

Executive Summary

This paper takes its cue from Justice Anthony Kennedy's concurrence in the 2002 case of Republican Party of Minnesota v. White. In *White* (discussed in greater detail in the body of the paper), Justice Kennedy wrote that in response to dynamics perceived to threaten the impartiality of the courts, states "may adopt recusal standards more rigorous than due process requires, and censure judges who violate these standards." The need for states to heed Justice Kennedy's advice was critical in 2002 — and has only become more critical in the years since.

The paper describes the increasing threats to the impartiality of America's state courts and argues that they have been spurred by two trends: the growing influence of money in judicial elections and the dismantling of codes of judicial ethics that once helped to preserve the distinctive character of the judiciary, even during the course of campaigns for the bench. While acknowledging that more sweeping — and controversial — measures are ultimately needed to fully address the emerging threats to impartial courts, this paper focuses on how judges, courts, legislators, and litigants can maximize the due process protection that stronger recusal rules potentially afford. Technically, there is a difference between disqualification and recusal — disqualification is mandatory, recusal is voluntary — but the difference is often blurred because in the many jurisdictions in which judges adjudicate challenges to their own qualification to sit, disqualification functions essentially as recusal. In this paper, we use the terms interchangeably but distinguish between mandatory and voluntary removal of a judge from a case.

We first describe the trends undermining public confidence in the courts and explain how, in a recent decision, the United States Supreme Court exacerbated the impact of those trends. Second, we explain why current recusal practice is marked by underuse and underenforcement. Third, we examine the case of Avery v. State Farm Mutual Insurance Company as a means of illustrating the real-world implications of the dynamics discussed in the first two parts of the paper. In *Avery*, the plaintiffs were unable to remove a judge who, during his campaign, received substantial financial support from individuals and organizations closely associated with the defendant, *while the case was pending* before the court.

Finally, we offer ten proposals to strengthen the fairness and legitimacy of state recusal systems. Some of the procedures we recommend are already in place in some states. Others are more novel and demanding. All would help protect due process. The ten proposals are as follows:

1. *Peremptory disqualification.* Just as the parties on both sides of criminal trials are permitted to strike a certain number of people from their jury pool without showing cause, so might litigants be allowed peremptory challenges of judges. About a third of the states already permit counsel to strike one judge per proceeding. Simplicity is a significant advantage of peremptory disqualification, but the potential for gamesmanship is a concern. We argue that the cost-benefit analysis militates in favor of a carefully-crafted provision.6

2. *Enhanced disclosure.* At the outset of litigation, judges could be required to disclose orally or in writing any facts, particularly those involving campaign statements and campaign contributions, that might plausibly be construed as bearing on their impartiality. Such a mandatory disclosure scheme would shift some of the costs of disqualification-related fact finding from the litigant to the state. It would also increase the reputational and professional cost to judges who fail to disclose pertinent information that later emerges through another source. To further enhance the disclosure of relevant information concerning disqualification, states could also provide a centralized system through which attorneys and their clients can review a judge's recusal history.

3. *Per se rules for campaign contributors.* To address the concern about judges who decline to recuse themselves when their campaign finances reasonably call into question their impartiality, the ABA recommends mandatory disqualification of any judge who has accepted large contributions (i.e., contributions over a pre-determined threshold amount) from a party appearing before her. The ABA's provision, however, has not been adopted by the states. We recommend a minor modification to the ABA's provision that should mollify concerns that may have created a hesitancy to adopt this sensible provision.

4. *Independent adjudication of disqualification motions.* The fact that judges in many jurisdictions decide on their own disqualification challenges, with little to no prospect of immediate review, is one of the most heavily criticized features of United States law in this area — and for good reason. Allowing judges to decide on their own disqualification motions is in tension not only with the guarantee of a neutral case arbiter, but also with states' express desire for objectivity in disqualification decisions.

5. *Transparent and reasoned decision-making.* All judges who rule on a disqualification motion should be required to explain their decision in writing or on the record, even if only briefly. Such a requirement would facilitate appellate review and ensure greater accountability for these decisions.

6. *De novo review on interlocutory appeal.* Making appellate review more searching would be less important if the other reforms on this list were adopted, but it would still provide a valuable safeguard against partiality. The United States Court of Appeals for the Seventh Circuit, the only federal appeals court to review recusal determinations de novo, offers one example of a court that has embraced enhanced review.

7. *Mechanisms for replacing disqualified judges.* If recusal is to provide a due process protection, rather than an invitation for gamesmanship, courts need to put in place efficient methods for replacing a disqualified judge. This is particularly true at the appellate level.

8. *Expanded commentary in the canons.* Expanding the canon commentary on recusal, while a "soft" and highly limited solution, would nonetheless offer relatively costless guidance for judges seeking to adhere to the highest ethical standards, even when not strictly required.

9. *Judicial education.* Seminars for judges that enable them to confront the standard critiques of disqualification law might provide another soft solution for invigorating its practice. Judges could be instructed on the underuse and underenforcement of disqualification motions, the social psychological research into bias, the importance of avoiding the appearance of partiality, and their own potential role in helping to reform recusal doctrines and court rules.

10. *Recusal advisory bodies.* Just as many states, bar associations, and other groups have created non-binding advisory bodies to serve as a resource for candidates on campaign-conduct questions, a similar model might be followed with respect to recusal. Advisory bodies could identify best practices and encourage judges to set high standards for themselves. Judges could be encouraged to seek guidance from the advisory body when faced with difficult issues of recusal. A judge accepting such advice could expect a public defense if a disgruntled party criticized a decision not to recuse.

We recognize that all of these proposals come with their own risks. On the one hand, strengthening disqualification rules may be a means to safeguard due process and public trust in the judiciary. On the other hand, strengthening these rules may increase administrative burdens and litigation delays, open new avenues for strategic behavior (such as judge shopping), and undermine a judge's duty to hear all cases. These tradeoffs demand that any solution be carefully designed and implemented, and we do not mean to minimize that task by providing only a cursory sketch of each option. But the looming crisis in judicial recusal means that reform is no longer an option; it is a necessity.

Introduction

While on a recent vacation, the pipes in your basement froze, flooding the interior and causing substantial damage to your home. Fortunately, you were covered by your home insurance policy. Or at least, so you thought. But the insurance company, citing a strained reading of your policy, refused to pay. After seeking legal advice, you decided to sue for the cost of repairs. The judge dismissed your case. Months later, you happened across a television commercial in which the judge, now running for re-election, rails against "the plaintiffs' lawyers and litigants responsible for the jackpot justice mentality that is costing us jobs and destroying our family values." You normally agree with such sentiments as a general matter. In suing, however, you wanted no jackpot, just a fair hearing and, ideally, the cost of restoring your home.

A few days later, a profile of the judge in the local paper lists the biggest contributors to his previous campaign, as well as the contributors to his current re-election bid. Your insurance company and the lawyers who represented it are near the top of each list. Neither you nor your lawyer, a solo practitioner, ever contributed to a judicial campaign. Numerous friends, expert and otherwise, have told you that while your case may have been a close call, it was by no means a slam dunk for the defense. Was justice done? Maybe you don't actually know, and think it's at least possible that it was. So let's rephrase. Does it *appear* to you that justice was done? Or, to borrow from the American Bar Association's standard for mandatory judicial recusal, "might" the judge's impartiality "reasonably" have been questioned? And would it affect your view on this if you knew that the judge was permitted to decide that question in his own case?

Unfortunately, in far too many state courtrooms around the country today, the above scenario is anything but hypothetical. The parties may be switched; the details are always unique; but the fundamental appearance of bias remains the same. Not only are the rules of recusal often too weak; those rules that do exist often go underenforced.

In many respects, recusal is an incomplete due process protection, a safeguard of last resort. More complete, *ex ante* solutions promoting fair and impartial courts—whether in the form of judicial selection methodology, campaign finance regulation, or the canons of conduct governing judicial speech—are likely to be more effective, but they are beyond the scope of this paper. This paper focuses on disqualification doctrines and procedures. It argues that the rules currently used by many judges are inadequate to protect litigants or preserve public trust and that, to safeguard their own independence, courts should consider a variety of reforms. Its aim is to help judges, courts, legislators, and litigants maximize the due process protection that recusal potentially affords. . . .

E. RECUSAL, JUDICIAL ELECTIONS, AND DUE PROCESS

The following case combines three themes we have met in this unit: the selection or election of judges, the recusal of judges, and two clashing constitutional values: the First Amendment and Due Process.

CAPERTON V. A. T. MASSEY COAL CO.

129 S. Ct. 2252 (2009)

Justice KENNEDY delivered the opinion of the Court.

In this case the Supreme Court of Appeals of West Virginia reversed a trial court judgment, which had entered a jury verdict of $50 million. Five justices heard the case, and the vote to reverse was 3 to 2. The question presented is whether the Due Process Clause of the Fourteenth Amendment was violated when one of the justices in the majority denied a recusal motion. The basis for the motion was that the justice had received campaign contributions in an extraordinary amount from, and through the efforts of, the board chairman and principal officer of the corporation found liable for the damages.

Under our precedents there are objective standards that require recusal when "the probability of actual bias on the part of the judge or decisionmaker is too high to be constitutionally tolerable." Withrow v. Larkin, 421 U.S. 35, 47 (1975). Applying those precedents, we find that, in all the circumstances of this case, due process requires recusal.

I

In August 2002 a West Virginia jury returned a verdict that found respondents A. T. Massey Coal Co. and its affiliates (hereinafter Massey) liable for fraudulent misrepresentation, concealment, and tortious interference with existing contractual relations. The jury awarded petitioners Hugh Caperton . . . (hereinafter Caperton) the sum of $50 million in compensatory and punitive damages. . . .

Don Blankenship is Massey's chairman, chief executive officer, and president. After the verdict but before the appeal, West Virginia held its 2004 judicial elections. Knowing the Supreme Court of Appeals of West Virginia would consider the appeal in the case, Blankenship decided to support an attorney who sought to replace Justice McGraw[,] a candidate for reelection to that court. The attorney who sought to replace him was Brent Benjamin.

In addition to contributing the $1,000 statutory maximum to Benjamin's campaign committee, Blankenship donated almost $ 2.5 million to "And For

The Sake Of The Kids," a political organization formed under 26 U.S.C. §527[, a section of the Internal Revenue Code permitting tax-exempt political organizations]. The §527 organization opposed McGraw and supported Benjamin. Blankenship's donations accounted for more than two-thirds of the total funds it raised. This was not all. Blankenship spent, in addition, just over $500,000 on independent expenditures—for direct mailings and letters soliciting donations as well as television and newspaper advertisements—"'to support . . . Brent Benjamin.'"

To provide some perspective, Blankenship's $3 million in contributions were more than the total amount spent by all other Benjamin supporters and three times the amount spent by Benjamin's own committee. Caperton contends that Blankenship spent $1 million more than the total amount spent by the campaign committees of both candidates combined.

Benjamin won. He received 382,036 votes (53.3%), and McGraw received 334,301 votes (46.7%).

In October 2005, before Massey filed its petition for appeal in West Virginia's highest court, Caperton moved to disqualify now-Justice Benjamin under the Due Process Clause and the West Virginia Code of Judicial Conduct, based on the conflict caused by Blankenship's campaign involvement. Justice Benjamin denied the motion in April 2006. He indicated that he "carefully considered the bases and accompanying exhibits proffered by the movants." But he found "no objective information . . . to show that this Justice has a bias for or against any litigant, that this Justice has prejudged the matters which comprise this litigation, or that this Justice will be anything but fair and impartial." In December 2006 Massey filed its petition for appeal to challenge the adverse jury verdict. The West Virginia Supreme Court of Appeals granted review.

In November 2007 that court reversed the $50 million verdict against Massey. The majority opinion, authored by then-Chief Justice Davis and joined by Justices Benjamin and Maynard, found that "Massey's conduct warranted the type of judgment rendered in this case." It reversed, nevertheless, based on two independent grounds—first, that a forum-selection clause contained in a contract to which Massey was not a party barred the suit in West Virginia, and, second, that res judicata barred the suit due to an out-of-state judgment to which Massey was not a party. Justice Starcher dissented, stating that the "majority's opinion is morally and legally wrong." Justice Albright also dissented, accusing the majority of "misapplying the law and introducing sweeping 'new law' into our jurisprudence that may well come back to haunt us."

Caperton sought rehearing, and the parties moved for disqualification of three of the five justices who decided the appeal. Photos had surfaced of Justice Maynard vacationing with Blankenship in the French Riviera while the case was pending. Justice Maynard granted Caperton's recusal motion. On the other side Justice Starcher granted Massey's recusal motion, apparently based on his public criticism of Blankenship's role in the 2004 elections. In his recusal memorandum Justice Starcher urged Justice Benjamin to recuse himself as well. He noted that "Blankenship's bestowal of his personal wealth, political tactics, and 'friendship' have created a cancer in the affairs of this Court." Justice Benjamin declined Justice Starcher's suggestion and denied Caperton's recusal motion.

The court granted rehearing. Justice Benjamin, now in the capacity of acting chief justice, selected Judges Cookman and Fox to replace the recused justices. Caperton moved a third time for disqualification, arguing that Justice Benjamin had failed to apply the correct standard under West Virginia law — i.e., whether "a reasonable and prudent person, knowing these objective facts, would harbor doubts about Justice Benjamin's ability to be fair and impartial." Caperton also included the results of a public opinion poll, which indicated that over 67% of West Virginians doubted Justice Benjamin would be fair and impartial. Justice Benjamin again refused to withdraw, noting that the "push poll" was "neither credible nor sufficiently reliable to serve as the basis for an elected judge's disqualification."

In April 2008 a divided court again reversed the jury verdict, and again it was a 3-to-2 decision. Justice Davis filed a modified version of his prior opinion, repeating the two earlier holdings. She was joined by Justice Benjamin and Judge Fox. Justice Albright, joined by Judge Cookman, dissented: "Not only is the majority opinion unsupported by the facts and existing case law, but it is also fundamentally unfair. Sadly, justice was neither honored nor served by the majority." The dissent also noted "genuine due process implications arising under federal law" with respect to Justice Benjamin's failure to recuse himself.

Four months later — a month after the petition for writ of certiorari was filed in this Court — Justice Benjamin filed a concurring opinion. He defended the merits of the majority opinion as well as his decision not to recuse. He rejected Caperton's challenge to his participation in the case under both the Due Process Clause and West Virginia law. Justice Benjamin reiterated that he had no " 'direct, personal, substantial, pecuniary interest' in this case.' " Adopting "a standard merely of 'appearances,' " he concluded, "seems little more than an invitation to subject West Virginia's justice system to the vagaries of the day — a framework in which predictability and stability yield to supposition, innuendo, half-truths, and partisan manipulations."

We granted certiorari.

II

It is axiomatic that "[a] fair trial in a fair tribunal is a basic requirement of due process." As the Court has recognized, however, "most matters relating to judicial disqualification [do] not rise to a constitutional level." The early and leading case on the subject is Tumey v. Ohio, 273 U.S. 510 (1927). There, the Court stated that "matters of kinship, personal bias, state policy, remoteness of interest, would seem generally to be matters merely of legislative discretion."

The *Tumey* Court concluded that the Due Process Clause incorporated the common-law rule that a judge must recuse himself when he has "a direct, personal, substantial, pecuniary interest" in a case. This rule reflects the maxim that "[n]o man is allowed to be a judge in his own cause; because his interest would certainly bias his judgment, and, not improbably, corrupt his integrity." The Federalist No. 10, p. 59 (J. Cooke ed. 1961) (J. Madison). Under this rule, "disqualification for bias or prejudice was not permitted"; those matters were left to statutes and judicial codes. Personal bias or prejudice "alone would not be sufficient basis for imposing a constitutional requirement under the Due Process Clause."

As new problems have emerged that were not discussed at common law, however, the Court has identified additional instances which, as an objective matter, require recusal. These are circumstances "in which experience teaches that the probability of actual bias on the part of the judge or decisionmaker is too high to be constitutionally tolerable." To place the present case in proper context, two instances where the Court has required recusal merit further discussion.

A

The first involved the emergence of local tribunals where a judge had a financial interest in the outcome of a case, although the interest was less than what would have been considered personal or direct at common law.

This was the problem addressed in *Tumey*. There, the mayor of a village had the authority to sit as a judge (with no jury) to try those accused of violating a state law prohibiting the possession of alcoholic beverages. Inherent in this structure were two potential conflicts. First, the mayor received a salary supplement for performing judicial duties, and the funds for that compensation derived from the fines assessed in a case. No fines were assessed upon acquittal. The mayor-judge thus received a salary supplement only if he convicted the defendant. Second, sums from the criminal fines were deposited to the village's general treasury fund for village improvements and repairs.

The Court held that the Due Process Clause required disqualification "both because of [the mayor-judge's] direct pecuniary interest in the outcome, and because of his official motive to convict and to graduate the fine to help the financial needs of the village." It so held despite observing that "[t]here are doubtless mayors who would not allow such a consideration as $12 costs in each case to affect their judgment in it." The Court articulated the controlling principle:

> Every procedure which would offer a possible temptation to the average man as a judge to forget the burden of proof required to convict the defendant, or which might lead him not to hold the balance nice, clear and true between the State and the accused, denies the latter due process of law.

The Court was thus concerned with more than the traditional common-law prohibition on direct pecuniary interest. It was also concerned with a more general concept of interests that tempt adjudicators to disregard neutrality.

This concern with conflicts resulting from financial incentives was elaborated in Ward v. Monroeville, 409 U.S. 57 (1972), which invalidated a conviction in another mayor's court. In *Monroeville*, unlike in *Tumey*, the mayor received no money; instead, the fines the mayor assessed went to the town's general fisc. The Court held that "[t]he fact that the mayor [in *Tumey*] shared directly in the fees and costs did not define the limits of the principle." The principle, instead, turned on the "'possible temptation'" the mayor might face; the mayor's "executive responsibilities for village finances may make him partisan to maintain the high level of contribution [to those finances] from the mayor's court." As the Court reiterated in another case that Term, "the [judge's] financial stake need not be as direct or positive as it appeared to be in *Tumey*." . . .

The Court in *Lavoie* further clarified the reach of the Due Process Clause regarding a judge's financial interest in a case. There, a justice had cast the deciding vote on the Alabama Supreme Court to uphold a punitive damages award against an insurance company for bad-faith refusal to pay a claim. At the time of his vote, the justice was the lead plaintiff in a nearly identical lawsuit pending in Alabama's lower courts. His deciding vote, this Court surmised, "undoubtedly 'raised the stakes'" for the insurance defendant in the justice's suit.

The Court stressed that it was "not required to decide whether in fact [the justice] was influenced." The proper constitutional inquiry is "whether sitting on the case then before the Supreme Court of Alabama 'would offer a possible temptation to the average . . . judge to . . . lead him not to hold the balance nice, clear and true.'" (quoting *Monroeville*, in turn quoting *Tumey*). The Court underscored that "what degree or kind of interest is sufficient to disqualify a judge from sitting 'cannot be defined with precision.'" In the Court's view, however, it was important that the test have an objective component.

The *Lavoie* Court proceeded to distinguish the state court justice's particular interest in the case, which required recusal, from interests that were not a constitutional concern. For instance, "while [the other] justices might conceivably have had a slight pecuniary interest" due to their potential membership in a class-action suit against their own insurance companies, that interest is "'too remote and insubstantial to violate the constitutional constraints.'"

B

The second instance requiring recusal that was not discussed at common law emerged in the criminal contempt context, where a judge had no pecuniary interest in the case but was challenged because of a conflict arising from his participation in an earlier proceeding. This Court characterized that first proceeding (perhaps pejoratively) as a "'one-man grand jury.'"

In that first proceeding, and as provided by state law, a judge examined witnesses to determine whether criminal charges should be brought. The judge called the two petitioners before him. One petitioner answered questions, but the judge found him untruthful and charged him with perjury. The second declined to answer on the ground that he did not have counsel with him, as state law seemed to permit. The judge charged him with contempt. The judge proceeded to try and convict both petitioners.

This Court set aside the convictions on grounds that the judge had a conflict of interest at the trial stage because of his earlier participation followed by his decision to charge them. The Due Process Clause required disqualification. The Court recited the general rule that "no man can be a judge in his own case," adding that "no man is permitted to try cases where he has an interest in the outcome." It noted that the disqualifying criteria "cannot be defined with precision. Circumstances and relationships must be considered." These circumstances and the prior relationship required recusal: Having been a part of [the one-man grand jury] process a judge cannot be, in the very nature of things, wholly disinterested in the conviction or acquittal of those accused." That is because "[a]s a practical matter it is difficult if not impossible for a judge to free himself from the influence of what took place in his 'grand-jury' secret session."

The *Murchison* Court was careful to distinguish the circumstances and the relationship from those where the Constitution would not require recusal. It noted that the single-judge grand jury is "more a part of the accusatory process than an ordinary lay grand juror," and that "adjudication by a trial judge of a contempt committed in [a judge's] presence in open court cannot be likened to the proceedings here." The judge's prior relationship with the defendant, as well as the information acquired from the prior proceeding, was of critical import.

Following *Murchison* the Court held in Mayberry v. Pennsylvania, 400 U.S. 455 (1971), "that by reason of the Due Process Clause of the Fourteenth Amendment a defendant in criminal contempt proceedings should be given a public trial before a judge other than the one reviled by the contemnor." The Court reiterated that this rule rests on the relationship between the judge and the defendant: "[A] judge, vilified as was this Pennsylvania judge, necessarily becomes embroiled in a running, bitter controversy. No one so cruelly slandered is likely to maintain that calm detachment necessary for fair adjudication."

Again, the Court considered the specific circumstances presented by the case. It noted that "not every attack on a judge . . . disqualifies him from sitting." The Court distinguished the case from Ungar v. Sarafite, 376 U.S. 575 (1964), in which the Court had "ruled that a lawyer's challenge, though 'disruptive, recalcitrant and disagreeable commentary,' was still not 'an insulting attack upon the integrity of the judge carrying such potential for bias as to require disqualification.'" The inquiry is an objective one. The Court asks not whether the judge is actually, subjectively biased, but whether the average judge in his position is "likely" to be neutral, or whether there is an unconstitutional "potential for bias."

III

Based on the principles described in these cases we turn to the issue before us. This problem arises in the context of judicial elections, a framework not presented in the precedents we have reviewed and discussed.

Caperton contends that Blankenship's pivotal role in getting Justice Benjamin elected created a constitutionally intolerable probability of actual bias. Though not a bribe or criminal influence, Justice Benjamin would nevertheless feel a debt of gratitude to Blankenship for his extraordinary efforts to get him elected. That temptation, Caperton claims, is as strong and inherent in human nature as was the conflict the Court confronted in *Tumey* and *Monroeville* when a mayor-judge (or the city) benefited financially from a defendant's conviction, as well as the conflict identified in Murchison and Mayberry when a judge was the object of a defendant's contempt.

Justice Benjamin was careful to address the recusal motions and explain his reasons why, on his view of the controlling standard, disqualification was not in order. In four separate opinions issued during the course of the appeal, he explained why no actual bias had been established. He found no basis for recusal because Caperton failed to provide "objective evidence" or "objective information," but merely "subjective belief" of bias. Nor could anyone "point to any actual conduct or activity on [his] part which could be termed 'improper.'" In other words, based on the facts presented by Caperton, Justice Benjamin conducted a probing search into his actual motives and inclinations; and he found none to be improper. We do not question his subjective findings of impartiality and propriety. Nor do we determine whether there was actual bias.

Following accepted principles of our legal tradition respecting the proper performance of judicial functions, judges often inquire into their subjective motives and purposes in the ordinary course of deciding a case. This does not mean the inquiry is a simple one. "The work of deciding cases goes on every day in hundreds of courts throughout the land. Any judge, one might suppose, would find it easy to describe the process which he had followed a thousand times and more. Nothing could be farther from the truth." B. Cardozo, The Nature of the Judicial Process 9 (1921).

The judge inquires into reasons that seem to be leading to a particular result. Precedent and stare decisis and the text and purpose of the law and the Constitution; logic and scholarship and experience and common sense; and fairness and disinterest and neutrality are among the factors at work. To bring coherence to the process, and to seek respect for the resulting judgment, judges often explain the reasons for their conclusions and rulings. There are instances when the introspection that often attends this process may reveal that what the judge had assumed to be a proper, controlling factor is not the real one at work. If the judge discovers that some personal bias or improper consideration seems to be the actuating cause of the decision or to be an influence so difficult to dispel that there is a real possibility of undermining neutrality, the judge may think it necessary to consider withdrawing from the case.

The difficulties of inquiring into actual bias, and the fact that the inquiry is often a private one, simply underscore the need for objective rules. Otherwise there may be no adequate protection against a judge who simply misreads or misapprehends the real motives at work in deciding the case. The judge's own inquiry into actual bias, then, is not one that the law can easily superintend or review, though actual bias, if disclosed, no doubt would be grounds for appropriate relief. In lieu of exclusive reliance on that personal inquiry, or on appellate review of the judge's determination respecting actual bias, the Due Process Clause has been implemented by objective standards that do not require proof of actual bias. In defining these standards the Court has asked whether, "under a realistic appraisal of psychological tendencies and human weakness," the interest "poses such a risk of actual bias or prejudgment that the practice must be forbidden if the guarantee of due process is to be adequately implemented."

We turn to the influence at issue in this case. Not every campaign contribution by a litigant or attorney creates a probability of bias that requires a judge's recusal, but this is an exceptional case. We conclude that there is a serious risk of actual bias — based on objective and reasonable perceptions — when a person with a personal stake in a particular case had a significant and disproportionate influence in placing the judge on the case by raising funds or directing the judge's election campaign when the case was pending or imminent. The inquiry centers on the contribution's relative size in comparison to the total amount of money contributed to the campaign, the total amount spent in the election, and the apparent effect such contribution had on the outcome of the election.

Applying this principle, we conclude that Blankenship's campaign efforts had a significant and disproportionate influence in placing Justice Benjamin on the case. Blankenship contributed some $3 million to unseat the incumbent and replace him with Benjamin. His contributions eclipsed the total amount spent by all other Benjamin supporters and exceeded by 300% the amount spent by Benjamin's campaign committee. Caperton claims Blankenship spent $1 million more than the total amount spent by the campaign committees of both candidates combined.

Massey responds that Blankenship's support, while significant, did not cause Benjamin's victory. In the end the people of West Virginia elected him, and they did so based on many reasons other than Blankenship's efforts. Massey points out that every major state newspaper, but one, endorsed Benjamin. It also contends that then-Justice McGraw cost himself the election by giving a speech during the campaign, a speech the opposition seized upon for its own advantage.

Justice Benjamin raised similar arguments. He asserted that "the outcome of the 2004 election was due primarily to [his own] campaign's message," as well as McGraw's "devastat[ing]" speech in which he "made a number of controversial claims which became a matter of statewide discussion in the media, on the internet, and elsewhere."

Whether Blankenship's campaign contributions were a necessary and sufficient cause of Benjamin's victory is not the proper inquiry. Much like determining whether a judge is actually biased, proving what ultimately drives the electorate to choose a particular candidate is a difficult endeavor, not likely to lend itself to a certain conclusion. This is particularly true where, as here, there is no procedure for judicial factfinding and the sole trier of fact is the one accused of bias. Due process requires an objective inquiry into whether the contributor's influence on the election under all the circumstances "would offer a possible temptation to the average . . . judge to . . . lead him not to hold the balance nice, clear and true." In an election decided by fewer than 50,000 votes (382,036 to 334,301), Blankenship's campaign contributions—in comparison to the total amount contributed to the campaign, as well as the total amount spent in the election—had a significant and disproportionate influence on the electoral outcome. And the risk that Blankenship's influence engendered actual bias is sufficiently substantial that it "must be forbidden if the guarantee of due process is to be adequately implemented."

The temporal relationship between the campaign contributions, the justice's election, and the pendency of the case is also critical. It was reasonably foreseeable, when the campaign contributions were made, that the pending case would be before the newly elected justice. The $50 million adverse jury verdict had been entered before the election, and the Supreme Court of Appeals was the next step once the state trial court dealt with post-trial motions. So it became at once apparent that, absent recusal, Justice Benjamin would review a judgment that cost his biggest donor's company $50 million. Although there is no allegation of a quid pro quo agreement, the fact remains that Blankenship's extraordinary contributions were made at a time when he had a vested stake in the outcome. Just as no man is allowed to be a judge in his own cause, similar fears of bias can arise when — without the consent of the other parties — a man chooses the judge in his own cause. And applying this principle to the judicial election process, there was here a serious, objective risk of actual bias that required Justice Benjamin's recusal.

Justice Benjamin did undertake an extensive search for actual bias. But, as we have indicated, that is just one step in the judicial process; objective standards may also require recusal whether or not actual bias exists or can be proved. Due process "may sometimes bar trial by judges who have no actual bias and who would do their very best to weigh the scales of justice equally between contending parties." The failure to consider objective standards requiring recusal is not consistent with the imperatives of due process. We find that Blankenship's significant and disproportionate influence — coupled with the temporal relationship between the election and the pending case — "offer a possible temptation to the average . . . judge to . . . lead him not to hold the balance nice, clear and true." On these extreme facts the probability of actual bias rises to an unconstitutional level.

IV

Our decision today addresses an extraordinary situation where the Constitution requires recusal. Massey and its amici predict that various adverse consequences will follow from recognizing a constitutional violation here — ranging from a flood of recusal motions to unnecessary interference with judicial elections. We disagree. The facts now before us are extreme by any measure. The parties point to no other instance involving judicial campaign contributions that presents a potential for bias comparable to the circumstances in this case.

It is true that extreme cases often test the bounds of established legal principles, and sometimes no administrable standard may be available to address the perceived wrong. But it is also true that extreme cases are more likely to cross constitutional limits, requiring this Court's intervention and formulation of objective standards. This is particularly true when due process is violated.

This Court's recusal cases are illustrative. In each case the Court dealt with extreme facts that created an unconstitutional probability of bias that " 'cannot be defined with precision.' " Yet the Court articulated an objective standard to protect the parties' basic right to a fair trial in a fair tribunal. The Court was careful to distinguish the extreme facts of the cases before it from those interests that would not rise to a constitutional level. In this case we do nothing more than what the Court has done before.

As such, it is worth noting the effects, or lack thereof, of the Court's prior decisions. Even though the standards announced in those cases raised questions similar to those that might be asked after our decision today, the

Court was not flooded with *Monroeville* or *Murchison* motions. That is perhaps due in part to the extreme facts those standards sought to address. Courts proved quite capable of applying the standards to less extreme situations.

One must also take into account the judicial reforms the States have implemented to eliminate even the appearance of partiality. Almost every State — West Virginia included — has adopted the American Bar Association's objective standard: "A judge shall avoid impropriety and the appearance of impropriety." ABA Annotated Model Code of Judicial Conduct, Canon 2 (2004); see Brief for American Bar Association as Amicus Curiae 14, and n. 29. The ABA Model Code's test for appearance of impropriety is "whether the conduct would create in reasonable minds a perception that the judge's ability to carry out judicial responsibilities with integrity, impartiality and competence is impaired."

The West Virginia Code of Judicial Conduct also requires a judge to "disqualify himself or herself in a proceeding in which the judge's impartiality might reasonably be questioned." Canon 3E(1); see also 28 U.S.C. §455(a) ("Any justice, judge, or magistrate judge of the United States shall disqualify himself in any proceeding in which his impartiality might reasonably be questioned"). Under Canon 3E(1), " '[t]he question of disqualification focuses on whether an objective assessment of the judge's conduct produces a reasonable question about impartiality, not on the judge's subjective perception of the ability to act fairly.' " Indeed, some States require recusal based on campaign contributions similar to those in this case.

These codes of conduct serve to maintain the integrity of the judiciary and the rule of law. The Conference of the Chief Justices has underscored that the codes are "[t]he principal safeguard against judicial campaign abuses" that threaten to imperil "public confidence in the fairness and integrity of the nation's elected judges." Brief for Conference of Chief Justices as Amicus Curiae 4, 11. This is a vital state interest:

> Courts, in our system, elaborate principles of law in the course of resolving disputes. The power and the prerogative of a court to perform this function rest, in the end, upon the respect accorded to its judgments. The citizen's respect for judgments depends in turn upon the issuing court's absolute probity. Judicial integrity is, in consequence, a state interest of the highest order.

Republican Party of Minn. v. White, 536 U.S. 765, 793(2002) (Kennedy, J., concurring). It is for this reason that States may choose to "adopt recusal standards more rigorous than due process requires."

"The Due Process Clause demarks only the outer boundaries of judicial disqualifications. Congress and the states, of course, remain free to impose more rigorous standards for judicial disqualification than those we find mandated here today." *Lavoie.* Because the codes of judicial conduct provide more protection than due process requires, most disputes over disqualification will be resolved without resort to the Constitution. Application of the constitutional standard implicated in this case will thus be confined to rare instances.

* * *

The judgment of the Supreme Court of Appeals of West Virginia is reversed, and the case is remanded for further proceedings not inconsistent with this opinion.

Chief Justice ROBERTS, with whom Justice SCALIA, Justice THOMAS, and Justice ALITO join, dissenting.

I, of course, share the majority's sincere concerns about the need to maintain a fair, independent, and impartial judiciary — and one that appears to be such. But I fear that the Court's decision will undermine rather than promote these values.

Until today, we have recognized exactly two situations in which the Federal Due Process Clause requires disqualification of a judge: when the judge has a financial interest in the outcome of the case, and when the judge is trying a defendant for certain criminal contempts. Vaguer notions of bias or the appearance of bias were never a basis for disqualification, either at common law or under our constitutional precedents. Those issues were instead addressed by legislation or court rules.

Today, however, the Court enlists the Due Process Clause to overturn a judge's failure to recuse because of a "probability of bias." Unlike the established grounds for disqualification, a "probability of bias" cannot be defined in any limited way. The Court's new "rule" provides no guidance to judges and litigants about when recusal will be constitutionally required. This will inevitably lead to an increase in allegations that judges are biased, however groundless those charges may be. The end result will do far more to erode public confidence in judicial impartiality than an isolated failure to recuse in a particular case. . . .

I . . .

In any given case, there are a number of factors that could give rise to a "probability" or "appearance" of bias: friendship with a party or lawyer, prior employment experience, membership in clubs or associations, prior speeches and writings, religious affiliation, and countless other considerations. We have never held that the Due Process Clause requires recusal for any of these reasons, even though they could be viewed as presenting a "probability of bias." Many state statutes require recusal based on a probability or appearance of bias, but "that alone would not be sufficient basis for imposing a constitutional requirement under the Due Process Clause." *Lavoie.* States are, of course, free to adopt broader recusal rules than the Constitution requires — and every State has — but these developments are not continuously incorporated into the Due Process Clause.

II

In departing from this clear line between when recusal is constitutionally required and when it is not, the majority repeatedly emphasizes the need for an "objective" standard. The majority's analysis is "objective" in that it does not inquire into Justice Benjamin's motives or decisionmaking process. But the standard the majority articulates — "probability of bias" — fails to provide clear, workable guidance for future cases. At the most basic level, it is unclear whether the new probability of bias standard is somehow limited to financial support in judicial elections, or applies to judicial recusal questions more generally.

But there are other fundamental questions as well. With little help from the majority, courts will now have to determine:

1. How much money is too much money? What level of contribution or expenditure gives rise to a "probability of bias"?
2. How do we determine whether a given expenditure is "disproportionate"? Disproportionate to what?
3. Are independent, non-coordinated expenditures treated the same as direct contributions to a candidate's campaign? What about contributions to independent outside groups supporting a candidate?
4. Does it matter whether the litigant has contributed to other candidates or made large expenditures in connection with other elections?
5. Does the amount at issue in the case matter? What if this case were an employment dispute with only $10,000 at stake? What if the plaintiffs only sought non-monetary relief such as an injunction or declaratory judgment?
6. Does the analysis change depending on whether the judge whose disqualification is sought sits on a trial court, appeals court, or state supreme court?
7. How long does the probability of bias last? Does the probability of bias diminish over time as the election recedes? Does it matter whether the judge plans to run for reelection?
8. What if the "disproportionately" large expenditure is made by an industry association, trade union, physicians' group, or the plaintiffs' bar? Must the judge recuse in all cases that affect the association's interests? Must the judge recuse in all cases in which a party or lawyer is a member of that group? Does it matter how much the litigant contributed to the association?
9. What if the case involves a social or ideological issue rather than a financial one? Must a judge recuse from cases involving, say, abortion rights if he has received "disproportionate" support from individuals who feel strongly about either side of that issue? If the supporter wants to help elect judges who are "tough on crime," must the judge recuse in all criminal cases?
10. What if the candidate draws "disproportionate" support from a particular racial, religious, ethnic, or other group, and the case involves an issue of particular importance to that group? . . .
19. If there is independent review of a judge's recusal decision, e.g., by a panel of other judges, does this completely foreclose a due process claim?

[Chief Justice Roberts's dissent listed, in all, forty questions thought to be unanswered by the majority opinion, concluding with one that looks back to earlier chapters in this book: "40. What if the parties settle a *Caperton* claim as part of a broader settlement of the case? Does that leave the judge with no way to salvage his reputation?"]

These are only a few uncertainties that quickly come to mind. . . .

III

A

To its credit, the Court seems to recognize that the inherently boundless nature of its new rule poses a problem. But the majority's only answer is that the present case is an "extreme" one, so there is no need to worry about other cases. . . .

But this is just so much whistling past the graveyard. Claims that have little chance of success are nonetheless frequently filed. The success rate for certiorari petitions before this Court is approximately 1.1%, and yet the previous Term some 8,241 were filed. Every one of the "Caperton motions" or appeals or §1983 actions will claim that the judge is biased, or probably biased, bringing the judge and the judicial system into disrepute. And all future litigants will assert that their case is really the most extreme thus far. . . .

B

And why is the Court so convinced that this is an extreme case? It is true that Don Blankenship spent a large amount of money in connection with this election. But this point cannot be emphasized strongly enough: Other than a $1,000 direct contribution from Blankenship, Justice Benjamin and his campaign had no control over how this money was spent. Campaigns go to great lengths to develop precise messages and strategies. An insensitive or ham-handed ad campaign by an independent third party might distort the campaign's message or cause a backlash against the candidate, even though the candidate was not responsible for the ads. . . .

Moreover, Blankenship's independent expenditures do not appear "grossly disproportionate" compared to other such expenditures in this very election. "And for the Sake of the Kids" — an independent group that received approximately two-thirds of its funding from Blankenship — spent $3,623,500 in connection with the election. But large independent expenditures were also made in support of Justice Benjamin's opponent. "Consumers for Justice" — an independent group that received large contributions from the plaintiffs' bar — spent approximately $2 million in this race. And Blankenship has made large expenditures in connection with several previous West Virginia elections, which undercuts any notion that his involvement in this election was "intended to influence the outcome" of particular pending litigation.

It is also far from clear that Blankenship's expenditures affected the outcome of this election. . . .

* * *

It is an old cliche, but sometimes the cure is worse than the disease. I am sure there are cases where a "probability of bias" should lead the prudent judge to step aside, but the judge fails to do so. Maybe this is one of them. But I believe that opening the door to recusal claims under the Due Process Clause, for an amorphous "probability of bias," will itself bring our judicial system into undeserved disrepute, and diminish the confidence of the American people in the fairness and integrity of their courts. I hope I am wrong.

I respectfully dissent.

Justice SCALIA, dissenting.

The principal purpose of this Court's exercise of its certiorari jurisdiction is to clarify the law. As the Chief Justice's dissent makes painfully clear, the principal consequence of today's decision is to create vast uncertainty with respect to a point of law that can be raised in all litigated cases in (at least) those 39 States that elect their judges. This course was urged upon us on grounds that it would preserve the public's confidence in the judicial system.

The decision will have the opposite effect. What above all else is eroding public confidence in the Nation's judicial system is the perception that litigation is just a game, that the party with the most resourceful lawyer can play it to win, that our seemingly interminable legal proceedings are wonderfully self-perpetuating but incapable of delivering real-world justice. The Court's opinion will reinforce that perception, adding to the vast arsenal of lawyerly gambits what will come to be known as the Caperton claim. . . .

A Talmudic maxim instructs with respect to the Scripture: "Turn it over, and turn it over, for all is therein." The Babylonian Talmud, Tractate Aboth, Ch. V, Mishnah 22 (I. Epstein ed. 1935). Divinely inspired text may contain the answers to all earthly questions, but the Due Process Clause most assuredly does not. The Court today continues its quixotic quest to right all wrongs and repair all imperfections through the Constitution. Alas, the quest cannot succeed — which is why some wrongs and imperfections have been called non-justiciable. In the best of all possible worlds, should judges sometimes recuse even where the clear commands of our prior due process law do not require it? Undoubtedly. The relevant question, however, is whether we do more good than harm by seeking to correct this imperfection through expansion of our constitutional mandate in a manner ungoverned by any discernable rule. The answer is obvious.

NOTE ON *CAPERTON*

1. Notice that the majority and the dissent do not fundamentally disagree about whether Judge Benjamin should have recused himself. They disagree instead about whether the Supreme Court has started down a treacherous path, whether, as one dissent has it "the cure," constitutionally mandating recusals, is worse than the "disease."

Why is there no disagreement about whether Judge Benjamin should have recused himself? He apparently had no personal ties to Blankenship, was an experienced lawyer, and was running for his office on his own "plat-form" before Blankenship made the campaign contributions. Under the majority's view of things, would a U.S. Supreme Court justice, plucked from obscurity by a president, be therefore bound to recuse himself in all cases important to the appointing administration? That certainly has not been the rule.

2. Does the dissent make too much of the line-drawing problem? In a number of areas—constitutional limits on punitive damages being just one—the court has enunciated rather vague standards and then, in a modest number of cases, worked out administrable rules. Is this situation different?

3. The day after *Caperton* was handed down, three major newspapers made it the subject of editorials. The *Wall Street Journal* bemoaned the decision as ham-handed meddling with state judiciaries by the Supreme Court, asserting that the author of the majority opinion favored judicial elitism over citizen voice in judicial selection. The *New York Times* applauded the decision as having secured the right to "honest justice," opining that "the only truly alarming thing about [the] decision is that it was not unanimous." *USA Today* took a third path, generally supporting the outcome and expressing the hope that the dangers exposed by the case would lead states to abandon judicial elections in favor of other selection systems.

A CONCLUDING NOTE

Many schools offer upper-level courses in complex litigation—surely a worthy topic of study. Think of this course as the converse: an exploration of the complex problems of apparently simple litigation. We have not dealt with nationwide class actions, multidistrict litigation, fancy choice of law problems, and the like. Instead, these materials have focused on the dynamics of "ordinary" litigation. As you have seen, such litigation can present the lawyer with very difficult decisions.

Some of those decisions are difficult because a developing lawsuit requires subtle evaluations of various risks. Some risks come from the everyday uncertainty about how a trier of fact will decide disputed facts. Other evaluations come from the "structure" of modern litigation. Look back on the eight hypothetical cases with which this book started. (See Chapter 1, Section C.) You will recognize that each deals with a problem explored in one of the four chapters: on the organization of the profession (cases 1, 3, 4, 5, 6); on the financing of litigation (cases 2, 5); on the evolving forms of settlement (cases 5, 6, 7); and on the selection, recusal and discipline of judges (case 8). Your study of these materials should enable you quickly to identify the source of the problem facing the hypothetical young lawyer and likely the way he can get himself out of or, in some instances, what he should have done to keep himself from getting into, the problem. Other difficult evaluations come from the interaction between chapters.

As you will have seen, the problems often do not have "solutions": good lawyers earn their keep not so much by "knowing the law" (although this trait is clearly helpful!) as from being able to evaluate competing risks. Should we seek to recuse this judge (who may be unsympathetic to our claim or defense), or will an unsuccessful motion to recuse make things even worse? Should we make (or accept) an offer to settle, recognizing that our case for liability against this defendant is thin, but it is the only assuredly solvent defendant in the case? And how should that decision be affected by our near-certainty that the primary and secondary insurers of the other defendant seem to be playing a game of "chicken" with each other: on the one hand that game is likely to force us to an expensive trial; on the other hand a later court *might* conclude that the insurers' failure to settle was in bad faith — with the result that they would be liable for an amount substantially greater than the coverage? Should we resist this discovery request — for which we have a plausible, although not an air-tight, legal basis — in the hopes that plaintiff's financing for the lawsuit will collapse? Or will our resistance drive the plaintiff to seek new and more robust financing, affecting not just this discovery request but the entire lawsuit? And, if we throw associate "person-power" at discovery in the case, we'll likely improve our chances of prevailing on the merits, but perhaps at the cost of losing some of the valuable young talent we've recruited to the firm: what should we do? Having a feel for such matters will, I hope, help you understand why "counselor" is not simply a fancy synonym for lawyer, but is rather a description of what good lawyers do. No course could expect to tell you how to "answer" questions like these. But this one should — I hope — give you an appreciation for the way in which the questions flow from the modern organization of practice.

The second lesson I hope you'll take away from the course is that there is no ideal form of practice: big firms, small firms, non-profits, and affinity groups all have characteristic advantages, and countervailing challenges. Your task, as you contemplate your career, is to identify the characteristics of practice that matter most to *you*, recognizing that you're making inevitable choices. Whatever choice you make — or whatever series of choices you make over the span of your professional career — this course should also enable you to recognize that all organizations delivering legal services operate in two markets. The first — the market for clients — exists regardless of whether the organization is for profit: government lawyers and legal aid organizations don't seek profits from practice, but they do need to have clients, and if they don't, their funding sources will dry up. The other market is that for legal talent — for you and your classmates. Legal organizations have to recruit, train, and retain legal talent to deliver services to their clients. And, as you know, their ability to do so is only partly a function of salary levels. Almost all lawyers entered the profession not just to earn a living but because the autonomy and the intellectual challenges of practice attracted them. If that autonomy or those challenges are degraded substantially, legal talent will move to greener pastures. So every organization that employs lawyers has to find its own balance of economic and non-economic incentives to succeed in this "second market." Rules of professional ethics place some limits on how organizations will meet this challenge: to use a simple example, they cannot increase the intellectual challenge of practice by asking the same lawyer to represent both sides of the same lawsuit! But within these boundaries, one can find many variations.

Not only practice organizations but even civil litigation itself can be understood as an effort to create a market — a market in claims. Most civil litigation is about the allocation of resources. Some of those resources are entirely and uncontroversially about money — how much should defendant have to pay if she breached the contract? Others, including many that appear to be about principle rather than principal, have resource allocation at their root. For example, litigation over the allegedly unconstitutional institutionalization of disabled children (Evans v. Jeff D.) involved a claim that the state of Idaho, which cared for the children, needed to devote more resources to the job—and that it needed to devote more resources as well to pay the lawyers who vindicated the children's claims. One of the great difficulties of practice flows from the circumstance that, even for many "simple" economic claims, even experts lack a firm sense of the "right price" for a settlement. The rules of the profession tell us that only the parties' agreement will strike that price—or, to put it another way—we know the right price only when the parties have told us what it is. But behind that truism lies a problem that's not so much ethical as empirical. Most clients, when faced with making or accepting a settlement offer, will quickly turn to their lawyers and ask "is this a fair offer?" The lawyer, after all, has more experience than most clients (insurers are an important exception) in valuing such claims. But lawyers, even experienced lawyers, turn out not to be reliably expert in such valuation.

So what? If a client thinks a claim is worth more—or less—than the lawyer does, a price determiner in a black robe sits ready to preside over a process that will "price" the dispute by adjudicating it. That can be a reassurance. It can also be frightening if one has low confidence in the judge and little power to replace him or her with a different arbiter. Many other countries have special educational tracks for aspiring judges, who, after appointment, operate under constant supervision and review. Not so in the United States: our judges come from the ranks of lawyers, and receive at most modest post-appointment training. That means the U.S. judge will have more experience of practice and its problems than will judges elsewhere, perhaps giving her a better "feel" for the pressures facing the lawyers before her. On the other hand, if the U.S. judge makes a mistake she is more likely to get away with it. U.S. judges operate under a significantly looser regime of supervision than their counterparts elsewhere. Not only the final judgment rule but also doctrines such as "abuse of discretion" and "clearly erroneous" add more insulation for the trial court's decisions.

* * *

The four chapters in this text explore the forces that drive civil litigation, and these forces interact. Lawyer and law firm demographics combine with professional rules to shape patterns of representation. For example, if insurers could not control settlement decisions of insureds, settlements would look different. If prohibitions on fee-sharing were strictly enforced, there would be fewer referrals by the plaintiffs' bar and less skillful representation by plaintiffs' lawyers. Lawyers and clients *invest* in litigation. Hourly fee clients invest directly in each litigation event. Contingent fees cause the lawyer (and the lawyer's other clients) to invest in each others' cases. Lawyers and clients make strategic choices in litigation. For example, the chance of an outlier damage verdict may lead a plaintiff represented on a contingent-fee basis to risk trial, which has chance of yielding nothing, but which could yield a high verdict. On the other side of the "v," the possibility of a bad-faith verdict may lead an insurer to cover damages greater than the policy limits. In making these choices, litigants are constantly looking over their shoulders at the judge, who represents both a possibility and a threat. For example, a public preference for "safety," may lead governors to appoint disproportionate numbers of former prosecutors as judges, who are then relatively unfamiliar with civil litigation issues — thereby increasing pressure on litigants to settle.

These themes of connectedness make civil litigation a constantly changing equilibrium. The identity of the client will affect the choice of a lawyer. The identity of the client may determine whether the lawyer can embark on that representation, and may block her from subsequent representation. The identity of the client and lawyer may determine the way in which the lawsuit will get financed, and that financing may help to determine whether and on what terms the case settles. Such settlement will also take account of the identity of the judge (including the judge's practice experience before taking the bench). The judge's pre-appointment experience, temperament, and perceived leanings will lead both parties to guess about what might happen at trial — the alternative to settlement. And predictions about trial may very well depend on the identity of the client, thus returning this circle to the place it began.

If this course has succeeded, you will have gained a preliminary understanding of this connectedness. You will also have gained a better understanding of why a number of considerations that seem to have little to do with "law" matter a great deal to experienced lawyers. And, finally, you will have gained a better sense of the shape of a profession you are about to enter.